GOVERNING STATES AND CITIES

GOVERNING STATES AND CITIES

David C. Saffell
Ohio Northern University

Harry Basehart
Salisbury State University

THE McGRAW-HILL COMPANIES, INC.
New York St. Louis San Francisco Auckland Bogotá Caracas Lisbon
London Madrid Mexico City Milan Montreal New Delhi
San Juan Singapore Sydney Tokyo Toronto

McGraw-Hill
A Division of The ***McGraw-Hill*** *Companies*

GOVERNING STATES AND CITIES

This book is printed on acid-free paper.

1 2 3 4 5 6 7 8 9 0 DOC DOC 9 0 9 8 7 6

ISBN 0-07-055000-X

This book was set in Times Roman by the Clarinda Company.
The editor was Lyn Uhl;
the production supervisor was Kathy Porzio;
the cover was designed by Christopher Brady;
cover photo: Frank Siteman/Tony Stone Images;
the photo editor was Inge King.
Project supervision was done by The Total Book.
R. R. Donnelley & Sons Company was printer and binder.

Library of Congress Cataloging in Publication Data

Saffell, David C., (date)
Governing states and cities/David C. Saffell, Harry Basehart.
p. cm.
Includes bibliographical references and index.
ISBN 0-07-055000-X
1. State governments—United States. 2. Municipal government—United States. 3. Federal government—United States. 4. Political participation—United States. 5. Urban policy—Uniited States.
I. Basehart, Harry. II. Title.
JK2408.S16 1997
353.9—dc20 96-15610

ABOUT THE AUTHORS

DAVID C. SAFFELL is professor of political science at Ohio Northern University. He received his Ph.D. in political science from the University of Minnesota. Dr. Saffell is the author of *State and Local Government: Politics and Public Policy*, fifth edition (McGraw-Hill). The author has been teaching the introductory course on state and local government to college students for over 25 years.

HARRY BASEHART is professor of political science at Salisbury State University. He received his Ph.D. in political science from The Ohio State University. He is a contributor to *Redistricting in the 1980s* and the author or coauthor of several articles on state legislatures that have appeared in *American Politics Quarterly* and *Legislative Studies Quarterly*. He also directs an internship program that places undergraduate students in the Maryland General Assembly and other state and local government agencies.

CONTENTS

PREFACE

This comprehensive textbook covers the broad spectrum of state and local government. It is an expanded and updated version of a more concise textbook, *State and Local Government: Politics and Public Policies,* 5th edition, also published by McGraw-Hill. The organization of chapters is designed to accommodate introductory courses taught in one semester or in one or two quarters. We begin with the study of constitutions and intergovernmental relations; proceed through the political process (parties, interest groups, and elections); discuss basic state government institutions (legislatures, governors, administrators, and courts); cover local government (cities, suburbs, counties, townships, and rural communities); and then conclude by examining the ways in which public policy is made in the areas of taxation, education, welfare, economic development, and the environment.

Our goal throughout the book is to answer "what difference does it make" questions. These include what difference does it make if state constitutions are long or streamlined, if political party systems are one-party or two-party competitive, if legislatures are professional or nonprofessional, if cities have elite or pluralist power structures, if states offer education vouchers, if governors have extensive formal powers, if states have the initiative process to make laws, and if states and localities compete in economic development. We seek to connect structure and process to public policy and to evaluate the nature of public policy outputs at all levels of government.

Political scientists described a "resurgence" of state and local governments in the 1980s, as they took the lead in political activism when faced with cutbacks in federal domestic policy initiatives. In the first half of the 1990s, states and cities faced severe financial distress. Many governments cut programs, laid off employees, and raised taxes. Now in the second half of the decade a growing national economy has put states in their best financial shape since the early 1980s. That's the good news. The possible bad news (or, as they say, "the challenge") for states and localities is that Congress may transfer responsibility for most domestic policy to the states. While Congress has pledged to return more money to states in the form of block grants and to cut federal mandates, states fear an overall reduction in federal financial assistance.

Finding the federal system in the midst of the greatest revolution of authority since the 1930s, we examine the ongoing changes in intergovernmental relations believing that states are better prepared than at any other time in their history to accept the transfer of programs and to provide services to their residents. But as state fiscal authority

Steven D. Gold warns, that does not mean states are magicians. If aid to states and localities is cut because it is a convenient way to balance the federal budget, then states will be hard put in the late 1990s to improve education, incarcerate more criminals, and protect the environment.

To help connect readers to the exciting reality of state and local government, we have included an article by Neal R. Peirce, the premier journalist writing about states and cities, in most chapters. To help give readers a more in-depth look at what political scientists and other scholars have to say about state and local government, we have a special boxed section in each chapter. These Scholarly Boxes focus on such topics as at-large elections, elasticity of cities, cumulative voting, party competition, the item veto, and state tax capacity. Key terms in the text appear in boldface type, and they are defined at the end of each chapter. There are also chapter summaries to give readers a review of the major points.

We have made every effort to include tables, graphs, and maps that contain the most current data available. While we discuss a number of issues that are in the news—such as community policing, reinventing government, term limits for state legislators, state-authorized gambling casinos, and the hiring of private contractors to operate public schools—our overriding concern is to give readers what introductory state and local government textbooks are supposed to deliver: an appreciation of the historical setting of subnational government, an understanding of how the primary institutions of government operate, an examination of how citizens participate in government, and an analysis of how these segments fit together to create public policy that affects our lives every day. If the most challenging public issues are to be dealt with effectively as we near the turn of the century, it is states and cities that will lead the way.

We want to acknowledge the help we received from those who reviewed the manuscript for this book. Their insights prompted us to make several organizational changes and they forced us to rethink issues raised in every chapter. Reviewers included: Edwin Benton, University of South Florida; Thad Beyle, University of North Carolina at Chapel Hill; William Culver, State University of New York at Plattsburgh; George Kiser, Illinois State University; Edgar LeDuc, University of Rhode Island; David Martin, Auburn University; John Portz, Northeastern University; Betty Rosser, Nicholls State University; Loran Smith, Washburn University; and John Straayer, Colorado State University.

At McGraw-Hill, Annette Bodzin, Monica Freedman, Bertrand Lummus, and Lyn Uhl provided the help and encouragement necessary to keep us on schedule and they directed the production of the book in ways that greatly improved the accuracy and look of the manuscript.

Others who provided assistance with the preparation of the manuscript include Barbara Roberts and Danielle Samrak at Ohio Northern University and Paula Hepburn at Salisbury State University.

David C. Saffell

Harry Basehart

GOVERNING STATES AND CITIES

1

THE SETTING OF STATE AND LOCAL GOVERNMENT

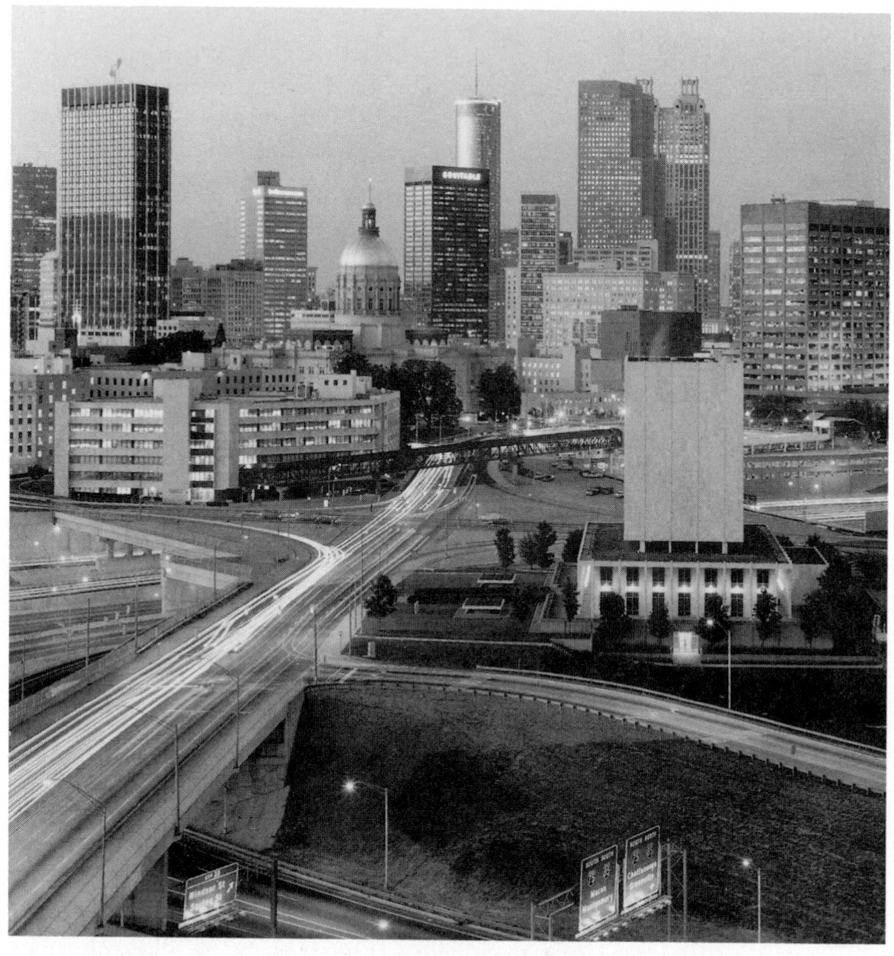

Kevin C. Rose/Courtesy of the Atlanta Convention and Visitors Bureau

STATE VITALITY

During this century, the role of the federal government in public policymaking has expanded to a degree unimagined in earlier times. In fact, today the federal government can act on virtually any policy issue affecting our lives.[1] In those areas where Washington has refrained from action—for example, domestic relations, property, and contracts—the absence of legislation has been a matter of federal restraint rather than lack of constitutional authority.

The states dominated American government in the nineteenth century and the first decade of this century. However, several events in the first half of this century relegated the states to a position of secondary importance. Ratification of the Sixteenth Amendment (relating to income tax) in 1913 gave the federal government much greater ability to raise money and to centralize policymaking. The Depression showed the weaknesses of the states in responding to the nation's economic problems and led to greater focus on the president as the center of government. World War II further strengthened the authority of the president and the centralization of power in Washington.

State reform has been taking place since the early twentieth century, but the negative image of corrupt and incompetent state government persisted (and with good reason) into the early 1960s.[2] Since the mid-1960s, over forty states have ratified new constitutions or made significant changes in existing ones. Governors' terms have been lengthened and their powers increased. Legislatures have become more professional (see Chapter 5) and more representative of urban interests, and nearly all meet in annual sessions. Court systems have been unified (see Chapter 8), and intermediate appellate courts have been added in many states. State bureaucrats are more professional, and the number of state employees under some form of merit system has increased from 50 percent in 1960 to nearly 80 percent (see Chapter 7). An increase in party competition in the states, coupled with legislative- and executive-branch changes, has led to more innovative policy. In addition, federal cuts in aid have caused local governments to look more to the states for financial help (see Chapter 2). Since 1980, states have shown a new creativity in several policy areas, including education, corrections, and hazardous waste disposal.

This resurgence of the states was well under way when Ronald Reagan was elected president in 1980. Reagan believed that the federal government had done too much and that more responsibility for policymaking should be turned over to the states. In addition, federal categorical grants-in-aid (see Chapter 2) were criticized by congressional conservatives and by state and local officials for their red tape and insensitivity to local problems. The timing of Reagan's changes in policy and philosophy thus caught the states at a point at which they were the most capable of assuming new policymaking responsibilities. Unfortunately, the states also found themselves without some of the financial assistance they had come to expect from the national government. By 1990 states and localities faced severe financial pressures brought on by the recession and cuts in federal funds. A majority of states raised taxes, spending was cut, and employees were furloughed or fired in the early 1990s.

By the mid-1990s the financial position of most states and cities had improved as the national economy rebounded. However, states faced even greater cutbacks in federal aid as Republicans in Congress sought to balance the federal budget. On the plus side for states, Republican control of Congress after the 1994 elections has resulted in a renewed commitment to the Reagan agenda of the 1980s to return power to the states. Early in 1995 Congress passed an unfunded mandates measure (see Chapter 2), making it harder for Congress to impose new requirements on state and local governments without providing federal money to pay for them. Republican governors and Republicans in Congress proposed more block grants to give states greater flexibility in dealing with health and welfare programs. In particular, they sought to limit the soaring costs of Medicaid.

Only a few domestic functions—control of natural resources, management of the postal service, space research, and air and water transportation—are predominantly the responsibility of the federal government. In most of those policy areas where responsibility is shared among federal, state, and local governments, the federal financial share was reduced in the 1980s. The share of total state and local spending paid for by Washington declined from 25 percent in the late 1970s to 17 percent in 1989, but it rose to 22 percent in 1992. Nearly 90 percent of all direct federal aid goes to states.[3] In comparison, the list of state responsibilities is long.

• *Education.* State and local governments administer public schools and colleges. The federal share of school expenditures rose from about 4.5 percent in 1960 to 9 percent in 1980. It declined to about 6 percent by 1991 and rose to 8 percent by 1995 under President Clinton.[4]

• *Transportation.* Highway routes and construction are largely determined by state and local governments. Federal grants make up about 30 percent of all highway and mass transit expenditures. Federal aid to mass transit declined from $4.6 billion in 1981 to $3.2 billion in 1994.

• *Welfare.* The states legislate welfare benefits paid to recipients and determine rules of eligibility. They also maintain homes for the aged, orphans, and the mentally ill. The federal government contributes about 55 percent of the cost of Aid to Families with Dependent Children (AFDC), the major nonmedical welfare program. Republican proposals call for federal welfare programs to be turned over to the states in block grants and for federal funding levels to decline.

• *Criminal justice.* In an overwhelming number of cases, criminal defendants are tried in state rather than federal courts. Nearly 95 percent of all persons in the United States engaged in law enforcement are employed by state and local governments. New York City has nearly as many law enforcement agents as do all the federal agencies. More than 90 percent of all prisoners are held in state prisons and jails. As we will see in Chapter 15, spending for corrections has been one of the fastest-growing items in state budgets in the 1990s. The federal share of funding for state and local police was about 13 percent in the early 1990s, while federal grants made up about 7 percent of state expenditures for corrections.

• *Commercial regulation.* Most regulation of industry, banking, and utilities is performed by the states.

• *Health.* States, cities, and counties run hospitals (New York City operates nearly twenty hospitals) and they subsidize private hospitals. Their health departments inspect and license various types of businesses. Public health programs try to prevent disease and their nurses visit the elderly. The fastest-growing state expense is Medicaid (medical benefits to low-income persons); the federal share of costs was 57 percent in 1992.

State and local governments now provide many services that previously were provided by private agencies or were not provided at all. The growth of technology has led to the creation of public utilities commissions to regulate electric, gas, and telephone service. State regulation extends from the disposal of waste materials to the preservation of historical sites. States license professions ranging from funeral directors to acupuncturists. Government services also have increased greatly as a higher percentage of our population has become urbanized. City residents require a host of services (health, police, sanitation) that were much less necessary when most of the population lived in rural areas. In addition, the concentration of large numbers of poor people in urban areas has contributed to the growth in public services. Since the Great Depression of the 1930s, public support of the poor (including racial and ethnic minorities) has expanded greatly.

The Advisory Commission on Intergovernmental Relations reports that in 1992 the states employed 3.86 million full-time workers, local governments employed 9.51 million, and the federal government employed 3.04 million civilians. Thus over 80 percent of all public civilian employees work for state and local governments. While state employment increased 34 percent in the 1970s, it had a more modest 10 percent gain in the 1980s. State and local employment figures were at all-time highs in 1992. Federal civilian employment dropped slightly in 1990, 1991, and 1992 to stand 67,000 below its post-World War II high of 3.114 million in 1989. Since World War II, there has been only one year, 1981, when state government employment decreased.

The states make significant monetary contributions to local governments—totaling $198 billion in 1992, up from $99 billion in 1983.[5] These payments represent about 28 percent of all state expenditures. If looked at as one program, local assistance would be the largest single state expenditure. There has been a virtually uninterrupted growth in state aid to localities in this century. This growth in state aid has been made possible by the changing nature of state tax systems, including the use of sales and income taxes. State aid also increased in the 1980s because the Reagan administration did away with a move that began in the 1960s to bypass the states and have federal grants go directly to the cities. By consolidating many categorical (specific purpose) grants into broader block grants and giving the block grants to the states, the federal government has given the states new authority and control over federal funds. (These grants are explained in Chapter 2.)

The shift of responsibility to the states has increased concern about state **mandates** to local governments. Mandates arise from statutes, court decisions, and administrative orders that demand action from a "subordinate" government. The number and cost of state mandates have increased substantially, and local officials have become increasingly upset about underfunded mandates. A key issue involves guidelines from the states regarding such matters as how to deal with the environment and public employees. Just as federal mandates put pressure on states, state mandates put financial pressure on cities and counties and they call into question the matter of local self-government. Although some states have reduced the burden of mandates on local

Why It Is Important to Teach State and Local Government

It is important to remember that during the Constitutional Convention there was never a question as to whether or not there would be states, but only if there was to be a national government. The balance of power between state and national governments may not be as much of a balance anymore, with the latter's power for all practical purposes unrestricted, but there remain important reasons for familiarizing our students with state and local governments.

It is at the subnational level that most people have contact with government. Most local services are people-related; the closeness of city hall and the ease of a local telephone call allow individuals the opportunity to observe government in action or to otherwise readily express their opinion on issues of direct interest to them. I often ask my students to imagine the three levels of government ceasing to exist as they arise one morning, and it is easy to see that the services first missed are local (water and sewage, traffic control, etc.). The most direct and intimate contact most people have with the national government is when they fill out their federal tax forms. Further, state and local governments offer even the introductory student the opportunity to conduct field work, to observe a city council or planning commission meeting, to interview a state or local director of finance. Such experiences can be extremely educational.

Both state and local governments have, on the whole, greatly modernized themselves over the past three decades. Many state legislatures are full time, governors' staffs have been expanded, and civil service requirements have upgraded the educational background of executive agencies at all staff levels. Local governments have full-time chief executives with professional staffs. The once corruptible county assessor has been replaced in many localities by systems analysts who use computer programs to reassess properties. We should no longer fear that an understanding of, or contact with, these governments will in some way warp our students' perspectives about politics and government.

Furthermore, some of the most challenging policy problems and issues are being confronted at the state and local level. Efforts to improve our educational system, to deal with the problems of the homeless, to combat drug use, to determine and provide an adequate level of service while staying within a balanced budget—the front line is at the subnational level. One of the most controversial issues of all, whether or not to take someone's life for the commission of a crime, has been left to states to decide on an individual basis.

Finally, students who wish to get involved with government, whether in a campaign, internship or career, will have a much better chance of meaningful participation if they have been taught the particular workings of state and local governments. A meaningful inclusion of these topics in an introductory course thus provides not only additional insight into the general functioning of politics and government, it also better prepares the student to exercise his or her citizenship.

Source: Bruce Wallin, "State and Local Governments Are American, Too," *Political Science Teacher,* Fall 1988, p. 3. Reprinted by permission.

governments, many continue to create new mandates even as they protest the imposition of federal mandates on themselves.

Current state vitality is part of a long history of innovative policymaking by state governments. Wisconsin serves as a classic example: In 1900–1914, that state initiated the direct primary, civil service regulations, a state income tax, conservation laws, and a variety of state regulatory commissions. In the past twenty years various states have been leaders in environmental protection, antidiscrimination, and community mental health.[6] More recently, several states have made significant changes in their health care systems, others have restructured education funding systems, and several states in the 1990s have streamlined their welfare systems.

As we will see in Chapter 7, a host of cities and counties across the country have been busy "reinventing government" by changing their budget processes; moving to prevent problems, such as crime and pollution, instead of treating symptoms; empowering citizens to manage public housing; privatizing public services; and establishing enterprises that make money. For example, some sewerage facilities are transforming sludge into fertilizer and selling it at a profit.

Much more so than federal government policy, what states and localities do directly affects everyday life. Not only do they have the major responsibility for education, crime, AIDS and other health problems, and welfare administration, these governments also determine public university tuition charges, the price of subway fares, where and when we can purchase alcoholic beverages, whether soda bottles are returnable, and how much we pay for electricity. Most of these issues, even those that may appear trivial, generate strong political reactions from groups that have economic or ideological interests in public policy outcomes.

Political activity within the states is another indication of vitality. The activities of political parties and the management of campaigns and elections occur mainly in state and local settings. All elected public officials, except the president, are selected by voters within the states. Political parties have their organizational base in the states, with their power lodged most firmly in county committees and city organizations. Many members of the U.S. Congress initially held state or local office. Once elected, many senators and representatives devote much of their time (and the time of their staff members) to "casework"—that is, representing the interests of their local constituents in dealing with federal agencies. In election campaigns they often focus their attention on local issues. In electing a multitude of state and local officials (plus participating in federal elections) and in deciding special ballot issues, such as higher tax rates for schools, voters experience a nearly continuous process of campaigns and elections. By holding the first presidential primary, New Hampshire exerts a disproportionate influence on national politics.

STATE POLICYMAKING

Economic Factors

Public policymaking is affected by a variety of factors operating outside the formal structure of state and local governments. A state's economic characteristics—including levels of urbanization, personal income, and education—influence political decision making as well as the nature of political participation and party competition.[7]

One example of the effects of economic factors on policymaking is in funding for education. Wealthy, urbanized states, such as Massachusetts, New Jersey, and New York, spend considerably more per capita on education than do less prosperous states. While wealthy states can obviously afford to spend more money per capita on social services than can poor states, their willingness to spend should be differentiated from their ability to spend. In education, some relatively poor states, such as Maine and Vermont, make a stronger effort to assist their schools than do some rich states (i.e., their educational spending as a proportion of personal income is greater than that of wealthier states). Yet poor states, particularly in the South, are still unable to match the per pupil expenditure of wealthier states, such as Delaware and Connecticut, where the tax effort (or burden) is significantly less. The term *tax burden* refers to taxes as a percentage of personal income; it expresses a relation between total taxes and total income in a state. The tax burden is lower than the national average in Connecticut because personal income is high while tax rates are relatively low.

The willingness to spend money is often tied to such political factors as the role of political parties, the influence of public opinion, and the leadership of the governor. These political factors operate at the margins of decision making and help to explain why differences in spending levels exist among rich states and why some poor states make substantially greater efforts than other poor states.[8] As we will see later in this chapter, willingness to spend money is also related to political culture and state tradition.

As far as political participation is concerned, party competition is usually stronger in the more wealthy, urbanized states, and voter turnout tends to be higher in those states as well. A few interest groups are more likely to dominate government in poor states, such as South Carolina and West Virginia, while in wealthier states a variety of interest groups tend to balance one another. The economically well-developed states have also been the most likely to adopt new policy ideas. Although there are many exceptions to economic explanations (see the two sections that follow), they do provide us with one of several useful approaches to understanding state politics.

Physical Setting

In a country as diverse as the United States, the physical environment affects the decisions of the state governments in many ways. Large states, such as Wyoming and Montana, often spend significantly more per capita to maintain their highways than do smaller states, such as Maryland and Massachusetts. In addition, the presence of natural resources may affect state policies significantly. Oil and natural gas interests have had a major impact on government in Oklahoma and Texas. For most of this century the Anaconda Company (copper) was the dominant political force in Montana. Unable to comply with new environmental standards in the 1970s, Anaconda ended all mining operations in Montana.[9] The distribution of water rights has had a tremendous influence on politics in such Western states as Arizona and California. Water shortage is a permanent circumstance in Los Angeles, where the annual rainfall is a scant 9 inches.

Farms and cities from Salt Lake City to San Diego are literally drinking the Colorado River dry. The existence of such geographical features as mountains, deserts, and lakes within a state may cause special problems and influence the allocation of state resources. Historically, physical features influenced the flow of migration and helped shape political institutions. For example, Utah is one of the most geographically isolated states, and Mormons chose to settle there largely for that reason.

Consider some of the physical features of California—features that subject its political decision makers to contrasting pressures from interest groups as well as force them to acquire knowledge about a wide array of technical matters. The state stretches for 650 miles, from the Mexican border to the Oregon state line. The Sierra Nevada Mountains extend for about 400 miles along the eastern border of the state. Temperatures range from harsh cold and deep snow in the High Sierras to unbearable heat in Death Valley. While northern California has ample water, southern California must import its water. The same state that has produced the Los Angeles freeway system also has the agriculturally rich Central Valley. The annual net farm income in California is nearly equal to the combined farm incomes of Iowa and Nebraska.

California is so physically and culturally diverse that a proposal has been made by a state legislator to divide it into three states—North, Central, and South.[10] Those who support division argue that the state is too large to be governed efficiently and that its residents are grossly underrepresented in the U.S. Senate. In addition, each state senator in California currently represents more people than do U.S. representatives. Under the U.S. Constitution, a state can be divided if its legislature and Congress agree. Historically, Vermont, Maine, Massachusetts, and Kentucky were carved out of existing states. Because Texas was an independent nation when it was annexed to the United States, it was given the right to divide itself into as many as five states.

Population size and the presence of large metropolitan areas also have important effects on state politics. In the mid-1970s, the financial problems of New York City threatened the fiscal stability of New York State and involved the governor in extended negotiations with private bankers and the federal government to help "save" New York City. In the 1990s the state's budget deficit has led to cuts for projects in New York City. City dwellers demand more services—health care, welfare, sanitation, recreation, slum clearance, public housing—than do residents of small towns. These demands are transmitted to state legislative and gubernatorial candidates, who cannot ignore city voters as they campaign for office. In New York, Illinois, Pennsylvania, and Michigan, to name a few, serious conflicts between major cities and the rest of the state have long existed within state government.

Due largely to their geographical location, several states have large immigrant populations that, they contend, place unfair financial burdens on them. About 85 percent of the nation's estimated 4 million illegal immigrants live in seven states—California, New York, Texas, Florida, Illinois, New Jersey, and Arizona. About 20 percent of all immigrants in the United States live in Los Angeles County and four surrounding counties, and one of four people in those five counties is foreign-born. Although many cross the 1,950-mile border with Mexico, nearly an equal number of immigrants arrive by air. More than 18 million *legal* immigrants came to the United States between 1965 and 1995. This was triple the number admitted in the previous thirty years.

While some contend that states overestimate the cost of illegal immigrants, a 1994 study by the Urban Institute showed that illegal immigrants cost states more than they contribute in taxes. Several states have sued the federal government to recover some of the costs of immigrants, and the politics of limiting immigration has become a major issue in California and Florida (see the reading by Neal R. Peirce that follows). In 1994 Californians overwhelmingly approved Proposition 187, which bars illegal aliens from receiving welfare, education, and nonemergency health services. An immediate legal challenge blocked its implementation, and it is expected to be tied up in the courts for several years. While Hispanics made up 25 percent of California's population in 1994, they constituted only about 8 percent of those voting on Proposition 187. In the mid-1990s there were an estimated 1.6 million illegal aliens in California and about 400,000 each in Florida and Texas. The Census Bureau projects that the percentage of Hispanics in the United States will increase from 9 percent in 1990 to 23 percent in 2050. As concern about immigrants has grown, nearly half the states have passed legislation declaring English the sole language of government.

Political Culture

While explanations based on economics and physical characteristics are helpful in understanding state politics, there remain a significant number of exceptions to the rule. Economic conditions do not explain the high levels of voter turnout in Montana, Idaho, Wyoming, and Utah, where levels of income and urbanization are below the national average. Some states with low levels of personal income, such as Louisiana and Oklahoma, provide surprisingly high welfare benefits. In contrast, while Nevada ranked ninth in per capita personal income in 1993, it ranked thirtieth in per pupil expenditure for education. In the next section, we will note some of the vast differences that exist even among states within the same geographical area.

Sometimes states that have similar economic and demographic characteristics are very different politically. A case in point is the adjacent states of Michigan and Ohio. They are alike in terms of population, industrialization, and urbanization. Both have many small towns and rich farmland. In both states, there is a high level of party competition. In both, organized labor is a strong political force. Yet Michigan has been a much more progressive state than Ohio. It has allocated proportionately greater expenditures for social welfare services, and it has experienced significantly less corruption in government. In Ohio, on the other hand, the **spoils system,** where political parties give public jobs to their supporters, has persisted and the political parties have avoided dealing with the issue.

Another example is the neighboring states of Vermont and New Hampshire. Both are small and predominantly rural. Yet Vermont, the poorer of the two states, ranks among the highest in terms of tax burden, while New Hampshire ranks among the lowest. Vermont has been a center of public-spirited activism, while New Hampshire is characterized as a stronghold of stingy government. Much of the reason for these differences appears to lie in the political cultures of the two states.

Political culture is defined by Daniel Elazar as "the particular pattern of orientation to political action in which each political system is embedded." Elazar notes that

The Ugly—but Inevitable—Debate

Neal R. Peirce

The political and press reaction ranged from skeptical to hostile when Republican Gov. Pete Wilson of California last summer took up the immigration issue, demanding that the federal government reimburse his state for the billions it's spending on services for illegal immigrants.

Wilson, the critics said, was desperately reaching for an issue to boost his dismal 13 per cent approval rating, brought on by California's deep recession and massive tax increases on his watch.

Wilson also had to face the suspicion of veiled racism that arises any time an Anglo politician starts blaming a big chunk of a state's ills on people of color.

Yet whatever Wilson's motives, he touched off a political chain reaction with implications both for immigration policy and for federal relations between Washington and the states.

Wilson started with a political demand that Washington pay the $3.1 billion that California says it will be spending this year to cover its costs for the education, health care and incarceration of illegal immigrants.

But Wilson is going further. He's also filing a series of lawsuits against the federal government in an effort to recover various costs California has incurred over the years because of Washington's failure to stop a flow of millions of illegal immigrants, most of them by way of illegal penetration across California's border with Mexico.

One of the lawsuits argues that California's inherent sovereignty and viability are threatened when federal inaction on the immigration front forces the state to raise billions of dollars a year to pay the costs. Such a huge unfunded mandate pressed down on the state, the suit says, turns the Constitution into "a suicide pact."

And now Wilson isn't nearly the loner on the immigration issue that he seemed to be last summer. Another Republican governor—J. Fife Symington III of Arizona—has also filed suit against the federal government. Arizona's action argues that the state could have been spared two new prisons if it weren't obliged to incarcerate 1,760 undocumented immigrant felons.

But any partisan tinge to the issue faded perceptibly on April 12 when Democratic Gov. Lawton Chiles of Florida filed his state's suit against the federal government. "Federal immigration policy," he said, "has created a nightmare for state and local government in Florida."

Chiles wants Washington to compensate Florida for the $1.5 billion the state expects to spend over the next two years to educate, imprison and provide health care for about 350,000 undocumented immigrants.

In late May, Gov. Ann W. Richards of Texas, another Democrat, joined the push for federal reimbursement. Texas plans legal action along the same lines, demanding reimbursement for the education, health care and imprisonment costs of illegal immigrants.

"The federal government has really got two choices," Richards said. "One is to enforce the immigration laws. The other is to pay for the costs if they don't."

Now the press for remedial federal action is being taken up by one of America's strongest champions of immigrants and their rights: Democratic Gov. Mario M. Cuomo of New York. Cuomo considered but rejected the idea of suing the federal government, even though he'd previously complained about the estimated $1 billion yearly cost that undocumented immigrants impose on his state. Cuomo said that he'd negotiate with the Clinton Administration for reimbursement.

Illinois has also chosen to lobby—not sue—Washington for more aid, though New Jersey may join Florida's suit.

Look at the demographic charts and it's easy to see why the pressure for action is mounting so rapidly in these states. California, Florida, Illinois, New York and Texas are home to 85 per cent of the nation's estimated 3.2 million illegal immigrants.

The Clinton Administration has now mounted a more aggressive border control program, especially along the U.S.-Mexican border, which may reflect the fact that the five states represent, together, a massive block of 166 electoral votes.

These days, there's increased talk in Washington of compensating states more for the bills they must foot because of illegal immigration. But assuming that border enforcement remains as haphazard as it is today, federal outlays of the order required to cover the states' full costs—in the many billions of dollars—are doubtful.

And so the likeliest result of the political chain reaction that Wilson set off may be much tougher border controls than this immigrant-founded nation—at least until now—has been willing to enforce.

The terms of the immigration debate are clearly shifting. We may not like the idea of high fences, klieg lights and semimilitary action along our borders. But the costs of porous borders, the idea that the United States can be an all-purpose escape valve for the Americas, and to some degree Asia, is finally coming into focus.

"We're moving into the first major national immigration debate in over 100 years," said Dan Stein of the Washington-based Federation for American Immigration Reform. "Most people are going to have to bloom where they're planted."

The sad fact is that by blindfolding itself to illegal immigration for so long, the United States invited today's fiscal standoff and crisis in federalism. Unfortunately, the debate will provide an opportunity for a lot of racist rhetoric to flourish.

Yet today's flow of illegal immigration is simply too great to ignore, the nation's wealth too limited to handle the consequences. A former official of the Immigration and Naturalization Service exaggerated—but not too greatly—when he suggested that the United States can "no longer educate, medicate, incarcerate and compensate all the illegals of the world."

Source: National Journal, July 16, 1994, p. 1700. Reprinted with permission of National Journal.

"the study of political culture is related to the study of culture as a whole."[11] Culture refers to a "way of life": It is learned behavior based on communication within a society. Political culture, says Elazar, sets limits on political behavior and provides subtle direction for political action. In the following analysis, political culture is understood to encompass political tradition and the rules governing political behavior. For students of state government, political culture helps explain differences in political attitudes and government concerns from state to state. In large part, political culture determines what policies can be expected from state government, the kinds of people who become active in political affairs, and the way in which the political game is played in particular states and their communities.

Each state has its own history and tradition, and this is reflected in differences in its population's concerns and attitudes toward political life. In many states, differences among nationalities are important to understanding politics. For example, Irish Catholics in Massachusetts and Jews in New York have played major roles in forming distinctive patterns of political participation in those states. The Civil War and Reconstruction left a lasting mark on the political systems of Southern and border states. The **Progressive movement** early in this century had a major impact on the political processes in Wisconsin, Minnesota, and the Dakotas. In particular, Progressivism created an intense distrust of party organizations and reliance on widespread citizen participation. Alaska and Hawaii have truly unique histories and cultures because of their geographical isolation and their mixtures of racial and ethnic groups. While residents of some states have a strong sense of identity with their state, it has been suggested that the dominant fact of political life in New Jersey is that residents do not and never did identify with their state.[13]

Elazar identifies three political cultures that can be found throughout the United States—**individualistic, traditional,** and **moralistic.**[14] These cultures have their roots in the three geographic regions of colonial America. The individualistic culture (I) developed in the business centers of New York, Philadelphia, and Baltimore; the traditional culture (T) developed in the plantation society of the Old South; and the moralistic culture (M) arose out of the tradition of Puritanism and town meetings in New England. As waves of settlers moved westward, these three cultures spread throughout the United States. In many instances, two or three cultures met, meshed together, and produced a variety of state and sectional cultural strains. In Illinois, Indiana, and Ohio, this mixing of political cultures produced complex politics and caused conflicts that have persisted over decades. The Scholarly Box that follows explains Daniel Elazar's concept of "the geology of political culture." This concept helps us understand the way in which political cultures have spread across the United States.

Politics in the three political cultures can be described with respect to (1) degree of political participation, (2) development of government bureaucracy, and (3) amount of government intervention in society. Of the three dimensions, degree of political participation (i.e., voter turnout and suffrage regulations) is the most consistent indicator of political culture. In individualistic political cultures, participation is limited because politics is viewed as just another means by which individuals may improve their economic and social position. Because corruption is accepted as a natural part of politics, its disclosure is unlikely to produce public protest. In moralistic cultures, political participation is regarded as the duty of each citizen in a political setting where government seeks to promote the public welfare of all persons. In traditional cultures, voter turnout is low and voting regulations are restrictive. Here government is controlled by an elite whose family and social position give it a "right" to govern. In many cases citizens are not even expected to vote. Corruption tends to be even more widespread in traditional than in individualistic states. This is so because politics is not oriented toward the **public interest,** and it is expected that payoffs will occur.

In traditionalistic South Carolina a very strong legislature developed, controlled by a few political leaders working with the state's two dominant business interests. *The State,* Columbia's newspaper, noted in 1991 that "through most of South Carolina's history, the people who set up and ran state government have had two main priorities: Keeping power out of the hands of black people. Keeping power out of the hands of everybody else."[15] As late as the 1940s, less than 10 percent of the eligible voters voted in presidential elections. The political culture of South Carolina is blamed for a scandal in which fifteen state legislators were indicted in 1991 for taking bribes from undercover FBI agents.

In regard to the development of government bureaucracy, individualistic cultures limit government functions and provide only those few basic services demanded by the public. While bureaucracy is distrusted because of its potential to encroach on private matters, it is often used to advance the personal goals of public officials. In moralistic cultures, bureaucracy typically is permitted to expand to provide the public with the wide range of services it demands. Here government commitment to the public good, honesty, and selflessness leads to low levels of corruption. Traditional cultures tend to be antibureaucratic, because a professional bureaucracy would interfere with the established pattern of personal relations developed by politicians.

In regard to government intervention into community affairs, both individualistic and traditional political cultures strive to protect private activities by limiting government intrusions. Government action in the individualistic political culture is largely limited to encouraging private economic initiative. In traditionalistic cultures government's role is limited to maintaining the existing social order. The moralistic culture, in contrast, fosters a definite commitment to government intervention; government is viewed as a positive force. Still, those who represent the moralistic political culture may oppose federal aid to some local projects because they favor community responsibility for local problem solving. **Communitarianism** (communal activism) often results in innovative new approaches to problems that may not be perceived by the general population. The moralistic political culture also differs from the other two cultures in that its political campaigns are marked by an emphasis on issues rather than personalities. Parties and interest groups are organized to direct policy in the public interest.

Each culture has made both positive and negative contributions. Elazar notes that the moralistic culture, although it has been a significant force in the American quest for the good society, tends toward fanaticism and narrow-mindedness—roughly parallel to groups that claim to have found the "true religion." In spite of widespread corruption, the individualistic culture of the Northeast and many large Midwestern cities did facilitate the assimilation of immigrant groups into American society. Moreover, some corruption occurs in all states and it does not necessarily affect the delivery of public services. Although the predominant traditional culture in the South has helped sustain racial discrimination and second-rate demagogues, it has also produced a significant number of first-rate national leaders and effective governors.

Elazar's groundbreaking theory has helped explain variations in public policy and political behavior. As we would expect, his typology has been subjected to a wide variety of tests. Critics have noted that Elazar has never adjusted the mapping of his three

SCHOLARLY BOX

THE "GEOLOGY" OF POLITICAL CULTURE

Political scientist Daniel Elazar uses the concept of cultural "geology" to illustrate how the three political subcultures (moralistic, traditionalistic, and individualistic) spread across the United States and subsequently were modified by local conditions.* In Elazar's descriptive words, as great streams of immigrants moved west and stopped in various places, they deposited their relatively clear-cut political cultures. In many cases, other populations stopped in the same locations and deposited their cultures. Sometimes these "deposits" were side by side, in other cases they were on top of each other, and in some cases they overlapped. Over time, external events, such as economic depressions, eroded these cultural traditions, or they may have modified or strengthened them. At any rate, the result was something like strata in exposed rock that's been blasted out for an interstate highway—a look into the past and present.

Elazar describes historic migration patterns from each of three regions along the East Coast. Puritans moved across New York and established a kind of greater New England in Michigan, Wisconsin, Minnesota, and Iowa, where the moralistic culture was deposited. Then they moved on to Oregon, Washington, and northern California. As Mormons, moralists settled Utah, and as abolitionists, they settled Kansas. Immigrants from the Middle Atlantic states moved across Pennsylvania and deposited their individualistic culture in parts of Ohio, Indiana, Illinois, and Missouri. They joined the gold rush to California and later settled areas along the Union Pacific railroad in the Great Plains. Southern migration went to Alabama and Mississippi and to the southern parts of Ohio and Illinois and on to Missouri. The traditionalist culture then spread through Texas, and across the southwest to central California.

Along the way various cultural mixes occurred. For example, moralistic Scotch-Irish emigrants were deflected south from Pennsylvania by the Appalachian Mountains where they settled in isolated southern mountain areas, such as the western Carolinas, and developed a special synthesis of traditional and moralistic culture. The Rocky Mountains also blocked direct migration, forcing migrants from all three cultures into valleys from Montana to Arizona. From 1818 to 1861 all three subcultures moved into Illinois, making it a microcosm of the entire United States as political cultures were layered on top of and adjacent to each other. The later arrival in Illinois of urban immigrants from Ireland, Italy, and Eastern Europe helped tip the overall state balance in favor of the individualist political culture.

Well-defined cultural patterns were established in California by the turn of the twentieth century. Yankee moralists settled in the south, Mid-Atlantic individualists moved to northern California, and central California attracted many southerners.

Present-day California illustrates the fact that recent migration has not followed a simple east to west path. Large numbers of Hispanics moved to southern California after World War II, and since the 1970s Asians have settled throughout the state. Asians have been more likely to live in northern California and join the individualist culture, while Hispanics have settled in areas influenced by the traditionalistic culture. In these cases, immigrants have reinforced existing cultural patterns, rather than bringing significant change with them.

The most pronounced break in the pattern of east to west migration has involved the North and South. Immediately after World War II large numbers of southern blacks moved north. This pattern soon was followed by the movement of white northerners to the South. At the same time, people across the country have been moving from central cities to suburbs.

Elazar points out that politicians in areas with changing cultures may have difficulty adjusting to their new circumstances. In particular, the change from individualistic to moralistic creates new standards of behavior for older politicians. Assimilation from one culture to another has been a reoccurring phenomena throughout American history, and it is this mosaic of cultural patterns that has defined American politics at any given point in time.

*See Daniel J. Elazar, *American Federalism: A View from the States,* 3d ed. (New York: Harper & Row, 1984), pp. 122–141; and Elazar, *The American Mosaic* (Boulder, Colo.: Westview Press, 1994), pp. 237–252.

subcultures, that what constitutes each subculture is a subjective judgment, and that his scheme relies on past behavior to predict current political behavior.[16]

As we have noted, political culture has been found to have a strong impact on political participation: It's higher in moralistic states. Moralistic states also are more likely to support social programs that are generous to the poor, and public officials in those states are less corrupt than in traditionalistic and individualistic states. While there is independent evidence linking political culture with policymaking and citizen participation, other factors that we explain in this chapter—economic factors, physical setting, and sectionalism—also affect state politics. Often it is difficult to isolate the impact of any one factor. Since economic factors are easier to quantify (that is, we have lots of economic data to examine), political culture often is used to explain state political behavior when social or economic factors are inadequate.

There is some evidence to suggest that distinctive state and local cultures are weakening because of population mobility, especially in the **Sunbelt** states—the fifteen states extending from southern California through Arizona, Texas, Florida and up the Atlantic coast to Virginia. The change has arisen because of the growing importance of the news media, especially television, nationwide and because federal grants have encouraged states to enact a variety of programs under which they can receive matching funds.

Sectionalism

States that are located adjacent to each other tend to share some persistent political similarities. States within particular areas, sharing a common cultural, economic, and historical background, exhibit clearly identifiable political tendencies. This is known as **sectionalism.** Major sections as defined by the U.S. Bureau of the Census are the Northeast, the North Central states, the South, and the West. Within each section we can identify several regions, such as the Southwest (West) and the Middle Atlantic (Northeast). The component states of the various sections and regions define problems and formulate public policy in a similar manner.

The *South,* which includes the eleven former Confederate states plus the border states of West Virginia, Kentucky, Delaware, Oklahoma, and Maryland, has long been the most clearly identifiable section of America. Throughout most of the South, there is widespread poverty, levels of educational attainment are generally low, and government functions are centralized at the state level. In the South, state governments often perform many of the government functions typically carried out by cities and counties in other sections of the country. As in other sections, it often is difficult to tell whether policy is influenced more by geographic location or by economic factors. Moreover, as in other sections, major exceptions to the general rule can be identified. For example, West Virginia has had a high level of interparty competition; considerable wealth exists in parts of Texas, Virginia, and Florida; and politics in Atlanta is vastly different from politics in Yazoo County, Mississippi.

From the Civil War until after World War II, the South remained solidly Democratic. Southern states began to vote for Republican presidential candidates in the 1950s and steadily elected more Republican governors, state legislators, and U.S. Congress members during the next three decades. In 1994, Republicans won a majority of U.S. House and Senate seats in the South, and they won elections in three southern states that had had Democratic governors. Republicans also made unprecedented gains in southern state legislatures in 1994. Although the South has undergone dramatic political and social change, "the Southern way of life" continues to bind southerners, black and white, together. Despite great urban growth, traditional courthouse politics in small town county seats continues to characterize the South more than any other section of the country.[17]

In the *Northeast* (the six New England states plus the Middle Atlantic states of New York, Pennsylvania, and New Jersey), most states share problems of congestion and industrialization. Levels of party competition and voter turnout are comparatively high. There is an emphasis on local government decision making stemming from the New England tradition of town meetings. As a result, government functions are much less centralized than in the South. On a regional basis, Boston continues to be the economic and educational hub of New England, while New York City dominates the Middle Atlantic states in terms of culture and business. In many Northeastern states a substantial number of children attend parochial schools. Yet major differences exist between the northern Northeastern states, which have been predominantly rural and Protestant (Maine, New Hampshire, and Vermont), and the southern Northeastern states, which have been predominantly urban and Catholic (Rhode Island, New York, Connecticut, Massachusetts, Pennsylvania, and New Jersey). There is a great contrast between the wealth of suburban Connecticut and the poverty of rural Maine and Vermont. Without military installations or large public works projects, Northeastern states lack a highly visible federal presence.

The eleven states of the *West* (including the Rocky Mountain, Desert, and Pacific Coast states), which comprise nearly 60 percent of the land mass of the continental United States, share problems of natural resource development, population diffusion, and water distribution. Most Western states have relied heavily on resource extraction with little economic diversity. This has produced a history of boom-or-bust economic cycles. Despite their political conservatism and dislike of the federal government, the Western states have depended heavily on federal aid, and government is the major employer in several of these states.[18] In eleven of the Western states, the federal government owns at least 28 percent of the land. The federal government owns 83 percent of the land in Nevada and 45 percent in California. As noted earlier, there is great geographical diversity in just one state, such as California, and there are vast cultural differences between residents of San Francisco and Salt Lake City. Thus, as with other sections of the country, we need to be careful about stereotyping the West. While there have been great population increases in metropolitan areas, such as Los Angeles, Las Vegas, Phoenix, and Seattle, other parts of the West have experienced population decline in the last twenty years. For example, Wyoming lost 3.4 percent of its population in the 1980s and became the nation's least populous state.

Typically, the Western states are marked by high levels of voter turnout and relatively weak party organizations. While Democratic-Republican competition is keen in state elections, these states have been strongly Republican in presidential elections. In the 1968 and 1972 presidential elections, Richard Nixon carried every Western state (except Washington in 1968). In 1976, Gerald Ford lost only Texas and Hawaii among all states west of Minnesota. In 1980 and 1984, Ronald Reagan carried all the Western states. And, in 1988, George Bush carried all the Western states except Washington and Oregon. In 1992, Bill Clinton won seven of the eleven Rocky Mountain and Pacific Coast states.

The *North Central* (Great Lakes and Great Plains) states each have a blend of agricultural, industrial, and urban areas. There is strong two-party competition and above-average wealth, particularly in the Great Lakes states. However, the twelve North Central states are the least homogeneous of the four sections. Because the North Central section borders on each of the other three sections, some of its regional areas share the characteristics found in other sections. As with the other sections, there are major internal contradictions. While politics in Indiana, Ohio, and Missouri often has centered on patronage, jobs, and personalities (a reflection of their Southern heritage), politics in Minnesota, Wisconsin, and Michigan has been issue-oriented and government has been essentially corruption-free.[19]

The Great Plains region includes parts of ten West and North Central states. It is where rainfall begins to stop and the tall grasses of the prairies become shorter. This area, with very hot summers and cold winters, has been called the Empty Quarter. While the overall Great Plains population has been slowly increasing, the rural population of the region has declined more than 15 percent since 1930.[20] Parts of the area are so desolate that some geographers have proposed that the remaining residents be removed and the federal government create a wildlife park called Buffalo Commons.

POPULATION SHIFTS AMONG SECTIONS

Americans are a highly mobile people, and movement from the cities to the suburbs and from one region to another has added a dynamic dimension to state politics. As of 1990, about 77 percent of Americans lived in metropolitan areas. There were a total of 284 **metropolitan statistical areas** (MSAs) in the United States in 1990. As defined by the Census Bureau since 1983, a county may qualify as an MSA if it contains a city of at least 50,000 population or if it contains an urbanized area of 50,000 or more population and a total metropolitan population of 100,000 or more. An MSA can be one county or group of counties. There is at least one MSA in every state. That the United States is becoming increasingly metropolitan can be seen in statistics showing that 56 percent of the population in 1950 lived in metropolitan areas and nearly 90 percent of the nation's population growth in the 1980s occurred in the thirty-nine largest metropolitan areas.

The density, heterogeneity, and interdependence of urban life have created obvious political problems in the areas of health, housing, and crime. The spread of the suburbs (in extreme cases creating vast, sprawling developments—as along the East Coast, southern California, and southern Lake Michigan) has fragmented government and made metropolitan planning and coordination extremely difficult. There are thirty-nine MSAs that have more than 1 million population and two with populations that exceed 10 million (see Table 1-1). Areas with more than 1 million residents are called consolidated metropolitan statistical areas. New Jersey is completely within MSAs and seven

TABLE 1-1 THE FORTY LARGEST METROPOLITAN AREAS, 1990

Metropolitan area	Total population (1,000)	Percent of total metropolitan population	
		Black	Hispanic origin
New York-Northern New Jersey-Long Island, NY-NJ-CT CMSA	18,087	18.2	15.4
Los Angeles-Anaheim-Riverside, CA CMSA	14,532	8.5	32.9
Chicago-Gary-Lake County (IL), IL-IN-WI CMSA	8,066	19.2	11.1
San Francisco-Oakland-San Jose, CA CMSA	6,253	8.6	15.5
Philadelphia-Wilmington-Trenton, PA-NJ-DE-MD CMSA	5,899	18.7	3.8
Detroit-Ann Arbor, MI CMSA	4,665	20.9	1.9
Boston-Lawrence-Salem, MA-NH CMSA	4,172	5.7	4.6
Washington, DC-MD-VA MSA	3,924	26.6	5.7
Dallas-Fort Worth, TX CMSA	3,885	14.3	13.4
Houston-Galveston-Brazoria, TX CMSA	3,711	17.9	20.8
Miami-Fort Lauderdale, FL CMSA	3,193	18.5	33.3
Atlanta, GA MSA	2,834	26.0	2.0
Cleveland-Akron-Lorain, OH CMSA	2,760	16.0	1.9
Seattle-Tacoma, WA CMSA	2,559	4.8	3.0
San Diego, CA MSA	2,498	6.4	20.4
Minneapolis-St. Paul, MN-WI MSA	2,464	3.6	1.5
St. Louis, MO-IL MSA	2,444	17.3	1.1
Baltimore, MD MSA	2,382	25.9	1.3
Pittsburgh-Beaver Valley, PA CMSA	2,243	8.0	0.6
Phoenix, AZ MSA	2,122	3.5	16.3
Tampa-St. Petersburg-Clearwater, FL MSA	2,068	9.0	6.7
Denver-Boulder, CO CMSA	1,848	5.3	12.2
Cincinnati-Hamilton, OH-KY-IN CMSA	1,744	11.7	0.5
Milwaukee-Racine, WI CMSA	1,607	13.3	3.8
Kansas City, MO-KS MSA	1,566	12.8	2.9
Sacramento, CA MSA	1,481	6.9	11.6
Portland-Vancouver, OR-WA CMSA	1,478	2.8	3.4
Norfolk-Virginia Beach-Newport News, VA MSA	1,396	28.5	2.3
Columbus, OH MSA	1,377	12.0	0.8
San Antonio, TX MSA	1,302	6.8	47.6
Indianapolis, IN MSA	1,250	13.8	0.9
New Orleans, LA MSA	1,239	34.7	4.3
Buffalo-Niagara Falls, NY CMSA	1,189	10.3	2.0
Charlotte-Gastonia-Rock Hill, NC-SC MSA	1,162	19.9	0.9
Providence-Pawtucket-Fall River, RI-MA CMSA	1,142	3.3	4.2
Hartford-New Britain-Middletown, CT CMSA	1,086	8.7	7.0
Orlando, FL MSA	1,073	12.4	9.0
Salt Lake City-Ogden, UT MSA	1,072	1.0	5.8
Rochester, NY MSA	1,002	9.4	3.1
Nashville, TN MSA	985	15.5	0.8

Source: U.S. Census Bureau.

other states are over 90 percent metropolitan. The increasing metropolitanization of our population masks the fact that Americans in this century have become less likely to live in large cities. For example, the percentage of our population living in cities over 1 million peaked in 1930. Currently a smaller percentage of people live in cities over 1 million than was the case in 1900. Curiously, more people in 1991 lived in towns with less than 10,000 population than lived in all cities with 500,000 or more people (see Figure 1-1). Another 66 million Americans (27 percent) lived outside the boundaries of incorporated or census-designated places. The least metropolitan state is Idaho (about 20 percent), followed by Vermont and Montana.

Particularly during the 1950s and 1960s, great numbers of lower-income Southern blacks and Appalachian whites moved into Northern cities such as Chicago, Detroit, and New York, greatly compounding the financial problems of those city governments. In the 1980s there was a large increase in the number of Asians and Hispanics in many American cities. For example, New York City's Hispanic population increased by 29 percent in the 1980s, and nearly 1,400 immigrants arrive each month in New York's Chinatown, the largest Chinese community in the Western Hemisphere. The INS estimates that 100,000 Chinese are smuggled into the country each year. At the same time, there has been an exodus of upper- and middle-class whites and of industries to the suburbs. Thus while the costs of public services multiplied, the tax base of many cities declined substantially. Currently, more than 80 percent of blacks and persons of Spanish origin live in MSAs.

FIGURE 1-1 Population in places by size of place, 1991 (includes incorporated and census designated places). [Reprinted with permission: George E. Hall and Courtenay M. Slater, *Places, Towns and Townships,* Lanham, Md.: Bernan Press, 1993 (copyright).]

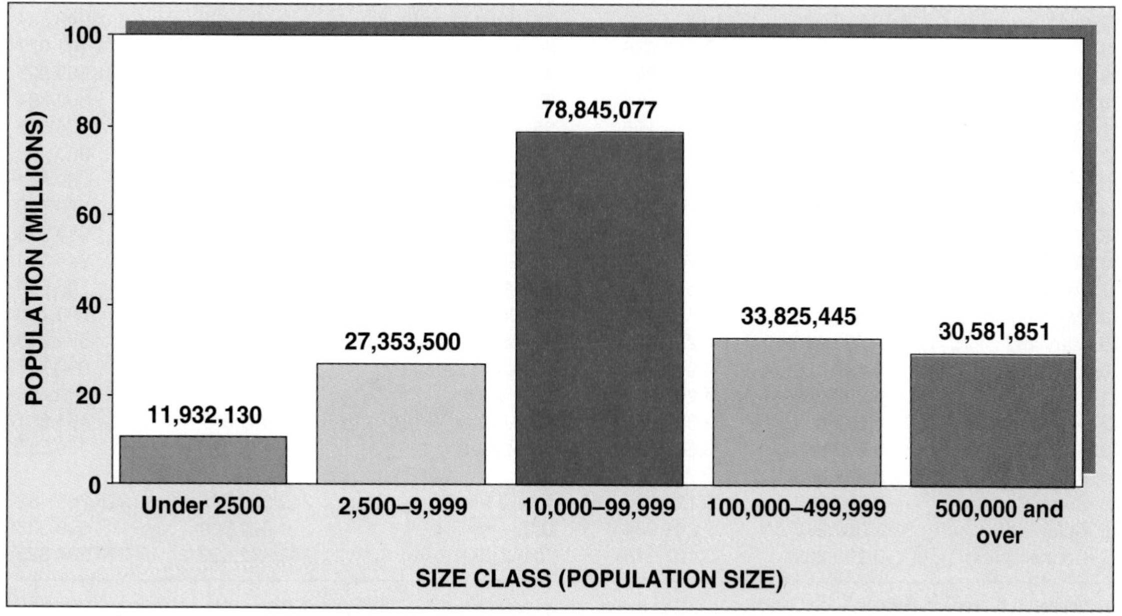

GROWTH IN THE SUNBELT

In 1976, the Census Bureau reported for the first time that a majority of the United States population lived in the South and the West. The growth in these states has been accompanied by a variety of political and economic problems. As in the 1970s, Nevada was the fastest-growing state in the 1980s (49 percent). It was followed in order by Arizona, Florida, California, Texas, and Utah, all up at least 18 percent. About 50 percent of the nation's population increase occurred in three states—California, Florida, and Texas. While only one state (Rhode Island) lost population in the 1970s, nine states, led by West Virginia (down 8.6 percent), lost population in the 1980s (see Table 1-2).

From 1940 through 1990, the population of Houston grew from 385,000 to 1,631,000; that of Phoenix from 65,000 to 968,400. San Diego gained 900,000 people, San Jose 714,000, and San Antonio 682,000. In that same period Chicago lost 714,000 people, Cleveland lost 373,000, and St. Louis lost over one-half its population (420,000). Virtually all the fastest-growing cities in the 1980s were mid-sized suburbs,

TABLE 1-2 STATE POPULATION CHANGES, 1990

Rank and state	1990	1980	Rank and state	1990	1980
1 California	29,839,250	23,667,902	**28** Oklahoma	3,157,604	3,025,290
2 New York	18,044,505	17,558,072	**29** Oregon	2,853,733	2,633,105
3 Texas	17,059,805	14,229,191	**30** Iowa	2,787,424	2,913,808
4 Florida	13,003,362	9,746,324	**31** Mississippi	2,586,443	2,520,638
5 Pennsylvania	11,924,710	11,863,895	**32** Kansas	2,485,600	2,363,679
6 Illinois	11,466,682	11,426,518	**33** Arkansas	2,362,239	2,286,435
7 Ohio	10,887,325	10,797,630	**34** West Virginia	1,801,625	1,949,644
8 Michigan	9,328,784	9,262,078	**35** Utah	1,727,784	1,461,037
9 New Jersey	7,748,634	7,364,823	**36** Nebraska	1,584,617	1,569,825
10 North Carolina	6,657,630	5,881,766	**37** New Mexico	1,521,779	1,302,894
11 Georgia	6,508,419	5,463,105	**38** Maine	1,233,223	1,124,660
12 Virginia	6,216,568	5,346,818	**39** Nevada	1,206,152	800,493
13 Massachusetts	6,029,051	5,737,037	**40** Hawaii	1,115,274	964,691
14 Indiana	5,564,228	5,490,224	**41** New Hampshire	1,113,915	920,610
15 Missouri	5,137,804	4,916,686	**42** Idaho	1,011,986	943,935
16 Wisconsin	4,906,745	4,705,767	**43** Rhode Island	1,005,984	947,154
17 Tennessee	4,896,641	4,591,120	**44** Montana	803,655	786,690
18 Washington	4,887,941	4,132,156	**45** South Dakota	699,999	690,768
19 Maryland	4,798,622	4,216,975	**46** Delaware	668,696	594,338
20 Minnesota	4,387,029	4,075,970	**47** North Dakota	641,364	652,717
21 Louisiana	4,238,216	4,205,900	**48** Vermont	564,964	511,456
22 Alabama	4,062,608	3,893,888	**49** Alaska	551,947	401,851
23 Kentucky	3,698,969	3,660,777	**50** Wyoming	455,975	469,557
24 Arizona	3,677,985	2,718,215			
25 South Carolina	3,505,707	3,121,820	Total states	249,022,783	225,866,492
26 Colorado	3,307,912	2,889,964	D.C.	609,909	638,333
27 Connecticut	3,295,669	3,107,576	Total U.S.	249,632,692	226,504,825

Source: U.S. Census Bureau.

close to interstate highways, and located in the Sunbelt. Of the twenty fastest-growing cities, eleven were in California (see Table 1-3). Curiously, several large Sunbelt cities, such as New Orleans, Louisville, Atlanta, and Memphis, lost population—because of either a downturn in the local economy (New Orleans) or a movement to the suburbs (Atlanta). Previously booming Denver lost 5 percent of its population in the 1980s (see Table 1-4). Population growth was especially strong in state capitals and in university towns across the country in the 1980s. Sunbelt state capitals with large state universities, such as Austin and Tallahassee, had especially strong growth. In many cases, state government generates jobs and helps the economy of an entire metropolitan area. In several instances, urban public universities have spurred economic growth and have become community social leaders. For example, the University of Alabama at Birmingham is the largest employer in the state and has about a $1 billion annual impact on the region.

A controversial issue with the U.S. Census is the undercount and adjustment of population figures. Census takers missed about 5 million Americans in 1990, and they missed black and Hispanic men at more than twice the national rate. This has major significance for cities such as Los Angeles and San Antonio, where minorities comprise a majority of the population and where the census count missed 3 to 5 percent of the population. Population adjustment would help cities gain seats in state legislatures and give them more federal and state aid. However, Secretary of Commerce Robert A. Mosbacher decided *not* to adjust the 1990 census. He argued that adjusted figures would be increasingly unreliable for smaller communities and would increase cynicism about government by suggesting that the census process could be manipulated by statisticians in Washington. In 1996 the Supreme Court ruled against adjusting the 1990 census to make up about 5 million people. Had the Court ordered the census adjustment, California and Arizona would have each gained a seat in Congress and Wisconsin and Pennsylvania would have lost a seat. In addition, state legislative districts might have been redrawn and the distribution of federal aid among the states would have been altered.

In his provocative book *Power Shift,* Kirkpatrick Sale vividly describes the political implications of this population shift.[21] Sale argues that America's southern rim, or Sunbelt, has come to dominate American politics, as population, manufacturing, and capital have moved form the North to the South. From 1960 to 1992, New York lost ten seats in Congress and Florida gained eleven. In 1960, California had thirty-two electoral votes, the same number as Pennsylvania; in 1992, California had fifty-four electoral votes, Pennsylvania only twenty-three. Congressional redistricting for 1992 resulted in a switch of nineteen seats. All the gainers, except Washington (one seat), were in the Sunbelt and all the losers were concentrated in a nearly unbroken line from Massachusetts west to Iowa. California, Texas, and Florida gained a total of fourteen seats.

Projections for the census in 2000 indicate that population trends from the past several decades will continue (see the Appendix). Nevada's population is expected to increase by 40 percent (its gain in the 1990s will be greater than the total population of Wyoming). California, Texas, and Florida each is projected to increase its population by about 18 percent, while the populations of most northern, industrial states will increase by less than 5 percent. Despite a weak economy and a host of natural disas-

TABLE 1-3 THE TWENTY FASTEST-GROWING CITIES AND LARGEST POPULATION LOSERS, 1980–1990

City	1980 population	1990 population	Percent gain
Mesa, Ariz.	152,404	288,091	88.98%
Rancho Cucamonga, Calif.	55,250	101,409	83.54%
Plano, Texas	72,331	128,713	77.95%
Irvine, Calif.	62,134	110,330	77.57%
Escondido, Calif.	64,355	108,635	68.81%
Oceanside, Calif.	76,698	128,398	67.41%
Bakersfield, Calif.	105,611	174,820	65.53%
Arlington, Texas	160,113	261,721	63.46%
Fresno, Calif.	217,491	354,202	62.91%
Chula Vista, Calif.	83,927	135,163	61.05%
Las Vegas	164,674	258,295	56.85%
Modesto, Calif.	106,963	164,730	54.01%
Tallahassee, Fla.	81,548	124,773	53.01%
Glendale, Ariz.	97,172	148,134	52.45%
Mesquite, Texas	67,053	101,484	51.35%
Ontario, Calif.	88,820	133,179	49.94%
Virginia Beach, Va.	262,199	393,069	49.91%
Scottsdale, Ariz.	88,622	130,069	46.77%
Santa Ana, Calif.	203,713	293,742	44.19%
Stockton, Calif.	148,283	210,943	42.26%
City	**1980 population**	**1990 population**	**Percent loss**
Gary, Ind.	151,968	116,646	–23.24%
Newark, N.J.	329,248	275,221	–16.41%
Detroit	1,203,368	1,027,974	–14.57%
Pittsburgh	423,959	369,879	–12.75%
St. Louis	452,801	396,685	–12.39%
Cleveland	573,822	505,616	–11.89%
Flint, Mich.	159,611	140,761	–11.81%
New Orleans	557,927	496,938	–10.87%
Warren, Mich.	161,134	144,864	–10.10%
Chattanooga, Tenn.	169,514	152,466	–10.08%
Louisville	298,694	269,063	–9.92%
Macon, Ga.	116,896	106,612	–8.80%
Erie, Pa.	119,123	108,718	–8.73%
Peoria, Ill.	124,160	113,504	–8.58%
Buffalo	357,870	328,123	–8.31%
Richmond, Va.	219,214	203,056	–7.37%
Chicago	3,005,072	2,783,726	–7.37%
Atlanta	425,022	394,017	–7.29%
Kansas City, Kan.	161,148	149,767	–7.06%
Birmingham, Ala.	284,413	265,968	–6.49%

Source: U.S. Census Bureau.

TABLE 1-4 THE THIRTY LARGEST CITIES, 1980–1990

1990 rank	1980 rank	City	1990 population	1980 population	Percent change
1	1	New York	7,322,564	7,071,639	3.5%
2	3	Los Angeles	3,485,398	2,968,528	17.4%
3	2	Chicago	2,783,726	3,005,072	–7.4%
4	5	Houston	1,630,553	1,595,138	2.2%
5	4	Philadelphia	1,585,577	1,688,210	–6.1%
6	8	San Diego	1,110,549	875,538	26.8%
7	6	Detroit	1,027,974	1,203,368	–14.6%
8	7	Dallas	1,006,877	904,599	11.3%
9	9	Phoenix	983,403	789,704	24.5%
10	11	San Antonio	935,933	785,940	19.1%
11	17	San Jose, Calif.	782,284	629,400	24.3%
12	12	Indianapolis	741,952	711,539	4.3%
13	10	Baltimore	736,014	786,741	–6.4%
14	13	San Francisco	723,959	678,974	6.6%
15	19	Jacksonville, Fla.	672,971	571,003	17.9%
16	20	Columbus, Ohio	632,910	565,021	12.0%
17	16	Milwaukee	628,088	636,297	–1.3%
18	14	Memphis	610,337	646,174	–5.5%
19	15	Washington	606,900	638,432	–4.9%
20	21	Boston	574,283	562,994	2.0%
21	23	Seattle	516,259	493,846	4.5%
22	28	El Paso	515,342	425,259	21.2%
23	25	Nashville	510,784	477,811	6.9%
24	18	Cleveland	505,616	573,822	–11.9%
25	22	New Orleans	496,938	557,927	–10.9%
26	24	Denver	467,610	492,686	–5.1%
27	42	Austin, Texas	465,622	345,164	34.6%
28	33	Fort Worth	447,619	385,164	16.2%
29	31	Oklahoma City	444,719	404,014	10.1%
30	35	Portland, Ore.	437,319	368,148	18.8%

Source: U.S. Census Bureau

ters, California is expected to gain about 5 million people in the 1990s, which is greater than the total 1990 population of thirty-six states. By the mid-1990s Texas had moved past New York to become the second largest state. The South is the nation's most populous section, and by the year 2020 the West will surpass the Midwest for second place. By 2020 California will have about 50 million people, making it nearly equal to the present-day populations of France, Great Britain, and Italy.

Another issue of concern is the flow of federal dollars to the Sunbelt. As the amount of federal grants has increased, competition among the states for federal dollars has grown intense. In general, Western and New England states receive the highest levels of federal expenditures per capita (see Table 1-5). Southern states receive the lowest levels of federal expenditures.

TABLE 1-5 FEDERAL AID TO STATE AND LOCAL GOVERNMENT, PER CAPITA, 1993

State	Per capita	State	Per capita
1 District of Columbia	$3,392.46	**26** Michigan	702.04
2 Alaska	1,583.02	**27** Ohio	695.74
3 Rhode Island	1,407.47	**28** California	693.18
4 Wyoming	1,371.52	**29** Oregon	692.37
5 New York	1,163.15	**30** South Carolina	692.10
6 Louisiana	1,121.55	**31** Nebraska	689.76
7 West Virginia	1,035.05	**32** Missouri	681.29
8 North Dakota	1,007.61	**33** Wisconsin	674.25
9 Montana	990.14	**34** Arizona	670.79
10 Vermont	966.81	**35** Illinois	670.70
11 New Mexico	949.10	**36** Maryland	666.59
12 Maine	941.15	**37** Indiana	653.33
13 Massachusetts	918.21	**38** Oklahoma	653.30
14 South Dakota	915.18	**39** Delaware	650.40
15 Mississippi	864.40	**40** Idaho	648.11
16 Hawaii	839.56	**41** North Carolina	647.62
17 Connecticut	821.04	**42** Georgia	637.32
18 Kentucky	802.46	**43** Kansas	635.28
19 New Jersey	785.55	**44** Utah	630.88
20 Tennessee	769.72	**45** Iowa	617.11
21 Arkansas	765.23	**46** Texas	612.01
UNITED STATES	745.65	**47** Colorado	591.50
22 Alabama	735.90	**48** New Hampshire	579.33
23 Minnesota	729.95	**49** Florida	554.04
24 Washington	708.29	**50** Nevada	552.06
25 Pennsylvania	706.89	**51** Virginia	453.73

Source: Edith Horner, ed., *Almanac of the 50 States* (Palo Alto, Calif.: Information Publications, 1995), p. 435.

CONSTITUTIONAL AND LEGAL LIMITS ON STATE ACTION

The U.S. Constitution on the one hand provides certain guarantees to the states and on the other hand imposes certain restrictions on state actions.[22] For example, political integrity is protected by federal constitutional provisions that states cannot be divided or consolidated without state legislative consent. In addition, amendments to the Constitution must be ratified by three-fourths of the states. The Constitution limits state action by denying to the states the power to coin money or pass **ex post facto laws.** Treaties with foreign nations are binding on the states as the law of the land; and the Constitution and all laws made under it are the supreme law of the land.

The American system of federalism (discussed in detail in Chapter 2) distributes power in such a way as to deny the central government authority in only a few areas. However, the central government must rely on the cooperation of state and local governments to achieve most of its objectives. As a result, there is a great deal of sharing in policymaking between the states and the federal government. Because the constitutional division of power between the states and the federal government is not precise, a dynamic relationship exists that allowed the federal government to move into many areas traditionally reserved to the states. Federal administrative actions, congressional statutes, and court decisions have imposed national standards that in some instances replace previously controlling local standards. Specifically, federal grants-in-aid (see Chapter 2) have given the national government the means to exercise powers concurrent with the states in many areas of policymaking.

Federal court decisions have limited state action from the earliest days of the republic. In ***McCulloch* v. *Maryland* (1819)** and ***Gibbons* v. *Ogden* (1824),** the Supreme Court supported the supremacy of national law and broadly interpreted congressional power in interstate commerce (these decisions are discussed in Chapter 2). More recently, decisions in the areas of civil rights, school integration, rights of criminal defendants, and voting qualifications have expanded federal authority while limiting that of the states. As an instrument of the national government, the Supreme Court, under Chief Justice John Marshall and in most instances since the late 1930s, has broadly construed the implied powers of Congress vis-à-vis the states and ignored the so-called reserved powers of the states (see the **Tenth Amendment**). Under court order, federal registrars have replaced local voting officials in Southern states and state legislatures have been ordered to reapportion themselves on the basis of "one man, one vote."

STATE CONSTITUTIONS

General Information

State constitutions prescribe the structure of government, the powers granted various public officials, terms of office and means of election, and the way in which constitutional amendments shall be enacted. Like the U.S. Constitution, state constitutions take precedence over any state laws that are in conflict with them.

It is difficult to generalize among the fifty state constitutions (see Table 1-6). The oldest is that of Massachusetts, adopted in 1780; Georgia, Illinois, Louisiana, Montana, and Virginia have adopted new constitutions since 1970. The 1982 constitution in Georgia replaced a document well known for its excessive length (48,000 words) and excessive amendments. The new Georgia constitution eliminated approximately 1,200 local amendments added by voters over the years.

Probably the most unusual of all state constitutions was a proposal for the new state of New Columbia, which was approved by voters of the District of Columbia in 1982; a revised document was submitted to Congress in 1987. The proposed government structure called for a unicameral legislature, permitted public employees to strike, guaranteed a right to employment, and gave state benefits to persons unable to work because of pregnancy. It was rejected by Congress.

While twenty states have had only one constitution, Louisiana has had eleven. The constitution of Alabama contains approximately 174,000 words, while the constitutions of five states have less than 10,000. Vermont has added 50 amendments to its 1793 constitution, while California has added more than 485 amendments. Most state constitutions were written in the nineteenth century, when government power was distrusted. Only eighteen are twentieth-century documents. The reform movement of the early twentieth century was reflected in modern constitutions that sought to limit par-

TABLE 1-6 GENERAL INFORMATION ON STATE CONSTITUTIONS
(As of January 1, 1994)

State or other jurisdiction	Number of constitutions*	Dates of adoption	Effective date of present constitution	Estimated length (number of words)	Number of amendments	
					Submitted to voters	Adopted
Alabama	6	1819, 1861, 1865, 1868, 1875, 1901	Nov. 28, 1901	174,000	783	556
Alaska	1	1956	Jan. 3, 1959	16,675 (a)	32	23
Arizona	1	1911	Feb. 14, 1912	28,876	215	119
Arkansas	5	1836, 1861, 1864, 1868, 1874	Oct. 30, 1874	40,720	171	81 (b)
California	2	1849, 1879	July 4, 1879	33,350	814	485
Colorado	1	1876	Aug. 1, 1876	45,679	254	124
Connecticut	4	1818 (c), 1965	Dec. 30, 1965	9,564	29	28
Delaware	4	1776, 1792, 1831, 1897	June 10, 1897	19,000	(d)	123
Florida	6	1839, 1861, 1865, 1868, 1886, 1968	Jan. 7, 1969	25,100	92	65
Georgia	10	1777, 1789, 1798, 1861, 1865, 1868, 1877, 1945, 1976, 1982	July 1, 1983	25,000	52 (e)	39
Hawaii	1 (f)	1950	Aug. 21, 1959	17,453	102	86
Idaho	1	1889	July 3, 1890	21,500	189	109
Illinois	4	1818, 1848, 1870, 1970	July 1, 1971	13,200	14	8
Indiana	2	1816, 1851	Nov. 1, 1851	9,377 (a)	70	38
Iowa	2	1846, 1857	Sept. 3, 1857	12,500	52	49 (g)
Kansas	1	1859	Jan. 29, 1861	11,865	118	90 (g)
Kentucky	4	1792, 1799, 1850, 1891	Sept. 28, 1891	23,500	65	32
Louisiana	11	1812, 1845, 1852, 1861, 1864, 1868, 1879, 1898, 1913, 1921, 1974	Jan. 1, 1975	51,448	92	54
Maine	1	1819	March 15, 1820	13,500	192	162 (h)
Maryland	4	1776, 1851, 1864, 1867	Oct. 5, 1867	41,349	238	205 (i)
Massachusetts	1	1780	Oct. 25, 1780	36,690 (j)	144	117
Michigan	4	1835, 1850, 1908, 1963	Jan. 1, 1964	20,000	51	17
Minnesota	1	1857	May 11, 1858	9,500	207	113
Mississippi	4	1817, 1832, 1869, 1890	Nov. 1, 1890	24,000	148	116
Missouri	4	1820, 1865, 1875, 1945	March 30, 1945	42,000	132	81
Montana	2	1889, 1972	July 1, 1973	11,866	32	18
Nebraska	2	1866, 1875	Oct. 12, 1875	20,048	293	197
Nevada	1	1864	Oct. 31, 1864	20,770	184	113 (g)
New Hampshire	2	1776, 1784	June 2, 1784	9,200	280 (k)	143 (k)
New Jersey	3	1776, 1844, 1947	Jan. 1, 1948	17,086	57	44
New Mexico	1	1911	Jan. 6, 1912	27,200	240	123
New York	4	1777, 1822, 1846, 1894	Jan. 1, 1895	80,000	280	213
North Carolina	3	1776, 1868, 1970	July 1, 1971	11,000	35	27
North Dakota	1	1889	Nov. 2, 1889	20,564	235 (l)	129 (l)

Ohio	2	1802, 1851	Sept. 1, 1851	36,900	253	151
Oklahoma	1	1907	Nov. 16, 1907	68,800	293 (m)	146 (m)
Oregon	1	1857	Feb. 14, 1859	26,090	383 (n)	(n)
Pennsylvania	5	1776, 1790, 1838, 1873, 1968 (n)	1968 (n)	21,675	26	56
Rhode Island	2	1842 (c)	May 2, 1843	19,026 (o)	102	36
South Carolina	7	1776, 1778, 1790, 1861, 1865, 1868, 1895	Jan. 1, 1896	22,500 (o)	648 (p)	463
South Dakota	1	1889	Nov. 2, 1889	23,300	191	99
Tennessee	3	1796, 1835, 1870	Feb. 23, 1870	15,300	55	32
Texas	5	1845, 1861, 1866, 1869, 1876	Feb. 15, 1876	76,000	518 (q)	353
Utah	1	1895	Jan. 4, 1896	11,000	131	82
Vermont	3	1777, 1786, 1793	July 9, 1793	6,600	208	50
Virginia	6	1776, 1830, 1851, 1869, 1902, 1970	July 1, 1971	18,500	28	23
Washington	1	1889	Nov. 11, 1889	29,400	158	88
West Virginia	2	1863, 1872	April 9, 1872	25,600	110	64
Wisconsin	1	1848	May 29, 1848	13,500	174	129 (g)
Wyoming	1	1889	July 10, 1890	31,800	102	61
American Samoa	2	1960, 1967	July 1, 1967	6,000	14	7
No. Mariana Islands	1	1977	Jan. 9, 1978	11,000	49 (r)	47 (r, s)
Puerto Rico	1	1952	July 25, 1952	9,280	6	6

Note: An authoritative revision of the number of words in each of the 50 state constitutions will be included in *The Book of the States, 1996–97.*

*The constitutions referred to in this table include those Civil War documents customarily listed by the individual states.

(a) Actual word count.

(b) Eight of the approved amendments have been superseded and are not printed in the current edition of the constitution. The total adopted does not include five amendments that were invalidated.

(c) Colonial charters with some alterations served as the first constitutions in Connecticut (1638, 1662) and in Rhode Island (1663).

(d) Proposed amendments are not submitted to the voters in Delaware.

(e) The new Georgia constitution eliminates the need for local amendments, which have been a long-term problem for state constitution makers.

(f) As a kingdom and a republic, Hawaii had five constitutions.

(g) The figure given includes amendments approved by the voters and later nullified by the state supreme court in Iowa (three), Kansas (one), Nevada (six) and Wisconsin (two).

(h) The figure does not include one amendment approved by the voters in 1967 that is inoperative until implemented by legislation.

(i) Two sets of identical amendments were on the ballot and adopted in the Maryland 1992 election. The four amendments are counted as two in the table.

(j) The printed constitution includes many provisions that have been annulled. The length of effective provisions is an estimated 24,122 words (12,400 annulled) in Massachusetts, and in Rhode Island before the "rewrite" of the constitution in 1986, it was 11,399 words (7,627 annulled).

(k) The constitution of 1784 was extensively revised in 1792. Figures show proposals and adoptions since the constitution was adopted in 1784.

(l) The figures do not include submission and approval of the constitution of 1889 itself and of Article XX; these are constitutional questions included in some counts of constitutional amendments and would add two to the figure in each column.

(m) The figures include five amendments submitted to and approved by the voters which were, by decisions of the Oklahoma or U.S. Supreme Courts, rendered inoperative or ruled invalid, unconstitutional, or illegally submitted.

(n) Certain sections of the constitution were revised by the limited constitutional convention of 1967–68. Amendments proposed and adopted are since 1968.

(o) Of the estimated length, approximately two-thirds is of general statewide effect; the remainder is local amendments.

(p) As of 1981, of the 626 proposed amendments submitted to the voters, 130 were of general statewide effect and 496 were local; the voters rejected 83 (12 statewide, 71 local). Of the remaining 543, the General Assembly refused to approve 100 (22 statewide, 78 local), and 443 (96 statewide, 347 local) were finally added to the constitution.

(q) The number of proposed amendments to the Texas Constitution exclude three proposed by the legislature but not placed on the ballot.

(r) The number of amendments is from 1984–1994.

(s) The total excludes one amendment ruled void by a federal district court.

Source: Copyright 1994–95 The Council of State Governments. Reprinted with permission from *The Book of the States 1994–95* (Lexington, Ky.: Council of State Governments, 1994), pp. 19–20.

tisan influences in government. More recent constitutions have strengthened the governors and unified state judicial systems.

In spite of their differences, a general framework of state constitutions can be presented. Most constitutions have a separate section to give effect to the doctrine of separation of powers. All state constitutions have a preamble and a bill of rights. Often these sections contain obsolete provisions. For example, according to the Pennsylvania and Tennessee preambles, a state officeholder must not only believe in God but also in a future state of rewards and punishments. And in seven of the bills of rights, the honorable art of dueling is at issue.

The newer constitutions, such as Alaska's and Hawaii's, omit any specific reference to the mutual exclusiveness of legislative and executive functions. Legislative articles have been strengthened in recent years so that most legislatures are considered to be in continuous session and empowered to meet annually. Executive articles limited the power of governors by creating large numbers of boards and commissions whose members often were independent of the governor. For example, before Michigan wrote a new constitution in 1963, the executive branch consisted of the governor, six major elected officials, twenty-three executive departments, four elected boards, sixty-four appointed boards and commissions, six ex-officio boards, and five retirement boards. Judicial articles typically have been marked by detail, multiplicity of courts, overlapping jurisdictions, and low salaries. Here, too, many amendments have been added to establish new courts, alter the way in which judges are selected, and create a unified state judicial system.

Other constitutional articles deal with suffrage and elections, local government, particular economic interests (such as farming), and amendments. Although most rules and regulations regarding voting have been established by the states, a series of amendments to the U.S. Constitution (Fifteenth, Seventeenth, Nineteenth, Twenty-third, Twenty-fourth, and Twenty-sixth) have provided a degree of uniformity throughout the nation. Nevertheless, a few interesting examples may be cited. In Vermont, for example, the constitution requires "quiet and peaceable behavior" as a voting qualification. In some Southern states before 1965, a person of "good character" might have been excused by the local voting registrar from taking a literacy test or complying with other regulations specifically established to disenfranchise blacks.

Most newer state constitutions have separate articles on policy areas, such as education and welfare. Recently, several states have made changes to eliminate gender-bias language in their constitutions. Most constitutions have a Miscellaneous or General Provisions article to lay out provisions that do not fit elsewhere or that apply to more than one section of the constitution.

There have been fewer constitutional amendments in the 1990s than in the past two decades, but the number of changes brought out by the initiative process in the 1990s has been at a record high.[23] Mississippi became the eighteenth state to permit the constitutional initiative, and Rhode Island and New Jersey have authorized the recall in the 1990s. About one-third of the amendments adopted by initiative in the 1992–1993 biennium dealt with lotteries and gambling. The most common legislative proposals were finance and taxation. Rights of crime victims were adopted in six states, and voters in Iowa defeated an equal rights amendment.

In contrast to the U.S. Constitution, most state constitutions are long, detailed, and heavily amended. There is a strong feeling that much of their detail should have been left to legislatures to determine by passing bills. While length and detail are not necessarily bad, these characteristics have had great political significance in the operation of state government. Excessive detail is due in part to the successful efforts of interest groups to have constitutions specifically recognize and protect their economic concerns. Indeed, constitutions are longest in those states with the strongest interest groups. Unless amended, these provisions may hinder government regulation as changes in society occur. Duane Lockard notes that the complexity of state constitutions invites litigation and thus plays into the hands of those resisting change.[24] Opponents can often challenge new laws on the grounds that some detail of constitutional procedure was not properly followed. State courts have often tended toward a narrow interpretation of state constitutions, particularly limiting legislative and executive authority. Indeed, Lockard suggests that courts have often been so opposed to change that they reach beyond specific to general provisions in order to invalidate laws.

Recently, state supreme courts have been forces for change, not obstruction. Several state courts have interpreted their own constitutions independently of the U.S. Constitution, especially in civil rights cases, to support reformist goals. We need to remember that state constitutions are changed by judicial interpretation as well as by amendments. Very detailed constitutions make it more likely that amendments will be added as circumstances change and explicit provisions leave less leeway for change through interpretation. As a result, length and detail beget greater length through amendments.

Many state constitutions reveal a strong suspicion of government power, and they act as roadblocks to change. In particular, constitutional restrictions on gubernatorial power have made activist government in the twentieth century difficult. In many of the constitutions written in the last century, governors were limited to two-year terms; legislatures met as infrequently as every other year and only for a limited period (sixty to ninety days); legislative salaries were specified; most state officials, such as the attorney general and auditor, were elected rather than appointed by the governor; significant restraints were placed on borrowing; many special interests were exempt from taxation; and reapportionment in some cases required constitutional amendment. As noted in Chapter 6, much of the history of state governors can be written in terms of constitutional amendments to give them powers comparable to those of the president of the United States.

State constitutions also impose major limitations on the powers of local governments, which legally are only subdivisions of the state. The government structure of cities, counties, and townships generally is prescribed by the states. State constitutions often delegate responsibility for certain services, such as police, fire, and health, to particular units of local government; but local taxes are prescribed and debt limits are established. All this, of course, adds to the detail of state constitutions. While there has been a concerted drive toward granting **home rule** to cities (in the form of charters that allow cities to adopt the kind of government structure they prefer and perform services as they see fit), in many cases local officials still must turn to state legislatures for approval of government programs (see Chapter 9).

Local governments are clearly subordinate to the state. In a classic statement, Judge John F. Dillon formulated **Dillon's Rule** (1868), which says that municipal corporations can exercise only those powers expressly granted by state constitutions and laws and those necessarily implied from granted powers. If there is any question about the exercise of power, it should be resolved in favor of the state. Although this rule has been accepted by the U.S. Supreme Court, Daniel Elazar notes that more than 80 percent of the states have rejected Dillon's Rule or have changed it to recognize the residual powers of local government.[25]

An effective state constitution—that is, one allowing government to take an active role in the initiation and implementation of policy—should include the following three fundamental characteristics.

1 It should be brief and to the point. Constitutions are not legislative codes; all they should do is establish the basic framework within which state officials can act.

2 It should make direct grants of authority so that the governor and legislators can be held accountable by the voters for their actions.

3 It should be receptive to orderly change. The amendment process should not be too cumbersome, and the constitution should include enforceable provisions on redrawing legislative districts. Unfortunately, legislators often have a built-in resistance to change, and voters often defeat new constitutions at the polls when they are asked to accept or reject in total a new constitution.

To most people, state constitutions are painfully boring documents. They are not read by those seeking examples of stirring phrases or eloquent prose style. However, as we shall see throughout this book, there are few if any problems of state government for which the suggested solution will not sooner or later run headlong into constitutional prohibitions, restrictions, or obstructions. Constitutions are necessarily conservative documents that limit the exercise of political power. Because of the nature of state constitutions, there has been a strong reform movement in this century to pass constitutional amendments aimed at increasing the power of legislators, governors, and judges and at providing an independent basis of power for local governments.

Amending Constitutions

There are four methods of changing state constitutions: legislative proposal, constitutional initiative, constitutional convention, and constitutional commission. **Legislative proposal** is available in all states, and it is by far the most commonly used means of change. In most states, a two-thirds or three-fifths vote of the legislature is required as the first step in approving an amendment. In seventeen states, only a majority vote is necessary. While most states require approval in only one legislative session, twelve require approval in two consecutive sessions. Following legislative approval, the amendment is typically placed on the ballot, where a majority vote is needed for ratification. Only Delaware does not require voter approval of amendments. State legislators initiate nearly 90 percent of all proposed amendments. Voters approve about 70 percent of legislative proposals submitted to them.

The **constitutional initiative** may be used in eighteen states. It allows proponents of reform to have suggestions for limited change placed on the ballot. The process is time-consuming and often expensive for reform groups, especially in large states. Still, the number of constitutional initiatives rose to all-time highs during the 1980s and 1990s. Proponents must first get signatures on an initiative proposal. In California, for example, the number required is 8 percent of the total number of voters for governor in the last election. In a few states, the signatures must come from people distributed across the state. In Massachusetts no more than one-fourth can come from any one county. As a final step, there is a referendum vote, in which most states require a majority vote on the amendment for it to be approved.

Sixteen states use a constitutional initiative in which citizens by petition propose amendments that go directly to the voters. Only Massachusetts and Mississippi employ an indirect initiative, which is submitted to the legislature before it is placed on the ballot. As the following explanation makes clear, the procedures for the new Mississippi indirect initiative are extremely complicated and restrictive.[25]

> The initiative is indirect because the measure must be submitted to the Legislature before it is placed on the ballot. The Legislature, which receives initiatives on the first day of the regular session, may adopt, amend or reject a proposal, or take no action. But whatever the Legislature does or does not do, a proposal, if it meets all the requirements outlined, will be placed on the ballot. However, ballot forms and choices depend on what course of action the Legislature takes. If no legislative action occurs in four months, or if the Legislature adopts the proposal without any changes, the measure goes on the ballot in its original form as received by the Legislature. If the Legislature amends the proposal, the original constitutional initiative and the amended version are both placed on the ballot. If the Legislature rejects the proposal and submits an alternative, both the original and the alternative will be on the ballot. A constitutional initiative is adopted only if it receives a majority of the votes on the proposition and at least 40 percent of the total vote cast in the election. In addition, a fiscal analysis must be attached to ballot measures; no more than five initiative proposals can be placed on a single ballot, and a defeated proposition cannot be considered again for two years.

Recently, two constitutional initiatives approved by the voters were overturned by the courts. In Colorado a state court struck down an initiative that would have restricted the rights of gays, lesbians, and bisexuals. The Arkansas Supreme Court invalidated an amendment that set term limits for members of Congress, and that decision was upheld by the U.S. Supreme Court in 1995. As we will see in Chapter 5, voters in sixteen states had approved constitutional initiatives limiting the terms of Congress members.

Constitutional commissions may be formed to study the state constitution and make recommendations for change, or their purpose may be to make arrangements for a constitutional convention. Only in Florida can a constitutional commission initiate and refer amendments to the voters. Most commissions have acted as study groups. Commission size varies from as few as five members to as many as fifty. Members are usually appointed by the governor, legislative leaders, and chief justice of the highest court in the state.

Constitutional conventions are the oldest method of changing constitutions. Conventions are called by state legislatures, and in some cases they must be authorized to meet by the voters. Fourteen states require a vote on the question of calling a convention. In several states a vote must occur every ten years, while in one case it is every twenty years. Delegates to conventions usually are elected on a nonpartisan basis from state legislative districts. In most instances delegates have been white, middle-aged, professional men. In some cases the state legislature convenes as a constitutional convention.

Conventions may approve amendments, or they may propose completely new constitutions. Not surprisingly, less extreme changes in constitutions are more likely to be approved by voters than entirely new documents. Louisiana convened a convention in 1992, the only one in the country since 1986. The most recently adopted new constitution was in Georgia in 1982.

THE STATES CONTRASTED AND COMPARED

This chapter has pointed out the great diversity among the states in terms of culture, socioeconomic characteristics, population, and geography. In the chapters that follow, the reader should develop a clearer picture of *similarities* among the states. Most states have virtually the same patterns of government structure—they have bicameral legislatures, organized by parties and by committees; their governors exercise similar constitutional powers in such areas as the budget and veto; and their judicial systems are organized in a common three- or two-tier arrangement of trial and appellate courts.

Although personalities differ and unique styles can be identified, political campaigns and elections proceed in the same general pattern in all the states. Particular circumstances dictate how each state and community will respond to demands for public policy. Yet every state must confront common problems in education, housing, transportation, welfare, health, and safety. Differences in political culture are becoming less distinct as people grow more mobile, as means of communication improve, and as an international economy develops.

Comparative analysis of politics in the fifty states reveals both similarities and differences. Because the states are alike in many ways, they offer social scientists the opportunity to make a wide range of comparisons. Because there also is great variety among the states and the thousands of local governments, it gives us the opportunity to study why structural and behavioral differences occur at particular times and under particular conditions. In the chapters that follow, the reader should be careful to note both similarities and differences among the states and relate this to particular patterns of policymaking.

SUMMARY

There has been a resurgence of state government, beginning with constitutional reform in the 1960s and extending into the 1990s as the predominant political mood in the country has favored the return of power to the states. Because states have had their federal assistance cut since the 1980s, they have been under strong pressure to maintain services without increasing taxes. In many states taxes were raised in the 1980s. Because cities have had their federal aid reduced, states have increased aid to local governments, placing even more strain on their budgets. In part, states have dealt with this dilemma by trying to "reinvent government" to produce better services for less money.

The nature of public policy varies greatly among the fifty states. Even states with similar economic and geographic circumstances may differ markedly in the amount of money they devote to particular policy areas. Differences in public policymaking are explained by examining the impact of the following factors on the states: levels of economic development, physical setting, political culture, and sectionalism. The Scholarly Box discusses how the concept of the geology of political culture helps explain the dispersion of the three political cultures—moralistic, traditionalistic, and individualistic—across the United States.

Shifts in population—to metropolitan areas, to suburbs, and to the South and West—have had major impacts on state policymaking since the end of World War II. Projections are that these population trends will continue well into the next century.

Public policymaking also is affected by state constitutions, which are conservative documents that have hindered change. Constitutional change mainly comes from legislative proposals for amendments and from direct initiatives in which the general public may recommend and approve amendments.

KEY TERMS

Communitarianism The support of cooperative or collectivist community action. This is positive government at the local level.

Constitutional commission A group selected to study state constitutions, propose changes, and prepare for a constitutional convention.

Constitutional convention A group of people selected to rewrite all or parts of a state constitution.

Constitutional initiative Means by which citizens can petition to have a proposed amendment put on the ballot for voter approval.

Dillon's Rule A general guideline formulated for courts in 1868 stating that municipal corporations can exercise only those powers specifically granted them by state constitutions and laws.

Ex post facto law A law that makes an act a crime although it was not a crime when committed, or increases the penalty for a crime after it was committed. The U.S. Constitution prohibits the federal government and the states from enacting such laws.

***Gibbons* v. *Ogden* (1824)** A Supreme Court decision that broadly interpreted the power of the national government to regulate commerce and thus limited state authority.

Home rule Power given local governments to draft charters and manage their own affairs; limits the ability of state legislatures to interfere in local affairs.

Individualistic culture A pattern of political orientation characterized by distrust of government bureaucracy, low levels of political participation, and above-average corruption in government. Often found in large cities.

Legislative proposal Means by which state legislators propose constitutional amendments, which then must be approved by the voters.

Mandates State statutes, court decisions, and administrative orders that demand action (and often expenditures) from cities and counties. Often they have been unfunded.

***McCulloch* v. *Maryland* (1819)** A Supreme Court decision that extended federal authority by supporting the creation of a national bank and ruling against state taxation of a federally established instrument.

Metropolitan statistical area (MSA) A population center of at least 50,000, generally consisting of a city and its immediate suburbs, together with adjacent communities that have close economic and social ties to the central city. First developed for the 1950 census.

Moralistic culture A pattern of political orientation characterized by high levels of political participation, support of government intervention in social and economic affairs, and little public corruption. Found in the upper Midwest and Far West.

Political culture The predominant way of thinking, feeling, and believing about the political system.

Progressive movement Reform in the early twentieth century that advocated government ownership of railroads, the right of labor to bargain collectively, and the use of direct-democracy techniques such as the initiative and recall.

Public interest Actions taken in the public interest to support measures that benefit the whole community rather than narrow economic interests.

Sectionalism The division of the nation into geographical areas, such as the South, in which the people share common cultural, economic, and historical backgrounds.

Spoils system Awarding government jobs to political supporters and friends. Now replaced in most cases by merit systems of government employment.

Sunbelt The area stretching east from southern California through the Southwest and South to Florida and north along the Atlantic coast to Virginia. It has been marked by exceptional population growth and economic development since World War II.

Tenth Amendment "The powers not delegated to the United States by the Constitution, nor prohibited by it to the States, are reserved to the States respectively, or to the people." This amendment was added to the Constitution to define the principle of federalism.

Traditional culture A pattern of political orientation characterized by low levels of political participation, little government interference in social and economic affairs, and a dislike of formal bureaucracy. Found predominantly in the South.

REFERENCES

1 See Michael Reagan and John G. Sanzone, *The New Federalism,* 2d ed. (New York: Oxford University Press, 1981), pp. 11–15. They note that "no sphere of life is beyond the reach of the national government" with the exception of the continuance of the state's present boundaries. Here the Constitution (Article IV, Section 3) provides that a state's boundaries cannot be changed without its consent. In *Garcia* v. *San Antonio*

Metropolitan Transit Authority (1985), Justice Brennan's majority opinion stated that "with rare exceptions" the Constitution does not impose affirmative limits on federal power to intrude in the affairs of state and local governments.

2 Larry Sabato, *Goodbye to Goodtime Charlie,* 2d ed. (Washington, D.C.: Congressional Quarterly Press, 1983), p. 8.

3 John Kincaid, "Developments in Federal-State Relations, 1992–93" in *The Book of the States 1994–95* (Lexington, Ky.: Council of State Governments, 1994), pp. 580–581.

4 All current statistics in this section are from U.S. Bureau of the Census, *Statistical Abstract of the United States, 1994* (Washington, D.C., 1994).

5 Henry S. Wulf, "State Aid to Local Governments, Fiscal 1992," *Book of the States, 1994–95,* p. 600.

6 See David C. Nice, *Policy Innovation in State Government* (Ames: Iowa State University Press, 1994).

7 See Thomas R. Dye, *Politics, Economics, and Public Policy: Policy Outcomes in the American States* (Chicago: Rand McNally, 1966). Dye regards urbanism, industrialism, and education, in addition to income, as economic measures. See also Dye, *Understanding Public Policy,* 8th ed. (Englewood Cliffs, N.J.: Prentice-Hall, 1995).

8 Virginia Gray, "Politics and Policy in the American States," in Virginia Gray, Herbert Jacob, and Kenneth N. Vines, eds., *Politics in the American States,* 4th ed. (Boston: Little, Brown, 1983), p. 20.

9 Thomas Payne, "Montana: From Copper Fiefdom to Pluralist Polity," in Ronald J. Hrebenar and Clive S. Thomas, eds., *Interest Group Politics in the American West* (Salt Lake City: University of Utah Press, 1987), p. 77.

10 Charles Price, "The Longshot Bid to Split California," *California Journal* (August 1992), pp. 387–391.

11 Daniel J. Elazar, *American Federalism: A View from the States,* 3d ed. (New York: Harper & Row, 1984), p. 109.

12 Daniel J. Elazar, *The American Mosaic* (Boulder, Colo.: Westview Press, 1994), pp. 3–4.

13 Maureen Moakley, "New Jersey," in Alan Rosenthal and Maureen Moakley, eds., *The Political Life of the American States* (New York: Praeger, 1984), pp. 219–220.

14 Elazar, *American Federalism,* pp. 114–122. As a handbook for further reading into the elements and patterns of political cultures and subcultures of the United States, see Daniel Elazar and Joseph Zikmund II, eds., *The Ecology of American Political Culture: Readings* (New York: Crowell, 1975). See also John Kincaid, ed., *Political Culture, Public Policy, and the American States* (Philadelphia: Institute for the Study of Human Issues, 1982).

15 Quoted in Peter Applebome, "Scandals Cloud Life in South Carolina," *The New York Times,* May 12, 1991, Sec. 1, p. 16.

16 See Joel Lieske, "Political Subcultures of the United States: A New Measure for Understanding Political Behavior." Paper delivered at the 1991 meeting of the Midwest Political Science Association.

17 Elazar, *The American Mosaic,* p. 140.

18 See Hrebenar and Thomas, eds., *Interest Group Politics in the American West,* p. 144.

19 See John H. Fenton, *Midwest Politics* (New York: Holt, Rinehart and Winston, 1966).

20 Dirk Johnson, "Life on the Great Plains: A Test of Survival Skills," *New York Times,* December 12, 1993, p. A17.

21 Kirkpatrick Sale, *Power Shift: The Rise of the Southern Rim* (New York: Random House, 1975).

22 Elazar, *American Federalism,* Chapter 2.
23 Janice C. May, "State Constitutions and Constitutional Revision, 1992–93" in *Book of the States 1994–95,* p. 2.
24 Duane Lockard, *The Politics of State and Local Government,* 3d ed. (New York: Macmillan, 1983), Chapter 4.
25 Elazar, *American Federalism,* p. 203.
26 May, "State Constitutions and Constitutional Revision, 1992–93," p. 3.

2

INTERGOVERNMENTAL RELATIONS

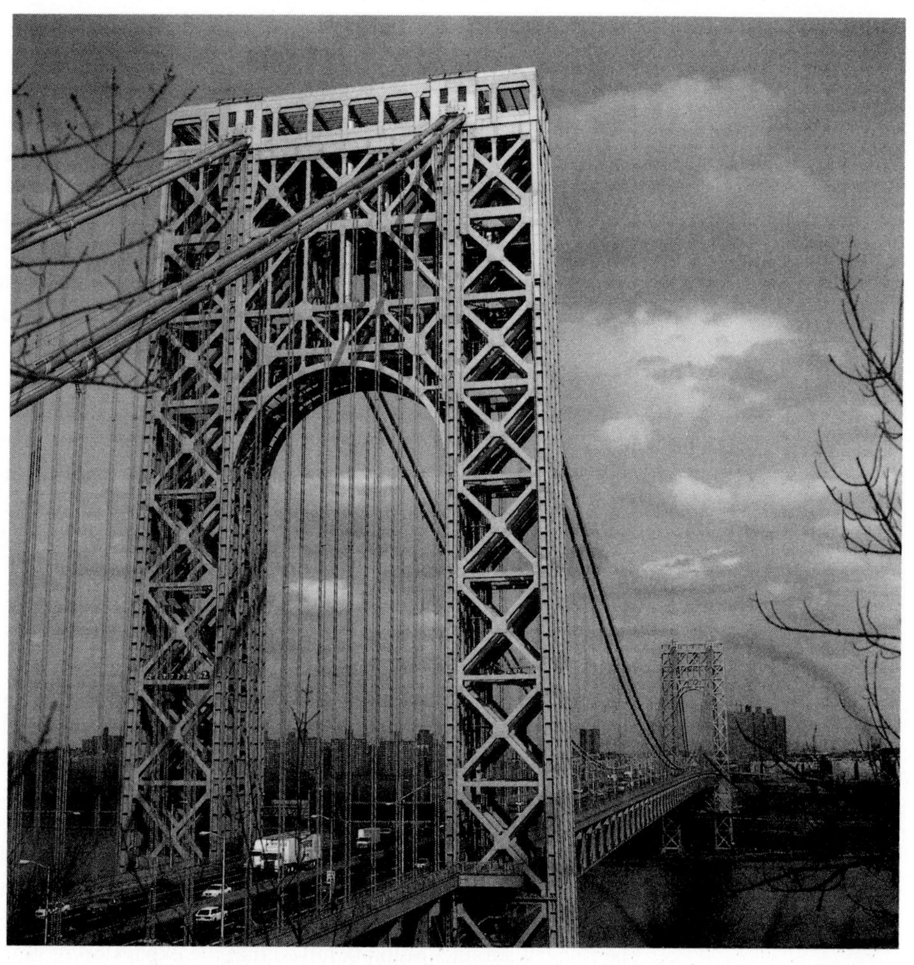

Photo courtesy of the Port Authority of NY and NJ

FEDERALISM AS A POLITICAL CONCEPT

Most textbooks in the past discussed federalism in terms of structure and legal principles. This approach stressed the constitutional division of authority and functions between the national government and the states. As such, it was a static view of power being assigned to units of government and remaining fixed over long periods of time. The current approach suggests a much more dynamic notion of intergovernmental relations. Thus interpretation focuses not on *structure* but on *politics.* According to this view, levels of government share authority and power in an interdependent and constantly changing relationship of joint action. Federalism is regarded, in part, as a state of mind. For example, although the national government has the *legal* authority to take a wide range of actions, it is constrained by political and social forces that support state autonomy and resist centralization. As we will see in each of the policymaking chapters (education, welfare, crime, economic development), the decentralized nature of our system has a powerful impact on how money is spent and how problems are addressed.

We need to be reminded that there never was a time when federal, state, and local government affairs were completely separate. The traditional analogy of the American federal system as a "layer cake," with clear divisions between layers of government, was never true. Instead, it is more accurate to speak of the federal system as a "marble cake," in which government functions are shared by all levels.[1] Cooperative efforts by federal, state, and local governments have become increasingly necessary in the last twenty years. A vast system of over 86,000 local governments fits together to serve a wide range of functions. There are about 3,043 counties; 19,300 municipalities; 16,670 townships and towns; 14,600 school districts; and 33,000 special districts. A suburban Pittsburgh resident, for example, may come under the jurisdiction of and pay taxes to nearly a dozen governments. In 1992 the Bureau of the Census reported that the number of local government units per state ranged from 6,809 in Illinois to 20 in Hawaii.

This sharing of functions is most clearly seen in federal grants-in-aid (which are discussed in detail later in this chapter). Most Americans favor the decentralization of power. At the same time, they want to solve problems. Grants-in-aid are a practical solution: The programs are funded by the national government but administered by state and local governments and even by nonprofit business firms. Virtually every function of local government has a counterpart federal program. As we shall see in this chapter, fiscal federalism provides the means by which the congressional majority's sense of basic policy needs directs and shapes public policymaking in states and cities.

The Reagan administration believed that the expansion of grants-in-aid in the 1960s and 1970s represented a serious overreaching of federal authority. It was concerned that the state and local governments had become too dependent on federal funds and that federal regulations had become too intrusive. Also, the Reagan administration was convinced that state and local aid was taking too high a percentage of the federal budget (it had reached an all-time high of 17 percent of all federal spending in 1978). As we shall see later in this chapter, Reagan's proposals to change the nature of intergovernmental relations fostered the impression that "federalism" was simply a code word for making budget cuts.[2] Although President George Bush continued to support the Reagan philosophy of limiting federal expenditures and giving more management responsibility to states and cities, funding for grants-in-aid increased substantially while he was in office. During his first year in office President Clinton met frequently with governors and mayors who were enthusiastic about the possibility of improved relations with Washington. However, the administration suffered an early defeat of its economic stimulus plan, and it was slow to fill positions in federal intergovernmental institutions, such as the Advisory Commission on Intergovernmental Relations (ACIR). Of course, the federal deficit made it difficult to propose new programs. By late 1993, the situation had improved. The Clinton administration released its National Performance Review (discussed later in this chapter), the president issued several executive orders on intergovernmental relations, and a new chair was named to the ACIR.

CREATION OF THE AMERICAN FEDERAL SYSTEM

The decision by the framers of the Constitution in 1787 to create a federal system of government may be viewed as a compromise between those who wanted to continue with a confederate form of government and those who wanted to change to a centralized system as existed in England. Under the Articles of Confederation, the national government lacked the authority to manage effectively the economic and international affairs of the nation. The population had strong loyalties to the states, and there was a general fear of centralized authority as it had been manifested in colonial America. A federal system offered unity without uniformity. By reserving to the states considerable power, it lessened the likelihood of centralized tyranny. A federal system seems appropriate for many developing countries because it is flexible and permits changes in the distribution of power among government units and in the balance of power without changing the fundamental charter of government.

A **federal system** may be distinguished from a **confederacy** in the following ways: (1) in a federal system, the central government is stronger than its member states in regard to the size of its budget and the scope of its jurisdiction; (2) in a federal system, national law is supreme; (3) in a federal system, the central government acts directly upon individuals in such matters as taxation and raising an army, whereas in a confederacy, the central government must act indirectly through the states when dealing with individual citizens; and (4) in a federal system, states may not withdraw from the union, but in a confederacy, they may secede.

A less flexible sort of system is the **unitary nation-state,** in which local governments can exercise only those powers given them by the central government. Unitary government exists in such nations as Great Britain, France, and Israel. In physically small countries, a unitary structure provides efficiency in dealing with national problems and ensures that national values will prevail. In the United States, cities and counties exist as extensions of state governments except when allowed home rule by state constitutional provisions.

As discussed in Chapter 1, the U.S. Constitution provides guarantees to the states and imposes limits on their actions. The powers of the states are limited because substantial powers are delegated to Congress, and the supremacy clause makes very clear the subordinate relationship of the states to the national government:

> This constitution, and the laws of the United States which shall be made in pursuance thereof; and all treaties made or which shall be made under the authority of the United States shall be the supreme law of the land; and the judges in every state shall be bound thereby, anything in the constitution or laws of any state to the contrary notwithstanding.

At the same time, certain constitutional powers are reserved to the states (e.g., ownership of property, regulations of domestic relations, control over local government) and some powers (such as passing ex post facto laws or **bills of attainder**) are denied to both the national and the state governments. To underline the limits of federal authority, the Tenth Amendment states:

> The powers not delegated to the United States by the Constitution, nor prohibited by it to the States, are reserved to the States respectively, or to the people.*

THE EVOLUTION OF AMERICAN FEDERALISM

Relationships among governments in the United States have been dynamic, rather than stable. Figure 2-1 illustrates the changes in the distribution of power between the states and the federal government, and the general expansion of government powers in the United States during the past 200 years. As conceived by the framers (Figure 2-1a), federal authority was limited largely to foreign affairs while state authority was relatively broad, and there was little overlap or cooperation between the two levels of government. Over time (Figure 2-1b), both federal and state authority have expanded, and federal activities are now greater than those of the states. The overlap in power between the states and the federal government has also expanded greatly. The loss of power has been in those areas originally reserved to the people. Expanded government activity and regulation in such areas as environmental control and occupational safety inevitably limit the authority of private persons and businesses.

The increase in federal authority has been the result of various factors. Congress has enacted legislation, and presidents have supported broad federal enforcement of laws and constitutional provisions. This, in turn, has led to a series of challenges in federal courts. As a result, federal courts (especially the Supreme Court) have acted as umpires in the federal system to decide where power should reside.

McCulloch v. *Maryland* (1819) was the first examination by the Supreme Court of state-federal relations. The background of the case is as follows: Maryland had levied a tax on notes issued by all banks not chartered by the state of Maryland. McCulloch, the cashier in the Baltimore branch of the United States Bank, refused to pay the tax, and Maryland brought suit against him. After losing in Maryland state courts, McCul-

*One view of the Tenth Amendment suggests that it reserves to the states all powers not specifically granted to the national government in the Constitution. However, such an interpretation ignores the elastic clause which follows the enumerated powers of Congress and states that Congress may "make all laws which shall be necessary and proper for carrying out the foregoing powers." The more widely accepted view of the Tenth Amendment, as expounded by the Supreme Court, is that it is simply a truism—"that all is retained which has not yet been surrendered." From this second perspective it follows that there is not a constitutionally binding permanent division of power between the national government and the states. In *United States* v. *Darby* (1941) the Supreme Court specifically repudiated the doctrine of dual federalism in favor of national supremacy.

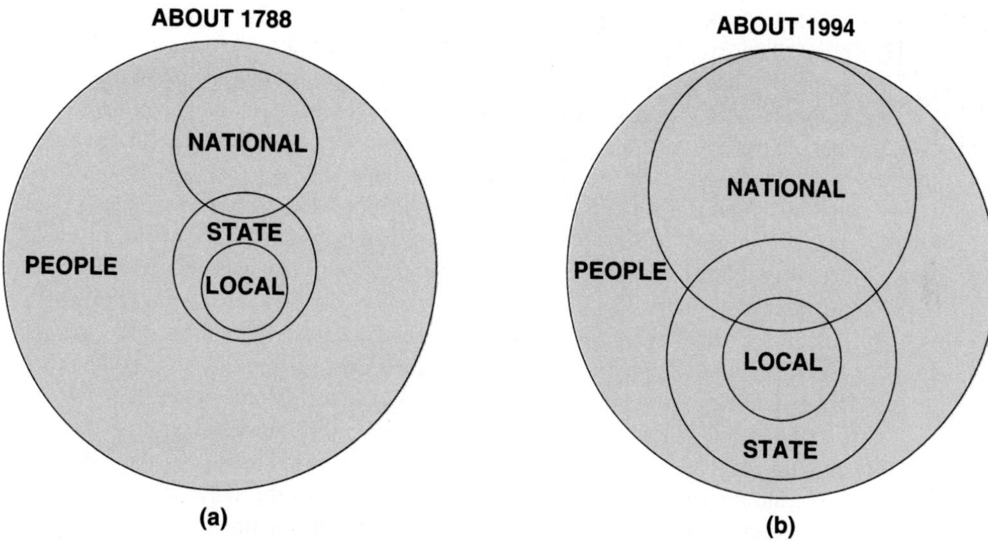

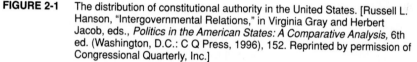

FIGURE 2-1 The distribution of constitutional authority in the United States. [Russell L. Hanson, "Intergovernmental Relations," in Virginia Gray and Herbert Jacob, eds., *Politics in the American States: A Comparative Analysis,* 6th ed. (Washington, D.C.: C Q Press, 1996), 152. Reprinted by permission of Congressional Quarterly, Inc.]

loch (as directed by the secretary of the treasury) appealed and the case was reviewed by the Supreme Court, headed by Chief Justice John Marshall.

Regarding the first issue—"Does Congress have the authority to charter a bank?"—the Court ruled that while this was not among the enumerated powers of Congress, it could be *implied* from the **"necessary and proper" clause** of the Constitution. Marshall reasoned that while the chartering of a bank was not absolutely indispensable in the performance of delegated Congressional responsibilities, it was, nevertheless, "convenient or useful to another objective." On the second issue—"Can the states tax an instrument of the national government?"—the Court ruled no. The power to tax, said the chief justice, is the power to destroy, and states cannot interfere with operations of the national government.

Shortly after *McCulloch,* the Marshall Court had another opportunity to rule in favor of a broad interpretation of national authority. *Gibbons* v. *Ogden* (1824) concerned the desire of New York and New Jersey to control shipping on the lower Hudson River. The states argued that the definition of **commerce** should be narrowly construed so as to include only direct dealings in commodities. Thus the regulation of shipping on inland waterways would be beyond the constitutional power of Congress. Marshall, however, ruled that the power of the national government to regulate commerce included all commercial activity. The Court stated: "This power, like all others vested in Congress, is complete in itself, may be exercised to its utmost extent, and acknowledges no limitations other than are prescribed in the Constitution."

The first federal money grants to states were made in 1837, when surplus funds were sent to the states with no restrictions regarding their use. Before that, federal land grants had been made to assist in the construction of schools, canals, roads, and railroads. The first Morrill Act, passed in 1862, provided land to states to establish agricultural colleges; these institutions became land-grant universities. Terms of the legislation foreshadowed more modern grants-in-aid because they required colleges to make annual reports and required governors to account for the use of federal funds.

Of course, the most serious threat to national authority came with the Civil War. Prior to 1860, John C. Calhoun proposed the concept of **concurrent majority.** In Calhoun's model each interest group (or state) had the right to decide independently whether to accept or reject national policy affecting it. Calhoun's idea was similar to the doctrine of **nullification,** under which each state could veto national legislation with which it disagreed.* Ultimately, the Southern states seceded from the Union. After the issue had been decided on the battlefield, the Supreme Court ruled in *Texas* v. *White* (1869) that: "Ours is an indestructible union, composed of indestructible states."

During the years between the Civil War and 1937, the Court followed the doctrine of **dual federalism,** in which the distribution of powers between the federal government and the states was seen as fixed. This meant that the states were allowed to operate within their own exclusive jurisdiction, and the national government could not intervene. In particular, the Court narrowly defined commerce so as to exclude manufacturing. The effect was to prevent the state and national governments from regulating such matters as wages, hours, and child labor.

Since 1937, the Court has reverted to the views of the Marshall era that the national government has broad authority under its implied powers and that the reserved powers under the Tenth Amendment do not limit national action (however, as we will see later in this chapter, the Court has acted to restrict federal authority in the 1990s). As a result, the modern Supreme Court has upheld provisions of the 1965 Voting Rights Act calling for federal registrars to replace state officials in several Southern states; it has ordered apportionment of both houses of state legislatures on the basis of population; and it has ordered busing to achieve racial integration in school districts where previously segregation was imposed by law.

During the 1920s, the federal government turned away from social concerns and the states were left to take action regarding such problems as care of dependent children. Federal domestic programs in the late 1920s were so limited that state spending was double federal spending.[3] Innovative state programs were used as models for new federal programs enacted under President Franklin D. Roosevelt's New Deal of the 1930s. The modern-day structure of categorical grants-in-aid came into being in the 1930s.[4] Federal aid was provided almost exclusively to states. It required them to submit plans for the use of the funds, to provide matching funds, and to allow federal audit and review of the programs. Under President Harry Truman, more federal aid went directly to local governments. Federal grants continued to expand under President Dwight Eisenhower, although there was some concern about the proper division of responsi-

*Following the passage of the Alien and Sedition Acts of 1798, the Jeffersonians developed the idea of "interposition." Under this doctrine, states were given the power to "interpose" themselves between their citizens and the national government if they believed that a national law affecting their citizens was unconstitutional. The Alien and Sedition Acts were repealed in 1801, and interposition was never reviewed by the courts.

bility between Washington and the states. Although federal aid tripled from 1952 to 1961 (reaching $7.3 billion), dramatic change in the federal system did not occur until the mid-1960s.

Expanding Federal Aid to States and Localities

From 1965 to 1969 federal aid to state and local governments nearly doubled, to $20.2 billion. Under President Lyndon Johnson's "creative federalism," over 200 new grant programs were created. In many cases, states were bypassed and aid went directly to cities, counties, school districts, and nonprofit organizations. Although the first two block grants (fairly general grants) were created in 1966 (Partnership in Health Act) and 1968 (Safe Streets Act), the Johnson administration relied heavily on categorical grants (grants made for a specific purpose) to further national objectives.

In the 1968 campaign, Richard Nixon stressed his commitment to return power to the states and to cut administrative red tape. In fact, however, federal grants grew from $24 billion in 1970 to nearly $50 billion in 1975. Nearly 100 new categorical grants were created under the Nixon and Ford administrations. Nixon's **"new federalism"** did, however, establish general revenue sharing, which gave state and local governments greater discretion and flexibility in spending federal funds. Three new block grants, giving recipients more freedom, were also established.

The 1970s were marked by several significant changes in intergovernmental relations. We have noted the continued growth of federal grants. Grant eligibility was extended to virtually all local governments and many nonprofit organizations. As a result, by 1980 about 30 percent of all federal aid bypassed state governments, compared with 8 percent in 1960. Federal aid became available for a host of projects (e.g., libraries, historic preservation, snow removal, and development of bikeways) that previously had been totally state-local responsibilities. Thus state-local reliance on the federal government grew significantly. More procedural strings were attached to grants-in-aid, and more substantive strings were added to block grants.

According to David B. Walker, cooperative federalism was replaced by "dysfunctional federalism," or congressional federalism, in the 1970s.[5] New federal regulations became more intricate and more pervasive than the conditions attached to grants in the 1950s and 1960s. Responding to pressure from government lobbyists, more money went directly to substate governments. These changes placed Congress at the center of intergovernmental relations. This, says Walker, is why Nixon's "new federalism" failed to change the relative power positions of the states and the federal government. The result was more managerial confusion and overloading of the intergovernmental network.

As president, Jimmy Carter spoke of a "new partnership" in referring to federal-state-local relations. Essentially, this was a return to Johnson's policies. Carter called for a greater urban focus, expanded intergovernmental programs, and a leadership role for the federal government. Categorical grants remained dominant, and the federal government maintained direct access to local governments. It is significant that there was a clear shift in federal aid policy in the second half of Carter's term. Carter pulled back from his urban aid proposals, and the national political mood (as evidenced in "tax revolts" across the country) began to call for cuts in government programs. This shift became a focal point of the Reagan administration.

Under Ronald Reagan's "new federalism" plan the first substantial effort was made to reduce the tide of centralization that had been growing since the 1930s. After his first year in office, Reagan cut federal aid to state and local governments by about $6.5 billion. About sixty categorical aid programs were dropped and more than seventy-seven others were consolidated into block grants. Essentially, the administration sought to retrench by cutting the federal budget and to "devolve" domestic programs back to state and local governments.

At the beginning of his second year in office, President Reagan announced plans to shift most domestic programs to state and local governments by 1990. Reagan's new "new federalism" program, if enacted, would have given the federal system its most dramatic change since the New Deal brought big government to Washington in the 1930s. In his 1982 State of the Union message, the president declared, "In a single stroke we will be accomplishing a realignment that will end cumbersome administration and spiraling costs at the federal level while we insure these programs will be more responsive to both the people they are meant to help and the people who pay for them." President Reagan called for the federal government to take full financial responsibility for Medicaid, while the states would take full responsibility for food stamps. In addition, forty other federally assisted programs were to be phased out over a period of several years and federal excise taxes would have been eliminated to encourage states to increase their taxes and fund the former federal aid programs. This proposal was consistent with Reagan's commitment to return power to the states, and it would have helped balance the federal budget.

These proposals were not even given serious considerations by Congress, and they were strongly attacked by Democrats and minority groups. In his 1983 State of the Union message, the president dropped the idea of transferring major federal programs to the states. By its second term the Reagan administration had lost much of its enthusiasm for radical reform of intergovernmental relations. Emphasis shifted to more conventional reform, such as reducing federal regulations regarding grant applications and evaluation.

The relative lack of success of Reagan's proposals can be attributed to several factors.[6] One was bad timing. The national recession and runaway inflation in 1982 diverted attention away from debate about the nature of American federalism, and it also put additional financial pressure on the states. Politically, many liberals in Congress wanted to maintain control over federal programs, and they resisted cuts in social services when the president was asking for money for military spending. At the state and local levels, governors called for a federal takeover of the Aid to Families of Dependent Children (AFDC) program, rather than devoting it to the states. They feared the Reagan proposal would increase the tax needs and burdens of the states. Mayors feared that states would not deliver federal funds that were designed to be used to finance the turnback programs. Politically, the administration was not able to build a coalition broad enough to support a revolutionary restructuring of our federal system, and it had less control over Congress after 1982.

The Reagan Legacy

Although President Reagan's "big swap" of federal-state programs did not occur, fundamental change did take place. States were given more control over the grant-in-aid program, and the federal government sent a clear signal to the states that they could not expect future federal initiatives in domestic policy. As we have seen, the shift to retrenchment in domestic spending began in the 1970s under the Carter administration. When Reagan took office in 1981, cuts were made in entitlement programs to the poor (Medicaid, food stamps, and Aid to Families with Dependent Children) and in operating grants to the states. In addition, the creation of new block grants gave the states greater flexibility in administrating federal funds. Despite cutbacks in federal aid, states continued to increase their spending until 1985.[7] After 1985, state spending on social programs became increasingly dependent on changes in the level of income of their residents.

Nathan and Doolittle state that Reagan's cuts in federal aid fell disproportionately on the poor.[8] Cuts were made in entitlement programs and public service, jobs for the poor were eliminated, child nutrition programs were reduced, funding for community development in large cities was diminished, aid to schools in low-income urban areas was reduced because of changes in block grants, and public housing rents increased. Thus most of the Reagan cuts came in federally controlled grant-in-aid programs. Where state governments play a stronger role, as in Medicaid policy, cuts were less substantial (see Chapter 14).

President Bush shared Reagan's view that more responsibility should be shifted to the states in the form of block grants and that federal domestic policy should be limited to a few areas where there was a "vital national interest." Still, federal grants-in-aid in constant dollars increased from $115 billion in 1988 to $182 billion in 1992, Bush's last year in office. The Advisory Commission on Intergovernmental Relations reports that there was a 20 percent jump in 1992, the largest yearly increase since 1973.

A major legacy of the Reagan-Bush administrations was the huge federal debt. Although the federal budget has had a deficit every year since 1969, the rate of growth was particularly steep in the 1980s. The size of the debt and the antitax sentiment of the Reagan-Bush years have made it very difficult to initiate new domestic programs in the 1990s. In response to these financial and political restraints Congress has effected change largely through unfunded mandates that require spending by state and local governments.

As explained by political scientist John Kincaid, the other predominant change in intergovernmental relations that started in the 1980s and continues in the 1990s is that federal policy increasingly has been aimed at persons rather than places.[9] Previously, federal aid was directed largely to state and local governments (places) because they were viewed as having primary responsibility for the well-being of citizens. Now proportionately more aid, including mandates, is given directly to individuals. In the 1960s and 1970s about one-third of federal grant funds were entitlement payments to individuals. This increased to 55 percent in 1989, and it is estimated to be 74 percent by 1997. In part this has occurred because members of Congress get reelected by gaining interest group support and by communicating directly with voters through the media, rather than by gaining the political support of state and local officials. Huge increases in Medicaid and other entitlement programs caused payments to individuals as a proportion of all federal grants to double from 1965 to 1995.

Clinton Programs

As a former governor, it was expected that President Bill Clinton would identify closely with the intergovernmental problems faced by states. During his first year in office President Clinton met frequently with state and local officials, and he placed Vice President Al Gore in charge of a review of federal-state relations. Because of the president's eagerness to invite governors to the White House for social occasions, but then exclude them from the policymaking process, the term "black tie" federalism has been applied to the Clinton administration.[10]

Although President Clinton issued an executive order on unfunded mandates shortly after he took office, he found mandates and preemptions convenient ways to support his domestic programs when the federal deficit made it difficult to find additional funding. For example, the Handgun Violence Prevention Act of 1993 (the Brady Bill) requires local law enforcement officers to conduct background checks on handgun purchasers, but it does not provide any money to cover the added expense. The Americans with Disabilities Act of 1993 requires state and local governments to make all new and renovated facilities accessible to the disabled, but it is an underfunded mandate that provides only part of the cost of compliance.

With the election in 1994 of a Republican Congress and the expectation of decreased federal aid to cities, the designation of nine **empowerment zones** and ninety-five enterprise communities (sixty urban and thirty rural) may have been the last big federal handout to urban areas in this decade. Under the Omnibus Reconciliation Act of 1993, empowerment zones are at the center of President Clinton's urban policy. In particular, the act provided federal grants of $100 million each to six large cities in which empowerment zones were identified in the most economically deprived neighborhoods. The money will be used to fight crime and poverty, create jobs, and encourage economic development. Three rural empowerment zones will receive $40 million each plus tax breaks. As part of the application process for the awards, cities and rural areas were asked to explain what they could do to help their most depressed areas if federal funds were made available. In Detroit, its successful application included a commitment from General Motors, Ford, and Chrysler to create over 3,000 jobs to invest nearly $2 billion in the enterprise zone. A consortium of Detroit universities pledged to focus the efforts of several of their academic departments on the enterprise zone.[11]

Vice President Gore's National Performance Review (NPR), reported in September 1993, had over 100 recommendations for change in federal-state relations. The broad goals of the NPR sounded a definite "reinventing government" theme (see Chapter 7) that included "cutting red tape, putting customers first, empowering employees to get results, cutting back to basics . . ."[12] Reflecting a desire for mission-driven government, the NPR stated, "In a perfect world, we would consolidate the 600 federal grant programs into broad funding pools, organized around major goals and desired outcomes—for example, safe and secure communities . . ."

Specifically, the NPR called for a **"bottom-up solution"** to the problem of grant fragmentation. It cited the failure of previous "top-down" proposals aimed at revamping all 600 federal grant programs from offices in Washington. Instead, state and local officials would be trusted to design solutions from the citizen-customer perspective. The National Performance Review noted, for example, that there are over 140 federal programs assisting children and their families, with funding coming from 10 federal departments and 2 independent agencies. After a grant has been awarded to a state or local agency, the recipient would have the power to consolidate all or part of that grant with other grants serving the same customers. These bottom-up solutions would have some limitations, such as requiring notification to the corresponding federal offices for small grants and federal approval if the grant is over $10 million.

The NPR called for ways to simplify and streamline procedures for state and local governments to comply with federal grant regulations. The report noted that about $19 billion in federal grant funds in 1993 were used to reimburse state and local governments for their administrative costs related to federal grants.

The Republican-controlled Congress in 1995 acted to devolve much more power to the states than had occurred under President Reagan in the 1980s. As will be discussed near the end of this chapter, Congress quickly passed a bill aimed at reducing the number of unfunded mandates. Legislation was approved late in 1995 to permit the states to set whatever speed limit they wished on interstate highways (or to choose not to post any limits) and to drop federal incentives that have encouraged states to adopt motorcycle helmet laws. In both cases it is up to the states to decide how they want to balance individual freedom against the need for public order. As discussed later in this chapter, the most significant proposals to rearrange state-federal relations came when Republicans wanted to turn over much of the administration of federal welfare and health care programs to the states in the form of block grants.

The Role of the Supreme Court

In the American federal system, the distribution of power between national and state governments has never been fixed. There has been a continual reshuffling of power, followed by considerable resistance when one level is forced by legislative or judicial action to give up power. For example, some states were reluctant to relinquish the authority to apportion their legislatures and integrate their schools. In 1985, the Supreme Court held in *Garcia* v. *San Antonio* that federal wage and hour standards apply to municipal and state workers and that the Tenth Amendment does not shield states from this federal regulation of "traditional government functions." That decision was reinforced in *South Carolina* v. *Baker* (1988), in which the Court ruled that Congress could tax interest on bonds sold by state and local governments.

When Congress passed the National Minimum Drinking Age Act in 1985, it included a provision that states would get reductions in federal highway funds if they did not raise the legal age for purchasing alcoholic beverages to 21. This was challenged as a violation of the Twenty-first Amendment (repeal of Prohibition), which some contended returned absolute control of alcoholic beverages to the states. In *South Dakota* v. *Dole* (1987) the Supreme Court held that even though Congress lacked the authority to raise the drinking age, it could attach an age requirement to a grant proposal because state participation was voluntary. To others it seemed coercive because states could not afford to give up sizable federal revenue. While South Dakota would have lost $8 million in 1988, Texas would have forfeited $100 million in highway aid. All states raised their drinking age to 21. In dissent, Justice Sandra Day O'Connor believed the legislation violated the Twenty-first Amendment, and she stated that the drinking age was not "sufficiently related to highway construction to justify conditioning funds appropriated for that purpose."

Earlier in this chapter we noted that beginning in the late 1930s the Supreme Court consistently supported broad federal power over the states. Several decisions since 1992 indicate that a four- or five-person group on the Court is committed to returning power to the states and limiting federal authority. In *United States* v. *Lopez* (1995) a five-person majority for the first time since 1936 overturned a federal law on the ground that it exceeded the Constitution's grant of authority to Congress to regulate interstate commerce. In *Lopez* the Court declared unconstitutional the Gun-Free School Zones Act of 1990 that made it a federal crime to possess a gun in close proximity to a school. The majority held that this was the responsibility of states, noting that many states already had approved gun-free zones around schools and that the law had "nothing to do with commerce." Shortly after *Lopez* was decided, the Court struck down state-imposed term limits for members of Congress. But it is noteworthy that writing for the dissent in *U.S. Term Limits* v. *Thorton* Justice Clarence Thomas argued that the federal government operates largely with the concurrence of the states on domestic matters. In another example of how 1930s' ideas about federal powers are making a comeback, Justice Sandra Day O'Connor resuscitated the Tenth Amendment when the Court in *New York* v. *United States* (1992) overturned a federal environmental law because it unconstitutionally infringed on state sovereignty.

Taking a much more extreme states rights position, Representative Helen Chenoweth (R, Idaho) suggested in 1995 that it was a violation of state constitutional provisions for federal fish and wildlife officials to be armed in Idaho without state approval. Her comments came shortly before the bombing of the federal building in Oklahoma City raised national concern about how the American people perceive the role of the federal government and its employees. In turn, the rise of militia groups in about two-thirds of the states has led antiviolence advocates to wonder why militia groups exist despite the fact that laws in forty-one states bar or regulate armed paramilitary groups. The Supreme Court has held that the Second Amendment grants states, *not individuals,* the right to form well-regulated militias.

CONTEMPORARY FEDERAL-STATE RELATIONS

The evolution of American federalism shows that the nation has moved from separate levels of government, acting almost as sovereign entities, to levels of government that interact and cooperate in an increasingly interdependent system. Intergovernmental relations involve interactions between the federal government and the states, between states, and between states and their localities.

Grants-in-Aid

We have briefly examined the changing relationships between the national government and the states. In large part, **grants-in-aid** have been the vehicle by which federal authority has greatly expanded since the early 1950s. **Fiscal federalism**—grants of money from the national government to the states and from the states to local governments—is at the center of intergovernmental relations and enables Congress to exert considerable influence over the states. For example, the threat of withholding funds from the states allowed Congress to set such national standards as the 55 m.p.h. speed limit and has led to increasing the legal age for drinking alcoholic beverages.

One argument for increased federal involvement in traditional state and local activities has been that it provides a degree of national uniformity (in the form of minimal standards) in a system divided by interstate competition. Also, because of great differences in state wealth, spending for such programs as education and public assistance varies greatly from one part of the country to another. Federal aid can make things more equal and provide more nearly uniform benefits by transferring money from rich states to poor states (the "Robin Hood effect"). As a result, the federal grants-in-aid program has provided a politically acceptable way of providing needed money to state and local governments while keeping the formal structure of federalism.

Increasingly in the 1950s and 1960s, both state and local governments were faced with pressing demands to solve social problems at a time when their financial base was either dwindling or expanding only a little. Cities often found state legislatures unwilling or unable to come to their aid. As a result, they turned directly to Congress for help. Congress responded to cities and states by greatly expanding the grants-in-aid programs already existing while keeping state and local administration of government programs. Grants provide the means by which the federal government exerts some effect on state programs without taking over the entire function and removing it from state or local control.

The federal grant program also grew as a result of the formation of **vertical coalitions.**[13] As explained by Thomas J. Anton, groups that were too weak politically to get what they wanted from local governments joined with similar groups across the country to persuade Congress to enact legislation that would support their goals. Anton comments that these relatively loose vertical coalitions often were able to demonstrate that a "problem" existed and to convince Congress to "spend some money and see what happens." The groups received grants and members of Congress could take credit for responding to needs in their districts. Of course, program administrators could expand their budgets and also appear responsive to societal needs. In this way categorical grants and vertical alliances led to alliances of administrators that have been referred to as **"picket-fence federalism"** (see the Scholarly Box).

Grants-in-aid are by no means new. They began with the Land Ordinance Act of 1785, which provided land grants for public schools in the developing Western territory. Throughout the nineteenth century, grants were made available for railroads and canals.

SCHOLARLY BOX

PICKET-FENCE FEDERALISM

This is a concept or model first developed by North Carolina governor Terry Sanford and expanded on by political scientist Deil S. Wright* to illustrate the power of and the relationships among national, state, and local administrators (program specialists) operating in various policy areas.

As federal grants-in-aid grew in the 1960s and 1970s, federal funding dominated program areas, but implementation was largely left to state and local administrators. Those persons in charge of libraries or mental health facilities developed close relationships with their counterparts in other levels of government. Each picket in the model illustrated below represents an alliance among program specialists that existed independently of the level of government (the horizontal lines) they served. While functional program specialists were united across government boundaries, they competed at each level of government against other program areas (for example, education versus hospitals) for grant money.

Competition among functional departments divided city, county, and state government, leading to the use of such descriptive terms as "balkanized bureaucracies." As we will see in Chapter 7, as administrators received higher proportions of their funds from Washington, they became less responsible to elected officials and to the general public and became known as "bureaucratic baronies."

Today, the picket-fence model has become a less accurate way to describe the federal system. This is because the bureaucratic maze of the 1970s and the lack of local political control have been mitigated by the

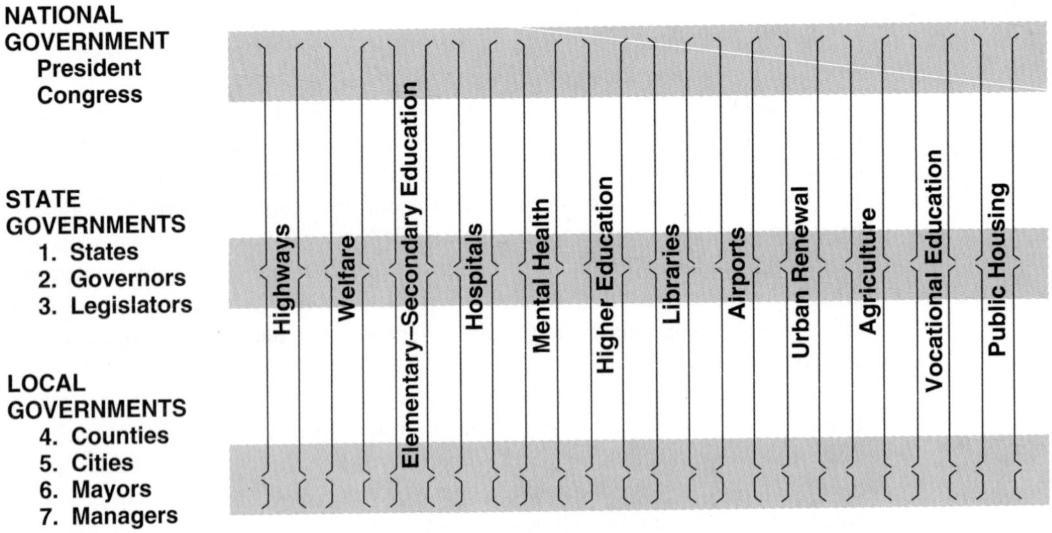

THE BIG SEVEN PUBLIC INTEREST GROUPS

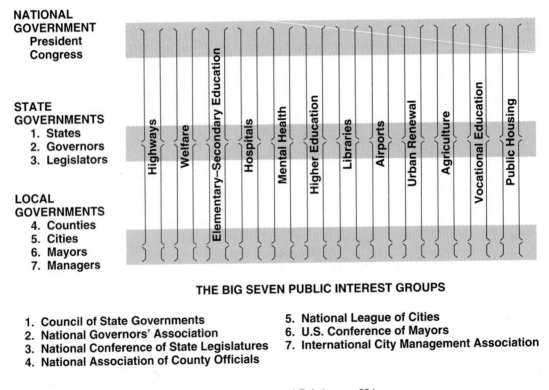

1. **Council of State Governments**
2. **National Governors' Association**
3. **National Conference of State Legislatures**
4. **National Association of County Officials**
5. **National League of Cities**
6. **U.S. Conference of Mayors**
7. **International City Management Association**

Source: (Deil S. Wright, *Understanding Intergovernmental Relations,* p. 83.)

increased use of block grants and by the exercise of more oversight of federal programs by local officials.

Deil S. Wright acknowledged several limits in the model, even as applied to the 1960s and 1970s. After all, any model is a simplification of reality. Wright noted that the "pickets" are broad categories, not specific programs. In fact, there might be 500 to 1,000 specific programs. The vertical pickets, with the national government at the top, were not meant to suggest an automatic hierarchy with national administrators at the top. National administrators, says Wright, seldom "control" state or local administrators. Nor does the model mean to imply that there is total agreement on issues among administrators working in the same policy area.

Still, the model reflects many aspects of federalism in the 1960s and 1970s, and until more extensive consolidation of grants occurs, it continues to give us a means of visualizing relationships within the intergovernmental system.

*Terry Sanford, *Storm over the States* (New York: McGraw-Hill, 1967), pp. 80–81; and Deil S. Wright, *Understanding Intergovernmental Relations,* 3d ed. (Pacific Grove, Calif.: Brooks/Cole, 1988), pp. 83–86.

However, they did not become politically significant until after World War II. In 1950, federal grants to state and local governments amounted to only $2 billion annually. By 1970, there were 530 grants-in-aid programs paying out about $24 billion every year. In spite of President Nixon's campaign oratory about decentralizing government, about 100 grant programs were created by the Nixon and Ford administrations. The federal grant program continued to increase sharply under the Carter administration.

In fiscal 1982, federal grants had their first absolute decline in more than twenty-five years (see Table 2-1). As noted earlier, this was consistent with President Reagan's desire to cut federal spending and reduce government regulation.

There are two types of federal grants. **Categorical grants** are made for specific purposes, such as job training, highway safety, prevention of juvenile delinquency, and agricultural extension. The recipient of such a grant has little choice about how the money is to be spent, so the federal government retains more control. Categorical grants made up about 80 percent of all federal grants in 1980. **Block grants** are much broader in their scope. They allow greater choice by the recipient, and they reduce or end matching requirements. For example, Community Development Small Cities Block Grants create a "package" of grants to deal with a series of problems previously covered by separate, categorical grants. As discussed in the next section, President Reagan's "new federalism" program stressed the development of block grants, and the Republican-controlled Congress has since 1995 strongly favored the use of block grants as a way to return power to the states.

Another way of categorizing grants is according to their terms for distribution. **Formula grants** are distributed to all eligible recipients on the basis of established guidelines. For example, in aid to the blind, all needy blind persons in every state can receive federal aid as a matter of "right." **Project grants,** however, require specific congressional approval; they are not distributed equally among all potential recipients. Instead, under grants such as urban renewal, specific programs are funded in only some of the areas in which problems exist. About two-thirds of all grants are project grants. In contrast to states, local governments receive most of their federal aid in proj-

TABLE 2-1 FEDERAL GRANTS-IN-AID IN RELATION TO STATE AND LOCAL OUTLAYS, TOTAL FEDERAL OUTLAYS AND GROSS DOMESTIC PRODUCT
1955–1994
(Billions)

	Federal grants-in-aid (current dollars)				
			As a percentage of		
Fiscal year[1]	Amount[2]	Percent increase or decrease (–)	Total state-local outlays[3]	Total federal outlays	Gross domestic product
1975	49.8	14.7	22.6	15.0	3.3
1976	59.1	18.7	24.1	15.9	3.5
1977	68.4	15.7	25.5	16.7	3.6
1978	77.9	13.9	26.5	17.0	3.6
1979	82.9	6.4	25.8	16.5	3.4
1980	91.5	10.4	25.8	15.5	3.5
1981	94.8	3.6	24.7	14.0	3.2
1982	88.2	–7.0	21.6	11.8	2.8
1983	92.5	4.9	21.3	11.4	2.8
1984	97.6	5.5	20.9	11.5	2.6
1985	105.9	8.5	20.9	11.2	2.7
1986	112.4	6.1	19.9	11.3	2.7
1987	108.4	–3.6	18.0	10.8	2.7
1988	115.3	6.4	17.7	10.8	2.4
1989	122.0	5.7	17.3	10.7	2.4
1990	135.4	11.0	19.4	10.8	2.5
1991	154.6	14.2	20.5	11.7	2.7
1992[r]	178.1	15.2	21.5	12.9	3.0
1993[r]	193.7	8.8	21.9	13.8	3.1
1994[e]	217.3	12.2	n.a.	14.6	3.3

n.a.—not available
[r]revised
[e]OMB estimate
Note: The number of federal grant programs funded was 132 in 1960, 379 in 1967, 426 in 1975, 404 in 1984, and 557 in 1992.
[1]For 1955–1976, fiscal years ending June 30; 1977 and later, fiscal years ending September 30.
[2]See *Special Analysis H* of the *1990 Budget of the United States* for explanation of differences between grant-in-aid figures published by the National Income and Product Accounts, Census, and OMB.
[3]As defined in the National Income and Product Accounts.
Source: Significant Features of Fiscal Federalism 1994, vol. 2 (Washington, D.C.: Advisory Commission on Intergovernmental Relations, 1994), p. 9.

ect grants. This means they must rely heavily on "grantsmanship" in obtaining categorical grants. A balance sheet evaluating the grants-in-aid system would contain the advantages and disadvantages shown in the table on p. 53.

Although states have the option of *not* participating in the grants-in-aid programs, there is strong pressure to take advantage of the opportunity to get programs for half cost or less. This, in turn, places a great financial burden on states (particularly poor

Grants-in-aid

Advantages	Disadvantages
1 Provide funds needed by state and local governments.	**1** Large number and complexity of grants imposes administrative burdens on recipients and leads to the development of large bureaucracies.
2 Help to equalize resources in rich and poor states.	**2** Uncoordinated grants often overlap or are at odds with one another.
3 Encourage local initiative and experimentation.	**3** They dull local initiative and distort planning by directing attention to available grants rather than proposing solutions for problems in fields not covered by grants.
4 Are based on the progressive tax structure of the federal government.	**4** Duration of grants is often too long or too short.
5 Can concentrate attention in a problem area and provide valuable technical assistance.	**5** They encourage "grantsmanship"—the ability to fill out the forms in a way that pleases federal officials.
6 Allow introduction into the federal system of national values and standards.	**6** Categorical grants leave little room for state and local discretion regarding expenditures and require increased federal supervision. Local elected officials have little control of the programs.

ones) to earmark much of their discretionary money as matching funds for grants-in-aid. This fiscal federalism also puts strong pressure (some would say coercion) on the states to comply with federal regulations. Earlier we said that states were pressured by Congress into raising the drinking age to 21. As also noted, more recent decisions by the Supreme Court suggest that states may receive more judicial protection against federal policymaking than had been the case from the late 1930s until the early 1990s.

Let us look at the *economic rationales* that support the entire grants-in-aid system. As noted earlier, it is easier to raise revenue at the national level than at the state and local levels. This is so because the federal tax structure is more elastic than that of the state and local governments. Federal revenues rise in direct proportion to overall economic growth in the United States. As a result, federal revenue expands greatly without any increase in tax rates. In contrast, state and local taxes are less elastic; they do not respond well to economic growth. Thus city councils and state legislatures must create new taxes or raise existing tax rates to get added funds necessary to respond to their constituents' demands for more services. In addition, federal taxes are more *progressive* than state and local taxes. (Chapter 12 deals more specifically with state and local financing.)

A second economic rationale for grants-in-aid is what some observers refer to as **spillover benefits.** This means that the benefits obtained from a program administered in one government area may extend into other government areas. Thus it seems fair that all who benefit should share in the cost. Education is an example of how spillover benefits work. If a person educated in New York or New Jersey, where per pupil spending is far greater than the national average, moves to a state such as Tennessee, where per capita spending for education is lower, the second state benefits from educational programs for which it has not paid. Federal grants that support education make certain that all states share in the cost of any single program by the national government.

An additional benefit of federal grants is that they have helped reduce corruption by requiring review of state and local financial records by federal auditors. A final economic rationale is that grants reduce unnecessary administrative expense by requiring recipients to improve their administrative structures.

Regarding *political* expediency, it may be easier to mount a national campaign for a mixed federal-state program than to manage campaigns throughout the fifty states. Labor, for example, has its membership centered in about one-third of the states. It therefore has little effect in many of the other state capitals. Yet labor's strong influence in urban, industrial states gives it a great deal of bargaining power with Congress and the president. It also exerts pressure on the national government to respond to such problems as poverty, community mental health, and environmental protection—problems that otherwise would not receive political support because of the unresponsiveness of local political elites. From another perspective, political scientist David Mayhew argues that categorical grants provide "particularized benefits" to congressional constituencies and thus allow members of Congress to claim credit for benefits in their districts.[14] Since this helps their chances for reelection, it is not surprising that members of Congress are reluctant to cut categoricals.

More and more, traditional state and local political problems can be viewed as having national implications. With an interdependent economy, including transportation and communications systems, most problems do not have a purely local impact. As a result, the federal system involves plans in which federal and state officials join in fighting such problems as air pollution and urban decay. Federal grants allow Congress to form national objectives, which are put into effect through cooperation between federal officials and state and local governments. Such grants have also been an effective way for strong presidents, such as Franklin D. Roosevelt and Lyndon Johnson, to centralize their political aims.

Despite presidential calls for consolidation and simplification, federal grants-in-aid increased 88 percent during the last six years of the Reagan-Bush administrations. Much of the increase was in matching grant entitlement programs for individuals, led by Medicaid and Aid to Families with Dependent Children (AFDC). Direct aid to state and local governments decreased during that period. At the same time, states faced rising costs for education, health care, and crime control, plus increased expenditures to comply with federal mandates.

In 1994 there were over 600 programs (totaling about $226 billion), and 75 percent (about 450) were grants of $50 million or less. Duplication abounds. For example, the Clinton administration's National Performance Review (NPR) stated that 10 departments and 2 independent agencies administered over 140 programs designed to help children and their families. Each program has its own set of rules and regulations. Because of competing, and often conflicting, federal rules, states are not free to integrate programs in a general service area to fit the special needs of residents. As a result, programs are operated by different agencies, often in different locations, by different people with varying degrees of expertise, and in accordance with different sets of rules and regulations.

The complex grant delivery system increases the administrative costs of states and localities. Nearly $20 billion of federal grant funds is used to reimburse states for direct and indirect administrative costs. Procedures could be greatly simplified to reduce costs. The NPR reported that states and localities must comply with eighteen cross-cutting federal requirements for each grant application, and there are other requirements not contained in the standard forms. Great disparities in administrative costs exist among the states. For example, in 1991 Alaska spent $300 per recipient to administer AFDC, Medicaid, and food stamps, while West Virginia spent $54 per recipient.

For those who worry that the acceptance of categorical grants with their rules and regulations has had a negative impact on the political traditions of states, political scientist Daniel J. Elazar has some reassurance. Elazar finds that states generally accept those federal programs that fit into their political cultures.[15] For example, Wisconsin's pioneering welfare programs became the model for federal programs in the 1930s. Minnesota's predisposition for positive governmental programs has led its members of Congress to support the initiation of federal health and welfare programs. On the other hand, program administrators in other states may use federal requirements to expand state programs or to create new ones. Thus states respond to federal programs in ways that reflect their political cultures.

Revenue Sharing

Dissatisfaction with the restrictiveness of grants-in-aid and a desire to return power to the states prompted the creation of revenue sharing. Essentially, **revenue sharing** was the return of federal tax money to states and localities, with minimum restrictions on its use, permitting the local decision-making process to determine which programs will be funded. Passage of a revenue-sharing bill was delayed for several reasons. First, the Vietnam War removed an expected federal revenue surplus. Second, liberals, including organized labor, feared that states would not "pass through" enough funds to cities. Third, Representative Wilbur Mills (then chairman of the House Committee on Ways and Means) delayed the bill. He argued that when one level of government spends money raised at another level, it encourages irresponsible behavior free from voter scrutiny. Once Mills's opposition was removed, the Nixon revenue-sharing plan—the State and Local Fiscal Assistance Act of 1972—was quickly approved.

The 1972 revenue-sharing act provided about $30 billion to be given to states and localities over a five-year period. Roughly one-third of the funds were allocated to the states, two-fifths to cities, and one-fourth to counties. (Special-purpose districts, such as school districts, were not eligible to receive these funds.) Some 39,000 government units received revenue-sharing money. The funds were given out under a very complex formula that looked at such factors as total population, state and local tax revenue, state income tax, personal per capita income, federal tax liabilities, and degree of urbanization. As a result, there was not a direct population equation.

In 1976, Congress overwhelmingly voted to extend the revenue-sharing program through September 30, 1980. Provisions under the 1976 act called for greater citizen participation in deciding how revenue-sharing funds would be spent. In 1980, another election year, mayors and governors strongly supported keeping the program at full funding. Early in the year, the Carter administration called for the termination of revenue sharing as part of a move to balance the federal budget. However, this position was later changed when it became clear that the budget would remain unbalanced. Congress extended revenue sharing, but only for local governments, where the financial need seemed greater than at the state level. President Reagan called for the elimination of revenue sharing as a way to reduce federal spending, and Congress ended all revenue sharing appropriations by 1988. Unfortunately for cities, concurrently with the end of revenue sharing came reductions in federal grants and a recession in the early 1990s. Many cities turned to increased user fees and to more state aid to compensate for the loss of federal money.

Block Grants

Earlier we considered block grants in contrast to categorical grants. More accurately, block grants may be thought of as a middle ground between categorical grants, which provide for strong congressional control, and general revenue sharing, which gives states greater independence. As such, block grants represent a balance between national goals and greater recipient flexibility.[16] Block grants are programs in which federal funds are provided to "general purpose governments" for use in a broad functional area, largely at the recipient's discretion.

Prior to 1981, only five block grants had been created. The oldest block grant still functioning is for education under Chapter Two of the Elementary and Secondary Education Act of 1965. No new block grants were enacted during the Ford and Carter administrations. Block grants approved in the 1960s and 1970s consolidated existing categorical grants, the aim being increased efficiency. Local officials were given greater control over selecting activities to be funded, and there were fewer federal regulations.

The Reagan administration abruptly reversed past practice in 1981 by converting fifty-seven categorical programs designed to achieve specific goals in health, education, transportation, and urban aid into nine block grants. These changes began with the 1982 fiscal year. President Reagan originally proposed consolidating eighty-six categorical grants into seven major block grants, but Congress retained many of the categoricals. Still, a substantial number of categorical grants were eliminated in the early 1980s. Overall, states received less money under the new system, but the Reagan administration argued that states would be compensated for that by being given greater flexibility to administer grants.

However, the amount of grant funds began to increase by the mid-1980s, and states lost some of the flexibility promised by block grants because of the growing use of **set-asides** in the late 1980s. Set-asides are provisions attached to block grants that designate a certain percentage of spending for special purposes. This has the effect of nationalizing public policy by creating similar priorities for spending across the country. Not surprisingly, states have objected to Congress attaching strings to block grants in a manner similar to categorical grants. From 1966 to 1995 twenty-three block grants were enacted and fifteen were still on the books in 1995. They totaled about $35 billion, compared to $200 billion in categorical grants.

Until 1995 all block grants involved capital or operating expenses. For the most part, they were collections of categorical grants, which had already been approved

Are Block Grants Really a Better Idea?

Neal R. Peirce

If a block grant loomed in front of you, would you recognize it? Most Americans wouldn't. They have some idea that block grants are big, sort of omnibus, go to state and local governments and ought to save money. If they're old enough, they remember that block grants have been kicking around in public debate since the Nixon presidency.

Whatever block grants lack in clear image, however, they're surely making up in popularity this year in Washington.

House Republicans, who are intent on cutting a massive $230 billion in federal spending out of domestic programs over seven years, aim to fold 336 categorical aid programs into block grants. The Senate has voted for $190 billion in such cuts, with committees instructed to combine hundreds of programs into block grants.

Even the Clinton Administration is straining to move in the same direction. It's urging the consolidation of 271 categorical aid programs into 27 so-called Performance Partnerships—clearly a form of block granting.

Since the Nixon Administration, block grants have been associated with the New Federalism. The common theme has been to repudiate Franklin D. Roosevelt's New Deal, defang Washington bureaucrats and give more programs and responsibilities to the states—and to save money in the process.

President Nixon managed to get the community development block grant (CDBG) program up and running—it's still a mainstay of federal aid for poor neighborhoods—plus the popular but ill-starred general revenue sharing program, which was eventually killed in the Reagan Administration.

President Reagan's famed 1981 Omnibus Budget Reconciliation Act created nine big block grants that incorporated 57 categorical aid programs. But the overall saving—less than $10 billion a year—was a pale shadow of what's now on the table.

At the same time, neither Nixon nor Reagan could stop the proliferation of small categorical aid programs—indeed, they increased by more than 100 under Presidents Nixon and Ford. Reagan's block grants got slowly "recategorized" with new congressional conditions.

At last count (by the Advisory Commission on Intergovernmental Relations), the federal government has 618 categorical aid programs—a historic high-water mark.

The obvious questions: Will history repeat itself? Will efforts to cut the federal behemoth down to size by handing more responsibilities to the states be frustrated again?

Maybe—but maybe not. The American people are more fed up with Washington and more dubious of its management capacities than ever before.

And the spending cuts being contemplated by the Republican-controlled Congress—whether or not they're large enough to make room for tax cuts—are of gargantuan proportions. They make Nixon look like a liberal, Reagan like a middle-of-the-roader.

And some of the spending cuts will hurt, maybe a lot. Earlier generations of block grants went to help meet the operating and capital expenses of state and local governments. This time, the human side will be targeted. Programs ranging from aid to families with dependent children to medicaid, and from infant nutrition to services for abused and neglected children, are to be converted into block grants and then cut back severely in size.

Education and training programs, economic development, Head Start, criminal justice, housing—all are to be converted into block grants and shrunk. Even Nixon's legacy, the CDBG program that sustains many community development and other grass-roots efforts, will be reduced 20–50 percent in the first year, and more in each successive year.

In the 1980s, when the Reagan Administration was cutting back, states were coming out of an economic recession, had lots of cash in their coffers and were able to make up for a good chunk of the federal cutbacks. Today, with states and cities strapped for funds and competing bitterly for new businesses, the prospects for that kind of relief are very dim.

Instead, the nation is seeing a "race to the bottom" by lawmakers in Washington and in the states who are scurrying to see how many government programs and opportunities can be choked off—and how fast.

Then there's the issue of state bureaucracies. They're often as bloated and hidebound as Washington's.

John DiIulio and Donald F. Kettl, writing earlier this year about the House GOP's Contract With America in a report for the Brookings Institution, offered a serious warning:

"The contract contains virtually no administrative fine print," they wrote. "The language of devolution does more to hide than highlight the administrative realities of federal-state relations."

So far, as Congress rushes headlong toward change, there's scarcely a hint of how those hard questions are being addressed. Where are sensible requirements for state matching funds or protections for vulnerable populations or protections for funds that have flowed to the nation's hardest-pressed inner cities?

It would be much more effective, says "reinventing government" guru David Osborne, if block grants were structured as "challenge grants," providing more assistance to states or localities that can show real performance—jobs actually created, job placements made, changes in family health or private investment leveraged.

And what about the new demographic realities of metropolitan America? States could be encouraged to give proportionately greater funds to "citistate" regions that can come up with smart plans and approaches—ways to put their turf differences aside and tap regionwide public and private resources for greater results.

And what about reforming federalism to connect estranged citizens with their government—is anyone in Congress thinking of that?

Washington should be using block grants to achieve reform that works, instead of just inflicting pain. Maybe Congress could do just that if it would only stop to think.

by Congress. The Republican-controlled Congress in 1995 proposed a major change in which need-based entitlements would be turned into block grants. The most dramatic proposals were to consolidate several welfare programs, including AFDC, into state block grants, with far less federal restrictions than were written into the categorical grants, and to turn much of Medicaid into block grants. Critics responded that this kind of devolutionary approach would leave poor people without an adequate safety net. For Republicans, welfare block grants would fit into their vision of federalism that calls for the assignment of many federal government responsibilities to state and local units.

In the preceding reading Neal R. Peirce questions the rush by Republicans and Democrats to create more block grants. Peirce fears that when Congress turns power over to the states to manage a host of social programs (as they did shortly after this article was published) and simultaneously cuts funding, some states will be unable or unwilling to continue funding the programs. Peirce notes that it is the inner-city poor who will suffer if this happens. He then suggests how Congress should act to reform federalism.

FEDERAL MANDATES AND PREEMPTIONS

Federal mandates are legal orders from Congress or administrative agencies that require state or local governments to perform a certain activity or to provide a service. While condition-of-aid provisions in categorical grants can be avoided by states and localities by simply not applying for the grant, mandates legally cannot be avoided and they can be enforced in court. States and localities have always been subject to mandates. The mandate problem has occurred since the late 1980s because of the cumulative effect of an increased number of mandates since the mid-1960s and because an increasing percentage of mandates are unfunded. As we will explain later, cities get a double hit from mandates imposed by Congress and by state legislatures. In addition, some federal mandates are placed on states that, in turn, pass them through to local governments.

Two bills passed by Congress in 1993 show the financial impact of mandates on state and local governments. First, the Family and Medical Leave Act requires private and public employers with fifty or more employees to allow up to twelve weeks of unpaid leave in any twelve-month period. Second, the National Voter Registration Act ("Motor-Voter Bill") mandates that state and local governments establish procedures to permit voter registration where individuals apply for drivers' licenses or by mail. It also permits, but doesn't require, state and local governments to use offices that provide public assistance, unemployment compensation, and services to the disabled as voter registration locations. Of course, some federal regulation is welcomed by local governments. The Brady handgun control bill, also passed in 1993, was supported by the National League of Cities.

As explained by Joseph F. Zimmerman, mandates need to be distinguished from **restraints,** which prevent action by a state or local government.[17] Like mandates, restraints can impose significant costs on local governments. For example, in 1982 Congress prohibited private and public employers from requiring nonpolicymaking employees to retire because of age. This restraint increases costs to the extent that governments cannot replace older workers with lower-paid younger workers.

Zimmerman notes that environmental mandates are the most expensive federal requirements imposed on local governments, and they have increased dramatically since the early 1970s. For example, new EPA standards in 1991 require cities to lower by tenfold the level of lead in drinking water. In many cases water suppliers have to replace service lines, and this imposes significant costs, especially on small local governments. At the other extreme, New York City has constructed a $600 million plant to comply with federal water filtration requirements. Other expensive mandates for states and localities include those dealing with underground storage tanks, asbestos abatement, and persons with disabilities.[18]

Unfunded mandates have been the biggest source of conflict between states and the federal government in the 1990s. Nearly thirty statutes were enacted in the 1980s that imposed new regulations or significantly expanded existing mandates. By the early 1990s over 170 pieces of federal legislation imposed mandates on state and local governments. Alice Rivlin has observed that:[19]

> The federal government's own fiscal weakness has not made it any less eager to tell states and localities what to do. Indeed, when its ability to make grants declined, the federal government turned increasingly to mandates as a way of controlling state and local activities without having to pay the bill. . . . Mandates add to citizen confusion about who is in charge. When the federal government makes rules for state and local officials to carry out, it is not clear to voters who should be blamed, either when the regulations are laxly enforced or when the cost of compliance is high.

In response to widespread criticism about mandates, President Clinton issued an executive order on unfunded mandates, and over thirty mandate-relief bills were introduced in Congress by the end of 1993. One of the first actions taken by the 104th Congress after Republicans gained control of the House and Senate in the 1994 elections was to pass the so-called unfunded mandates bill. The bill had broad support among Republicans and Democrats, and it was backed by President Clinton. The bill forces Congress to define the costs and to vote on individual mandates, but it does not prohibit Congress from imposing new mandates. It does not apply to existing legislation, and it will not apply to bills, such as the Clean Water Act, when they come up for reauthorization. Still, it will reduce some of the financial burden placed on states. To the extent that Congress will be less likely to impose regulations if it has to pay the costs, the bill is part of a broader Republican party attack on federal power.

In addition to mandates, restraints, and restrictions in federal grants, **preemption** is another means of federal intervention into state and local affairs. Here Congress nullifies certain state and local laws totally or partially. Congress enacted only thirty preemption statutes before 1900, and the number remained low until the 1970s.[20] The major increase came when President Reagan signed into law over ninety preemption bills in the 1980s.

Various types of total preemption range from those removing all regulatory power from states to those that encourage states to cooperate in enforcing a statute. As Zimmerman notes, "The states have been stripped of their powers to engage in economic regulation of airlines, buses, and trucking companies, establish a compulsory retirement age for their employees except for policy-makers, or regulate bankruptcies."

Since the mid-1960s, partial preemption statutes have had a greater impact on federal-state relations than total preemption statutes. Congress has enacted minimum standards for partial preemption to give a framework for new regulatory programs. This has increased the interdependence of states and the federal government because states develop regulations and then negotiate with federal officials to implement the plans within minimum standards set by a federal agency, such as the EPA. Only if a state fails to carry out regulation will the federal government step in to assume complete control.

While partial preemptions usually have resulted in state cooperation, states resent federal intrusion and they have lobbied for relief. However, only ten preemption relief bills were approved from 1965 to the early 1990s. Zimmerman notes that Congress tends to enact preemption statutes and then amends them when faced with political opposition. When preemption is considered with mandates, Zimmerman believes that Congress has changed since 1965 from a generous supplier of funds (grants-in-aid) to a preemptor imposing costs that have the potential for bankrupting many small local governments and fiscally strained cities by the year 2000.[21] Particularly in regard to small governments, Zimmerman recommends that Congress should show more restraint in imposing mandates, and it should at least partially reimburse governments for mandated costs.

Although federal aid as a percentage of all state and local expenditures declined from an all-time high of 27 percent in 1978 to 22 percent in 1992, the federal government actually became *more* intrusive in state and local affairs. This is due to the increase in mandates and preemptions plus the fact, as noted earlier, that federal aid increasingly has bypassed state and local governments to go directly to individuals. The "persons not places" phenomenon has meant that federal payments to individuals gradually have exceeded grants to state and local governments.[22] As this has happened, states and cities often have been treated as just another special interest group seeking funds from the federal government.

HORIZONTAL FEDERALISM: INTERSTATE COOPERATION

The U.S. Constitution attempts to encourage cooperation among the states in the following ways:

1 States are to give "*full faith and credit* . . . to the public acts, records, and judicial proceedings of every other state." This clause requires a state to recognize the validity of civil actions, such as a contract for sale of property, which originate in another state. In the area of domestic relations—divorce, child custody, alimony—the situation is complicated by state refusal on occasion to accept as binding civil judgments of other states.

2 States are to extend to residents of other states all **"privileges and immunities"** granted their own residents. This includes allowing residents of one state to acquire property, enter into contracts, and have access to the courts in a second state. It does

not include the extension of political rights such as voting and jury service. In 1984 the Supreme Court held that New Hampshire could not exclude nonresidents from admission to the bar and the practice of law.

3 States are to return to another state fugitives who have fled from justice. It is the governor who signs **extradition** papers to deliver a fugitive to the state having jurisdiction over the criminal act. Although governors usually comply with requests for extradition, the Supreme Court during the Civil War ruled that this was a matter of executive discretion and a governor may refuse to deliver a fugitive upon request from another state. More recently the Court held that states must return fugitives. In 1934, Congress made it a federal crime to cross state lines to avoid prosecution or imprisonment.

4 States may enter into **compacts** with one another provided that Congress approves. There has been only one case in which congressional approval of a proposed interstate compact was denied. A state cannot withdraw from a compact unless the other-party states agree. The provisions of compacts take precedence over any state laws that conflict with their provisions.

The most significant use of interstate compacts has developed since World War II. Only 35 compacts were created between 1783 and 1920. There were 58 by 1940. Between 1941 and 1975, however, more than 100 compacts were enacted and the coverage was broadened. There are now over 120 compacts in effect dealing with the management of problems that cross state lines, such as transportation, environmental protection, taxes, and health care. The best-known interstate compact is the Port Authority of New York and New Jersey, established in 1921, which controls much of the transportation in greater New York City. Beginning with the Delaware Basin Commission in 1961, the federal government has joined with states—here Delaware, New York, New Jersey, and Pennsylvania—in "federal-interstates." More than thirty compacts are open to participation nationwide. Although the growth of interstate compacts has slowed, new compacts have been formed in recent years dealing with such areas as hazardous waste and natural resources management. In most instances compacts are viewed as a way to improve problem solving without involving the federal government.

States also cooperate through the exchange of information. An ever-growing number of associations—governors, attorneys general, welfare officials, lieutenant governors—hold regular conferences. Many of these organizations are associated with the Council of State Governments, which provides a framework of organization and also publishes materials (including *The Book of the States*) on a wide range of state government issues. State and local police cooperate with each other and with the FIB in the exchange of information regarding criminals. Some states have developed reciprocal programs in higher education. For example, residents of northwestern Ohio can attend Eastern Michigan University and pay Michigan in-state tuition. In turn, residents of southeastern Michigan can attend the University of Toledo and pay Ohio in-state tuition.

In spite of the availability of formal means of cooperation, interstate relations often are marked by *competition* and *conflict,* rather than by accommodation. In the field of taxation, states sometimes cite their low tax rates as a means of luring businesses from other states. Increasingly, environmental issues are causing interstate conflict. These include disposal of hazardous waste, dumping of pollutants in waterways, and acid rain in New England that is caused by air pollution in the Midwest.

In spite of federal encouragement of cooperation, the states differ considerably. For example, even though legislators and attorneys general attend regular conferences, and even though the National Conference of the Commissioners on Uniform Law has existed since 1892, there remains a significant lack of uniformity in commercial law. Differences also exist in divorce laws, legal marriage age, and voting residency requirements. At one time, California legislators attempted (unsuccessfully) to bar paupers from moving into their state. Truckers are confronted with a variety of state rules regulating lights, load limits, and licensing as they travel cross-country. One might expect that in a "reasonable" system such confusion would have been eliminated by now. However, in the name of federalism Americans continue to support state and local autonomy and are therefore willing to live with the inconveniences that inevitably result.

STATE-LOCAL RELATIONS

As we have seen, states and cities in the United States exist in a unitary relationship. Thus, unlike the federal government's relations with the states, each state can coerce its cities to comply with policy objectives. For example, in the Aid to Families with Dependent Children (AFDC) program, federal matching funds are made available to states and their participation is voluntary. Because of fiscal incentives, all states participate in the program. However, states have considerable control because they are free to establish eligibility requirements and benefits beyond federal minimum standards. On the other hand, states may require localities to administer the AFDC program and contribute to its costs. When states also limit the ability of cities to raise revenue through taxation and they impose mandates on them, this creates severe financial stress.[23]

We have noted a decline in federal aid to state and local governments in the 1980s and then an increase in the early 1990s. The bad news for cities and counties is that much of the federal increase has been for entitlements to individuals that require them to provide benefits under federal guidelines and much of the increase in federal spending has gone to states. The part of municipal budgets provided by federal funds fell from 16 to 8 percent through the 1980s. Counties were hit just as hard. While local governments receive four times more state aid than federal aid (30 percent of local revenue comes from states), 60 percent of state aid is for education (see Table 2-2). Only one-eighth of traditional municipal services are supported by state funds.[24] As states experience their own financial problems, they pass costs along to cities and to counties and they cut assistance.

There are wide variations in levels of state aid, depending on such factors as tradition of centralization or decentralization of services. For example, the state of Hawaii totally administers and finances its elementary and secondary education system, while in New Hampshire virtually all education funding is a local responsibility. Seven states

TABLE 2-2 STATE INTERGOVERNMENTAL EXPENDITURES TO LOCAL GOVERNMENTS, BY FUNCTION, SELECTED YEARS 1954–1992 (Millions)

Fiscal year	Total	Annual percentage change	General support	Corrections	Education	Health	Highways	Public welfare	Other[2]
1975	51,978	13.1	5,129	103	31,110	n.a.	3,225	8,101	4,310
1976	57,858	11.3	5,674	120	34,084	n.a.	3,241	9,476	5,263
1977	62,470	8.0	6,373	123	36,975	n.a.	3,631	10,133	5,235
1978	67,287	7.7	6,819	118	40,125	n.a.	3,821	10,047	6,356
1979	75,975	12.9	8,224	195	46,206	n.a.	4,149	10,146	7,055
1980	84,505	11.2	8,644	237	52,688	n.a.	4,383	10,977	7,576
1981	93,180	10.3	9,570	277	57,257	n.a.	4,751	12,882	8,441
1982	98,743	6.0	10,044	366	60,684	n.a.	5,028	13,744	8,877
1983	101,309	2.6	10,364	456	63,118	n.a.	5,277	13,091	9,003
1984	108,373	7.0	10,745	571	67,485	3,363	5,687	13,628	6,894
1985	121,571	12.2	12,320	801	74,937	4,342	6,019	14,629	8,524
1986	131,966	8.6	13,384	915	81,929	4,609	6,470	16,298	8,360
1987	141,426	7.2	14,245	932	88,253	4,875	6,785	17,331	9,004
1988	151,662	7.2	14,897	1,016	95,391	5,407	6,949	17,665	10,338
1989	165,506	9.1	15,750	1,192	104,601	6,229	7,376	19,614	10,743
1990[r]	175,096	5.8	16,565	1,369	109,251	7,157	7,784	21,770	11,200
1991[r]	186,469	6.5	16,977	1,433	116,109	7,292	8,126	24,341	12,191
1992	201,313	8.0	16,368	1,689	124,920	6,360	8,481	29,512	13,983

[r]revised
[1]Average annual change from 1954 to 1964.
[2]Includes transit subsidies, sewerage, corrections, housing and community development, and other.
ACIR computations based on U.S. Department of Commerce, Bureau of the Census, *State Government Finances.*
Source: Significant Features of Fiscal Federalism 1994, vol. 2 (Washington, D.C.: Advisory Commission on Intergovernmental Relations, 1994), p. 10.

in 1992 distributed over $1,000 per capita in state aid, while five provided less than $500. Because Hawaii runs the educational system, it does not give education funds to local school districts, and as a result, it distributed only $110 per capita of state aid in 1992. Alaska and Wyoming rank first and second in the amount of state aid provided, reflecting the need to serve widely dispersed populations and the availability of severance tax revenue to fund programs.

As in federal-state relations, states pass financial burdens on to localities by the use of mandates and preemptions. Like the states, localities oppose mandates (especially unfunded mandates) because they distort local planning, limit their managerial flexibility, and impose costs. In particular, health care, education, and environmental mandates can overwhelm local resources. States impose more mandates on cities than does the federal government, and often expensive federal mandates are passed on to cities by states. Political scientist David Berman points out that local administrators may *welcome* some mandates that call on them to carry out politically unpopular programs, such as public housing, that they personally believe are the right thing to do.

Berman notes that "perhaps the most striking aspect of intergovernmental politics in 1993 . . . was increased evidence that local officials are willing and able to fight challenges to their authority and well being."[25] Political pressure has led states to enact legislation to ease the burden of mandates. Over forty states have set up commissions to estimate the cost imposed on localities by state legislation, and about thirty states require at least partial reimbursement of mandated costs. For example, in California the legislature must pay the cost of mandates or give localities the authority to raise taxes. In 1990 Florida voters approved a constitutional amendment that unfunded mandates can take effect only if approved by a two-thirds vote in both houses of the legislature. Since then the legislature has enacted far fewer mandates. Voters in Maine approved a constitutional amendment in 1992 that requires the state to provide 90 percent of the cost of mandates. As a result of this "combat federalism," relatively few new state mandates were imposed on local governments in the early 1990s.

State preemption refers to mandates that prohibit local governments from taking certain actions. Often preemptions are enacted in response to pressure from groups that want to avoid or minimize taxation or regulation. For example, businesses that manufacture pesticides have been successful in preventing local governments from regulating the use of pesticides. Largely because of pressure from the National Rifle Association, thirty states prohibit local governments from enacting gun control ordinances.

While state legislators criticize federal control of states, both Republican and Democratic legislators resist turning over political power to cities and counties. In part, this is because business groups (refer to preemptions) prefer to deal with one government rather than fight battles across the state. Legally, states have nearly unlimited authority to direct city and county governments by various rules, regulations, and mandates.

If states wanted to help localities, they could, of course, stop unfunded mandates and resist passing restrictive legislation. They also could assume responsibility for programs currently funded by localities. As we will see in Chapter 8, states have been centralizing control of courts and corrections. Although cities would like more discretion to raise taxes, they risk incurring the wrath of local taxpayers if states grant them authority to raise new sources of revenue. Federal *and* state mandates illustrate the mistrust between levels of government in our federal system. Federal officials mistrust the ability of the states to make good decisions, especially when it comes to protecting the interests of the poor, and, in turn, state officials don't trust city and county governments to act in the best interests of the public. States criticize the federal government, and cities and counties criticize the states, both arguing that remote officials in Washington and in state capitals do not understand what it is like to govern on a daily basis.

FEDERALISM EVALUATED

Critics of federalism offer a number of serious changes. Some suggest that because it gave Southern states independent power federalism helped foster racism in America;[26] that the states cannot deal effectively with social problems that cross state boundaries; that relations between states are marked more by conflict than by cooperation; that the unequal distribution of wealth among the states creates a system in which social benefits vary greatly from state to state; and that with more than 80,000 units of government, duplication of effort is unavoidable and makes it difficult for citizens to hold officials accountable for their actions.

In this chapter we have examined the lack of cooperation and the unequal distribution of social services among the states. We have noted that states have delayed and often obstructed national policy directions. Perhaps federalism means there will be too much attention directed to local matters. What level of government should address specific problems in our society has been the most persistent and divisive fundamental political issue throughout American history.

Considering the defects of the American federal system, the reader might well ask, "Why not scrap it and create a unitary system?" Centralization of authority under a unitary form of government might produce more efficiency in operating social programs and in overcoming racial discrimination.[27] The problem is that a unitary system might actually create more problems than it would solve.

Lockard argues that a unitary government might not be able to cope with controversial problems now left largely to the states. Of course, a unitary government could impose policies with a narrow ideological bent on a national basis. The misuse of the FBI and CIA by the Nixon administration shows how close the nation came to the establishment of a police state even under federalism. In a unitary system, a president seeking power might more easily have succeeded when directing a national police force. A unitary system possibly would create an even more dehumanized and routinized bureaucracy than already exists in city halls and county courthouses.

As we shall see in Chapter 11, Americans are questioning more and more the growth and centralization of government authority. Smaller units of government permit more citizens to participate and make possible greater economic control for residents of urban areas. While few people would favor conversion to a confederate form of government, there has been a strong movement led by the political right since the early 1980s to reduce the centralization of power that has occurred within our federal system. The evolution of American federalism shows periodic movement along a continuum that extends from very centralized to very decentralized (that is, state-centered) federalism.

Recently there have been calls for sorting out responsibilities between the states and the federal government in a way that clearly would limit federal authority. In a book written before she joined the Clinton administration, Alice Rivlin suggested that we rethink federalism and "divide the job" in such a way that the federal government limits its domestic agenda primarily to reforming the nation's health financing system.[28] States would take charge of such areas as education, housing, pollution control, infrastructure, and economic development. Rivlin bases her recommendations on the belief that states have increased their competence in recent years and thus are better able to deal with this federal devolution of tasks. She also sees this as a way to reduce the federal deficit, and she believes that the national government should devote more attention to international affairs. Under the Rivlin plan, states would strengthen their tax systems and establish common shared taxes that would help limit interstate competition.

During the Clinton transition period of 1992–1993, David Osborne argued that the federal government should not act unless (1) the problem needs an interstate solution, (2) uniform national standards are required, (3) the absence of national standards would lead to "destructive competition" among the states, or (4) redistribution across state lines is required to solve local problems.[29]

Federal systems offer a number of benefits.[30] These include the flexibility to respond to regional differences; the prevention of abuse of power because no single group is likely to gain control of government at the state and local levels; the encouragement of innovation by testing new ideas at the local level; the creation of many centers of power to resolve conflict and to handle administrative burdens; the stimulation of competition among levels of government that encourages policy innovation; and, as James Madison predicted, the prevention of abuse of power because it is nearly impossible for a single group to gain control of government at all levels. Of course, most of these benefits will occur only if state and local governments are energetic and respond to public demands. As we shall see throughout this book, there is strong evidence that the states have made the necessary structural changes and that elected officials have sufficient personal commitment to enable them to respond effectively to their policy needs.

SUMMARY

American federalism has evolved from a decentralized (state-centered) system, at the time of its creation until the first part of the twentieth century, to an increasingly centralized system. This expansion of power in Washington reached its high point in the 1960s and 1970s. President Reagan's call for a "new federalism" in the 1980s and the Clinton administration's efforts at devolution of power, which were accelerated by demands for "less government" by congressional Republicans, have led to a shift of government responsibilities to the states and to reductions in federal government spending for many domestic programs.

Much of the increase in federal power in the 1960s, 1970s, and 1980s was accomplished by the expansion of federal grants-in-aid and by the use of unfunded federal mandates. The use of block grants, beginning in the 1970s and expanded in the 1990s, and congressional action to limit unfunded mandates have contributed to a reduction of power in Washington that promises to continue into the next century.

Relations among states and between states and cities also have been marked by conflict and by the centralization of power in state capitals. State aid to localities has increased in recent years, and states also have used unfunded mandates to require certain actions by cities and counties.

KEY TERMS

Bill of attainder A legislative act that determines the guilt of an individual and hands down punishment without a trial. The United States Constitution prohibits the national government and the states from taking such action.

Block grants Grants made to cover broad, general areas of policy, such as health care, which allow the recipient freedom in the allocation of funds.

Bottom-up solution Permitting states and localities to combine and shape federal grants to meet their special needs.

Categorical grants Grants made for a specific purpose; the recipient has little choice in deciding how to spend the money.

Commerce The buying and selling of commodities, transportation, and commercial exchange.

Compacts Arrangements made by two or more states to cooperate in the management of a common problem, such as flood control.

Concurrent majority A proposal made by John C. Calhoun prior to the Civil War that all segments of the country must concur in decisions of the national government. If concurrence is lacking, individual states may accept or reject national decisions. This concept has been accepted only by extreme supporters of states' rights.

Confederacy A loose organization of independent states in which the central unit of government (unlike in a federation) cannot act directly upon individuals.

Dual federalism The belief that the powers of the states and the national government are fixed and that grants of power to the national government do not destroy power reserved to the states. This doctrine has been rejected by the Supreme Court.

Empowerment zones Distressed areas that receive federal grants and tax breaks to fight poverty and to encourage economic development.

Extradition The return of a fugitive to the state in which it is alleged that he or she committed a crime. This is done at the discretion of the governor.

Federal system A system in which a national government shares power with state and regional governments; supremacy rests with the national government.

Fiscal federalism The use of federal funds (often the threat to cut them off) to force states to take actions favored by Congress.

Formula grants Grants made available to everyone who qualifies under the guidelines established for eligibility, such as blind persons.

Grants-in-aid Federal programs in which funds are made available by Congress to state and local governments. The recipient must accept prescribed standards and usually must make a contribution from its own funds. States provide grants to local governments.

"Necessary and proper" clause The so-called elastic clause of the U.S. Constitution, which allows Congress broad authority to carry out its enumerated powers.

"New federalism" A way of viewing federalism that focuses on political interrelationships rather than on government structure. Stresses cooperation among government units.

Nullification As supported by Southern states prior to the Civil War, the doctrine that individual states might declare a national law null and void and secede from the Union. This was based on the belief that the states are the final judges of their authority.

Picket-fence federalism A model showing the interrelationships among program specialists at the local, state, and national levels of government.

Preemption The power of Congress to nullify certain state and local government laws and regulations totally or partially.

"Privileges and immunities" The provision of the U.S. Constitution that compels states to extend to residents of other states the same legal rights, such as the right to enter into contracts, as they extend to their own residents. Some *political* rights may be denied to out-of-state residents.

Project grants Grants that require specific congressional approval; not every unit of government that is generally qualified will receive funds.

Revenue sharing A federal program of returning tax dollars to state and local governments to be spent largely as they desire; this contrasts with grants-in-aid, under which money must be spent for specific programs as approved by the federal government. Revenue sharing ended in 1986.

Restraints Federal or state regulations that prevent action by other governments.

Set-asides Provisions attached to block grants that require a certain percentage of funds to be spent for a specific purpose.

Spillover benefits The benefits of a federal program in one state that "spill over" and benefit a second state.

Unitary nation-state A system in which states or regional governments can exercise only those powers given them by the central unit of government—as in Great Britain.

Vertical coalitions Groups that form at different levels of government across the country in order to persuade Congress to create grants that will support a particular policy area.

REFERENCES

1 See Morton Grodzins, "Centralization and Decentralization in the American Federal System," in Robert A. Goldwin, ed., *A Nation of States* (Chicago: Rand McNally, 1963).

2 David R. Beam, "New Federalism, Old Realities: The Reagan Administration and Intergovernmental Reform," in Lester M. Salamon and Michael S. Lund, eds., *The Reagan Presidency and the Governing of America* (Washington, D.C.: The Urban Institute, 1984), p. 423.

3 Russell L. Hanson, "Intergovernmental Relations," in Virginia Gray and Herbert Jacob, eds., *Politics in the American States,* 6th ed. (Washington, D.C.: C Q Press, 1996), p. 46.

4 Richard P. Nathan, Fred C. Doolittle, et al., *Reagan and the States* (Princeton, N.J.: Princeton University Press, 1987), p. 31.

5 David B. Walker, "Dysfunctional Federalism—The Congress and Intergovernmental Relations," *State Government,* vol. 54, no. 2 (1981).

6 Peter M. Benda and Charles H. Levine, "Reagan and the Bureaucracy: The Bequest, the Promise, and the Legacy," in Charles O. Jones, ed., *The Reagan Legacy: Promise and Performance* (Chatham, N.J.: Chatham House, 1988), p. 123.

7 J. Edwin Benton, "The Effects of Changes in Federal Aid on State and Local Spending," *Publius* (Winter 1992), p. 81.

8 Nathan, Doolittle, Fred C. Doolittle, et. al., *Reagan and the States* (Princeton, N.J.: Princeton University Press, 1987), p. 45.

9 John Kincaid, "Developments in Federal-State Relations, 1992–93," *Book of the States, 1994–95* (Lexington, Ky.: Council of State Governments, 1994), p. 580.

10 Ann O'M. Bowman and Michael A. Pagano, "The State of American Federalism, 1993–1994," *Publius* (Summer 1994), p. 1.

11 Neal R. Peirce, "The Power of Entitlement Zones," *National Journal* (February 4, 1995), p. 315.

12 "Creating a Government That Works Better and Costs Less" (Washington, D.C.: U.S. Government Printing Office, 1993), p. 1. Also see Bill Clinton and Al Gore, *Putting People First* (New York: Times Books, 1992); and William A. Galston and Geoffrey L. Tibbets, "Reinventing Federalism: The Clinton/Gore Program for a New Partnership among the Federal, State, Local, and Tribal Governments," *Publius* (Summer 1994), pp. 23–48.

13 See Thomas J. Anton, *American Federalism and Public Policy: How the System Works* (New York: Random House, 1989), pp. 83–85.

14 David Mayhew, *Congress: The Electoral Connection* (New Haven, Conn.: Yale University Press, 1974), p. 129.

15 Daniel J. Elazar, *The American Mosaic* (Boulder, Colo.: Westview Press, 1994), pp. 281–282.

16 Michael D. Reagan and John G. Sanzone, *The New Federalism,* 2d ed. (New York: Oxford University Press, 1981), pp. 124–125.

17 Joseph F. Zimmerman, "Financing National Policy through Mandates," *National Civic Review* (Summer–Fall, 1992), p. 366.

18 John Kincaid, "Developments in Federal-State Relations, 1992–93," p. 580. Also see Timothy J. Conlon and David R. Beam, "Federal Mandates: The Record of Reform and Future Prospects," *Intergovernmental Perspective* (Fall 1992), pp. 7–11.

19 Alice Rivlin, *Reviving the American Dream* (Washington, D.C.: The Brookings Institution, 1992), p. 107.

20 Joseph F. Zimmerman, "Congressional Regulation of Subnational Governments," *PS: Political Science & Politics* (June 1993), pp. 178–179. Also see Joseph F. Zimmerman, "Federal Preemption under Reagan's New Federalism," *Publius* (Winter 1991), pp. 7–28.

21 Joseph F. Zimmerman, "Congressional Regulation of Subnational Governments," p. 180.

22 John Kincaid, "From Cooperation to Coercion in American Federalism: Housing, Fragmentation and Preemption, 1780–1992," *The Journal of Law and Politics* (Winter 1993), pp. 333–430.

23 Russell L. Hanson, "Intergovernmental Relations," pp. 60–61.

24 David R. Berman, "State-Local Relations: Patterns, Politics, and Problems" in *The Municipal Year Book 1994,* p. 62.

25 Ibid., p. 59.

26 William H. Riker, *Federalism: Origin, Operation, Significance* (Boston: Little, Brown, 1964), p. 155.

27 Duane Lockard, *The Perverted Priorities of American Politics,* 2d ed. (New York: Macmillan, 1976), pp. 125–128.

28 Alice Rivlin, *Reviving the American Dream,* pp. 110–125.

29 David Osborne, "A New Federal Compact: Sorting Out Washington's Proper Role," in Will Marshall and Martin Schram, eds., *Mandate for Change* (New York: Berkley Books, 1993).

30 See David C. Nice, *Federalism: The Politics of Intergovernmental Relations* (New York: St. Martin's Press, 1987), pp. 13–16.

3

POLITICAL PARTIES AND INTEREST GROUPS

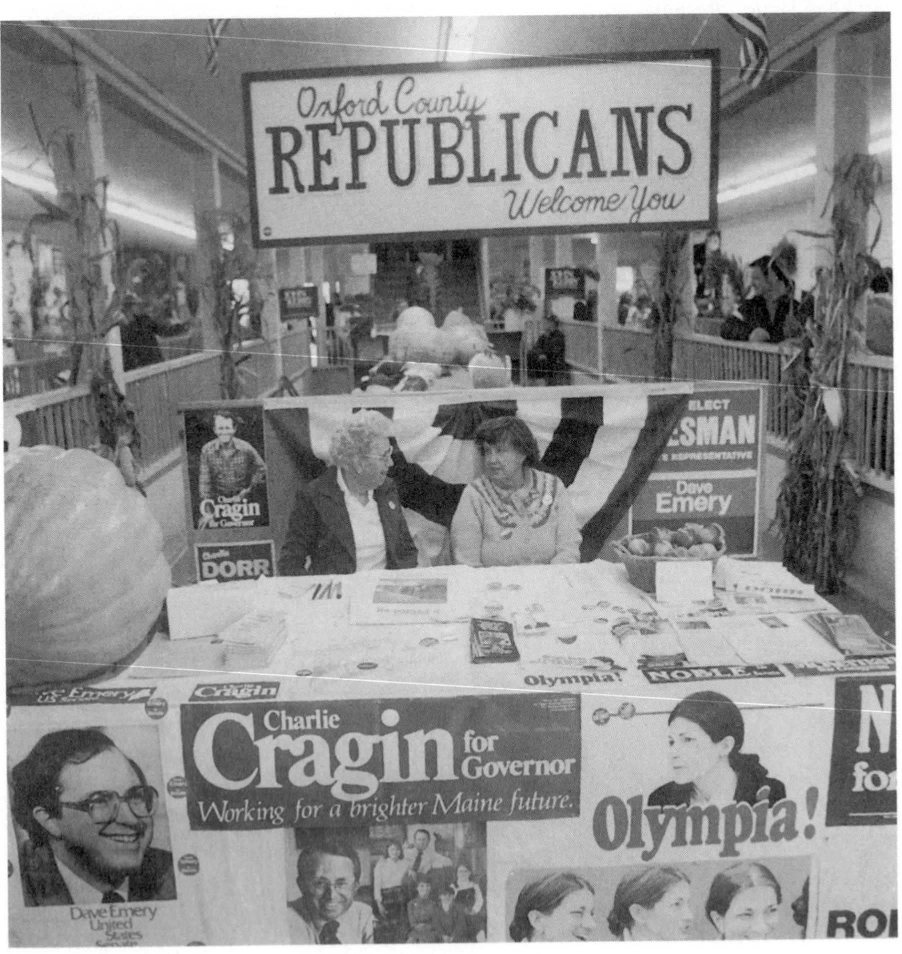

Mike Mazzaschi/Stock, Boston

Linking citizens to government is a function shared by political parties and interest groups. Political parties do this by running candidates for office during an election campaign who advocate certain programs and then implement these programs after being elected by the voters. Interest groups perform the linkage function by organizing citizens with similar views in a specific policy area and then presenting these views to government officials.

Still, there are more differences than similarities between parties and interest groups. Most significantly, interest groups—in the United States, at least—do not contest elections by running candidates for office. Although they may work within parties to have a favorite candidate nominated and endorse and work to elect candidates in the general election who will support their goals, they do not run their own candidates for office nor do they serve as symbols of voter loyalty.

Second, although political parties are committed exclusively to political action, interest groups engage in both political and nonpolitical activity. For example, while the American Medical Association (AMA) makes major financial contributions to political campaigns, it also maintains a variety of professional services for physicians. In regard to political activities, the two major parties take positions on a vast array of social and economic issues confronting the nation or the state. Interest groups, in contrast, are often concerned about only a single issue or a limited number of policy matters. Because of their broad commitment to public policies and their concern for winning elections, parties must appeal to the broadest possible spectrum of the electorate. The political positions taken by interest groups are much less inclusive, and their appeal is often limited to a small percentage of the American people. Because of their more narrowly defined goals and greater unity among members, interest groups generally have been more effective representatives of particular points of view than political parties.[1]

This chapter focuses on (1) changes in party organization and activities, (2) interest group growth and tactics, and (3) the influence parties and interest groups have in state politics and policymaking. For political parties, the increasing number of states that have two competitive parties will be of particular interest. And for interest groups, we will pay special attention to the ethics of lobbying.

POLITICAL PARTIES

Parties as Organizations

Legal Basis The U.S. Constitution does not mention political parties, and Congress has made little effort to regulate them. As a result, states are relatively free to restrict party activity by provisions in their constitutions and laws. On occasion, however, the U.S. Supreme Court has found some state regulations unconstitutional.

State regulation of parties can be divided into three periods. The first period, from the founding of parties through the beginning of the 1880s, contained no regulation, since parties were considered to be private political associations.

The second period, characterized by extensive regulation of parties, started in the 1880s and lasted into the 1970s. Some of the first laws to affect parties were those that adopted, beginning in 1888, the secret ballot system, also known as the Australian ballot. It was a reform measure aimed at reducing the hold that corrupt political machines had on the governments of many cities and states (see Chapter 9). Prior to the secret ballot, voters orally indicated the candidates they supported or they would deposit a ballot in the ballot box that had been printed by one of the parties and contained only the names of its candidates. Either practice led to voter intimidation and bribery. The new secret ballot system consisted of a ballot prepared by the state that listed all parties and candidates and, as its name implied, was marked in private by the voter.[2] Later reforms in the Progressive period (1900–1920) were directed to parties' internal structure and procedures. Also, states began requiring parties to use the direct primary to nominate candidates for elected office. This was an important change, as will be discussed shortly, because it undercuts the parties' ability to control who was nominated.

State regulations and party practices that prevented minority groups from voting in primary elections in many Southern states were appealed to the U.S. Supreme Court. For example, the practice of the Texas Democratic party of excluding blacks from primary elections was declared unconstitutional, as was the practice of Democrats in a Texas county of excluding blacks from participating in a preprimary straw ballot used by an informal group known as the Jaybird Democratic Association to determine who they would support in the primary.[3]

The third period of state regulation, which began in the 1970s and continues today, is actually one of deregulation, with the idea that political parties should be treated as private associations, as they once were. This is not to say that states no longer regulate parties; they do. But the necessity of some of these regulations is being questioned because they are viewed as contributing to the weakening of political parties as a link between voters and their government.[4] The U.S. Supreme Court has again entered the picture and declared some state party regulations unconstitutional. A Connecticut law that limited participation in a party's primary to voters registered with that party was overturned by the Court because it was in conflict with how one party wanted to run its primaries. The Republican party of Connecticut, which wanted to open its primary to voters registered as independents, challenged the law. The Court concluded that the Republican party's decision on who could vote in its primary could not be overridden by state law.[5] Republicans hoped that independents who voted in their party's primary would vote for Republican candidates in the general election and might eventually join the party, resulting in a stronger organization.

A major obstacle to party activity in California was eliminated when laws prohibiting parties from endorsing candidates in primary elections and regulating various aspects of the internal governance of the parties were overturned by the Court.[6]

How far will this deregulation trend go? Will political parties be completely deregulated? This seems unlikely because some regulations benefit the Democratic and Republican parties, and they will work hard to keep them. "Sore-loser" laws in many states, for example, help the two major parties by prohibiting a candidate who loses in a primary election from running in the general election as an independent or even as the nominee of another party.

Structure of State Parties The structure of state political parties follows that of voting districts, beginning with the smallest voting district, the **precinct.** An example of how one state party is organized is found in Figure 3-1. Rank-and-file party supporters are at the bottom, and the state party chairperson is at the top. (Of course, each party has its own organization.) Today, this is usually not a hierarchical structure, in which power flows from top to bottom. Each level operates somewhat independently of those units above and below it.

State party chairs and the state party committees are selected according to state laws or, in the absence of such laws, party rules. In over forty states, members of state committees are selected by committee members at local levels or by delegates to party conventions. The remaining states select state committee members in primary elections. The formal means of selecting state party chairs are by the state committee or by state conventions; however, the actual choice, as will be discussed in the section on Party Organization Today, is frequently influenced by the state's governor.[7]

The structure of county party organization also varies among the states. In the more common pattern, the precinct committeeperson is elected either by a precinct **caucus** or by voters in the party's primary election. The precinct committeeperson becomes a member of the county committee, which elects the county chairperson. In other states, the ward is the lowest level of organization that has a leader elected by the party's rank and file. The elected ward leaders compose the county committee and elect the county chairperson. Still another pattern is where members of a county committee are the lowest level of elected party officials. In the latter two cases, if precincts are organized, it is done by appointment by the ward or county chairperson.

Organizational Change A discussion of party organizations cannot proceed without brief reference to the gradual decline of what are now called **traditional party organizations.** Traditional party organizations, according to David Mayhew, had strong leaders who obtained the nomination and election of their favored candidates to a variety of local and state government offices through the use of material incentives or **patronage** (jobs and government contracts, for example).[8] (One type of traditional party organization, the urban political machine, is discussed in Chapter 9.) Although these organizations are frequently discussed by political scientists as if they existed everywhere in the first half of the twentieth century, this is not accurate. James Reichley notes that traditional party organizations were usually present in older industrial states reaching from New England to Illinois. In states where the Progressive movement was strong—from the upper Midwestern states of Wisconsin and Minnesota extending to Pacific Coast states—party organizations were typically weak. The dominance of the Democratic party in Southern states "produced a politics of faction rather than of party, and state party organizations were largely irrelevant."[9]

Supreme Court decisions limiting the use of patronage have been an important factor causing the decline of traditional party organizations. In *Elrod* v. *Burns* (1976) the Court held that in most instances it was unconstitutional to fire employees simply because they did not support the party in power. During the 1960s, the governor of Pennsylvania could fill more than 40,000 jobs on a political basis; by 1988, the number was only 2,000.[10]

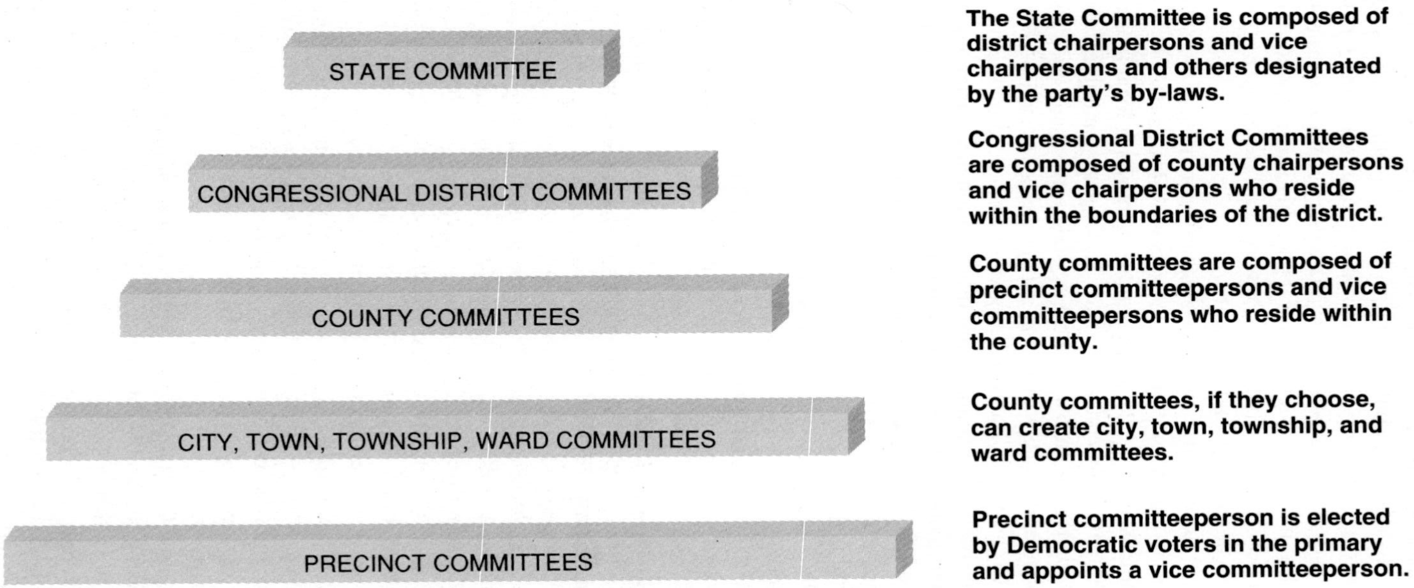

STATE COMMITTEE	**The State Committee is composed of district chairpersons and vice chairpersons and others designated by the party's by-laws.**
CONGRESSIONAL DISTRICT COMMITTEES	**Congressional District Committees are composed of county chairpersons and vice chairpersons who reside within the boundaries of the district.**
COUNTY COMMITTEES	**County committees are composed of precinct committeepersons and vice committeepersons who reside within the county.**
CITY, TOWN, TOWNSHIP, WARD COMMITTEES	**County committees, if they choose, can create city, town, township, and ward committees.**
PRECINCT COMMITTEES	**Precinct committeeperson is elected by Democratic voters in the primary and appoints a vice committeeperson.**

FIGURE 3-1 Democratic party organization in Indiana. (*Rules of the Indiana Democratic Party,* March 1994.)

Party Organization Today This section will discuss the growing importance of state party organizations in recent years. However, it is important to keep in mind the earlier status of a state's parties. Obviously, as just mentioned, party organizations were traditionally weak in Southern and Progressive Era states, so there is little doubt they are stronger there today. In the traditional party organization states, most are stronger today than they were at their low point in the 1970s, but they will probably never be as strong as they were earlier in the twentieth century.

State parties in almost all states now have a permanent headquarters, annual budgets in election years that average close to $1 million, and a professional staff organized into several sections such as finance, political, communications, field operations, and clerical. In addition to the position of state party chair, which is usually not a paid position, there is a paid, full-time executive director in all of the state parties. The headquarters of the Florida Republican party, one of the best organized and funded, "operates with a budget of $6 million and is packed with computer hardware, telephone banks, and printing facilities."[11]

John Bibby calls today's state parties "service-oriented" organizations that provide important services to local parties and candidates.[12] Party-building activities include regular programs to raise money, maintaining voter identification lists, and conducting public opinion polls for the development of campaign strategy. Candidates' personal campaign organizations, especially in statewide races, make most of the decisions about individual campaigns, but state parties are increasingly providing services to candidates: training of campaign volunteers, assistance in polling, and get-out-the-vote drives.

How many and how well these activities are performed by a state party will depend in part on the relationship between the party chairperson and the governor, when they are of the same party. Frequently, a governor will be responsible for the election of a chairperson, and when this happens, he or she serves as the governor's agent and tries to control the party and have it fight the governor's battles.[13] Sometimes the chairperson is more independent of the governor, especially if the office was achieved on his or her own efforts. While this chairperson may cooperate with the governor, he or she can devote more time to broad-based party activities. Of course, half of the chairpersons are members of the party that does not control the governor's office (the out-party) and would also tend to engage in party-building activities.

Although state-level party organizations are important, party politics is dominated in most parts of the country by county committees. Paul Allen Beck and Frank Sorauf suggest that the county party committee is important because the county as a governmental unit elects a large number of public officials; its officials still control some political patronage, although significantly less than in the past; the boundaries of many larger electoral units, such as congressional and state legislative districts, frequently follow county lines; and county chairpersons usually serve as members of the state committee.[14]

Great diversity in the organizational strength and activity of parties exists at the county level. A few are well funded with a paid executive director and permanent headquarters, but most are part-time, voluntary operations without paid staff, permanent headquarters, an annual budget, or even a telephone listing.[15] Sometimes, just finding an intelligent and energetic person to become Republican or Democratic county chairperson is a difficult task. Still, these committees may undertake a number of activities, especially during elections (See Table 3-1).

Activities presently performed by state and local parties appear to be routine, and one may wonder whether they affect the outcomes of elections. Overall, studies show that a well-organized county party has a positive, though minor, effect on the share of the vote received by its candidates. However, in certain situations a well-organized party can make a greater difference. This is true in counties where the party occupies a minority status, that is, a party that wins few or no elections. In these counties, the better organized parties will run candidates for every elected office on the ballot (a full slate of candidates), resulting in an increase in the number of votes their candidates receive, even at the congressional level. Also, it is likely that a minority party with a strong organization may have a greater effect on election results when longtime incumbents retire or a sudden swing in the mood of the voters goes against the dominant party.[16] A well-organized minority party is capable of taking advantage of these situations. Finally, party organization is an important factor in determining how much competition exists between the parties in elections to statewide offices: The better organized the parties, the more competitive the Democratic and Republican parties are.[17]

People active in a political party, from precinct committeepersons to state party chairs, are often classified as **professionals** or **amateurs.** Amateurs are usually more reform-minded, more interested in advocating certain issue positions and supporting candidates who take the same positions. They enter politics because of their desire to further particular political causes. Professionals are more interested in winning elections and are therefore more willing to compromise issue positions if that is what it takes to win. They are less concerned about their parties' candidates taking clear positions on the issues. The Christian Coalition is the most recent example of an issue-oriented group that has been winning control of state party executive committees so that

TABLE 3-1 ACTIVITY LEVELS OF COUNTY PARTY COMMITTEES, 1984
(In Percentages)

Activity	Republicans	Democrats
Chair works at least 6 hours per week	87	81
County Committee meets at least bimonthly	62	64
Involved in candidate recruitment for county offices	81	76
Participates in planning and strategy meetings with candidate campaign organizations for county offices	87	84
Arranges fund-raising events	83	80
Organizes telephone campaigns	78	76
Distributes posters or lawn signs	81	83
Sends mailings to voters	75	66

Source: James L. Gibson, John P. Frendreis, and Laura L. Vertz, "Party Dynamics in the 1980s: Change in County Party Organizational Strength, 1980–1984," *American Journal of Political Science* 33 (February 1989), pp. 73–74. Adapted by permission of the Midwest Political Science Association.

they can advance a conservative agenda. The Christian Coalition has gained considerable influence in the Republican parties in Iowa, Minnesota, New Mexico, Oregon, South Carolina, and Texas.[18]

Because the amateur style emphasizes issues over party, there has been speculation that it might severely weaken party organizations, but there is no real evidence that this has occurred.[19] In fact, politically active groups would not try to gain control of party organizations if they didn't think they were important in the political process. Nevertheless, differing styles are a source of tension and conflict within party organizations.

Parties and the Nomination of Candidates

The nomination process is crucial to voters because it narrows a voter's choices down to the candidates, usually two, who will appear on the general election ballot. It is also crucial to parties because candidates' images and stands on policy issues will be identified as those of their party, and if the nominated candidates are unsuccessful in the general election, the party will fail to gain control of the government and shape public policy. The importance of the nomination process is summed up by the statement "who can make nominations is the owner of the party."[20]

The Direct Primary Until the beginning of the twentieth century, parties were free from any interference in controlling the nomination of candidates. In the early days of the American republic, this was accomplished by a party caucus—the party's elected members of the state senate and house of representatives. By the mid-nineteenth century, statewide nominations were made by state party conventions composed of delegates selected at county conventions. In 1903, Wisconsin instituted by law the **direct primary** to nominate candidates. The direct primary is an election in which voters decide a party's nominees for the general election, rather than indirectly by selecting delegates to attend party conventions and decide on nominees. The spread of the direct primary (by 1917 most states had adopted it) weakened party organizations. This, of course, is just what its advocates, members of the Progressive movement, intended. They wanted to open the political process by removing the monopoly of power held by party leaders to handpick candidates and to even direct their behavior once they were elected to office. Today, no state uses only the convention method to nominate candidates, but a few Southern states (Alabama, Georgia, South Carolina, and Virginia[21]) allow the party to choose each election year whether to use a convention or a primary. Although laws regulating nominations and primary elections vary among the fifty states and will sometimes even vary office by office, they all must cover how a person places his or her name on the primary ballot as a candidate for the party's nomination and who is allowed to vote in the primary.[22]

Access to the Primary Ballot Candidates normally gain access to the ballot by obtaining a certain number of signatures on a petition or paying a modest filing fee. Seven states, however, use this stage of the nominating process as an opportunity for parties to gain back some of the influence they have lost over nominations. They do this by allowing preprimary endorsements by state party conventions. It is a procedure that is written into law in these states. The specifics vary with parties playing a rather strong role in Utah where a candidate receiving more than 70 percent of the convention vote is declared the nominee and no primary is held. Otherwise, the top two candidates in convention voting are placed on the primary ballot. In other states, the names of the endorsed candidates will appear automatically on the primary ballot while others seeking the nomination will have to gather signatures on petitions. Sometimes the endorsement is simply an endorsement and does not affect access to the ballot.

During the 1960s and 1970s, these endorsements had substantial influence in determining who was nominated (endorsed candidates won contested primaries close to 80 percent of the time). The success rate of endorsed candidates between 1982 and 1994 has dropped to the 40 percent level. Malcolm Jewell suggests there is no single explanation for the decline in success of party-endorsed candidates. But some of the endorsed candidates have lost to opponents who had little political experience, which is actually appealing to many voters at this time, or had ample campaign funds to spend on television ads to counter the party endorsement.[23] In a study of 1982 gubernatorial nominations, Sarah Morehouse concluded that in convention endorsing states, party support is more important than how much money candidates spend in winning the endorsement and in the primary that may follow.[24]

Types of Primaries Who is allowed to vote in primary elections? One might think all registered voters are eligible to vote in primary elections, but this is usually not the case. Party organizations in many states want only voters who think of themselves as Democrats or Republicans, in other words, who have some commitment to the party, to decide the nominees of their party. Others argue that voters should have the freedom to vote for the person they perceive as the best candidate, and that the party affiliation of the voter and candidate is immaterial. In devising primary rules states have sided with one or the other of these two positions, and some have managed to fall in between. Several political scientists have developed elaborate schemes to classify state primaries. Nevertheless, the familiar closed and open, along with Washington's blanket primary and Louisiana's open elections system, make for the simplest presentation. These categories are described below with attention paid to whether and when a voter must indicate his or her party choice.

Closed primaries are used in twenty-seven states. Voters declare a party preference in advance and can vote only in that party's primary. States vary in terms of how far in advance voters need to declare their party preference or affiliation. Most require voters who want to change their party to do so several months in advance of the primary election. Others have more flexibility in changing parties. Iowa, for example, allows voters to switch registration on the day of the election, although a record is kept of the party a voter registers with. States that allow voters to change registration on election day are very similar to open primaries.

Open primaries are used in twenty-one states. Voters do not declare a party preference in advance and may choose either a Republican or a Democratic ballot, that is, vote in either party's primary. While some states require voters to express publicly a preference for the ballot of a party at the polls, in others voters can decide which party's primary they will vote in in the privacy of the voting booth. (Either way it is possible for the supporters of one party to vote in the other party's primary. This is known as crossover voting.)

A *blanket primary* is used in the state of Washington. This primary allows maximum choice. It goes a step further than open primaries by allowing voters to decide office by office which party's primary they will vote in. Voters can vote in the Democratic primary for governor and then in the Republican primary for state senate, moving back and forth between the parties by office. The only restriction is that voters can vote in only one party's primary for each office.

A unique *open elections* law,[25] adopted in 1975, is used in Louisiana. All candidates for an office, regardless of party affiliation, are required to appear on the same ballot. Candidates may, and usually do, list their party affiliation. If one of the candidates receives a majority of the votes cast, that candidate is declared elected and the general election is canceled. If no one has a majority, the top two candidates run against each other in the general election. This allows for the possibility that the two candidates could be affiliated with the same party, both Democrats or both Republicans. This happened in the 1987 gubernatorial race when two Democrats ran against each other. The effect of this system has been to help incumbents who, because of their name recognition, frequently win a majority in the first election. Also, at least initially the law resulted in fewer Republicans, the minority party in Louisiana, contesting state legislative contests. The fact that a minority party may not have a chance to contest general elections makes the open elections a bad choice; it will undoubtedly discourage the development of two strong parties.

In most states the winner of the primary is the candidate who receives the most votes (plurality), even if it is not a majority. In many Southern states, however, a majority vote is required. This has led to **runoff primaries,** a second primary between the top two candidates if no one received a majority in the first. The runoff primary was instituted in the South when the Democratic party was dominant and winning the Democratic primary was tantamount to being elected. The runoff required candidates to receive support of a majority of the Democrats. The rise of the Republican party has put more importance on the general election and decreased participation in the Democratic primary.[26] Some civil rights organizations claim that runoff primaries are discriminatory. They argue that fewer whites voting in the Democratic primary, and splitting their votes among two or three white candidates, has increased the importance of the black vote and made it possible for a single black candidate to win a plurality in the first primary. The runoff will usually have a black candidate facing a white candidate, and with the support of all of the white voters the white candidate receives a majority of the vote and the nomination. Thus far, courts have not declared runoff primaries unconstitutional.

Party Competition in the States

Political scientists have devoted considerable attention to the level of competition between the Democratic and Republican parties in the states (see the Scholarly Box

SCHOLARLY BOX

MEASURING INTERPARTY COMPETITION IN THE STATES

Defining party competition is not difficult, but actually applying it to state elections is another story. **Party competition** is the idea that the parties' candidates (usually Democratic and Republican) have close to an equal chance in winning any given election. But how do we identify how competitive each of the fifty states is?

Probably the first thing that comes to mind is that the vote percentage candidates receive would be a good indicator of competition. For example, an election where one candidate has 52 percent of the vote and the other candidate 48 percent would be competitive because the results are so close; an election where the winning candidate receives 70 percent and the losing candidate 30 percent would be noncompetitive, or safe for the majority party. A decision must be made on exactly what percentage of the vote received by the winner makes an election noncompetitive. Is it 70 percent, or 65 percent, or even 60 percent? Of course, a middle category between competitive and noncompetitive could be created.

The next factor to consider is not as easy: What elected offices should we include? We are interested in state politics, so elections for president and U.S. Congress are of little interest. Certainly, elections for the governor's office should be included. To avoid measuring party competition of gubernatorial elections only, another political office needs to be included, for example, state legislative elections. Using both gubernatorial and legislative elections would be a good combination to measure party competition at the state level. But there is a problem: Collecting election statistics on 50 governors is not difficult; collecting the same statistics on over 7,500 state legislators is. Instead of collecting data on legislative elections, many political scientists use the percentage of seats the parties control in the legislature as an indicator of competition. This information is much easier to obtain.

The last question to answer in measuring party competition concerns time. Is it enough to look at one election, say the most recent? Or are data needed from several elections? And if so, how many? The problem with one election is that it may be atypical. A scandal, for example, may cause the incumbent party to lose in a close race even though it won previous elections with comfortable margins. It is better to use several elections that cover a period of twelve to sixteen years. Any more than that will cause a different problem by yielding results that might obscure recent trends.

entitled Measuring Interparty Competition in the States). And even more time has been spent on attempting to identify the effects of parties on the kind of policies states adopt.

Classifying the States Regardless of measurement techniques employed to determine the degree of competitiveness, states are usually grouped into a number of categories that identify those where Republicans dominate elections, those with competitive elections, and those where Democrats dominate elections. Our classification is for 1982 through 1994 elections and is based on definitions developed by Malcolm Jewell and David Olson that we have modified to take into account the large number of competitive states that have emerged recently.[27] (Jewell and Olson, analyzing the 1965–1988 time period, identified thirty-two states as competitive.) For Figure 3-2, the competitive category has been expanded from one to three so that we can determine if a state leans to one party or the other. The majority and dominant categories were merged into one category. The categories are described below:

Dominant/majority. In a majority party state, one party is consistently more successful in winning elections to state offices. Both parties seriously contest elections for

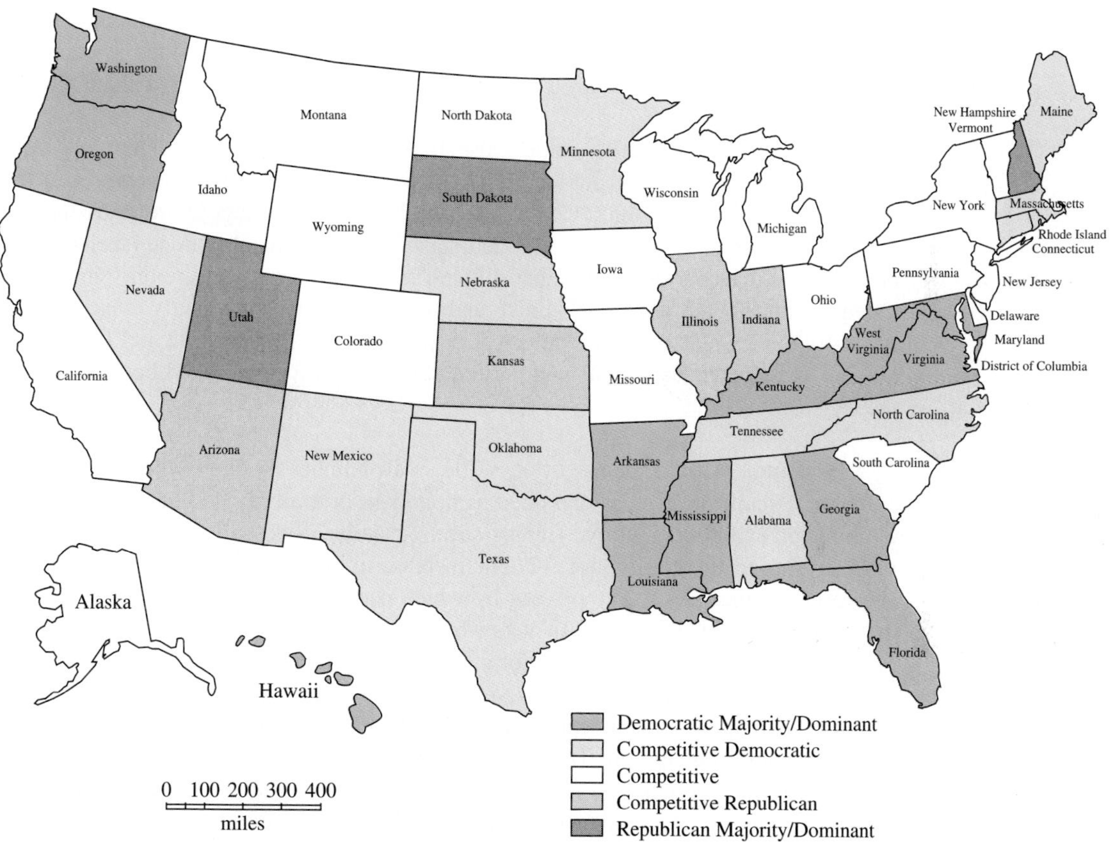

FIGURE 3-2 Patterns of party competition in the states, 1976–1994. [This is an updated version of a map of party competition in the states that appeared in Malcolm E. Jewell and David M. Olson, *Political Parties and Elections in American States,* 3d ed. (Chicago, Ill.: The Dorsey Press, 1988), p. 29.]

the governor's office and for control of the house and senate. However, the majority party controls the governor's office more than two-thirds of the time, and its candidates usually receive approximately 60 percent of the vote. And the majority party controls the senate and house more than two-thirds of the time, and the proportion of the seats it wins is usually under three-fourths of the total. Also in this category are a few states labeled one-party dominant because one party always or almost always wins the election for governor, receiving over two-thirds the total vote cast. The party that wins the governor's office also always wins control of the state house and senate with a majority that frequently exceeds three-fourths of the total number of seats. Democratic-dominant states are Arkansas, Georgia, Hawaii, Kentucky, and Maryland. New Hampshire is the only Republican-dominant state.

Competitive leaning. Both parties win elections to state offices, but one party does just slightly better. Typically, in these states the Democratic and Republican parties divide control of the governor's office, but one is more consistent in winning control of both houses of the legislature. Competitive leaning states are classified as competitive Democratic or competitive Republican to indicate which party has a slight advantage.

Competitive. Both parties come close to sharing equally the winning of state offices. Democratic and Republican parties divide control of the governor's office close to one-half of the time. Control of both houses of the legislature is frequently divided between the parties as is the membership in each chamber. Also labeled competitive are a handful of states rather difficult to classify: states where one party consistently controls the governor's office and the other party consistently controls both houses of the legislature. Colorado is a perfect example. Between 1982 and 1994, governors were always Democrats and the Republicans always controlled both houses of the legislature.

The Trends toward Competition The small number of states where the Democratic or Republican party is classified as dominant or majority and the large number of competitive and competitive leaning states (usually called two-party states) are the most striking features of Figure 3-2. The increase in the number of competitive states is a recent phenomenon. The process by which party competition develops in a state may be described as follows: (1) Voters who consistently supported the dominant party begin to split their tickets and vote for some minority party candidates in national and state elections; (2) voters (especially younger persons) begin to shift their party identification, perhaps first to independent and then to the minority party; and (3) voters shift their party registration. This is not an automatic process, and a wide variety of factors may work to retard change. In states with closed primaries, voters will be more hesitant to change registration because the winner of the dominant party's primary almost always wins the general election, meaning that the only real choice a voter has is in this party's primary. Republicans have been frequently frustrated in the South because Democratic incumbents compile fairly conservative records, giving the people little incentive to switch parties. Earl and Merle Black note that Democratic candidates for statewide office try to distance themselves from the liberal image of the national Democratic party. They campaign on platforms that combine conservative (support of budgetary restraint and school prayer) and progressive (support for improving the educational system and environmental protection) themes.[28]

However, the Republican party doesn't feel quite as frustrated in the South after the 1994 elections. The antigovernment, anti-Democratic tide that swept the Republicans to control of both houses of the United States Congress for the first time in forty years also helped Republican candidates in Southern states. Republican gains were equally historic in state elections in the South where, for the first time in the twentieth century, the party won control of a majority of the governorships. Although Democrats still control most of the state legislatures, the Republicans won a majority of the seats in North Carolina's House of Representatives and the Florida Senate, again for the first time in the twentieth century. Another indication of growing Republican strength is that two of the newly elected Republican governors were previously members of the Democratic party. In fact, both had been elected as Democrats: Fob James, Jr., was

Democratic governor of Alabama (1979–1983), and David Beasley was a Democratic member of the South Carolina state legislature. Now, both are Republicans and governors!

Third Parties It is easy to dismiss third parties and conclude that Democrats and Republicans have a complete monopoly on state politics; there is a near monopoly, but not complete. From 1950 to 1988, only one state (Maine) had an independent governor. In 1990, independent governors were elected in two states, and in 1994, an independent governor was again elected in Maine. Some states have a history of active minor parties. Minnesota's Farmer-Labor party won gubernatorial elections early in the twentieth century and eventually merged with the Democratic party. The official name of the Democratic party in Minnesota is still the Democratic Farmer-Labor party (DFL). In recent years, support for the Liberal and Conservative parties has been as high as 9 percent in New York and 7 percent for the Libertarian party in Alaska. In general, support for minor parties has been strongest in Western states and weakest in the South.[29] A pro-environment party, known as the Green party, has been active in some Western states, notably New Mexico.

Do Competitive Parties Affect Public Policies?

While it is generally taken for granted that competitive, two-party states are preferable to one-party states, political scientists disagree regarding the effects of competition on government performance. This debate was framed by V. O. Key in his classic book, *Southern Politics in State and Nation.*[30] Key analyzed the politics of Southern states in the late 1940s, noting that the South's one-party politics did not raise important issues during election campaigns, discouraged voter participation, and resulted in governments adopting policies that ignored the needs of the "have-nots" (lower socioeconomic groups).[31] Two-party politics, Key believed, would raise more important issues because the parties would tend to represent different socioeconomic classes. The presence of these issues in elections and governing would increase voter participation. In addition, close electoral competition between the parties would force one of them to offer some policies favored by the have-nots so that they could win their votes.

Some political scientists adapted Key's framework by using interparty competition to study all fifty states, but they did not always agree with his conclusions. Studies by Thomas Dye indicated that education, welfare, taxation, and highway programs appear to be more closely related to economic factors in the states than the degree of party competition. In other words, states with greater wealth spend more money on various programs regardless of levels of competition. Dye concludes that "party competition itself does not necessarily cause more liberal welfare policies."[32] In fact, some observers even went so far as to argue that politics was really unimportant in the making of policy.

Unfortunately, analyzing all fifty states, although a good idea, frequently pushes researchers to rely on a few statistical indicators of each state's politics and policy that in all likelihood do not accurately reflect its political history and perhaps not even the current context of policymaking. They have underestimated the important role of political parties. However, recent research is providing new evidence that parties do affect policymaking.

Sarah McCally Morehouse looked more closely at the possible effects of interparty competition and concluded that it is not so much the degree of competition but the cohesiveness of political parties that influences policy outcomes in the states. Morehouse found that in states with *cohesive parties*—where the governor heads the state ticket and other candidates run on an established platform—the quality and distribution of public services are improved.[33]

Robert Brown concludes that greater state policy benefits for the have-nots are found in states where the electoral base of the Democratic party tends to be a coalition of low-income persons, union members, and Catholics.[34] (Brown's study will be discussed in more detail in Chapter 13.) Using a similar approach in a study of California and New York, Dwyre and her associates add more evidence for the importance of parties in policymaking when they have different electoral bases. This study concludes that the "disorganized" decision-making process in California is the principal cause of policies that have placed a greater state and local tax burden on low-income groups (have-nots) than in New York, where the process is more "organized." California's decision-making process is one where parties are minor actors. Many decisions are made through the use of ballot initiatives (see Chapter 4) with temporary coalitions forming around them. These coalitions are composed of various interests but not political parties; they exist for that single issue and then disappear. New York's decision-making process is one where parties are major actors having clear differences in their electoral bases, with the Democratic party representing the interests of the have-nots.[35] Party members in the legislature are reasonably cohesive in advancing the interests of their electoral base. Brown, Dwyre, and her colleagues, by examining the electoral bases of parties, are focusing on a crucial and frequently neglected part of Key's arguments.

Another problem with studies that have found economic factors of prime importance in policymaking is that they were usually *cross-sectional;* that is, the data were collected for fifty states at one point in time and then the states were compared with each other. James Garand has utilized a *longitudinal* approach, collecting data on each state at different points in time. In other words, the data reflect characteristics of each state at several points during a twenty-year period. As a result, he was able to examine the effect of political changes on policy within states. Garand finds, for example, that a change in the party that controls state government does have a substantial impact on spending priorities, especially on the money spent for education.[36]

Further evidence that parties matter in the making of policy comes from a study that finds state party elites have different **ideologies,** that is, beliefs about the purpose and role of government. Although it is frequently claimed that there is not a "dime's worth" of difference between the Democratic and Republican parties, this bit of conventional wisdom appears to be wrong. Erikson, Wright, and McIver[37] have developed a "party elite ideology" score for both parties in forty-six states. The term *party elite* refers to Democrats and Republicans who occupy reasonably high-level positions such as national convention delegates, local party chairpersons, and state legislators.

The attitudes of state party elites on various issues result in a conservative/liberal classification scheme. These traditional labels in American politics have defined liberals as those favoring an active role for government and conservatives as favoring a limited role for government, definitions that are probably too simple for today's complex issues. Today's **liberals** believe government should act to assist the economically disadvantaged and racial minority groups, but they are less willing to have government take an active role intervening on moral and social issues such as abortion and prayer in public schools. **Conservatives** still oppose government intervention in economic areas and in actively assisting minority groups, but they favor government action on many moral and social issues, for example, making abortions illegal and requiring prayer in public schools.

Overall, Republican party elites tend to be conservative and Democrats tend to be liberal (see Table 3-2). Variations exist by state and region. This is noticeable in the Democratic party where a number of Southern state party elites are classified as "conservative" and only one state (Maryland) is labeled as "most liberal." The largest concentration of "most liberal" Democratic party elites is in the Northeast. In the Republican party, the "most conservative" are found in the South and West. No state Republican party is classified as liberal, not even in the more liberal Northeast. Differences within the parties are evident also. Ideologically, Connecticut Democrats ("most liberal") have about as much in common with Georgia Democrats ("conservative") as they do with Connecticut Republicans ("conservative").

Although these variations are important, it should be remembered that in each state the Republican party is always more conservative than the Democratic party. State Democratic and Republican party elites do have different beliefs on public policy issues.

INTEREST GROUPS

Only about 25 percent of American adults have ever worked for a political party or for a candidate in an election, and fewer than 10 percent have been members of a political club or organization. In contrast, about 60 percent of the American people are members of organized interest groups, which take stands on various public issues and try to affect government decision making.

Since the 1960s, there has been a significant expansion in virtually all states in the number of groups that are politically active. While interest groups representing business, labor, and agriculture continue to be important, new groups representing women, minorities, the elderly, and focusing on specific issues such as abortion, gun control, smoking, tourism, and environmental protection have become increasingly active and influential. Also, greater economic diversity in the states (such as the growth of the telecommunications industry) has caused the creation of new groups in the private economic sector. Education and public employee unions have become much more politically active and powerful in the states.

Interest Group Tactics

Interest groups are involved in all stages of political activity but usually focus on state legislatures where they work to have bills adopted or defeated. A 1990 Associated

TABLE 3-2 IDEOLOGIES OF STATE PARTY ELITES

Region/state	Score Dem./Rep.	Region/state	Score Dem./Rep.
Northeast		**South**	
Connecticut	ML/C	Alabama	C/C
Massachusetts	ML/C	Arkansas	C/MC
New Hampshire	ML/C	Delaware	L/C
New Jersey	ML/C	Florida	L/MC
New York	ML/C	Georgia	C/MC
Pennsylvania	L/C	Kentucky	L/C
Rhode Island	L/C	Louisiana	C/MC
Vermont	ML/C	Maryland	ML/C
		Mississippi	C/MC
		North Carolina	L/MC
		Oklahoma	C/MC
		South Carolina	L/MC
		Tennessee	L/MC
		Texas	L/MC
		Virginia	L/MC
		West Virginia	L/MC
Midwest		**West**	
Illinois	L/C	Arizona	ML/C
Indiana	L/C	California	ML/C
Iowa	ML/C	Colorado	ML/C
Kansas	ML/C	Idaho	L/MC
Michigan	ML/C	Montana	L/MC
Minnesota	ML/C	New Mexico	L/MC
Missouri	L/MC	Oregon	ML/C
North Dakota	ML/C	Utah	L/MC
Ohio	ML/C	Washington	ML/C
South Dakota	ML/MC	Wyoming	L/MC
Wisconsin	ML/C		

The classification scheme is MC = most conservative, C = conservative, L = liberal, and ML = most liberal. Data are not available for Alaska, Hawaii, Nebraska, and Nevada.

Source: Robert S. Erikson, Gerald C. Wright, and John McIver, *State House Democracy: Public Opinion and Policy in the American States* (New York: Cambridge University Press, 1993), p. 103. Reprinted by permission of Cambridge University Press.

Press survey found that registered lobbyists outnumbered legislators by a margin of 6 to 1.[38] Before discussing specific tactics, it should be noted that in many instances the most successful interest groups are those whose basic strategy is defensive: They wish to preserve the status quo rather than initiate change. Many legislators live by the adage, "If it ain't broke, don't fix it." The status quo represents previous political compromises. This means interest groups advocating a new policy must first show that something is so wrong that it must be fixed before they can effectively argue for their proposed solution. For convenience, interest group tactics may be divided into three categories: public relations, electioneering, and lobbying.

Public Relations Campaigns Interest groups can use public relations campaigns to help create a favorable image of themselves and to generate support on specific issues. These campaigns include press conferences, advertising, radio and television interviews, and news releases. Because there is a close connection between public relations campaigns and commercial advertising, groups representing the business community have an advantage in expertise and available personnel, not to mention money. Sometimes the media give favorable coverage on issues that are popular with the public such as environmental protection, and this can help groups that are not well financed. Alan Rosenthal reports that an environmental group in New Jersey received considerable media attention when it created a visual event for television by announcing the results of pollution studies at contaminated waste sites.[39]

Electioneering Interest groups may participate in political campaigns by providing assistance to political parties or individual candidates. Some groups may assume a position of neutrality and support candidates from both parties if they support the group's goals. Others may be closely tied to partisan politics. Labor unions, for example, are intimately connected to the Democratic party in most of the large, industrial states, such as California, Illinois, Michigan, New Jersey, New York, Ohio, and Pennsylvania.

Interest groups provide an opportunity for candidates to acquire friendships and build reputations. Most candidates are members of several groups, and they believe they can translate friendship into votes. Candidates may be invited to appear before the group, or they may respond to questionnaires that seek to identify candidates' positions on issues that are of concern to the group. More directly, interest groups may provide staff assistance in running a campaign. Mailing lists of members, office material, and equipment also can be made available for candidates' use.

Money is probably the most important resource an interest group can provide candidates. Although many states still allow corporations and labor unions to contribute money legally to campaigns, PACs **(political action committees),** which are sponsored by interest groups, have expanded in the states just as they have at the national level. PACs, created specifically to raise and distribute money to political campaigns, have become the dominant source of campaign funds in virtually all states as election campaigns have become more and more expensive. According to Rosenthal, PACs contribute money to political campaigns to (1) help elect candidates who are considered friends; (2) show support for those who are likely to be reelected, especially if they are in a legislative leadership position such as committee chair; and (3) gain or improve access to legislators.[40]

PACs raise money through personal contact and direct mail appeals. Some corporations and labor unions even use voluntary payroll deduction; teachers' unions are particularly good at rasing money. The Minnesota Education Association automatically receives $10 from every member, unless he or she indicates otherwise.[41] Incumbents are the prime beneficiaries of PAC money, sometimes receiving up to 80 percent of PAC contributions. Frequently, they ignore party labels and give money to incumbents of both parties and "go with the power."

Lobbying At a third stage in the political process interest groups use **lobbying** to communicate specific policy goals more directly to legislators. Communication may be in the form of testimony before legislative committees or, more indirectly, by establishing contacts in a social setting. In state legislatures with a large professional staff it is often as important to communicate with the members of the legislator's staff as it is with the legislator. If lobbyists can convince a staff member that their policy position is the correct one, then the staff member may be able to convince his or her boss.

Thomas and Hrebenar have identified five categories of lobbyists in the states:

In-house lobbyists. Employees of organizations who have titles such as vice president of public affairs or director of government relations and as part of their job devote at least some of their time to lobbying. They represent only one client, and that is their employer. Examples are state chambers of commerce or large corporations. This category represents nearly 40 to 50 percent of all state lobbyists.

Government lobbyists or legislative liaisons. Employees of state, local, and federal agencies who represent their agencies to the legislature. These are sometimes called the "hidden lobbies" because many states do not require government employees to register as lobbyists. State universities, for example, usually have a vice president of state relations (or a similar title) whose real job is to lobby the legislature. This category contains 25 to 40 percent of all lobbyists.

Contract lobbyists. Also known as independent lobbyists or "hired guns." They are hired for a fee to lobby and will represent a number of clients, ranging from less than ten to thirty or forty. Contract lobbyists sometimes work by themselves or with partners in law firms; either way they are a growing presence in state capitals. They represent 15 to 25 percent of all lobbyists.

Citizen lobbyists. These lobbyists represent citizen or community organizations on a part-time and volunteer basis. They rarely represent more than one organization at a time. Perhaps 10 to 20 percent of all lobbyists fit into this category.

"Hobbyists." These are self-styled lobbyists who act on their own behalf to support pet projects and are not designated to act on the behalf of any organization. The number of "hobbyists" (perhaps 5 percent) is hard to estimate because few are required to register by law.[42]

After laws are passed, interest-group activity continues as lobbyists contact executive branch administrators, who are usually given considerable discretion in executing the law. Administrators interact very little with the general public, and they have a tendency to identify very closely with the goals of the groups they are supposed to oversee. As noted in Chapter 1, detailed state constitutions invite litigation by opponents charging that a new law violates part of the constitution. This provides yet another tactic for interest groups that hope to negate laws or render their provisions meaningless through narrow judicial interpretation. Beginning in the 1980s, interest groups have increased their participation in state court litigation, and a greater variety of interest groups are using litigation as means of shaping policy. Business, religious, and civil rights organizations are continuing to use litigation strategies, and educational and health groups are using it more than they have in the past.[43] In some states, pro-smoking groups are going to court to challenge the legality of government regulations banning smoking in various places such as work areas.

Power of Interest Groups

While no state today is run by one or two interests, as once was the case in Montana with the Anaconda Copper Company, Thomas and Hrebenar believe that the increased number of interest groups and the fragmentation of the business community have not lessened the overall power of interest groups. In addition, the need for more campaign money and the rise of PACs to furnish it have increased the power of interest groups.

One way to look at interest group power is to compare interest groups to political parties. In other words, are interest groups or political parties dominant in the making and implementing of policy in a state? It should be assumed that interest groups are always important in the making of policy and the real question is the extent of their power, or dominance.[44] Strong political parties can exert some control over the process of making policy and reduce the ability of interest groups to dominate it. Because parties represent broader constituencies than interest groups, it is also more likely that the public can have a voice in policy deliberations. Table 3-3 classifies the states according to the impact on policymaking made by interest groups. States with the "dominant" classification have an interest group system that has overwhelming influence on policymaking. Interest groups in "complementary" states have to work with other participants such as political parties. The "subordinate" category is where interest groups have little impact on policymaking; no state fits into this category. The two mixed categories ("dominant/complementary" and "complementary/subordinate") contain states that alternate between the two categories or are evolving from one to the next.

Ethics of Lobbying

Can lobbyists buy a legislator's vote? It does occur, but not often. During the past ten years a number of lobbyists and legislators have been found guilty of taking money for their votes. Prosecutions occurred in Alabama, Arizona, California, Kentucky, New York, and South Carolina. Many of these indictments and convictions were the result of federal investigations. Still, given the total number of lobbyists and legislators, the actual number of instances of bribery is very small. This is not to underestimate the importance of this kind of corruption because its effect on public confidence in government can be devastating. After a corruption probe in Arizona was made public, a survey found that over 70 percent of the people interviewed believed that a legislator would take a bribe if offered one.[45]

Nevertheless, the more significant problem centers on how the decisions legislators make are affected by campaign contributions from PACs and gifts and free entertainment from lobbyists. The effect of PACs in making campaign contributions was noted earlier. In addition, many legislators accept gifts and free entertainment from lobbyists that include tickets to sporting events, hunting trips, and dinners and drinks during the legislative session. Lobbyists also hold receptions where members of their interest group can be present to talk with legislators. Alan Rosenthal reports that during one session of the Colorado legislature, members "were invited to forty-eight cocktail parties, forty-four lunches, forty breakfasts, nineteen dinners, and twenty-three other functions during their six-month session."[46]

TABLE 3-3 CLASSIFICATION OF THE FIFTY STATES ACCORDING TO THE OVERALL IMPACT OF INTEREST GROUPS

Impact of interest groups				
Dominant (7)	**Dominant/ complementary** (21)	**Complementary** (17)	**Complementary/ subordinate** (5)	**Subordinate** (0)
Alabama	Arizona	Colorado	Delaware	
Florida	Arkansas	Connecticut	Minnesota	
Louisiana	Alaska	Indiana	Rhode Island	
New Mexico	California	Maine	South Dakota	
Nevada	Georgia	Maryland	Vermont	
South Carolina	Hawaii	Massachusetts		
West Virginia	Idaho	Michigan		
	Illinois	Missouri		
	Iowa	New Hampshire		
	Kansas	New Jersey		
	Kentucky	New York		
	Mississippi	North Carolina		
	Montana	North Dakota		
	Nebraska	Pennsylvania		
	Ohio	Utah		
	Oklahoma	Washington		
	Oregon	Wisconsin		
	Tennessee			
	Texas			
	Virginia			
	Wyoming			

Source: Clive S. Thomas and Ronald J. Hrebenar, "Interest Groups in the States," in Virginia Gray and Herbert Jacob, eds., *Politics in the American States: A Comparative Analysis,* 6th ed. (Washington, D.C.: CQ Press, 1996), 152. Reprinted by permission of Congressional Quarterly, Inc.

What does all of this buy? One view is that lobbyists are only buying access to legislators; they want to ensure that when they need five minutes with a legislator, they can get it. Or when a legislator has twenty phone messages, their call is one of the three that will actually be returned. Tickets to games and free food and drinks at receptions, it is argued, are not given with the expectation that lobbyists are actually buying a vote; they are only buying access. An alternative view is that access is close to influence. And if money is needed to have access, then interest groups that can mount a well-financed lobbying operation have an advantage over groups with less money. According to Common Cause, the "result is that public policy decisions may be based solely on who has money and access to government officials, rather than on whether the policy is in the public's interest."[47]

On the other hand, it may not be necessary to determine if access is simply access or if access is influence. It may be much simpler than that: Is there a legitimate reason for legislators to receive free tickets, dinners, drinks, and whatever else comes their way (or they ask for)? We believe public confidence in government requires the elimination of activities that can be interpreted as buying influence, and that is the way many states are moving. New laws regulating interest groups and lobbyists are being adopted in the states and usually take the form of (1) registration by lobbyists and disclosure of lobbying expenditures, (2) limitation on PAC campaign contributions, (3) identification of public officials who receive gifts from lobbyists and a limitation on such gifts, (4) a ban on lobbyists making campaign contributions while the legislature is in session, and (5) financial disclosure statements by public officials.

SUMMARY

Political parties and interest groups continue to be important links between citizens and their government. As has been noted in this chapter, state political party organizations have moved out of the doldrums they were in during the 1970s and are providing more services to candidates running for elected government positions, even though they may never again control the nominating process the way traditional party organizations did. Fewer states are dominated by one party; the trend among the states is toward two competitive parties. The Democratic party's grip on the South is rapidly weakening, especially in races for the governor's office and sometimes even in state legislative races. This is of some importance because recent research concludes that changes in party control of state government affect state policies such as spending priorities. And state parties with different electoral bases frequently adopt policies that are in the interests of the "have-nots." The party that controls state government does make a difference!

Accompanying the growth of state government in policymaking has been the growth in the number of interest groups and the variety of interests they represent. Interest groups use various tactics in presenting their views to legislators and in working to have favorable policies enacted. All of these tactics can help advance their position, although having their own lobbyist or hiring one may be the most effective way. Vote-buying scandals in a few state legislatures, along with media attention on the money interest groups contribute to political campaigns and spend on entertaining legislators, though legal, have pushed many states to enact new laws that further regulate what lobbyists can do.

KEY TERMS

Amateurs Party members who are issue-oriented and often unwilling to compromise their beliefs to achieve party unity.

Caucus A meeting of rank-and-file members of a party to select a precinct committee person. More generally, a meeting attended only by party members or party officials to conduct business relating to party affairs.

Closed primary A primary in which voting is restricted to those registered as members of a particular political party.

Conservatives Individuals who oppose government intervention in economic areas and to actively assist minority groups but favor government action on many moral and social issues.

Direct primary An election in which voters determine who the candidates will be in the general election. Today, almost all political parties nominate their candidates in a primary election.

Ideology Individuals' basic beliefs concerning the purpose of government and government's role in society.

Liberals Individuals who believe government should act to assist the economically disadvantaged and racial minority groups but are less willing to have government take an active role regulating moral and social issues.

Lobbying Action to change the content of bills or bring about their defeat or passage by communicating specific policy goals directly to legislators.

Open primary A primary in which voters participate regardless of their party registration.

Party competition The relationship between political parties in a state in which both parties' candidates (usually Democratic and Republican) have close to an equal chance of winning any given election.

Patronage Appointing individuals to government jobs or granting contracts and other special favors on the basis of party loyalty.

Political action committees Committees, usually sponsored by interest groups, created to raise and distribute money to political campaigns.

Precinct The basic unit for voting in elections and for party activity and organization. Usually contains 200 to 1,000 people and one polling place. In larger cities, several precincts together constitute a ward.

Professionals Party members who are willing to compromise on issues to accomplish their main goal of winning elections.

Runoff primary A second primary that is held if no candidate wins a majority of the total vote in the first primary election. Used almost exclusively in Southern states.

Traditional party organizations Party organizations that existed from about 1875 through 1950 with strong leaders who used patronage to reward party members who worked for the nomination and election of the candidates favored by the party leaders.

REFERENCES

1 Clive S. Thomas and Ronald J. Hrebenar, "Interest Groups in the States," in *Politics in the American States,* 5th ed., Virginia Gray, Herbert Jacob, and Robert B. Albritton, eds. (Glenview, Ill.: Scott, Foresman/Little, Brown, 1990), p. 127.

2 Jerrold G. Rusk, "The Effect of the Australian Ballot Reform on Split Ticket Voting: 1876–1908," in *Controversies in American Voting Behavior,* Richard G. Niemi and Herbert F. Weisberg, eds. (San Francisco: W. H. Freeman, 1976), pp. 485–488.

3 Leon Epstein, *Political Parties in the American Mold* (Madison: The University of Wisconsin Press, 1986), pp. 174–179. The two U.S. Supreme Court cases are *Smith* v. *Allright,* 321 U.S. 649 (1944) and *Terry* v. *Adams* 345 U.S. 461 (1953).

4 An excellent analysis of the effect of state laws on the political parties can be found in Kay Lawson, "How State Laws Undermine Parties," in *Elections American Style,* A. James Reichley, ed. (Washington, D.C.: The Brookings Institution, 1987), pp. 240–260.

5 *Tashjian* v. *Republican Party of Connecticut,* 479 U.S. 208 (1986).

6 *Eu* v. *San Francisco County Democratic Central Committee,* 489 U.S. 214 (1989).
7 L. Sandy Maisel, *Parties and Elections in America: The Electoral Process,* 2d ed. (New York: McGraw-Hill, 1993), pp. 60–61.
8 David R. Mayhew, *Placing Parties in American Politics* (Princeton, N.J.: Princeton University Press, 1986), pp. 19–23.
9 Reichley, *The Life of the Parties: A History of American Political Parties* (New York: Free Press, 1992), p. 382.
10 Ibid., p. 384.
11 John F. Bibby, "State Party Organizations: Coping and Adapting," *The Parties Respond: Changes in American Parties and Campaigns,* 2d ed., L. Sandy Maisel, ed. (Boulder, Colo.: Westview Press, 1994), p. 30; Reichley, *The Life of the Parties,* p. 388.
12 Bibby, "State Party Organizations," p. 29.
13 Robert J. Huckshorn, "State Party Leaders," in *Political Parties and Elections in the United States: An Encyclopedia,* L. Sandy Maisel and Charles Bassett, eds. (New York: Garland Publishing, 1991), pp. 1059–1060.
14 Paul Allen Beck and Frank J. Sorauf, *Party Politics in America,* 6th ed. (Glenview, Ill.: Scott, Foresman, 1988), p. 79.
15 John F. Bibby, *Politics, Parties, and Elections in America* (Chicago: Nelson-Hall Publishers, 1992), pp. 107–109; James L. Gibson, "County Party Organization," in *Political Parties and Elections,* Maisel and Bassett, eds., pp. 206–211.
16 John P. Frendreis, James L. Gibson, and Laura L. Vertz, "The Electoral Relevance of Local Party Organizations," *American Political Science Review* 84 (March 1990), pp. 228–233.
17 Samuel C. Patterson and Gregory A. Calderia, "The Etiology of Partisan Competition," *American Political Science Review* 78 (September 1984), pp. 701–703.
18 Sidney Blumenthal, "Letter from Washington: Christian Soldiers," *The New Yorker* 18 (July 1994), pp. 31–37.
19 Bibby, *Politics, Parties and Elections,* pp. 116–118.
20 E. E. Schattschneider, *Party Government* (New York: Holt, Rinehart and Winston, 1942), p. 1, quoted in Bibby, *Politics, Parties, and Elections,* p. 8.
21 Bibby, p. 131.
22 Maisel, *Parties and Elections in America,* pp. 151–160.
23 Malcolm E. Jewell, "State Party Endorsements of Gubernatorial Candidates Declining in Effectiveness," *Comparative State Politics* 16 (June 1995), pp. 10–12.
24 Sarah M. Morehouse, "Money versus Party Effort: Nominating for Governor," *American Journal of Political Science* 34 (August 1990), pp. 717–719.
25 Louisiana's nomination process is sometimes classified as "nonpartisan," meaning no party names are on the ballot. (Also, the "nonpartisan" is placed in quotes indicating that it is somehow different from the normal nonpartisan election.) This seems incorrect for Louisiana because party names are allowed in both the first and second elections. The open elections name has been used by Kazee and Hadley and is more appropriate. See Charles D. Hadley, "The Impact of the Louisiana Open Elections System Reform," *State Government* 58, no. 4 (1986), pp. 152–156; Thomas A. Kazee, "The Impact of Electoral Reform: 'Open Elections' and the Louisiana Party System," *Publius* 13 (Winter 1983), pp. 131–139.
26 Bibby, *Politics, Parties, and Elections,* p. 137.
27 Malcolm Jewell and David Olson, *Political Parties and American States,* 3d ed. (Chicago, Ill.: The Dorsey Press, 1988), pp. 28–30.

28 Earl Black and Merle Black, *Politics and Society in the South* (Cambridge, Mass.: Harvard University Press, 1987), p. 287.

29 Euel Elliott, Gerald S. Gryski, and Bruce Reed, "Minor Party Support in State Legislative Elections," *State and Local Government Review* 22 (Fall 1990), pp. 123–125.

30 V. O. Key, Jr., *Southern Politics* (New York: Vintage Books, 1949), pp. 15–18, 298–311. For an analysis of Key's work, see *V. O. Key, Jr., and the Study of American Politics,* Milton C. Cummings, ed. (Washington, D.C.: American Political Science Association, 1988). David Mayhew's "Why Did V. O. Key Draw Back from His 'Have-Nots' Claim?" in the Cummings monograph is excellent.

31 Key, *Southern Politics,* pp. 307–310.

32 Thomas R. Dye, *Politics in States and Communities,* 7th ed. (Englewood Cliffs, N.J.: Prentice-Hall, 1991), p. 135.

33 Sarah McCally Morehouse, *State Politics, Parties and Policy* (New York: Holt, Rinehart and Winston, 1981), p. 88.

34 Robert D. Brown, "Party Cleavages and Welfare Effort in the American States," *American Political Science Review* 89 (March 1995), pp. 23–33.

35 Diana Dwyre, Mark O'Gorman, Jeffrey M. Stonecash, and Rosalie Young, "Disorganized Politics and the Have-Nots: Politics and Taxes in New York and California," *Polity* 27 (Fall 1994), pp. 26–27.

36 James C. Garand, "Partisan Change and Shifting Expenditure Priorities in the American States, 1945–1978," *American Politics Quarterly* 13 (October 1985), pp. 370–371.

37 Robert S. Erikson, Gerald C. Wright, and John McIver, *Statehouse Democracy: Public Opinion and Policy in the American States* (New York: Cambridge University Press, 1993).

38 Associated Press, June 25, 1990, quoted in Common Cause, *State Issue Brief: Lobby Disclosure Reform in the States* (Washington, D.C.: Common Cause, 1993), p. 4.

39 Alan Rosenthal, *The Third House* (Washington, D.C.: Congressional Quarterly Press, 1993), p. 170.

40 Ibid., p. 136.

41 Ibid., p. 134.

42 Clive S. Thomas and Ronald J. Hrebenar, "Interest Groups in the States," in *Politics in the American States,* 5th ed., Virginia Gray, Herbert Jacob, and Robert B. Albritton, eds. (Glenview, Ill.: Scott, Foresman/Little, Brown, 1990), pp. 149–151; Alan Rosenthal, *The Third House,* pp. 21–23.

43 Lee Epstein, "Exploring the Participation of Organized Interests in State Court Litigation," *Political Research Quarterly* 47 (June 1994), pp. 341–348.

44 Clive S. Thomas and Ronald J. Hrebenar, "Interest Group Power in State Politics: A Complex Phenomenon," *Comparative State Politics* 15 (June 1994), pp. 13–15.

45 Susan Biemesderfer, "Making Laws, Breaking Laws," *State Legislatures* (April 1991), p. 18.

46 Rosenthal, *The Third House,* p. 95.

47 Common Cause, *State Issue Brief: Lobby Disclosure,* p. 2.

4

POLITICAL PARTICIPATION AND ELECTIONS

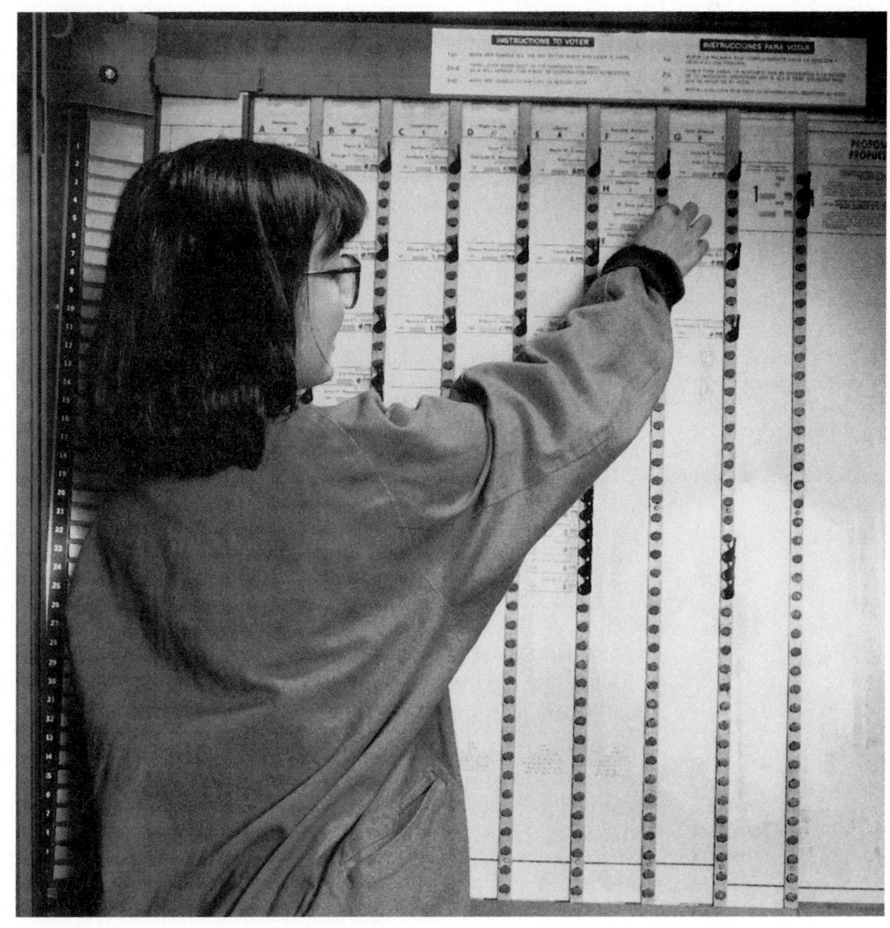

Grant LeDuc/Stock, Boston

Participating in politics is frequently thought of as simply voting every two or four years for candidates running for various offices. Political scientists take a broader approach and define **political participation** as "actions through which ordinary members of a political system influence or attempt to influence outcomes."[1] For this definition, voting in elections is one example, but so are other acts such as demonstrating, contributing money to candidates or interest groups, signing petitions, and writing letters to government officials. Two other elements in this definition should be emphasized. The concept of political participation refers to actions of ordinary citizens, not those involved in politics and government in elected positions or as a career. And *outcomes* is a general term referring to policies adopted by government officials.

This chapter focuses on the types of political participation, with special emphasis on voter turnout and a prerequisite of voting—registration. Recent efforts to encourage and broaden citizen participation at the local level will be discussed. The cost of election campaigns and state regulations governing campaign finance will be considered. The characteristics of particular elections—such as those for governors, mayors, legislators, and judges who are elected—will be discussed in chapters that focus on the institutions these officials are a part of. Finally, the initiative, referendum, and recall, which establish a unique opportunity for citizens to have a direct voice in governing, will be examined in detail.

POLITICAL PARTICIPATION

How much do Americans participate in politics? Is the level of participation declining? What kinds of political acts do Americans engage in? Verba, Schlozman, and Brady present **survey research** data on fourteen acts of participation, gathered on the American public, for two different years, 1967 and 1987, that help to provide answers to these questions. Their data are in Table 4-1 and are worth discussing in some detail.

The often mentioned decline in voting since 1960 is reflected in questions that asked about participation in presidential and local elections. Regular voting in both types of elections has decreased. There is a decline in the percentage of respondents who are members of a political club, and there is no change in those who report attending political meetings or rallies—both campaign-related activities. However, the decline in voting is *not* found in other acts of political participation. This is the case even in some that are related to campaigns and voting, such as persuading others how to vote and contributing money to a party or candidate, which has increased by 77 percent!

When it comes to political activity not related to campaigns and elections, the rate of participation has increased. This is true of citizens who contact public officials concerning a problem that relates only to them or to their immediate family (particularized contacting), such as fixing the pothole in the street in front of their house. And it is true of citizens whose contacts focus on problems that are more public in nature where government action might affect the entire community (issue-based contacting).[2] Also, participation has increased in the community category where local citizens come together to solve local problems.

TABLE 4-1 POLITICAL PARTICIPATION IN THE UNITED STATES, 1967 AND 1987

Specific activity	1967	1987	Absolute change	Relative change
Voting				
Regular voting in presidential elections	66	58	−8	−12
Always vote in local elections	47	35	−12	−26
Campaign				
Persuade others how to vote	28	32	+4	+14
Actively work for party or candidate	26	27	+1	+4
Attend political meeting or rally	19	19	0	0
Contribute money to party or candidate	13	23	+10	+77
Member of political club	8	4	−4	−50
Contact				
Contact local official: issue-based	14	24	+10	+71
Contact state or national official: issue-based	11	22	+11	+100
Contact local official: particularized	7	10	+3	+43
Contact state or national official: particularized	6	7	+1	+17
Community				
Work with others on local problem	30	34	+4	+13
Active membership in community problem-solving organization	31	34	+3	+10
Form group to help solve local problem	14	17	+3	+21

Note: The "Absolute Change" column heading refers to the actual difference between 1967 and 1987 percentages; the "Relative Change" column heading refers to the proportional change between the percentages.

Source: 1967 data, Verba and Nie, *Participation in America,* data file. 1987 data, National Opinion Research Center, General Social Survey. Reprinted by permission of the publisher from *Voice and Equality: Civic Voluntarism in American Politics* by Sidney Verba, Kay Lehman Schlozman, and Henry E. Brady, Cambridge, Mass.: Harvard University Press, © 1995 by the President and Fellows of Harvard College.

Although not shown in Table 4-1, another important finding concerning state and local participation is reported by Verba, Schlozman, and Brady:

> Fully 92 percent of those who are in any way politically active beyond voting engaged in some activity with a state or local focus—for example, campaigned for a state or local candidate, contacted a state or local official, or sat on a local governing board.[3]

Even though voting in elections is declining, it is still the political act that citizens engage in most frequently. However, before citizens can vote, they must register by filling out a voter registration application form for the local board of elections; this results in their names being placed on a list of eligible voters and their assignment to a polling place. This sounds simple enough, but state voter registration procedures have involved considerable controversy over the years.

African-Americans and the Right to Vote

Historically, procedures and requirements in Southern states in particular made it difficult for African-Americans to register; in essence they were discriminatory against African-Americans and other minority groups. This has changed greatly over the past thirty years. Sometimes states made changes on their own; other times, only after being pressured by the federal government.

Voter turnout among African-Americans in the South was dramatically altered when the U.S. Congress adopted the **Voting Rights Act of 1965.** Beginning in the 1890s, Southern states enacted various laws, including a literacy test requirement, aimed at preventing blacks from registering to vote but still allowing all whites to register. Over the years these laws became quite complex in the procedures used to accomplish this goal. Basically, local registration officials were given considerable discretion in deciding who to register. Illiterate whites could register because an "understanding clause" allowed potential voters to interpret a section of the Constitution after it was read to them. And for whites their interpretation was always correct. Black citizens who were literate and correctly interpreted the Constitution could still be kept from registering if, in the opinion of the registration official, they failed a "good character" requirement.[4]

A county or state was covered by the Voting Rights Act if it met the guidelines of a "triggering formula": (1) A literacy test was in use as of November 1, 1964, and (2) fewer than 50 percent of the eligible voters were registered or cast ballots in the 1964 presidential election. If a county or state met these conditions, and it was almost exclusively those in the South that did, the U.S. attorney general was empowered to abolish the literacy tests and replace local registration officials with federal agents who would register voters under federal procedures. The act effectively ended literacy tests, and they were permanently banned nationwide in 1975. Because of voluntary compliance in registering voters, federal registrars were sent to only a few counties in the South.

The Voting Rights Act also barred covered jurisdictions from making any changes affecting voting unless they received approval from the U.S. attorney general or the U.S. District Court for the District of Columbia. This meant that government actions such as drawing new district lines for members of legislative bodies or the annexation of additional land by a city that changed its racial composition had to be "precleared" at the federal level before they could be implemented.

The results of the Voting Rights Act are impressive: Nearly 1 million blacks were added to voter registration lists in Deep South states. In the period from 1964 to 1968, for example, the percentage of voting-age blacks registered in Mississippi increased from 6.7 to 59.4. The U.S. Justice Department, charged with implementing the act, estimated that within 5 years after its passage as many blacks had registered in Alabama, Mississippi, Georgia, Louisiana, North Carolina, and South Carolina as in the previous 100 years.[5]

Amendments in 1975 extended coverage of the Voting Rights Act to language minorities—Asian-Americans, American Indians, Alaskan natives, and Hispanic Americans—if one group made up more than 5 percent of the voting-age population in the jurisdiction and if voter turnout was below 50 percent in the 1972 presidential election.

Voting Rights Today

Prior to the renewal of the Voting Rights Act in 1982, a debate exploded over whether those suing under the act had to prove that a defendant had intended to discriminate.

Civil rights groups protested that intent would be difficult to prove and that, in any case, discrimination even if it is not deliberate still adversely affects blacks, Hispanics, and other minorities. The 1982 amendments resolved this controversy by prohibiting any voting practice or procedure, regardless of intent, that results in discrimination. As a consequence, the Voting Rights Act today deals with subtle forms of discrimination that occur when election laws and bloc voting combine to keep minorities from winning elective positions. This is called **minority vote dilution;** it can and does occur in jurisdictions throughout the United States and not just those in the South. Examples of minority vote dilution are especially evident at the local government level where city or county councils use at-large elections; that is, all council members are elected from only one district, and its boundaries are coterminous with those of the city or county. If voting in a county with a population 51 percent white and 49 percent one or more minority groups is polarized—minority voters vote for minority candidates, and white voters vote for white candidates—100 percent of the council members will be white, all elected with 51 percent of the vote, and all minority candidates will lose, with 49 percent of the vote. Even though the minority population is almost as large as that of the whites, no minorities will be elected to the council. After being sued under the Voting Rights Act, many local governments, with at-large elections and a history of no minorities running in or winning these elections, have been forced to adopt single-member districts. These increase the likelihood of members of minority groups winning office because boundary lines are drawn so that the minority will be a majority of the voters in at least one district. (See the Scholarly Box entitled Lani Guinier and Cumulative Voting.)

Additional Changes in Voter Registration

During the 1970s and 1980s, other registration requirements such as living in a state for at least one year and appearing in person at the election board's headquarters to register have been eliminated. Most states require residency of only ten to thirty days before an election, over half the states allow mail registration, and many give voters the opportunity to register when they obtain or renew their driver's license or apply for certain types of public assistance. (The latter is frequently referred to as "motor-voter" registration.) Although many states have been easing registration procedures on their own, Congress in 1993 enacted a **National Voter Registration Act** that expanded federal control over voter registration. This act requires all states to adopt mail and motor-voter registration procedures. In addition, state laws that purge voters, that is, cancel their registration solely for failure to vote at least once during a specified period of time, are prohibited.[8]

Governors in a few states are refusing to implement the motor-voter law, and some are challenging it in federal courts. They argue that it is another unfunded mandate (see Chapter 2); California officials estimate that it will take close to $20 million from the state treasury to implement motor-voter. They also argue that the federal government infringes on state authority by telling specific state agencies, which have nothing to do with elections, that they are to handle the additional responsibility of registering voters.[9]

SCHOLARLY BOX

LANI GUINIER AND CUMULATIVE VOTING

Lani Guinier, nominated in 1993 by President Bill Clinton to become assistant attorney general for civil rights, never achieved that position. Guinier's nomination was withdrawn by President Clinton when her ideas on ways to ensure participation of African-Americans in the governing process were attacked by critics, who also gave her the title of "Quota Queen."

Guinier believed that majority rule was not democratic if it excluded certain groups from the process of making decisions.[6] One of the changes in election procedures she advocated was the adoption of **cumulative voting.** This way of voting, she and others argued, could counter minority vote dilution in at-large election systems without creating single-member districts.

What is cumulative voting? First, cumulative voting requires that candidates be elected from at-large districts. It would be possible in large cities to have several at-large districts with each electing three to five council members. More likely to occur, especially in cities and counties with smaller populations, would be one at-large district that has boundaries identical with the city or county. (Even though voting rights suits have required many communities to abandon at-large districts in favor of single-member districts, at-large districts are still widely used to elect members of local legislatures.) The second and most important characteristic of cumulative voting is the way in which voters can use their votes. If there are five seats to be filled, an at-large election decided by plurality vote allows voters to give one vote to each of five candidates. Under cumulative voting, voters can distribute their five votes any way they want. For example, a voter could give one vote to five candidates, five votes to one candidate, or something in between such as two votes to one candidate and three to another. This method of voting allows members of a minority to concentrate their five votes on one candidate, increasing the chances that their candidate will win.

Although cumulative voting is not widely used in the United States, it has been adopted for elections in Peoria, Illinois; Cambridge, Massachusetts; Alamogordo, New Mexico; and several Alabama towns. Most studies of cumulative voting conclude that members of minority groups usually allocate their votes to a single candidate. In Alamogordo, it was first used in 1987 and was critical to the election of the first Hispanic candidate to the city council.[7]

In states where the law has been implemented, early reports indicate that as many as 2 million new voters have been registered. And contrary to the long-standing fear of Republicans, it is not a bonanza of new registrants for the Democratic party; voters are registering as independents much more frequently than party officials expected. In the South, in particular, many voters are registering as independents and "may well represent partial conversions by people abandoning traditional Democratic ties but simply unwilling to jump all the way over to the Republican side in one step."[10] In Kentucky, a strong Democratic state, independents make up 25 percent of new registrants, while in 1992 only 3 percent of voters were registered as independents.[11]

Three states have gone even further in easing registration requirements: Maine, Minnesota, and Wisconsin have made registration as easy as voting by permitting registration on election day. Registration and voting become a one-step process, with both completed at the same time. A study of these states concludes that on average they have a voter turnout rate that is 5 percent higher than states that do not have a one-step process.[12] Nevertheless, concern about the potential for voting fraud with election day registration has prevented most states from adopting it. (The National Voter Registration Act exempted from its coverage states with election day registration. As a result, the states of Idaho, New Hampshire, and Wyoming have quickly adopted it.)

Voter Turnout in Gubernatorial Elections

In recent gubernatorial elections, turnout has ranged from a low of 30 percent (Georgia and Kentucky) to a high of almost 85 percent (Utah). (For comparative purposes, remember that 55 percent of the voting-age population voted in the 1992 presidential election, and turnout was even lower in 1988. In 1994, turnout for congressional elections was 38 percent.)

A close examination of Table 4-2 reveals several patterns: (1) States that elect governors in the same years that presidents are elected have higher turnout than states that elect governors in nonpresidential years. Over two-thirds of the states that held elections in 1992 had over 50 percent turnout, while only 15 percent of the states with elections in nonpresidential years reached that level. Presidential elections stimulate voter interest, increasing the number of people who go to the polls. (2) The effect of presidential elections also can be found in New Hampshire, Rhode Island, and Vermont, where two-year gubernatorial terms cause elections to alternate between presidential and nonpresidential years. Turnout declined by at least 10 percentage points when nonpresidential years were compared with presidential years, and in New Hampshire the decline was considerably more. (3) Although the relationship between turnout and region is not perfect, states in the West tend to have the highest turnout and states in the South the lowest with Midwestern and Northeastern states in the middle.

As noted in Chapter 1, political culture affects voter turnout. States with a moralistic culture consistently lead the nation in rates of turnout. In these states individuals have the strongest belief that they can accomplish something positive through the political process. Traditional states have the lowest turnout, and individualistic states fall in the middle.[13] Citizens residing in moralistic political culture states tend to have a higher sense of citizen duty and the resulting feeling that it is their duty to vote. They also have a higher sense of **political efficacy;** that is, they believe their vote will make a difference and that they can influence policymaking. All of these individual attitudes correlate positively with high levels of voting. Finally, recent research, done before the enactment of the National Voter Registration Act, discovered that moralistic states have laws that make it easier for citizens to register to vote and traditionalistic cultures have more restrictive registration laws.[14]

Voter turnout is even lower in local (city and county) elections—often under 30 percent. (See Table 4-1. Surveys of 1967 and 1987 show lower participation in local elections than in presidential, and the decline over time is greater in local elections than in presidential.) A variety of factors are responsible, including the lack of media attention paid to these elections, the absence of opponents to challenge incumbents in many races, and frequently the large number of positions to be filled by election. In most cases, there is little excitement because local officials deal largely with such noncontroversial issues as road repair and other basic services. In most small towns, officials avoid controversy and support the status quo. Campaigns are low-key events and center on name identification.

TABLE 4-2 VOTER TURNOUT IN RECENT GUBERNATORIAL ELECTIONS

1991	1992	1993	1994	
Louisiana 57.8	Utah 84.5	New Jersey 40.1	South Dakota 59.7	Hawaii 41.0
Mississippi 38.2	Montana 69.6	Virginia 36.7	Wyoming 58.3	Ohio 40.0
Kentucky 30.0	North Dakota 65.3		Maine 53.6	Arkansas 39.4
	Vermont* 64.6		Minnesota 51.5	Pennsylvania 39.1
	New Hampshire* 60.5		Idaho 51.2	New Mexico 38.9
	Washington 59.5		Vermont* 47.8	Florida 38.5
	Rhode Island* 56.1		Nebraska 47.6	Alabama 38.0
	Missouri 54.1		Massachusetts 47.0	Tennessee 37.7
	Indiana 53.3		Iowa 46.7	New York 37.1
	West Virginia 48.7		Connecticut 45.8	New Hampshire* 36.8
	Delaware 45.7		Rhode Island* 45.6	Maryland 36.3
	North Carolina 41.8		Alaska 44.3	Illinois 35.3
			Michigan 44.1	Nevada 34.1
			Kansas 43.4	South Carolina 34.0
			Oklahoma 41.6	California 33.8
			Wisconsin 41.4	Texas 33.4
			Oregon 41.2	Georgia 29.9
			Colorado 41.1	

*These states elect governors every two years. A recent Rhode Island constitutional amendment changed the gubernatorial term from two to four years beginning in 1994.

Note: Percentages are calculated by dividing the total number of votes cast by the voting-age population, eighteen years and older.

Source: Voting-age population: Current Population Reports, P25-1085, P25-1117, *Projections of the Voting-Age Population* (Washington, D.C.: U.S. Bureau of the Census). Gubernatorial vote for 1994: *Congressional Quarterly Weekly Report* (Washington, D.C.: Congressional Quarterly, 1994), November 12, 1994, pp. 3301–3308. Figures for 1993, 1992, and 1991: *Statistical Abstract of the United States: 1994* (Washington, D.C.: U.S. Bureau of the Census, 1994), p. 282.

Beyond Voting

The New England town meeting, where citizens come together to make decisions for the community, is the ideal of democratic decision making. Today, however, the size of most local governments and the complexity of issues they face would seem to make it impractical for everyone to come together at one time to make decisions. Nevertheless, there are a number of political scientists and governmental leaders who think that ways must be found to increase citizen participation in government, that is, create **strong democracy.**[15] They argue that this may not be possible in national and state politics because of problems of distance and size, but that it is possible in local governments. The goal is to rebuild citizenship in the United States, which means getting people to participate in "public forums where they can work with their neighbors to solve the problems of their community."[16] (See the reading on "civic journalism.")

Of course, the many demands on people's time lead one to question whether they would participate in these forums. Berry, Portney, and Thomson, after studying five cities, conclude that effective citizen participation can occur through neighborhood-based associations, containing 2,000 to 5,000 people, if they meet the criteria of breadth and depth.

Breadth of participation is the extent to which every citizen is offered the opportunity to take part in the deliberations of their neighborhood association. This involves conducting an extensive outreach effort detailing information on the time and place of meetings and issues to be discussed. Efforts to keep citizens informed should be continuous, perhaps involving the publication of a monthly neighborhood newspaper describing the association's activities. This type of effort requires a commitment of financial resources and staff from the local governmental unit that the associations are a part of. *Depth of participation* is the extent to which citizens, working through associations, actually influence local governmental policies. Citizens should have a say, at least, in how land is used and how government funds are spent in their neighborhoods.[17]

Again, at the heart of strong democracy is the idea that citizenship, people participating in the making of decisions that affect themselves and their community, is much more than simply voting. In fact, voting is frequently viewed not as an act that empowers individuals but one that takes the power to decide from them and delegates it to a few elected leaders.[18] Neighborhood assemblies, it is believed, "conducted as an open and ongoing forum for the discussion of a flexible and citizen-generated agenda,"[19] can provide an institutional framework for effective citizen participation.

FINANCING AND REGULATION OF ELECTION CAMPAIGNS

The exploding growth of campaign spending is reflected in Figure 4-1. Gubernatorial races, of course, are the most expensive at the state and local level. According to Beyle, the average cost of gubernatorial elections in twelve states in 1992 was just over $5 million. Campaigns in Missouri and North Carolina were both over $13 million, and these are not even large states. The 1990 races in Texas and California were over $50 million each.[20] State legislative elections in large states such as California can be enormously expensive; candidates spent $78.9 million in 1988 campaigns for the California legislature. Candidates running for seats in state senates spent in the primary and general election, in the late 1980s, as much as $447,000 (Florida), $378,000 (New Jersey), and $237,000 (Washington).[21]

Civic Journalism: A New Genre

Neal R. Peirce

A new way of covering the news—one that deemphasizes conflict and political machinations and stresses citizens' concerns and ideas about solving problems—may soon be coming to a newspaper or television station near you.

Or it may already have arrived. With remarkable speed, a wave of "civic" or "public" journalism is spreading from coast to coast.

Civic journalism is a revulsion against the rituals that have become an inescapable part of how the news media cover election campaigns—among them "horse race" polling, "soundbite" reportage and television attack ads.

The *Wichita Eagle* (Kan.) and *Charlotte Observer* (N.C.) blazed the trail in their 1992 election coverage, switching the focus of their campaign coverage to issues that their readers—through opinion surveys and in-depth interviews—said concerned them the most. Top billing went to the positions of candidates on citizen-identified issues rather than stories flowing from political charges and countercharges and reporters following the normal "insider" games.

Candidates quickly learned that a new day had dawned. When then-Sen. Terry Sanford, D-N.C., said that he wasn't ready to state a position on the environment, the *Observer* (working in partnership with WSOU-TV) told him that it would leave white space beside his name. Sanford quickly relented.

In 1992, the *Eagle* launched a "People Project" of even broader import. Through surveys and extensive interviews, citizens focused on problems that local government seemed unable to solve—faltering schools, crime and the lure of gangs, family and neighborhood tensions and health care.

The *Eagle* carefully reported and analyzed each problem and then printed pages containing the dates and times of community forums, plus lists of groups working on solutions to those problems. The newspaper's role, according to its editor, Davis Merritt Jr., is to provide "a huge and accessible marketplace where ideas can be formed and exchanged—not simply ideas about what's wrong, but ideas about solutions.

Now, as the 1994 elections approach, a flood of newspapers and television and radio stations are moving to the new coverage style. In Florida, an unprecedented combine of six newspapers is conducting joint statewide polls to identify issues on the minds of voters and preparing to grill gubernatorial candidates on those issues. The six—critics call them the "cartel"—are *The Miami Herald,* the *St. Petersburg Times,* the *Tallahassee Democrat,* the *Florida Times-Union* (Jacksonville), the *Bradenton Herald* and the *Boca Raton News.*

In California, the *San Francisco Examiner,* working jointly with KQED public radio and KRON-TV, has confronted gubernatorial candidates with "Voice of the Voter" questions identified in citizen polls. A very reluctant Kathleen Brown—then the front-runner in and later the winner of the Democratic primary—found herself obliged to engage in a televised debate with her opponents. The clincher: an argument that by staying out, she'd be avoiding questions posed directly by voters.

The *Examiner* and its partners have made it clear that they don't intend to neglect their basic investigative watchdog role, in and out of the election season.

Some journalists deride the idea of putting the views of citizens at the center of election coverage. In a column for *California Journal,* Susan Rasky, a former reporter for *The New York Times,* called the "Voice of the Voter" effort "pseudo-journalism" and "a perhaps well-intentioned but ultimately harebrained notion." The "dirty little truth" acknowledged by reporters and politicians, she wrote, is that the "vox populi may not be all it's cracked up to be"—that voters, for example, often want contradictory things.

Rasky's quote pinpoints the issue. The public journalism community, observes Jay Rosen of New York University, believes firmly "that average citizens are capable of intelligent judgment, mature understanding and rational choice if offered the opportunity."

If polls show that citizens have inconsistent goals—longer criminal sentences but no new prisons, for example—then public journalism's expanded issue discussions should foster more-realistic debates.

A healthy free press and a strong civic culture—"binding people to their communities, drawing them into politics and public affairs"—are interdependent, insist Rosen and Edward Miller of the Poynter Institute for Media Studies (which owns the *St. Petersburg Times*). Voters, they say, need "to see 'the system' as theirs—public property rather than the playground of insiders or political professionals."

Buying into those ideas, National Public Radio has signed up 86 of its member stations to approach this year's elections by surveying voter attitudes, holding community forums and working with local newspapers and television stations to produce lively, ongoing political coverage with a heavy dose of citizen participation.

Such newspapers as *The Boston Globe, Dallas Morning News* and *Seattle Times* are to collaborate with NPR in the effort, with support from the Poynter Institute and the Center for Civic Journalism, which was recently created by the Pew Charitable Trusts, a Philadelphia-based philanthropy. The Radio and Television News Directors Association has also bought into the effort, and in June it sponsored a forum on community journalism at Northwestern University's Medill School of Journalism. Twice the expected 30 attendees, from newspapers and stations nationwide, signed on.

One could argue that the newspapers and radio and TV stations are chiefly interested in civic journalism to attract readers and viewers. That's a particularly big worry for newspapers, which continue to lose readership and today are read by only half as many 18–29-year-olds as in 1968.

But civic journalism is arguably more than that. It's an opening wedge of editors and broadcasters to "reengineer" their operations and reinforce the focus that they should always have: the needs and concerns of all citizens, not just as consumers but as participants in the democratic process.

Source: National Journal, July 2, 1994, p. 1585. Reprinted with permission of National Journal.

Such large sums of money are difficult to raise if they come in amounts of $10 and $20, so candidates typically turn to the business community (if they are Republicans) or to labor unions or teachers' associations (if they are Democrats). Unlike the federal government about half the states permit corporations to make campaign contributions

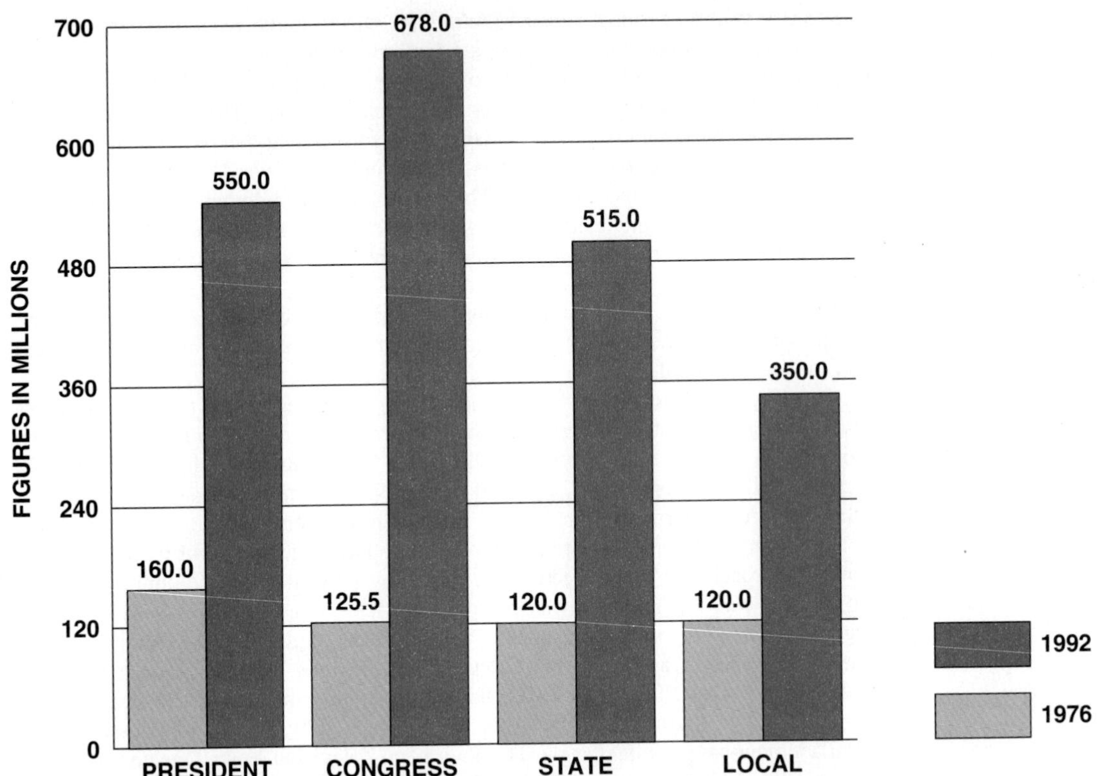

FIGURE 4-1 Increases in campaign spending, 1976–1992. [Herbert E. Alexander, *Reform and Reality: The Financing of State and Local Campaigns* (New York: The Twentieth Century Fund Press, 1991), p. 7. Reprinted with permission of the Twentieth Century Fund, New York. Campaign spending costs for 1992 were provided by the Citizens' Research Foundation.]

directly from their profits. Many states allow labor unions to make contributions directly from their treasuries. Candidates also use dinners, mail solicitation, and cocktail parties to raise funds, especially in smaller states where campaigning is not as expensive.

As noted in Chapter 3, PACs have raised and distributed increasingly greater amounts of money to campaigns in the past ten years. A study of state legislative candidates in several states found that on average PAC contributions made up anywhere from 13 to 43 percent of the total funds candidates raised.[22]

Campaign Contributions: Disclosure and Limits

State laws regulating campaign finance are as varied as the fifty states. Recent efforts to more closely regulate the financing of campaigns originated as a response to a number of developments: the national Watergate scandal in the early 1970s, the public's view that politicians are too beholden to campaign contributions from special interests, and, occasionally, campaign financing scandals in individual states.

Almost all states made major changes in their election laws in the 1970s, beginning with candidates disclosing the source of their campaign funds and expenditures. Comprehensive and timely **disclosure laws** can help the public learn what interests are supporting a candidate before elections are held. If all contributors and the size of contributions are made public, ideally, voters have the opportunity to vote against a candidate who is receiving money from groups they don't support. Disclosure could even reduce the influence of special interests because candidates may not want to act in ways that appear to be responding to interests that gave them money. While all states have disclosure laws, unfortunately, their quality varies. To be useful, disclosure reports should contain information on the amount of money contributed, the contributor's occupation, and his or her place of employment. Reports from candidates for state office should be readily available at intervals before and after the election at the state election office and, in the case of legislative candidates, also at the county board of elections.[23]

Contribution limits are another way states regulate campaign financing. Over half the states limit how much individuals can contribute. These limits tend to fall in the range of $1,000 to $2,000 per candidate per election and force candidates to raise smaller amounts of money from a greater number of people, reducing dependence on a few contributors who donate large sums of money. States that allow labor unions and corporations to make contributions usually place limits on them as well. Most states limit PAC contributions, and a few have placed limits on the percentage of a candidate's contributions that can come from PACs.

Public Funding of Campaigns

Public Funding of candidates' campaigns or political parties is a reform idea being tried in twenty-two states. New Jersey's public financing law, one of the nation's most successful, was adopted in 1974 a few months before Congress decided that presidential campaigns should be publicly funded. New Jersey's law covers only gubernatorial candidates. To qualify for public funds, a candidate must raise $150,000 from private contributors; then he or she receives $2 in public funding for every $1 from private sources. By accepting public funds, candidates agree to limit how much money they will spend in the election (expenditure limit) and to participate in two debates in the primary and general election. It should be noted that candidates do not have to accept public funding. If they choose, they can run their campaign entirely from private contributions. New Jersey's law has reduced the importance of special interest money and has encouraged candidates to run in the primary who might not have done so without the promise of public funds.[24]

The Supreme Court in *Buckley* v. *Valeo* (1976) found campaign expenditure limits imposed by state legislatures or Congress to be unconstitutional. The Court ruled that spending money in a political campaign was a form of speech and was therefore protected by the First Amendment to the U.S. Constitution. At the same time the Court allowed the setting of expenditure limits if they are a condition of accepting public funding. In other words, the only legal way to limit spending is to tie it to public funds.

Public funding of campaigns is not a universal success; notable exceptions are New Jersey, Minnesota, and Wisconsin. (Minnesota and Wisconsin extend public funds to state legislative campaigns, as well as to gubernatorial.) Of course, public funding is not possible if funds are not available, and that is the nub of the problem. Most states rely on state income taxes to generate revenues for funding of campaigns. The most popular method is an "add-on" tax, whereby a taxpayer donates, depending on the state, anywhere from $1 to $25. Because this adds on to the taxes an individual must pay, participation is very low. No state has had participation higher than 2 percent of its taxpayers. Other states use the "tax checkoff," which allows voters to designate $1 to $5 of their taxes to public financing. The contribution is not added on to their taxes but is taken out of what they already owe. Participation is higher than in the add-on states, around 16 percent in 1988.[25] Still, little money is raised to distribute to candidates, and with the exception of New Jersey, states have been unwilling to use money from their budgets to supplement taxpayer designated funds. (Minnesota and Wisconsin both use the tax checkoff.) Maryland has had an on-and-off relationship with public financing. In the post-Watergate period, it passed a comprehensive law but repealed it when several years of the add-on tax raised enough money to offer public funding only to gubernatorial candidates in the 1994 election. Then in 1995, after many observers concluded that public funding was a success, the legislature readopted it for gubernatorial elections using the add-on tax. If the past is any guide, it could take close to ten years to raise enough money to finance one gubernatorial election.

It is ironic that public displeasure with candidates raising money from special interests has not produced public willingness to support a system of public funding based on relatively small contributions from all or almost all taxpayers. An average-sized state with 1 million taxpayers and a $25 tax checkoff could raise $25 million a year, more than enough to finance gubernatorial elections every four years and perhaps state legislative elections as well.

INITIATIVE, REFERENDUM, AND RECALL

As will be noted in Chapter 5, the 1960s and 1970s marked the most extensive restructuring of state legislatures in American history. These revitalized institutions, it was contended, would enact legislation desired by a majority of the people, which in turn would restore public faith in representative bodies. Yet the 1970s saw a renewal of interest in the techniques of direct democracy—initiative, referendum, and recall—by which citizens are able to bypass legislatures and act directly.

Extent of Direct Democracy in the United States

State and local election laws differ from federal laws in that they often permit the use of the initiative, referendum, and recall. Although these techniques were available in colonial America and their use can be traced back to ancient Greece, they are largely a product of the Progressive movement in the early twentieth century. These reformers distrusted partisan politicians and wished to introduce the means by which citizens could check government excess and incompetence. Because of widespread corruption and incompetence, turn-of-the-century reformers had good reason to want to bypass legislatures. States using these techniques today are identified in Figure 4-2.

Although tax limitation proposals, such as Proposition 13 in California, were widely publicized, citizens in many states have been actively involved with other initiative issues such as nuclear power regulation, the death penalty, and, more recently, term limitations for state legislators and members of the United States Congress.

Use of the initiative continues unabated. In the 1994 general election, voters in twenty-two states determined the fate of seventy initiatives, more than in any year since 1932, including the much publicized Proposition 187 in California. This measure, which prohibits illegal immigrants from receiving public benefits, was approved

FIGURE 4-2 Citizen-initiated initiative, referendum, and recall at the state level. [Thomas E. Cronin, *Direct Democracy: The Politics of Initiative, Referendum, and Recall,* A Twentieth Century Fund Book (Cambridge, Mass.: Harvard University Press, 1989), p. 47. Reprinted with permission of the Twentieth Century Fund, New York. Map has been updated to reflect Mississippi's adoption of the initiative in 1993.]

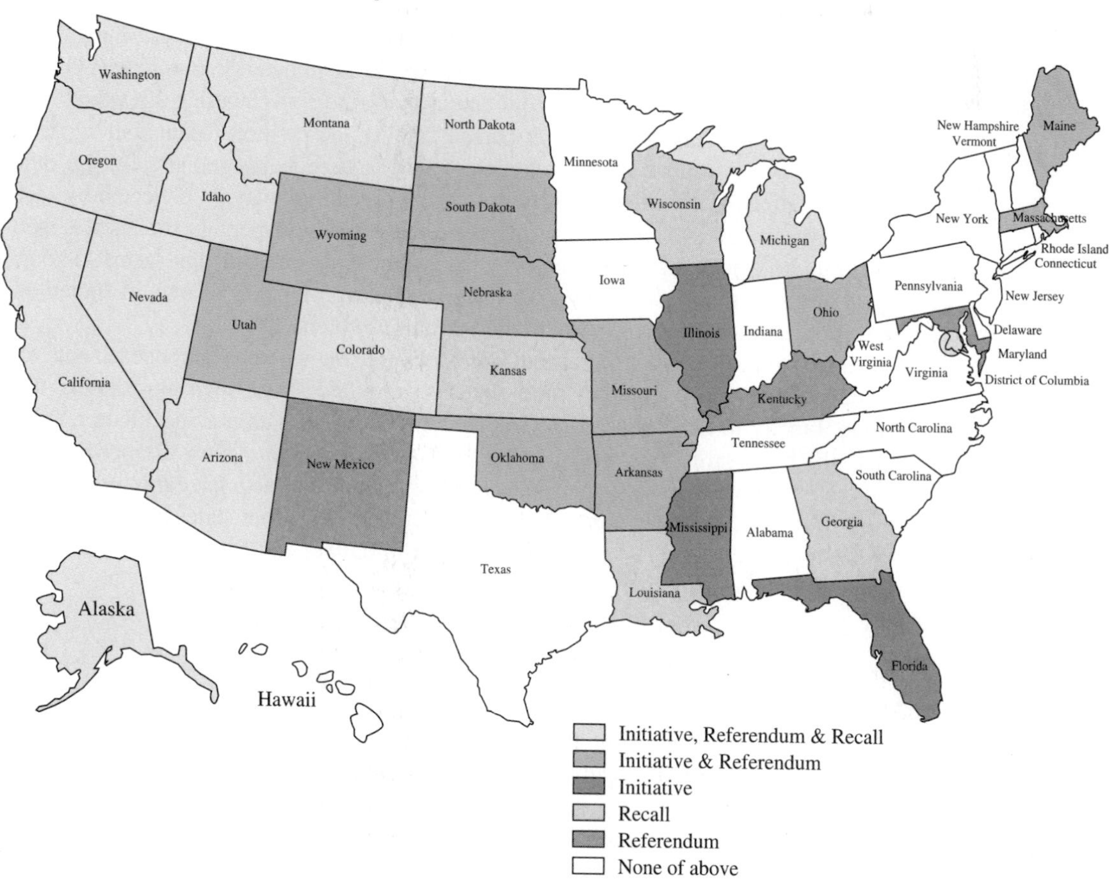

by California voters, but its constitutionality has been challenged in the courts.[26] Oregon passed a "Death with Dignity Act," legally recognizing physician-assisted suicide of the terminally ill. The constitutionality of this measure also is being challenged in the courts. Arizona residents voted to finance health care for the poor by increasing the tax on cigarettes.[27]

The Initiative Process

The **initiative** is a technique whereby citizens can propose new laws or changes in state constitutions and determine by their votes in an election whether the proposal will be adopted; proposals are actually placed on the ballot for voter approval. The *direct initiative* allows voters to bypass the legislature and place proposals directly on the ballot. Twenty states have the direct initiative to propose new laws and/or changes in the constitution. The vast majority of these states are located west of the Mississippi River, where political parties are weaker and nonpartisan good-government groups have been stronger than in the East.[28]

Petitions to place a proposal on the ballot are circulated, and if a certain percentage of registered voters (usually about 10 percent) sign the petition within a designated period of time, the proposal will be on the ballot in the next election. Laws regulating how petitions can be circulated are an important factor in determining the level of difficulty in using the initiative. A requirement that a person gathering signatures on a petition must actually witness each person signing the petition means that signature gathering will consume a large amount of time and probably money. On the other hand, the process is easier in California, where signatures may be collected by mail, and in Washington, where petitions may be printed in newspapers. In some states, petitions can be placed on bulletin boards where almost anyone can sign them. Although these methods sound easy, they frequently yield a high number of invalid signatures, that is, signatures of people who are not registered voters.[29]

Another type of initiative is the *indirect initiative,* whereby a proposal with the required number of signatures must first be submitted to the legislature rather than going directly to the voters. If the legislature fails to act within a specified period of time, the proposal is then placed on the ballot for voter approval or disapproval. The indirect initiative is used in nine states, including five that also have the direct initiative. (To avoid confusion, remember that a total of twenty-four states have some form of the initiative; twenty states have the direct initiative, and five of these states also have the indirect initiative; four states have only the indirect initiative.)

The Referendum Process

A **referendum** gives voters the opportunity to have the final say on issues that a legislature already has decided. Twenty-three states have a *popular* or *petition referendum* where, after voters gather the required number of signatures on petitions, a newly enacted law must win the approval of the voters at the next election. If the law is not approved by the voters, it does not go into effect. The popular referendum, because of citizens signing petitions and citizens voting on a measure, is easily confused with the direct initiative. The important difference between the two is the source of the issue that appears on the ballot. With the direct initiative, the issue being voted on is a proposal for a new law that is put forth by a number of citizens. With the popular referendum, the issue being voted on is a law that was just approved by the legislature and signed by the governor.

The more common referendum procedure is *submission by the legislature.* Here the legislature, after adopting a law, directs that it be placed on the ballot for final approval or disapproval by the voters. Also, some issues, in a slight variation of the submission by the legislature process, may be required by state constitutions or local charters to automatically go to the voters. Examples are amendments to state constitutions and financial (tax and bond) issues.

The Recall Process

The **recall,** a procedure to remove an elected public official from office before his or her term officially ends, is the least used and least available of the three techniques of direct democracy. Only fifteen state constitutions include a provision for a statewide recall. In addition, fifteen other states allow local recall. States that allow a recall tend to be the same states that have the initiative and referendum. Of course, this is because the recall is the product of the same Progressive movement as the initiative and referendum and is similar in that it shows a distrust of elected officials.

Under recall procedures, voters circulate petitions calling for the removal of an elected official. The percentage of valid signatures required to call a special election is usually high, about 25 percent of the vote cast for the office in the last election. If a sufficient number of signatures is obtained, the recall election is held and the voters choose either to keep the official or to remove him or her from office. If the majority of voters approve the recall, a successor may be chosen on the recall ballot or in a subsequent special election.

Recalls occur more frequently, though they are still the exception rather than the rule, in local politics where the targets are mayors, members of city councils, and school boards. Only one governor has been recalled, Lynn Frazier of North Dakota in 1922. (He was subsequently elected to the U.S. Senate from North Dakota.) Recall does not require that an elected official be accused of a criminal action; voters' dissatisfaction with an official's performance may be enough. In 1984, Michigan voters, unhappy with a large tax increase, successfully recalled several state legislators and changed party control of the legislature as a result.[30] The recall cannot be used against judges in some states, where it is considered to impair an independent judiciary. In other states, judges can and have been recalled.

Initiative and Referendum Evaluated

The direct initiative and popular referendum were adopted to counter the influence of special interests on legislators and to give citizens more control over the making of laws. However, some question whether today's practice of direct democracy is actually achieving these goals. To support their position they cite the fact that interest groups, not grassroots organizations composed of average citizens, are the dominant users of the initiative and referendum. Just organizing and financing a petition drive is expensive. Even with dedicated volunteers circulating petitions, it may cost $250,000 to gather the signatures needed to qualify an initiative for the ballot.[31] Of course, interest groups are well equipped with organizing skills and financial resources. Groups do not have to know a lot about running an initiative campaign because they can hire "professional managers, petition circulators, media consultants, pollsters, direct-mail specialists and lawyers."[32] Paid petitioners frequently work with at least three separate initiatives, approaching citizens and asking them to sign as many as they agree with. Price reports that in California two professional petitioning organizations, usually referred to as signature companies, were responsible for 75 percent of the initiatives on the California ballot between 1982 and 1992.[33] In addition, a study of recent elections in California reveals that two-thirds of the money spent in initiative campaigns came from business interests and two-thirds of all money donated came in amounts of $100,000 or more.[34]

Money is important in getting a proposal on the ballot, but the side that spends the most money is not always the side that wins support of the voters. For example, in 1988, when over $140 million was spent on initiative campaigns in California, five competing auto insurance initiatives were voted on and the only one approved had lower campaign expenditures made on its behalf than the other four. Overall, the effect of money in initiative campaigns is this: If *opponents* spend more, or if spending is roughly equal, the measure is defeated more than 80 percent of the time. If *proponents* spend substantially more money, they will win about 50 percent of the time.[35] Between 1981 and 1994, voters rejected 55 percent of initiatives appearing on statewide ballots (see Table 4-3).

The growing importance of money in the initiative process has caused some experts on direct democracy to call for the adoption of safeguards to ensure that citizens can "exercise the judgment required to make direct democracy live up to its potential."[36] Cronin suggests that all states and localities with the initiative and referendum must also have mandatory financial disclosure laws of all contributions of $200 or more during and after an initiative campaign. As with election campaigns, this will help the public learn how a measure got on the ballot and who is supporting it and who is opposing it. Disclosure will help voters judge who stands to benefit most if a measure is adopted. Excessive contributions from a single source would be a clue to voters that they should look closely at a measure's potential impact.

Another safeguard would be a required official information pamphlet for voters that would contain 100-word summaries of ballot measures that are easily read and understood by voters with no more than a high school education. Pamphlets would also contain basic arguments for and against the proposal and the full text of the measure. Massachusetts, Oregon, and Washington use such pamphlets, and voters often mention that they were important in their voting decisions.[37]

Finally, placing a limit on the number of ballot measures voters must decide on in any one election may be necessary. Eighteen measures appearing on the same ballot, as happened in Oregon in 1994, are so many that very few people could be expected to vote intelligently on all of them.

TABLE 4-3 NUMBER OF STATEWIDE INITIATIVES APPEARING ON THE BALLOT, BY STATE: 1981–1994

State	Initiatives on ballot	Initiatives approved by voters
Alaska	13	7
Arizona	24	10
Arkansas	11	6
California	70	32
Colorado	32	11
Florida	9	6
Idaho	8	5
Illinois	0	0
Maine	18	12
Massachusetts	22	11
Michigan	10	3
Missouri	12	7
Montana	19	7
Nebraska	7	4
Nevada	11	7
North Dakota	19	5
Ohio	14	4
Oklahoma	6	5
Oregon	60	24
South Dakota	16	9
Utah	7	0
Washington	24	12
Wyoming	6	3
Total	418	190

Source: Initiative and Referendum Analysis (June 1992), p. 1. Updated through 1994 with information furnished by Public Affairs Research Institute of New Jersey. Reprinted by permission of Public Affairs Research Institute of New Jersey.

SUMMARY

American citizens can participate in state and local politics in a number of ways—from voting to forming a group to work on a local problem. Discriminatory voter registration requirements have been eliminated by the Voting Rights Act of 1965. And many states, even before the passage of the 1993 National Voter Registration law, acted on their own to make voter registration less burdensome by adopting mail and "motor-voter" procedures. Although voter turnout in elections has been declining, states with the following characteristics consistently have the highest turnout: state elections held at the same time as presidential elections, a moralistic political culture, and less restrictive voter registration laws.

Running political campaigns for elected office is increasingly expensive, especially in large states. Even before the start of this explosive growth, states were attempting to regulate the influence of large financial contributors through laws that limit the size of contributions and require candidates to disclose information about the source of contributions and expenditures. Public funding of campaigns, which could reduce a candidate's reliance on private contributors, has had limited success because most states rely on the "add-on" tax to generate funds and taxpayer participation has been very low.

The initiative, referendum, and recall are procedures that allow citizens to propose laws, to make decisions on laws they have proposed or their legislatures have proposed, and to remove elected officials from office before they have finished their terms. These procedures are used in many state and local governments, but by no means all. Progressive Era reformers hoped these techniques of direct democracy would be a way for ordinary citizens to enact laws without the influence of special interests that characterizes legislatures. Contrary to their expectations, well-financed interest groups are using these techniques with increasing frequency to advance their goals.

KEY TERMS

Contribution limits Limits on the amount of money contributors can give to political campaigns. Typically, individuals are limited to $1,000 or $2,000 per candidate per election (primary and general).

Cumulative voting A method of voting, used by a few local governments in the United States, whereby members of a legislative body such as a city council run at large and voters have as many votes as there are members to be elected. Voters can give all of their votes to one candidate or divide their votes among as many candidates as they wish.

Disclosure laws Laws that require candidates for elected office to disclose on a timely basis the financial contributions, contributors, and expenditures associated with their campaign.

Initiative A procedure whereby citizens can bypass elected officials and propose new statutes, or changes in state constitutions or local government charters; these proposals are placed on the ballot for voter approval.

Minority vote dilution Occurs when voting strength of an ethnic or racial minority group protected by the Voting Rights Act is diminished by election laws or procedures and the bloc voting of a majority group.

National Voter Registration Act A 1993 federal law that requires all states to have mail and "motor-voter" registration procedures. The constitutionality of this law is being challenged by a few states.

Political efficacy The belief of individuals that they can influence government decisions and policies.

Political participation Actions through which citizens influence or attempt to influence policies adopted by government officials.

Public funding The use of public funds to finance political campaigns of candidates for various state or local offices. Candidates usually raise some money from private sources, which is then matched with public funds. Approximately twenty states have some form of public funding.

Recall A procedure whereby petitions are circulated calling for the removal of a public official from office. If a sufficient number of signatures is obtained, an election is held in which voters decide whether to keep the official in office.

Referendum A procedure that allows citizens to decide through an election if a proposal passed by a legislative body will actually become law.

Strong democracy Citizens participating on a continuing basis in neighborhood-based public forums to identify and solve problems in their community.

Survey research A means of data collection that asks respondents, who are a representative sample of a larger population, questions about their political attitudes and behavior.

Voting Rights Act of 1965 A federal law that significantly helped to increase voter turnout in the South by suspending literacy tests. Amendments to the act prohibit any practice that discriminates against voters who are members of certain designated minority groups such as African-Americans, Hispanic Americans, Asian-Americans, and American Indians.

REFERENCES

1 Jack H. Nagel, *Participation* (Englewood Cliffs, N.J.: Prentice-Hall, 1987), p. 1.

2 Sidney Verba and Norman H. Nie, *Participation in America: Political Democracy and Social Equality* (New York: Harper & Row, 1972), pp. 66–67.

3 Sidney Verba, Kay Lehman Schlozman, and Henry E. Brady, *Voice and Equality: Civic Voluntarism in American Politics* (Cambridge, Mass.: Harvard University Press, 1995), p. 66.

4 V. O. Key, Jr., *Southern Politics in State and Nation* (New York: Alfred A. Knopf, 1949), pp. 556–577.

5 Chandler Davidson, "The Voting Rights Act: A Brief History," in *Controversies in Minority Voting,* Bernard Grofman and Chandler Davidson, eds. (Washington, D.C.: The Brookings Institution, 1992), p. 21.

6 Lani Guinier, "Who's Afraid of Lani Guinier," *New York Times Magazine,* February 27, 1994, pp. 54–66.

7 Richard L. Cole, Richard L. Engstrom, and Delbert A. Taebel, "Cumulative Voting and Minority Representation: An Analysis of the Alamogordo, New Mexico Experience," presented at the 1988 annual meeting of the American Political Science Association.

8 Richard G. Smolka and Ronald D. Michaelson, "Election Legislation, 1992–93" in *Book of the States, 1994–95* (Lexington, Ky.: Council of State Governments, 1994), pp. 204–208.

9 Richard G. Smolka, "Motor-Voter Collisions," *State Government News* 38 (April 1995), pp. 9–10.

10 Geoff Earle, "Motor Trouble for Democrats," *Governing* 9 (August 1995), p. 26.

11 Ibid., pp. 25–26.

12 Mark J. Fenster, "The Impact of Allowing Day of Registration Voting on Turnout in U.S. Elections from 1960 to 1992," *American Politics Quarterly* 22 (January 1994), p. 84.

13 Daniel J. Elazar, *American Federalism: A View from the States,* 3d ed. (New York: Harper & Row, 1984), pp. 152–153.

14 James D. King, "Political Culture, Registration Laws, and Voter Turnout Among the American States," *Publius: The Journal of Federalism* 24 (Fall 1994), pp. 115–127.

15 The term *strong democracy* is frequently found in the literature on citizen participation in the affairs of local communities. The idea is presented fully in Benjamin R. Barber, *Strong Democracy* (Berkeley: University of California Press, 1984).

16 Jeffrey M. Berry, Kent E. Portney, and Ken Thomson, *The Rebirth of Urban Democracy* (Washington, D.C.: The Brookings Institution, 1993), p. 2.
17 Ibid., pp. 54–70.
18 Ibid., p. 145.
19 Ibid., p. 270.
20 Thad L. Beyle, "The 1992 Gubernatorial Elections," *Comparative State Politics* 15 (February 1994), p. 28.
21 Herbert E. Alexander, *Reform and Reality: The Financing of State and Local Campaigns* (New York: The Twentieth Century Fund Press, 1991), p. 6.
22 Frederick M. Hermann and Ronald D. Michaelson, "Financing State and Local Elections: Recent Developments," in *Book of the States, 1994–95* (Lexington, Ky.: Council of State Governments, 1994), p. 229. This information is based on William E. Cassie, Joel A. Thompson, and Malcolm E. Jewell, "The Pattern of PAC Contributions in Legislative Elections: An Eleven State Analysis," presented at the Annual Meeting of the American Political Science Association, 1992, Chicago, Ill.
23 Alexander, *Reform and Reality,* pp. 76–77.
24 Ibid., pp. 30–32.
25 Ibid., p. 42.
26 Karen Foerstel, "Voters Favor Term Limits, Reject Tax Restrictions," *Congressional Quarterly Weekly Reports,* November 12, 1994, p. 3251.
27 An excellent summary of 1994 ballot measures is available in Thomas E. Cronin, "Direct Democracy—1994," Everett Carll Ladd, ed., *America at the Polls 1994* (Storrs, Conn.: The Roper Center for Public Opinion Research, 1995), pp. 112–125.
28 Charles M. Price, "The Initiative: A Comparative Analysis and Reassessment of a Western Phenomenon," *Western Political Quarterly* 28 (June 1975), pp. 243–262.
29 David Kehler and Robert M. Stern, "Initiatives in the 1980s and 1990s," *Book of the States, 1994–95* (Lexington, Ky.: Council of State Governments, 1994), pp. 279–281.
30 Jack C. Plano and Milton Greenberg, *The American Political Dictionary,* 9th ed. (Orlando, Fla.: Harcourt Brace Jovanovich College Publishers, 1993), p. 102.
31 Charles M. Price, "Signing for Fun and Profit: The Business of Gathering Petition Signatures," *1994–1995 Annual—California Government and Politics* (Sacramento, Calif.: California Journal Press, 1994), p. 77.
32 Martha Angle, "Initiatives: Vox Populi or Professional Ploy," *Congressional Quarterly Weekly Report,* October 15, 1994, p. 2982.
33 Price, "Signing for Fun and Profit," p. 76.
34 David B. Magleby, "Direct Legislation in the American States," in *Referendums around the World,* David Butler and Austin Ranney, eds. (Washington, D.C.: The AEI Press, 1994), p. 243.
35 Ibid, p. 250.
36 Thomas E. Cronin, *Direct Democracy: The Politics of Initiative, Referendum, and Recall* (Cambridge, Mass.: Harvard University Press, 1989), p. 233.
37 Ibid., p. 238.

5

STATE LEGISLATURES

Howard Dratch/The Image Works

In a period of twenty-five years, from 1965 to 1990, state legislatures, in some respects, have come full circle. Before the mid-1960s, they were dominated by rural political interests and were described as holdovers from the nineteenth century, when many state constitutions were written and the public wanted a limited role for state government. Only twenty legislatures met in annual sessions back then. Being a legislator was a part-time activity performed by individuals who viewed themselves as citizen legislators. They had little, if any, staff and usually did not even have offices in the state capitol building. Sessions were short, and a large number of members voluntarily left after serving one or two terms. By the beginning of the 1960s, state legislatures were criticized as "sometime governments: their presence is rarely felt or rarely missed."[1]

Change began in 1965, following the Supreme Court's rulings on legislative apportionment, which diminished the legislative representation of rural areas and increased the representation of cities and their suburbs. Furthermore, studies conducted by universities and especially the Citizens Conference on State Legislatures recommended significant reforms including more frequent sessions, higher salaries for members, and more staff assistance.[2] Being a legislator, in other words, should be a full-time job; professional legislators, not citizen legislators, were needed. In the 1980s, President Reagan's "new federalism" also helped to energize state legislatures by reducing the federal government's role in domestic policy. Legislatures frequently became the focal point for initiatives in areas such as education, the environment, and welfare.

By 1990, however, the public was dismayed. Professional legislators were present in many states, but now they were viewed by the public as more interested in advancing their legislative careers than pursuing the interests of the people who elected them. The most visible manifestation of the public's mood was the term limits movement that hoped to keep legislators accountable to voters by allowing only a few terms of service, thus no professional or career legislators.

This chapter will examine the primary source of these changes—the reapportionment revolution—and how legislative redistricting is handled today, along with a look at running campaigns to be elected to a legislature. The basic structure and degree of professionalization of legislatures will be described as well as the characteristics of today's legislators. The term limits movement and arguments for and against it will be considered. Finally, the functions of legislatures and the role of parties and leaders in the legislative process will be discussed.

APPORTIONMENT AND DISTRICTING

Before legislators can be elected, there must be districts containing voters they can represent. Creating legislative districts is accomplished through apportionment and districting. Some confusion exists in the meaning of these terms, so a brief definition of each is needed. **Apportionment** refers to how the number of seats in a legislative body is distributed within a state's boundaries. Historically, population and units of local government (such as counties) have been the most important factors in apportionment. **Districting** is the process of drawing boundaries on a map that delineates the geographic areas—the districts—from which representatives will be elected.[3] Normally when we see the terms *reapportionment* and *redistricting* in newspapers or hear them on television it means that they are being done again after the federal government's decennial census.[4]

The Reapportionment Revolution

Before 1962, the term **malapportionment** was used to describe state legislatures. Simply put, malapportionment meant that legislators from some districts represented more people than legislators from other districts. In part, this problem was caused by the legislatures' failure to change boundaries as population growth and shifts occurred; some state constitutions required reapportionment on a regular basis, but these provisions were ignored. As a result, cities (and minority groups living in them) were underrepresented in legislatures dominated by rural and small town interests. Before 1962, for example, Alabama and Tennessee had not reapportioned since 1901, and Vermont's house and senate apportionment had not been changed since the adoption of the state constitution in 1793!

State senates were particularly malapportioned because representation was apportioned to political subdivisions in the state, usually counties. This meant that counties, regardless of population, would each elect a state senator.

Illustrations of malapportionment could easily fill an entire book, but a few examples will do. Some legislative chambers were so malapportioned that the population represented by a majority of the legislators was only a fraction of the state's total population. In California, 10.7 percent of the state's population elected a majority of the members of the state senate in the early 1960s: One senator represented 6 million people and another represented only 14,294 people. In Vermont, 11.9 percent of the state's population elected a majority of the members of the state's house of representatives: One representative served a district with 24 people while another served a district with 35,531 people. Equal representation to each county was guaranteed in the senates of eight states and to each town in the lower house of Vermont.

The federal courts were of no help to those who wanted states to reapportion; the Supreme Court had ruled that malapportionment was a political question, meaning that change would have to come through the action of legislators themselves rather than by decisions from federal or state courts. This, of course, had the practical effect of producing no change since legislators were unlikely to risk voting themselves out of a job by adopting a new apportionment scheme.

In ***Baker* v. *Carr*** (1962), however, the Supreme Court changed course and ruled that federal courts have jurisdiction in cases challenging malapportionment. The Court concluded that malapportioned state legislatures may violate the equal protection clause of the Fourteenth Amendment. The reapportionment revolution was started. *Baker* v. *Carr* opened the flood gates, and suits challenging apportionment schemes that had been used for decades quickly appeared in every state. But it was not clear what would be acceptable to the Court. Would states be required to make extensive changes? In ***Reynolds* v. *Sims*** (1964), the Court answered this question by ruling that *both* houses of state legislatures must be apportioned on the basis of population—that is, "one person, one vote." By including state senates, the Court rejected the federal analogy of having one house of a state legislature, like the U.S. Senate, apportioned on the basis of geography or governmental units rather than population. The Court held that counties and cities within the states are not "sovereign entities" as are the states themselves, concluding that "legislators represent people, not trees or acres."

Although the Supreme Court demands almost exact population equality in the drawing districts for the U.S. Congress, it permits greater flexibility in state legislative redistricting. In ***Mahan* v. *Howell*** (1973), the Court approved a Virginia plan in which the number of people in one district was 6.8 percent under the average size of all house districts and one district was 9.6 percent over. The Court suggested that applying the "absolute equality" test to state legislative redistricting might impair the normal functioning of state and local governments.

Effects of the Reapportionment Revolution

By 1968, every state had reapportioned at least one house of its legislature since the *Baker* v. *Carr* decision, and redistricting was implemented in every state following the 1970 census. Several consequences of reapportionment can be noted, but the verdict still is not in regarding its effects on the nature of public policy. The following consequences were generally identified throughout the country:

1 Younger, better-educated people, often with little political experience, have been elected to state legislatures.

2 The number of urban and especially suburban representatives is markedly increased. In some Southern states where cities had been grossly underrepresented, urban representation has increased by a factor of ten. There also has been an increase in the number of African-American legislators in both the North and the South.

3 Democrats have gained some seats, but the impact on party strength has been less than Republicans feared.

Most political scientists are cautious in regard to the policy implications of reapportionment. However, the more urban and suburban representatives there are in a state legislature, the more likely it will be as a body to take liberal positions on such matters as housing, welfare, education, and mass transit. In a few states, however, new suburban legislators have joined with rural legislators in opposing liberal social policies.

Some statistical studies indicate that reapportionment is associated with higher spending for education, public health, hospitals, and highways. Reapportioned legislatures were found to be more responsive to majority views on civil rights, gun control, and public employee labor rights. State legislators believe that policy has become more liberal and more urban oriented.[5]

A major factor limiting the impact of reapportionment on policymaking is that within metropolitan areas, legislators are often strongly divided between city and suburbs, African-Americans and whites, Republicans and Democrats. In contrast, rural legislators are more homogeneous (white, Protestant, and Republican) and thus constitute a much more effective voting bloc than metropolitan legislators.

Legislative Redistricting Today

Although federal and state courts are important actors in the redistricting process, it needs to be remembered that the responsibility of drawing district lines does not belong to the courts. In most states, it is the state legislature that must draw the new lines. As noted earlier, this means that those who will be directly affected by where lines are placed are also the ones who draw them. Districting plans are contained in a bill and go through the normal legislative process of passage through both houses and approval of the governor before becoming law. This is done in the first or second year of each decade, as soon as population figures are available from the federal decennial census.

If one party controls the governor's office and both houses of the legislature, it will be able to create districts as it wants them—probably protecting members of its party and attempting to win a few seats from the minority party. Drawing lines in this manner is called **gerrymandering** (see Figure 5-1). With computer technology and sophisticated databases, creating districts nearly equal in population and still helping your party's candidates is not difficult. The Supreme Court ventured into the partisan gerrymandering question in ***Davis* v. *Bandemer*** (1986). For the first time, the Court held that gerrymandering may violate the Constitution. However, in this instance (the case involved a districting plan for the Indiana legislature) the majority held that relying on a single election was inadequate to make a judgment that unconstitutional gerrymandering had occurred. Because the decision did not set definite guidelines for defining a gerrymander, it left the matter very unclear. *Davis* v. *Bandemer* placed a heavy burden of proof on those seeking to show that a violation has occurred. It still remains to be seen whether this ruling, as interpreted in future cases, will have any effect on gerrymandering.

If party control of the governor's office and the legislature is divided, a districting plan may emerge that is a compromise and protects the incumbents of both parties. Years of divided government in New York have led to a unique arrangement whereby the party that controls each house develops its own plan for that chamber. The assembly Democrats draw lines for the assembly, and senate Republicans draw lines for the senate. Then each house approves the work of the other, and they are signed by the governor. Compromise is not always the outcome of divided government. In 1992, a deadlock developed in California between the Republican governor (Pete Wilson) and the Democratic legislature, causing the state court to intervene and draw its own redistricting plan.[6]

A few states have taken redistricting out of the hands of the legislature and given it to a commission, but it is almost impossible to take the politics out completely. Commissions often yield bipartisan gerrymandered plans that protect the incumbents of both parties. This occurs in Pennsylvania where a commission has four members appointed by the majority and minority leaders of the senate and house of representatives. These four then select the fifth member, who serves as the chairperson.[7] Iowa has a unique approach where a legislative staff office (the Legislative Service Bureau) prepares a new districting plan following specific criteria such as population equality, contiguous territory connected by roads, and maintaining the unity of county and city boundaries. Voter registration addresses of incumbents and other political information cannot be considered in drawing the lines. The legislature, along with the governor, still retains approval in a series of steps. The first proposed plan must be accepted or rejected by the legislature. If it is rejected, the Legislative Service Bureau develops a second plan, which can be accepted or rejected. If it is rejected, a third plan is presented that the legislature can accept, reject, or modify.[8] The advantage of this process

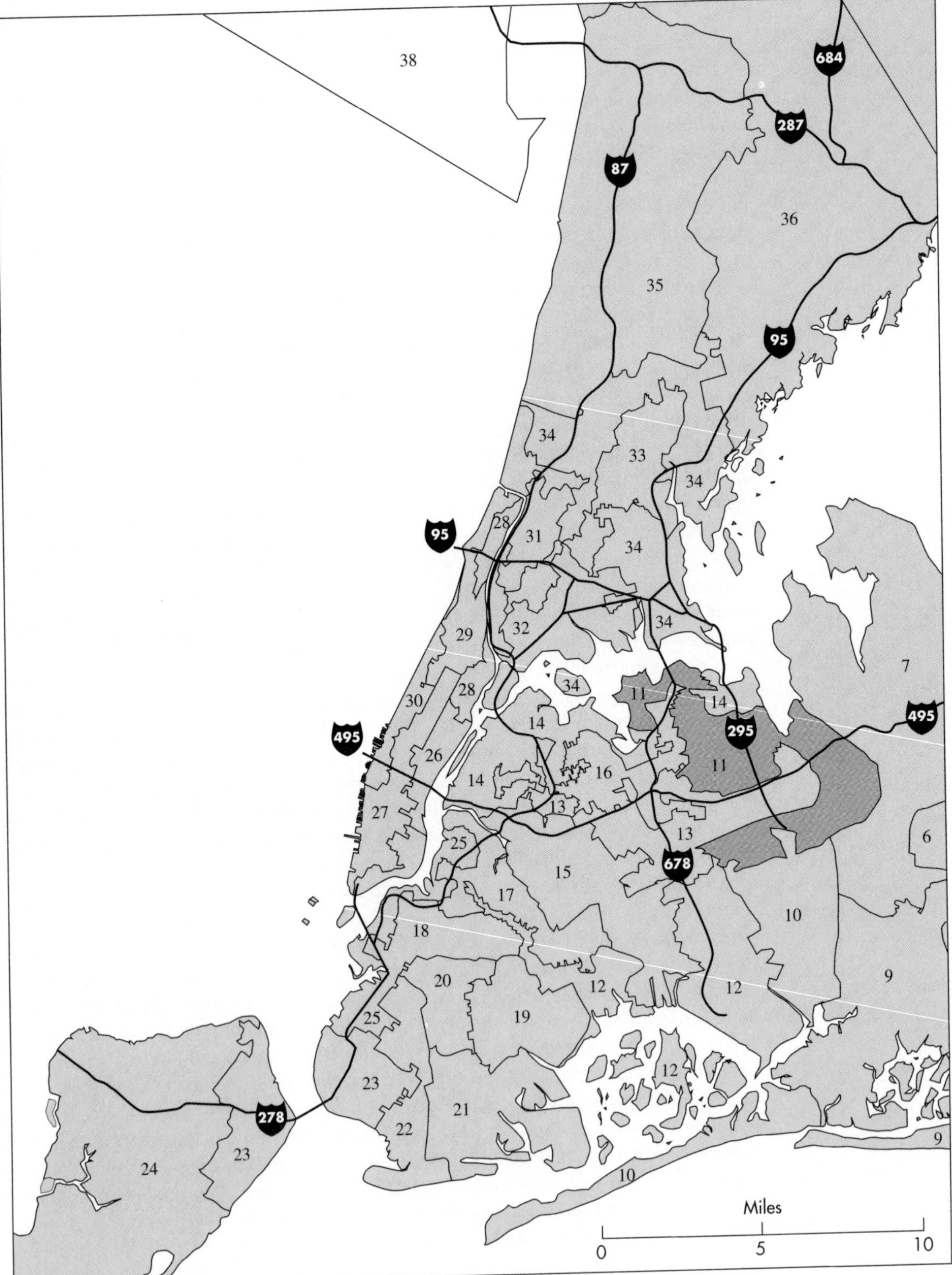

38
684
287
87
36
35
95
34
33
34
95
28
31
34
29
32
34
7
28
34
11
14
30
14
495
295
495
26
11
16
14
13
27
13
6
25
678
15
17
10
18
20
12
12
9
19
25
12
23
21
278
22
9
23
24
10
Miles
0
5
10

is that these plans carry some weight with the public and the news media because they come from a neutral office using neutral and nonpolitical criteria to draw the lines. In addition, the majority party may be subject to criticism for rejecting three plans only to end up adopting its own plan.

Legislative redistricting plans also are subject to the 1982 amendments to section 2 of the Voting Rights Act, discussed in Chapter 4. Plans that dilute the voting strength of minority groups are prohibited.[9] To avoid court challenges after the 1990 census, most states with a substantial minority population drew a number of districts where members of a minority group were in the majority. This is frequently referred to as "affirmative gerrymandering." Perhaps the most interesting court decision in the 1990s involved a congressional redistricting case, *Shaw* v. *Reno* (1993), which concludes that under certain conditions the creation of majority minority districts could be a form of reverse discrimination and unconstitutional.

RUNNING FOR THE LEGISLATURE

Every two years, over 14,000 people may run for state legislative seats. Most have had a long-term interest in politics, and many come from politically active families. In the past, legislative candidates were selected by party officials. Today, candidates tend to be **self-starters,** who actively seek their party's nomination by deciding on their own to run in the primary. More than in the past, legislators cite commitment to issues as a reason for running.[10]

A recent study of ten states finds that close to half of the candidates are from "broker careers"; that is, they are in occupations that require them to negotiate, bargain, and convince. Examples of such private careers are lawyers, teachers, real estate agents, and owners and operators of business establishments.[11] Candidates consciously weigh their opportunity costs.[12] The risks, including some sacrifice of their private careers and of time spent with their families, are balanced against increases in social esteem and political influence. Of course, the opportunity costs include the chances of winning, the presence of an incumbent, and the financial cost of running a campaign.

The strategies of individual campaigns differ greatly depending on the nature of the district. District size varies from about 744,000 people in California senate districts and 372,000 in California house districts to 15,100 in Wyoming senate districts and 2,770 in New Hampshire house districts. Urban house districts may be small geo-

FIGURE 5-1 Gerrymandering in the 1990s. This map highlights the 11th district of the New York State Senate, which is located in New York City. Lines for this district, along with other senate and assembly districts, were drawn in 1991–1992. The 11th district was represented by an incumbent Republican, and the new lines were drawn to help him win reelection by placing more conservative white voters in his district. The lines also twist around minority areas, which helped to create one or two districts where minority candidates had a strong possibility of winning elections. [William Lilley III, Laurence J. DeFranco, and William M. Diefenderfer III, *The Almanac of State Legislatures* (Washington, D.C.: Congressional Quarterly Inc., 1994). Description of New York's redistricting process can be found in Sam Howe Verhovek, "Making a Puzzle of the Political Pie," *The New York Times,* January 25, 1992, p. 1. Reprinted by permission of Congressional Quarterly Inc.]

graphically, while many rural senate districts are very large. Campaigning in single-member districts differs from that in multimember districts, where two or three legislators are elected from the same district and candidates frequently urge voters to vote for a "slate" consisting of all the Democratic candidates or all the Republican candidates. The use of multimember districts to elect all or a portion of the membership has declined dramatically in the last twenty years; today ten states use multimember districts in the house, and only four use them in the senate.

Strategy will also vary depending on the presence of an incumbent on the ballot and the relative strength of the political parties. As in congressional races, most legislative races are not very competitive. That is, the majority party in the district can count on winning by a margin of over 55 percent.

Because political parties are usually weak, most legislative candidates are on their own and need to develop a personal following that will volunteer for campaign work. However, in the few states where parties are strong, party leaders often play a major role in recruiting candidates to run. In several states, legislative leaders, often the house speaker, control as much as $2 or $3 million that they can allot to their party's candidates.

The level of professionalism in campaigns varies greatly across the country. In large states, such as California, races are often professionally managed, with widespread use of television and mass mailings. In most states, however, races are very informal, with the focus on face-to-face contact.

Campaigns are valued because they provide an opportunity for candidates to educate voters on the issues of the day. Tom Loftus, former speaker of the Wisconsin State Assembly, argues that campaigns, especially those involving face-to-face contact with the voters, can also educate the candidate. Loftus says:

> All the handshaking, all the pleasantries exchanged, help make a politician representative. If you talk with people at their doors, on the threshold of their homes, and glimpse their families and perhaps their furniture and the pictures on the walls, you will begin to see their dreams realized and not realized, and you will begin to understand your prospective constituents.[13]

In large states the campaigns of incumbent legislators are becoming more like campaigns for seats in the U.S. House of Representatives. Many incumbents become preoccupied with the next election and are continually campaigning or raising money to finance their campaign. When this happens, legislators may not give their full attention to the lawmaking functions. Salmore and Salmore call this the *congressionalization* of state legislative campaigns.[14]

The number of members who leave a legislature at the end of their term and are replaced by newly elected members is called **membership turnover.** Turnover rates have been on a long-term decline in almost all states (see Table 5-1). The most likely cause of this decline is a drop in the proportion of members that leave voluntarily, that is, simply decide not to run again. A study of eighteen states found that it is not unusual for 70 to 80 percent of incumbents to run for reelection, and incumbents who decide to run are less likely to face an opponent in the general election than they were a few years ago.[15] Even with this decline in turnover, many states still have a considerable number of new members after an election.

TABLE 5-1 MEMBERSHIP TURNOVER IN STATE LEGISLATURES, 1992

State	Senate			House		
	Total number of members	Number of membership changes	Percentage change of total	Total number of members	Number of membership changes	Percentage change of total
Alabama	35 (a)	2	6	105 (a)	2	2
Alaska	20	14	70	40	23	58
Arizona	30	11	37	60	29	48
Arkansas	35	4	11	100	19	19
California	40	9	23	80	32	40
Colorado	35	8	23	65	23	35
Connecticut	36	12	33	151	57	38
Delaware	21	1	5	41	8	20
Florida	40	19	48	120	48	40
Georgia	56	24	43	180	67	37
Hawaii	25	5	20	51	10	20
Idaho	35 (b)	(b)	(b)	70 (b)	(b)	(b)
Illinois	59	23	39	118	49	42
Indiana	50	9	18	100	24	24
Iowa	50	12	24	100	37	37
Kansas	40	22	55	125	47	38
Kentucky	38	6	16	100	19	19
Louisiana	39 (c)	15	38	105 (c)	41	39
Maine	35	16	46	151	52	34
Maryland	47 (a)	2	4	141 (a)	7	5
Massachusetts	40	15	38	160	36	23
Michigan	38 (a)	3	8	110	29	26
Minnesota	67	17	25	134	33	25
Mississippi	52 (c)	28	54	122 (c)	50	41
Missouri	34	8	24	163	48	29
Montana	50	12	24	100	31	31
Nebraska	49	15	31		Unicameral	
Nevada	21	5	24	42	17	40
New Hampshire	24	8	33	400	154	39
New Jersey	40 (c)	13	33	80 (c)	33	41
New Mexico	42	17	40	70	12	17
New York	61	8	13	150	31	21
North Carolina	50	13	26	120	43	36
North Dakota	49 (d)	(d)	(d)	98 (d)	(d)	(d)
Ohio	33	4	12	99	21	21
Oklahoma	48	6	13	101	18	18
Oregon	30	8	27	60	19	32
Pennsylvania	50	2	4	203	37	18
Rhode Island	50	16	32	100	38	38
South Carolina	46	17	37	124	43	35
South Dakota	35	16	46	70	29	41
Tennessee	33	5	15	99	19	19
Texas	31	9	29	150	41	27
Utah	29	8	28	75	31	41
Vermont	30	12	40	150	53	35
Virginia	40 (c)	15	38	100 (c)	25	25
Washington	49	16	33	98	38	39
West Virginia	34	6	18	100	31	31
Wisconsin	33	7	21	99	26	26
Wyoming	30	14	47	60 (e)	(e)	(e)

Note: Turnover calculated after 1992 legislative elections. Data were obtained by comparing the 1991–92 and 1993–94 editions of *State Elective Officials and the Legislatures,* published by The Council of State Governments.

(a) No election in 1992.

(b) As a result of redistricting, membership of the Idaho Legislature decreased: Senate—from 42 to 35 members, House—from 84 to 70 members. Turnover cannot be determined using method employed here.

(c) Election held in 1991.

(d) As a result of redistricting, membership of the North Dakota Legislative Assembly decreased: Senate—from 53 to 49 members, House—from 106 to 98 members. Turnover cannot be determined using method employed here.

(e) As a result of redistricting, membership of the Wyoming House decreased from 64 to 60 members. Turnover cannot be determined using method employed here.

Source: The Council of State Governments, *The Book of the States: 1994–95 Edition* (Lexington, Ky.: The Council of State Governments, 1994), p. 115.

A PROFILE OF LEGISLATORS AND LEGISLATURES

Legislators

According to a survey of 900 state legislators, the average legislator is 49.4 years old, is married, has 2.4 children, and first ran for office at the age of 38. Over 80 percent are college graduates, and one-third report an annual family income between $60,000 and $85,000. Most continue to live in the state where they were born, and many live in the cities and towns where they grew up.[16] Attorney is the most common occupational background (about 16 percent). This figure is approximately 6 percentage points lower than it was in 1976.[17]

Although most legislators are white males, the number of African-American and women legislators has increased significantly in the past twenty-five years. Today more than 20 percent are women and close to 8 percent are black (see Figure 5-2). The number of women is five times as many as in the 1960s, and the number of African-American has doubled since then.

FIGURE 5-2 Percentage of African-Americans and women in state legislatures. ["CAWP Fact Sheet: Women in Elective Office, 1995" (New Brunswick, N.J.: Center for the American Woman and Politics). Percentages for African-American legislators for 1975 to 1981 are from biennial editions of *National Roster of Black Elected Officials* (Washington, D.C.: Joint Center for Political Studies); percentages for 1983 to 1995 are from biennial editions of *Black Elected Officials* (New York: UNIPUB and Joint Center for Political Studies).]

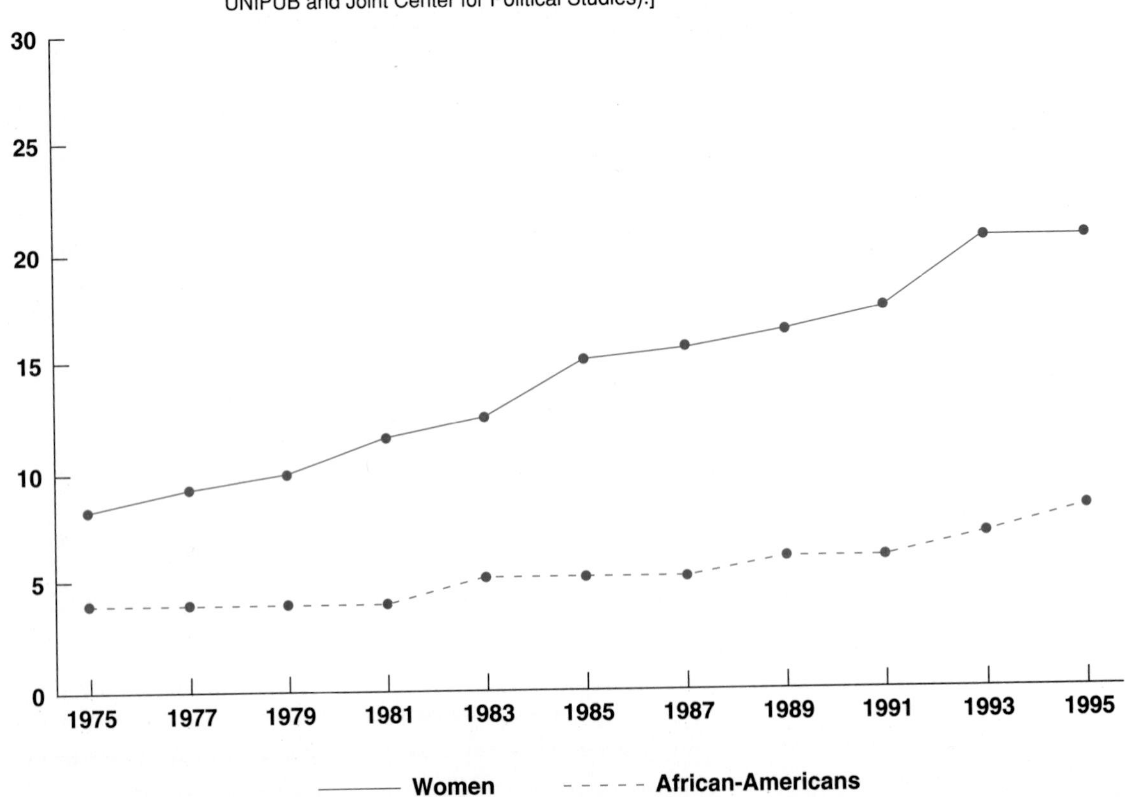

Another important distinction is how legislators themselves view their job. Do they see themselves as full-time (professional) legislators or as part-time (citizen) legislators? In a 1993 study 15 percent of those queried reported that being a legislator was their sole occupation, up from 3 percent in 1976. If legislators who listed themselves as retirees, students, and homemakers are included, the number of full-time lawmakers jumps to 24 percent. Over half of the legislators in Massachusetts, Michigan, New York, Pennsylvania, and Wisconsin consider themselves professional or career legislators. (Keep in mind that this study is reporting how legislators describe the legislative job. A categorization of state *legislatures* according to degree of professionalization will be presented shortly.)

Basic Structure of Legislatures

With the exception of Nebraska, every state has a **bicameral** (two-house) legislature. The strong bicameral tradition originated when most legislatures in colonial America adopted the upper and lower house model of the British Parliament. (But Georgia, Pennsylvania, and Vermont had unicameral legislatures in the eighteenth century.) The U.S. Constitution, of course, provides for two chambers, a House and Senate, and this influenced the states. In the early years, many state legislatures included an economic class aspect, in which extra property requirements were imposed for service in the state upper chamber. Concern over a unicameral legislature is reflected in John Adams's warning that "a single assembly is liable to all the vices, follies, and frailties of an individual; subject to fits of humor, starts of passion, flights of enthusiasms, partialities or prejudices, consequently productive of hasty results and absurd judgments."

It is significant that separation of powers did not exist in the early state governments. Governors had little power and were often appointed by the legislature. Legislatures exercised broad powers of economic management and occasionally even overrode the courts in some property-dispute cases. In such circumstances, a bicameral legislature offered greater protection against the abuse of power and undue influence by strong interest groups. As noted in the discussion of reapportionment, having two legislative chambers made it possible for the state to apportion one on the basis of geography, rather than population, and thus protect rural, conservative interests.

Due largely to the well-organized campaign of Senator George Norris, Nebraska adopted a **unicameral** (one-house) legislature in 1934. Although no state has followed Nebraska's lead, it is not outlandish to suggest that unicameral plans could be adopted in other states. Jesse Unruh, speaker of the California Assembly in the 1960s, believed that the most effective way to improve state government is to have one legislative house in each state. Unruh plainly puts the question: "Does any corporation have *two* boards of directors? Would there be any point to it?" Unruh suggests that three major benefits would result from the adoption of unicameralism. First, the delay and buck-passing found in bicameral legislatures would be lessened, making it easier to enact "progressive" legislation. Second, there would be an economic saving once duplication of costs in terms of staff time was eliminated and the total number of legislators was reduced. (The costs for lobbyists would also be reduced.) Third, a unicameral legislature would be more visible to the public and would help restore public confidence in state legislatures.

The case for unicameralism has been made at several recent state constitutional conventions. Although the idea appears logical to many academics, and as a cost savings measure it should be attractive to today's public demanding more efficient and less costly government, arguments for unicameralism have failed to move politicians who fear radical change and the loss of a large number of legislative seats. The longstanding tradition of bicameralism will undoubtedly continue, with the Nebraska experiment serving only to illustrate the exception to the rule.

The number of members of state legislatures varies, with the senates having the smaller membership. Size of upper houses varies from 20 in Alaska to 67 in Minnesota. New Hampshire has 400 members in its lower house to represent 1.1 million people, while California has 80 members to represent over 30 million people. In a majority of states (twenty-nine), the lower house has 100 or more members, and in several others, the number is 98 or 99. In thirty-three states, the upper house has at least 35 members.

Although most students of state government conclude that legislatures are too large, it is difficult to say what the ideal size should be because there are advantages and disadvantages to both small and large. Large bodies often become impersonal and more dedicated to staging debates than to taking action. On the other hand, in larger bodies the representational function, to be discussed shortly, is generally improved as legislators represent smaller numbers of people. There is also evidence that larger legislatures are more efficient because of their greater specialization in committees. A disadvantage of small legislatures is that members have a tendency to become too cozy in a kind of social club atmosphere. Moreover, racial and ethnic minorities are less likely to be represented among the members of small legislatures.

As a practical matter the size of legislative bodies does not change very often. Nevertheless, marginal changes will occasionally be made in the size of a legislature to facilitate reapportionment and redistricting. More unusual is the action taken by Rhode Island voters in 1994 when they reduced the size of the senate from 50 members to 37 and the house from 100 to 75. (This change will take place in 2002, the first election after the census in 2000.)

Length of terms also varies among the states. The most common pattern is for representatives to serve two-year terms and senators four-year terms. Terms in the senate are usually staggered with half of the members elected every two years. Maryland is an exception to the normal pattern. In Maryland, all members of both houses, along with the governor, are elected for four-year terms at the same election; this provides voters the opportunity, if they desire, to vote in a large number of new faces in one single election. (Limitations on number of terms will be discussed later in this chapter.)

Professional Legislatures

The professionalization of state legislatures, which began in the aftermath of the reapportionment revolution, sometimes involved changes in state constitutions and sometimes simply changes in legislative procedures and rules. The goal was to give legislatures the capability to deal with complex problems facing modern state government as a coequal of the states' governors. Higher legislative salaries, longer legislative sessions, and more legislative staff were the most important factors in **professionalization.** (See the Scholarly Box entitled The Diversity of State Legislatures.) On the average, salaries are higher, sessions are longer, and staff is larger today than thirty years ago.

Legislative salaries range from $100 per year in New Hampshire to $57,500 per year in New York; in most states, members of each house receive equal pay. In five states (all with low pay), salaries are still set by state constitutions. Ten states pay legislators over $30,000 per year; however, several states, including Texas, still pay them less than $10,000. In all but five states, legislators receive a per diem allowance for living expenses when the legislature is in session, and forty-two states provide extra compensation for legislative leaders.

TERM LIMITS

State legislators, as with most public officials and the institutions they are a part of, have not escaped the public's growing dissatisfaction with government, as was noted earlier. Professional legislators are increasingly viewed as part of the problem. It is in this environment that the **term limits movement** was born. In 1990, initiatives were placed on the ballot in California, Colorado, and Oklahoma, limiting the number of terms a citizen could serve in the legislature. The initiatives passed in all three states. Other states, especially those with the initiative process, quickly followed so that by the end of 1994, twenty-one states had term limits for members of the state legislature. (See Figure 5-4.) All but one of these states (Utah) limited legislative terms through the initiative process.

Term limits adopted by Oklahoma voters are among the most restrictive, limiting a legislator during his or her lifetime to no more than twelve years of service in either or both houses. California law allows no more than six years in the house and eight years in the senate. In almost all states, these provisions apply to members who are elected immediately after the law is adopted; in other words, terms served in the legislature prior to the adoption of the law do not count toward the number of allowable terms.

Although the idea of term limits is supported by voters and has been approved by overwhelming margins in initiative states, political scientists are divided as to whether it will improve the governing process. The proponents argue that limiting the length of time individuals can serve will break up the "culture of ruling" that is present in every state legislature and capital. This culture is based on the interaction of legislators with other legislators, lobbyists, and executive branch officials, all of whom are in the "business of regulating other people's lives or spending other people's money."[18] The professional legislature has provided the means for members to become career legislators: higher salaries, more staff, and larger office space. Of course, legislators must be reelected or it is not a career, but this is not a problem, say the proponents of term limits, because PACs and other special interests provide campaign funds. This culture has a harmful impact because legislators are primarily interested in keeping themselves in office. To do this they cater to special interests, and the interests of the voters they are elected to represent are forgotten.

Opponents argue that term limits violate one of the basic principles of democracy, that "the people choose their representatives and tell them when to leave."[19] People, not

SCHOLARLY BOX

THE DIVERSITY OF STATE LEGISLATURES

Although political scientists place great emphasis on the trend toward more professional state legislatures, it should be remembered that a great deal of diversity still exists among the legislatures of the fifty states. Karl Kurtz has categorized all state legislatures based on three important indicators of professionalization: salaries of legislators, length of sessions, and number of staff. This results in three categories of state legislatures (see Figure 5-3). The first category consists of nine states in which the job of a legislator is full-time, staffs are large, and salaries are relatively high. At the other extreme is the third category, containing sixteen state legislatures that spend much less time in session, have low-paid citizen legislators, and support small staffs. In between these two categories is a group of twenty-five states in the second category: They have characteristics from the two extremes or fall in the middle on all three indicators.

It is clear that a state's population affects the category in which it is placed. States in the first category—California, New Jersey, New York, along with states in the Great Lakes region—have large populations. States with smaller populations, especially those in the Rocky Mountains and New England, tend to be in the third category. Political culture is important, also. No Southern state is in the first category, even though Texas and Florida are among the top ten population states. This is due, in part, to a traditionalist political culture and a distrust of an activist government.[20]

Large and diverse states probably need professional legislators who can devote full time or close to full time to the problems of governing such states, but small and medium-sized states may get along fine with part-time legislators. Although the trend during the 1970s and 1980s was toward professional legislators, it is frequently argued today that people who combine being a legislator for part of the year with another occupation for part of the year may better represent their constituents. The National Conference of State Legislatures concludes that the desire for more full-time, professional legislatures must be balanced with the benefits of part-time citizen bodies.[21]

Length of legislative sessions, usually established in state constitutions, still varies greatly among the states. Today, most state legislatures hold annual sessions; only seven have biennial sessions. States with annual sessions may have limits on how many days they can meet. At one extreme, the New Mexico legislature meets for sixty calendar days for one year and thirty calendar days the next, so that at most, the legislature is in session from mid-January to mid-March. Sixteen states, usually those with large populations, have no constitutional limitations on the length of regular sessions. The supporters of professional legislatures oppose session restrictions, which were originally established in the nineteenth century to prevent interference with planting time and harvest and to guard against the irresponsible enactment of too much legislation.

Because the demands of contemporary state government frequently require longer sessions than allowed in the constitution, thirty legislatures can call themselves into special session without action by the governor. Legislatures also make greater use of the interim period, that is, the time between sessions. The creation of study committees and the authorization of standing committees to hold hearings and develop ideas for legislation increase the time spent on legislative work without increasing the number of days in session.[22] Kurtz concludes that all of these changes allow legislatures to deliberate more effectively and make the legislative branch more independent."[23]

The growth and development of legislative staff has been called the "cornerstone of the modern legislature."[24] With increased staff, a legislature is better able to initiate its own programs and to work with the governor in developing the state's budget. Legislative staff is valuable because it provides legislators with information that is independently gathered and evaluated, information that is less dependent on the executive branch and lobbyists.

The first staffs, in the 1940s and 1950s, were part of a legislative council, a central nonpartisan staff that provided bill drafting and policy research for all legislators. Specialized staff to deal with budget and other financial information was added next. In the 1980s, partisan staff for legislative leaders and party caucuses developed, and in a few states professional staffing—beyond administrative and clerical support—was added for individual legislators. Today, the number of full-time and session-only staff working in state legislatures is more than 33,000.[25]

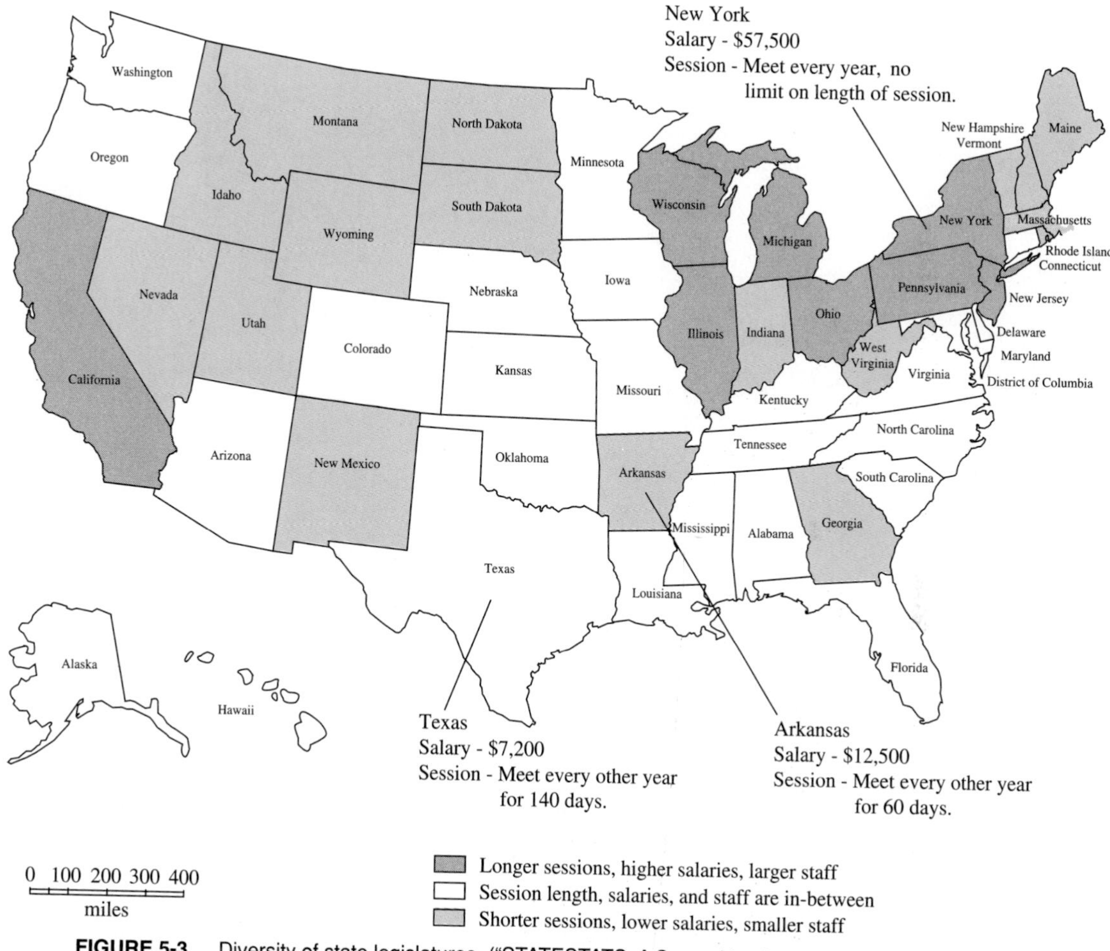

FIGURE 5-3 Diversity of state legislatures. ("STATESTATS: A Second Look at the Cost of Legislatures," *State Legislatures,* November 1994, p. 7. Reprinted with permission from the National Conference of State Legislatures, 1994. Information on New York, Texas, and Arkansas is from Sam Howe Verhovek, "With Power Shift, State Lawmakers See New Demands," *The New York Times,* September 24, 1995, p. 24.)

arbitrary limits, should make this decision. Furthermore, experienced legislators develop a knowledge of issues that frequently makes them more of an expert than career civil servants in the executive branch, especially in complicated budgetary matters.

Arguments as to how term limits will affect the influence of special interests are of particular importance, and here the sides disagree completely. Proponents have argued that term limits will reduce the influence of special interests because legislators, not planning on a legislative career, will have less interest in winning the next election and less interest in doing the bidding of special interests so that they can raise needed campaign funds. Opponents argue that special interests will be more influential under term

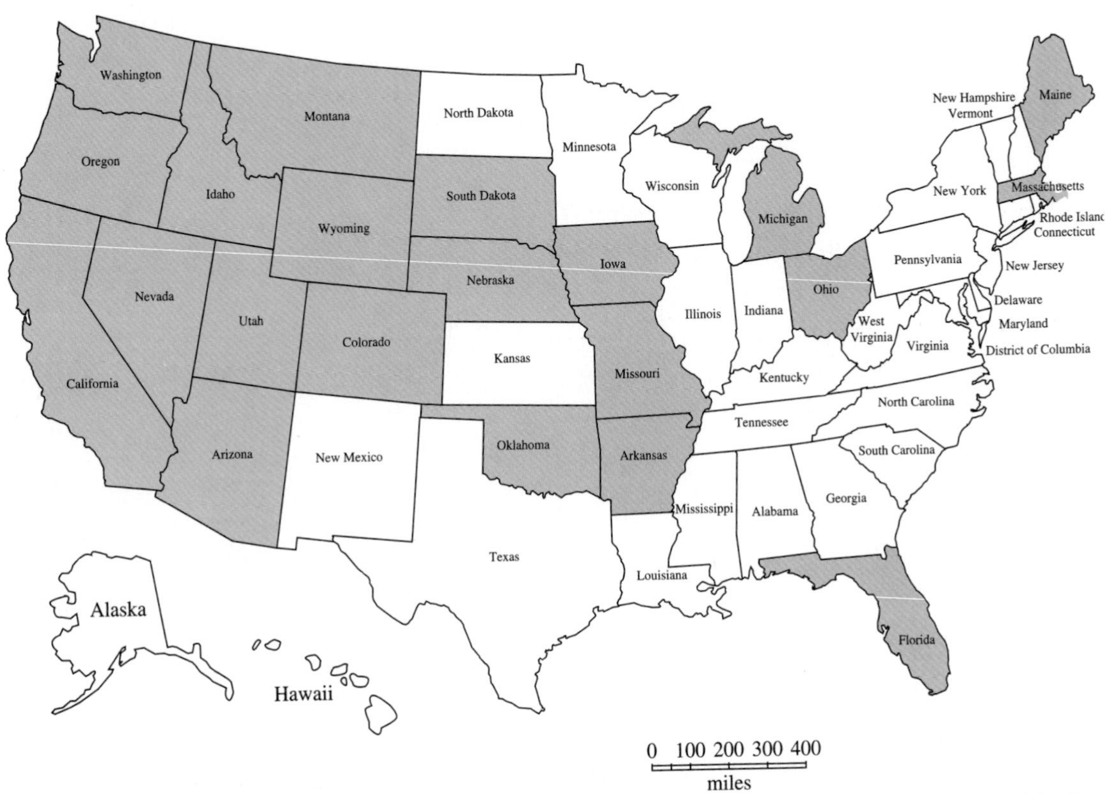

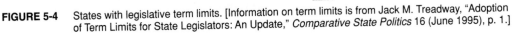

FIGURE 5-4 States with legislative term limits. [Information on term limits is from Jack M. Treadway, "Adoption of Term Limits for State Legislators: An Update," *Comparative State Politics* 16 (June 1995), p. 1.]

limits. What will really happen is that legislators will have to rely on the lobbyists' knowledge of issues. Of course, their knowledge is always based on their clients' perspectives.[26] Thus, the influence of special interests will only increase.

The term limits debate has been intense, yet may be misdirected in targeting state legislatures. If legislatures are out of touch with their constituents, it is not for a lack of new members. Although turnover has been declining for a number of years, a healthy rate of turnover still exists in most states (see Table 5-1). One study found that over 70 percent of the legislators, from both lower and upper houses, in 1979 were not members ten years later, a time period that is only two years longer than most of the limits that have been adopted. Similar turnover exists among legislative leaders. During a recent ten-year period, the turnover rate of senate presidents and house speakers was close to 90 percent.[27]

It needs to be noted that the antigovernment mood has affected, to some extent, the other two key components in the professionalization of state legislatures: session length and size of staff. Voters have approved reduction in length of sessions in Alaska, Colorado, and Oklahoma. There even has been some discussion that legislatures should return to biennial sessions! The growth of legislative staff has slowed, and in some cases declined. California's Proposition 140, which established term limits, also mandated a $115 million ceiling on legislative expenditures, resulting in a 38 percent cut in the legislature's budget and the elimination of 600 staff positions.[28]

FUNCTIONS OF STATE LEGISLATURES

The accomplishments of state legislatures can be measured by the way in which they perform three basic functions: representation, policymaking, and oversight.

Individual legislators must represent the interests of their constituents. They frequently respond to their demands for policy changes, and if they cannot, they usually are called upon by their constituents to explain why. Legislators provide service functions by helping people in their dealings with state administrative agencies and by answering other personal requests from constituents.

Policymaking

The most important function of the state legislature is to participate in making policy by passing laws. A self-respecting legislature should not be content merely to deal with the governor's legislative program or routinely approve members' bills. It has a responsibility to initiate action and to consider seriously a wide variety of proposals dealing with the most important and controversial problems of the day—abortion, crime, welfare, and education, to name a few.

In reality, policy initiation, that is, priorities and ideas for legislation, remains largely the function of state governors. The lawmaking process is best for deliberation, discussion, marginal changes, and delay or defeat of bills rather than the initiation of policy. Under the best of circumstances, legislators share their lawmaking power with the governor. More will be said of the governor's role in policymaking and influence on the legislature in Chapter 6.

In making public policy, each legislator is confronted with a wide range of issues, from the trivial (whether the ladybug should be designated the "state insect" in Ohio) to the enormously complex (the annual general expenditures for California, which are over $80 billion).

In general, all state legislatures follow a similar procedure for passing bills into laws. (Of course, in Nebraska bills are considered only by the one house.) Once a bill has been introduced in the upper or lower house, it is assigned to a committee. The committee holds public hearings and then meets to discuss and possibly amend the bill. If committee action is favorable, the bill is reported out and placed on the chamber's calendar. If party organization is strong, the bill is discussed at a regular caucus of the party's legislators and a position is agreed upon before the whole chamber considers the bill. The bill is then given a second reading on the floor (its introduction constitutes a first reading), following which there is debate, amendments are offered, and a vote is taken on passage. After a usual delay of one calendar day, a third reading occurs and a final vote is taken. If the vote is affirmative, the bill then

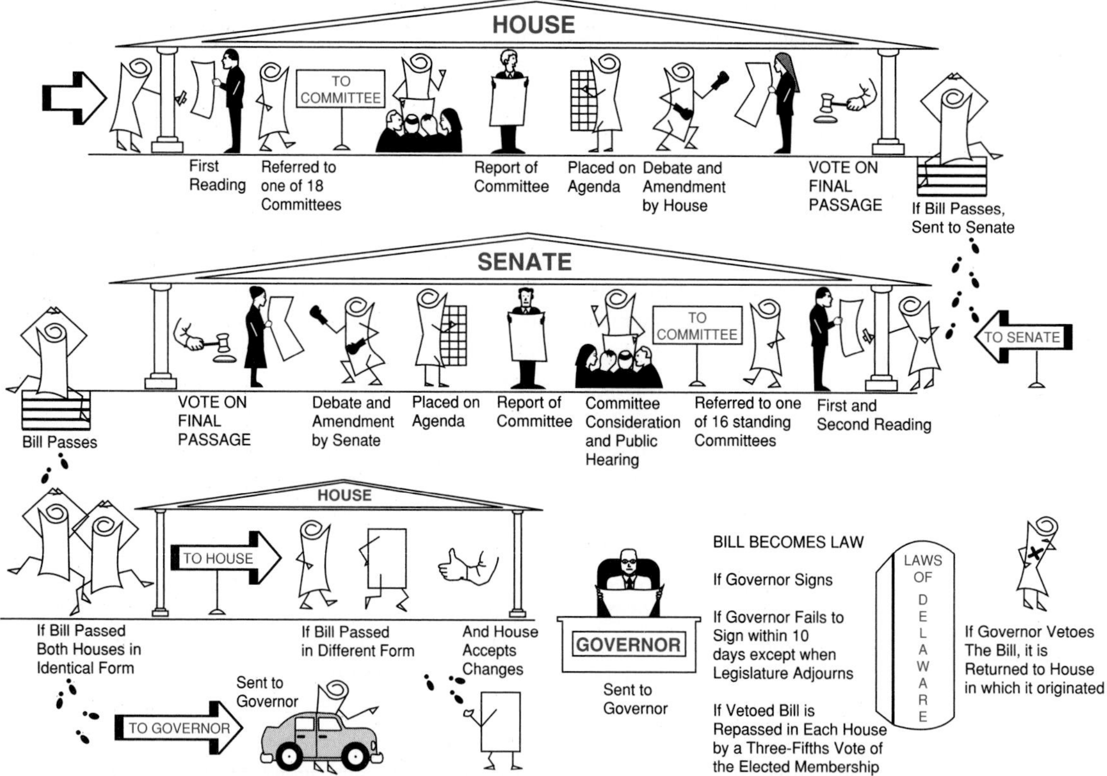

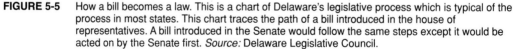

FIGURE 5-5 How a bill becomes a law. This is a chart of Delaware's legislative process which is typical of the process in most states. This chart traces the path of a bill introduced in the house of representatives. A bill introduced in the Senate would follow the same steps except it would be acted on by the Senate first. *Source:* Delaware Legislative Council.

moves to the other legislative chamber, where the process of committee and floor action is repeated. If the second chamber approves the bill without amendment, it goes to the governor for his or her signature. If the bill is approved in a different form by each house, a conference committee is appointed to work out an agreement and both houses must approve the conference report before the bill is sent to the governor. (See Figure 5-5.)

Legislative Oversight

With the growth of gubernatorial power (see Chapter 6) and the expansion of state administrative bureaucracies, legislatures have struggled to find ways to check executive authority. Because their attention tends to be focused on immediate policy issues, such as school finance or taxes, legislators find it difficult to conduct long-range review **(legislative oversight)** of the executive branch. For example, the real challenge in budgeting often comes after legislative approval, when allotment procedures and executive transfers can change legislative intent.

Legislative oversight takes many forms.[29] Legislators are constantly being asked by constituents for help in dealing with state agencies. In responding to a particular problem, legislators may be prompted to review in more general terms how an agency is performing. In the budget process, several committees—appropriations, ways and means, and finance—review requests from state agencies, and this allows legislators to examine how well the agencies are performing. After funds have been appropriated and programs have been enacted, legislatures are devoting more time to evaluation. More than forty states have an auditor selected by the legislature to evaluate programs in terms of effectiveness and efficiency.

Since the mid-1970s a majority of the states have enacted **sunset laws,** which call for the termination of specified executive agencies unless the legislature formally reviews and extends their programs. At one time thirty-six states had enacted such laws, but six states repealed them and six others allowed the laws to lapse into inactivity.[30] Generally the agencies that have been terminated have been minor and had lost their usefulness. Most states also have provisions for legislative review of administrative rules and regulations that have been established by state agencies.

LEGISLATIVE POLITICS

Committees

The average state senate has fifteen standing committees and the average house has nineteen. These committees are established on a subject basis to consider bills introduced by legislators and to monitor the activities of particular administrative agencies. The trend in recent years has been to reduce the number of committees. Nevertheless, a considerable range still exists among the states: Maryland has the fewest committees, with six in the senate and seven in the house; New York has the highest number of committees in a senate, thirty-two, and Missouri the highest in the house, forty-two. Connecticut, Maine, and Massachusetts have joint committees; that is, there is only one set of committees and they have members from both the senate and the house. As in Congress, the fate of bills is determined in committee where many die for lack of action. The number of bills introduced in each two-year session is over 190,000, with about 43,000 (23 percent) actually being approved by the legislature. The number of bills introduced during the average biennium is from a low of 1,000 in states such as Alaska and Colorado to a high of more than 30,000 in New York.[31] A few states limit the number of bills that members can introduce. For example, Colorado legislators are limited to introducing six bills the first year and four bills in the second year of each session.

The role of committees in reducing the legislative work load by providing a division of labor varies among the states. In Illinois, a significant number of bills are not reported to a committee at all, and most bills sent to committee are subsequently reported to the floor. In other states, two to three committees may deal with 25 percent of all legislation.[32] In thirteen states, committees are required to report out all bills referred to them, but this rule gets only technical compliance.[33]

Political Parties

A basic goal of political parties in a legislature is to produce the votes necessary to pass specific bills. However, the degree to which parties are successful in controlling their members' votes varies greatly among the states. In urban, industrial states with strong two-party systems, party control of voting behavior is clearly evident. Frequently, in these states parties will **caucus** on a regular basis to determine a party position on various pieces of legislation.

In Pennsylvania, Ohio, and Michigan, where parties follow a clear urban-rural alignment, party cohesion is strong. In states such as California and Missouri, where Democrats and Republicans are not divided sharply along urban-rural lines, party cohesion is weak. Also, in California there is a strong tradition of nonpartisanship in which legislators do not wish to be perceived as captives of their party. Daily caucuses occur in about 15 percent of state legislatures while about half the states have weekly caucuses. There seems to be less direct influence by interest groups on legislators in states that have strong party cohesion.

For the most part, however, party control has been weakening as legislators become more independent from state and local party organizations and as voters become more independent and less likely to vote a straight party ticket.

Leaders

In the lower house, a speaker, elected by a vote of the entire membership, is the presiding officer. Where political parties are strong, each party nominates its own candidate for speaker and the nominee of the majority wins in a straight party-line vote. The speaker elected by a party vote is the presiding officer and the effective leader of the majority party. Even though the speaker's party has a position with the title of majority leader, this position is not as powerful as that of speaker.

Where parties are weak, as in some Southern states, or where a **bipartisan coalition** has ousted an entrenched speaker, candidates for speaker will seek support from members of both parties. In 1989, the Florida senate was run by a bipartisan coalition. In North Carolina and Connecticut, Democrats and Republicans joined forces to replace longtime speakers. Still, this type of coalition is infrequent.

Identifying the most important leader in a state senate is more difficult than in the house. In over half of the states the lieutenant governor presides over the senate, following the federal arrangement where the vice president is the president of the Senate. Because the lieutenant governor is elected by the voters and not by the senators, his or her influence in the senate is minimal in most cases; the effective leader is the president pro tem, who is elected by the majority party. If the lieutenant governor has no constitutional responsibilities in the senate, the presiding officer is elected by the entire membership, usually in a party-line vote, and has the title of president of the senate.[34]

How do these leaders affect the legislative process? Jewell and Whicker, in a major study of legislative leadership in the states, identify a number of roles:

1 *Gatekeepers* in the lawmaking process who can use their power to delay or block the adoption of a proposed law.

2 *Coalition builders* and *negotiators* who can put together majority support for a proposal that will determine whether it is enacted in the form it was introduced or becomes a "watered-down" version.

3 *Communicators* to the public of legislative intent. By communicating their own interpretations of the how and why of new laws they can aid public understanding and acceptance.[35]

Legislative leaders have a considerable number of specific powers they can rely on in performing these roles. A major one is control over appointing legislators to committees. This can be used as patronage, where members who have been loyal to the leadership are assigned to the more important committees. Committee assignments also have a policy dimension because leaders can appoint members to a committee who have policy views similar to theirs on bills that come before that committee. Leaders can also decide not to reappoint legislators to a committee because most states do not have a written or unwritten rule that gives legislators the right to reappointment.

Legislative leaders also appoint committee chairs. Because chairs owe their position to the leaders, they are much more likely to cooperate with them in speeding or slowing the movement of key bills through their committees and in keeping unwanted amendments from being adopted.[36]

Traditionally, state legislative committees have been viewed as less influential in the making of laws than their U.S. Congress counterparts. For the most part, this has been true because state legislative leaders' appointing power is much greater than that of congressional leaders. (This may not be as true after the 1994 congressional elections where the Republican party won a majority of the seats in the House of Representatives and elected Newt Gingrich as Speaker. Gingrich played a major role in appointing new committee chairs.) In addition, unlike Congress many states have short legislative sessions that make it difficult to carefully review bills and suggest amendments. High membership turnover or the frequent transfer of legislators from one committee to another, again unlike Congress but characteristic of many states, hinders the development of expertise in a given subject area.

However, in state legislatures that have become more professional their committees have also become stronger, making them more like Congress. Lower turnover allows members to stay on the same committees for a longer period of time and to develop expertise on bills that come before them. The same is true for committee chairs. When this happens, committees tend to become more independent of party leaders. Even though the leaders still control committee appointments, it may only give them "influence over the broad direction in which the committee moves . . . the leader cannot solve differences over specific legislation by a constant threat to remove members from the committee."[37]

In fact, Jewell and Whicker conclude that legislative **leadership style** is changing. The *command* style of leadership is not as common as it used to be. Command-style leaders limit decision making to a single small group of leaders, minimize participation by rank-and-file legislators, and have a high need to control the behavior of others. Conflict is viewed as a challenge to their leadership. They are likely to use the threat of punishment (for example, removal from a committee) to pressure members to support the party line.

More prevalent today are the *coordinating* and *consensus* leadership styles. Coordinating-style leaders usually harmonize the decision making of various small groups of leaders. When conflict occurs, this type of leader tries to resolve it through negotiation and is more likely to use rewards rather than the threat of punishment. Rank-and-file legislators occasionally participate in decision making. Consensus-style leaders have a low need to control the behavior of others and use accommodation to resolve conflict. Rank-and-file legislators are encouraged to participate in decision making. Debate, discussion, and developing a consensus that a large number of party members can support replace the use of rewards and punishment to gain adherence to the party line.[38]

SUMMARY

In the recent history of state legislatures, the reapportionment revolution is a landmark event. Supreme Court decisions in the 1960s ruled that both the lower and the upper houses of state legislatures were to be apportioned on the basis of population. With the resulting shift in legislative power from rural to urban and suburban areas, many states began a process of professionalizing their legislatures so that they could deal more effectively with problems associated with the complexity of modern-day life.

State legislators tend to be white men, but the number of legislators who are women, African-Americans, and members of minority groups has increased substantially since 1975. State legislatures are quite diverse. Some are professional, with longer sessions, higher salaries for their members, and a larger staff. At the other extreme are legislatures with short sessions, lower salaries, and a smaller staff; their members are usually called citizen legislators. Most legislatures fall in between the professional and citizen types.

The term limits movement, to some extent an expression of the public's dissatisfaction with government and career politicians, has limited the number of terms an individual can serve in the legislatures of twenty states.

State legislatures have a number of functions, including representation (individual legislators representing the interests of their constituents), lawmaking (making policy through the passage of laws), and legislative oversight (reviewing the performance of executive branch agencies). Governors are important in lawmaking because of the key role they play in the initiation of policies that are considered by the legislature.

Decision making in legislatures centers around committees, parties, and leaders. Leaders perform a number of roles, including gatekeeping and coalition building, and have powers such as control over the appointment of committee chairs that allow them to influence the making of decisions, even with the general decline in the strength of allegiance legislators have to their parties. Today's legislative leaders use a coordinating and consensus style of leadership more than a command style.

KEY TERMS

Apportionment Deciding how seats in a state legislature will be distributed within a state's boundaries. The principal criterion of apportionment today is population.

***Baker* v. *Carr* (1962)** Supreme Court announced that federal courts have jurisdiction in cases challenging malapportioned state legislatures because they may violate the equal protection clause of the Fourteenth Amendment.

Bicameral A legislature with two chambers, generically referred to as the lower house and the upper house. Official names are usually the house of representatives and the senate. In some states the lower house is called the assembly or house of delegates.

Bipartisan coalition Cooperation between Democratic and Republican legislators in decisions made in the legislature.

Caucus A meeting of political party members to determine a party position on various pieces of legislation.

***Davis* v. *Bandemer* (1986)** Supreme Court for the first time ruled that gerrymandering by political parties may violate the Constitution. But in this case from Indiana, the Court did not find the state legislative districting plan unconstitutional.

Districting Process of drawing boundaries on a map that delineates the geographic area of each legislative district. Since the reapportionment decisions of the 1960s, districting occurs after each federal decennial census.

Gerrymandering Drawing of legislative district lines so as to increase the likelihood that members of the party drawing the lines will win more legislative seats. Usually occurs when the governor's office and both houses of the legislature are controlled by the same party.

Leadership style Extent to which legislative leaders desire to control the behavior of other members and how they react to conflict. Coordinating and consensus styles of leadership are replacing the command style.

Legislative oversight Review by the legislature of the performance of executive branch agencies in administering the laws and programs approved by the legislature.

***Mahan* v. *Howell* (1973)** Supreme Court decision that gives states a little flexibility in meeting the population equality standard in the drawing of district lines for state legislatures. Exact population equality is more important for congressional districts.

Malapportionment A characteristic of state legislatures where a legislator from an urban district represented more people than a legislator from a rural district. Malapportioned legislatures were declared unconstitutional by the U.S. Supreme Court in the early 1960s.

Membership turnover Percentage of members who leave a legislature at the end of their term and are replaced by newly elected members. For this statistic, the reason a legislator leaves, voluntarily by not running again or through electoral defeat, is unimportant.

Professionalization State legislatures that stay in session longer, have higher salaries for their members, and support a large legislative staff. Movement for professional legislatures started at the time of the reapportionment revolution; the goal was to create legislatures that could more effectively handle the complex problems of governing in the latter half of the twentieth century.

***Reynolds* v. *Sims* (1964)** Supreme Court ruled that both houses of a state legislature must be apportioned on the basis of population and that districts must be substantially equal in population: "one person, one vote."

Self-starters Candidates who decide to run on their own initiative without strong encouragement from political parties or interest groups.

Sunset laws Laws passed by state legislatures providing that the powers of specified executive agencies will expire after a certain date unless renewed by the legislature.

Term limits movement Started in 1990 in California, Colorado, and Oklahoma, where voters approved limits to the number of terms individuals can serve as state legislators. Term limits in California, six years in the house and eight years in the senate, are fairly typical of term limit states.

Unicameral A legislature with a single chamber or house. Nebraska has the only state legislature with a single chamber, which is called the senate.

REFERENCES

1 See John Burns, *The Sometime Governments* (New York: Bantam Books, 1971), p. 32.

2 Rich Jones, "State Legislatures," *The Book of the States 1994–95* (Lexington, Ky.: Council of State Governments, 1994), p. 98.

3 Leroy Hardy, Alan Heslop, and George S. Blair, "Introduction," in *Redistricting in the 1980's,* Leroy Hardy, Alan Heslop, and George Blair, eds. (Claremont, Calif.: Rose Institute of State and Local Government, 1993), pp. 1–4.

4 Newspaper and television reporters frequently use the term *redistricting* to refer to the drawing of new congressional district boundaries and *reapportionment* to refer to the drawing of new state legislative district boundaries. Although this usage is not exact, it conveniently distinguishes the two processes.

5 See Timothy O'Rourke, *The Impact of Reapportionment* (New Brunswick, N.J.: Transaction Books, 1980); and David C. Saffell "Reapportionment and Public Policy: State Legislators' Perspectives," *Policy Studies Journal* 9 (Special #3 1980–1981).

6 For an overview of 1991–1992 redistricting in several states, see Harry Basehart and John Comer, "Redistricting and Incumbent Reelection Success in Five State Legislatures," presented at the Hendricks Symposium, April 8–9, 1994, University of Nebraska. Information on New York can be found in Kevin Sack, "The Great Incumbency Machine," *New York Times Magazine,* September 27, 1992, p. 54; for California, see Philip Hager, "How Panel Redrew the Political Map," *Los Angeles Times,* December 8, 1991, p. A3.

7 Harry Basehart, "Pennsylvania," in *Redistricting in the 1980's,* Leroy Hardy, Alan Heslop, and George Blair, eds. (Claremont, Calif.: Rose Institute of State and Local Government, 1993), pp. 217–221.

8 Rex Honey and Douglas Deane Jones, "Iowa," *Redistricting in the 1980's,* Leroy Hardy, Alan Heslop, and George Blair, eds. (Claremont, Calif.: Rose Institute of State and Local Government, 1993), pp. 97–102.

9 Laughlin McDonald, "1982 Amendments of Section 2," in *Controversies in Minority Voting: The Voting Rights Act in Perspective,* Bernard Grofman and Chandler Davidson, eds. (Washington, D.C.: The Brookings Institution, 1992), p. 69.

10 Lillian C. Woo, "Today's Legislators: Who They Are and Why They Run," *State Legislatures* (April 1994), p. 29.

11 Emily Van Dunk, "Who Runs for State Legislative Office? A Look at Candidates for Citizen and Professional Legislatures," presented at the 1994 Annual Meeting of the Midwest Political Science Association, April 14–16, Chicago, Ill.

12 Alan Rosenthal, *Legislative Life* (New York: Harper & Row, 1981), pp. 101–112.
13 Tom Loftus, *The Art of Legislative Politics* (Washington, D.C.: CQ Press, 1994), p. 10.
14 Barbara G. Salmore and Stephen A. Salmore, "The Transformation of State Electoral Politics," in *The State of the States,* Carl Van Horn, ed. (Washington, D.C.: CQ Press, 1989), pp. 188–194.
15 David Breaux and Malcolm Jewell, "Winning Big: The Incumbency Advantage in State Legislative Races," in *Changing Patterns in State Legislative Careers,* Gary F. Moncrief and Joel A. Thompson, eds. (Ann Arbor: The University of Michigan Press, 1992), p. 104.
16 Woo, "Today's Legislators," p. 28.
17 Jones, "State Legislatures," p. 100.
18 Edward H. Crane, "Six and Twelve: The Case for Serious Term Limits," *National Civic Review* (Summer 1991), pp. 252–253.
19 Cal Ledbetter, Jr., "Limiting Legislative Terms Is a Bad Idea," *National Civic Review* (Summer 1991), p. 244.
20 Karl Kurtz, "Understanding the Diversity of American State Legislatures," *Extension of Remarks* (June 1992), p. 3.
21 Ibid.
22 Ibid.
23 Ibid., p. 4.
24 Rich Jones, "The State Legislatures," in *The Book of the States 1992–93* (Lexington, Ky.: Council of State Governments, 1992), p. 129.
25 Ibid., p. 131.
26 Charles Price, "Advocacy in the Age of Term Limits: Lobbying after Proposition 140," in *1994–1995 Annual California Government and Politics,* Thomas R. Hoeber and Charles M. Price, eds. (Sacramento, Calif.: California Journal Press, 1994), p. 56.
27 Thad Beyle and Rich Jones, "Term Limits in the States," in *The Book of the States 1994–95* (Lexington, Ky.: Council of State Governments, 1994), p. 31.
28 Jones, "State Legislatures," 1994, p. 103.
29 Alan Rosenthal, "Legislative Oversight and the Balance of Power in State Government," *State Government* 56, no. 3 (1983), pp. 93–95.
30 Thad L. Beyle, "The Executive Branch: Organization and Issues, 1988–89," *The Book of the States 1990–91* (Lexington, Ky.: Council of State Governments, 1990), p. 78.
31 Jones, "State Legislatures," 1994, pp. 101–102.
32 Rosenthal, *Legislative Life,* p. 195.
33 William J. Keefe and Morris S. Ogul, *The Legislative Process,* 7th ed. (Englewood Cliffs, N.J.: Prentice-Hall, 1989), p. 194.
34 Malcolm E. Jewell and Marcia Lynn Whicker, *Legislative Leadership in the American States* (Ann Arbor: The University of Michigan Press, 1994), pp. 58–59.
35 Ibid., pp. 26–27.
36 Ibid., pp. 89–95.
37 Ibid., p. 96.
38 Ibid., pp. 125–130.

6

GOVERNORS

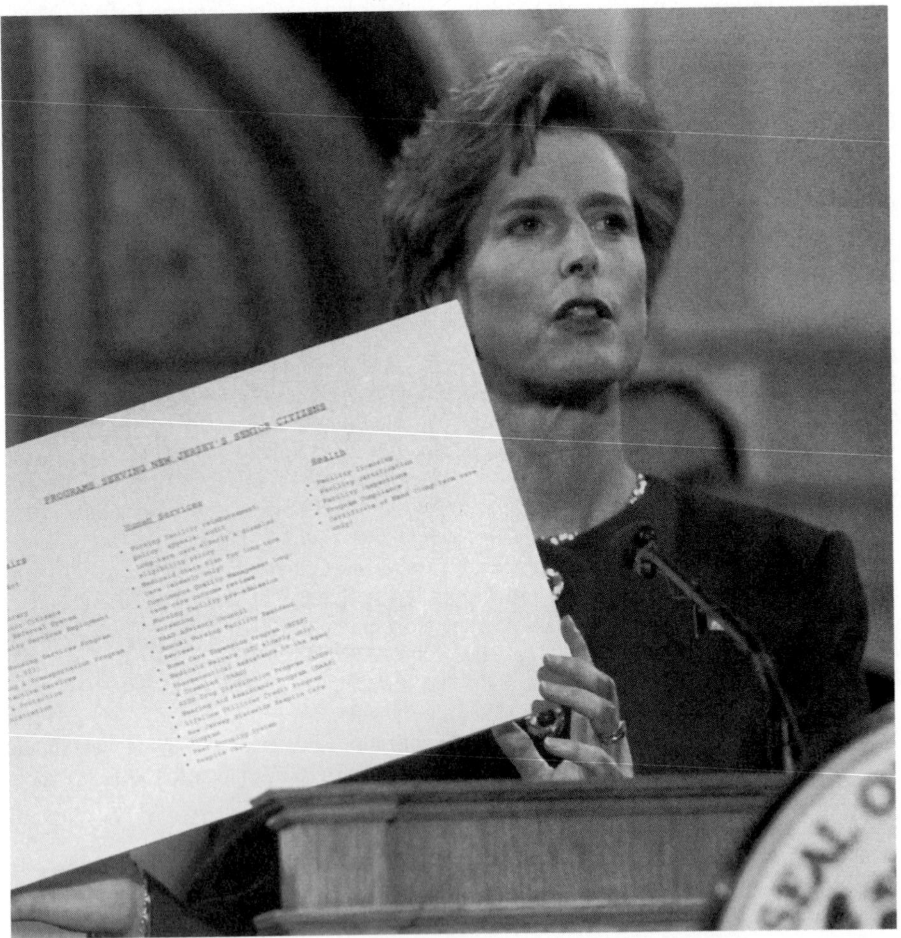

Charles Rex Arbogast/AP/Wide World Photos

Today's governors, even more than in the past, are major policy actors, attracting attention to their policy initiatives not only within their states but from outside as well. A measure of their increased prestige is found in the fact that of the last four presidents only George Bush was not a governor. Jimmy Carter was governor of Georgia, Ronald Reagan was governor of California, and Bill Clinton was governor of Arkansas. This contrasts with the period between the end of World War II and 1976 when no president was previously a governor. Recently, some members have even left their seats in Congress, where they were reasonably sure of reelection, to run for governor in their state. This has happened a number of times: Pete Wilson ran for governor of California in 1990 while still a member of the U.S. Senate and resigned his seat after winning the election. Lawton Chiles retired from the U.S. Senate in 1986, citing "burnout," only to run and win the governor's office in Florida in 1990. Both Wilson and Chiles were reelected in 1994. An interesting twist on this development occurred in Delaware in 1992 when the Republican governor decided to run for Delaware's only seat in the U.S. House of Representatives and the Democratic congressman decided to run for governor. Both were elected!

This chapter briefly traces the history of the governor's office and identifies salient factors in gubernatorial elections and the characteristics of governors. The governor's roles and the roles of other elected officials in the executive branch are explained. The focus is on the governors' formal and informal powers and their prominence in the making of policy.

HISTORICAL DEVELOPMENT OF THE GOVERNOR'S OFFICE

Governors have not always been prominent in state politics. When the early state constitutions were written, all governmental power was distrusted, but executives were particularly suspect because of the colonial experience under King George III of England. Consequently, the legislative branch dominated early state government: In most of the original states the legislature chose the governor, who served a one-year term. In only one state did the governor have the veto power. Virginia did not elect its governor until 1851.

During the **Jacksonian democracy era,** which began with the election to the presidency of Andrew Jackson in 1828, the prestige of chief executives was enhanced. Jacksonian democracy emphasized political and social equality, government by the "common man" over government by an aristocracy, that is, those who inherited their wealth and social position. Popular election was viewed as the best way to fill other executive offices such as attorney general and treasurer. Pushed by the disclosure of legislative corruption and incompetence, states extended the terms of governors, usually to two years, and added the veto power. Toward the end of the nineteenth century, legislatures, responding to urban residents who were demanding more services, created new executive branch agencies. In New York, there were only ten state agencies in 1800; by 1900 the number had increased to eighty-one. Typically, these agencies were administered by boards and commissions that had at least part of their members appointed by the legislature.[1] The executive branch of state government was becoming an administrative nightmare.

Twentieth-century reforms fall under the heading of **administrative efficiency,** meaning to centralize administrative authority and responsibility in the hands of one person—the governor. Boards and commissions were consolidated into a more manageable number of departments headed by a secretary appointed by the governor. Urbanization, the Great Depression, and the growth of federal programs administered by the states placed increasing burdens on state governments. To meet these responsibilities, gubernatorial powers, including the adoption of four-year terms, have gradually increased. Changes were made by state constitutional conventions or by legislative action. Reapportionment reduced the influence of rural legislators, who historically were hostile toward executive authority. Another factor helping to strengthen the role of governors has been the general acceptance of the view that chief executives should maximize their powers in the manner of Franklin D. Roosevelt. The presidential model still continues to have a strong influence on people's willingness to support strong executive authority at the state level and on people's expectations that governors should be able to solve problems.

GOVERNORS AND POLICYMAKING

A number of studies have documented the rise of American governors as policymakers, even policy innovators.[2] The cover of one of these books proclaims that "a new breed of governor creates models for national growth,"[3] and concludes that a governor's ideas can reach beyond his or her state to affect other states and the nation. Thad Beyle notes that creating "innovative approaches, and bragging about them, has become a way of political life for the governors."[4] (See the Scholarly Box entitled Governor William Winter: Policy Innovator.)

Since the 1980s, states and governors are frequently in the forefront of domestic policymaking, especially in education and welfare (see Chapters 13 and 14). During the 1960s and 1970s, governors were not even invited to federal policy conferences in Washington. Washington policymakers were interested in solving the problems of the cities and decided to deal directly with mayors of cities rather than governors of states. With the election of Ronald Reagan (1980), cuts in federal financial assistance and efforts to return control over programs to the states have increased the importance of the governor, a trend that appears certain to continue in the 1990s.

WHO BECOMES GOVERNOR?

The image of the typical governor as a white male lawyer in his late forties is still fairly accurate, but it should not obscure the slowly increasing diversity of political leaders who are now becoming governors. The main source of diversity is the election of more women to the governor's office. In 1990, women were elected governors in three states: Joan Finney, Kansas; Barbara Roberts, Oregon; Ann Richards, Texas. These women were Democrats. In 1993, Christine Todd Whitman, a Republican, was elected governor of New Jersey. However, news in 1994 on women candidates was mixed: A large number of women (six) were gubernatorial candidates, but they all lost including Ann Richards, the only woman governor seeking reelection. Other losers

SCHOLARLY BOX

GOVERNOR WILLIAM WINTER: POLICY INNOVATOR[5]

William Winter, governor of Mississippi (1980–1984), illustrates how governors can bring about new policies, in this case reform of Mississippi's public education system. Winter was convinced that the problems of unemployment and high welfare case loads in Mississippi were caused by the low quality of the state's public schools. Previous governors paid little attention to educational policy, which was really set by the state superintendent of education who was elected by the state's voters. Winter started his reform efforts by appointing a panel of business, education, and legislative leaders to evaluate the status of education and to make recommendations to him. The recommendations—including free kindergarten, increased teacher salaries, enforcement of compulsory school attendance, and improved curriculum standards—became part of an education reform package the governor sent to the legislature. The proposal carried a $100 million price tag that could only be paid for with an increase in state taxes. Selling education reform to the legislature was made even more difficult because of race. After the U.S. Supreme Court declared segregated public schools unconstitutional and ordered school integration, whites in many counties in Mississippi left public schools and established segregated academies, leaving public schools mostly black. Many white legislators were not interested in raising taxes so that more money could be spent on public schools that were mainly attended by blacks. For almost two years little progress was made in gaining legislative approval. Winter then decided he would use his constitutional powers to call a special session of the legislature where he would again seek passage of his reforms. Before the session convened, he decided he had to sell his proposals to the citizens of Mississippi and then mobilize them to put pressure on legislators. Forums were held throughout the state, petitions were signed, PTA leaders were organized, and funds were raised for radio and television advertising. This "full court press" worked, and the legislature passed the governor's education reform package. Kaplan and O'Brien note that "at a time when it seemed impossible to accomplish anything, Winter accomplished major reform of Mississippi's schools and educational values."[6]

were in California, Iowa, and Wyoming. All of these candidates were Democrats; the two Republican women seeking the governor's office lost in heavily Democratic Hawaii and Maryland. As of 1995, nineteen women were serving as lieutenant governors and nine as attorneys general; a large number of women are well-placed to run for governor over the next few years.

The first African-American elected governor was L. Douglas Wilder of Virginia (1989–1993). In Idaho, Democrat Larry EchoHawk lost in his bid to become the first Native American to be elected governor. EchoHawk had an early lead in the race but could not escape the anti-Democratic mood of voters in 1994.

In states with strong party organizations (e.g., Illinois and Massachusetts), a pattern of service in the state legislature and in a statewide elective position such as lieutenant governor, attorney general, or secretary of state is achieved prior to running for governor. For example, Jim Edgar, Republican governor of Illinois, started as a staff intern in the state legislature. He failed on his first try to win a seat in the Illinois House of Representatives but succeeded the second time (1976). Prior to completing his second legislative term, he moved to the executive branch to direct the governor's office of legislative relations. Edgar then received an interim appointment as secretary of state of Illinois, and later was elected to this position (1982).[7] Edgar ran for governor and was elected in 1990, and reelected in 1994.

The influence of media politics in gubernatorial elections is increasing. Thad Beyle suggests that those "who already have name recognition from previous political campaigns, or positions they hold, have an advantage as do those who can afford to run expensive campaigns."[8] The last positions held by thirty-two newly elected governors[9] who took office between 1990 and 1993 are listed below:

- Fifteen (47 percent) statewide elective positions
- Six (19 percent) members of Congress
- Six (19 percent) "outsider" candidates
- Five (15 percent) miscellaneous category, such as a state-level appointive position, mayor, or federal attorney

Who are the outsider candidates? Outsiders are candidates who do not work their way up the political career ladder one rung at a time but make their first run for elective office by starting at the top. They usually have widespread name recognition because of success in the business world, or money to buy name recognition through paid advertising, or both. Fife Symington, elected governor of Arizona in 1990, is an example of an outsider. He was a successful businessman, accumulating a personal fortune estimated at $12 million while the head of a real estate development company. Symington, active in nonpolitical community activities such as arts councils and charitable foundations, was not completely unknown to the Republican party because his wife, Ann Pritzlaff Symington, came from a politically active family. With a crowded field of five candidates, Symington won the Republican gubernatorial primary. The general election was a close contest with no candidate winning a *majority* of the votes cast as required by a new Arizona law. A runoff election was held between the top two vote-getters, Symington and a Democratic candidate. During the runoff, Symington outspent his opponent by a ratio of 2 to 1 and won the election.[10] Symington was reelected in 1994. A successful business career and personal wealth do not guarantee election to the governor's office, but it does allow a person to skip holding office in a city or county council and in the state legislature and to go immediately after the highest elected position in a state. (Governor Symington ran into difficulty with his personal finances after his reelection and filed for bankruptcy in 1995.)

RUNNING FOR THE GOVERNOR'S OFFICE

The Incumbency Factor

Incumbency is always a good place to start in identifying factors that determine who wins an election. Data gathered by Beyle show that between 1970 and 1991, incumbent governors were *eligible* to seek another term in 78 percent of the elections. (Most governors are subject to term limits, which will be examined in more detail later in this chapter.) What happened in these elections where incumbents were eligible to run?

- 74 percent of the incumbents decided to run.
- 73 percent of the incumbents who decided to run were reelected.

These two percentages are not as high as those found for members of the U.S. Congress, which are normally in the 80 percent range and sometimes even higher. Nevertheless, the percentages for governor are moderately high.

Squire and Fastnow compare the election environment of incumbent governors and U.S. senators and conclude that it is different. Voters are more likely to know and have an opinion of their governor than of their senators. News about governors in newspapers appears much more frequently than news about senators. But better known does not translate into better liked: Governors receive less favorable job performance ratings than senators. Consequently, voters are more likely to vote for a challenger to an incumbent governor than for a challenger to an incumbent senator.[11] Overall, there have always been a number of new faces among the nation's fifty governors after elections are held.[12]

Incumbent reelection success between 1992 and 1995 is presented in Table 6-1. The pattern for 1992–1995 contains similarities and differences when compared with the 1970–1991 time period. The percentage of incumbents eligible to run is about the same for both periods (81 percent versus 78 percent). The percentage who decided to run is *less* in 1992–1995 than in the earlier time period (58 percent versus 74 percent). And the percentage of incumbents who won is *larger* in 1992–1995 (84 percent versus 73 percent). A trend may be emerging of fewer incumbents running for reelection, but incumbents who run are winning reelection at a slightly higher rate.

The Electoral Context

State elections are becoming increasingly autonomous affairs, that is, separate from the issues and personalities of national elections that occur at the same time. To a large degree, this is happening because many gubernatorial elections are held when there are no presidential elections (see Chapter 4); this reduces the likelihood that voters' eval-

TABLE 6-1 INCUMBENT REELECTION SUCCESS IN GUBERNATORIAL ELECTIONS, 1992–1995

Year	Number of races	Eligible to run	Did run	Won
1992	12	75%	44%	100%
		(9)	(4)	(4)
1993	2	50%	100%	0%
		(1)	(1)	(0)
1994	36	83%	63%	84%
		(30)	(19)	(16)
1995	3	100%	33%	100%
		(3)	(1)	(1)
Percentages, 1992–1995		81%	58%	84%
Total number of cases, 1992–1995	53	(43)	(25)	(21)

Source: Data for 1992 and 1993 are from Thad Beyle, "The Governors, 1992–93," in *The Book of the States, 1994–95* (Lexington, Ky.: The Council of State Governments, 1994), p. 37; 1994 data are from "1994 Election Results," *Congressional Quarterly Weekly Report,* November 12, 1994, pp. 3301–3308; and 1995 data are from "Democrats Warmed by a Touch of Southern Hospitality," *Congressional Quarterly Weekly Report,* November 11, 1995, p. 3474.

uations of both parties' presidential candidates will affect their evaluation of gubernatorial candidates. During the 1980s, for example, voters were prone to elect Democratic governors but Republican presidents.[13]

As often happens, just about the time political scientists have evidence to support a generalization, a political event occurs that runs counter to the generalization. In this case, the event is the 1994 midterm elections. As noted in Chapter 3, 1994 elections resulted in huge loses for the Democratic party. Not only did the Republican party win new majorities in the U.S. Senate and House of Representatives but it also made significant gains in governors' offices and state legislative seats (see Table 6-2). It is hard to escape the conclusion that voters were intent on throwing out Democrats at the national and state level. In 1994, voters' evaluations of the national scene affected their evaluations and votes at the state level, contrary to most recent elections.

Voters' perceptions of state economic conditions also affect the reelection success of incumbent governors; this is called **retrospective voting.** If voters think their state's economy is performing poorly in relation to that of other states or of the nation as a whole, they tend to blame the person sitting in the governor's office. If the economy is doing well, voters give credit to the governor. Although we usually think economic conditions are primarily affected by national policies, it seems that governors, by working to attract businesses to their state through tax incentives and other devices (see Chapter 16), are being viewed by voters as managers of the health of the economy in their state.[14]

In recent years, many incumbents running for reelection have encountered a dilemma because they frequently face an electorate that seems to want both increased services and lower taxes. If they balance the state budget but do not increase services, they may lose in their bid for reelection. If they increase services and raise taxes to pay for them, they again may lose in their bid for reelection. Finally, if they increase services but do not raise adequate revenues, they may be labeled financially irresponsible, which again may cost them reelection.

TABLE 6-2 REPUBLICAN GAINS IN ELECTED POSITIONS AT THE NATIONAL AND STATE LEVELS, 1992 TO 1994*

	Republicans in			
Year	U.S. Senate	U.S. House	Governors	State legislatures
1992	44%	41%	38%	41%
1994	53%	53%	60%	48%
Change	+9	+12	+22	+7

Source: Congressional Quarterly Weekly Reports, November 12, 1994, pp. 3232, 3240, 3247; and Rob Gurwitt, "The Strains of Power," *Governing* 8 (February 1995), p. 21.

*Figures in this table are the percentage of the total number of legislative members or governors who are members of the Republican party.

ROLES OF THE GOVERNOR

Chief of State

As chief of state, the governor performs a variety of ceremonial functions and acts as official spokesperson for the people of the state. Ceremonial functions include dedicating new highways and bridges, attending funerals and weddings, greeting distinguished visitors to the state capitol, proclaiming special days or weeks, and attending football games. Although much of this activity appears trivial and undoubtedly bores many governors, it does reap political rewards in terms of publicity and image building.

In this role of official spokesperson, the governor can speak in a highly moralistic tone. This approach was effective in the area of civil rights when governors were able to promote social justice by their actions as well as by their words. For example, in his inaugural speech, Governor Jimmy Carter of Georgia (1971–1975) stated, "I say to you quite frankly that the time for racial discrimination is over." Carter went on to appoint African-Americans to important positions in state government and to place a portrait of Martin Luther King, Jr., in the statehouse.

As we mentioned earlier, governors are acting as economic advocates for their states, expending time and energy to lure business and manufacturing concerns from other states and to encourage plant investment from foreign corporations. For example, Tom Carper, Democratic governor of Delaware, traveled to Michigan and spent a day making a pitch to executives of Chrysler and Volkswagen of America, hoping to keep them involved in the Delaware economy. Carper said that his state was prepared to pay for retraining Chrysler's Delaware employees if they decided to build a new sport-utility vehicle there. Volkswagen officials, who were considering moving their import operations out of the Port of Wilmington, were told about plans to upgrade the port.[15] This type of activity is fairly typical of today's governors.

Commander-in-Chief

Although governors do not command a navy with nuclear-powered submarines or an air force with intercontinental ballistic missiles, they do have a commander-in-chief role as head of their state's National Guard (formerly called the state militia) until it is called into service by the president. The U.S. Constitution provides for a cooperative system in which states appoint officers (the state adjutant general is their commander) and Congress organizes, arms, and finances the Guard. Since 1916, the former militias have been organized as an auxiliary of the regular army subject to substantial national control. As its civilian commander-in-chief, the governor may call the Guard into service for such emergencies as floods, tornadoes, or urban riots. The president may also call the Guard into service, at which time state control ends. Control of the Guard allowed some governors to become involved in foreign affairs by refusing to send their state troops to Central America for training exercises in 1986. In response, Congress passed a bill to prohibit governors from interfering with overseas troop deployment.

The record of the Guard in responding to civil disturbances has ranged from adequate to disastrous. Prior to World War II, the Guard often was used brutally to break up racial disturbances, labor strikes, and prison riots. Perhaps the most noteworthy incident occurred in Ohio in 1970 when Ohio National Guardsmen killed four students and injured others in responding to a demonstration against the Vietnam War at Kent State University. On a more positive note, the Guard has been effective (often invaluable) when dealing with natural disasters. Also, with Guardsmen posted on nearly every corner, looting quickly diminished after two days of rioting in Los Angeles in 1992. The Los Angeles police clearly had lost control of the situation.

Chief Administrator

As chief administrator, the governor is responsible for the management of all state administrative agencies. As was noted, the governor's administrative authority in the early part of the twentieth century was not equal to the responsibility associated with a person who is a chief executive. Agencies in the executive branch were actually controlled by boards or commissions with several members. This meant that if a governor wanted an agency to take some action, he or she would first have to convince the members of the board, because it was the board that had direct control over the agency's activities. This awkward administrative arrangement occurs less frequently today because administrative efficiency reforms have eliminated boards and commissions and reduced the number of agencies by consolidating them into a smaller number of departments.[16] More and more states have moved to a **cabinet** form of executive branch organization that concentrates authority and responsibility in the hands of the governor and creates a cabinet of department secretaries appointed by the governor who individually administer a department and collectively advise the governor.[17]

Because of the increasing complexity of state government and the ever-broadening responsibilities of their office, governors have surrounded themselves with expanding numbers of *staff personnel* who provide both political and administrative assistance. In a large state a governor's staff of perhaps 100 people will include a press secretary, an executive secretary, a legal adviser, a speechwriter, a director of the budget, a commissioner of administration, and others assigned by the political party. Some staff will work as liaison with state, local, and federal agencies and as liaison to the state legislature to help guide the governor's program through the legislative process. Staff personnel tend to be young (in their thirties) and politically ambitious. Many are lawyers, and most staff members previously worked in the governor's campaign or in the campaigns of other candidates in their party.

In addition to serving in an administrative capacity, the governor's staff provides other more political services. The staff:

1 Serves as a research office to provide information and to help shape the governor's position on a wide range of policy issues

2 Serves as public relations specialists to do such things as write press releases and keep the governor posted on political developments that may affect how citizens perceive the governor

3 Handles the important tasks of answering the mail, controlling the governor's schedule, and determining who sees the governor

As with the president, the governor must guard against the dangers of an overprotective staff that isolates him or her from the world beyond the office.

According to Martha Wagner Weinberg, reformers have often suggested that if governors would only adopt modern business management techniques, they would be able to manage public affairs much more effectively.[18] She believes, however, that this assumption overlooks some major differences between governors and private sector chief executives. The governor's management task is much more difficult because the environment in which his or her decisions are made is more complex and less controllable. Even compared with large private businesses, the operations of states such as New York and California, or even Nebraska, are much more complex in terms of budget, number of personnel, and variety of functions.

Differences exist between managing state government and private enterprise that relate more directly to the political process. Governors must share power with legislative and judicial branches, and they must operate with a federal system in which the national government has substantial power. In addition, governors constantly keep in mind how management decisions might affect their future political aspirations.

Does Salary Equal Responsibility?

Over the years, increased responsibilities have brought higher salaries for governors. Today, ten governors make over $100,000 per year, with New York having the highest paid governor at $130,000. Most salaries are in the $80,000 to $90,000 range. The lowest paid governor ($55,850) is in Montana. Governors usually have access to a number of perquisites including an official residence and transportation in state-supplied automobiles and airplanes.

Are governors paid too much? If they are compared to chief executive officers of large corporations, the answer is probably no. For example, Table 6-3 compares the governor of North Carolina to the chief executive officer of Xerox. They oversee budgets of almost equal size, and North Carolina's governor oversees substantially more employees; but the most significant difference is in compensation. The governor does

TABLE 6-3 COMPARISON ON SELECTED CHARACTERISTICS OF GOVERNOR OF NORTH CAROLINA AND THE CEO OF XEROX CORPORATION

	Number of employees	Revenue (in billions)	Salary	Bonus
Xerox Corporation	87,600	$17.8	$700,000	$775,000
North Carolina	127,279	$17.7	$93,777	None

Source: The Book of the States, 1994–95 (Lexington, Ky.: The Council of State Governments, 1994), pp. 53, 339, 442; "500 Largest U.S. Corporations," *Fortune* 15 (May 1995), pp. F-1, F-30; Andrew E. Serwer, "Pay Day! Pay Day! What CEOs Make," *Fortune* 14 (June 1993), p. 104.

not receive a bonus, and the salary is only 13 percent of the salary paid to the CEO of Xerox. This is not to argue that all governors need a big pay raise, simply that they are not overcompensated when compared to the private sector.

OTHER STATEWIDE ELECTED EXECUTIVES

Unlike the national level, where the president and vice president are the only popularly elected officials, most states continue to fill several executive branch positions through election. As of 1992, there were 304 statewide elected executives, including governors and lieutenant governors. Many political scientists argue that the governor and lieutenant governor should be the only statewide elected executives. Electing more creates a **long ballot** where voters must vote for offices and candidates they know little about. It also creates agencies that to some extent are independent of the governor because they also have their own executive who has been elected by the voters.[19] Consequently, having a large number of separately elected officials (SEOs) is viewed as reducing a governor's influence in the executive branch. Brief descriptions of officials that are typically elected and their duties follow.

Lieutenant Governor

The basic responsibilities of the lieutenant governor are comparable to those of the vice president of the United States: to be first in line to succeed the governor in the event of the governor's death and in twenty states to be presiding officer of the state senate when it is in session (see Chapter 5). In the eight states that do not have a lieutenant governor, the first in the line of succession is usually the secretary of state.

When a governor is out of the state, many lieutenant governors become acting governor. This is an important difference when compared with the vice presidency, because vice presidents do not become acting president when the president is out of the country. A 1992 survey that was responded to by close to half of the lieutenant governors found that many had served as acting governor; the average length of time was forty-six days. During this time, some of the lieutenant governors had signed bills into law, reviewed pending executions, and made other important decisions.[20]

Still, the job of lieutenant governor will be determined largely by what the governor wants the lieutenant governor to do. Governors frequently consult their lieutenant governors when appointing administrators to head executive branch agencies and often use them as policy advisers.[21]

For a long time states elected governors and lieutenant governors separately, which meant that a governor might have to deal with a politically ambitious lieutenant governor of the opposite party. However, thirty-one states now have joint nomination and joint election of these two officials.

Attorney General

As the state's chief legal officer, the attorney general represents the state in legal disputes and serves as the legal adviser to the governor and other executive branch employees. Curiously, in about half the states, the attorney general does not have to be a licensed attorney. Attorneys general are popularly elected in forty-three states, chosen by the governor in five states, chosen by the legislature in one state, and chosen by the state supreme court in one state. Although a part of the executive branch, they can become involved in battles with governors. An extreme example is when the attorney general of Arizona was a leader in the move to impeach Governor Evan Mecham in 1986–1987.

In most states, the attorney general is the second most powerful political figure in state office. His or her power stems in large part from the ability to initiate prosecution in well-publicized criminal and civil cases. In addition, when the governor, the legislature, administrative agencies, county attorneys, or city attorneys ask the attorney general for advice regarding an interpretation of state law, the attorney general's opinion generally has the force of law unless challenged in court. The attorney general's office often serves as a state headquarters for consumer complaints about faulty merchandise or misleading advertising.

In many instances, the attorney general heads the largest law office in the state. This ability to appoint hundreds of young lawyers to serve in state government gives the attorney general a substantial power base should he or she choose to run for governor or senator after those attorneys have gained experience and moved into private practice around the state. Several attorneys general have gone on to become governors and well-known national political figures. They include Robert LaFollette of Wisconsin, Thomas Dewey of New York, and more recently Bill Clinton of Arkansas.

Secretary of State

The duties of secretary of state are to keep records—such as the state constitution, constitutional amendments, legislative acts, and mortgages—and to supervise both federal and state elections. They are elected in thirty-eight states and selected by either the governor or the legislature in eleven states; Alaska does not have such a position. Secretaries of state receive statements of candidacy for public office, oversee the printing of ballots, and certify election results. Because secretaries of state are basically record keepers, many proposals call for the transfer of these duties to regular administrative departments. In recent years, several secretaries of state have become governors. These include Jerry Brown of California, Jay Rockefeller of West Virginia, and Barbara Roberts of Oregon. Over twenty secretaries of state have become governor this century, but many do not have further political ambitions. For example, Thad Eure retired in 1989 as secretary of state of North Carolina after fifty-two years in office.

Treasurer, Auditor, and Controller

A number of functions involving the handling of money generated from taxes are divided among several officials, and it is difficult to find more than a handful of states that do it the same way. A state treasurer is usually responsible for tax collection, the safekeeping of state funds, and the actual spending of money. Treasurers are elected in thirty-eight states and chosen by the governor or legislature in others. **Postaudit,** a review after money is spent to see if it was spent according to legislative intent and without corruption, is the responsibility of the state auditor. Auditors are elected in twenty-five states and chosen by the governor or legislature in others. In a few states the auditor is called the controller. **Preaudit** is the approval of spending before it actually takes place and is normally done by the controller. The controller is elected in only nine states; appointment by an agency head (such as the department of finance) is becoming more common.

The treasurer, auditor, and controller will not be found in every state, but the functions they perform will be done by some office. The administrative efficiency school argues that all, or most, of these functions should be centralized in one office headed by a gubernatorial appointee. This would make the governor clearly responsible for the performance of these functions.

FORMAL POWERS OF THE GOVERNOR

In a much cited analysis of governors, Joseph A. Schlesinger studied formal gubernatorial powers and developed an overall measure of the relative power of governors in the fifty states.[22] **Formal powers** are those powers that can be found in a state's constitution or statutes. The more important powers are those dealing with tenure potential, appointment of executive branch officials, control over preparing the budget, and ability to veto legislation.

Tenure Potential

As noted earlier in this chapter, governors historically have had short terms of office. In ten of the original thirteen states, the governor was limited to a term of one year. States moved first to two-year terms (by the 1840s) and gradually to four-year terms, which today can be found in forty-eight states. Recently, Arkansas and Rhode Island switched to four-year terms, leaving only New Hampshire and Vermont with two-year terms. As far as length of term is concerned, governors with four-year terms are high on tenure potential.

Another side of tenure potential is term limits, which has recently been an important issue with state legislators (see Chapter 5). A few states follow the model of the Twenty-second Amendment to the U.S. Constitution, which says that a person can be elected only twice to the presidency. In these states, governors can serve only two terms; for obvious reasons this type of term limitation is known as an absolute two-term limit. Other states limit the number of *consecutive* terms, usually two, so that it is possible to serve two four-year terms, leave the office for one term, and then serve another two terms. Of course, other examples of restraints can be found: Wyoming limits governors to eight years out of any sixteen, and Utah allows three consecutive terms. Only Virginia has a one-term limit. Overall, governors are relatively equal in tenure potential:

- Thirty-eight states have four-year terms and some form of restraint on reelection.
- Ten four-year term states and two states with two-year terms have no restraint of any kind on reelection.

Of course, governors with four-year terms and no restraint on reelection have the highest tenure potential.

Tenure potential is a measure of the possible number of years a governor could stay in office. Why is tenure potential important to a governor's power? The ability to succeed oneself in office means that the governor will not become a **lame duck,** that is, have diminished power because he or she will soon leave office and cannot run again. Legislators cannot ignore a governor in the fourth year of his or her term if he or she may run for reelection and win and be around another four years. Also, a four-year term allows governors time to prove themselves: Policies enacted during their first two years (e.g., something controversial such as a tax increase) can be evaluated by reelection time two years later (whether any benefits have been produced by the tax increase).

Appointing Power

Governors' **appointing power** is strongest when they alone can name people to head (usually called a secretary or director) the more important agencies in the executive branch such as corrections, public safety, education, agriculture, environment, and economic development. Appointive power diminishes when one or two houses of the legislature must approve appointments or if the appointment is made by a department director. If the position is elective or is filled by a board or commission, then the governor's formal power is reduced.

Gubernatorial appointive power varies greatly among the states. Almost all appointments by the governor of Virginia must be approved by both houses of the legislature. In Massachusetts, boards appoint many administrative officials, while in Georgia, the governor appoints a large number of them. Not only is there variation among states but there is also variation within states. Even in states where the governor's appointing authority is strong, some appointments will need the approval of the senate and some will probably be made by a board or commission acting on its own.

A strong appointing power is important because governors free to appoint officials to top-level posts in the executive branch can select people whose political views are similar to theirs and who will feel a sense of obligation to the governor who appointed them. This will help a governor obtain action on his or her priorities.

Budgetary Power

Early in the twentieth century, most states instituted an **executive budget.** This means that the governor and officials appointed directly by the governor have full responsibility to *prepare* the state budget. Governors' staffs almost always include a budget director and professional assistants. The budget staff reviews requests for funds from all state agencies and, with the governor exercising final approval, prepares a budget that is then acted upon by the legislature (see Chapter 7). In only six states (four of them in the South) does the governor share responsibility for budget preparation with civil service appointees or with the legislature. A governor's **budgetary power** is determined largely by the presence or absence of the executive budget.

Even when governors have strong formal powers, they find their control does not give them complete discretion in proposing where money should be spent because more than 50 percent of the budget must provide funds for specific purposes (such as gasoline taxes for highway construction and maintenance).

Veto Power

Governors are participants in the legislative process because they must sign bills passed by the legislature before they can become state law. (Only the governor of North Carolina does not have a veto.) Governors **veto** a bill by returning it to the legislature unsigned, along with their objections. The veto makes the governor a participant in the legislative process. If the legislature votes to override a veto, the bill becomes law without the governor's signature.

Seven states give the governor a third option to signing or vetoing a bill. It is usually called an **amendatory veto** and allows the governor to return a bill to the legislature with suggested amendments. If the legislature agrees to these amendments, the bill will become law.

Budget problems, again growing out of the Great Depression, brought an expansion of veto power that gave governors a way to avoid the difficult choice of accepting or rejecting an entire appropriations bill. The power of the **item veto** permits governors in forty-three states to veto individual items in appropriation bills. Governors in ten states have a reduction veto for reducing specific items in appropriations bills without vetoing the line item entirely. (See the Scholarly Box entitled Should the President Have the Item Veto?) The veto power is a measure of the extent to which governors can reject bills and appropriation items that have passed the legislature.

An extreme example of the veto power is found in Wisconsin where Republican Governor Tommy Thompson (1987–), taking literally his constitutional power to veto appropriation bills "in whole or in part," has changed the meaning of a sentence by vetoing words such as "shall" and "not." Thompson has even struck out individual letters to make new words, and new laws. Local commentators have labeled this the "Vanna White veto" (named after Vanna White, who appears on the television show "Wheel of Fortune"). A recent constitutional amendment has somewhat lessened the veto power of the governor in Wisconsin.[23]

Typically, the governor's veto must be overridden by at least a two-thirds vote of the elected membership of both houses of the legislature (some states specify two-thirds of the members present on an override vote rather than elected membership). This means that the governor's veto will be sustained if he or she can persuade only a small percentage of the legislators in one house not to vote to override. Two-thirds vote is normally required to override an item veto, also.

Tommy Thompson may hold the record for vetoes with close to 1,500 in eight years,[24] and he can continue to add to that number because he was reelected to another four-year term in 1994. A fifty-state average finds that governors veto only about 5 percent of the bills that pass the legislature, and very few (4 percent) of these vetoes are overridden by the legislature. The number of vetoes increases dramatically if the

SCHOLARLY BOX

SHOULD THE PRESIDENT HAVE THE ITEM VETO?[25]

Recent presidents, along with some members of Congress, have argued that the president of the United States should be given the power of the item veto. After all, it is argued, forty-three governors have this power. Why not the president? In 1995, the Republican-controlled Congress debated several bills that would give the president an item veto, although the specific procedures would differ from those of the gubernatorial item veto.

The advocates of the presidential item veto see it as an important tool to reduce spending by the federal government and thus reduce the federal deficit. The idea behind a presidential item veto is simple: Members of Congress spend money on projects that are important to their constituents; more often than not these projects have little value to the nation and do nothing but increase the national debt. Congress has even forced the Pentagon to buy airplanes it really did not want because the plane's manufacturing plant was located in the district or state of an important member of the U.S. House of Representatives or Senate. The president, it is argued, is the only political leader who can stop this kind of spending because the president's constituency is the nation. The president will support spending that is only in the national interest.

Evidence from the states suggests, however, that the use of the item veto by governors has not really reduced state spending. Governors actually use the item veto to pursue their own policy and political objectives. For example, governors veto expenditures they think are bad policy or veto projects simply because they are favored by legislators who do not belong to the governor's party. One observer concludes: "Although the item veto may have an effect on the budget, that effect is much more likely to be to substitute the governor's priorities for those of the legislature than to reduce spending."[26] Consequently, many political analysts oppose the presidential item veto. They argue that it would considerably weaken Congress's strong power over appropriations.

It is difficult to make predictions about the effect of the presidential item veto, in part because the environment of its use at the state level is different from that at the federal level. For example, since most state constitutions require the legislature to adopt a balanced budget, it may not be all that surprising that the use of the item veto by governors has not had much impact on total spending. Perhaps the item veto in the hands of a president who has spending reduction as a top priority could help to achieve that goal. Nevertheless, it would be in Congress's institutional interest to reduce spending on its own rather than give the president a new tool that may considerably enhance presidential power.

governor's office and legislature are controlled by different parties. James Thompson, Republican governor of Illinois (1977–1991), vetoed one out of every three bills sent to him by a Democratic legislature.[27] And, in most states, if the governor's party has at least one-third of the seats, it is unlikely that vetoes will be overridden.

Oftentimes a governor's threat of a veto can cause legislators to change the content of a bill before they finish acting on it. Unfortunately, no statistics are compiled on the number of times governors threaten to veto and with what success, but it is another tool skillful governors can use to persuade legislators to modify bills so that they are more to their liking. Recently, the newly elected governor of Maryland (1995–), Parris Glendening, used the threat of a veto to negotiate changes in a smoking ban that the Maryland legislature was attempting to weaken. The legislature wanted to allow smoking in hotels, motels, and all businesses with a liquor license, including restaurants. The governor wanted a more comprehensive ban and threatened to veto the bill if it contained the exemptions the legislature wanted. A compromise was reached that gave each side some of what it wanted. For example, in restaurants smoking is banned in the eating areas but allowed in the bar and adjacent areas.[28]

A Revised Index of Gubernatorial Power

Thad Beyle has updated and expanded Schlesinger's work on the formal powers of the governor. Beyle includes the four powers discussed above, adds two more—the number of separately elected officials in the executive branch and the party that controls the legislature—and then compares the *institutional* powers of the governors in all fifty states. States are rated on a scale of 1 to 5, with 5 representing governors who have the strongest power. The results, including an overall average for each state, are in Table 6-4.

The states of Maryland (4.3 on the five-point scale), West Virginia (4.2), Hawaii (4.1), New York (4.1), and New Jersey (4.0) give their governors the strongest powers. And governors in North Carolina (2.5) and South Carolina (2.5) have the weakest institutional powers. Overall, governors are strongest on veto power (4.4) and weakest on appointment power (2.8).[29]

LEGISLATIVE LEADERSHIP

Identifying formal powers of governors is important, but it does not reveal what happens when men and women use these powers during their tenure, especially in their relationship with the legislative branch where only one of the formal powers—the veto—can be used directly. Also, lists of formal powers measure only *potential* effectiveness. Bad economic times, for example, may seriously limit the initiatives taken by a governor even though he or she may have considerable formal power. But the most effective opposition to a governor's efforts to change policies resides right in the capitol building with the governor—the state legislature. Governors must persuade the legislature that what they want to accomplish is what the legislature, or at least a majority of its members, should want to accomplish also.

Alan Rosenthal suggests a number of additional powers, some formal and some informal, that contribute to a governor's success as a legislative leader: the power of initiation, the power of publicity, and the power of party.[30] Informal powers are not found in constitutional or statutory law. **Informal powers** refer to things such as the skill a governor brings to negotiating and bargaining and the ability to communicate through the media.[31]

Power of Initiation

State constitutions authorize governors to recommend measures to the legislature that they think should become law. This may seem to be rather innocuous, but it is the basis of the power of initiation. Initiation is the ability to set the policy agenda for the state, that is, to identify those issues that need to be addressed first. Governors begin the process of setting the agenda in their inaugural address, delivered at the start of their term. In this address governors can set out broad themes and goals for their new administration and, because of media attention to the event, can communicate to the people. Annual "state of the state" messages from the governor to the legislature are more specific than inaugural addresses. These messages contain the governor's priorities for the upcoming legislative session and are referred to as the governor's

TABLE 6-4 INSTITUTIONAL POWERS OF THE GOVERNORSHIP, 1994

State	Institutional power						Score	State	Institutional power						Score
	SEOs[a]	Tenure[b]	Appoint[c]	Budget[d]	Veto[e]	Party[f]	Total ÷6[g]		SEOs[a]	Tenure[b]	Appoint[c]	Budget[d]	Veto[e]	Party[f]	Total ÷6[g]
Ala.	1	4	2.5	3	4	5	3.3	Nebr.	3	4	3	4	5	3	3.7
Alaska	5	4	3	3	5	1	3.5	Nev.	2	4	3	3	2	3	2.8
Ariz.	2	4	2.5	3	5	4	3.4	N.H.	5	2	3	3	2	4	3.2
Ark.	2	4	2.5	3	4	5	3.4	N.J.	5	4	3	3	5	4	4.0
Calif.	1	4	3	3	5	2	3.0	N.Mex.	3	4	3	2	5	4	3.5
Colo.	3	4	3	2	5	2	3.2	N.Y.	4	5	3.5	4	5	3	4.1
Conn.	4	5	3	3	5	1	3.5	N.C.	1	4	3	3	0	4	2.5
Del.	2	4	3	3	5	3	3.3	N.Dak.	3	5	2.5	3	5	3	3.6
Fla.	3	4	1.5	3	5	3	3.3	Ohio	3	4	5	3	5	3	3.8
Ga.	1	4	1.5	3	5	4	3.1	Okla.	1	4	1	3	5	4	3.0
Hawaii	5	4	2.5	3	5	5	4.1	Oreg.	3	4	2.5	3	5	3	3.4
Idaho	2	5	2	3	5	2	3.2	Pa.	4	4	4.5	3	5	3	3.9
Ill.	3	5	2.5	3	5	3	3.6	R.I.	3	5	4	3	2	5	3.7
Ind.	3	4	4	3	1	3	3.0	S.C.	1	4	2	1	5	2	2.5
Iowa	4	5	3	3	5	3	3.8	S.Dak.	3	4	3.5	3	5	3	3.6
Kans.	3	4	3	3	5	2	3.3	Tenn.	4	4	4	3	4	4	3.8
Ky.	4	4	3	2	4	4	3.5	Tex.	1	5	1	1	5	4	2.8
La.	1	4	3	2	5	5	3.3	Utah	3	4.5	2.5	3	5	3	3.5
Maine	5	4	3.5	3	2	2	3.3	Vt.	3	2	2.5	3	2	3	2.6
Md.	4	4	2.5	5	5	5	4.3	Va.	3	3	3.5	3	5	2	3.3
Mass.	4	5	1	3	5	1	3.2	Wash.	1	4	2.5	3	5	4	3.3
Mich.	3	4	3.5	3	5	3	3.6	W.Va.	3	4	4	5	4	5	4.2
Minn.	4	5	2.5	3	5	2	3.6	Wis.	3	5	2	3	5	3	3.5
Miss.	3	4	2	3	5	1	3.0	Wyo.	2	4	3.5	3	5	2	3.3
Mo.	3	4	2.5	3	5	4	3.6								
Mont.	3	4	2	3	5	3	3.3	Average	2.9	4.1	2.8	3.0	4.4	3.2	3.4

[a]Based on which of certain offices (attorney general, agriculture, auditor, K-12 education, insurance, labor, lieutenant governor, public utilities authority, secretary of state, and treasurer) are filled by a separately elected official (SEO). Scoring is as follows: 5 points = only governor or governor/lieutenant governor team elected statewide; 4 = same team with some process officials (attorney general, secretary of state, treasurer, and auditor) separately elected; 3 = team and some process officials with a major policy official (education, public utilities), or governor (no team) and four or more process and minor elected officials (agriculture, insurance, labor); 2 = governor (no team) with six or fewer officials and a major policy official; 1 = governor (no team) with seven or more process and major policy officials.

[b]Limits on governors' terms scored as follows: 5 = four-year term, no reelection restraint; 4.5 = four-year term, only three terms permitted; 4 = four-year term, two terms permitted; 3 = four-year term, no consecutive reelection permitted; 2 = two-year term, no reelection restraint; 1 = two-year term, only two terms permitted.

[c]Governor's appointment power in six major areas (corrections, K-12 education, health, highways, public utilities regulation, and welfare) in each state scored as follows: 5 = governor appoints alone; 4 = governor appoints and a board, council, or the legislature must approve; 3 = someone else appoints and governor approves/shares in appointment; 2 = someone else appoints and governor and others (legislature) approve; 1 = someone else appoints alone; 0 = separately elected or selected by legislature.

[d]Governor's ability to develop budget and legislature's ability to change budget scored as follows: 5 = governor has full responsibility for developing budget and legislature may not increase it; 4 = governor has same responsibility, but legislature can increase budget by special majority vote or subject it to item veto; 3 = governor has same responsibility, but legislature has unlimited power to change it; 2 = governor shares budget development responsibility, but legislature has unlimited power to change budget; 1 = governor shares budget responsibility with other elected official(s), and legislature has unlimited power to change budget.

[e]Governor's ability to veto legislation and legislature's veto override mechanism are scored as follows: 5 = item veto, with votes of three-fifths of elected legislators or two-thirds of legislators present needed to override; 4.5 = item veto, with majority of elected legislators needed to override, except for appropriations bills when votes of two-thirds of those elected are needed; 4 = item veto, with majority of elected legislators needed to override; 3 = item veto, with majority of legislators present needed to override; 2 = no item veto, but a special legislative majority needed to override; 1 = no item veto, and only simple legislative majority needed to override; 0 = no veto of any kind.

[f]Measures congruence of partisan control of executive and legislative branches and is scored as follows: 5 = governor's party has substantial majority (75 percent or more) in both houses; 4 = governor's party has simple majority in both houses, or simple majority in one house and substantial majority in other house; 3 = split party control or nonpartisan legislature; 2 = governor's party in simple minority in both houses, or simple minority in one house and substantial minority in other house; 1 = governor's party in substantial minority in both houses.

[g]The six separate institutional powers scores for each governorship totaled and divided by 6 to stay within a 5-point scale framework.

Source: Thad L. Beyle, "Enhancing Executive Leadership in the States," *State and Local Government Review* 27 (Winter 1995), p. 29. Reprinted by permission of the author and the Carl Vinson Institute of Government, University of Georgia.

legislative program. These proposals are general statements that will have to be drafted into bills and introduced by legislators, usually members of the leadership, and then considered by both houses. The fact that a bill is part of the governor's legislative program guarantees that it will receive serious consideration by the legislature and, in most cases, increases the likelihood that the bill will become law. Governors may also focus attention on a particular issue by calling the legislature into special session to deal with politically difficult problems. Because many legislatures meet for short regular sessions, the ability to call members back into session gives governors a means of exerting considerable pressure on legislators who are reluctant to face an issue.

Governors can influence the agenda through the creation of commissions or task forces to study a problem and make recommendations to solve it. Members of this type of commission are appointed by the governor and represent the governor's office and relevant interest groups. They may also contain key legislators and distinguished private citizens. Commission recommendations usually support the policy direction the governor wants to take: After all, it is the governor who created the commission. Because the commission works over several months, it is quite likely that it will attract media attention, which also may create some public support for its final product. In addition, members of the commission can be helpful in lobbying for legislative approval of the recommendations. The commission approach sounds easy, but it takes a skillful governor to balance the membership so that it is not viewed as a group that will simply get out the rubber stamp and "approve" everything the governor wants. If this is the case, the commission will be viewed as too one-sided, and it will be of little help in gaining legislative support of the governor's ideas. Rosenthal notes that commissions were popular in many public education reforms in the 1980s. Bill Clinton, as governor of Arkansas, used recommendations from a legislatively created committee on educational standards, chaired by his wife, Hillary Rodham Clinton, to pass a tax increase to pay for improvements in primary and secondary education.[32]

Power of Publicity

Governors have the power of publicity—the ability to command broad attention.[33] In today's media-conscious world, political leaders must communicate with people through the media, particularly television. Here, the governor has an advantage over the legislature because the governor is a single person and is much easier for the media to focus on. The legislature, with a presiding officer for each chamber and a large number of committee chairs, is simply more difficult to report on. The knowledge that almost anything a governor says will be picked up by the media can help governors develop public support for their proposals.

John G. Rowland, governor of Connecticut (1995–), after only three months in office was called a master of the media by supporters and critics. Rowland makes himself readily available to the media, schedules news conferences and speeches late in the day so that they can be carried live on the evening television news shows at 5:30, and usually stays to do live interviews for the 6:00 news. He has taken on one of Connecticut's major newspapers, *The Hartford Courant,* by telling voters not to believe what it reports. Rowland plans to communicate his conservative views through other media such as television, where it is easier to talk directly to the voters.[34]

The power of publicity is similar to the power of initiation in that it sounds easy to do. Every governor should simply go directly to the public and, with public backing, get everything he or she wants through the legislature. But it is not that easy, even if governors have the requisite communication skills. Rosenthal cautions that governors cannot "make use of this power on each and every issue; to do so would be self-defeating, for at some point they would no longer be taken seriously by the press or public."[35] Governors cannot continuously try to drum up public support and expect that the public will always respond.

Power of Party

In a manner similar to the president, all governors are party leaders, though not in the sense that they occupy a formal position in their party's organization. Rather, they are the informal head of their party by virtue of the fact that they occupy the highest elected position in the state. At one time governors working with the chairperson of their state party could maintain **party discipline** in the legislature through the use of patronage appointments to fill state jobs and the promise of help from the party in primary and general elections. But those days are long gone in most states: Patronage appointments are fewer, and candidates frequently run for the legislature without the help of anyone in their party.

Still, party leadership is of some importance to a governor. Legislators are more likely to support governors of their own party and oppose governors who belong to the other party. Members of the party share a common association, frequently share similar ideas on the role of government, and sometimes share specific policy preferences.[36] Even with more and more legislative candidates running their own campaigns, a governor who runs strongly at the top of the ticket in the general election can pull some of the party's candidates along to victory. And after the election is over, legislators in the governor's party have some incentive to support the governor's proposals so that he or she is able to do something other than squabble with the legislature, which will drive down the governor's popularity and could harm the reelection chances of the legislators as well as the governor. It is in their interests to have their governor look good to the public. On the other hand, if the governor's popularity drops, party support can quickly erode.

SUMMARY

The importance of governors in the making of state policy has grown steadily during the twentieth century. Many governors deserve the name of policy innovator because they bring about significant change in policies in their states and even affect the direction of change followed by governors of other states.

Governors are primarily white males, with diversity coming from the election of a few women rather than members of minority groups. Governors usually have served in other elected positions before their first election to the governor's office, although a number of "outsiders" with no prior political experience have succeeded in winning the office. Incumbent governors running for reelection will probably win, but because voters are more critical of their performance than they are of, for example, incumbent

U.S. senators, they are more likely to vote for challengers to governors than challengers to senators.

All governors perform roles that make them official spokespersons for their states, commanders of their states' National Guard units, and managers of administrative agencies in the executive branch.

Today's governors have considerable formal powers, including control over preparing the state's budget, the authority to veto bills passed by the legislature, and, in many states, the ability to veto specific items in appropriation bills. Still, for governors to have their greatest impact on state policies they need the support of members of the state legislature. To succeed in this task, governors must use their informal powers: initiation, publicity, and party.

KEY TERMS

Administrative efficiency A twentieth-century reform that seeks to concentrate executive power in the hands of state governors by reducing and consolidating executive branch agencies and by giving the governor power to appoint administrators to head the newly formed agencies.

Amendatory veto An alternative to vetoing a bill that permits governors to return the bill to the legislature with suggested amendments. If the legislature agrees to the amendments, the bill will become law. It is used in only seven states.

Appointing power A formal power of the governor's office that measures whether a governor alone can name persons to head important agencies in the executive branch or whether someone else such as the legislature must be consulted.

Budgetary power A formal power of the governor that measures a governor's control over the budget process, especially the preparation of the budget.

Cabinet A form of executive branch organization used in many states today. Authority and responsibility are concentrated in the hands of the governor. The governor appoints department secretaries, who individually administer a department and collectively advise the governor.

Executive budget A budget that is prepared by the governor or officials appointed by the governor. This budget will be submitted to the state legislature for its approval.

Formal powers Gubernatorial powers that have a legal basis; that is, they can be found in a state's constitution or statutes. The degree to which a governor can control the budgetary process is an example of a formal power.

Informal powers Gubernatorial powers based on skill in negotiating, bargaining, building political support, dealing with party members in the legislature, and communicating to the public. Informal powers are not found in constitutional or statutory law.

Item veto A power possessed by most governors that allows them to veto a section or item in an appropriation bill but enables the rest of the bill to become law.

Jacksonian democracy era A period associated with the election of Andrew Jackson as president in 1828 and marked by an increase in democratic procedures, including universal male suffrage, direct election of many public officials, and short terms of office.

Lame duck Generally used to refer to an elected official who is nearing the end of his or her term of office and is not running for reelection. Earlier use was more limited in terms of the time period during which an elected official was considered a lame duck, specifically the time between the election at which an incumbent does not run or is not reelected and the day he or she actually leaves office.

Long ballot A ballot that has a large number of offices to be filled. It emerged during the Jacksonian democracy era when many state offices in the executive branch were filled by popular election.

Party discipline A high percentage of legislators voting with their party on roll call votes. Party discipline can help governors enact their legislative programs, but is more difficult to maintain today than in the past.

Postaudit A check, usually by the state auditor, to see if state agencies have spent money as intended by the legislature.

Preaudit Approval of expenditures, usually by the controller, before they are made.

Retrospective voting Basing a vote for governor on how well the state's economy performed under the incumbent governor.

Tenure potential A formal power of the governor that measures how long it is possible for a person to stay in the governor's office. A short term of office and restrictions on the number of reelections permitted reduce tenure potential.

Veto When a governor prevents a bill from becoming law by not signing it. The unsigned bill is returned to the legislature with the governor's objections. If an extraordinary majority agrees, veto can be overridden.

Veto power A formal power of governors that measures the extent to which they can reject bills and appropriation items that have passed the legislature.

REFERENCES

1 Larry Sabato, *Goodbye to Good-Time Charlie: The American Governorship Transformed,* 2d ed. (Washington, D.C.: CQ Press, 1983), pp. 5–7.

2 These include Eric B. Herzik and Brent W. Brown, *Gubernatorial Leadership and State Policy* (New York: Greenwood Press, 1991); and Marshall Kaplan and Sue O'Brien, *The Governors and the New Federalism* (Boulder, Colo.: Westview Press, 1991).

3 David Osborne, *Laboratories of Democracy* (Boston: Harvard Business School Press, 1990).

4 Thad Beyle, "The Governor as Innovator in the Federal System," *Publius* (Summer 1988), p. 152.

5 This box is based on Kaplan and O'Brien, *Governors,* pp. 23–25.

6 Ibid., p. 28.

7 Samuel K. Gove, "Illinois: Jim Edgar, the New Governor from the Old Party," in *Governors and Hard Times,* Thad Beyle, ed. (Washington, D.C.: CQ Press, 1992), pp. 108–109.

8 Thad L. Beyle, "The Governors, 1992–93," *The Book of the States 1994–95* (Lexington, Ky.: Council of State Governments, 1995), p. 38.

9 The term *newly elected governors* excludes incumbent governors who were reelected. It includes governors elected for the first time and former governors, that is, those who have been governor but were not an incumbent governor during this time period.

10 Ruth S. Jones and Katheryn A. Lehman, "Arizona: The CEO Approach of J. Fife Symington III," in *Governors and Hard Times,* Thad Beyle, ed. (Washington, D.C.: CQ Press, 1992) p. 33.

11 Peverill Squire and Christina Fastnow, "Comparing Gubernatorial and Senatorial Elections," *Political Research Quarterly* (September 1994), pp. 703–720.
12 Thad L. Beyle, "The Governors, 1992–93," p. 36.
13 Mark E. Tompkins, "Have Gubernatorial Elections Become More Distinctive Contests?" *Journal of Politics* 50 (1988), pp. 192–205.
14 Lonna Rae Atkeson and Randall W. Partin, "Economic and Referendum Voting: A Comparison of Gubernatorial and Senatorial Elections," *American Political Science Review* 89 (March 1995), pp. 99–107.
15 Neil Cornish, "A Drive for Jobs," *Wilmington News-Journal,* March 30, 1995, p. 1.
16 James K. Conant, "Executive Branch Reorganization in the States, 1965–1991," *The Book of the States 1992–93* (Lexington, Ky.: Council of State Governments, 1993), pp. 64–73.
17 Keon S. Chi, "Trends in Executive Reorganization," *The Journal of State Government* 72 (April–June 1992), p. 34.
18 Martha Wagner Weinberg, *Managing the State* (Cambridge, Mass.: MIT Press, 1977), pp. 6, 21–23.
19 Ibid., p. 36.
20 Daniel G. Cox, "Second Thoughts about the Second Banana," *State Government News* 37 (September 1994), pp. 29–33.
21 Ibid.
22 Joseph A. Schlesinger, "The Politics of the Executive," in Herbert Jacob and Kenneth N. Vines, eds., *Politics in the American States,* 2d ed. (Boston, Mass.: Little, Brown, 1971), pp. 222–234.
23 "Tommy Thompson," by Norman Atkins, *New York Times Magazine,* January 15, 1995, p. 25.
24 Ibid.
25 Useful essays on the item veto at the state level and arguments for and against its adoption at the national level are contained in *Congressional Digest* 65 (February 1993).
26 Robert D. Reischauer, "Should Congress Grant the President Line Item Veto or Expanded Rescission Authority? Con," *Congressional Digest* 65 (February 1993), p. 57.
27 Alan Rosenthal, *Governors and Legislatures: Contending Powers* (Washington, D.C.: CQ Press, 1990), p. 9.
28 Marina Sarris, "Smoking Deal Eases Ban for Bars, Hotels," *Baltimore Sun,* March 28, 1995, p. 1A.
29 Thad L. Beyle, "Enhancing Executive Leadership in the States," *State and Local Government Review* 27 (Winter 1995), p. 28.
30 Rosenthal, *Governors and Legislatures,* pp. 6–9, 17–20, 24–27.
31 Robert E. Crew, Jr., "Understanding Gubernatorial Behavior: A Framework for Analysis," in *Governors and Hard Times,* Thad Beyle, ed. (Washington, D.C.: CQ Press, 1992) p. 21.
32 Rosenthal, *Governors and Legislatures,* pp. 110–112.
33 Ibid., p. 25.
34 Jonathan Rabinovitz, "Governor Styles Himself as a Regular Guy," *The New York Times,* March 19, 1995, p. 44.
35 Rosenthal, *Governors and Legislatures,* pp. 26–27.
36 Ibid., pp. 18–19.

7

STATE AND URBAN BUREAUCRACY

Tom Cheek/Stock, Boston

STATE AND LOCAL GOVERNMENT EMPLOYMENT

As discussed in Chapter 1, the scope of state government activities has increased greatly in recent years. As a result, state and local payrolls and numbers of employees now far outstrip those of the federal government. In 1992, state governments employed about 4.6 million workers, compared to 3 million federal civilian employees and 11 million local employees. Nearly one-quarter of state employees worked part-time.[1] About 40 percent of state workers are in higher education, and over one-half the local employment is in elementary and secondary education (see Tables 7-1 and 7-2). State employment increased about 1.5 million from 1982 to 1992, with the largest jump (90 percent) coming in correctional employees. During that same time federal employment remained nearly constant (see Figure 7-1). This expansion has, of course, placed increasing burdens of responsibility on governors, who historically have been denied strong formal powers as chief administrators. States have responded by giving governors control of budget preparation and by increasing gubernatorial power to appoint and remove officials.

Financial hardships in recent years have placed severe burdens on most state bureaucracies. Budget cuts have led to employee layoffs and staff reductions. In the face of a loss of federal funding and opposition to tax increases, there has been a demand for increased services to deal with problems such as crime, drug abuse, and environmental protection. As a result, state bureaucracies have been required to do more even though their budgets have stayed the same or have been cut.[2]

State, city, and county administration is closely tied to decisions made in Washington. Some state agencies receive over 50 percent of their funds from the federal government, and few do not get any federal money. As noted in Chapter 2, even while federal funding has declined in the past decade, mandates from Washington have

TABLE 7-1 TOTAL STATE GOVERNMENT EMPLOYMENT: OCTOBER 1992, 1982

	1992 Total employment	Percent of total	1992 Change 1982–92	% Change 1982–92
Total state	4,594,635	100.00%	850,570	22.72%
Higher education	1,909,022	41.55%	409,489	27.31%
Hospitals	554,560	12.07%	(9,712)	–1.72%
Health	166,888	3.63%	49,413	42.06%
Social insurance admin.	118,143	2.57%	6,193	5.53%
Highways	261,362	5.69%	17,003	6.96%
Police	86,606	1.88%	10,514	13.82%
Corrections	347,985	7.57%	164,781	89.94%
Natural resources	164,333	3.58%	9,216	5.94%
Financial admin.	150,612	3.28%	32,755	27.79%
Judicial and legal	113,548	2.47%	38,883	52.08%
Other government	51,753	1.13%	8,649	20.07%

Source: The Book of States, 1994–95 (Lexington, KY: Council of State Govenments, 1994), p.436.

TABLE 7-2 TOTAL LOCAL GOVERNMENT EMPLOYMENT: OCTOBER 1992, 1982

	1992 Total employment	Percent of total	Change 1982–92	% Change 1982–92
Total local	11,103,221	100.00%	1,854,140	20.05%
Elementary and secondary education	5,727,103	51.58%	996,018	21.05%
Police	683,468	6.16%	89,520	15.07%
Fire	343,985	3.10%	46,149	15.49%
Corrections	194,697	1.75%	93,184	91.80%
Highways	299,763	2.70%	18,013	6.39%
Hospitals	608,476	5.48%	9,403	1.57%
Parks and recreation	275,600	2.48%	64,673	30.66%
Judicial and legal	209,295	1.88%	74,630	55.42%
Health	214,288	1.93%	83,880	64.32%
Utilities	430,459	3.88%	68,482	18.92%
Water supply	155,988	1.40%	29,489	23.31%
Electric power	78,451	0.71%	12,059	18.16%
Gas supply	10,561	0.10%	1,465	16.11%
Transit	185,459	1.67%	25,469	15.92%

Source: The Book of the States, 1994–95 (Lexington, Ky.: Council of State Governments, 1994), p. 436.

increased. In addition, the expansion of block grants has given state officials more responsibility for administering programs. For example, in 1995 Congress transferred nearly the entire federal welfare program to the states. The new federalism legacy of the 1980s is that more programs are provided by and funded by state and local governments. As federal funds have decreased, state grants to local governments have increased, and this means that states must devote more attention to monitoring how local governments spend money.

THE NATURE OF BUREAUCRACY

Bureaucracy refers to large, complex organizations characterized by a chain of command, a hierarchy of offices with specific tasks, formal rules of behavior, and job appointment based on some form of competitive examination. This general definition applies to all levels of government, as well as to other entities such as churches and universities that have a hierarchy of offices.

Like most words, *bureaucracy* has a neutral meaning, here stemming from its connection to bureaus, or departments ("desks" in French). Yet even a brief dictionary explanation of the term may refer to "inflexible routine" and to "red tape." Many readers will quickly connect bureaucrats to state motor vehicle departments or college registrars' offices. After waiting in long lines in those offices we often are frustrated by clerks who, because they are "just going by the book," refuse to cut us any slack in

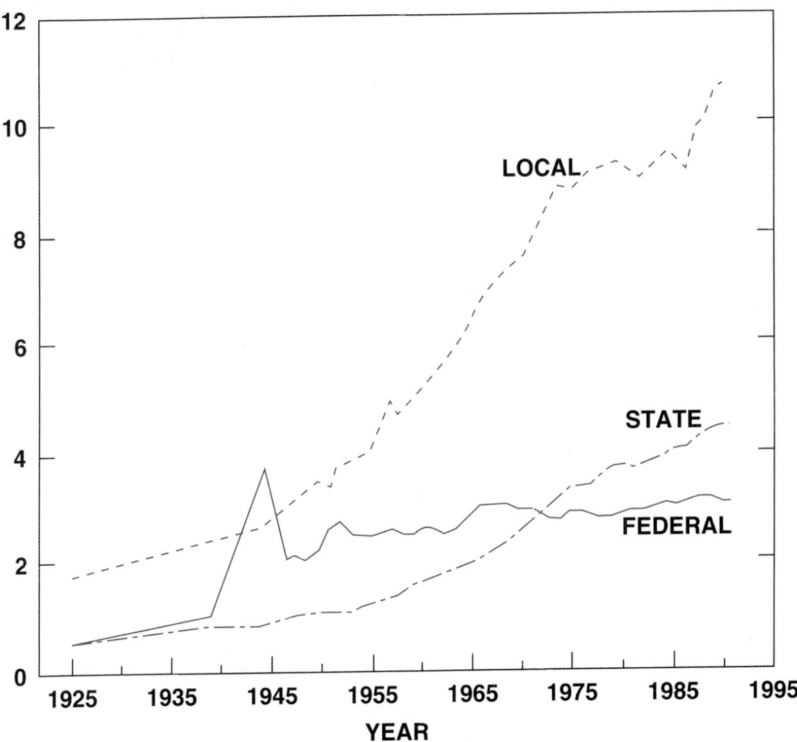

FIGURE 7-1 Number of federal, state, and local government employees, 1929–1991. [1929–1944, 1949, 1952, 1954, 1959, 1964, 1969–1988: U.S. Advisory Commission on Intergovernmental Relations, *Significant Features of Fiscal Federalism, 1990,* vol. 2 (Washington, D.C.: U.S. Advisory Commission on Intergovernmental Relations, 1990), p. 177; 1989–1990: *1992,* p. 230; other years: U.S. Bureau of the Census, *Historical Statistics of the United States,* Series Y189–198 (Washington, D.C.: U.S. Government Printing Office, 1975), p. 1100.]

complete compliance with their regulations. Of more serious consequence, ethnic and racial minorities complain that government bureaucrats seldom understand their needs and thus they are not responsive to their problems.

Lest we become unfairly critical of the system, we need to remember that in most instances the public is reasonably well satisfied with their bureaucratic encounters.[3] We also need to remember that a century ago bureaucracy meant something positive.[4] The creation of bureaucratic government was in large part a response to the mismanagement of cities by political machines (see Chapter 9). Bosses distributed jobs and public contracts to their political friends, and they often ignored the basic needs of growing cities, such as sanitation and transportation. Graft was commonplace when machines demanded a percentage of all contracts awarded by the city.

The *Progressive movement* of the late nineteenth century sought to rid cities of these ills through a series of reforms. To lessen the effects of *patronage* they created *civil service* systems with written examinations and protections against arbitrary firing. To weaken the political power of bosses they reduced elective offices with the "short ballot," which helped concentrate authority. To further integrate the executive branch, to insulate government from politics, and to have cities run more like businesses, they invented the city manager form of government. In other words, they put in place a bureaucratic model.

Classic View of Bureaucracy

As classically explained by German sociologist Max Weber, the "ideal" type of organization has the following characteristics:[5]

1 Hierarchy
2 Recruitment and promotion based on competence
3 Use of rules and regulations
4 Fixed areas of official jurisdiction
5 Development of a career system
6 Impersonality in the performance of duties

Hierarchy usually is illustrated by a pyramid (see Figure 7-2) in which there are a large number of workers at the lower levels who are directed by orders from the top so that there is a unity of command.[6] Rules are formal (written) and informal (handed down by custom among the lower-level bureaucrats). At their best, rules treat everyone "equally" under the law; at their worst, rules may be used as an excuse not to comply with a request that would inconvenience bureaucrats.

Problems with the Bureaucratic Model

In a hierarchy (and most organizations are hierarchical) there is specialization of knowledge and specialization by function. Authority is to be commensurate with

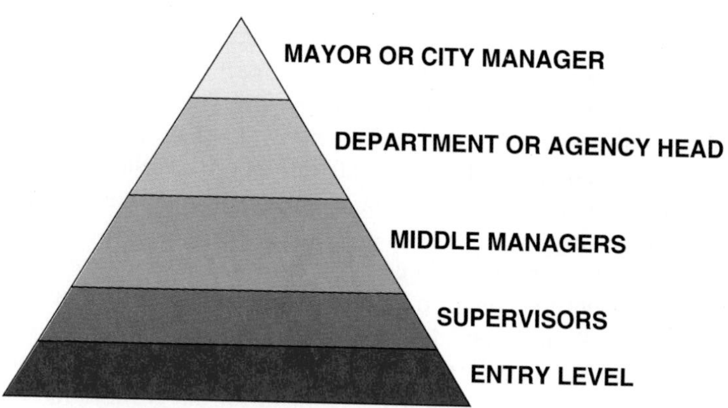

FIGURE 7-2 Hierarchy of city government.

responsibility. In large organizations virtually no one understands all facets of activities, and within departments personnel perform specialized tasks. Critics such as Osborne and Graebler believe this leads to a lack of overall coordination, and it often means that clients face a maze of offices in which rigid rules make it difficult to deliver services that match the needs of clients.

Development of a career system refers to the professionalization of government bureaucrats. They are recruited through a merit system and often have received advanced training or education before they are hired. Once on the job they join professional associations and they develop a set of expectations about how their jobs are performed. In government bureaucracies professionalization may lead to a middle-class bias that makes it difficult for officials to understand the problems of the poor and racial minorities. In any event, bureaucracies tend toward the impersonal delivery of services in which any special client needs are subordinated to the rules and regulations of the organization.

Osborne and Graebler note that for many years the bureaucratic model worked well. Considering what they replaced, government bureaucracies provided a sense of fairness and equity. Political favoritism was removed from service delivery, and basic urban facilities—such as roads, bridges, and sewers—were constructed in growing cities.[7] The system was especially successful in the stressful years of the Depression and World War II. Goals were clear, tasks were straightforward, and most people were willing to work as cogs in giant machines. As the United States changed to a **postindustrial society,** there were more demands for flexibility in service delivery and there were calls for citizen empowerment. As we will see later in this chapter, dissatisfaction with the bureaucratic model has led to calls to reinvent government by empowering communities to take charge of their government rather than to be served by it.

REORGANIZATION OF GOVERNMENT

Despite recent changes, governors continue to be limited as administrators by the fragmented nature of state government. Most states failed to develop well-organized administrative structures because of the piecemeal growth of bureaucracy. As new functions were given to the states, the easiest response was to create a new state agency as visible proof to concerned citizens and interest groups that the state was "doing something" about the problem. Under these circumstances, the duties of each agency were not clearly defined and the jurisdiction of new agencies often overlapped with that of already established agencies. Large cities had similar problems of fragmented organization. However, city reform came earlier than did state reform because of the adoption of strong-mayor–council and council-manager plans at the beginning of this century.

Because of the desire to take politics out of state government, many agencies were placed under the control of boards and commissions that acted independently of the governor. Agencies and departments performing similar tasks were nevertheless separated from one another with no one to serve as a coordinator. Communication between agencies was limited, and it was difficult for the governor or the legislature to know what the agencies were doing or who was responsible for their actions. Mergers were opposed by bureaucrats who sought to protect their jobs and by interest groups that were being aided by agencies they had helped create. At their peak in the 1950s, many states had more than 100 boards, commissions, and departments. There were even stories of dead men being appointed to serve on obscure boards.

The movement for administrative reform began in the 1890s but did not take hold in state government until after 1920, when administrative reorganization in Illinois under Governor Frank Lowden became known around the country. State commissions on **reorganization** were appointed in several states, although there were few instances of substantial reform. The basic goal of the early reformers was to reduce the number of agencies and bring them more directly under the control of the governor. There was a general attempt to upgrade the bureaucracy by creating civil service commissions for merit appointment and by developing the executive budget. Following World War II and the report of the **Hoover Commission** on the federal level, there was a revival of interest in structural reorganization.

Comprehensive reorganization has occurred recently in Iowa and South Carolina. For example, in 1993 South Carolina reduced the number of state agencies from seventy-nine to seventeen and eliminated many boards and commissions.[8] Typically, reform has been more incremental, with states collapsing boards and commissions into a cabinet model similar to that used by the president (see Table 7-3). Currently, three-fourths of governors have cabinets, which range in size from six to thirty members.

The state of Ohio in 1994 had over 450 separate boards and commissions, an increase of over 60 percent since 1980. They included the Underground Parking Commission and the Board of Embalmers and Funeral Directors. Soon after he became governor, George Voinovich proposed the elimination of twenty-three state boards and commissions, and he proposed a committee to review the continuation of existing agencies. One of his targets was the Amusement Ride Safety Advisory Board, whose existence was immediately defended by the state legislator whose bill had created the board.

In the past twenty years reorganization has been the most common response to correcting the problems of bureaucracy. Political scientist Richard C. Elling speaks of the "religion of reorganization" in which twenty-six states completed organizational restructuring from 1965 to 1991.[9] Typically states consolidate several similar agencies into one larger functional unit, such as transportation or welfare. The goal is to reduce duplication of services and to centralize administration in the hands of fewer department heads. In turn, governors are strengthened by giving them the power to appoint the heads of these reorganized superagencies. Reformers contend that these changes will bring about more effective service delivery and that they will increase the accountability of bureaucrats to the public. As Elling notes, reorganization usually is supported by governors, the media, and "good-government" groups that long have criticized the lack of businesslike practices in government.

Because state administration is a highly *politicized* process, these apparently logical goals of centralization have met with strong resistance in virtually every state. Interest groups often prefer separation because of the strong control they have been able to maintain over state agencies. State legislators are able to use separate agencies to their political advantage, and they are inherently suspicious of moves to strengthen the gov-

TABLE 7-3 STATE OF OHIO CABINET DEPARTMENT HEADS, 1996

The director of administrative services
The director of aging
The director of agriculture
The director of office of budget and management
The director of commerce
The director of development
The administrator of employment services
The director of environmental protection agency
The director of health
The director of highway safety
The director of human services
The director of insurance
The director of mental health
The director of mental retardation and developmental disabilities
The director of natural resources
The chairman of public utilities commission
The director of rehabilitation and correction
The tax commissioner
The director of transportation
The director of youth commission

The superintendent of public instruction, the administrative head of another major department within the executive branch, is appointed by and serves at the pleasure of the State Board of Education.

The appointive powers of the governor are extensive, including not only the heads of the departments listed above, but also the adjutant general and members of most of the boards and commissions provided by statute, and some heads of divisions within departments as well. In some instances the advice and consent of the senate is required for confirmation of the governor's appointees.

ernor. Finally, by requiring specific allocation of matching funds to support categorical grants, federal grants-in-aid have encouraged separate agencies.

Reorganization seldom has resulted in saving states money.[10] However, reorganizers argue that the main benefits will be more efficiency and more effective service delivery. Yet even here studies have shown that some services are provided best by small agencies in which a particular function is not subordinated to the main activities of the larger department. Even collegial administration (organizations headed by boards or commissions) may be as effective as single-headed departments. After his study of Texas, where collegial administration is very common, Charles Goodsell concluded that collegial administration has two major positive justifications.[11] It can improve the demographic and geographic representation of administration, and it has the ability to absorb political heat because of its representativeness. Goodsell believes that both legislators and career bureaucrats can "get off the hook" from constituent or interest-group demands by referring critics to the independence of boards or commissions. Governors can sidestep attacks by arguing that a problem is out of their hands.

Clearly, reorganization does not always lead to greater efficiency or accountability. Centralization of authority may not work well for all organizations.[12] Still, the extreme decentralization of state government, often bordering on chaos, has led to a lack of accountability, and to the extent that problems remain, good-government groups will continue to push for reorganization. Politically, it is in the best interest of governors to be able to consolidate their power through reorganization plans.

PERSONNEL PRACTICES

The *personnel systems* of agencies also affect their culture and expectations of employee behavior. Some agencies may discourage awarding middle-management positions to outsiders, while others encourage transfers with experience in other types of organizations. When there is a strong preference to promote from within the agency, the bureaucrats who attain supervisory posts tend to be rigid and less open to new ideas than are relative newcomers to the agency.

Personnel practices also include determination of the kinds of people selected for government positions. Since the 1960s, the use of affirmative action programs has led to increased hiring of women and minorities in many government departments. In the past, ethnic background and/or political party connections played a major role in creating informal hiring qualifications that effectively screened applicants for jobs in many city departments.

An agency's culture (and its policy implementation) is influenced by the **professional ideology** of its employees. For example, social workers continue to place a strong emphasis on working with individual clients, whereas reformers contend that group political action is a more effective way to deal with problems of the poor. In addition, professional codes of conduct may serve as a check on the abuse of administrative power.

As in any organization, newly hired employees in government agencies undergo a period of socialization, in which they learn how they are expected to act within the framework of their agency's culture. Those who deviate from established norms will usually encounter difficulty in working with their peers, and they may be denied promotions by their superiors. Although some agencies are program-oriented and encourage innovation, most are conservative in their opposition to change.

Top-level bureaucrats frequently influence policymaking because of their expertise and professionalism. Bureaucrats testify before legislative committees, and they meet informally with legislators to help draft legislation. However, their most significant role in the policy process is in implementation. Particularly in large executive establishments, bureaucratic autonomy is increased because chief executives simply cannot know what each agency is doing. Bureaucrats may implement orders in a very formalistic manner without any personal enthusiasm; they may delay implementation by sticking closely to all administrative regulations; or they may refuse outright to follow legislative or executive directions. As a result, reluctant or hostile administrators can create major difficulties for governors and mayors, and they can alter substantially the intention of legislators.

As will be discussed in Chapter 9, urban political machines used patronage jobs as an effective means to maintain political control. In Chicago, for example, thousands of city employees could be counted on to work for the machine in order to ensure the continuation of their jobs. Of course, those city employees had relatives who would vote for the machine's candidates.

Merit Systems

The value of patronage began to decline as urban residents progressed to better paying jobs in private business and when the reform movement began to press for a **merit system** of civil service. Reformers argued that if workers were appointed by civil service commissions that developed competitive examinations, the system would be insulated from partisan politics and it would lead to "a competent corps of politically neutral civil servants."[13]

Elling notes that states moved slowly to implement civil service reform. It was not until the late 1930s that states were required by the federal government to put employees whose salaries were partially paid by federal grant funds under merit arrangements. Where machines remained in operation, cities moved even more slowly to institute merit appointment.

As noted earlier, civil service systems have been broadly criticized in recent years. While the bureaucratic model worked well to limit specific abuses fifty years ago, it has created new problems for contemporary government. In the 1930s government employees were not unionized and courts had not acted to protect workers from wrongful discharge. Much of what civil service was designed to prevent has been ruled illegal or made unlikely to happen by collective bargaining agreements.

Osborne and Graebler contend that civil service rules can hamstring most personnel managers.[14] Unlike private businesses where interviews and references are used to make hiring decisions, governments often must take the person with the highest score or one of the top three scorers on written examinations, even though they may otherwise be unsuited for the position. Because the process takes so long, the high scorers may accept another job during the six months or so that it takes between testing and hiring. Job classifications, which set pay levels, are determined by how long employees have worked, not by how well they have performed. When employees reach the top of their pay range, they cannot earn more money unless they are promoted into a new classification.

It is extremely difficult to fire government employees because of the need to document poor performance and the lengthy appeals process. For example, *The New York Times* reports that it costs about $200,000, including arbitration fees and the salary of the accused, and it takes an average of 476 days in New York state to fully prosecute a teacher charged with misconduct.[15] Because civil service employees usually can bump those with less seniority, when layoffs occur, it is younger workers who lose their jobs.

Many civil service problems are being addressed by states and cities. The testing process has been streamlined. Questions have been revised to relate more closely to job skills, and departments have been given more freedom to choose among high-scoring candidates. Several states have established "broadband" job classifications in which hundreds of categories are greatly reduced with distinctions made between levels of expertise, or bands. As part of the reorganization process, management of the civil service system in most states has been shifted from semi-independent commissions to personnel departments whose heads are appointed by the governor. Similar to changes in the federal government, several states have established a senior executive level in which employees are given less job security but their pay and promotion are based on merit performance. Civil service systems have been abolished in some cities, and the state of Texas has never had a civil service system.

As with university professors' tenure, critics of civil service suggest that the system perpetuates mediocrity and makes it nearly impossible to fire so-called deadwood. In fact, the percentage of employees fired by governments is about the same as among private industrial employers. Still, stories often appear in the media about incompetent government workers whose continuance on the public payroll seems to defy all logic.

Collective Bargaining

An easy explanation is to blame unions for protecting the incompetent. While public employee unions clearly seek to protect job security, **collective bargaining** contracts explain only a small part of the problem since about 60 percent of city employees and 70 percent of state workers are not members of unions. The major reason it is difficult to fire public employees is that they are protected by a wide range of constitutional guarantees.[16] Oftentimes management is at fault for failing to document an employee's performance, and there is good reason to guard against arbitrary or capricious decisions to fire people. Several states, including New York where public employee unions are very strong, have established "expedited arbitration" procedures in which disputes are heard within thirty days of a firing and an arbitrator makes a decision immediately.

While only about 10 percent of government employees were unionized in 1960, nearly one-third were members of collective bargaining units by the mid-1970s. About 60 percent of police were unionized by 1975. These increases occurred because of employee demand, weak employer resistance, and the passage of protective legislation.[17] Public unionization has leveled off since the mid-1970s as a result of changes in the distribution of public employees, more management resistance, and a decrease in interunion competition in organizing campaigns. Both public and private unions faced major obstacles in the 1980s. The firing of striking federal air traffic controllers by the Reagan administration encouraged antiunion sentiment. In the 1990s financial difficulties have led some public unions to agree to wage concessions in return for job security.

One result of the increase in union membership in the 1970s was that strikes or slowdowns by city workers occurred in areas where they previously were viewed as illegitimate by public employees. While unions have encouraged militancy in demands for higher salaries, they also have reinforced the natural inclination of bureaucrats to support the status quo. Unions seek to ensure that department routines and regulations, particularly in dealing with personnel problems (hiring, grievance procedures, and dismissal), remain unchanged.

As in the private sector, a group of government employees votes to unionize and usually affiliates with a national union. For example, the police in Ada, Ohio, voted 4 to 1 in 1993 to unionize and to affiliate with the Fraternal Order of Police. The bargaining unit then negotiates a master contract that spells out such matters as pay, hours, fringe benefits, and grievance procedures. Most agreements stress seniority rights, meaning that longtime employees are protected from staff reductions.

Since the mid-1980s about forty states have engaged in some form of negotiations with their employees, but serious collective bargaining is followed only in about half the states. Unionization is most likely to occur in Northeastern and Great Lakes states, where private sector unions are strongest. In Connecticut and New York, more than 80 percent of state employees are in bargaining units. At the other extreme, there are about a dozen states (all in the South and West) where no state employees are in bargaining units. The most prominent organizations are the National Education Association; the American Federation of Teachers; and the American Federation of State, County, and Municipal Employees, which ranks second behind the Teamsters as the largest labor union in the United States. Organizational activities have been particularly successful in large cities in recent years. Just over 50 percent of all city firefighters belong to unions, and nearly 30 percent of public hospital workers are unionized. As will be seen in Chapter 12, the demands of public employee unions in New York City played a significant role in the city's financial crisis of 1975–1976. New York City, however, is an unusual case. Evidence across the country suggests that unionization increases wages of state employees about 5 percent and that unionization and merit principles are not incompatible. Although strikes by public employees are illegal in most states, job actions have occurred in many cities when groups such as firefighters and police officers have "sick-ins" (e.g., cases of the "blue flu") as a means of expressing their demands on city officials. In many cases, state law stipulates that public employee labor disputes must go to arbitration.

Women and Minorities

Merit systems and collective bargaining agreements can affect gender and race discrimination to the extent that they protect the status quo through the seniority system and by strict reliance on test scores for hiring. While the Supreme Court has upheld seniority-based layoffs even when they adversely affect women and minorities (*Firefighters Local 1784* v. *Stotts,* 1984), it also has upheld affirmative action plans in which women with lower test scores than men have been promoted in order to have more women in job classifications where they historically have been significantly underrepresented (*Johnson* v. *Transportation Agency, Santa Clara County, California,* 1987).

Stratification of women and minorities in lower-level positions has been a persistent problem in government employment. Even when members of these groups get top administrative positions, it often is in a narrow range of social service agencies. While the impact of affirmative action on employment patterns has been modest, changes also are occurring as government agencies alter their recruiting procedures and as they promote more women and minorities to middle management positions.

Public sector unions in health care and clerical services, where there are high percentages of women, have been strong supporters of **comparable worth.** Because women often have been limited to lower-level job classifications, advocates of comparable worth argue that pay ranges should be equalized for jobs that are of equal (comparable) worth to the organization. For example, it might be argued that the skill and educational requirements of nurses give them a worth to the employer comparable to that of accountants. This differs from the widely accepted concept of "equal pay for equal work" because comparable worth is based on the proposition that women have been channeled into different jobs than men and that those positions have consistently been undervalued by employers.

Critics of comparable worth contend that the concept is too vague to be workable and that it would undercut traditional market forces. Federal courts have not used comparable worth to support equity in pay disputes. However, a handful of states have adopted comparable worth plans for their employees. In a period of budget cuts, legislators are unlikely to approve plans that raise state payroll costs.

Changes in civil service procedures, implementation of affirmative action plans, political pressure for change, and the presence of more enlightened government managers have combined to increase the representativeness of state and local bureaucracy over the past twenty years. In fact, the bureaucracy long has included a much larger percentage of racial and ethnic minorities and women than is found in elected bodies.

OVERSIGHT OF THE BUREAUCRACY

Roles of Governors and Legislators

Governors are responsible for management of all state administrative agencies, but as we have noted, their power has been limited by a host of factors. These include a fragmented system of boards and commissions with independent administrators, civil service procedures that set hiring and firing guidelines, and the demands of public employee unions. As government grows, governors are limited by the sheer size of bureaucratic systems with thousands of employees. Elling notes that because state government is so large, governors must pick their spots to intervene.[18] Often intervention comes in agencies where some kind of crisis has occurred. Of course, this is not the ideal form of management. Governors have tried to anticipate problems better and manage more effectively by surrounding themselves with larger personal staffs and, as we have noted, by expanding the number of positions over which they have direct control by reorganization.

Legislators have struggled to keep up with the complexity of state administration and with growing staffs that enlarge gubernatorial administrative and political power. As in Congress, most legislative oversight is done by committees, and in large part, it is through the budgetary process. Legislators also oversee by means of the legislative veto, sunset laws, and review of administrative rules (see Chapter 5). As noted in the Scholarly Box, use of the legislative veto has declined following a Supreme Court decision in 1983. And, as we have noted, sunset laws have not been very effective.

Budgeting

State budget preparations operate in a manner similar to the congressional process. They are executive-centered with responsibility for formulation fixed in an office of budget and management, whose head is appointed by the governor. Governors form a budget as a spending and policy document and send it to the legislature for review and adoption. In recent years legislatures, like Congress, have added staff and have made

SCHOLARLY BOX

LEGISLATIVE VETO

Congress began to use the legislative veto in the 1930s. Its use expanded in the 1970s, and state legislatures increasingly implemented various forms of the process during the same period of time. The legislative veto permitted Congress to pass bills giving general powers to administrative agencies and then to review and veto the specific way in which those powers were implemented by bureaucrats. In some cases, passing vague laws allowed members of Congress to avoid political heat and later to veto action if it proved to be unpopular. A legislative veto could be put into effect by a majority vote of one house, by both houses, or by a single committee.

In a 1983 decision *(INS* v. *Chadha),* the Supreme Court said the legislative veto was unconstitutional because it violated the separation of powers between the legislative and executive branches. Since then Congress has devised several ways (quasi-legislative vetoes) that permit it to overrule administrative actions but still comply with the Court's directive that congressional policy directions be more explicit.

State legislatures have used a variety of means to exercise legislative vetoes.* Rosenthal reports that in Wisconsin standing committees can approve, object, or request changes in rules proposed by administrative agencies. If an agency refuses to comply, a standing committee takes the matter to a joint committee for review of the rules application. Decisions of the joint committee to overturn administrative actions are subject to a gubernatorial veto. In other states the objections of a joint committee alone can nullify, or veto, administrative rulings.

Legislative vetoes have been popular because legislators were concerned that administrators were using too much discretion in formulating rules and regulations. In effect, legislators believed administrators were making policy and this was leading to a loss of legislative control over the executive branch.

Governors have objected to the legislative veto, and suits asserting that the process violated separation of power clauses in state constitutions were filed before *Chadha* was decided in 1983. State courts often have sided with governors, saying that if legislators disapprove of administrative actions, they need to pass specific bills that set the guidelines they favor. In response, the use of the legislative veto has declined. Rosenthal reports that Connecticut and Iowa have approved constitutional amendments that authorize legislative vetoes if both houses act on the matter. In several other states such amendments, proposed by the legislature, have been defeated.

States have established a number of alternative ways to control administrative rule making. In some, the governor is required to approve regulations before they go into effect. In others, administrative review offices have been set up to check agency behavior. Such procedures seem to restrain administrative discretion, and they increase the legislature's involvement in administrative matters.

*See Alan Rosenthal, *Governors and Legislatures: Contending Powers* (Washington: Congressional Quarterly Press, 1990), pp. 182–186.

use of computerized information systems. Because of their skilled staff, many legislatures are able to develop independent sources of financial information.[19] As a result, appropriations committees and their subcommittees now are able to analyze governors' budgets much more carefully by using their own revenue projections. Hearings are held and negotiations proceed with the governor's office before the budget moves to the house and senate for approval.

Effective legislative or executive administrative oversight is strongly influenced by the type of budget process that the state employs. **Incremental budgeting**—the traditional system—provides little opportunity for overall review or program evaluation. Budgeting is based on last year's figures, which were the result of previous political compromises. Agencies make requests for a few new programs, and they routinely overstate the amount of money they need. Governors make some cuts and legislators cut some more. As a result, old programs are seldom reviewed, little innovation occurs, legislators can point to their efforts to keep spending down, and agencies usually get about what they need to run their programs.

In the 1960s, some states and cities attempted to adopt a **program-planning-budgeting system** (PPBS), in which expenditures are placed together in a comprehensive program package, such as improved environmental quality or the control and reduction of crime. Instead of having to justify specific line items in their budget requests (as in traditional budgeting), under PPBS departments are forced to justify appropriation requests in terms of program objectives. That is, they must link the political ends of their programs to economic means. In some cases, program performance is quantitatively assessed to determine the most effective use of money to attain program goals. Under such a system, there is continuous evaluation and feedback to measure the effectiveness of programs in meeting the needs of the public.

Program-planning-budgeting is a very time-consuming process, requiring accurate data on program efficiency and impact. In the highly political environment of state government, it faced strong opposition from legislators and from interest groups who benefited from incremental budgeting. Although no government has completely implemented PPBS, a majority of states continue to use some modified form of the process.

In spite of the failure to implement PPBS, the experiments with it have produced some valuable spin-off benefits to budgeting. One of the most publicized has been **zero-based budgeting** (ZBB), in which each department must justify all appropriations items each year. The budget is broken down into units, called decision packages, prepared by managers at each level, which cover every existing proposed activity of each department. This approach encourages greater policy orientation, because out-of-date programs are dropped instead of being continued as existing budget items that are not questioned once they become part of a department's established budget. In some cases, departments rank their programs in order of priority and set performance levels for all programs.

Even at its high point in the 1970s and early 1980s, ZBB was less widely adopted than program-planning-budgeting. It was used by Governor Jimmy Carter in Georgia, in Delaware and New Jersey, and in a number of cities, especially in the West. Like PPBS, ZBB continues to be used in modified forms. For example, the governor of Iowa in the early 1990s proposed a complete budget review of every department on a five-year cycle. Aaron Wildavsky noted that in all cases the "zero" is ignored and the base grows to 80 or 90 percent of the last year's budget.[20] As this happens, the process reverts to incremental budgeting. We will discuss other budget innovations in the concluding section of this chapter.

URBAN BUREAUCRACY

So far we have focused on the administration of state government and the roles of governors and legislators. However, much of what was said about the nature of bureaucracy and about personnel practices applies equally to state and local governments. We now turn to city government and the roles of mayors as chief executives.

As noted earlier, much of the impetus for reform and the move to bureaucratic government in the late nineteenth century was prompted by the abuses of urban political machines. However, we also have argued that the adoption of these reforms led to a number of unintended consequences, including an impersonal, middle-class bias in the delivery of government services. As a result, city residents found few bureaucrats who were responsive to their needs. Political scientist Theodore Lowi speaks of the "new machines"—powerful urban service bureaucracies protected by civil service rules, receiving substantial amounts of money from federal and state sources, and thus not responsible to elected city officials or to the general public.[21]

Control of urban government also is made difficult because many street-level bureaucrats have broad discretion in how they perform their jobs. Contrary to what the hierarchical model suggests, people at the bottom of the bureaucracy—those who deal directly with the public—effectively make policy by deciding how public services will be dispensed.[22] As Ross and Levine point out, because they often are understaffed and must make quick decisions, bureaucrats such as police officers and welfare workers often use shortcuts, including categorizing clients or rationing services to them. Police look for the "wrong" type of person in a neighborhood, and welfare clients often have to wait a long time before receiving services. Bureaucrats see clients in terms of group identification, while citizens seek personal attention to their problems.

The success of many urban programs rests with how well lower-level bureaucrats perform their jobs and how well their supervisors monitor their activities. Major problems include efficiency (how much it costs to produce a service), effectiveness (how well government is able to meet the objectives or goals of its programs), and equity (to what extent services are provided fairly to all residents). While it is easy to argue that poor and minority neighborhoods do not receive the same level of service delivery as more upscale areas, several studies indicate that age of buildings and density of population are more closely related to service delivery levels than racial or class characteristics.[23]

Criticism of service levels and budget cuts in recent years have led to a host of proposals for alternative ways to provide urban services. We turn to those in the conclusion of the chapter.

REINVENTING GOVERNMENT

Best-selling authors David Osborne and Ted Graebler point out that the last time we "reinvented" government in the United States was during the Progressive era early in this century and again in the New Deal of the 1930s. Earlier we evaluated the impact of Progressive reforms on state and local government. Now that we are in a *postindustrial,* knowledge-based, global economy, Osborne and Graebler believe it is time to make major changes in government at all levels.[24] They use the term **"entrepreneurial government"** to describe a new model that uses resources in different ways to maximize productivity and effectiveness. In this new order, the bureaucratic model would be replaced by more flexible, responsive organizations that empower citizens rather than serve them.

Entrepreneurial governments, which are operating to various degrees in many cities across the country, function on the basis of several main principles. In their ideal form, entrepreneurial governments act in the following ways. They encourage competition among service providers by privatizing services or contracting them out. They empower citizens by encouraging them to take control of services through such means as public housing resident advisory boards, ballot initiatives, and community-oriented policing. They focus on outcomes by creating goals for government and measuring how well agencies perform their tasks. (The box on pages 184–185 describes how a variety of organizations are listening to and responding to their customers.) They treat citizens as valued customers with individual needs. They earn money by charging fees or by ownership of businesses, such as cable television systems. They anticipate problems, believing that an ounce of prevention is worth a pound of cure. For example, they believe that fire departments should be rewarded more for fire prevention than for their fast response time after a fire occurs.

Privatization

The Progressives championed service delivery by bureaucracies as a means to eliminate the corruption of payoffs to political machines for contracts awarded by the city to private businesses and as a means to ensure that everyone was treated the same, rather than given preferential attention because of political connections. As a result, we created a series of government monopolies—schools, garbage collection, utilities—to avoid waste and duplication.

Even when they are not conscious of reinventing government, many communities have discovered they can save money when service providers compete for public business. As a result, **privatization** has become increasingly common in the 1990s. As explained by E. S. Savas, it can appear in several forms.[25] Perhaps the most familiar is contracting with private firms to perform a service previously done by government employees. This includes managing prisons, providing janitorial services, operating homeless shelters, and collecting taxes. Privatization also includes contracting with not-for-profit agencies to provide a service such as meals-on-wheels, forming neighborhood security patrols, selling off publicly owned businesses, and giving housing vouchers to the poor. Since competition is central to the ideas of Osborne and Graebler, privatization has been strongly associated with the reinventing government movement. In terms used by Osborne and Graebler, privatization separates steering from rowing in local government. Public officials set policy goals and monitor private providers of services (steer), while nongovernmental employees perform day-to-day tasks (row).

The increase in federal and state mandates is a major factor that has led cities to contract out for services. In particular, environmental mandates for such things as toxic waste cleanup require a level of technical expertise and the use of sophisticated equipment that often are beyond the capabilities of local governments.

Advocates of privatization, such as E. S. Savas, argue that it can substantially reduce service delivery costs. Political scientist James Q. Wilson agrees that private

LISTENING TO THE VOICE OF THE CUSTOMER

There are dozens of different ways to listen to the voice of the customer:

Customer surveys. In addition to the organizations described in the text, we have seen customer surveys used by Phoenix, Sunnyvale, and Orlando, Florida; by the Massachusetts Bay Transportation Authority, the Housing Authority of Louisville, the Michigan Commerce Department, and the New York Department of Labor; by court systems in Michigan, Washington State, and Los Angeles; and by the Naperville, Illinois, police department.

Customer follow-up. Fox Valley Technical College and the Michigan Modernization Service have surveyed their customers six months, a year, or two years after they were served to see whether the service actually yielded the desired results. Fox Valley even plans a follow-up survey after five years.

Community surveys. These are even more common than customer surveys. Every year, many cities—including Visalia, Sunnyvale, Fairfield, St. Petersburg, Dayton, and Dallas—survey their residents to see what they like and dislike about their city and their government. The International City Managers Association has even published a how-to book called *Citizen Surveys.*

Customer contact. Police Chief David Couper of Madison spends one month of every year in the field, working as a frontline police officer. Florida TaxWatch has recommended that "every state employee who does not have direct contact with the public should spend a minimum of two days a year in direct contact service." Minnesota's STEP program urged managers to sit in the service areas of their offices to talk with customers, and to ask frontline employees what they heard from customers and how service could be improved.

Customer contact reports. Madison's Experimental Police District gives customer feedback directly to the employee who served the customer.

Customer councils. Several housing authorities, including Louisville's, use resident councils to stay in touch with their customers. The Michigan Modernization Service used a customer council to give it feedback, particularly on new ideas.

Focus groups. Common in industry and in political campaigns, focus groups bring customers together to discuss a product, service, or issue. The consulting firm Jobs for the Future discovered through focus groups that people in Indiana reacted negatively to the phrase *job training program,* because it implied there was something wrong with them. They preferred *career development opportunities,* because it implied respect for their potential.

Customer interviews. Michigan's Literacy Task Force interviewed 130 people—both providers and customers—to find out what kind of adult education and job training system Michigan needed. It discovered that social problems—issues of motivation, attitude, and expectations—were a greater obstacle than lack of programs. And it learned that many Michigan workers saw "going back to school" as a traumatic idea and associated visiting government service offices with receiving welfare or unemployment—"something successful people just don't do."

Electronic mail. In Santa Monica, California, citizens can use the city's Public Electronic Network to communicate directly with any department. Staff members are expected to respond to any request within 24 hours. Citizens can hook up through their own computers, or they can use public terminals located throughout the city.

firms usually are more efficient, but he cautions that publicly owned utilities may have lower costs than private organizations.[26] Osborne and Graebler note that where private providers do not have to compete, they may be as inefficient as public monopolies.

In addition to saving money, *proponents* of privatization contend that it is consistent with free market ideology, it reduces the size of government, it forces providers to be more responsive to customer needs, it rewards innovation, it avoids the rigidities of civil service, and it introduces successful private management ideas to the public sec-

LISTENING TO THE VOICE OF THE CUSTOMER (continued)

Customer service training. Many governments, including Madison, Phoenix, Wisconsin, and Arkansas, now offer customer service training to their employees. San Antonio has developed an interesting wrinkle: its Yes, It Is My Problem initiative encourages city employees to solve citizens' problems in one phone call, rather than bouncing them from agency to agency.

Test marketing. Customer-oriented governments test new services to see if people like them before imposing them on everyone. The Phoenix Department of Public Works tested its one-person, automatic side-loading trucks with 90 homes; when it found 96 percent liked the service, it adopted the system citywide. The Minnesota Department of Natural Resources tested the use of credit cards in one park before accepting them statewide.

Quality guarantees. At least a dozen community colleges in Michigan guarantee their training to industry. West Virginia's Guaranteed Work Force Program retrains employees at no cost, to employer specifications, if employers are not satisfied. Many high schools in Colorado and West Virginia guarantee qualifying graduates to employers; if the graduate has problems with some basic skill needed on the job, the high school will bring him or her up to speed for free.

Inspectors. The New York City Taxi Commission sends inspectors out as undercover passengers to police the behavior of New York's taxi drivers. Private firms routinely send professional service raters out to check the quality of their banks, supermarkets, and restaurants. An entire industry has grown up to provide this service on contract.

Ombudsmen. Some customer-driven governments create an ombudsman, so citizens have someone they can call who will work with the offending department to straighten out the problem. Peter Drucker calls ombudsmen "the hygiene of organizations—or at least their toothbrush." Sweden, which invented the idea, even has a national ombudsman—as do the rest of the Scandinavian countries and most of the British Commonwealth. In the United States, at least 15 states, cities, and counties had ombudsmen by 1988.

Complaint tracking systems. Many cities have systems that track responses to inquiries and complaints, to improve the city's response time. With Phoenix's computerized system, city council members can see whether citizens in their district are getting the answers they need from city departments.

800 numbers. Governor William Donald Schaefer in Maryland set up a red-tape telephone hotline on which citizens can report cases of bureaucratic mismanagement. The Michigan Commerce Department uses 800 numbers to make it easy for businesses to call. The Georgia Public Service Commission set up 800 numbers so all residents could call their county officials for free.

Suggestion boxes or forms. The open-ended question asked by the Madison Police Department's customer survey is in effect a suggestion box. Fox Valley Tech has 23 suggestion boxes on its campus. The Michigan Treasury Department puts a suggestion box right on its tax forms.

Source: David Osborne and Ted Graebler, *Reinventing Government* (Reading, Mass.: Addison-Wesley, 1992), pp. 177–179.

tor. Where public agencies have successfully competed for contracts against private businesses, the morale of public employees is greatly improved.

Opponents contend that when the costs of monitoring contracts are considered, service delivery may be more expensive under privatization. Contracting, they argue, encourages "lowballing," where private firms bid low and then raise their charges to cover the real costs of the service. When costs are lower, opponents believe it often is because providers cut corners in their services and they pay workers lower salaries. There are concerns that private companies will not be sufficiently committed to affirmative action in hiring workers and that services may not be provided equitably to minority groups. When law enforcement is privatized (see Chapter 15), there is special concern that civil liberties will be abused. Not surprisingly, public employee unions fear that privatization will lead to a loss of jobs and/or lower wages and benefits. In large cities, such as Chicago, African-Americans have taken a substantial hit because they hold a disproportionately high percentage of service and maintenance jobs and those are the most likely to be privatized.[27] As under machine rule, there still is the danger of favoritism in awarding contracts.

Most of the pitfalls of privatization can be avoided by careful wording of contracts and by close supervision of the providers. For example, rather than automatically accepting the lowest bid, cities may use the "lowest responsible bid." City auditors' offices can ensure that bidding is truly competitive and can monitor contractors' performance. As in Phoenix, cities may wish to retain some public delivery of a service, such as garbage collection, even when the majority of the service is provided by private organizations. Contracts can encourage private companies to hire displaced city workers or cities can assure public employees that they will not be laid off because of privatization. In a word, cities need to manage competition by defining clearly what they want done, by evaluating performance, and by penalizing those who do not provide services at the expected levels. As Chicago mayor Richard M. Daley has stated, "People want services without higher taxes, and they don't care who gives it to them."[28]

According to a 1992 survey, 90 percent of state agencies have privatized some of their services. The most frequently privatized services are custodial, food, clerical, and security. Increasingly, states also are privatizing the professional services of engineers and architects. While over 90 percent of privatization is done by contracting out, states also provide vouchers, especially for social services, and they enter into partnerships with private groups. Exclusive use of public employees is highest in providing public safety operations, such as fire and police, but contracts are used for every service that local governments perform.[29] However, cities have made minimal use of alternative service delivery, other than contracting out.

Total Quality Management

Total quality management (TQM) is a business management philosophy most closely identified with W. Edwards Demming and first put into practice by Japanese business. TQM, sometimes called quality improvement (QI), uses performance data to identify problems and then gives employees the tools they can use to identify root causes and develop solutions. The primary tenets of TQM as it applies to government can be listed as follows.[30]

1 The customer is the ultimate determiner of quality.

2 Preventing variability is the key to producing high-quality products. Control charts should be used to track quality in the production process.

3 Quality results from people working together within systems, not from individual efforts. When quality declines, it usually is because the system is not working well, rather than the fault of individuals. A good system should lead *all* workers to perform well. If this were the case, organizations would *not* use merit pay to reward individuals.

4 Quality requires continuous improvement of inputs and processes. As customer expectations rise, so must product quality.

5 Quality improvement requires effective worker participation.

6 Quality requires a total organizational commitment.

While TQM acquired a near cultlike status among its supporters by the late 1980s, it also has its critics.[31] In part, criticism has been directed at "orthodox" TQM that was designed for routine manufacturing processes. Its tenets are more difficult to apply to government *services,* which are much more labor-intensive than in manufacturing. For example, uniformity of service output (tenet 2) is more appropriate as a manufacturing production goal than in service delivery where it often is appropriate to treat individuals differently. Moreover, government customers evaluate service on the basis of results (how quickly did the police respond to my call?) *and* on the behavior and appearance of the person delivering them (how courteous was the police officer and how well dressed was he or she?).

While pleasing business customers usually is a direct relationship (does an automobile perform well, and is its cost fair?), it is not easy even to identify government customers (tenet 1). For example, are the customers of an environmental protection agency the businesses it regulates or the groups that lobby for greater environmental protection? If it is a combination of both groups, then what weight should be assigned to each of their interests? Often in government service delivery there are competing clients with contrary demands and the general public may be inattentive or totally absent. Thus government agencies often face a conflict between the needs and demands of their direct customers (clients) and their ultimate customers (the general public). The buyers (taxpayers) often are not the clients.

TQM requires a strong organizational culture (tenets 3, 4, 5, and 6), and this is more difficult to achieve in government than in private business because government offices usually experience greater turnover among top managers and they must contend with a variety of outside political forces.

Orthodox TQM could do more harm than good if it focuses too strongly on the demands of direct clients. Thus in government, adjustments need to be made to focus on the general public and to consider the broader political environment in which the agency operates. Reformed TQM that considers client feedback, tracks performance, seeks continuous improvement, and empowers its workers certainly can help improve government performance. Major barriers to its implementation include turnover of political leaders; union opposition; lack of support from top management; and the inability to shift workers, evaluate programs, and document savings.[32]

TQM utilizes many of the budget strategies discussed earlier in this chapter. It includes the concept of "benchmarking"—measuring performance against the best performing units, both within the department and in other departments or in other cities or counties. Performance guides are developed for each program to measure progress toward goals, and funds are allotted to agencies based on how well they meet their goals. While this may seem too much like business school rhetoric to have practical applications in the world of partisan politics and benchmaking has been one of the least used quality improvement techniques, some form of TQM is being implemented in over half the states.[33] South Carolina, which began using TQM in 1988, claims that the state has earned an additional $2 million by identifying strategies to deposit money more quickly and thereby increase its interest income. This came about because of teamwork and decentralized decision making as part of the state's TQM program.

As shown in Table 7-4, state personnel directors report that TQM was the second most important issue facing their states in the first half of the 1990s. In the second half of the decade they projected that TQM will decrease slightly in importance but remain a major issue. Note that privatization is expected to become a much more important issue.

Reengineering Government

Reengineering government is a step beyond TQM in the quest to reinvent government.[34] In this management approach organizations are urged to break away from old rules and fundamental assumptions and redesign themselves around desired outcomes, rather than around functions or departments. Instead of having specialists working in separate departments, reengineering proposes that problems be solved by teams that cut across traditional functional lines. Organizations become "seamless" in the sense that barriers between departments are eliminated.[35] As discussed in Chapter 15, community policing, where several city departments cooperate to help make neighborhoods more safe, is an example of how walls can be torn down between bureaucratic agencies. It also is an example of how hard this is to do.

TABLE 7-4 MOST IMPORTANT ISSUES FACING STATE PERSONNEL DIRECTORS

Past five years:
- 1 Downsizing
- 2 Total quality management
- 3 Federal mandates
- *4 Budget cuts
- *4 Civil service reform
- *4 Health-care costs
- *4 Pay for performance

Next five years:
- 1 Downsizing
- 2 Compensation reform
- 3 Privatization
- *4 Technology
- *4 Pay for performance
- *4 Total quality management

*—tied

Source: Survey by CSG and the National Association of State Personnel Executives, January 1995.
From: State Trends Bulletin (February–March 1995), p. 1.

As in the private sector, government agencies are encouraged to provide quick, one-stop service to customers. It is the difference between the college registration process of the 1950s, when students spent hours waiting in lines in the gym or they went around to individual departments, and registration in the 1990s, where students phone from their residences to register and do not have to worry about being told two weeks later that they have been closed out of classes.[36]

While reengineering may mean "downsizing," it does not automatically mean the reduction of jobs or a move to more automation.[37] Nor should it be used synonymously with "restructuring." The focus is more on how work is done than on how organizations are structured.

Budget Reforms

Entrepreneurial government uses a variety of approaches to budgeting along with such broad-based concepts as total quality management and management by results. It calls for a change from rule-driven bureaucracies to **mission-driven organizations.** Mission-driven organizations define their desired outcomes (that is, the fundamental purpose of the organization) and then try to measure how well they achieve their goals. Much of this process is done through budgeting. In order to anticipate problems, entrepreneurial government recommends long-term budgeting that projects costs and revenues over a ten-year period. The basic idea is that money will be spent on those activities that move government toward its measurable goals, such as cleaner air or lower infant mortality.

More specifically, entrepreneurial government recommends budget systems in which managers can respond more quickly to changing circumstances. Traditional line items within departmental budgets would be eliminated to permit managers to shift resources as needed. Departments would be encouraged to save money (traditionally departments lose any funds they do not spend in a fiscal year and then risk having their next year's budget cut) by being allowed to keep what they do not spend from one year to the next. As a department builds up savings, it could use that money to make large purchases and do it much more quickly than under traditional budgeting. "Spend it or lose it" gives way to "save it and invest."[38]

Reinventing Government Evaluated

Reinventing government strategies seemed to be everywhere in the early 1990s. (See the Neal R. Peirce article for a description of reinventing government in Philadelphia.) President Clinton put Vice President Al Gore in charge of the federal program, and hundreds of activists in states, counties, cities, and school districts were eager to change their governments. While few persons would argue that long-term strategic planning, outcomes-based budgeting, and citizen empowerment are bad, some programs have been reined in by politicians and voters who feel they have been carried to their illogical extremes. Innovation makes some persons uncomfortable, and partisan political concerns may prevent otherwise rational budgeting changes from being implemented.

Philadelphia Rec Department an Example of "Reinventing" Government

Neal R. Peirce

Philadelphia—If you're wondering what "reinventing government" in America's states and cities is all about, check out this city's recreation department and especially its commissioner of the last 16 months, Michael DiBerardinis.

DiBerardinis was a community activist and organizer for 15 years in Philadelphia's gritty inner-city Kensington and Fishtown neighborhoods before being tapped by incoming Mayor Edward Rendell to take over a thoroughly battered city "rec department."

Hit by Philadelphia's devastating budget cutbacks, the department had seen its worker rolls slump from 1,200 in 1983 to 500 in 1992. Many of the community recreation centers around the city were in ramshackle condition, some close to abandonment. Only a few of the swimming pools—safety valve for kids through long, hot summers in poor neighborhoods—were getting opened early in the summer or at all.

To make things worse, the last rec commissioner, Delores Andy, had distinguished herself chiefly for working up so much weekend and holiday overtime that she demanded a $19,537 kiss-off payment when Rendell dumped her.

DiBerardinis was Rendell's pick because, the mayor said, he wanted someone to fight for the department "like no one else ever fought for it before." The selection of DiBerardinis looked ideal—a bundle of energy who'd picked up a fighting spirit from a militant trade unionist father, a social conscience from the Jesuits at St. Joseph's University, and firsthand knowledge of the city from years of working with kids in tough neighborhoods and from running (albeit unsuccessfully) for political offices.

But energy, conscience and knowing the territory won't, alone, cut the mustard in the resource-scarce '90s. There's a critical role for the so-called "reinvention" principles in today's governments—being entrepreneurial, treating citizens like valued customers, involving employees and citizens in setting an organization's mission and priorities, delegating authority and then holding managers accountable for results.

One of DiBerardinis' first moves was to energize the department's largely dormant network of advisory committees—parents, volunteer coaches and neighbors—at each of the recreation centers. A manual outlining the department's responsibility to the advisory committees, and theirs to the department, was written by a team of department officials and local committee members: It was a strategy, says DiBerardinis, "to involve the citizenry in the department in a real direct way, mirrored in how we deal with our employees as well."

The scandal of closed and late-opening swimming pools, caused both by the uncaring management of past years and fund shortages, was high on DiBerardinis' list. He communicated the urgency of prompt openings to all his managers; then he launched a campaign for corporate sponsorship and support. Advisory committees held fundraisers; the *Philadelphia Daily News* ran coupons for citizens to send in contributions. In 1991, not a single pool was open by July 1 and many never opened at all; in 1992, all but two of the system's 80 pools opened promptly in June.

The department's slogan had been "Life, Enjoy It." "Kind of stupid for these times," DiBerardinis notes. He and his colleagues went to work on a new mission statement, focused around active involvement of neighborhood residents and organizations and taking on social issues important to young people. A new and improved slogan surfaced—"Building Youth, Building Neighborhoods."

Recreation department staff and advisory councils started to get intensive training—in how to recruit volunteers, how to raise money, how to galvanize community support. DiBerardinis instructed all his managers to spend more time in the field, staying close to problems. Rank-and-file workers were involved in internal committees focused on problems that used to be the sole purview of management. A retreat centered around five issues employees had said were important to them.

The new esprit de corps in his recreation department is clearly what Mayor Rendell would like to achieve across the entire lumbering city bureaucracy he now heads. Rendell last October did win an historic agreement with his municipal unions to pare costs and keep the city moving on a five-year fiscal plan to pull it back from the brink of bankruptcy.

But now Rendell and his department heads need ways to reach out to and motivate city workers, even as the workers are obliged to accept the idea of fewer raises, fewer holidays and less protective work rules. In some parts of Philadelphia government, such as the scandal-ridden and inefficient Philadelphia Housing Authority, hope of constructive change still seems light-years away. Reform is slow, too, in the deeply troubled human services department.

But in other departments, new lights of hope and reform are being lit, just as in DiBerardinis' recreation department. Philadelphia is also getting ready to launch a big strategic planning effort to move beyond fiscal crisis and focus on its big economic and social challenges.

The new "reinvention" principles don't get spread across whole governments quickly or easily; too often hidebound managers, civil service or union contract work rules stand in the way. But in times of doom and gloom about whether government can work at all, the reinvention experiments are beacons of new possibilities.

Source: Washington Post Writers Group, 1993.

Curiously, the city in which entrepreneurial government found the greatest acceptance in the 1980s has changed direction in the 1990s. As its city manager for eight years, Ted Graebler helped make Visalia, California, the "most entrepreneurial city in America." Aided by a group of well-educated managers, many recruited from other parts of the country, Graebler and his successor as city manager reinvented government in their central California city of 75,000 people. Visalia's mission-driven budget was only two pages long, the city bought a minor league baseball team, and it established an award for "the year's most spectacular failure."

After Graebler left Visalia, the city got involved in a project to build a hotel and redevelop land on the edge of downtown.[39] As the city's share of the project's cost soared, criticism forced the city manager to resign. New city council members who opposed entrepreneurial government were elected, and they appointed a city manager who as police chief under Graebler had not embraced entrepreneurial government.

Even in its heyday, Visalia illustrates the need to take a moderate approach to reinventing government. While the process was exciting to its professional managers, many townspeople felt cut off from their government (this was despite constant surveys to listen to the voices of Visalia's customers). The city had over 100 task forces, which led to a lot of talking but limited government efficiency. When Graebler proposed that the city sell fire insurance as a way to make money, there was strong and effective opposition from the business community. Of course, nothing succeeds like success. Had a more financially secure developer been found to manage the hotel project, a political backlash might not have occurred. In fact, the hotel was built and it is operating successfully.

While some may dismiss reinventing government as faddish rhetoric, it seems likely that many of its concepts will be implemented by state and local governments in the late 1990s as they search for ways to maintain and improve service levels without increasing costs and taxes.

Here are some recent examples of redesigning government that show us how officials at all levels are changing the old ways of doing business: (1) After an extensive review of state government that led to streamlining departments and agencies, New Jersey estimates it saved nearly $2 billion in two years under Governor James Florio. (2) "Oregon Benchmarks" is a serious effort by that state to measure progress in more than 270 areas. A Progress Board plots how well objectives are achieved, and it sets priorities within the benchmarks.[40] (3) The Lansing (Michigan) Housing Commission has established Computer Learning Centers in public housing projects where children can sharpen their academic skills after school hours.[41]

SUMMARY

The number of state and local employees and the amount of spending by those governments have been increasing as federal funding has been cut back.

While we are critical of "bloated bureaucracy," we need to remember that the creation of bureaucratic organizations in the late nineteenth century was part of a reform movement to deal with the evils of political patronage. Specific reforms such as the creation of civil service rules are now criticized because they are believed to hamstring managers.

Governors typically have had limited powers as chief administrators, and the sheer size of the bureaucracy inhibits their ability to oversee state government operations. Legislators have sought to control the bureaucracy through the budget process and legislative vetoes. While budget techniques have improved, there are serious questions regarding the constitutionality of legislative vetoes. Unionization and newer issues such as gender equality have made personnel management more complicated.

Urban bureaucracies are described as the "new machines"—powerful groups that are protected from effective control by elected officials and by the general public.

Authors David Osborne and Ted Graebler suggest that we need to "reinvent government" in order to control the bureaucracy and improve government efficiency. To do that, they recommend privatizing some public services, changing budget procedures, and using total quality management (TQM) techniques. The chapter reading by Neal Peirce looks at reinventing government in Philadelphia.

KEY TERMS

Bureaucracy Large, complex organizations with a chain of command and a hierarchy of offices.

Collective bargaining Negotiating the terms of employment between labor and management, resulting in a contract.

Comparable worth The belief that salaries should be equalized for jobs that are different but are of comparable (equal) worth to the organization.

Entrepreneurial government Concentrates on earning, not just spending; seeks to prevent, rather than cure; seeks to structure the marketplace to achieve its ends.

Hoover Commission Study of the federal executive branch conducted in 1949; it recommended the consolidation of many federal agencies.

Incremental budgeting Basing the current budget largely on last year's budget.

Merit system Making appointments to public office on the basis of the ability to perform assigned tasks. This system uses scores on competitive examinations as the basis for hiring and promoting.

Mission-driven organizations The commonsense idea that the guiding force behind what government does is its fundamental purpose. This contrasts with rule-driven organizations that, according to Osborne and Graebler, are larger, less innovative, and less flexible.

Postindustrial society Contemporary economy of the United States that is based on the provision of services rather than industrial manufacturing.

Privatization Turning over the management of public services to the private sector. Includes contracting out, using vouchers, and selling off public enterprises.

Professional ideology Codes of conduct, based on membership in professional associations, which influence the behavior of public officials.

Program-planning-budgeting system A budget technique in which government agencies must justify specific requests for appropriations in terms of how well particular programs are achieving their intended goals.

Reinventing government As popularized by Osborne and Graebler, it refers to a call to move from bureaucratic government to a new system that emphasizes citizen empowerment and competition.

Reorganization Changes in administrative structure that often consolidate departments and promote more centralized control of bureaucracy.

Total quality management Strategy adapted from private business to set goals, measure performance, and develop solutions.

Zero-based budgeting A technique that breaks down each government agency into its individual functions and analyzes each function annually. Thus each agency's budget starts at zero and builds in programs only if they can be justified each year by the agency.

REFERENCES

1 Meredith DeHart, "Government Employment in 1992," *The Book of the States, 1994* (Lexington, Ky.: Council of State Governments, 1994), p. 435.

2 Richard C. Elling, "Bureaucracy: Maligned Yet Essential," in Virginia Gray and Herbert Jacob, eds., *Politics in the American States,* 6th ed. (Washington: Congressional Quarterly Press, 1996), p. 288.

3 See Charles T. Goodsell, *The Case for Bureaucracy: A Public Administration Polemic,* 3d ed. (Chatham, N.J.: Chatham House, 1994), Chapter 2.

4 David Osborne and Ted Graebler, *Reinventing Government* (Reading, Mass.: Addison-Wesley, 1992), p. 12.

5 H. H. Gerth and C. Wright Mills, eds., *From Max Weber: Essays in Sociology* (New York: Oxford University Press, 1946), pp. 196–204.

6 Bernard H. Ross and Myron A. Levine, *Urban Politics: Power in Metropolitan America,* 5th ed. (Itasca, Ill.: F. E. Peacock, 1996), pp. 251–252.

7 Osborne and Graebler, *Reinventing Government,* p. 14.

8 Julie C. Olberding, "Reforming State Management and Personnel Systems," *The Book of the States, 1994–95,* p. 407.

9 Elling, "Bureaucracy," p. 293.

10 James K. Conant, "In the Shadow of Wilson and Brownlow: Executive Branch Reorganization in the States, 1965–1987," *Public Administration Review* (September–October 1988), p. 895.

11 Charles T. Goodsell, "Collegial State Administration: Design for Today?" *Western Political Quarterly* (September 1981), pp. 455–460.

12 B. Boseman and M. Crow, "Organizational Theory and State Government Structure: Are There Lessons Worth Learning?" *State Government* (1986), pp. 144–151.

13 Elling, "Bureaucracy," p. 297.

14 Osborne and Graebler, *Reinventing Government,* p. 125.

15 Sam Dillon, "Teacher Tenure: Rights vs. Discipline," *The New York Times,* June 28, 1994, p. 1.

16 Jonathan Walters, "The Fine Art of Firing the Incompetent," *Governing* (June 1994), p. 36.

17 Timothy D. Chandler and Timothy A. Judge, "Collective Bargaining with Police Unions," in *The Municipal Year Book 1993* (Washington: International City/County Management Association, 1993), pp. 34–43.

18 Elling, "Bureaucracy," p. 308.

19 Alan Rosenthal, *Governors and Legislatures: Contending Powers* (Washington: Congressional Quarterly Press, 1990), p. 141.

20 Aaron Wildavsky, *The New Politics of the Budgetary Process,* 2d ed. (New York: HarperCollins, 1992), p. 439.

21 Theodore Lowi, "Machine Politics—Old and New," *Public Interest* (Fall 1967), p. 86.

22 Ross and Levine, *Urban Politics,* p. 253.

23 See Robert C. Lineberry, *Equality and Urban Policy: The Distribution of Municipal Services* (Beverly Hills, Calif.: Sage Publications, 1977) for a report on San Antonio, Texas.

24 Osborne and Graebler, *Reinventing Government,* Preface.

25 E. S. Savas, *Privatization: The Key to Better Government* (Chatham, N.J.: Chatham House, 1987), p. 3.

26 James Q. Wilson, *Bureaucracy: What Government Agencies Do and Why They Do It* (New York: Basic Books, 1989), pp. 350–351.

27 Charles Mahtesian, "Taking Chicago Private," *Governing* (April 1994), p. 31.
28 See John Donahue, *The Privatization Decision* (New York: Basic Books, 1990).
29 Rowan Miranda and Karlyn Anderson, "Alternative Service Delivery in Local Government, 1982–1992," in *The Municipal Year Book 1994* (Washington: International City/County Management Association, 1994), p. 28.
30 James E. Swiss, "Adapting Total Quality Management (TQM) to Government," *Public Administration Review* (July–August 1992), pp. 357–358.
31 See Jonathan Walters, "The Cult of Total Quality," *Governing* (May 1992), pp. 38–42.
32 Swiss, "Adapting Total Quality," p. 359.
33 Jonathan P. West, Evan M. Berman, and Mike E. Milakovich, "Total Quality Management in Local Government," *The Municipal Year Book 1994* (Washington: International City/County Management Association, 1994), p. 22.
34 Peter F. Drucker, "Really Reinventing Government," *Atlantic Monthly* (February 1995), pp. 49–61.
35 Russell M. Linden, *Seamless Government: A Practical Guide to Reengineering in the Public Sector* (San Francisco: Jossey-Bass, 1994).
36 "A Guide to Reengineering Government," *Governing* (May 1995), p. 72.
37 Michael Hammer, "Reengineering Work: Don't Automate, Obliterate," *Harvard Business Review* (July–August 1990), pp. 104–112.
38 Olberding, "Reforming State Management," p. 407.
39 See Rob Gurwitt, "Entrepreneurial Government: The Morning After," *Governing* (May 1994), pp. 34–40.
40 "Innovations 1994: Government At Its Best," *Governing* (October 1994), pp. 38–39.
41 "1993 Innovations in State and Local Government" (New York: Ford Foundation, 1993), p. 10. Also see James P. Troxel, ed., *Government That Works: Profiles of People Making a Difference* (Alexandria, Va.: Miles River Press, 1995).

8

STATE COURT SYSTEMS

S. Tanaka/The Picture Cube

State courts deal with those issues that most directly affect people's everyday lives. Most criminal cases are decided in state courts because most crimes are violations of state laws. Virtually all cases dealing with domestic relations—divorce, adoption, child custody—are heard by state courts. Questions of property ownership, contracts, zoning, wills and estates, and automobile accidents all originate in state courts. Americans appeared in court in 1993 about 100 million times, and 99 million of those appearances were in state courts. For example, courts in California handled about 2 million new civil cases and 1 million criminal cases in 1991. State courts process nearly five times as many appeals as the federal court system.

The legal system of the United States is complicated by a federal structure that permits a variety of laws and courts, rather than specifying a unified plan. Throughout the country, state law is the basic law. In the United States, federal law is drafted for specific purposes and **common law** is interpreted individually by each state.* In such a situation, both state and federal courts are bound by state law unless a state statute has been superseded by federal law or is in conflict with the Constitution.

The system is made even more complex by the dual nature of state and federal courts. Unlike many other federal systems, in the United States both the states and the federal government have a complete set of trial and appellate courts. Although federal courts are concerned only with cases that raise federal issues (i.e., involve the interpretation of federal laws or the U.S. Constitution), the jurisdiction of state and federal courts occasionally overlaps. In some civil suits this gives plaintiffs the choice of initiating action in a state or federal court, and in some criminal cases it means the defendant may be tried in both state and federal courts. State courts are inferior to federal courts in the sense that decisions of state supreme courts can be reviewed and overturned by the U.S. Supreme Court. However, the Supreme Court annually reviews only a handful of the millions of state court decisions.

Although there have been significant organizational reforms in state court systems in the past twenty years, the judicial branch has not been changed as much as the legislative and executive branches. As we will see in this chapter, current issues being addressed include reduction of delay, selection of judges, the role of women and minorities in the courts, and alternative resolutions to disputes.

STATE COURT ORGANIZATION

The historical development of state court systems is strikingly similar to the development of state and local bureaucracy as discussed in Chapter 7. In the nineteenth century, the forces of urbanization and industrialization created a myriad of social and economic problems. Crowded cities led to increases in crime and juvenile delinquency and to the breakup of families. Landlord-tenant relations caused conflicts that were resolved by lawsuits. Questions of employer liability for personal injury and property

*Common law is judge-made law that originated in England from decisions shaped according to existing custom. Decisions were reapplied in similar situations (precedents) and, over a period of time, became common to the nation. English common law formed the basis of legal proceedings in the American states—except in Louisiana, where French legal traditions were used—and it has been preserved over the years. Common law also serves as the basis for much federal constitutional and statutory law.

damage opened new areas in the law. The use of automobiles created traffic law problems; and, of course, accident claims placed a heavy burden on local courts.

The response of many states was to create new courts, just as new boards and commissions were added to cope with regulatory problems. As with the bureaucracy, courts expanded in an unplanned manner. Their jurisdiction often overlapped, and each court acted independently of others.* New courts included those for juvenile and family relations, small claims, and traffic. Each court had its own rules of procedure, and the nature of decisions varied among courts with similar jurisdiction. As with state administrative structures, much of the history of twentieth-century court organization can be written in terms of reform attempts to unify and streamline complex state court systems.

At the extremes, some states have fully consolidated their courts, while others continue to operate very complex, fragmented court systems. Illinois (see Figure 8-1) represents a state that has streamlined its court system to a very basic form. In Illinois there is a single set of trial courts that handle major and minor trials. In contrast, Indiana (see Figure 8-2) has a traditional court system with eleven different courts. New York's court system is even more complicated than Indiana's. While many states have simplified their court systems, typically several different types of trial courts remain at the state level.

Trial Courts

Minor trial courts are limited to hearing less serious criminal and civil cases. Municipal courts, for example, often hear only criminal misdemeanor cases where the punishment is a fine or a jail sentence of less than six months. They hear civil suits where there is a limit of $500 to $1,000 in damages being sought. Civil cases relate to the private rights of individuals, while criminal law regulates individual conduct and is enforced by the government. When a case is appealed from these courts, a new trial is held *(trial de novo)* without reference to the first proceeding.

At the bottom rung of **trial courts,** many states have abolished justices of the peace and courts presided over by mayors and magistrates. These have been replaced by county or municipal courts. Justices of the peace settled local traffic law violations, issued warrants for arrest and search, and performed marriages. In some states, they did not receive a base salary but were paid a percentage of fines collected. This led to the classic "kangaroo court," in which the justice and local police officers cooperated in the profitable business of setting speed traps and sharing the fines. Mayors' courts have operated in a fashion similar to justices of the peace, with many small-town mayors meting out "justice" in a very personal manner.

In most states minor trial courts are highly decentralized.[1] There are many municipal courts in urban areas and a variety of county courts in rural areas. Then there are

*A 1931 study found there were 556 independent courts in Chicago, of which 505 were justice of the peace courts. Cited in Henry R. Glick and Kenneth N. Vines, *State Court Systems* (Englewood Cliffs, N.J.: Prentice-Hall, 1973), p. 25. In such a situation, court costs, reputation of judges, and speed of securing a decision were considered in deciding which court to use. Justices of the peace competed for business and would often trade favorable decisions for continued use of their courts.

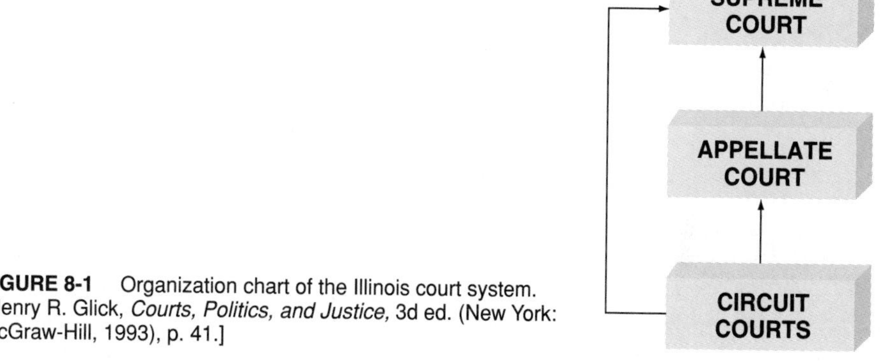

FIGURE 8-1 Organization chart of the Illinois court system. [Henry R. Glick, *Courts, Politics, and Justice,* 3d ed. (New York: McGraw-Hill, 1993), p. 41.]

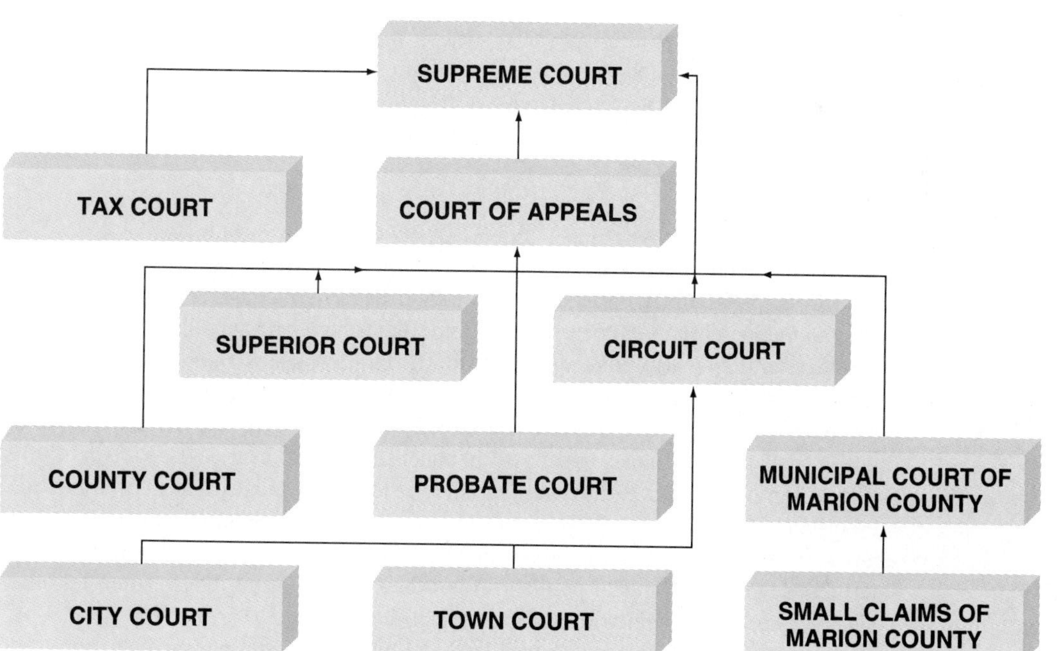

FIGURE 8-2 Organization chart of the Indiana court system. [Henry R. Glick, *Courts, Politics, and Justice,* 3d ed. (New York: McGraw-Hill, 1993), p. 41.]

separate trial courts to perform specific judicial functions, such as small claims or juvenile crime. Only a few states have a single set of minor courts. Often where trial courts are consolidated, there are still separate criminal and civil divisions.

"Justice" in minor trial courts often is quick and routine. Defendants appear, they plead guilty or **no contest *(nolo contendere),*** a fine is set, and the court proceeds to the next case. When defendants plead "no contest," it is in effect an admission of guilt without stating so formally. The defendant does not admit civil liability. This can be very important in traffic accidents where a civil suit for damages may follow the criminal traffic violation. While penalties technically are the same as for a plea of guilty, judges may be more lenient in some circumstances.[2] Often, administrative personnel other than judges preside over these cases.

Major trial courts handle felony criminal cases and civil cases involving large amounts of money. From 1984 to 1990, total felony filings in the states increased over 50 percent. Because felony cases place the strongest demands on trial courts, this increase has made effective case management critical if courts are to function well with limits on new personnel. Most often major trial courts—known as district courts, superior courts, or common pleas courts—are established at the county level. While they are less fragmented than minor trial courts, major trial courts typically have divisions to hear such specialized cases as divorce proceedings and probate of wills. As noted earlier, when cases are appealed from municipal courts, they usually are retried in a major trial court. Some states have grouped county courts into circuit courts, and judges are moved around the circuit. However, that kind of consolidation remains the exception in a system where local control is highly valued. Few decisions are appealed from major trial courts, and thus for most litigants they are, in fact, courts of first and last resort.

Appellate Courts

Early in this century most states had only a supreme court to which all cases were appealed. By 1991, thirty-eight states had established intermediate **courts of appeal** to deal with the increased volume of cases. Some states have one appellate court; in other states there are several regional appellate courts. In a few states, intermediate appellate courts are divided between criminal and civil divisions. Even where these intermediate courts do exist, some cases proceed directly from trial courts to the state supreme court. Appellate court judges usually sit in panels of three to hear cases. Parties to suits (litigants) are successful if they can convince at least two judges that their arguments are correct. In a majority of cases appeals are mandatory, meaning that intermediate court of appeals judges can exercise little control over their docket. In some states intermediate courts of appeal publish few of their opinions and judges often let other colleagues speak for them with little review of the opinion.[3]

All states have a *supreme court* that hears appeals from intermediate courts of appeal and, occasionally, appeals directly from major trial courts. State supreme courts have from five to nine justices, who generally sit *en banc* (all together) to hear cases (see Table 8-1). While state supreme courts do not have as much discretion over which cases to hear as the U.S. Supreme Court, their discretion is so broad that most appeals are rejected.

An ultimate power for state supreme courts and for the U.S. Supreme Court is the ability to declare legislative acts unconstitutional. The use of **judicial review** by state supreme courts, that is, to overrule acts passed by state legislatures, is about as frequent as it is for the U.S. Supreme Court to overrule acts passed by Congress.[4] Political scientist Henry Glick points out that the percentage of challenged state laws declared unconstitutional varies greatly among state supreme courts. For example, in a recent five-year period the North Carolina supreme court overruled only one law, while twenty-five state laws were declared unconstitutional by the Georgia supreme court.

Like the U.S. Supreme Court, state supreme courts schedule oral arguments and then meet in private conference to decide cases. Unlike the U. S. Supreme Court, in many state supreme courts opinion assignments are made on a rotating basis among the justices, and this reduces the power of the chief justice. While chief justices in both systems are one among equals in deciding cases, they may play a dominant role in leading the discussion of cases in conference, and they also have special administrative powers over their court system.

In contrast to the U.S. Supreme Court, there are relatively few dissents among judges in state supreme court decisions. Several factors help explain this apparent lack of conflict. First, legal tradition supports unanimity in order to present clear policy guidelines. Second, appellate courts often assign one judge to research the case and write the opinion. In such circumstances, the other judges are likely to concur, since they have not paid close attention to the case. Moreover, because of the nature of their interaction in a small group setting, there is a need to maintain congenial personal relations.

In contrast to legislators, judges are more likely to be drawn from a homogeneous upper-class or middle-class background, which means they tend to share similar perspectives on many legal issues. In 1991 women constituted about 11 percent of all state appellate judges, and only twelve states had any African-Americans on their supreme courts.[5]

REFORM OF STATE COURTS

The structure of state courts can have an important political impact on a variety of groups. Particularly in urban areas, courts have massive backlogs of cases, a situation that directly influences the administration of justice. In the past thirty years, the number of cases filed and disposed of has increased by 1,000 percent. Because they are unable to make *bail* (money or credit deposited with the court to get an arrested person temporarily released on the assurance that he or she will appear for trial), large numbers of people charged with crimes, but assumed innocent until proven guilty, are forced to spend months in county jails waiting for their cases to appear on the court calendar. Forced to exist in overcrowded, outdated facilities, many prisoners have suffered physical hardships, and a variety of suits have been initiated by civil liberties groups to force improvements in jail conditions. These same groups have protested against the bail system, which forces indigents to await trial in jail, and they have complained vigorously about judicial sentencing practices in which different penalties, ranging from probation to several years in prison, are given to individuals who have committed similar offenses. The backlog of cases has also led to the widespread use of **plea bargaining** (discussed in the following section), in which the accused are encouraged to plead guilty to lesser charges in return for the promise of leniency in sentencing. As a result, seemingly routine court decisions have had serious cumulative effects on the administration of criminal justice.

TABLE 8-1 STATE COURTS OF LAST RESORT

State or other jurisdiction	Name of court	Justices chosen (a): At large	Justices chosen (a): By district	No. of judges (b)	Term in years (c)	Chief justice: Method of selection	Chief justice: Term of service as chief justice
Alabama	S.C.	*		9	6	Popular election	6 years
Alaska	S.C.	*		5	10	By court	3 years (d)
Arizona	S.C.	*		5	6	By court	5 years
Arkansas	S.C.	*		7	8	Popular election	8 years
California	S.C.	*		7	12	Appointed by governor (e)	12 years
Colorado	S.C.	*		7	10	By court	At pleasure of court
Connecticut	S.C.	*		7	8	Nominated by governor, appointed by General Assembly	8 years
Delaware	S.C.	*		5	12	Appointed by governor with consent of Senate	12 years
Florida	S.C.	*		7	6	By court	2 years
Georgia	S.C.	*		7	6	By court	4 years
Hawaii	S.C.	*		5	10	Appointed by governor, with consent of Senate	10 years
Idaho	S.C.	*		5	6	By court	4 years
Illinois	S.C.		*	7	10	By court	3 years
Indiana	S.C.	*		5	10 (f)	Selected by Judicial Nominating Commission from S.C. members	5 years
Iowa	S.C.	*		9	8	By court	Remainder of term or 8 years
Kansas	S.C.	*		7	6	By seniority of service (g)	Remainder of term
Kentucky	S.C.		*	7	8	By court	4 years
Louisiana	S.C.		*	7	10	By seniority of service	Remainder of term
Maine	S.J.C.	*		7	7	Appointed by governor, with consent of Senate	7 years
Maryland	C.A.		*	7	10	Designated by governor	Remainder of term
Massachusetts	S.J.C.	*		7	To age 70	Appointed by governor	To age 70
Michigan	S.C.	*		7	8	By court	2 years
Minnesota	S.C.	*		7	6	Popular election	6 years
Mississippi	S.C.		*	9	8	By seniority of service	Remainder of term
Missouri	S.C.	*		7	12	By court	2 years
Montana	S.C.	*		7	8	Popular election	8 years
Nebraska	S.C.		* (h)	7	6	Appointed by governor from Judicial Nominating Commission	Remainder of term
Nevada	S.C.	*		5	6	Rotation by seniority (i)	1–2 years
New Hampshire	S.C.	*		5	To age 70	Appointed by governor and Council	To age 70
New Jersey	S.C.	*		7	7 (j)	Appointed by governor, with consent of Senate	Remainder of term
New Mexico	S.C.	*		5	8	By court	2 years

New York	C.A.	*		7	14 (j)	Appointed by governor from Judicial Nomination Commission with consent of Senate	14 years (j)
North Carolina	S.C.	*		7	8	Popular election	8 years
North Dakota	S.C.	*		5	10	By Supreme and district court judges	5 years (k)
Ohio	S.C.	*		7	6	Popular election	6 years
Oklahoma	S.C.		*	9	6	By court	2 years
	C.C.A		*	5	6	By court	2 years
Oregon	S.C.	*		7	6	By court	6 years
Pennsylvania	S.C.	*		7	10	Rotation by seniority	Remainder of term
Rhode Island	S.C.	*		5	Life	By legislature	Life
South Carolina	S.C.	*		5	10	Joint public vote of General Assembly	10 years
South Dakota	S.C.		* (l)	5	8	By court	4 years
Tennessee	S.C.	*		5	8	By court	18 months
Texas	S.C.	*		9	6	Popular election	6 years
	C.C.A.	*		9	6	Popular election (m)	6 years (m)
Utah	S.C.	*		5	10 (n)	By court	4 years
Vermont	S.C.	*		5	6	Appointed by governor from Judicial Nomination Commission with consent of Senate	6 years
Virginia	S.C.	*		7	12	By seniority of service	Remainder of term
Washington	S.C.	*		9	6	By seniority of service	2 years
West Virginia	S.C.A.	*		5	12	Rotation by seniority	1 year
Wisconsin	S.C.	*		7	10	By seniority of service (o)	Remainder of term or until declined
Wyoming	S.C.	*		5	8	By court	2 years
Dist. of Columbia	C.A.	*		9	15	Designated by Mayor from Judicial Nominating Commission	4 years
American Samoa	H.C.	*		8 (p)	(q)	Appointed by Secretary of the Interior	(q)
Puerto Rico	S.C.	*		7	To age 70	Appointed by Governor with consent of Senate	To age 70

Sources: National Center for State Courts, *State Court Caseload Statistics: Annual Report 1992* (released 1994) and *State Court Organization 1993;* state constitutions and statutes.

Key:

S.C.—Supreme Court
S.C.A.—Supreme Court of Appeals
S.J.C.—Supreme Judicial Court
C.A.—Court of Appeals
C.C.A.—Court of Criminal Appeals
H.C.—High Court

(a) See Table 4.4, "Selection and Retention of Judges," for details.
(b) Number includes chief justice.
(c) The initial term may be shorter.
(d) A justice may serve more than one term as chief justice, but may not serve consecutive terms in that position.
(e) Subsequently, must run on record for retention.
(f) Initial two years; retention 10 years.
(g) If two or more qualify, then senior in age.
(h) Chief justice chosen statewide; associate judges chosen by district.
(i) If two or more qualify, then determined by lot.
(j) May be reappointed to age 70.
(k) Or expiration of term, whichever is first.
(l) Initially chosen by district; retention determined statewide.
(m) Presiding judge of Court of Criminal Appeals.
(n) Initial three years; retention 10 years.
(o) If two or more qualify, then justice with least number of years remaining in term.
(p) Chief judges and associate judges sit on appellate and trial divisions.
(q) For good behavior.

From: The Book of the States, 1994–95 (Lexington, Ky.: Council of State Governments, 1994), pp. 184–185.

The variety of courts operating under different rules of procedure within a single county results in confusion and unequal application of the law. The quality of "justice" may depend largely on how successful attorneys are in steering cases to courts presided over by friendly judges. Trial judges function independently of one another, and there are few effective controls that can be applied to them by appellate courts.

Faced with such a situation, reformers have called for an integrated system in which the number of separate courts would be greatly reduced and the problem of overlapping jurisdiction eliminated. Reformers would place all judges under the general supervision of the chief justice of their state in order to ensure uniform practices and standards of conduct. As will be seen later in this chapter, reformers would also like to eliminate the use of judgeships as political patronage.

Consolidation

Structural reform includes both the **consolidation of courts** and the **centralization of courts.** Only a few states have consolidated their court system into a single set of courts that handle all trial court litigation. Most continue to have a number of specialized courts with their own procedures. As noted earlier, Indiana has eleven kinds of trial courts. States have been more successful in centralizing or unifying their court system under an administrative judge who controls work loads, makes staff assignments, and determines budgets. A majority of states have assumed all or most of the funding of court systems. Only a few states, such as Hawaii, have consolidated *and* centralized their courts. At the other extreme, the court system in Indiana is nonconsolidated and decentralized. Relations among state courts are never as simple as suggested in Figure 8-1. Judges in so-called lower courts seldom are under close supervision from higher courts.[6]

In addition to streamlining the structure of courts, unified judicial systems also include centralizing authority with the state supreme court to budget for all courts; to manage the case load of courts statewide, including the use of retired judges; and to be responsible for disciplining attorneys and judges. In such cases, the chief justice becomes an administrator responsible for the operation of courts across the state.

Reform is difficult to accomplish because traditional court practices benefit groups, such as lawyers and political parties, that have substantial political influence. Opposition also comes from legislators and judges who believe their existing power would be diminished by the elimination of the current maze of courts and the independence it provides to local judges. However, since 1978 all states have had a court administration office, and some states monitor courts and shift judges to respond to case loads across the state.

Proponents of consolidation argue that fragmented court systems are inefficient and that overlapping court jurisdiction often is confusing. Opponents counter that it is desirable for courts to have the flexibility to adapt to unique needs of the local area. Proponents of centralized control contend that when each court makes its own procedural rules, "justice" may vary greatly among courts that are independent of each other. State supreme court justices favor centralization because it increases their power, but local judges and government officials want to maintain community control.

Even when court systems have administrators under supreme court control, their power over local courts varies greatly, and some courts may continue to operate independently of statewide authority.[7]

In the 1990s, financing has become the "hottest" issue in court unification. Most states have moved from the traditional pattern of local financing to statewide systems aimed at greater equalization of resources. While a handful of states have shifted completely to state funding, most local courts continue to receive financial support from state and local authorities. As states control a higher percentage of court expenditures (appropriations for the judiciary average about 1 percent of state budgets) and more unification occurs, judicial personnel must make greater efforts to lobby state legislators and to cooperate with them.

Political scientist Lawrence Baum concludes that court unification may not produce the benefits its proponents proclaim.[8] Even in consolidated systems individual courts and judges may retain substantial autonomy and efficiency may be more closely related to the work habits of individual judges than to court structure. If cases are disposed of more quickly, it may be at the expense of careful review. Many people believe that courts *should* be influenced by external politics in order to maintain public accountability. Although nearly all state court systems have become more unified in recent years, no state is totally unified, and it is unlikely that major changes will occur in the near future.

Access to Courts

Judicial reform has stressed better access to the courts. Many people are effectively denied access because of legal costs. Many states do not require public defender systems statewide. Even when they exist, public defender offices are often underfunded, and budgets for paying court-appointed counsel were cut in the 1980s. Most researchers conclude that public defenders are more effective than court-appointed attorneys, who may have little criminal court experience. In general, however, defending the poor is not a high priority for state and local governments. The United States is the only Western democracy in which civil litigants are not guaranteed legal counsel.

In addition to issues dealing with legal counsel, states have taken a number of other steps to improve access to courts in both criminal and civil proceedings. These include training and certifying court interpreters for those with limited English skills; enforcement of the Americans with Disabilities Act; examination of racial, ethnic, and gender bias in the courts; the use of alternative dispute resolution, such as mediation and arbitration; expansion of night courts; and the creation of family courts. Family courts consolidate all matters concerning families—divorce, child custody, adoption, and domestic violence—into a single court.[9] If access is improved, it will, of course, increase the case loads of courts that are already crowded. As state courts have become more active participants in social change, public attitudes about them and easier access to courts have become more important issues.[10]

Access to crowded courts in civil matters is increasingly aided by the use of mediation and arbitration. In **mediation** an impartial third party assists the disputants in reaching a voluntary settlement. Usually the process is nonadversarial, meaning that there is no attempt to determine right or wrong, but instead the parties seek to reach a mutual agreement among a selection of alternative solutions. **Arbitration** calls for one or more persons to hear the arguments in a dispute, review the evidence, and reach a decision, or award. The parties agree ahead of time to be bound by the decision. Arbitration long has been used in labor disputes. More recently court-annexed arbitration has been used in which judges refer civil suits to private arbitrators, who render prompt decisions. If the losing party does not accept the arbitrator's decision, then a trial can be held in the regular court system. In a similar process, a few cities have moved lesser criminal cases to special judges who settle disputes without a jury. California has pioneered in the use of a "private" judicial system in which the parties hire a retired judge to resolve their dispute. Judge Wapner from the television program "The People's Court" is the most famous private judge.

TRIAL COURT PROCEDURES

A popular view of the administration of justice is that of the classic adversary system in which the attorney (say, Perry Mason) battles valiantly on behalf of his or her clients. There is always a jury, a narrow-minded prosecutor, and a white-haired judge who wields even control as the attorneys take turns objecting to the irrelevant, immaterial, and leading questions of their worthy opponent. In such a setting, justice always triumphs as the defendant is exonerated and the guilty person is dramatically exposed. In fact, however, most legal issues are settled without a trial when the defendant pleads guilty and the judge issues a sentence.

Plea Bargaining

Only about 10 percent of all criminal cases come to trial. Most are settled in pretrial negotiations among the defendant, the prosecutor, and the judge. This arrangement—*plea bargaining*—in which the defendant pleads guilty in return for a reduced charge and, most likely, a less severe penalty, is dominated by the prosecutor. Defense attorneys typically approach prosecutors to see what kind of bargain they can reach. Because prosecutors and defense attorneys know more about the details of a case, judges often defer to them for factual information and sentencing guidelines. As we would expect, cases most likely to be bargained are those where there is strong evidence against the defendant and the charges are not serious.[11] Still, prosecutors may not want to bargain some cases where they are very confident they will win at trial.

Plea bargaining is a common practice because it appears to benefit each of the interested parties. *Defendants* plead guilty because they receive a reduction of charge (e.g., from aggravated murder to manslaughter); a reduction in length of sentence; a chance for probation; or some combination of these agreements that results in softening the potential damage of the original charge. *Prosecutors* seek to avoid time-consuming trials, and they also wish to keep their conviction rates high. In some cases, the prosecutor may have obtained evidence illegally or may wish to protect informants by keeping them from taking the witness stand; he or she is therefore willing to trade a trial with its doubtful outcome for the sure thing of a guilty plea to a reduced charge. Attorneys for both sides like pretrial settlements because they can control the flow of information. Witnesses are not questioned, and they are not subject to the strict rules of trial procedure. *Judges,* concerned with avoiding delay and backlogs, encourage plea bargaining as a speedy way to dispose of cases. The *police* benefit because they do not have to appear in court as witnesses during their off-duty hours. Plea bargaining also helps the police "clear" cases and therefore bolsters their image as successful crime fighters. This was acknowledged as a judicial fact of life by the U.S. Supreme Court in *Santobello* v. *New York* (1971). While the *Santobello* decision recognizes the need for plea bargaining, it also requires that judges make sure that defendants understand the agreements.

Plea bargaining is a quick and efficient means of disposing of legal disputes. Given the existing structure of the courts and the limited number of judges, the legal system in most states would rapidly break down if even half the criminal defendants pleaded not guilty and demanded a jury trial. At the present time, many defendants are convinced that they will be in for a rough time if they do not cooperate with the police and plead guilty rather than having their cases come to trial.

Plea bargaining has been going on for more than 100 years, and it is not a technique that developed in response to a heavy criminal work load in big cities. In fact, evidence suggests that heavy work loads do not cause plea bargaining.[12] Plea bargaining is widespread in rural counties that have low crime rates, and in some cities with heavy case loads it is used relatively little. Researchers suggest that the use of plea bargaining is closely tied to the closeness of interaction among members of the courtroom work group—judges, lawyers, and prosecutors.[13] Since these officials often work closely together for a year or more, personal relations develop and they seek more informal solutions for cases. Pretrial settlements in civil cases are a product of the same circumstances that lead to plea bargaining in criminal cases. In both situations settlement helps courtroom work groups achieve several goals. As Eisenstein and Jacob show, plea bargaining reduces uncertainty for all parties, it helps maintain the cohesion of the work group, and it makes the court look good to the general public by showing that it can dispose of cases quickly and that "justice" is done. In other words, criminals are caught and punished.

In spite of its appealing characteristics, plea bargaining has many disturbing consequences. In plea bargaining, the procedures are invisible and informal. Records are not kept of conversations, and decisions seldom are reviewed by higher courts to determine if the defendant really was guilty as charged. There is a strong potential for coercion as the prosecutor pressures the defendant. Illegally obtained evidence that might be held inadmissible in a court is never questioned. Often the unsuspecting defendant is simply advised by his or her court-appointed attorney to plead guilty, thereby saving the attorney time and allowing him or her to collect an easy fee. Some bargains appear to be too lenient and thus benefit criminal defendants. In other instances, defendants risk much harsher sentences if they insist on their right to go to trial, and thus they may accept a plea bargain even when the case against them is relatively weak.

Given the broad criticism of plea bargaining, it is not surprising that there have been calls to abolish it. Indeed, some state and local governments have experimented with strict limits on plea bargaining. However, most have reinstated it rather quickly.

As noted earlier, close-knit courtroom work groups encourage plea bargaining, and in most cases it is clear that the defendant is guilty. Several states and the federal government have passed new laws requiring mandatory minimum sentencing for certain crimes (see Chapter 15). This would eliminate plea bargaining in those instances. However, prosecutors often refuse to charge defendants with crimes that require a mandatory sentence because it limits their power to bargain.

In civil cases, there is typically an even greater delay than in criminal cases. In urban areas it may be several years before a case comes to trial. Trial court delay may be caused by a variety of factors. These include lax continuance policies that allow lawyers to control the pace of litigation, lack of adequate case monitoring by the court system, and lack of commitment by judges to control their dockets.[14] Delay is a major factor leading to out-of-court settlements, in which the two parties agree to a financial resolution of their dispute. Many civil suits involve personal injury in which the plaintiff has accumulated substantial medical bills. Because of the pressure of medical and legal expenses, plaintiffs may choose to settle before a trial date arrives. The defendant (often an insurance company) can usually better afford the costs incurred in delay but may wish to settle privately, being aware of exorbitant awards made by juries in cases where physical injury has resulted in the permanent loss of sight or limb.

When the full range of legal procedures is employed, the following patterns in civil and criminal cases can be identified as common among the states.

Civil Disputes

The procedure in a **civil dispute** is as follows:

1 The plaintiff (the complainant, the one who brings suit) approaches a lawyer, who requests the clerk of the proper court to issue a *writ of summons.* This writ, delivered by a deputy sheriff, directs the defendant to appear in court to answer the plaintiff's charges. Increasingly, private process servers perform this task. Failure to appear will result in the defendant losing the judgment by default.

2 Once the summons is delivered, the plaintiff files a *complaint* stating his or her cause of action and establishing that the court has jurisdiction and can provide a remedy in his or her dispute. The complaint is filed with the clerk of courts, who then has a copy delivered to the defendant along with a notice that the complaint is to be answered by a certain date. The defendant may admit to the charges, deny some or all of the charges, or argue that the charges do not raise a sufficient legal issue for the case to come to court. The judge will rule on the defendant's response and, unless he or she has admitted guilt, will allow the defendant to file a more detailed answer. This process of charge and response and possible countercharge by the defendant may continue for an extended period of time. When all complaints are answered and all pleadings filed, the issue is "joined" and the attorneys prepare for trial.

3 *Preliminary motions* are made and the case then lies dormant for several months (or years) as the trial date approaches. During the delay, negotiation takes place in an attempt to settle the dispute out of court. More than two-thirds of the cases filed never get beyond the preliminary stages, and in fact many cases are filed with no intention of pushing them to trial. Because lawyers in many civil cases are compensated on a contingency basis (they receive from 25 to 40 percent of the award), they push for out-of-court settlements to be sure of receiving some payment and to save the time and effort of going to trial. Shortly before the trial date, **pretrial conferences** are held in which the judge meets with attorneys for each side in an attempt to clarify and simplify the issues to those in contention.

4 If a settlement cannot be reached privately, the case goes to *trial.* Often a jury trial is waived, although plaintiffs in personal injury cases may prefer a jury rather than having the case heard by a judge, who they believe will be less generous. The judge or jury will decide which party was legally at fault and will also determine the amount of damages to be awarded. It is possible to appeal the verdict to a higher court.

Criminal Disputes

The procedure in a **criminal dispute** is as follows:

1 Before any arrests are made, the police must secure a *warrant.* A magistrate issues the warrant directing a search or the apprehension of a suspect, having received a sworn statement that there is probable cause to believe that a crime has been committed by a particular person at a given time and place. If the warrant authorizes a search, it must state clearly the place to be searched and the material to be seized.

2 Following his or her arrest, the defendant is brought before a magistrate (often a municipal judge) for a *preliminary hearing.* The purpose of this hearing is to determine if the prosecution has sufficient evidence to hold the accused and, if so, to set bail.

3 The prosecutor proceeds to determine the strength of his or her case. In many states, the prosecutor (district attorney) simply files a statement (the "information") with the appropriate court, which *indicts* or formally accuses a person of the commission of a crime. In other states, the prosecutor presents evidence that a serious crime has been committed to a **grand jury.*** If the grand jury finds sufficient reason to believe the accused committed the crime for which he or she is charged, it will return a "true bill" that indicts the accused, who then is bound over for trial.

4 When both the defendant and the prosecutor are ready for trial, the defendant is brought to court for **arraignment.** The charges are read and a plea of guilty or not guilty is entered. A plea of no contest *(nolo contendere)* is treated essentially the same as a guilty plea.

5 At the *trial* stage, the defendant in most states may waive the right to a jury trial and have the case heard by a judge. If the defendant is found guilty by a judge or jury, it is the judge who determines the sentence. Traditionally, judges were given broad dis-

*The *grand jury* is a body of twelve to twenty-five members whose purposes are inquisitorial and accusatorial. It is contrasted with a *petit jury,* usually of twelve persons, but at least six, which determines guilt or innocence. The grand jury meets in secret and decides by a majority vote. On occasion, it may conduct its own investigations into official misconduct. The grand jury has the power to subpoena witnesses and records and to compel testimony under oath. It usually follows the dictates of the prosecutor. Because grand juries are expensive and time-consuming, they have been abolished in many states.

cretion between minimum and maximum penalties for specific crimes. Of course, the defendant may appeal a guilty verdict.

Juries

Juries have been mentioned in the discussion of both civil and criminal disputes, and a few words of explanation are in order. A group of potential jury persons (a *venire*) is selected by lot, usually from voting lists or drivers' licenses. These people are called into court as jury cases arise and are examined *(voir dire)* regarding their qualifications to return an impartial verdict in the case at hand.

Charges have been made that the jury system underrepresents minorities. Because African-Americans and Hispanics are less likely than whites to be registered to vote, driver's license lists are increasingly used to pick jury members. However, these lists tend to underrepresent older persons, and many who live in large urban areas do not have driver's licenses. Minorities also may be disadvantaged by changes in trial location. In the highly publicized Rodney King case there was a change of venue from Los Angeles, where his alleged beating by police took place, to the nearly all-white suburb of Simi Valley, where it was unlikely there would be any African-American jurors. In 1986 *(Batson* v. *Kentucky)* the Supreme Court held that prosecutors may not use their peremptory challenges (where potential jury members may be rejected without any reason, as contrasted with dismissal "for cause" where attorneys have reason to believe a potential juror may be biased) to exclude members based on race. In 1994, this ruling was extended to prevent exclusion based on gender in *J.E.B.* v. *Alabama.* Critics of small juries—six or eight members—contend that they are more likely than twelve-member juries to exclude minorities and they are less likely to have a minority point of view.[15]

Concern about juries extends beyond matters of race and gender to proposals that would make jurors more active participants in trials. Some courts are experimenting by allowing jurors to ask questions and to take notes. One-day, one-trial terms of jury duty with more pay can make jury service more attractive by reducing the inconvenience of long trials.

In spite of the importance attached to the jury system, it is not employed as often as one might expect. In some jurisdictions, as many as 90 percent of all people charged with criminal offenses plead guilty. Of those going to trial, roughly half opt to have their cases heard by a judge. Although the Constitution guarantees the right to a jury trial in criminal and civil cases, fewer than 10 percent nationwide of those charged with a criminal offense demand a jury trial. Juries are not required for all cases, and typically criminal misdemeanors and various civil actions—divorce, small claims, landlord-tenant disputes—are heard by judges alone. Juvenile defendants are not automatically guaranteed jury trials.

Compared with judge-tried cases, jury trials are longer, cost more, and involve more people. Most research indicates that judge and jury decisions are remarkably similar. A major study of the American jury system found that judges agreed with jury verdicts 80 percent of the time. When there was disagreement, the jury tended to be more lenient than the judge and more willing to consider a social, as opposed to a strictly legal, definition of guilt.[16] Despite the decline in its use, the jury remains a basic protection of citizens against the overreach of official power.

JUDICIAL SELECTION

The way in which state court systems function is influenced strongly by the quality of judicial personnel. In turn, the type of judge presiding in courtrooms across the country is influenced by the ways in which judges are selected. Judicial selection is a highly political process that affects very directly the interests of the most powerful partisan forces in states and communities. Political parties use judgeships as a source of patronage. Lawyers and their bar associations are very much involved in the selection process. Not only are the judgeships themselves prized positions, but judges are able to spread the patronage further by assigning counsel in criminal cases, by naming administrators of estates where a will does not exist, and by appointing numerous minor court officials.

Each of the thirteen original states selected judges by either legislative or gubernatorial appointment. By the 1830s the popular democracy movement associated with Andrew Jackson began pushing states to elect judges. The concurrent rise of political parties meant that the selection and recruitment of judges were done by powerful new political party leaders in many large cities.[17] The Progressive movement in the second half of the nineteenth century reacted against political parties by moving to nonpartisan judicial elections. A feeling of dissatisfaction with both election and appointment of judges led the American Judicature Society, founded in 1913, to propose a plan in which judicial nominating commissions would recommend judicial candidates to governors. From this came the Missouri Plan, which will be discussed later.

Several selection systems are currently used by the fifty states—election, appointment by governors, appointment by legislatures, merit plans, and various combinations of these basic plans (see Table 8-2). Several states use one system for trial judges and another for appellate judges, and there may be special systems for minor trial judges. Currently, thirty-three states use a merit system to select judges at least at one court level. Trial judges are more likely to be elected than are appellate judges.

Election continues to be the most popular way of selecting judges. Judges are on the ballot along with a variety of other officials, and parties participate by endorsing candidates and managing nominations. Even when nonpartisan systems are used, parties often play a dominant role. In Ohio, for example, judges are chosen in nonpartisan general elections, but partisan primaries are conducted in which judges' party affiliations are clearly stated. Partisan election (election by party label) is most likely to occur in the South. In most cases judicial elections are nearly invisible to voters. They get lower voter turnouts than legislative or executive elections.

In many instances, judges resign before their term of office expires. This allows the governor to make an interim appointment. Typically, incumbent judges stand an excellent chance of being reelected. In addition to low turnout, often there are no opposition candidates in judicial elections.

In nine states, the governor *appoints* some judges in a manner similar to the presidential selection of federal judges. Usually the legislature confirms the appointment,

TABLE 8-2 PRINCIPAL METHODS OF JUDICIAL SELECTION FOR STATE COURTS

Partisan election	Nonpartisan election	Legislative election	Gubernatorial appointment	Merit plan
Alabama[a]	Georgia[a]	Connecticut[a]	California	Alaska
Arkansas	Idaho[a]	Rhode Island[c]	Delaware	Arizona[a]
Illinois[a]	Kentucky	South Carolina[a]	Maine[a]	Colorado[a]
Mississippi[a]	Louisiana	Virginia	Massachusetts	Florida[a,b]
New Mexico	Michigan[a]		New Hampshire	Hawaii
North Carolina[b]	Minnesota		New Jersey[a]	Indiana[a]
Pennsylvania[a]	Montana		New York[a,d]	Iowa[a]
Tennessee[a,b]	Nevada			Kansas[a]
Texas[a]	North Dakota			Maryland
West Virginia	Ohio[a]			Missouri[a]
Oregon[a]				Nebraska
Washington[a]				Oklahoma[a,b]
Wisconsin[a]				South Dakota[a]
				Utah
				Vermont
				Wyoming[a]

[a]Minor court judges chosen by other methods.
[b]Most but not all major judicial positions selected this way.
[c]Supreme Court justices only.
[d]Appellate judges only.
Source: Council of State Governments, *The Book of the States, 1994–95* (Lexington, Ky.: Council of State Governments, 1994), pp. 190–192.

and a strong role is played by interest groups to influence nominations. In a few states, the legislature appoints judges. In those cases, the governor often plays a major role in controlling the legislature's choices.

Merit Systems

Most states adopting new plans of judicial selection since the 1930s have chosen some form of *merit system.* These plans are based on a selection process first instituted by California in 1934 and made popular by Missouri in 1940. The goal of merit plans is to remove judicial selection from the influence of partisan politics and to select judges on the basis of ability, in large part as determined by lawyers and sitting judges.

The **Missouri Plan** operates as follows. Whenever a judicial vacancy arises, the governor appoints an individual from a list of acceptable names submitted by a commission. There are three commissions in Missouri to nominate judges for three types of courts. The commissions are composed of lawyers, ordinary citizens, and a sitting judge. The lawyers are elected by all the lawyers in the court's district; the lay citizens are appointed by the governor; and the judge is the presiding judge of the court of appeal in that area. In California, the governor's appointments are subject to confirmation by a state commission. After a judge has served for a period of time, his or her name appears on the ballot and the voters check yes or no. If the vote is no, the selection process begins again. If the vote is yes, the judge's name will appear on future ballots, again without an opponent, and the voters will decide if they wish the judge to remain in office.

Contrary to the arguments of good-government groups, most studies indicate that merit plans do *not* produce judges who differ substantially from those who are elected or appointed. They have not had better legal qualifications nor have they decided cases in a noticeably different manner from judges selected by other methods. None of the selection systems increases the number of women or minority judges. In the most comprehensive review of the Missouri Plan, the authors note that "governors have used their appointments to reward friends or past political supporters and have implemented the plan very largely from a personal and political viewpoint."[18] Under this plan, only one judge has been given a no vote by the citizens of Missouri. Turnout usually is low in retention elections, and few judges have been voted out of office in states with merit plans. In California, no judge had been voted out of office since the plan was implemented in 1934 until chief justice Rose Elizabeth Bird and two justices were overwhelmingly denied reconfirmation in 1986. In 1994 the vote against three justices on the California supreme court averaged a surprisingly high 41 percent. Merit systems do not remove partisan considerations from the judiciary, nor do they make judicial elections different from elections for other public offices. For example, the 1986 judicial retention election in California was as high-spending and personally contentious as any gubernatorial partisan election. Moreover, while Governor Jerry Brown (1975–1983) had appointed a series of liberals to the California supreme court, his Republican successor George Deukmejian (1983–1991) was able to recast the court with a strong conservative majority.

Regardless of the method of selection, partisan politics plays a major role in the selection of judges. Even in Missouri, governors have appointed most judges from their own party. In nonpartisan elections, parties are usually active in primary elections, and they are often directly involved in general elections. Interest groups are active participants in every selection plan. Governors tend to draw a high percentage of their appointments from current and past members of the state legislature. Under both partisan and merit systems, judges seem equally objective and equally attuned to popular sentiment in their states.

In the 1980s voters in several states defeated proposals to move to merit systems of judicial selection. In general, the proponents and opponents of merit selection among the states have been similar. Proponents include various good-government groups, such as the League of Women Voters; bar associations; and business groups. Opponents include trial lawyers, labor unions, and minorities. Political parties often are split on merit selection depending on how they have fared under an electoral system.[19]

Judicial Elections

We have seen that in practice judges selected by merit plans enjoy a lifetime of service, although they are subject to periodic approval at the polls. Incumbent judges usually face little opposition. Often lawyers are reluctant to challenge sitting judges, and low-level campaigns favor incumbents running against challengers who are not well known to the general public. Incumbent judges are even less likely to be defeated in nonpartisan elections where party identification cannot be used as a voting clue. When incumbents are defeated, oftentimes there have been allegations of immoral conduct or incompetence that have been played up by the local media.[20] Unlike federal judges, few state judges are given life tenure in a single appointment and few states give their governors sole power to appoint judges. For appellate courts, the typical length of a term is five to twelve years. Generally, terms of trial judges are shorter, averaging four to eight years. Long terms are believed to be beneficial because they help ensure judicial independence.

Minority lawyers and politicians favor election because they believe members of their racial or ethnic group are less likely to be selected as judges under a merit system. However, they prefer that judges be elected from small, single-member districts where it is more likely that a majority of voters will be minorities than is the case in at-large districts that compose an entire city or county. Their position has been helped by the Supreme Court's rulings in *Clark* v. *Roemer* (1991) and in *Chisom* v. *Roemer* (1991) that provisions of the Voting Rights Act of 1982 are applicable to judicial elections because judges, like legislators, serve as "representatives" of the people. In *Chisom,* it was contended that Louisiana's system of electing some state supreme court judges from multimember (at-large) districts diluted the voting strength of African-Americans. Because 1982 Voting Rights Act amendments prescribe an "effects test" to determine if government actions have impaired the ability of minorities to influence the outcome of elections (this is most often seen in the way in which legislative boundaries are drawn), if minorities can show that existing electoral systems have had the effect of limiting or excluding the selection of minority judges, states will be forced to change their election districts. The key change in the 1982 amendments was that plaintiffs no longer had to prove that government officials "intended" to weaken the political power of minorities. In *Chisom,* Justice Stevens stated a clear preference for the merit selection of judges.

Discipline and Removal of Judges

All state judges serve for at least four years. Terms range up to fourteen years (in New York). In Rhode Island, judges have life appointments, and in a few states appointment is to age seventy. Only in rare instances have judges been removed, or even disciplined, during their term in office. Most states have constitutional provisions for impeachment, but the process (which involves securing valid signatures on petitions and holding trials) is time-consuming and very expensive. Few judges have been impeached and removed from office. Seven states permit judicial recall; but even fewer judges have been recalled than have been impeached.

Not only are these traditional means of removal time-consuming and costly, but they also are often perceived as overly harsh penalties for the alleged offenses. As a result, judges with serious problems frequently escape removal because voters or legislatures are reluctant to take such drastic action. Occasionally judges resign when threatened with impeachment.

A more practical solution to dealing with problems of judicial incompetence or unethical behavior has been the creation of judicial tenure commissions composed of lawyers, judges, and citizens. They investigate complaints, hold hearings, and impose penalties ranging from temporary suspension to removal. Over thirty states have judicial commissions. Most are patterned after the California Commission of Judicial Qualifications, which was created in 1961. The California commission has nine members (five judges appointed by the state supreme court, two lawyers selected by the state bar association, and two citizens appointed by the governor and approved by the senate) and receives over 300 complaints a year. If it believes a judge has acted unprofessionally, the commission issues a report to the state supreme court, which can discipline or remove an offending judge. In many instances judges have resigned or retired while under investigation.

THE POLICYMAKING ROLE OF STATE COURTS

Court decisions are important in the study of state government because they do much more than decide narrow legal issues between two parties.[21] Decisions of state courts significantly affect the nature of public policy in a variety of ways. For example, court decisions concerning environmental protection have important economic as well as ecological consequences; decisions regarding legislative apportionment or the eligibility of a governor to run for reelection directly affect the success of political parties; decisions reviewing the constitutionality of state statutes covering such matters as abortion and capital punishment literally involve questions of life and death for the state's citizens; decisions interpreting rights of criminal defendants may allow convicted felons to be freed; decisions concerning state tax policies affect the distribution of individual wealth and they may also affect the type of education made available in the state's schools and colleges.

In a few celebrated cases, state courts make policy by deciding issues not previously considered by the judicial system. Innovative decisions are more likely to come from appellate courts than from trial courts.[22] This is so because appellate judges have broader powers and jurisdiction than trial judges, and they are less limited by the status quo. The written opinions of state appellate judges are often cited by judges in other states, and this of course broadens their policymaking impact. Trial courts usually deal with narrow problems that only affect specific individuals.

Innovative decisions, in which major policy implications derive from a single case, clearly are exceptional. More often, judicial policy is made by a series of decisions in apparently routine cases. Over a period of time, for example, decisions regarding sentencing of criminals may affect conditions in jails and, more fundamentally, may influence the rate of crime. Decisions may have a ripple effect as interested parties become aware of the kinds of decisions being handed down by certain courts. In this respect, environmentalists may be encouraged by court decisions to concentrate on litigation rather than on legislative lobbying or media appeals to achieve their goals. Trial court judges often develop innovative solutions to deal with old and new problems. As will be discussed in Chapter 15, in recent years local criminal courts have been especially innovative in creating alternative sentencing to imprisonment.

The nature of court decisions (and therefore the nature of court policymaking) is affected by the personal characteristics of judges and by the type of selection plan employed. One study found that Democratic and Republican judges decided cases in ways that correspond with their political party's position on certain issues.[23] For example, Democrats were more likely to vote for the defense in criminal cases; for labor unions in labor-management cases; and for tenants in landlord-tenant cases. In states where judges are appointed, their voting behavior typically does not follow closely the established positions of political parties. In other states, such as Michigan, the selection is highly partisan and judges' decisions tend to run parallel to party lines.

The majority of the U.S. Supreme Court since the mid-1980s has favored a hands-off approach to the law, preferring to let elected officials in Congress and the states take the lead. The Court has been deciding fewer cases in the 1990s—down about 25 percent from the 1980s—and the most interesting cases often are the ones the Court refuses to hear. As the U.S. Supreme Court has moved to the periphery, especially on civil liberties and civil rights cases, this has encouraged litigants to rely more heavily on state constitutions by filing cases in state courts. Judges in the states have responded by supporting greater protection of individual liberties than would be likely under federal provisions.[24] Increased judicial activism (policymaking) can be seen in Florida, where the state constitution has an explicit right to privacy and those provisions have been used to invalidate restrictive abortion regulations that were approved by the state legislature (see the discussion of judicial activism and restraint in the Scholarly Box). New Jersey's supreme court overturned the state's public education financing system, calling on the legislature to allocate more money to economically disadvantaged districts. While state courts continue to rely on the national Constitution in most instances, in recent years they have added state constitutional protections in the areas of privacy, criminal law, and school financing.

The area of education presents a good example of how inaction by the U.S. Supreme Court can lead to state court policymaking. Since the Supreme Court has declined to address the issue of how schools are financed, holding that education is not a fundamental right protected by the Constitution, state courts have played the major policymaking role in this area. Basing their decisions on state constitutions, they have forced state legislatures to revamp the ways in which they fund education.

THE IMPACT OF SUPREME COURT DECISIONS ON THE STATES: CRIMINAL RIGHTS AND ABORTION

Criminal procedures in state trial courts and state criminal statutes have been directly affected by a series of Supreme Court decisions beginning in the early 1960s. The activist Warren Court overturned a number of state court decisions, ruling that the constitutional rights of criminal defendants had not been adequately protected by state officials. In the course of these decisions, the Supreme Court nationalized (i.e., made applicable as limits on state officials) provisions of the Fourth, Fifth, Sixth, and Eighth amendments to the U.S. Constitution. Although the Supreme Court of the 1980s and 1990s has tended to defer to the states and has become less supportive of civil liberties in those cases it does decide, the Court has not directly overturned any of the Warren Court's major decisions of the 1960s. In fact, the Burger Court of the 1970s *expanded* some earlier rulings on the right to reproductive freedom and freedom of expression.[25] A brief review of leading decisions since 1960 follows.

SCHOLARLY BOX

JUDICIAL ACTIVISM AND RESTRAINT

Judicial activism and **judicial restraint** refer to the extent that judges "make policy." While judges have always made decisions that have led to new public policies, recent controversy involves the extent to which this should happen.

Activism can take several forms.* These include court opinions that overturn precedent set in past decisions dealing with issues similar to the case at hand (the doctrine of *stare decisis* calls on courts to let decided cases stand). While that may happen in dramatic fashion when a court overturns a well-known precedent, activism also can include incremental change through a series of seemingly routine decisions by trial courts. When courts declare legislative acts unconstitutional (the use of judicial review), this is seen as the most extreme kind of activism.

If a court mandates reform of its state's property tax system for funding public education or if it calls for a substantial increase in welfare benefits, it may be criticized for assuming powers that should be exercised by legislators. Those unhappy with the nature of court-directed policy, whether that policy is liberal or conservative, are likely to call on courts to exercise restraint. In recent years, conservatives have been most critical of activism and have called on judges to limit their opinions to an interpretation of what the writers of constitutions intended governments to do.

Some activism is inevitable as courts are presented with a wide range of new social issues. These include such biomedical questions as gene splitting, surrogate motherhood, and euthanasia. In addition, an increasing number of state courts are using state constitutions to extend individual rights at a time when the U.S. Supreme Court's exercise of restraint has led it to decide fewer cases (often ducking some issues altogether) and to upholding constraints on individual liberties.

Even if one strongly favors judicial activism, it is well to remember that courts are limited as policymakers by several factors. First, they cannot act until a situation has been presented to them. Unlike legislatures, courts cannot anticipate problems, but often act after serious damage has been done. Also, unlike legislatures, courts lack the staff for gathering social and economic information. Because they are limited to deciding cases on narrow grounds, a specific decision may not be applicable in other similar circumstances. The judicial process leads to yes or no answers (defendants are either guilty or innocent), while the legislative process leads to compromise. Finally, courts must rely on the executive branch to enforce decisions. Because they seek compliance with their rulings, courts may practice restraint rather than risk widespread noncompliance and a concurrent loss of legitimacy.

*See Henry R. Glick, *Courts, Politics, and Justice* (New York: McGraw-Hill, 1993), pp. 369–370.

In *Mapp* v. *Ohio* (1961), the Supreme Court ruled that the Fourth Amendment (which guarantees freedom from illegal search and seizure) extends to state as well as federal officials. In other words, the police could no longer seize evidence illegally (i.e., without a proper search warrant) and then have that material introduced during a trial to support the prosecutor's case. In *Miranda* v. *Arizona* (1966), the Court ruled that when state officials take individuals into custody, they must warn them that they have the right to remain silent (Fifth Amendment), that anything they say may be held against them (Fifth Amendment), that they have the right to an attorney (Sixth Amendment), and that if they cannot afford an attorney one will be provided for them. In both *Mapp* and *Miranda,* the Court overruled state convictions on the grounds that the defendants had been denied due process of the law as guaranteed by the Fourteenth Amendment. Although the U.S. Supreme Court has not directly overturned its rulings in *Mapp* or *Miranda,* since the mid-1980s it has created exceptions that clearly weaken these rules and permit greater flexibility by state and local law enforcement officers.

For example, *Mapp* has been weakened by the concept that if the police act in "good faith" and later discover a warrant is defective, the evidence seized still can be used in court. Regarding *Miranda,* the Court has adopted a "public safety" exception that allows rules to be bypassed if they might delay immediate recovery of a dangerous weapon. In 1991 the Court held that a coerced confession introduced at trial does not necessarily overturn a conviction. It can be excused as a "harmless error" if other independent evidence supports a conviction. The Rehnquist Court of the late 1980s and 1990s has been very deferential to federalism, allowing states broad authority to establish criminal procedure policies. For example, in 1993 the Court held that a police officer may seize drugs that are not immediately identifiable (that is, in "plain view") if they are felt through a suspect's clothing. In 1995 the Court held that the police should knock to announce themselves before entering a house to execute a search warrant. However, the unanimous opinion noted that there may be "reasonable" exceptions if there is the likelihood of violence or the immediate destruction of evidence.

Although the Supreme Court has weakened some U.S. constitutional protections, many state courts have used state constitutions to protect civil liberties. For example, the New Jersey supreme court rejected the good-faith exception rule in *United States* v. *Leon* by holding that the **exclusionary rule** is "embedded" in the state's legal system.

In *Gideon* v. *Wainwright* (1963) the Supreme Court held that states must provide free legal counsel to indigent defendants accused of felonies. Later, in *Argersinger* v. *Hamlin* (1972), the Court extended the right to court-appointed counsel to include those charged with misdemeanors so long as they faced the possibility of imprisonment. Before the *Gideon* decision, most states already provided free legal counsel to poor defendants. However, these two decisions have placed considerable financial burdens on state and local governments to provide lawyers in criminal cases. By 1968, four-fifths of all defendants in New York City were provided with free lawyers. Two systems for providing counsel to indigent defendants have been used by local governments: assigned counsel from among lawyers in private practice, and public defenders who are paid salaries by public or quasi-public agencies to handle the defense of poor people. In many cities, neighborhood legal-assistance offices, funded by grants from the federal government, provide a third type of counsel to indigents.

The Supreme Court has also ruled that juvenile defendants have a right to legal counsel. *In re Gault* (1967) extended essentially the same basic rights to defendants in juvenile court—right to counsel, right to confront and cross-examine witnesses, privilege against self-incrimination, right to appeal—as are provided adults in the regular court system.

Occasionally a Supreme Court decision will affect the administration of justice in virtually every state, necessitating a revision of criminal statutes across the country. This has occurred in the areas of capital punishment and abortion. In *Furman* v. *Georgia* (1972) a badly divided Court (5 to 4) overruled the imposition of the death penalty in Georgia, declaring that it constituted cruel and unusual punishment in violation of the Eighth and Fourteenth amendments. Since 1972, most states have rewritten their capital punishment statutes in an attempt to institute the death penalty within limits acceptable to the Court. In 1976, the Court upheld capital punishment in Georgia, Florida, and Texas, where statutes allow the judge or jury to set the death penalty after considering mitigating factors. At the same time, the Court struck down mandatory death penalty statutes in North Carolina and Louisiana. In 1977, the Court ruled that capital punishment could not be imposed for the crime of rape. The Court has held that opponents of the death penalty can be excluded from trial juries in capital cases.

In general, the Court has deferred to state legislative decisions and ruled in favor of state capital punishment procedures since the 1980s (see Chapter 15). For example, in 1987 it upheld the death penalty in Georgia, even though statistics showed that African-Americans were much more likely to be executed than whites. In 1989 the justices agreed that the Eighth Amendment does not bar absolutely the execution of murderers with mental deficiencies or the execution of sixteen- and seventeen-year-old murderers. In both opinions Justice Sandra Day O'Connor cast critical votes with the 5-to-4 majority. In 1991 the Court set limits on the number of petitions that could be filed by death row inmates, hoping to speed up the process of execution. In *Tennessee* v. *Middlebrook* (1993) the Supreme Court held that a defendant who is sentenced to death and presents new evidence of his or her innocence is not ordinarily entitled to a new trial unless the evidence is "truly persuasive."

Three cases involving the use of juries illustrate the Court's willingness to allow state experimentation with unorthodox practices in criminal procedures. In *Williams* v. *Florida* (1970), the Court upheld the conviction of a criminal defendant in Florida who was tried by a six-person jury as allowed under Florida law in all cases except capital offenses. In *Apodaca* v. *Oregon* (1972), the Court upheld the conviction of a defendant when the jury had voted 10 to 2, the minimum margin necessary under Oregon law, that he was guilty. In 1981, the Court upheld camera coverage of trials in Florida, and since that time most states have permitted television coverage of court proceedings.

In *Roe* v. *Wade* (1973) the Supreme Court overturned a Texas statute that made it a felony for anyone to destroy a fetus except "on medical advice for the purpose of saving the life of the mother." Since the Texas statute was typical of those in effect in most states, statutes have been rewritten to allow state control of abortions *after* the third month of pregnancy. Then, in 1977, the Court ruled that state and local governments could choose whether or not to finance abortions for nontherapeutic reasons under Medicaid. In 1980, the Court upheld a congressional ban on federal payments through Medicaid for abortion even to those women for whom the procedure is medically indicated. In one of its most significant abortion decisions since 1973, the Court in *Webster* v. *Reproductive Health Services* (1989) upheld several provisions of a Missouri statute that limited abortion rights. Stopping just short of overturning *Roe* v. *Wade,* the majority in *Webster* sustained provisions making it "unlawful for any public facility to be used for the purpose of performing or assisting an abortion not necessary to save the life of the mother" and "unlawful for any public employee . . . to perform or assist in an abortion not necessary to save the life of the mother."

Webster invited states to adopt more restrictions on the availability of abortions, and many responded by passing parental notification or consent laws and establishing waiting periods before an abortion could be performed. As of 1993, about half the states required minor women to get parental consent to have an abortion. Over 400,000 women under the age of 18 become pregnant every year, and about 180,000 of them choose to have an abortion.[26]

In decisions after *Webster,* the Supreme Court in 1990 upheld a Minnesota law requiring teenage girls to notify both parents or get judicial permission before having an abortion, and in *Planned Parenthood of Southeast Pennsylvania* v. *Carey* (1992) the Court voted to uphold all of Pennsylvania's restrictions on abortion, except for a requirement of spousal notification. Only a bare majority of justices stood against expressly overturning *Roe* v. *Wade* and permitting states to ban abortions at any stage of pregnancy.

President Bill Clinton used the twentieth anniversary of *Roe* v. *Wade* in 1993 to issue a series of directives to remove restrictions on abortions in federal facilities. In 1994 the Supreme Court ruled that violence at abortion clinics can be challenged under a federal antiracketeering statute. This was followed by a ruling in *Madsen* v. *Women's Health Center* (1994) that upheld a court-ordered 36-foot buffer zone to restrict antiabortion protesters and to ensure access to abortion clinics.

With the addition of a clear conservative majority since 1986, the Supreme Court has become increasingly deferential to the states. As we have seen, the Court has been willing to accept state experimentation in the areas of criminal procedures, the death penalty, and abortion. A curious aspect of this approach by the Supreme Court can be seen in *Cruzan* v. *Missouri* (1990), the so-called right-to-die case. In a 5-to-4 opinion the Court upheld the right of a state to establish procedures by which people can express their desire not to be kept alive by artificial means. The majority agreed with the state of Missouri's argument that Nancy Cruzan's parents had not shown clear evidence of their daughter's wishes. In a concurring opinion Justice O'Connor noted that "the more challenging task of crafting appropriate procedures for safeguarding incompetent's liberty interests is entrusted to the laboratory of the states."

The *Cruzan* and *Webster* decisions give states the opportunity to demonstrate how well they can deal with controversial issues and shape public policy.[27] At the same time, this passive role by the U.S. Supreme Court allows losers to pursue their objectives in other forums.[28] For example, Nancy Cruzan's parents brought additional evidence of her desire not to remain in a comatose state to another trial court hearing, and subsequently the feeding tubes were withdrawn. Once abortion became a state legislative issue, pro-choice activists gained strength in several states.

While we have limited our discussion here to criminal rights and abortion cases, throughout this book we refer to many other areas in which Supreme Court opinions have a direct impact on the states. These include legislative districting, school desegregation, affirmative action, environmental protection, religion in public places, and, as decided in 1995, the right to test for drugs in public schools and the right to distribute anonymous campaign literature.

SUMMARY

States typically have three-tiered court systems composed of fragmented trial courts, intermediate courts of appeal, and a supreme court. While state supreme courts hear and decide cases in ways similar to the U.S. Supreme Court, they often differ in that the power of state chief justices is less and there are fewer dissenting opinions.

Reform has centered on consolidation and centralization of state trial and appellate courts. Other reforms include providing better access to the courts and the use of alternative dispute resolution, including arbitration and mediation.

Criminal procedures are strongly influenced by plea bargaining, in which all interested parties seem to benefit. The prevalence of plea bargaining is affected by the cohesiveness of courtroom work groups, whose members seek to reduce uncertainty and avoid time-consuming trials.

States have experimented with the size of juries and the use of nonunanimous juries in criminal trials. While there are few jury trials, concern remains about the competence of jury members to understand complex legal issues.

Academics have devoted a great deal of time to studying procedures by which judges are selected—election, appointment, and merit. Their conclusions are that the method of selection has, at best, a limited impact on the quality of judges and the nature of their opinions. There also is long-standing debate over the role of courts as policymakers, with opinion divided regarding the extent to which courts should create new policy by overturning precedents and by ruling against the constitutionality of state laws.

KEY TERMS

Arbitration Operates like mediation, but parties agree ahead of time to be bound by the arbitrator's decision. In arbitration, decisions are enforceable in court.

Arraignment The stage in a criminal proceeding in which the defendant is brought before a judge to hear the formal charges and to enter a plea of guilty or not guilty.

Centralization of courts Control of courts under the direction of the chief justice of the state supreme court, who assigns cases and manages work loads for a more efficient system of justice.

Civil disputes Normally legal disputes in which the parties are private citizens or private organizations.

Common law Law that has developed from a series of decisions by judges in similar situations. In the United States, there is no federal common law, but common law exists within state judicial systems. American common law originated in England, and it forms the basis of legal procedures in all states except Louisiana.

Consolidation of courts The process of streamlining court systems into a single set of trial courts.

Courts of appeal Those courts that review the proceedings of trial courts to determine if significant legal errors have occurred.

Criminal disputes Legal disputes in which the state prosecutes people accused of violating criminal codes. Criminal law includes felonies (serious crimes for which the penalty is imprisonment) and misdemeanors (less serious offenses for which the maximum penalty is a fine or short jail sentence).

Exclusionary rule As established in *Mapp* v. *Ohio,* it precludes illegally seized evidence from being used against a defendant in a trial.

Grand jury A body of twelve to twenty-five people that considers evidence brought by a prosecutor concerning the commission of a serious crime. Grand juries do not determine guilt or innocence; they determine only whether a matter should go to trial.

Judicial activism When courts engage in policymaking, typically to reflect the current values of the American people. **Judicial restraint** is when courts defer to legislators and executives by upholding their policies and not introducing the judges' own policy preferences.

Judicial review The ability of a state court to hold unconstitutional any law or action by a public official that it deems to be in conflict with the state constitution.

Mediation Process in which a neutral third party listens to both sides of a dispute, tries to identify areas of common concern, and proposes a solution. This is a nonadversarial process.

Missouri Plan A method of selecting judges in which the governor makes an appointment from a list of three names prepared by a commission. After the judges have served for a period of time, their names appear on the ballot unopposed for the voters to retain or remove them on the basis of their record.

No contest *(nolo contendere)* Literally, "I do not wish to contend." In effect, the defendant pleads guilty to a criminal charge without stating so formally.

Plea bargaining An arrangement between the prosecutor and the defendant in which the defendant agrees to plead guilty if the prosecutor will reduce the charges and recommend a lighter sentence.

Pretrial conference A meeting between the judge and attorneys in civil cases to clarify the issues about to come to trial and to determine if the conflict can be settled out of court.

Trial courts Courts that conduct examinations of the facts presented by plaintiffs and defendants to resolve criminal and civil conflicts. This is the first step in the process of trial and appeal. In criminal cases, the state is always the plaintiff, initiating the legal proceedings.

REFERENCES

1 Lawrence Baum, *American Courts,* 3d ed. (Boston: Houghton Mifflin, 1994), p. 45.

2 Henry J. Abraham, *The Judicial Process,* 6th ed. (New York: Oxford University Press, 1993), p. 135.

3 Henry R. Glick, *Courts, Politics, and Justice,* 3d ed. (New York: McGraw-Hill, 1993), p. 338.

4 Ibid., pp. 371–372.

5 Herbert Jacob, "Courts: The Least Visible Branch," in Virginia Gray and Herbert Jacob, eds., *Politics in the American States,* 6th ed. (Washington: Congressional Quarterly Press, 1996), p. 266.

6 Ibid., p. 254.

7 Baum, *American Courts,* p. 51.

8 Ibid., pp. 52–53.

9 Erick B. Low, "Accessing the Judicial System: The States' Response," *The Book of the States, 1994–95* (Lexington, Ky.: Council of State Governments, 1994), pp. 168–176.

10 Kenneth G. Pankey, Jr., "The State of the Judiciary," *The Book of the States, 1992–93* (Lexington, Ky.: Council of State Governments, 1992), p. 210.

11 Glick, *Courts, Politics, and Justice,* pp. 230–231.

12 Ibid., p. 232.

13 See James Eisenstein and Herbert Jacob, *Felony Justice* (Boston: Little, Brown, 1977).
14 Erick B. Low, "State of the Judiciary," in *The Book of the States 1988–89* (Lexington, Ky.: Council of State Governments, 1988), p. 149.
15 Kathleen Sylvester, "Putting the Jury on Trial," *Governing* (March 1993), pp. 40–41.
16 Harry Kalven and Hans Zeizel, *The American Jury* (Boston: Little, Brown, 1966).
17 Anthony Champagne and Judith Haydel, eds., *Judicial Reform in the States* (Lanham, Md.: University Press of America, 1993), p. 6.
18 Richard A. Watson and Ronald G. Downing, *The Politics of Bench and Bar: Judicial Selection under the Missouri Nonpartisan Court Plan* (New York: Wiley, 1969), pp. 338–339. Also see Barbara L. Graham, "Do Judicial Systems Matter? A Study of Black Representation on State Courts," *American Politics Quarterly* (July 1990), pp. 316–336.
19 See Champagne and Haydel, *Judicial Reform in the States,* p. 185.
20 Philip L. Dubois, "Voting Cues in Nonpartisan Trial Court Elections," *Law and Society Review* (Vol. 18, No. 3, 1984), p. 426.
21 See Herbert Jacob, *Justice in America,* 4th ed. (Boston: Little, Brown, 1984), Chapter 3.
22 Glick, *Courts, Politics, and Justice,* p. 386.
23 Stuart Nagel, "Political Party Affiliation and Judges' Decisions," *American Political Science Review,* 1961, pp. 843–860.
24 See Stanley H. Friedelbaum, "The 'New' Judicial Federalism," *The Book of the States, 1992–93* (Lexington, Ky.: Council of State Governments, 1992), pp. 247–255.
25 See Vincent Blasi, ed., *The Burger Court: The Counterrevolution That Wasn't* (New Haven, Conn.: Yale University Press, 1983).
26 Kathleen Sylvester, "Making Families Talk about Abortion," *Governing* (April 1993), pp. 22–23.
27 Elder Witt, "On Issues of State Power, the Supreme Court Seems to Be of Two Minds," *Governing,* October 1990, p. 64.
28 Neil Skeme, "The Supreme Court's Passive Policy Role," *Congressional Quarterly Weekly Report,* March 23, 1991, p. 778.

9

THE STRUCTURE OF LOCAL GOVERNMENT

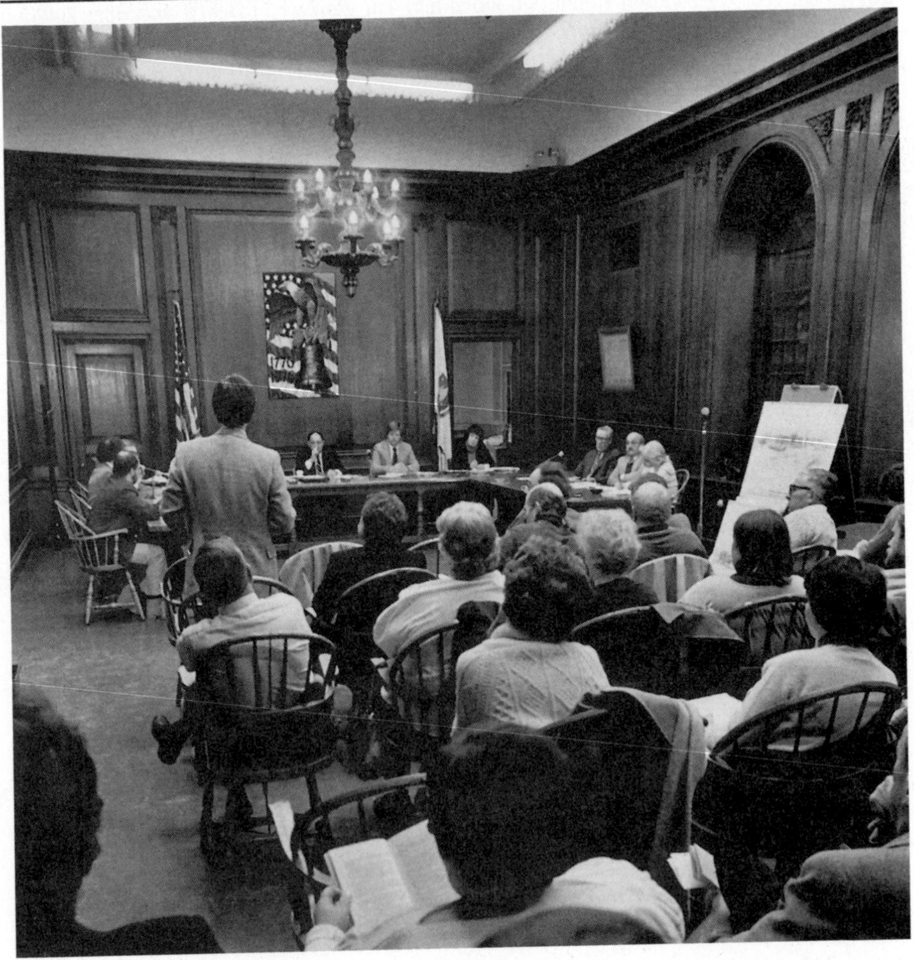

Walter S. Silver/The Picture Cube

This is the first of three chapters dealing with cities, suburbs, and metropolitan areas. As we begin to examine urban politics, the reading by Neal R. Peirce directs our attention to how some universities are responding to urban problems. Too often, many of our great universities have resembled cultural islands surrounded by violent and decaying inner-city neighborhoods. Conflicts inevitably occurred as universities sought to acquire more land, in part to serve as a buffer zone against the outside world. Increasingly universities across the country are doing more than studying urban problems: They are trying to solve them. This article examines how academia is tackling the urban crisis in Baltimore. Whether they reside in large cities or small towns, readers should consider what kind of commitment their universities are making to improve their communities.

CITIES IN THE NINETEENTH CENTURY

Throughout the nineteenth century most Americans lived in small towns and on farms. Not until 1920 did the census show that a majority of Americans lived in cities. In 1840 the United States had a population of about 17 million, of whom only 1.8 million lived in urban areas. No city had more than 500,000 people. Chicago had a population of 29,000 in 1850 and ranked as the nation's twentieth largest city.

By 1880 European immigration helped push the total population to 50 million, and within the United States people increasingly were drawn away from rural areas to new industrial jobs in cities. The industrial revolution and new technology such as the elevator made cities greater centers of opportunity and helped increase population density. In addition, improved sanitation made cities more livable. For example, as late as 1878 yellow fever reduced the population of Memphis from 50,000 to 20,000 as thousands died and even more people fled the city.

Still, in 1880 only 28 percent of Americans lived in urban areas. While the population of New York City had soared to 1.9 million, no other city had more than 850,000 people. In 1880, many cities in the South and West were scarcely more than small towns. Atlanta had a population of 37,000; Houston 16,000; and Los Angeles 123,000. Historian Richard Hofstadter describes the United States in 1880 as rural, Yankee, and Protestant.[1] Until then, immigrants had had relatively little impact on American political life.

Before the Civil War most city governments provided few public services beyond fire, police, and street maintenance. Urban power often was held by an elite group of higher-economic-status Protestants. All cities had some form of mayor-council government in which the power of mayors typically was very limited. The heads of many departments, even police and fire, were separately elected in a system of decentralized, fragmented government. So long as city populations remained small and homogeneous and demands for services were limited, this system worked satisfactorily. But with rapid population growth cities faced severe problems of rising crime, unsafe sanitation, inadequate transportation, and labor unrest by the 1870s.

Government structure and processes are not neutral. The bias in the late nineteenth century in urban America in terms of who benefited from public services clearly was on the side of the old-family elites who had dominated cities from their earliest days. It was time for change.

Academia Tackles the Urban Crisis

Neal R. Peirce

Baltimore—America's colleges and universities, to hear Sargent Shriver talk, must shake their ivory tower ways and start acting more like fire departments.

"Fire departments go where the fire is; universities need to bring the intellectual resources of their faculty, plus the altruistic motivations of their students, to bear on the fire consuming our cities," Shriver, the Kennedy brother-in-law who's remembered as the first director of the nation's war on poverty in the 1960s, said.

But Shriver is doing more than talking up a new role for the nation's colleges and universities. He's part of an ambitious effort, unveiled in December, to coalesce the 10 public and private universities of the Baltimore region in what's billed as America's first multi-university consortium designed to attack urban problems.

The lead university in the group is the University of Maryland (Baltimore County), where a new Shriver Center, named in honor of Shriver and his wife, Eunice Kennedy Shriver, will focus on training and deploying students to learn firsthand, as volunteers in an array of service programs, the problems of troubled city and suburban neighborhoods.

Mobilizing idealistic young people has been a hallmark of organized efforts by the Kennedy family for years. Shriver, for example, had a hand in the creation of the Peace Corps, the Job Corps and VISTA (Volunteers in Service to America).

The Shrivers' son, Mark, founded and runs the Baltimore-based Choice program, in which young college graduates work around-the-clock with neglected and oftentimes delinquent boys and girls, aiming to save them from the streets and get them headed toward productive lives.

The Shriver Center will provide an academic home base for the Choice program and two offshoot efforts, which are focused on job training and preventing students from dropping out of middle schools. The center will also be home to the new Shriver Peaceworker program, under which returning Peace Corps volunteers serve as university teaching assistants and try to relate their experiences in Third World countries to the conditions of American cities.

But the Shriver Center's outreach is supposed to embrace more than youth service and experiential learning, according to Freeman Hrabowski, the president of the University of Maryland (Baltimore County). There'll be a close connection, he said, to faculty research and course design. Staff from every discipline, from social work to engineering to education, will be encouraged to work interactively with students who are willing to become engaged in the laboratory of the city.

If that suggests a shattering of academia's ivory tower, the Baltimore effort is supposed to go even one giant step further. It will seek to engage faculty from a constellation of universities in the area, ranging from proud, nationally prestigious Johns Hopkins to blue-collar, historically black Morgan State and Coppin State.

The presidents of the 10 Baltimore-area universities agreed quickly to form a Presidents' Council and join the urban outreach effort. Key factors in the speed with which the agreement was reached may have been the Shrivers' involvement and respect for

Hrabowski, a distinguished African-American educator. The motivation clearly wasn't money, because no big endowment is in prospect.

In most cities, cooperative consortiums among universities have tended to come a cropper because of faculty jealousies and turf protection. Shriver believes that these and related problems would, in all likelihood, block a similar agreement among institutions of higher learning in cities such as New York, Los Angeles and Chicago.

Many colleges and universities in the greater Baltimore area already have strong urban studies and outreach programs, some of them run collaboratively.

Another explanation: The times are changing. Lenneal Henderson, the director of the William Donald Schaefer Center for Public Policy at the University of Baltimore, suggested that each Baltimore-area college and university is beginning to recognize its direct stake in surviving in an increasingly perilous urban environment.

For one thing, Henderson said, their customer bases of future students are being steadily eroded by the family dissolution, crime, poverty and illiteracy that are running wild in the inner city and now infecting more and more suburbs.

Maybe the "American Establishment" is perceiving the same dangers. It's unlikely that the Shriver name alone, for example, would have prompted such figures as former Defense Secretary and World Bank president Robert S. McNamara, television commentator Bill Moyers and psychologist Robert Coles to join the Shriver Center's advisory committee.

The chairman of the advisory committee is Ernest L. Boyer, the president of the Washington-based Carnegie Foundation for the Advancement of Teaching, who said that Baltimore's combination of scholarship and community service should provide a "laboratory for urban renewal" and perhaps even "a model for renewal of the nation."

None of that's a guarantee of success, of course. It will take a lot of new inducements to get teams of ambitious faculty members—top medical school physicians, for example—to focus on such basic problems as public health for poor people.

Another barrier could be negative reactions from black inner-city communities if they aren't adequately consulted on initiatives and get the idea that phalanxes of white students are being sent in to "save" them.

But the leaders of the Shriver Center sound too smart to let that happen. And the benefits to the nation could be immense if even one metropolitan region begins to succeed at realizing Shriver's dream of "putting together an area's best brains with its best hearts" as a way to begin extinguishing the flames that have been ravaging the foundations of urban America's social order.

Source: National Journal, January 29, 1994, p. 254. Reprinted with permission of National Journal.

URBAN POLITICAL MACHINES

I seen my opportunities and I took 'em.

George Washington Plunkett,
Tammany Hall politician in New York

Two things you can't let an opponent get away with—telling lies about you or telling the truth about you.

Anonymous Chicago politician

The structure of city government in the late nineteenth century severely restricted the ability of Americans to respond effectively to urban problems. Simply put, in many cities no one was in charge. Mayors and councils were hamstrung by a lack of formal power and by a fragmented system of government. At the same time, the structure of government helped move many cities toward extreme centralization in the form of the urban political machine.[2]

While the use of the long ballot (a product of Jacksonian democracy) to elect a long list of candidates, often running independently of the mayor and of each other, led to fragmentation of city and county government and to voter confusion, it also gave the machine the opportunity to control elections and centralize power. The use of the **spoils system** gave winning candidates the ability to award government jobs to their supporters and often put incompetents in administrative positions, and it was tailor-made to help political machines gain votes and control government. Council elections by districts, rather than at large by all voters in the city, helped machines by focusing elections on small areas where an ethnic group beholden to the machine often constituted a majority of the population. Although the goal of Jacksonian democracy (1829–1837) was to give political power to the common people, it often helped promote boss control by the use of the long ballot and the belief that not only was the common man qualified to vote, but he also was qualified to staff the government.

Fred I. Greenstein notes that nineteenth-century political machines developed because of five major factors:

1 In the second half of the nineteenth century, the American urban population increased sixfold. This increase in population created a need for improvement in such public services as transportation, public health, firefighting, and police.

2 The structure of city government, marked by weak mayors and the presence of many elected officials, made it virtually impossible for the city to respond to the challenges of growth by upgrading public services and assuming the management of urban life.

3 From 1860 until World War I, more than 25 million immigrants came to the United States and most of them settled in cities. There was an almost complete absence of social planning to meet the needs of these dependent people.

4 Businesses increasingly needed public services, such as street repair, and they also needed freedom from strict enforcement of ordinances controlling such matters as job safety and waste disposal.

5 Oftentimes, immigrants were naturalized and registered to vote soon after arriving in this country. Their votes were easily purchased by the machines.[3]

The party machine operated by providing employment (patronage jobs), financial assistance, and recognition to the urban poor. The machine was organized with the boss, assisted by ward leaders and precinct captains, presiding over a well-disciplined party. Precinct captains were responsible for an area of several city blocks, containing about 600 voters. Ward leaders were often city councilors and were responsible for the several precincts that made up their ward. Although the machine bosses were often the mayors, sometimes they were nonelected people who operated behind the scenes to control local government (see Figure 9-1).

While the classic power of the machine derived from its control of patronage jobs, it could also help the poor by securing jobs in private business or by acting as a friend in court. The party secured votes (often simply because of friendship established between the precinct captains and their neighbors) and limited nominations to its own politicians. The machine assured itself continuance in office, it centralized public decision making, and it provided much-needed social services (e.g., shelter for residents of an apartment gutted by fire) at a time when government assumed little responsibility for social welfare.

The main goal of political machines was to win elections by providing basic services to voters.[4] In many cases, as in Boston, machines went beyond providing basic services to build parks, modernize roads, and, in general, redevelop the city. By helping voters acquire jobs, food, and housing in an era before public welfare was widespread, the machine encouraged voter support for its candidates. More fundamentally, it may also have prevented political uprisings among immigrants. Because machine politicians had little interest in political ideology, they seldom developed broad policy goals. As in the case of the more modern Daley machine in Chicago, most bosses were described as brokers who chose among policies developed by others. For policy to be carried out it was absolutely critical that the boss put his stamp of approval on it.

Early political machines were greatly aided by the arrival of new waves of immigrants in the period from 1880 to 1920. As immigrants settled into Eastern cities, local governments were unprepared to deal with their needs. Machines quickly realized that by extending favors to people who put relatively little value on their right to vote, they could gain the support of these new Americans. For many immigrants, party work led

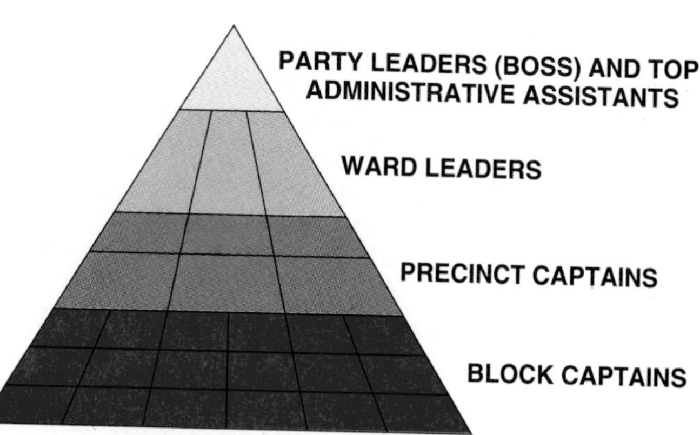

FIGURE 9-1 Political machine organization chart. [*Source:* Bernard H. Ross and Myron A. Levine, *Urban Politics: Power in Metropolitan America,* 5th ed. (Itasca, Ill.: F. E. Peacock Publishers, 1996), p. 147. Reproduced by permission of the publisher.]

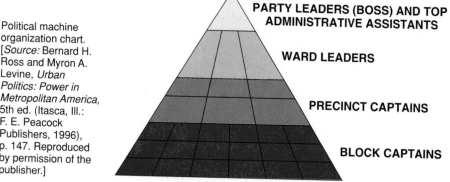

to economic and social advancement in communities where opportunities for them were very limited. More recently, African-Americans and Hispanics have given machines new opportunities to help dependent people, even though there are a host of public welfare programs. These new immigrants to Northern cities, such as Chicago, still needed help finding their way through a maze of public bureaucracies, and the procurement of federal grants could be used by cities to help minority inner-city neighborhoods. However, we need to remember that political machines dominated many Southern and Midwestern cities early in this century where there were relatively few new immigrants. In those cases machines relied on the working-class poor for much of their support.

The Democratic party organization in Chicago has been the most celebrated example of a contemporary political machine. Richard J. Daley was first elected mayor in 1955 as a reform candidate. As mayor of Chicago and chairman of the Cook County Democratic party, Daley is estimated to have controlled as many as 30,000 public jobs and perhaps 10,000 private jobs.[5] Most of the key projects supported by Daley—road building, a new airport, a convention hall—were noncontroversial and benefited the county as well as the city. Although several of his associates went to jail in the 1970s for graft, Daley did not fall victim to personal greed. He died in office in 1976 and was replaced as mayor by a handpicked member of the city council.

The machine had been losing power since the late 1960s. It began with violence at the 1968 Democratic party convention and was followed in the mid-1970s by the defection of members of the growing African-American community. Daley's successor was defeated in a 1979 primary election when Democratic leadership splintered. In 1983 African-American U.S. Congressman Harold Washington defeated the incumbent mayor, Jane Byrne, in a primary election. As mayor, Washington faced strong opposition from white ethnic members of council (aldermen), many of whom had been part of the Daley organization. After being largely ignored by Daley in the 1960s and 1970s, African-American and Hispanic community groups gained new access to government in the 1980s. Washington died in office in 1988 and an African-American alderman, Eugene Sawyer, was named to replace him. However, he was defeated in a 1989 special election by Richard M. Daley, son of Richard J. Daley.

Richard M. Daley inherited a political legacy marked by racial division, a generation gap, and a split between the old machine politics and the new media politics.[6] Daley's campaigns have stressed racial fairness, and he has been able to use new technology—polling and the media—to replace the old machine. Richard M. Daley's campaign manager, David Wilhelm, became chairman of the Democratic National Committee; and his brother, William M. Daley, managed the Clinton campaign to gain congressional approval of the North American Free Trade Agreement in 1993. Daley was easily reelected to a third term in 1995. He won about 25 percent of the African-American vote in the Democratic primary against a African-American opponent.

THE REFORM MOVEMENT

Structural Changes

Reformers were very successful in changing the structure of government, and this led to the fall of many machines. By the early twentieth century reformers, or so-called

good-government organizations, had invented and put into operation civil service commissions, direct primary elections, nonpartisan elections, and at-large elections. The change to a merit system (civil service) for public employment hit the machines especially hard. New York City's George Washington Plunkitt denounced the civil service as "the curse of the nation." Curiously, as noted in Chapter 7, reinventing government reformers in the 1990s also criticize the civil service. Primary elections limited the ability of the machine to handpick candidates for office, and the creation of city managers meant that professional, nonpolitical administrators would act independently of the machine.

It was anticipated that a switch from elections by wards to at-large elections would elevate the tone of elections, produce better candidates, and break the local bias of ward elections. Today, about 60 percent of all cities have at-large elections. No change ever receives universal acclaim: Current reformers argue that at-large elections hurt minorities by diluting their vote in citywide elections. They also contend that at-large elections produce long ballots that make intelligent voting difficult and that these elections weaken legislator-constituency links (see the Scholarly Box).

Reformers changed the way elections were run by instituting voter registration. Machines had relied on "repeaters," those who voted several times in the same election, and registration in advance provided a list of voters who could be checked on election day to make repeat voting less likely. Registration also had the effect of lowering turnout among low-income, less-educated residents by creating a process that they often did not understand.

In addition to primary elections, reformers opened the political process even wider with the introduction of the initiative, referendum, and recall, which are discussed in Chapter 5. These same reformers created the position of city manager, which is discussed later in this chapter.

While changes in the structure of local government had significant adverse effects on political machines, several other factors combined to weaken them. In the 1920s government policy severely limited immigration. Without new arrivals machines lost their supply of new voters. Meanwhile, second and third generation immigrants moved into the middle class and lost their ties to machines. Even among lower-class residents, the availability of federal welfare programs, beginning in the 1930s, eliminated another machine resource. No longer able to attract voters by giving out food baskets, the most machines could do was to take political credit for government programs or to help direct people to apply for public assistance.[7] In some cities machine leaders were prosecuted on corruption charges as voters began to hold politicians to higher standards.

In many ways, political machines were victims of their own success. As urban residents became better educated and better off financially, patronage jobs ceased to be attractive and they moved to better-paying jobs in private business. Individuals began to place a greater value on their vote and were less willing to tolerate corruption in government. The move to a short ballot helped focus political accountability, and it ended a kind of "farm league" of minor offices that the long ballot provided to machines. It was a combination of structural reforms *and* changing economic and social conditions that brought down many machines.

More recently, machine politics in Chicago and across the county has been dealt a setback by two Supreme Court decisions limiting the use of patronage. In *Elrod* v. *Burns*

SCHOLARLY BOX

AT-LARGE ELECTIONS

As reformers saw it, electing council members at-large (by all voters in a city) would change their focus from narrow interests affecting only members' districts to the broader (more important) interests of the entire city. And they believed that at-large elections would attract higher-quality candidates who could run well in citywide elections. Also, this change was intended to weaken the ability of machines to direct benefits to the poor through their systems of ward (district) organizations.

In large part these objectives were achieved. For example, studies show that council members in at-large cities have higher levels of education and more prestige occupations than council members in district cities. Machines weakened and collapsed under a barrage of electoral reforms. But there have been unintended consequences as well.

At-large elections have a class bias. Because racial and ethnic minority groups tend to be concentrated in distinct neighborhoods, it is likely that several black, Hispanic, or Italian council members will be elected in district systems. In at-large cities these minorities may be outvoted by the city's majority population. This is more likely if the size of the at-large council is substantially smaller than in the typical district city.

Several cases have come to the Supreme Court in which plaintiffs have contended that at-large elections unconstitutionally dilute the political strength of black voters. In a 1973 decision involving Mobile, Alabama, the Supreme Court held that while the city's at-large system underrepresented blacks (no black had ever been elected to the city council even though blacks made up 35 percent of Mobile's population), plaintiffs had not shown that there was an *intent* to discriminate, and therefore the at-large system was not unconstitutional.

The impact of the *Mobile* decision was weakened in 1982 when the Supreme Court ruled against an at-large election system in Burke County, Georgia, where no blacks had ever been elected commissioner even though blacks constituted 50 percent of the county's population. Circumstantial evidence was viewed by the Court as strong enough to imply intent. Later that year Congress changed the concept of "intent" by amending the Voting Rights Act to state that the "totality of circumstances" should determine whether or not an electoral system exhibited unconstitutional discrimination. These two actions strongly suggested that plaintiffs would be more successful in challenging election systems since the burden of proof was lessened.

However, more recent decisions indicate that the Supreme Court is interpreting the Voting Rights Act in ways that protect existing election arrangements. For example, revisiting Georgia county government in 1994 the Court upheld an unusual single-commissioner form of government, used by eleven counties in Georgia, in which one commissioner exercises all legislative and executive functions for the county. Blacks in Bleckley County argued that the system violated the Voting Rights Act, pointing out that in a county with 20 percent black population no black had even run for commissioner. Plaintiffs sought the creation of a multimember commission as a remedy. The Supreme Court ruled that the size of a local governing body could not be challenged under the Voting Rights Act. In 1993 the Court upheld a Florida reapportionment plan that plaintiffs contended had diluted the Hispanic vote and thus violated the Voting Rights Act. The Court said that the Voting Rights Act does not require state legislative districting plans to maximize the electoral potential of minority voters.

At-large systems present other controversies. They tend to increase costs by forcing candidates to run expensive citywide campaigns, and this, of course, disadvantages poorer candidates. Some research indicates that women candidates fare better in at-large elections than in district elections, while other studies have found that successful women candidates in district systems believed they would not have been elected if they had run at large. These women cited their involvement in neighborhood organizations as a way to enter city politics.

Political scientist John J. Harrigan discusses "revisionist thought on at-large elections."* Some researchers have concluded that court decisions in the 1970s and 1980s corrected the most flagrant problems in at-large elections and that blacks actually are helped by that system. This position suggests that district elections may provide only token representation to blacks and that white members from overwhelmingly white districts have little reason to respond to black needs. Others have found that while the discriminatory effects of at-large elections have been reduced, more minority council members are still elected in district systems.

*John J. Harrigan, *Political Change in the Metropolis,* 5th ed. (New York: Harper Collins, 1993), pp. 140–141.

(1976) the Court held that two non-civil-service employees of the newly elected Cook County (Illinois) sheriff had been improperly fired simply because they did not support the party in power. In *Rutan* v. *Illinois Republican Party* (1990), the Court decided that party affiliation could not be a factor in hiring, promoting, or transferring state employees. This decision affected the treatment of 60,000 employees in Illinois and has led to changes in personnel practices in several states and cities. In his dissent, Justice Antonin Scalia lamented the weakening of political parties and suggested that we continue to use patronage as a means of supporting the two-party system. *Rutan* was a 5–4 decision with the majority opinion written by former Justice William Brennan.

The Impact of Reform on Public Policy

While structural reforms clearly led to the demise of many political machines, their impact on how cities raised money and on how they spent money is less clear. In a pioneering study of 200 cities, political scientists Robert L. Lineberry and Edmund G. Fowler found that reformed cities spent less and had lower taxes than unreformed cities.[8] Moreover, they found that reformed governments were much less responsive to the needs of racial and ethnic minorities in their cities. More recent research has been divided on spending and responsiveness, with some concluding that there is little difference in policy among reformed and unreformed cities.[9] Still, many researchers believe that minority groups get better representation in district elections in a partisan system than in nonpartisan, at-large elections. One problem in studying the impact of structural reforms is that cities have adopted a variety of changes that are not clearly part of one model or the other.

In many instances **structural reformers** had little faith in the ability of the people to make good judgments about their government. They wanted cities to be run by an educated, upper-class elite. This suggests that reformed governments might not be sensitive to the needs of the underclass. However, there also were **social reformers** who sought to help the working class by keeping the price of utilities low and increasing the proportion of taxes paid by business. Social reformers included such colorful mayors as Samuel "Golden Rule" Jones in Toledo and Hazen Pingree in Detroit.

THE LEGAL POSITION OF CITIES

Because cities and counties are not mentioned in the United States Constitution, they fall under the control of states. This means that local powers are provided by state constitutions or by acts of state legislatures.

Local governments are clearly subordinate to the state. In a classic statement, Judge John F. Dillon formulated **Dillon's Rule** (1868), which says that municipal corporations can exercise only those powers expressly granted by state constitutions and laws and those necessarily implied from granted powers. If there is any question about the exercise of power, it should be resolved in favor of the state. Although this rule has been accepted by the U.S. Supreme Court, Daniel Elazar notes that more than 80 percent of the states have rejected Dillon's Rule or have changed it to recognize the residual powers of local government.[10]

The powers that cities have under state law are spelled out under general statutes or in **city charters.** Until the 1850s, legislatures issued a special act or specific charter to explain the structure of government for individual cities. Because this was a time-consuming process, state legislatures moved to establish classified charters in which cities are put in general classes according to population. Under this system larger cities typically have a broader range of powers than smaller cities. When a city's population increases, it does not automatically move into another classification but must wait for some formal procedure to be followed. Many states use optional charters in which voters can choose among several plans—mayor-council, manager-council, or commission—when a new city is incorporated.

Most states now provide home-rule charters for cities and counties, and two-thirds of cities with populations over 2,500 have adopted home-rule charters. This modifies the traditional subordinate relationship of cities to states by permitting cities to draft and approve their own charters. Home-rule cities are free to enact their own laws so long as they are not contrary to state law. There also is the recognition of implied powers for cities to do anything so long as it is not prohibited by state law. Variations in home-rule provisions among the states mean that in some states there is extensive local discretion and in others local choices are very limited. In states with constitutional home rule, cities can adopt whatever form of charter they wish without getting legislative approval to spell out details. In other states, legislative home rule can be withdrawn or amended by a vote of the legislature. A few states have "self-enforcing" home-rule provisions that permit cities to bypass state legislatures and enact home rule for themselves. In the other cases, cities must get legislative approval to have home rule.

Even when home-rule powers are extensive and self-enforcing, cities are by no means free from state supervision. State legislatures still can interfere in local matters if they raise statewide concerns, and Dillon's Rule means that courts will resolve disputes between state and local laws in favor of the state. Political scientist Daniel Elazar contends that home rule has not significantly altered the relationship between cities and states because most local activities have been defined as concerns of state governments.[11] For example, Elazar notes that the Colorado constitution grants home rule to all cities with over 2,000 population. This gives Colorado cities full power over local activities, and the state can intervene only in issues of "state concern." However, the Colorado legislature has held that whenever state funds are involved, the state can intervene in local matters. While home-rule cities and counties do have greater power to determine the structure of their governments, they clearly have not become independent of state control.

The good-government reform movement, beginning about 1890, placed great emphasis on charter revision. Reformers called for home rule and simplification of city government as means to improve municipal administration. Political scientist Duane Lockard notes that these early reformers thought the key to improved city government was structural, not political. Thus their focus was not on the social and political character of cities but on charters. As Lockard states, "Nothing is more characteristic of twentieth-century thinking about municipal government than the constant—sometimes almost evangelic—effort to find the right, *ideal* form of government."[12] As we will see in the following sections, the search for the "ideal" structure led urban reformers early in this century to the commission and council-manager forms of government.

FORMS OF CITY GOVERNMENT

Weak-Mayor–Council Plan

Until the 1870s, American cities operated with **weak-mayor–council plans** of government. As with early state government, city government structure was strongly affected by skepticism about politicians and about government. At a time when local government performed few functions and city officials were coordinated by party organizations, people were afraid to give substantial power to a single executive.

In a weak-mayor–council system, the council is both a legislative and an executive body (see Figure 9-2). Council members appoint administrative officials; they make policy; they serve as ex-officio members of boards; and they prepare the budget. The mayor is "weak" because of a lack of effective executive power. The authority to appoint is restricted, and the authority to remove is often altogether lacking. Often the mayor cannot veto ordinances passed by the city council. In cities with weak mayors, no single person is charged with overall responsibility for government action. Other executive officials are independently elected (there is a long ballot that often is not understood by voters), and a number of boards and commissions are not controlled by the mayor. Since no one is in charge of the overall affairs of a city, vot-

FIGURE 9-2 Hypothetical weak-mayor–council plan.

VOTERS
MAYOR
COUNCIL
AUDITOR
CITY ATTORNEY
PUBLIC WORKS
PARKS
UTILITIES
PLANNING COMMISSION
Council has both legislative and executive authority. Council must consent to mayor's appointments of department heads. Mayor's power of removal restricted. Council has primary control over the budget. Some department heads are appointed directly by council.
Appointive power

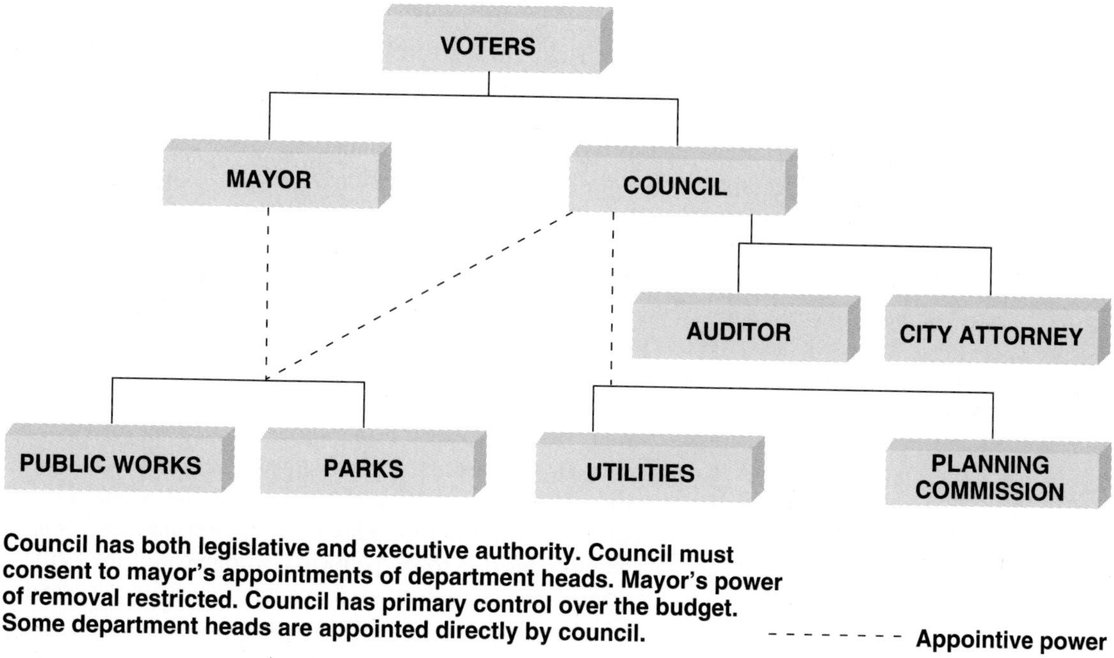

ers do not know who to blame when things go wrong. No one coordinates all public policies in a city, and no one can be held directly accountable when there are service breakdowns.

The weak-mayor system does have some advantages. City departments are free to act without undue political pressure from the mayor. If voters are concerned about the misuse of executive power, the weak-mayor system creates strong checks by the council and by independent boards. In many cases structurally weak mayors have been powerful political forces in their cities, but they must depend on informal factors such as their personal appeal or the strength of their political party.

Although the reform movement succeeded in strengthening the formal powers of many mayors early in this century (most cities with political machines had weak mayors), the weak-mayor–council system continues to be used in many small cities and in some large cities. Minneapolis, Los Angeles, Houston, and Seattle have weak mayors. In Houston, for example, the mayor cannot veto council actions, and in other cities the council or an independent budget director, not the mayor, prepares a budget.

Strong-Mayor–Council Plan

Under the **strong-mayor–council plan,** there is a short ballot. The mayor controls the budget, has broad power to appoint and remove city officials, and can veto ordinances passed by the council. Strong mayors are directly elected by the voters and usually have four-year terms with the possibility of reelection (see Figure 9-3). The council confirms appointments, and it usually controls the appropriations process. The mayor's legal position provides a firm base for political leadership, and the mayor is constantly in the limelight. In most cities the "strong" mayor is, in fact, a compromise between a weak and a very strong system.

This plan is used in most large cities where a complex administrative structure requires firm leadership and direction. Most cities with more than 1 million population have a strong-mayor–council system. Problems arise when voters expect too much from the mayor and find it easy to blame that individual for whatever goes wrong in the city. Often, those politicians who are effective campaigners lack the administrative skills to manage the day-to-day affairs of a large city. To offset this shortcoming of the system, many cities with strong mayors, including Los Angeles, have established the position of **chief administrative officer** (CAO). Appointed by the mayor, this professional person is given broad authority to manage the financial affairs of the city. In a few cities the CAO is a permanent position that carries over from one administration to another. In most cases, it is subject to appointment by the mayor.[13] In New York City the mayor selects several deputy mayors who function like the CAO concept.

As with governors, "strong" formal powers do not guarantee that mayors will be effective leaders in their cities. They need to have personal leadership capabilities, and even the strongest mayors usually lack some formal powers that they would like to have in an ideal situation. Likewise, mayors with weak formal power may be "strong" leaders because they are carefully tuned in to the political environment of their cities. This means that to be recognized as the political leader of his or her city, *all* mayors must exercise power beyond what is provided in their city charters.

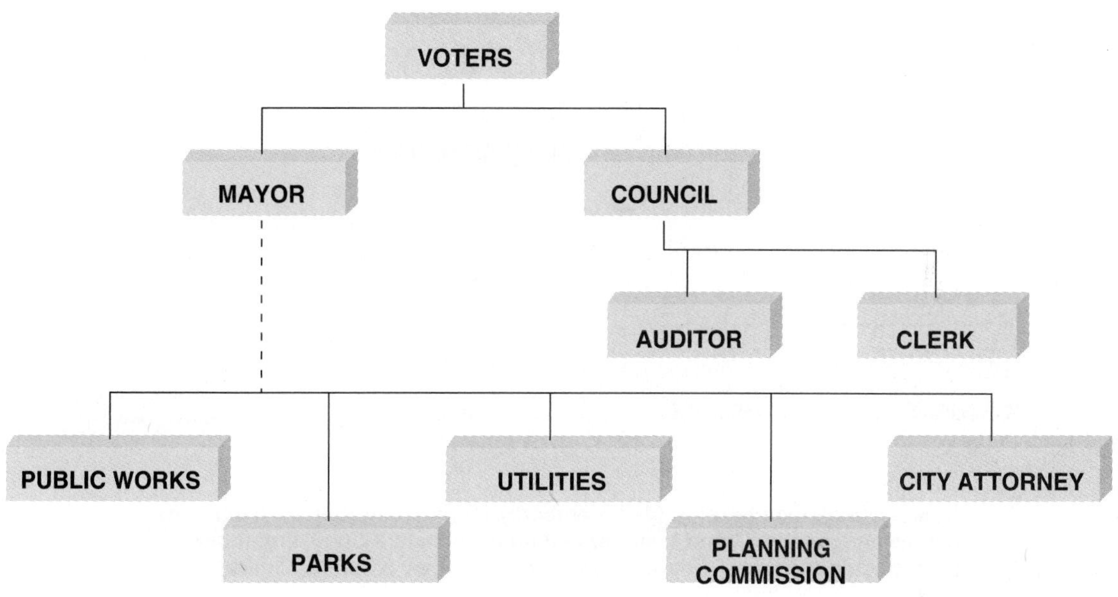

Mayor has strong administrative authority. Mayor appoints and dismisses department heads. Mayor prepares the budget. Short ballot.

- - - - - - **Appointive power**

FIGURE 9-3 Hypothetical strong-mayor–council plan.

Commission Plan

A few cities use a **commission form of government,** in which several (usually three to nine) commissioners, elected at large, exercise both legislative and executive authority. The commissioners are organized as heads of various city departments (public works, parks, finance), and they also act collectively to pass ordinances and control spending (see Figure 9-4). Often a mayor is selected from among the commissioners, but his or her duties are largely ceremonial.

After its initiation in Galveston, Texas, in 1903, use of the commission plan spread quickly, and by 1917 it was in operation in about 500 cities. Dallas, Houston, and Fort Worth were among the first cities to have commissions, and several other big cities, including Pittsburgh and Buffalo, adopted the plan early in this century. As recently as 1970, about 200 cities had commission forms of government. By 1990 the number dropped to 175, and in 1995 there were 163 cities with commissions (see Table 9-1). Only nine of the cities with commissions had populations of 50,000 or more.[14] In most states there are not any city commissions at all. Even Galveston now has a manager form of government. The Voting Rights Act has made the commission form with its at-large voting an endangered species of city government.

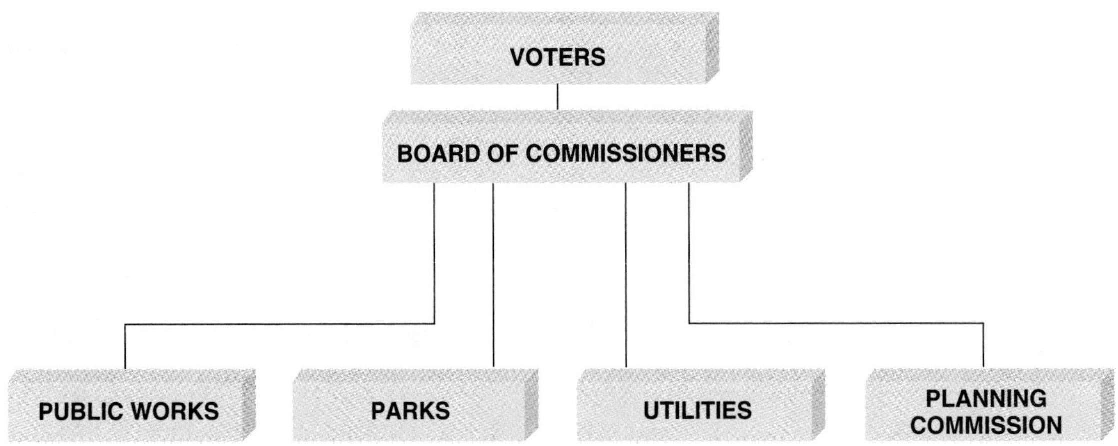

Usually small membership (4–7 members). Commissioners each serve as department heads. Commissioners sit as a legislative body. Often one commissioner acts as mayor (power equal to other commissioners).

FIGURE 9-4 Hypothetical commission plan.

The commission plan has many disadvantages. Because it does not provide for the separation of powers, it places little control on spending and administration. In most cities it is difficult to attract top-quality persons to serve as commissioners, and thus government business is often in the hands of amateurs. Without a chief executive, it is difficult to pinpoint responsibility. The small size of the commission does not foster debate and criticism, and it encourages a fraternity of tolerance. City commissioners often practice a mutual hands-off policy from one another's functional areas, and each moves in his or her own direction without overall coordination.

Council-Manager Plan

The council-manager plan originated early in the twentieth century as part of the Progressive movement. Reformers sought to eliminate corruption from city hall by removing administration from partisan politics. Their answer was to replace the mayor with a professional administrator appointed by the council. Among the early city reformers was Richard S. Childs, who founded the national short-ballot organization in 1909. A short ballot implied consolidation of elected offices, and from this followed Childs's manager plan to provide professional or "businesslike" administration. In many cases, plans calling for a **city manager** were accompanied by the initiation of nonpartisan elections.

In 1914 Dayton, Ohio, was the first city of substantial size to adopt the council-manager plan. By 1918 there were nearly 100 cities with managers, and counties began to adopt the system in the 1930s. By 1994, nearly 3,000 U.S. cities and coun-

TABLE 9-1 FORM OF GOVERNMENT AND CITY POPULATION

Classification	All cities	Cities 2,500 & over	Cities 5,000 & over	Cities 10,000 & over	Cities 25,000 & over	Cities 50,000 & over	Cities 100,000 & over	Cities 250,000 & over	Cities 500,000 & over	Cities over 1,000,000
Form of government										
Mayor-council	3,555	3,294	2,038	1,118	440	201	83	36	20	6
Council-manager	3,030	2,738	2,173	1,468	722	319	106	26	5	2
Commission	163	156	118	81	26	9	3	6	2	
Town meeting	411	364	233	105	7	0				
Rep. town meeting	72	71	60	45	20	4				

Source: Municipal Year Book 1995 (Washington, D.C.: International City/County Management Association, 1995), p. xii.

ties had managers, and the plan was in use in over 100 cities in Canada. The plan is particularly adaptable to medium-size cities (25,000 to 250,000). Small towns often find it too expensive to hire a full-time manager, and in many large cities the council-manager system is opposed by strong labor unions and minority groups, who often believe the manager has a pro-business bias. Still, an increasing number of large cities, especially in the South and West, have managers.

In most cases there is a small council, elected at large, which hires a manager (see Figure 9-5). In the past, managers were often civil engineers. Now they are likely to be people trained in public administration. The manager serves at the pleasure of the council in a relationship similar to that of a superintendent of schools and the board of education. A mayor may be selected from among the council members to perform ceremonial duties. In nearly half the cities with a manager there is a popularly elected mayor.

Where mayors coexist with managers, the mayor often has more power than the formal model suggests.[15] For example, Boynton and Wright found that mayors of several large cities often played a strong role in appointing department heads and in shaping the council's agenda. When mayors' actions conflict with the model, managers may complain about the overreach of power. More often, however, there is a sense of teamwork between the mayor and the manager.

FIGURE 9-5 Hypothetical council-manager plan.

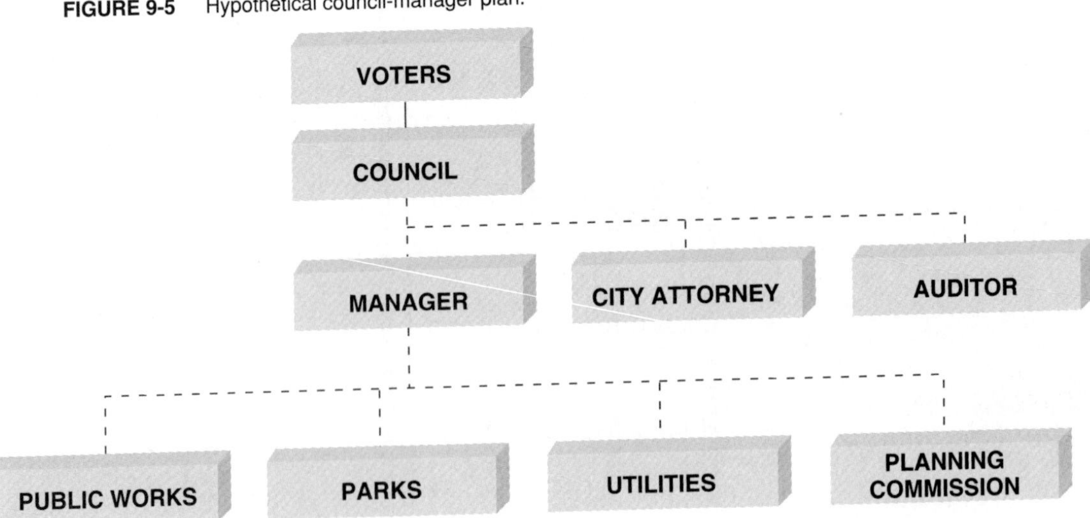

Usually small council (5–7 members). Often nonpartisan elections.
Council members make policy and oversee city administration.
Full-time professional manager. Budget prepared by the manager.
Mayor usually has only ceremonial power.

- - - - - - - - Appointive power

Where cities have changed from a council-manager system with a weak mayor to a strong mayor system, it often has been out of frustration that no one really is in charge. For example, Toledo, Ohio, made the switch in the early 1990s in the hope that a strong mayor could halt the long economic decline of the city. Toledo voters approved a charter change after a campaign for a strong mayor was led by the city's major newspaper. As in some other cities, Toledo also moved to a mixed election system for council, combining district and at-large elections.

Typically managers are involved in presenting proposals to council members and working for their adoption. Increasingly managers see a policymaking role for themselves, and patterns of liberal or conservative policy solutions can be associated with particular managers.[16] The duties of most managers include preparing the city budget, supervising the hiring and firing of city personnel, and negotiating with labor unions. Managers are expert advisers, providing information to city councils.

Much of the political science literature suggests that managers are most likely to be found in cities whose population is predominantly white, Protestant, white collar, middle class, college educated, growing, and mobile. But Thomas R. Dye and Susan A. MacManus, in testing these assumptions, found that the presence of a city manager is only weakly related to population size, economic class, race, religion, and the age of the city.[17] The best indicator of a manager form of government was ethnicity, or the percentage of foreign-born residents in a city. The lower the percentage of foreign-born, the greater the likelihood of a city having a manager. Council-manager cities require a consensus about politics, and often this is lacking in multicultural cities. Dye and MacManus did discover that managers are likely to be found in newer, fast-growing cities with mobile populations. This description fits many suburban communities, and it is there that continuing support for creating council-manager forms of government is to be found. For example, most of the commuter suburbs of Westchester County, New York, have managers.

In general, medium-size cities in the Northeast and Midwest tend to have strong mayors, while Sunbelt cities have managers. In growth areas of the South and Southwest, planning for streets and water lines are priorities, and the council-manager plan seems to work well. In the Northeast and Midwest, the priority is on responding to a variety of racial and ethnic groups, and the strong-mayor–council system has worked well in those circumstances.

Although some reformers have overstated the impact of the manager system (in particular, they fail to understand that "politics" cannot be eliminated and that the struggle for power will not disappear once partisan labels are removed), it has provided efficient, accountable government in many cities. Weaknesses stem from the nature of individual managers—it is difficult to attract competent, experienced people, and the manager must maintain a middle-of-the-road position in which he or she avoids, on the one hand, setting policy and, on the other hand, simply running errands for the council.

Some managers have had a tendency to become very closely identified with business and professional interests in their community. Because of this perceived bias, organized labor in many cities has opposed the creation of a manager plan. There has also been opposition from African-Americans and other minorities who believe their interests will be better served in nonreformed cities where the mayor's office may be more responsive to citizen demands. Also cities with managers may lack effective political leadership because of the weak position of the mayor.

TERMS OF OFFICE FOR LOCAL OFFICIALS

In a survey by DeSantis and Renner, about half the responding cities indicated that their mayors had terms of four years or more.[18] About one-third had two-year terms, 15 percent had one-year terms, and 4 percent had three-year terms. The larger the city, the more likely it was to give its mayor a four-year term. Four-year terms also predominated among mayor-council cities, while only about one-third of council-manager cities had four-year terms. Geographically, only in Pacific Coast states (37.6 percent) did more than 20 percent of cities report one-year terms for mayors.

While most cities reported four-year terms for council members, there was a significant difference in length of terms between cities with at-large elections and those with elections by district. Among council members elected at large 70 percent had four-year terms, 22 percent had two-year terms, and 7 percent were elected to three-year terms. When council members were elected by district, 59 percent had four-year terms.

As noted in Chapter 5, there has been a strong movement nationwide in the 1990s to limit terms of state legislators. This has not occurred in cities. DeSantis and Renner found that among cities with populations over 25,000, only 11 percent had term limits for mayors. And the percentage declined as population declined. Only 8.4 percent of cities reported having term limits for council members.

The apparent lack of local interest in term limits may be closely related to the higher rate of turnover among local officials, compared to state legislators and members of Congress. Nearly half the council members in the surveyed cities were in their first term, and the average tenure for mayors was 5.4 years. The turnover in city managers was 29 percent in a one-year period.

The apparent high level of turnover (and thus low level of term limits) among local officeholders can be attributed to several factors. As DeSantis and Renner note:[19]

> The advantages of incumbency, for example, may not be as strong given that incumbents' name recognition is likely to be lower, their constituencies smaller, and campaign costs lower than at other levels. It may be comparatively easy (from both an organizational and financial perspective) to successfully challenge an incumbent under these circumstances. It is also possible that the tendency for local public service positions to be part-time and volunteer, rather than full-time and career, results in more voluntary turnover of incumbents and less longevity than at other levels of government.

COUNTIES, TOWNSHIPS, AND TOWNS

Counties

There were 3,043 counties in 1990. Of those, 25 had a population over 1 million, 65 had between 500,000 and 1 million, and 291 had populations of less than 5,000.

Nearly 700 counties were located in metropolitan statistical areas. Counties are found in all states except Connecticut and Rhode Island (Louisiana calls them "parishes" and Alaska, "boroughs"), although they have never been important in the New England states, where the town remains the basic unit of local government. The size and number of counties vary greatly. Delaware and Hawaii have only 3 counties each, while Texas has 254. San Bernardino County, California (20,000 square miles), is larger than Vermont and New Hampshire combined. In contrast to Los Angeles, Cook (Chicago), and Harris (Houston) counties—each of which has over 3 million people—there are about 700 rural counties with populations of less than 10,000. Alaska, Arizona, and New Mexico each created a new county in the 1980s. Counties are the creatures of the state, with their existence often spelled out in state constitutions.

Traditionally, most counties have been administered by a three- or five-member board of commissioners. In a few states, such as Illinois and Wisconsin, there are large governing boards with ten or more members. Commissioners often share administrative duties and some legislative responsibilities with independently elected officials that include auditors, treasures, clerks-of-court, sheriffs, engineers, prosecutors, and coroners. Commissioners' legislative functions include adopting a budget and setting tax rates. As executives they appoint some county employees and supervise county road work. While the Voting Rights Act has prompted more district elections, the more common pattern is at-large election of commissioners within the county.

The organization of county government has been widely criticized.[20] The absence of a chief executive in the commission plan often has meant that there is inadequate supervision and coordination of the numerous county departments. A system designed for rural, small-town America has not had the flexibility to adapt to the needs of urbanized, metropolitan populations.

Reformers have favored alternative forms of county government with appointed or elected executives. Change has come because the home-rule movement has allowed counties to pick among several types of structures that centralize administrative responsibility. Nearly one-fourth of all counties, including many urban counties, have a commission-administrator form of government in which the commissioners appoint an administrator; or they have a council-elected executive with two branches of government—the executive and the legislative (the council). County administrators (a plan similar to cities with a CAO) are sometimes called county managers, chief administrative officers, or executive directors. They serve at the pleasure of the board. While administrators' powers vary, they include budget preparation, appointment of some department heads, and supervision of some departments. Executives who are elected by the voters have more substantial powers, which may include the ability to veto legislation approved by the county board. Elected executives are found in about one-fourth as many counties as administrators. Typically, voters elect fewer county officials under this structure than is the case in the commission form of government.

Counties traditionally have performed a wide variety of functions in the areas of health, welfare, education, criminal justice, maintenance of roads, and record keeping. In recent years they have been given additional functions as the administrative units for various federal and state programs. Although rural counties have traditionally been the most important unit of government within their geographical areas, urban counties have been gaining significant authority. In some states, home-rule charters allow counties to perform functions that previously were city responsibilities. These include water supply, library services, sewage disposal, flood control, and management of airports. This has been especially true in Southern states where counties traditionally have been more powerful than cities.[21] As will be discussed in Chapter 11, strong urban counties can serve as a kind of metropolitan government by providing a wide range of services traditionally associated with cities.

Counties that are neither urban nor rural—so-called 50-50 areas (they are 50 miles from a metropolitan area, and they have populations around 50,000)—are experiencing new demands from affluent families who are moving away from cities but still want many urban services.

Towns

The **town** continues to be the basic form of local government in New England states. In colonial America, a "town" included a village and its surrounding farms. Over time, some New England urban areas have incorporated and withdrawn from towns, but towns as governmental units continue to be a combination of urban areas and the surrounding countryside. As one example, while New Hampshire has only 10 counties and 13 municipalities, it has 221 towns. It is here that the fabled town meeting met to levy taxes, determine how money would be spent, and elect the next year's "selectmen." The selectmen acted in a manner similar to county commissioners to oversee the administration of schools, roads, health, and welfare.

Because attendance at many town meetings has declined, a representative town meeting plan has been devised in some towns whereby voters choose a large number of citizens (around 100) to attend the town meeting and represent their views. School consolidation also has limited the responsibilities of town governments. In many instances, the administration of local services has been turned over to a town manager.

Townships

The **township** functions as an intermediate form of government in the Middle Atlantic and Midwestern states. In much of the Midwest, townships were carefully laid out in 6-mile squares, with thirty-six 1-mile square sections. These surveyor's townships did not become political townships until later when local government was organized. As a result, not all political townships are neat 6-mile squares. Midwest counties were designed so that no one would be more than a day's driving time from the county seat, and the township hall was within an hour's buggy ride. Unlike towns, townships are primarily rural, not a combination of rural and urban areas. Also, townships are not the principal unit of government in any state in which they are found. Although they make up most of several Midwestern and Middle Atlantic states—such as Pennsylvania, Ohio, and Kansas—only parts of other states, such as Illinois and the Dakotas, have townships. While a few townships have had annual meetings that are similar to New England town meetings, most elect trustees to act as legislators, as well as administrators. Some elect a chief executive, commonly known as a supervisor. Many rural townships have transferred much of their authority (e.g., repair of roads and bridges) to counties.

In most Midwestern states all land area not incorporated into municipalities lies within the jurisdiction of townships. The township, typically with three elected trustees, may levy taxes and sue and be sued. In a few wealthy suburban areas (in Pennsylvania and Kansas, for example) townships have gained powers nearly equal to those of cities. Township powers can grow as new businesses locate in unincorporated areas adjacent to cities and as the population of those areas increases.

Collectively, townships may have surprising political power in a state. When we consider that many Midwestern counties are divided into more than a dozen townships, this means that some states have over 1,000 townships, with over 3,000 trustees. Because annexation presents a direct threat to their power, townships have lobbied in Ohio for a requirement that township land cannot be annexed without trustee approval. Of course, counties also have statewide organizations to lobby, and cities join state municipal leagues that present a unified effort to represent their interests in the state legislature.

SUMMARY

The United States remained a predominantly rural and small-town society throughout most of the nineteenth century. Industrialization and increased immigration helped swell urban populations in the last quarter of the nineteenth century, and political machines soon dominated government in many Eastern cities. The goal of machines was to win elections by providing good, basic public services. But corruption was widespread.

The power of urban machines decreased by the 1920s as reformers succeeded in creating such structural changes as at-large elections, nonpartisan elections, and the city manager form of government. Some big-city machines, such as in Chicago, persisted into the 1960s, and a few remain in operation. Critics charge that several Progressive reforms that weakened machines have politically disadvantaged African-American and Hispanics.

The traditionally weak legal position of cities has been strengthened by the approval of home-rule charters. Charter reform also has led cities to change from weak-mayor structures to commissions, strong mayors, and city managers. Managers have been especially attractive to newer suburban communities.

Counties typically have commission forms of government. In recent years, reformers have called for appointed or elected county executives, and many urban counties now have chief administrative officers. While counties always have performed a wide range of services, urban counties increasingly have assumed more power as managers of services on a metropolitanwide basis.

KEY TERMS

Chief administrative officer An adviser to mayors who is usually responsible for budgeting and personnel. Also found in some counties.

City charters Legal documents from the state that set forth powers of self-government for cities.

City manager A professional administrator, appointed by the city council, whose responsibilities include personnel management and the preparation of a city budget. Performs the administrative tasks typically assigned to a mayor.

Commission form of government City government structure that gives both legislative and executive power to a small group of elected commissioners.

Dillon's Rule A restrictive judicial interpretation stating that municipal corporations can exercise only those powers specifically granted to them by state constitutions and laws.

Good-government organizations Reform groups early in the twentieth century that favored structural reform of city government, nonpartisanship, and merit selection of public employees.

Social reformers Early twentieth-century reformers who wanted to extend government services to the needy. Social reformers were less elitist than **structural reformers** and had greater faith in the ability of the people to govern themselves.

Spoils system "To the victor belong the spoils." This philosophy permitted winning parties to dismiss public employees and replace them with party loyalists. It also permitted parties to give profitable public contracts to their supporters.

Strong-mayor–council plan A system of local government in which the mayor exercises broad administrative authority. Found in most large cities.

Weak-mayor–council plan A system of local government in which the mayor has limited administrative authority (particularly concerning the budget and personnel) and the council performs both legislative and executive duties.

Town A unit of local government in New England that includes an urban center and its surrounding rural area. Performs functions similar to those of cities and counties in other states.

Township A unit of local government found principally in the Middle Atlantic and Midwestern states. Midwestern townships typically cover 36 square miles and exclude municipal areas. Township responsibilities include law enforcement and maintenance of roads.

REFERENCES

1 Richard Hofstadter, *The Age of Reform* (New York: Vintage Books, 1955).

2 Tari Renner and Victor S. DeSantis, "Contemporary Patterns and Trends in Municipal Government Structure," in *The Municipal Year Book 1993* (Washington, D.C.: International City/Council Management Association, 1993), p. 59.

3 Fred I. Greenstein, *The American Party System and the American People,* 2d ed. (Englewood Cliffs, N.J.: Prentice-Hall, 1970).

4 Bernard H. Ross and Myron A. Levine, *Urban Politics: Power in Metropolitan America,* 5th ed. (Itasca, Ill.: F. E. Peacock Publishers, 1996), p. 147.

5 Milton Rakove, *Don't Make No Waves . . . Don't Back No Losers: An Insider's Analysis of the Daley Machine* (Bloomington: Indiana University Press, 1975).

6 Sidney Blumenthal, "The Making of a Machine," *The New Yorker* (November 29, 1993).

7 Ross and Levine, *Urban Politics,* p. 162.

8 Robert L. Lineberry and Edmund G. Fowler, "Reformism and Public Policy in American Cities," *American Political Science Review* (September 1967), pp. 701–716.

9 Susan Welch and Timothy Bledsoe, *Urban Reform and Its Consequences* (Chicago: University of Chicago Press, 1988), p. 101.

10 Daniel J. Elazar, *American Federalism: A View from the States,* 3d ed. (New York: Harper & Row, 1984), p. 203.

11 Daniel J. Elazar, *The American Mosaic* (Boulder, Colo.: Westview Press, 1994), p. 287.

12 Duane Lockard, *The Politics of State and Local Government,* 2d ed. (New York: Macmillan, 1969), p. 111.

13 Ross and Levine, *Urban Politics,* p. 123.

14 *The Municipal Year Book 1995* (Washington, D.C.: International City/County Management Association, 1995), p. xii.

15 Robert P. Boynton and Deil S. Wright, "Mayor-Manager Relations in Large Council-Manager Cities: A Reinterpretation," *Public Administration Review* (January–February 1971), pp. 28–35.

16 David N. Ammons and Charldean Newell, "City Managers Don't Make Policy: A Lie, Let's Face It," *National Civic Review,* March–April 1988, pp. 124–132.

17 Thomas R. Dye and Susan A. MacManus, "Predicting City Government Structure," *American Journal of Political Science,* May 1976, p. 260.

18 Victor S. DeSantis and Tari Renner, "Term Limits and Turnover among Local Officials," in *The Municipal Yearbook 1993,* pp. 36–38.

19 Ibid., p. 36.

20 See Herbert S. Duncombe, *Modern County Government* (Washington: National Association of Counties, 1977), Chapter 2.

21 See David R. Berman, ed., *County Government in an Era of Change* (Westport, Conn.: Greenwood Press, 1993).

10

THE POLITICAL DYNAMICS OF URBAN AREAS

Eric Risberg/AP/Wide World Photos

In Chapter 9 we looked at the "nuts and bolts" of local governments—charters, forms of city government, and electoral systems. Now we turn to the political dynamics of cities—the leadership style of mayors, the roles played by council members and interest groups, and the ways citizens participate in the political process. We want to know who local leaders are and how they go about energizing a city. For cities to prosper there needs to be a vision for the future, a plan for action, and the ability to get people to work together for outcomes that will benefit the entire community. In the last section of this chapter we examine the questions, "Who has power in local communities, and how is that power exercised?" As classically phrased by Harold Lasswell, we want to know "who gets what, when, how" in the political process.[1]

THE ROLE OF MAYORS

Mayors, like governors and presidents, play a variety of roles. As the ceremonial head of the city, the mayor greets distinguished visitors to the city, attends endless rounds of dinners, and issues proclamations. These activities help give mayors visibility, and they build up political goodwill. As chief administrators, mayors oversee the work of city employees and prepare an executive budget. They are limited in this function, however, by the presence of independent boards and commissions and other officials who are separately elected. As chief legislators, mayors often exercise strong control over the agenda considered by the council, and they may veto ordinances passed by the council. Increasingly, mayors act as chief city ambassador, devoting a great deal of time to meetings at the state capital and in Washington. Many cities have full-time lobbyists in Washington, and others act through the United States Conference of Mayors and the National League of Cities.

The powers of mayors are often weak, and the problems of big cities—crime, drugs, homelessness—seem to defy solutions. More recent financial cutbacks by the federal government and the states have placed additional burdens on city administrations. The complex of urban problems has led some scholars to conclude that cities are "ungovernable."[2] In many cases, urban social problems seem to be intractable. At best, it has been suggested that we can find only partial solutions to such troubling problems as drug abuse and teenage pregnancy. Moreover, as discussed in Chapter 9, the limited formal powers given mayors make it especially difficult to have a unified, centralized effect by cities to attack their problems.

Most mayors lack strong formal authority, even when operating under a strong-mayor system. When big-city mayors must contend with a weak-mayor system, many of them simply cease to function as chief executives. The following exchange between Mayor Samuel Yorty of Los Angeles and Senator Abraham Ribicoff of Connecticut during a congressional hearing makes it abundantly clear that the mayor's authority was nearly nonexistent.

> *Senator Ribicoff:* As I listened to your testimony, Mayor Yorty, I have made some notes. This morning you have really waived authority and responsibility in the following areas: schools, welfare, transportation, employment, health, and housing,

which leaves you as the head of the city basically with a ceremonial function, police, and recreation.
Mayor Yorty: That is right, and fire.
Senator Ribicoff: And fire.
Mayor Yorty: Yes.
Senator Ribicoff: Collecting sewage?
Mayor Yorty: Sanitation; that is right.
Senator Ribicoff: In other words, basically you lack jurisdiction, authority, responsibility for what makes a city move?
Mayor Yorty: That is exactly it.[3]

Before we give up on mayors, we need to consider the impact that personality and style can have on their ability to lead cities. As we noted in Chapter 9, weak formal powers do not necessarily make weak mayors. Nor, of course, do strong formal powers guarantee that mayors will be effective leaders. Objective resources are just part of the power equation.

The ways in which mayors carry out their formal duties depend in large part on their style of leadership. At one extreme is the **passive caretaker.**[4] Mayors of this sort take very little initiative, preferring to have private groups agree on projects, which they may endorse. These mayors make little effort to influence policy by offering a vision for the future. Instead, they tend to deal with problems one at a time in terms of whatever "comes up." Their basic concern is to maintain city services and make as few waves as possible. In some instances, the caretaker mayor may excel at ceremonial duties—cutting ribbons, welcoming conventions—and thus improve the image of the city. In some instances, the *only* parts of the job that seem to interest mayors are its ceremonial aspects.

At the other extreme are **entrepreneur mayors,** who have a clear vision of where their cities should go. These mayors surround themselves with large staffs, and they actively seek to build political coalitions in order to get broad support to implement their programs. Mayors of this sort want to exert strong leadership over their councils and the entire city. For example, Mayor Fiorello La Guardia of New York City (1933–1945) believed that "*his* policies should prevail in *every* area of government activity." Of course, some activist mayors may not be able to accomplish much in the way of substantive policy change. Douglas Yates cites the example of John Lindsay, who as mayor of New York City in the 1960s was a crusader for change but accomplished only a limited amount.[5]

The **opportunistic policy broker** style of mayor stands between these two extremes. While these mayors do not wish to dominate all city activities, neither do they wish to handle only housekeeping responsibilities. Richard J. Daley of Chicago is described as a classic broker politician who chose from policy proposals put forth by individuals outside city hall. It was, however, only Mayor Daley's "seal of approval" that could put the proposals into operation.

The power of mayors, even more than the power of the president, rests in their ability to persuade through the use of public relations approaches, the mass media, and bargaining among various urban interests. If mayors are effective as persuaders, they can overcome many of the handicaps of weak formal authority—as did Richard Lee of New Haven, Connecticut. In a classic study of political power, Lee was described as "not [being at] the peak of a pyramid but rather at the center of intersecting circles."[6] He rarely commanded. He negotiated, cajoled, exhorted, beguiled, charmed, pressed, appealed, reasoned, promised, insisted, demanded, even threatened; but he most needed support from other leaders who simply could not be commanded. Because the mayor did not dare command, he had to bargain.

Although it is difficult to generalize about the backgrounds and attitudes of mayors, case studies have discovered historical patterns in selected cities. In Chicago, for example, most mayors since 1930 have been Catholic, and all have risen through the ranks of the local party organization. In San Francisco and St. Louis, local businesspeople with outgoing personalities have most often been elected mayor. Until recently, the office of mayor seldom was a stepping-stone to statewide office or to Congress. Mayors of big cities built up too many liabilities, or they were not sufficiently well-known across the state even to be taken seriously as candidates for governor. By the 1980s this image of mayors had changed, and several were elected governor. These include Pete Wilson, mayor of San Diego, and George Voinovich, mayor of Cleveland. Although Voinovich lost a U.S. Senate race in 1988, he was elected governor of Ohio in 1990 and reelected in 1994 with a record 72 percent of the vote. As mayor of San Diego, Pete Wilson transformed the office into an effective force to manage rapid population growth, even though San Diego had a city manager form of government. Wilson was narrowly elected governor of California in 1990 and then was reelected by a comfortable margin in a nationally watched 1994 campaign.

Running for Mayor

Because of the great diversity of cities, it is impossible to generalize about mayoral campaigns. For example, running for mayor of Chicago differs greatly from running for mayor of San Francisco. Small-town campaigns in one-party areas or with nonpartisan elections obviously are very different from highly partisan elections in large or medium-size cities. This section will focus on new techniques used by mayoral candidates in cities of more than 100,000 population.

Mayoral candidates in large cities are using many of the same techniques—polling, television advertisements, direct mail—as gubernatorial candidates to build their images. As a result, campaign costs have skyrocketed. The use of new techniques and the employment of political consultants to manage campaigns are common in most big-city elections. In large Northern cities, old-time bosses have lost power because candidates can use television effectively to go directly to the voters. The use of these techniques has been particularly helpful to Republican candidates running in cities where their party never has had a strong organization.

As in statewide campaigns, political action committees have begun to contribute to mayoral campaigns. Typically mayoral candidates have received the bulk of their funds from businesses, real estate developers, and labor unions. Real estate investors and developers continue to be a major source of funding in fast-growing Sunbelt cities. Labor unions usually support Democratic candidates. Increasingly the American Federation of State, County, and Municipal Employees of the AFL-CIO has been a major force in city elections through endorsements and financial contributions.

Because nearly 70 percent of cities have nonpartisan elections, the personality of the candidates will be even more important than in gubernatorial elections. In addition, many cities with nonpartisan elections also have city managers and few, if any, patronage jobs. This means that mayoral candidates must rely on volunteer workers who cannot be promised jobs or other special favors if their candidate is elected.

Minority and Women Mayors

Minority mayors constitute an increasingly large category of individuals who, while they have different styles of leadership, face similar problems. Since 1980, blacks have served as mayors of many of the nation's largest cities—Atlanta, Baltimore, Cleveland, Dallas, Denver, Kansas City, Los Angeles, New Orleans, St. Louis, San Francisco, Seattle, and Washington, D.C. In the early 1990s there were over 300 cities with black mayors. Table 10-1 shows the significant increase in black elected officials at all levels of government. The first generation of black mayors, led by Carl Stokes in Cleveland and Richard Hatcher in Gary, Indiana, both elected in 1967, served in predominantly black cities. The major focus of their administrations was the "**political incorporation** of blacks."[7] That is, they sought to use city government as a means to empower blacks and other minorities in the political and civic life of their communities. Most studies of cities with black mayors have found that after their election blacks have gotten more municipal jobs and black contractors have benefited from affirmative action programs to award city contracts to minority businesses.[8] In particular, this can be seen in Detroit where longtime mayor Coleman Young began a policy of giving preferential treatment to local businesses over firms outside the city.

The second generation of black mayors includes several elected in cities where blacks make up less than one-third the population. These include Seattle, Denver, Kansas City, and Minneapolis (Tom Bradley in multiracial Los Angeles was a major exception—a first-generation black mayor elected in a city where blacks were less than 15 percent of the population). From 1967 to 1993 black candidates were elected mayor in seventy cities with populations of 50,000 or more even though in about 80 percent of those cities there was not a black majority population. In fact, in 30 percent of the cities less than one-third the residents were black.[9] In such cases, black mayoral candidates obviously must forge coalitions to get the support of white voters. Once in office, their goals tend to focus more on broad economic development, rather than on black incorporation. Even in predominantly black cities, such as Detroit and Cleveland, successful second-generation black mayoral candidates have deracialized their campaigns and then altered the focus of their administrations.

Still, many big cities remain racially polarized. In Memphis, which is 55 percent black, W. W. Hernton was elected mayor in 1991 by a margin of 142 votes. He received 99 percent of the black vote, while his white opponent, a former mayor, got 97 percent of the white vote. This may have been the most racially polarized vote in

TABLE 10-1 BLACK ELECTED OFFICIALS, BY CATEGORY OF OFFICE, 1970–1992

Year	Federal	State	Substate regional	County	Municipal	Judicial, law enforcement	Education	Total
1970	10	169	—	92	623	213	362	1,469
1971	14	202	—	120	785	274	465	1,860
1972	14	210	—	176	932	263	669	2,264
1973	16	240	—	211	1,053	334	767	2,621
1974	17	239	—	242	1,360	340	793	2,991
1975	18	281	—	305	1,573	387	939	3,503
1976	18	281	30	355	1,889	412	994	3,979
1977	17	299	33	381	2,083	447	1,051	4,311
1978	17	299	26	410	2,159	454	1,138	4,503
1979	17	313	25	398	2,224	486	1,144	4,607
1980	17	323	25	451	2,356	526	1,214	4,912
1981	18	341	30	449	2,384	549	1,267	5,038
1982	18	336	35	465	2,477	563	1,266	5,160
1983	21	379	29	496	2,697	607	1,377	5,606
1984[a]	21	389	30	518	2,735	636	1,371	5,700
1985	20	396	32	611	2,898	661	1,438	6,056
1986	20	400	31	681	3,112	676	1,504	6,424
1987	23	417	23	724	3,219	728	1,547	6,681
1988	23	413	22	742	3,341	738	1,550	6,829
1989	24	424	18	793	3,595	760	1,612	7,226
1990	24	423	18	810	3,671	769	1,655	7,370
1991	26	458	15	810	3,683	847	1,638	7,480
1992	26	484	15	857	3,697	847	1,623	7,552[b]

Note: "—" indicates not available. Figures are for January of the year indicated.
[a]The 1984 figures reflect blacks who took office during the seven-month period between July 1, 1983, and January 30, 1984.
[b]Total includes two shadow senators and one shadow representative from the District of Columbia.
Source: Joint Center for Political and Economic Studies, *Focus,* March 1993.
From: Harold W. Stanley and Richard G. Neimi, *Vital Statistics on American Politics,* 4th ed. (Washington, D.C.: Congressional Quarterly Press, 1994), p. 399.

big-city history. Following a drug conviction in 1990, Marion Barry was returned as mayor of Washington, D.C., in 1994 in a campaign accurately described as "in your face" racial polarization. Barry's white Republican opponent, Carol Schwartz, received a surprisingly high 42 percent of the vote resulting from high turnout in white neighborhoods and stronger than expected support from blacks.

In virtually all cities, once black mayors are in office they need to work with the predominantly white business community in order to further economic development for blacks. Some black mayors find it difficult to maintain an effective balance between catering to their black electoral constituency and forging alliances with upper-class white bankers and merchants. If they seem to be working too closely with the white business community, they are criticized by blacks for "selling out." If they alienate the white business establishment, black mayors risk even more white businesses moving out of their cities. As in Detroit, affluent white suburbs prosper, while the city loses people and jobs.

TABLE 10-2 WOMEN IN CITY GOVERNMENT

Seattle was the first major city to elect a woman mayor. Bertha Landes, who had served as president of the city council, was elected mayor of Seattle in 1926.[1] The largest U.S. city yet to elect a woman mayor is Chicago, where Jane Byrne (D) served from 1979 to 1983. Past women mayors elected to serve among the 100 largest cities have included:[2]

City	Name	Party[3]	Years served
Austin, TX	Carole McClellan	D	1977–1983
Chicago, IL	Jane Byrne	D	1979–1983
Cincinnati, OH	Bobbie Stern	NP	1975–76/78–79
Charlotte, NC	Sue Myrick	R	1987–1991
Corpus Christi, TX	Betty Turner	NP	1987–1991
Dallas, TX	Annette Strauss	NP	1987–1991
El Paso, TX	Suzie Azar	NP	1989–1991
Garland, TX	Ruth Nicholson	NP	1988–1990
Hartford, CT	Ann Uccello	R	1967–1971
Honolulu, HI	Eileen Anderson	D	1981–1985
Houston, TX	Kathy Whitmire	NP	1982–1992
Huntington Beach, CA	Norma B. Gibbs	R	1975–1976
Huntington Beach, CA	Ruth Bailey	R	1984–1985
Lincoln, NE	Helen Boosalis	D	1975–1983
Little Rock, AR	Lottie Shackelford	NP	1987–1988
Long Beach, CA	Eunice Sato	R	1980–1982
Oklahoma City, OK	Patience Latting	D	1971–1983
Phoenix, AZ	Margaret Hance	R	1974–76/78–80
Portland, OR	Dorothy Lee	R	1949–1952
Richmond, VA	Eleanor Sheppard	NP	1962–1964
Richmond, VA	Geline Williams	NP	1988–1990
Sacramento, CA	Belle Cooledge	NP	1948–1949
St. Petersburg, FL	Corinne Freeman	R	1978–1985
San Antonio, TX	Lila Cockrell	NP	1975–1981/1989–1991
San Francisco, CA	Dianne Feinstein	D	1978–1988
San Jose, CA	Janet Gray Hayes	D	1974–1982
Seattle, WA	Bertha Landes	NP	1926–1928
Spokane, WA	Vicki McNeill	NP	1986–1988
Stockton, CA	Barbara Fass	NP	1985–1990
Toledo, OH	Donna Owens	R	1983–1989
Worcester, MA	Sara Robertson	D	1982–1983

(*continued on next page*)

In addition to blacks, a few large, predominantly Hispanic cities, mainly in Texas and Florida, have elected Hispanic mayors. Occasionally, as in Denver and San Diego, predominantly Anglo cities have elected Hispanic mayors. Hispanics are much less segregated than blacks, and their relatively greater population dispersion lessens their potential for political power in American cities. Among the largest cities, only in San Antonio, El Paso, and Miami do Hispanics constitute more than half the population.

A third change has been the election of increasing numbers of women mayors, including several blacks. Since 1979 women have been elected mayor in such widely

TABLE 10-2 (Continued)

Elected in 1887, Susanna Salter of Argonia, KS was the first woman mayor in the United States; she was paid one dollar for a year of service.[1]

The first black woman to serve as mayor of a city with a population over 100,000 was Loretta Glickman; she was chosen as mayor of Pasadena, CA in 1982.

Women have presided over both major national organizations of municipal officials. Five women have served as presidents of the National League of Cities: Glenda Hood, Orlando, FL Commissioner 1992; Pamela Plumb, Portland, ME Councilor, 1988; Cathy Reynolds, Denver, CO City Councilwoman-at-Large, 1987; Jessie Rattley, Newport News, VA City Councilwoman, 1980; and Phyllis Lamphere, Seattle, WA City Council President, 1977. Two women have served as president of the U.S. Conference of Mayors: Kathy Whitmire, Houston, TX Mayor, 1989–1990; and Helen Boosalis, Lincoln, NE Mayor, 1981–1982.

Data from a 1981 Center for the American Woman and Politics survey of women in elected office show:[4]

(1) Women mayors and council members are most frequently between the ages of 40 and 59. (2) More than half of all women mayors and council members hold jobs outside of the home at the same time they are serving in office. (3) Most women mayors and council members who list occupations outside the home are in professional/technical or clerical/secretarial fields. More than 10% of the women municipal officials are elementary or secondary school teachers, by far the most common single occupation listed by the women. (4) More than half of all women mayors and council members have had at least some college education. (5) More than 3/4 of all women mayors and council members are currently married, and of those, almost all report that their husbands are supportive of their political careers. (6) Fewer than half of all women mayors and council members have children younger than 12 years old.

[1] *Women in American Politics,* Martin Gruberg (Oshkosh, Wis.: Academia Press, 1968).
[2] List may be incomplete. U.S. Bureau of the Census data on city population was used to determine the 100 largest cities during the years each woman served.
[3] NP indicates mayoral election is nonpartisan.
[4] From a series of CAWP studies entitled "Bringing More Women into Public Office," conducted under a grant from the Charles H. Revson Foundation.
Source: Fact Sheet (New Brunswick, N.J.: Center for the American Woman and Politics, National Information Bank on Women in Public Office, Eagleton Institute of Politics, Rutgers University, March 1992).

dispersed big cities as Chicago, San Francisco, San Diego, Fort Worth, Portland, Minneapolis, Houston, Pittsburgh, Washington, D.C., Salt Lake City, and Las Vegas (see Table 10-2). In 1994, 18 of the nation's 100 largest cities had women mayors. Of the 971 mayors of cities with over 30,000 population, 18 percent were women. About 21 percent of all council members in cities with over 10,000 were women in 1993.[10] The Center for the American Woman and Politics reports that the percentage of women holding municipal and township offices more than tripled from 1975 to 1985, rising from 4 to 14.3 percent. Seattle in 1926 was the first major city to elect a woman mayor. Pasadena, California, in 1982 was the first city with over 100,000 to elect a black woman mayor.

Paralleling the experience of blacks in cities with black mayors, research shows that the election of women mayors has led to more jobs for women in the municipal workforce. Being mayor of a large city seldom offers long-term job security, regardless of race or gender. While Kathy Whitmore was reelected mayor of Houston five times,

Jane Byrne in Chicago and Sharon Pratt Kelly in Washington, D.C., served only one term after being unable to respond effectively to problems facing their cities. Several blacks, including Coleman Young in Detroit and Marion Barry, served multiple terms; but Louis Stokes, the pioneering black mayor of Cleveland, was defeated in his first bid for reelection.

While mayors of big cities have overwhelmingly been Democrats—virtually all black and Hispanic mayors have been Democrats—an interesting feature of the early 1990s was the election of Republican mayors in the nation's two largest cities, New York and Los Angeles. The success of Republican candidates at the state and national levels in 1994 suggests that more Republicans are likely to be elected mayors of large cities whose populations are not overwhelmingly black.

THE ROLE OF CITY COUNCIL MEMBERS

If it is dangerous to make generalizations about fifty state legislatures, the pitfalls clearly are multiplied when presenting an overview of councils in nearly 20,000 municipalities. Councils vary in size from fifty members in Chicago to six in Dallas and seven in San Diego and Indianapolis. Councils tend to be small (five to nine members) where there is a city manager form of government and larger where there is a mayor-council system. Larger councils are elected by wards and often are more concerned about representing district interests than smaller councils. Smaller councils act more quickly on policy matters than larger, more deliberative bodies. Of course, in commission plans the mayor is a member of the council.

In most cities, council members (or aldermen) devote only part of their time to city business and continue their full-time employment, often in local business or, in large cities, as lawyers. Typically, their pay reflects this part-time service and is nominal. Only in the largest cities are council members paid well and do they devote full time to their public employment.

Currently almost all city councils are unicameral, although at the turn of the century many large cities had bicameral councils. At that time it also was common to elect council members by wards. As noted in Chapter 9, until passage of the Voting Rights Act there had been a trend toward at-large elections in all but the largest cities as well as a trend toward nonpartisan elections. Reformers believe that at-large elections lessen the inclination toward a parochial outlook and logrolling, which are common in cities with ward elections. *Logrolling* refers to the trading of votes among council members to achieve passage of projects of interest to one another. However, as noted earlier, blacks and ethnic minorities are disadvantaged by at-large elections, in which their voting strength is diluted. The typical council member is a man who owns a small business and is only slightly better educated and more affluent than his constituents.

Council meetings usually are presided over by the mayor. In small towns sessions may be once or twice a month, while in large cities councils meet at least once a week. In the past small-town councils often met informally before regular sessions, resolved issues privately, and then voted unanimously in public sessions. State **"sunshine laws"** have forced councils to have open meetings on nearly all matters. Small towns hold public hearings at which residents can informally address council issues and decisions may be made quickly following a hearing. In most cities large or small, councils respond to matters at hand, such as dog control problems, but they seldom set long-range goals for the city.

When council members exhibit low levels of professionalization (and this is widespread in large and small cities), it is easy for the mayor or city manager to dominate their decision making. It also is common for city councils to act on behalf of strong local interests such as realtors, builders, or main-street merchants when making city policy. The degree of council participation in decision making is greatly affected by the form of city government (see Chapter 9). Where there is a weak-mayor system or a commission system, the council will have considerable formal authority. In cities with strong mayors or managers, the basic function of council members is often to act as representatives to bring complaints to the attention of city hall. In most cities, councils are passive and seldom act as policy innovators. Their most common role is to oppose rather than to propose policy. Because turnover is high and voter participation low, it is difficult to hold council members accountable by threatening to defeat them in the next election. Many retire before the end of their term, allowing the mayor to appoint a successor, who then has the advantage of incumbency in the next election. In such a situation, the general public is limited in its ability to influence public policy through legislative representatives.

The composition of large and many medium-size city councils is changing as more minorities and women are elected. Blacks dominate city councils in many large cities, and those cities are very likely to have black mayors. Nationally, women constitute about 15 percent of city council members. Women are most likely to be underrepresented in Southern cities, where one study reported that 73 percent of medium-to-large cities in Alabama did not have any women on their councils.[11]

Political scientist Joseph F. Zimmerman notes that there are still a few legal barriers to the election of minorities and blacks on city councils.[12] Where cities have closed primaries, party leaders can control whose names appear on the primary ballot and access by women and minorities may be limited. Outdated city charters that do not provide for the initiative and recall limit citizens' ability to make council members responsive to their demands, and this may protect white male incumbents. A major barrier to the election of blacks and minorities is simply that there are not many opportunities to run in open-seat elections. To the extent that councils are small and their members most often are reelected, the chances for *all* newcomers are limited.

Increasing the size of councils and having more elections by wards would help elect more blacks and probably more women. The reform movement created small councils, elected at-large. More recently, some cities have responded to demands from minorities by keeping the at-large seats but adding several seats elected by wards. Zimmerman also suggests the creation of two-tiered councils, in which the second tier would be neighborhood (subcity) councils. At least for the initial neighborhood election, blacks and women would not have to challenge incumbents. Other proposals for cumulative voting or proportional representation are difficult for voters to understand and unlikely to be implemented.

R. Darcy reports that political party elites cannot be blamed for keeping women out of local political office.[13] Nor is there evidence that voters will not support women candidates. Instead, Darcy, like Zimmerman, concludes that the most significant barrier to women holding more political offices is the large number of male incumbents and their relatively slow turnover. More women need to be nominated to run for office, and electoral systems that give substantial advantages to incumbents need to be changed.

As city councils become less homogeneous, conflict increases among members. And sunshine laws that require open meetings have lessened the ability of council members to resolve their differences out of public view. If cities continue to move away from small at-large councils, this too will increase factionalism. In many larger cities council members are complaining about the same pressures that state legislators face—more interest group pressure, higher campaign costs, and more time devoted to the job.

URBAN INTEREST GROUPS

Interest groups operate in much the same way in large cities as in state legislatures. The difference is that the same groups are not equally active in state capitols and city halls. Lobbyists representing real estate groups, downtown merchants, and liquor dealers have been more influential at the city level than at the state level. Farmers, of course, direct their communication to state legislators and governors.

Urban interest groups may be classified as follows:

1 *Occupational interests.* Groups are organized on the basis of common work, trade, or business interests. Often individual occupations are organized in trade associations or professional societies. In most cities there are "peak associations" such as chambers of commerce and central labor councils.

2 *Problem-oriented interests.* Some groups come together to solve a particular social problem. This category includes groups dealing with housing, parks, schools, or welfare problems.

3 *Neighborhood interests.* These groups are most often concerned with local, territorial issues. In the past, they were usually found in upper-class areas where residents wanted to preserve the character of their neighborhood. Since the mid-1960s, community-action groups have been formed in many inner-city neighborhoods to support such causes as day-care and health-care centers.

4 *Good-government interests.* These are reform or improvement groups such as city clubs and the League of Women Voters.

The strength of urban interest groups comes from their willingness to take action, their pooled resources, and their numbers. Business groups often form nonpartisan research organizations to study a local problem. Their emphasis on expertise and their nonpartisan stance give them a high level of respectability. Although the poor find it much more difficult to organize than the affluent, they have been effective in many cities. Their tactics include legal action (instigating class-action suits), constant pressure on city officials to follow their own rules, and the threat of violence. Political organizer Saul Alinsky speaks of making the "enemy" live up to its own set of rules.[14] For example, by mastering the rules for welfare eligibility, neighborhood organizers can influence city officials to alter the way in which they administer the welfare program. We will discuss citizen participation more in the next section.

As we have noted in Chapter 9, the reform movement in American cities has been aided by a variety of so-called good-government groups. These citizens' groups have lobbied for lower taxes and lower city expenditures, and they have supported reform goals such as a council-manager plan, professional civil service, and nonpartisan elections. The League of Women Voters has also worked for these objectives.

Where strong party organizations do not exist, downtown merchants are often the dominant force in city politics. They are concerned about such matters as lower taxes, increased downtown parking, and zoning restrictions. The local chamber of commerce frequently speaks for all business interests. Banks and public utilities also exert pressure on local government. Matters related to business regulation, taxation, zoning, and housing are of utmost importance to each of these business groups. Contractors, who may do business with the city and who are affected by the city's inspection policies, engage in substantial lobbying.

Organized labor often lobbies for public policies that are opposed by the business community. These include subsidized public transportation, public housing, rent control, and higher wages for city employees. On some occasions, however, labor and business present a common front. For example, both support large construction projects that provide jobs and stimulate the local economy and highway construction. In recent years, unions representing city workers have had a major influence on city budgets, and they have utilized strikes to push for their demands. As discussed in Chapter 7, the increasing amount of privatization of city services has been strongly opposed by municipal unions. Because of the financial difficulties faced by many large cities, the bargaining position of public employee unions has been weakened. Indeed, the unions have been blamed for creating financial crises as wages grow and pension funds expand.

CITIZEN PARTICIPATION

Low levels of voter turnout in the United States, as discussed in Chapter 4, long have been a source of concern. While voter turnout patterns in city elections follow national patterns in terms of age, income, and education, the percentage of eligible voters who vote is even lower than for state elections and much lower than in national elections. On the average, turnout in municipal elections is below 30 percent. Of course, turnout varies greatly among cities. It tends to be lower in cities that have nonpartisan elections than in those with partisan elections. Remember that nonpartisan cities are likely to have city managers and at-large elections. In addition, city ballots often are complicated by having a large number of referenda, and there is a strong likelihood, up to 50 percent, of **ballot roll-off** (nonvoting) on referenda.

Thirty percent voter turnout (and in many cases turnout is much lower) means that sixteen percent of the eligible voters determine election outcomes. Given that those with low incomes are less likely to vote than those with higher incomes and more education, this means that an upper-class elite often exercises disproportionate power in local elections.

Of course, there are many other forms of political activity besides voting. We have discussed membership in interest groups, where, as with voting, there is a definite upper-class bias. Traditionally, high-status people have been the most likely to join groups, and among interest groups there has been a pro-business bias.[15] As a result, consumers, minorities, and those favoring broad governmental reform have been underrepresented among interest groups.

As discussed in Chapter 7, a noteworthy feature of urban interest groups has been their close ties to administrative bureaucracies. Interest groups have joined with their related municipal bureaucracies to form **"functional fiefdoms."**[16] These fiefdoms often operate largely outside the control of mayors (especially weak mayors), council members, and the general public. To the extent that they represent business interests such as building contractors or real estate agents working with city planning departments, they have extended the upper-class bias of the system. Moreover, professionally trained bureaucrats often have been unaware of neighborhood problems and individual problems of urban minority residents.

The upper-class bias of the interest-group system has been reduced in recent years as the poor, women, minorities, and nonbusiness groups have been better represented by **"public interest"** (or ideologically motivated) **organizations.** In addition, strong mayors can counteract the power of functional fiefdoms by centralizing power in their offices.

Neighborhood Groups

Many people whose voting records are not good and who seldom get involved in political campaign activity may still be active in community affairs. Political scientists Sidney Verba and Norman H. Nie described such persons as **"communalists."**[17] Communalists' activities involve a high degree of personal initiative, they often are not involved in partisan politics, and they have a strong sense of community contribution.

Here, too, there has been a white upper-class bias. Higher-status good-government groups long have pressed for structural reform. More recently, middle-class citizen associations have created block-watch programs, and they have opposed development that threatens the environmental quality of their neighborhoods. These are the NIMBY groups—not in my backyard.

As noted earlier, social activists, such as Saul Alinsky, have successfully organized ghetto residents to push for better housing, day care, and other neighborhood programs. Some tenant organizations have succeeded in improving conditions in public housing projects, and in a few instances they have taken over the management of their properties. Other inner-city residents have confronted drug dealers and assumed responsibility for the community's safety. In the reading for this chapter Neal R. Peirce describes the way in which neighborhood organizations are operating in Richmond, Jersey City, and Tampa. Peirce raises the question of how such organizations will affect the traditional role of constituency service by city council members.

While broader-based citizen participation offers exciting possibilities for cities, it also presents problems. If more people must be consulted and accommodated before decisions are made, this may delay action and it will extend already fragmented government structure. Cities must find ways to delegate meaningful authority to field offices, while maintaining policy control and oversight back in city hall.[18]

Minority Participation

Since the 1960s, the political participation of blacks has undergone significant changes. Change began with urban riots in the 1960s. After a large-scale black uprising in the Watts area of Los Angeles in 1965, riots spread to many other cities, including Cleveland and Detroit, in 1966 and 1967. Hundreds of racial disorders took place in small cities in this time period, and then major rioting exploded in the aftermath of the 1968 assassination of Martin Luther King. While often touched off by seemingly routine contact between the police and blacks, the underlying cause of the riots in several cities has been traced to long-standing racial discrimination and the resultant feeling of powerlessness by inner-city blacks.

Congress responded by trying to revitalize its community action program. As enacted in 1964, the **Economic Opportunity Act** called for "maximum feasible participation" by local residents in community action agencies, such as the Model Cities Program. However, many community activists protested that they had been shut out of these programs by local political leaders. While new federal guidelines encouraged broader political participation, cities across the country created advisory neighborhood commissions, and they tried to decentralize government by putting field offices in poor neighborhoods. These attempts to institutionalize citizen participation met with varying degrees of success. If large numbers of minority residents seldom were activated, municipal bureaucrats did become more sensitized to the needs of the poor and minorities.

More significant empowerment of minority communities has come at the ballot box. Under the protection of the Voting Rights Act of 1965, black voter registration in the South dramatically increased by the early 1970s. As the population of many large cities, North and South, became predominantly black, it was inevitable that more black mayors and council members would be elected. As noted earlier, black mayors have brought more blacks into city government as administrators, and this has increased minority access to decision making throughout city government. The 1995 election of Willie Brown as the first black mayor of San Francisco promises to change its previous pattern of decision making.

Yet as political scientist Clarence N. Stone has pointed out, this change has not meant greater access to government for lower-class blacks nor has it meant that poor inner-city neighborhoods have benefited from new public works projects.[19] To the contrary, the minority underclass in our nation's largest cities often finds that conditions have worsened. While cities build new convention centers, inner-city crime rates soar, schools deteriorate, and infant mortality rates resemble those in Third World countries.

THE NATURE OF COMMUNITY POWER

Elitists and Pluralists

The discussion of citizen participation repeatedly has raised questions about the nature of political power in cities. Is power typically held by the relatively small groups that control city halls and own downtown businesses, or is it more widely dispersed among various groups? Are the poor and minorities effectively shut out of community decision making? Regardless of who has political power, how is power exercised? Who

Some Cities (Finally) Are Listening Up

Neal R. Peirce

Several smart cities are turning to an obvious source—their own neighborhoods and citizens—as partners in solving the tough municipal problems of the 1990s.

Robert Bobb, the city manager of Richmond, Va., recently told *The Public Innovator* that "citizens are literally taking over city halls to get their needs met." Bobb is a member of the city management profession, which has traditionally thought that it had the best technocratic answers to local problems.

But it was Bobb's recognition that there's a limit to how responsive the bureaucrats in city government can be that led to Richmond's "Neighborhood Team Process." The city is divided into nine neighborhood-based districts, each with its own team to monitor pressing needs—from crack houses to potholes to tree trimming—and spark action.

Since 1988, more than 500 individuals and organizations in Richmond have participated in the teams, each of which has a broad cross section of citizens, business people, city officials and not-for-profit and civic organizations. The city officials on the teams pledge to take action on most issues within 30 days—before the citizen groups' next meetings.

In June, the team in Richmond's Braddock neighborhood capped off four years of working intensively with municipal employees—and cajoling members of the city council—to open a brand new park and fitness trail on what had been four acres of vacant city-owned land.

Jersey City, N.J., under Republican Mayor Bret Schundler, is about to pioneer an approach under which its citizens will be allowed to pick which firms they want to clean streets, repair roads and remove graffiti in their neighborhoods.

The first yearly outdoor maintenance pageant will be held at the Jersey City Armory this autumn. Maintenance, cleanup and repair firms will be given exhibit space to advertise and otherwise strut their stuff. Citizens will be invited to come in and kick tires—mix among the exhibits, talk directly with the competing contractors.

The residents will then get ballots to pick their preferred contractor, keyed to which of Jersey City's 33 "neighborhood improvement districts" they live in. The winner for each district will get a one-year contract. The company must agree to have a representative attend neighborhood association meetings throughout the year and to maintain a toll-free telephone number for citizen requests and complaints.

To keep the competition lively, no single vendor will get contracts for more than 30 per cent of the neighborhoods in Jersey City. City inspectors will monitor the work of all contractors, and the city will wisely reserve the right to terminate contracts with firms that fail to perform.

In Tampa, Fla., two-term Mayor Sandra Freedman has seen a wave of public support build behind Steve LaBour, her neighborhood ombudsman, whom she charged with making sure that grass-roots concerns reach individual departments and the city council.

Last spring, Tampa held a huge "neighborhood convention" in its handsome downtown convention center. Some 3,000 citizens turned out for the event, which featured booths and exhibits sponsored by city departments and individual neighborhoods.

The scene was government access at its most direct: Police officers, firefighters and the folks from sanitary sewers and water conservation explaining their programs. The neighborhood-based "Paint Your Heart Out, Tampa" program—which aids disabled elderly homeowners—had a booth. And the city attorney and chief labor negotiator sat behind a table hawking mugs and T-shirts advertising Tampa's "Year of the Neighborhood."

The idea, according to ombudsman LaBour, was a kind of city "open house" to make it easier for Tampa's citizens and neighborhood organizations to learn about many of the city government's departments and to get to know some of the people who run them. Workshops were held to brief neighborhood organizations on various city activities and to get feedback. And members of the neighborhood organizations had their first chance to talk among themselves and mix with city officials in a social setting.

Tampa is one of those fast-growth southern cities that never had the depth and richness of neighborhood organizations characteristic of so many Northeast and Midwest cities. But with plenty of encouragement from city hall, the number of neighborhood organizations in Tampa has grown in just five years from 21 to 54.

At the spring convention, it was clear that the movers and shakers of Tampa's neighborhood organizations—in both affluent and lower-income areas—felt that their groups had gained status, become more permanent, were getting attention and would remain a force even when their ally, Mayor Freedman, leaves office.

An unresolved issue in cities such as Richmond, Jersey City and Tampa is whether such close, hands-on work with neighborhoods by mayors, city managers and other municipal officials will eventually eclipse the traditional constituent services of city council members—which historically have been a major source of strength for many politicians. The new neighborhood service areas in all three cities ignore, for the most part, the boundaries of city council districts.

So far, though, city councils don't seem to be complaining about the new generation of direct links between city hall and neighborhoods. And one can argue that council members already have enough on their hands, dealing as they must with budget stringencies, difficult federal and state mandates and their cities' relationships with the other communities in their metropolitan regions.

What is clear is that mayors and professional managers are getting the point that an increasingly restive and demanding populace has to be reached and worked with where it lives—in the neighborhoods.

Source: National Journal, September 10, 1994, p. 2099. Reprinted with permission of National Journal.

---

wins and who loses? Is there a clear pattern of bias? And for academics, differences of opinion remain regarding how to define and measure community power.

Community Power Structures

Political scientists and sociologists have studied community power structures in great detail, and their conclusions are nearly as numerous as the individual cities and towns studied. Generally speaking, the researchers fall into one of two categories: the **elitists** (who find that a few top leaders form a power structure that dominates decision making) and the **pluralists** (who object to the idea of a **power structure** and instead view power as a process that is shared by a variety of competing groups).

In the classic elitist studies,[20] community power is believed to be concentrated in the hands of a few old families and business leaders. Community leadership is viewed as a rigid system in which those at the top are a relatively permanent group. There is a one-way flow of power, with the elite dictating policy to subordinates. In many cases, the "power elite" does not exercise control openly but operates by manipulating more visible public officials. Although there are occasional disagreements among the elite membership, their common economic interests unite them on most basic issues. In such a system, public opinion and elections have little effect on policymaking. In the elite model, as posited by Floyd Hunter in his study of Atlanta and by the Lynds in their study of Muncie, Indiana, government structure (strong or weak mayors, city managers) is nearly inconsequential. Instead, the economic structure of a community determines power relationships.

Critics charge that there is more conflict among top business leaders than the Lynds or Hunter suggest.[21] Still, *at the time* these studies were made, their conclusions, if a bit exaggerated, may have been correct. Many U.S. cities—such as Pittsburgh, Atlanta, and Gary, Indiana—early in this century were dominated by a single industry or small group of business persons, or even by a single family. As urban populations have become more heterogeneous, we would expect power relationships to change.

Pluralist studies,[22] on the other hand, are usually the work of political scientists. Pluralists conclude that power is shared by a variety of groups that are in conflict with one another. The groups are often short-lived—they form around an issue and then disappear. Thus pluralists do not see a power structure existing; rather, they perceive a fluid system of leadership. Persons or groups who dominate decision making in one area are seldom equally effective in other areas. In the pluralist model, public decisions are influenced by public opinion, and elections are an important means of transferring power from one group to another.

Even in machine-dominated Chicago, political scientist Edward Banfield found that there was not a hierarchical power structure with the mayor at the top.[23] Instead, Richard J. Daley acted as a broker among various interest groups in the city. Daley's preference was to allow interest groups to resolve issues among themselves, and then he would support their consensus opinion. Power in a large city such as Chicago also illustrates the point made by pluralists that while a city's elite business community may have the *potential* to control political affairs, its members seldom have the unity or the desire to exercise dominating power.

As one might expect, elitists and pluralists are critical of each other's methodology. Pluralists charge that elitists begin by assuming the existence of power relations. Elitists often rely on an interview method in which the respondents are asked, "Who has power in Gotham City?" Such a *reputational* approach, suggest the pluralists, often results in confusing groups with high potential for power (i.e., groups that have high status) with groups that actually exercise power. If obvious leaders do not emerge in their studies, elitists can resort to the argument that there are top leaders simply operating behind the scenes. A great many people believe that "they"—bankers, merchants, old families—run cities, so the elitist argument has strong appeal: It is simple, dramatic, and "realistic."

Elitists argue that the pluralist method of focusing on decision making has some major drawbacks. They contend that "key decisions" are not easily selected for analysis, and they suggest that an observer cannot always be sure whose interests have prevailed in those situations selected. Furthermore, elitists note that political influence is not always seen in the public decision-making process. Those with power may be able to exclude an issue from public discussion altogether and thus exercise control through prevention of decision making.[24] The ability to keep issues off local political agendas is, of course, the ultimate power that individuals or groups can exercise. However, it is very difficult to study nonevents. Finally, even pluralists agree that it is difficult to *compare* power in different situations. Thus the exercise of power on a zoning decision may differ greatly from the exercise of power on a decision regarding water fluoridation.

It is crucial to the pluralist model that many people in many small groups participate in public decision making. Yet even the leading pluralist, Robert A. Dahl, concedes that in many cases only a handful of leaders participate in decision making in such areas as urban renewal, party nominations, and public school matters. Although 60 percent of the American people belong to interest groups, it is significant that those most likely to be participants are white, better educated, and middle class. And two of every five Americans are not represented directly by any group. Regarding this last point, public interest groups such as Common Cause are serving the purpose of representing many consumer groups that previously did not have a voice in government decision making.

Alternative Explanations

As the study of community power has evolved, other more complex interpretations of power have emerged. Cities where pluralistic or elite structures were found have been revisited. Reputational approaches have been applied in cities where decision-making approaches were used, and the reverse has been done. Reputational *and* decision-making approaches have been applied concurrently in the same communities. And new approaches have been developed. The following are some of the major interpretations of community power that followed the early, now classic, studies.

Neo-Marxists believe that global economic markets determine the fate of cities. In this view, older industrial cities such as Detroit and Cleveland have become obsolete as world markets have changed. Major economic enterprises have changed from labor-intensive manufacturing to capital-intensive, high-tech operations. These new enterprises do not require the large concentrations of workers that were found in older cities, and city government is no longer needed by businesses to provide the infrastructure formerly required to support manufacturing plants and their workers who lived nearby.

Since capital can move—for example, many businesses have abandoned Detroit and moved to Sunbelt cities—cities are at the mercy of global economic demands.[25]

Older cities are forced to compete in a situation where the businesses hold the upper hand and newer cities lure this mobile capital with lower taxes and less government regulation.

While the neo-Marxist argument of economic determinism seems appealing in its simplicity, more in-depth case studies of cities reveal that economic development is more complicated. Public agencies have considerable independence even when a single industry dominates a city. Moreover, recent experience in many old industrial cities shows that their obituaries were premature. Much of the economic growth of the 1990s has been in the Midwest, while California and Texas have had rising rates of unemployment and low growth.

Urban specialist Paul Peterson also recognizes the power that business leaders have in a system where capital is very mobile. Since cities cannot afford to have businesses move, Peterson sees a **unitary interest** among all urban elements—government, business, and ordinary residents—to promote economic development.[26] In his model, local government nearly abdicates all responsibilities except pursuing economic development. Most controversially, Peterson believes that the battle for economic competition among communities is so all-consuming that cities should not divert their attention and resources from it by providing more than the most minimal welfare services. Welfare expenditures should be assumed by the national government. Thus there should be a recognition of "city limits" in terms of the ability of public agencies to solve all the city's problems.

Criticism of Peterson's views centers on the fact that most, if not all, cities have not been reduced to serving as agents for big business.[27] What is in the self-interest of business leaders may not be in the best interests of ordinary residents, whose neighborhood organizations often oppose development plans. Nor do all businesses benefit from all economic development projects. Thus a unitary interest may not exist. Of course, there also are humanitarian criticisms of Peterson's views concerning welfare. Like the neo-Marxist theories, unitary interest theory is very deterministic, presupposing that all elements will join together to prevent a major employer from leaving the city.

A third view of community power has been put forward by Clarence Stone. Stone believes that upper-strata groups (business and institutional elites) exercise **systemic power** in cities because mayors and other government officials need their support to stay in power.[28] This elite group initiates pro-business development projects that are in its best interest. The poor and middle class, who are unorganized and lack access to public officials, are left out of the decision-making process. Public officials are drawn to upper-strata interests who can give them a feeling of power and importance. Stone believes that mayors may anticipate the elites' reactions before decisions are made. Thus the power of elites often is covert.

Mayors stay in office, says Stone, by convincing the public that everyone in the city will benefit from these elite economic decisions. In this case there is not a unitary interest, but a "regime of systemic power." While some regimes concentrate on downtown development, others permit the city to fund neighborhood service projects. In the latter case, much depends on the inclination and the power of the mayor to be able to convince large developers to help fund neighborhood programs. Stone defines an

SCHOLARLY BOX

THE POLETOWN DECISION

When General Motors announced in 1980 that it was closing two of its Detroit factories and that it intended to build more modern facilities elsewhere, city officials moved quickly to keep GM in Detroit by finding a site to build a new plant.* Of several sites offered, one in the Poletown neighborhood was the only acceptable alternative to GM. The city acquired the property despite protests from residents who wanted the project scaled down. Within two years 1,500 homes, 2 schools, a hospital, and 16 churches were demolished and over 3,400 residents were relocated. The cost to Detroit was about $200 million. The new plant was given a 50 percent tax abatement for twelve years.

How and why did the city agree to take these extraordinary actions to benefit General Motors? Each of the approaches to community power that we have discussed offers a possible explanation.

Elitists would argue that Poletown was a classic case of a dominant business corporation holding sway over a city. Detroit was willing to spend millions of dollars without having a firm commitment from GM that it would produce the number of jobs (6,000) it promised.

Pluralists could contend that it was the city of Detroit that took the first steps to keep GM from leaving town. General Motors would not have considered the Poletown location if it were not for Mayor Coleman Young's persistence. The mayor worked closely with GM, but he also considered the interests of the United Auto Workers Union and the jobs that would be given to black and white residents of Detroit. From this perspective, city government was not simply acting out a role predetermined by global market conditions. Rather, the interaction of various groups produced a plan of action. Many black residents of Poletown were pleased with the generous settlements they received when they sold their property, and they felt empowered by the mayor's willingness to involve them in the decision-making process.

Neo-Marxists would view Poletown as a reflection of the class struggle in which Detroit acted in the tradition of older industrial cities to provide the infrastructure desired by business. The city placed itself between GM and the residents of Poletown, and its administration was willing to destroy a large neighborhood in order to meet GM's specifications.

In the unitary interest model, the Poletown decision seems to have worked to the best interests of all concerned. GM got a good deal to build a new plant, jobs stayed in Detroit, and Mayor Coleman Young was able to take credit for supporting the economic base of the city.

As a study in systemic power, Poletown shows Mayor Young aligning himself with the most powerful upper-strata power player in Detroit—General Motors. Then the mayor would be viewed as going out to convince the city's residents that he had acted in their best long-term interests.

Whether or not we agree that there was a kind of economic determinism operating in Detroit or that business (elite) interests dominated the Poletown decision, GM clearly exercised considerable power. Which theory do you think best explains the decision made to destroy the Poletown neighborhood? Can you think of cases in other cities where this same kind of analysis can be applied?

*See Bernard H. Ross and Myron Levine, *Urban Politics: Power in Metropolitan America,* 5th ed. (Itasca, Ill.: F. E. Peacock, 1996), pp. 89–92; and Bryan D. Jones and Lynn W. Bachelor (with Carter Wilson), *The Sustaining Hand: Community Leadership and Corporate Power* (Lawrence: University of Kansas Press, 1986).

urban regime as "the informal arrangements by which public bodies and private interests function together in order to be able to make and carry out governing decisions."[29] In his study of Atlanta, Stone found a unified business elite engaged in regime building. This elite set the terms of civic cooperation, and it incorporated the black middle class into the mainstream of economic and civic life in Atlanta. An interesting feature of Atlanta was the inclination of groups in positions of community responsibility, including the black middle class, to pull back from conflict with the business elite and seek accommodation.

From our overview of community power, it is clear that there is not a consensus among academics regarding the best way to explain the structure of community power. Of course, we would expect that studies of different cities would come to different conclusions about who has power and about how public decisions are made in different locations and in different periods of time. However, when different researchers study the same city or even the same decision-making situation in a given city, they often have come to different conclusions. The preceding Scholarly Box uses the decision in the early 1980s to build a new General Motors assembly plant in the Poletown neighborhood of Detroit to illustrate how each of the major community power theories can be applied to explain the same event.

SUMMARY

The political dynamics of urban areas are the result of the interactions of many players—mayors, council members, political party loyalists, and members of interest groups.

Mayors play a variety of roles, ranging from passive caretakers to entrepreneurs. In big cities, mayoral candidates utilize many of the same techniques that are employed in gubernatorial campaigns. Increasingly, blacks and women have been winning elections for mayor. While many blacks have been elected in cities with majority white populations, other cities with black majorities and black mayors remain racially polarized.

In most cities, being a council member is a part-time job, and the council is often dominated by the mayor or manager. Certain electoral reforms, as discussed in Chapter 9, have made it difficult for women and blacks to get elected to city councils.

While voter turnout in local elections tends to be very low, residents are more likely to participate in interest groups or in neighborhood organizations. Still, participation by members of minority groups remains low.

Given the relatively low levels of citizen participation, some scholars have concluded that a small "power elite" often dominates city politics. Others counter that power is divided among a number of groups in communities, or that a "regime of systemic power," consisting of public officials and business leaders, acts to support economic development and neighborhood service projects.

KEY TERMS

Ballot roll-off Tendency for fewer votes to be cast as voters move through a long list of candidates and issues in elections.

Communalists Persons who participate actively in community affairs but often are not involved in partisan politics. They come disproportionately from among those with college educations and high incomes.

Economic Opportunity Act of 1964 This was at the center of President Lyndon Johnson's war on poverty. It created the Job Corps and several community action programs.

Elitists Those who believe that a few top leaders form a power structure that dominates government decision making.

Entrepreneur mayors Dominant mayors who have a vision of where their cities should go and the ability to form political coalitions to accomplish their goals.

Functional fiefdoms City bureaucracies that conduct their specialized operations with considerable independence from outside authorities. They inhibit city leadership by fragmenting services among competing agencies.

Neo-Marxists New (recent) Marxists who believe that human history has been a struggle between the exploited working class and the owners of capital. They believe that economic development in cities drives public decisions.

Opportunistic policy broker A mayor who considers proposals initiated by various groups in the city and supports those he wishes to be implemented.

Passive caretaker A mayor who takes little initiative, preferring to have interest groups endorse public projects. The mayor takes care of such matters as snow removal and street maintenance.

Pluralists Those who believe that political power is shared by a large number of competing groups rather than concentrated in an elite.

Political incorporation Using city government to empower minority groups by giving them jobs or awarding them public contracts.

Power structure An "establishment" composed of the elite members (those with wealth, family status, or political power) who dominate a community.

Public interest organizations Groups that are motivated to action by a concern for the good of the whole community.

Sunshine laws Requirements that government bodies (city councils, county commissioners) hold their formal business meetings open to the public. Typically, meetings can be closed only for personnel evaluations.

Systemic power The concept that business and institutional elites exercise power over an entire city. It is believed that mayors identify with this elite and support upper-strata interests in the city.

Unitary interest Belief that business, government, and ordinary citizens share a common (unitary) interest to support economic development for the good of the entire city.

REFERENCES

1 Harold Lasswell, *Politics: Who Gets What, When, How* (New York: Meridian Books, 1958).

2 Douglas Yates, *The Ungovernable City* (Cambridge, Mass.: MIT Press, 1977), p. 5.

3 Quoted in Jay S. Goodman, *The Dynamics of Urban Government and Politics* (New York: Macmillan, 1975), p. 315.

4 See John P. Kotter and Paul R. Lawrence, *Mayors in Action: Five Approaches to Urban Governance* (New York: Wiley Interscience, 1974), Chapter 7.

5 Yates, *The Ungovernable City.*
6 Robert A. Dahl, *Who Governs? Democracy and Power in an American City* (New Haven, Conn.: Yale University Press, 1961), p. 204.
7 This term was first discussed by Rufus P. Browning, Dale R. Marshall, and David H. Tabb in *Protest Is Not Enough* (Berkeley: University of California Press, 1984).
8 See Peter K. Eisinger, "Black Mayors and the Policy of Racial Advancement," in William C. McReedy, ed., *Culture, Ethnicity, and Identity* (New York: Academic Press, 1983), pp. 95–109.
9 Abigail Thernstrom, "Redistricting, in Black and White," *New York Times,* December 7, 1994, p. A 17.
10 "Women in Elective Office," Center for the American Woman in Politics (New Brunswick, N.J., 1995).
11 Susan A. MacManus and Charles S. Bullock, "Women on Southern City Councils: A Decade of Change," *Journal of Political Science* (Spring 1989), pp. 32–49.
12 Joseph F. Zimmerman, "Enhancing Representational Equity in Cities," in Wilma Rule and Joseph F. Zimmerman, eds., *United States Electoral Systems: Their Impact on Women and Minorities* (New York: Praeger, 1992), pp. 209–210.
13 R. Darcy, "Electoral Barriers to Women," in *United States Electoral Systems,* pp. 221–223.
14 Saul Alinsky, *Rules for Radicals* (New York: Random House, 1972), pp. 128, 138.
15 See E. E. Schottschneider, *The Semisovereign People* (New York: Holt, Rinehart and Winston, 1960).
16 Theodore Lowi, *At the Pleasure of the Mayor* (New York: Free Press, 1964), Chapter 7.
17 Sidney Verba and Norman H. Nie, *Participation in America: Political Democracy and Social Equality* (New York: Harper & Row, 1972), p. 86.
18 Bernard H. Ross and Myron A. Levine, *Urban Politics: Power in Metropolitan America,* 5th ed. (Itasca, Ill.: F. E. Peacock, 1996), p. 243.
19 Clarence N. Stone, "Race and Regime in Atlanta," in Rufus P. Browning et al., eds., *Racial Politics in American Cities* (New York: Longman, 1991), pp. 125–139.
20 Robert Lynd and Helen Lynd, *Middletown* (New York: Harcourt, Brace, and World, 1929); Robert Lynd and Helen Lynd, *Middletown in Transition* (New York: Harcourt, Brace, and World, 1937); Floyd Hunter, *Community Power Structure* (Chapel Hill: University of North Carolina Press, 1953); and W. Lloyd Warner et al., *Democracy in Jonesville* (New York: Harper & Row, 1949).
21 See Nelson Polsby, *Community Power and Political Theory* (New Haven, Conn.: Yale University Press, 1963).
22 Robert A. Dahl, *Who Governs?* (New Haven: Yale University Press, 1964); Aaron Wildavsky, *Leadership in a Small Town* (Totowa, N.J.: Bedminister Press, 1964); Frank J. Munger, *Decisions in Syracuse* (Bloomington: Indiana University Press, 1961); Robert Agger, Daniel Goldrich, and Bert Swanson, *The Rulers and the Ruled* (New York: Wiley, 1964); and Robert Presthus, *Men at the Top* (New York: Oxford University Press, 1964).
23 Edward C. Banfield, *Political Influence* (New York: Free Press, 1965).
24 Peter Bachrach and Morton S. Baratz, *Power and Poverty: Theory and Practice* (New York: Oxford University Press, 1970).
25 Richard Child Hill, "Fiscal Collapse and Political Struggle in Decaying Central Cities in the United States," in William K. Tabb and Larry Sawyers, eds., *Marxism and the Metropolis* (New York: Oxford University Press, 1978), pp. 213–240.

26 Paul Peterson, *City Limits* (Chicago: University of Chicago Press, 1981).
27 See Clarence N. Stone, "Summing Up: Urban Regimes, Development Policy, and Political Arrangements," in Clarence Stone and Heywood T. Sanders, eds., *The Politics of Urban Development* (Lawrence: University of Kansas Press, 1987).
28 Clarence N. Stone, "Systemic Power in Community Decision-Making: A Restatement of Stratification Theory," *American Political Science Review* (December 1980), pp. 978–990.
29 Clarence N. Stone, *Regime Politics: Governing Atlanta, 1946–1988* (Lawrence: University of Kansas Press, 1989), p. 6.

11

POLITICS BEYOND CITY LIMITS

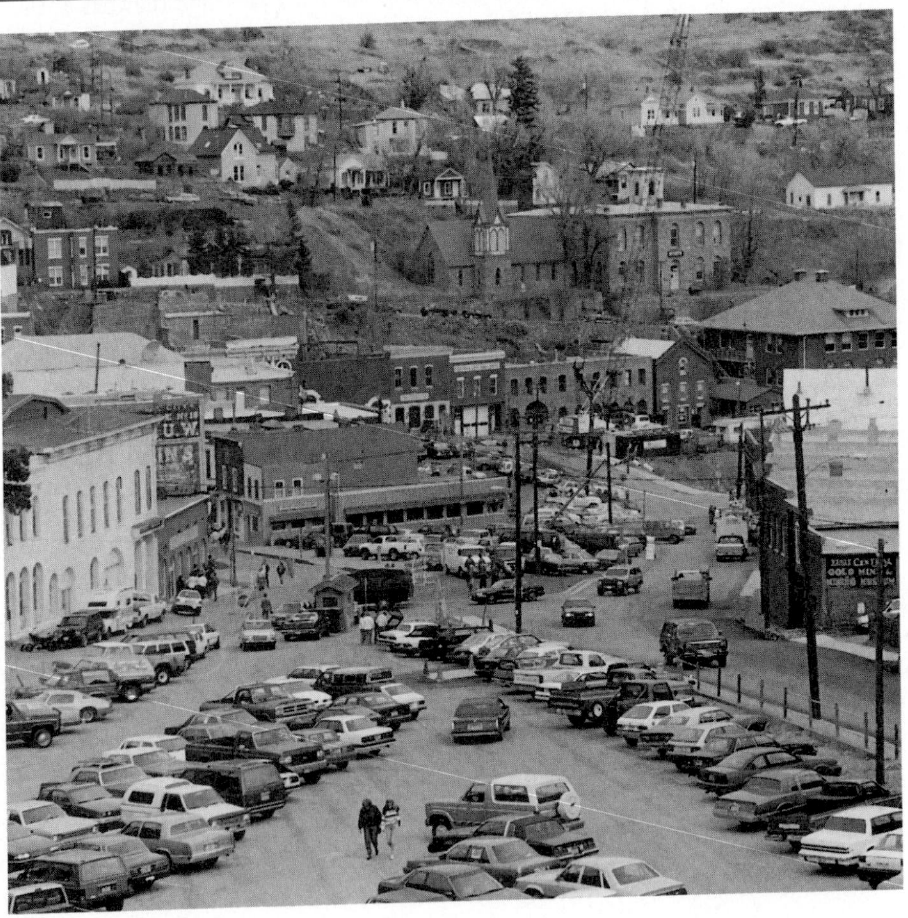

Eric Neurath/Stock, Boston

In the past two chapters we discussed urban government structure and political activity, largely as they occur in central cities. We now turn our attention beyond those city limits to look at politics in suburbs, small towns, and rural areas. The 1920 census showed that the United States had changed from a predominantly small-town, rural society in the nineteenth century to a predominantly urban society. As noted in Chapter 1, urbanization of the United States has increased to the point where currently about 80 percent of Americans live in metropolitan statistical areas.

Clearly, we have become a largely urbanized people. Yet more of us live *outside* central cities than within them. The 1990 census showed that for the first time in our history more than half the population of metropolitan areas was suburban. Moreover, because metropolitan statistical areas include whole counties adjacent to a central city or contiguous cities of 50,000 people, many residents of MSAs actually live in small towns that are not suburban or they live in rural areas. Of course, 20 percent of Americans live outside MSAs.

Our primary concern in this chapter is to examine politics in suburbia to see how it differs from big-city politics and to see how suburban communities interact with each other. The prevailing view of the suburbs in the 1950s was that they were a homogeneous group of bedroom communities whose white, upper- and middle-class residents voted Republican and limited their concern for social issues to their local schools.[1] While this picture was oversimplified even in the 1950s, suburbs have become increasingly diverse. By the 1970s the idealized version of these communities differed greatly from reality. After examining contemporary suburban life, we will look at ways in which metropolitan areas are attempting to create order where literally hundreds of overlapping governments have fragmented the political process. Then we will travel farther away from central cities to examine life in small-town and rural America.

URBAN SPRAWL: CAUSES AND EFFECTS

As political scientist John J. Harrigan notes, central cities could have grown by annexing areas on their fringes where population was growing.[2] Instead, cities became surrounded by autonomous suburban communities whose residents sought the advantages of a small-town setting close to the economic and cultural opportunities of the central city. As recently as 1950, 70 percent of metropolitan area populations lived in central cities. In 1990, 60 percent lived in the suburbs, and the majority of jobs had moved there also.

The mobility afforded by widespread automobile ownership after World War II and the construction of new highways helped to accelerate suburban growth. A host of federal government policies—including the interstate highway system, lower-interest home loans insured by the Federal Housing Administration, tax codes that permitted deductions for home mortgage interest, and grants to build hospitals and sewerage plants—encouraged Americans to move to the suburbs in the 1950s.

Earlier decisions made by private businesses also facilitated population movement away from central cities. Faced with labor unrest near the end of the nineteenth century, many businesses relocated their plants to the suburbs as a way to isolate workers and to control union activities. Credit institutions often practiced **redlining** in which they refused to make loans for construction in certain parts of cities they considered too risky. Depressed areas of cities grew worse as new or rehabilitated housing was not funded. Often this policy was strongly influenced by racial factors. The lack of acceptable central city housing led to the exodus of the middle-class to the suburbs as government policy made it easier for them to buy houses.

Fragmented Government

As people have moved farther away from the central city, **urban sprawl** has created a maze of government units over which there is little or no coordination or control by a central authority. The New York City metropolitan area, for example, extends over more than twenty counties in three states and includes more than 18 million people. Even though population growth in metropolitan New York City increased only 5 percent in the last twenty-five years, the amount of developed land in the area increased 60 percent. The Chicago metropolitan area contains over 1,100 government units. Phoenix in 1940 had a population of 65,000 within a 10-square-mile area. Currently it has a population of about 1 million in a 386-square-mile area. In addition, suburban sprawl has led to the expansion of Tempe, Mesa, Scottsdale, Paradise Valley, and other new Arizona cities.

Suffolk County, one of the two counties that make up Long Island, New York, presents an excellent example of extreme fragmentation.[3] The county has ten towns, thirty villages, seventy-one school districts, and ninety-two fire districts. It contains Dering Harbor, population twenty-eight, the smallest incorporated village in New York State. One attorney in Suffolk County describes himself as a kind of municipal Sherpa, guiding out-of-county businesses through the maze of government regulations on the island.

As noted in Chapter 1, by 1980 about three-fourths of all Americans lived in **metropolitan areas.** In 1990 there were 284 metropolitan areas in the United States. This was a substantial increase from the 212 metropolitan areas identified by the Bureau of the Census in 1960 and the 243 identified in 1970. About 42 percent of the nation's growth in the 1980s was in the fifteen largest consolidated metropolitan areas (see Table 11-1). More than one in three Americans lives in one of these fifteen areas. Much of the growth, even in Sunbelt areas such as Phoenix, was on the fringes where housing is less expensive. Overall in the 1980s metropolitan areas grew by 11.6 percent, while nonmetropolitan population growth was 3.9 percent.

The *fragmentation* of metropolitan government makes it extremely difficult to establish responsibility for metropolitan area policy. In addition, public services suffer because small units are unable to provide many specialized services; there is duplication of services when many governments independently operate facilities such as sewage-disposal and water plants; and it is difficult to deal with the many problems—pollution, mass transit, crime, traffic congestion—that extend over several community boundary lines. While affluent suburbs can spend vast sums of money for education, central cities face a declining tax base and an increasing demand for services. Property tax *rates* may be higher in a central city than in its more affluent suburbs. At the same time, many suburban governments need to spend relatively little money for crime con-

TABLE 11-1 THE FIFTEEN LARGEST METROPOLITAN AREAS, 1980–1990

Consolidated metropolitan area	1980	1990	Change
New York City	17,539,532	18,087,251	+ 3.1%
Los Angeles–Anaheim–Riverside	11,497,349	14,531,529	+26.4
Chicago–Gary–Lake County	7,937,290	8,065,633	+ 1.6
San Francisco–Oakland–San Jose	5,367,900	6,253,311	+16.5
Philadelphia–Wilmington–Trenton	5,680,509	5,899,345	+ 3.9
Detroit–Ann Arbor	4,752,764	4,665,236	− 1.8
Boston–Lawrence–Salem	3,971,792	4,171,643	+ 5.0
Washington–Maryland–Virginia	3,250,921	3,923,574	+20.7
Dallas–Fort Worth	2,930,568	3,885,415	+32.6
Houston–Galveston–Brazoria	3,099,942	3,711,043	+19.7
Miami–Fort Lauderdale	2,643,766	3,192,582	+20.8
Atlanta	2,138,136	2,833,511	+32.5
Cleveland–Akron–Lorain	2,834,062	2,759,823	− 2.6
Seattle–Tacoma	2,093,285	2,559,164	+22.3
San Diego	1,861,846	2,498,016	+34.2

Source: U.S. Census Bureau, 1991.

trol or public health. However, there are many middle-class suburbs that increasingly must deal with social and economic problems similar to those confronting central cities.

Fragmentation has numerous other consequences.[4] Significant racial imbalance occurs because outer-ring suburbs remain predominantly white, while the central city and, increasingly, inner-ring suburbs have large black and Hispanic populations. Suburban land-use regulations drive up the cost of new construction, and this leads to a shortage of housing in central cities when low-income persons are forced to stay within city limits. Suburbs that restrict the growth of *all* types of housing units force development on the suburban fringe, thus adding to the existing urban sprawl. Suburbs that restrict growth push development out farther, and this destroys more green space. Because suburban residents value their independence, they strongly resist metropolitan-wide government or other means of coordination.

A recent manifestation of "small-town sprawl" has been the building of so-called superstores just beyond town limits.[5] These stores have much the same impact on small towns that regional shopping centers have had on larger cities. Superstores drain off sales from downtown businesses, and their profits go to corporate headquarters far removed from the community. They pave over farm fields and lead to the location of other businesses on the fringes of small towns. When these "Big Box" stores close (K-Mart closed nearly 200 stores in 1994 and 1995), towns are left with an oversized building and its parking lot and probably a downtown with empty storefronts.

Cities versus Suburbs

An increasing trend since the 1980s has been the expansion of **satellite cities** on the fringes of metropolitan areas.[6] Although cities such as West Palm Beach (Miami),

Scottsdale (Phoenix), and White Plains (New York) are related to the central city, they are employment centers in their own right and often have downtowns and cultural complexes that are quite separate from the core city. Residents of these satellites may have little direct contact with the central city.

There have been both push and pull effects regarding patterns of residence. While suburbs have "pulled" residents out of cities with their promise of a better life, residents of central cities have also been "pushed out" because of a variety of city problems. Migrants from large cities most often mention crime as their major reason for leaving. Rundown schools, drugs, pollution, high taxes, and the rising cost of living are other factors that push people to the suburbs. As the percentage of blacks and Hispanics increases in central cities, a clear undercurrent of racism also influences whites to flee to predominantly white suburbs. In large cities, people also sense a loss of community feeling and often find it difficult to participate in government decision making.

As we have noted, it is a mistake to think of all suburbs as white, upper-class, bedroom communities surrounding central cities. Only about one-third of all suburbs are accurately described as residential or *dormitory.* The other two-thirds are *employing* and *mixed* suburbs, which combine dormitory and employment functions. In addition, suburbs range from being working class in character to being enclaves for wealthy exurbanites far removed from the central city. Some suburbs can be categorized by a specific function they perform, such as having a racetrack or having a large number of bars and nightclubs.[7] As some suburbs that were built just after World War II age, they begin to take on many of the same characteristics of older central cities.

When middle-class families and industry leave, the city's tax base shrinks, and this occurs at a time when welfare, police, and public health expenses are increasing. Yet great *private wealth* remains in the nation's largest cities. Ira Sharkansky describes an "irony of urban wealth" in which there is "the juxtaposition of enormous wealth in the private sector with apparent poverty in the public sector."[8] Urban wealth, says Sharkansky, attracts the untrained and unsuccessful who seek a better way of life. Unlike the early twentieth-century immigrants, today's urban poor find few jobs for unskilled workers, and union control of apprenticeship programs makes it difficult to acquire trade skills. In addition, young blacks are particularly frustrated and alienated when they encounter a substantial gap between real and anticipated social and economic gains. Inner-city neighborhoods continue to deteriorate, even as downtown development projects create spectacular new buildings. For example, Cleveland's poverty rate has remained around 40 percent despite the construction of new sports facilities and new downtown office buildings.

Still, there is increasing evidence to indicate that life in cities has actually improved. In places such as Boston and Baltimore, middle-class people have returned to live in the city, and new shopping areas such as Boston's Quincy Market are flourishing. The Society Hill–Market Street East area in Philadelphia is another example of a successful renewal effort. Downtowns are being preserved in virtually all cities. This is in contrast to the mid-1960s, when some 1,600 federally supported urban renewal projects in 800 cities often were bulldozing historic neighborhoods.[9] Federal tax laws now encourage preservation, and cities are putting a priority on downtown development. Unfortunately, as upscale renovation has lured white suburbanites back to inner cities, the increased costs have driven blacks and Hispanics to other urban neighborhoods.

Cities and their suburbs exist in a state of natural hostility. Most fundamentally, there is a substantial difference in life styles between residents of the two areas. Although it would be very misleading to picture Grosse Pointe, Beverly Hills, Shaker Heights, and Scarsdale as "typical" suburbs, suburbanites in Northern and Western states are better educated, have higher incomes, and are more likely to hold white-collar jobs than are central-city dwellers. In suburbia, life centers around single-family units and there is a strong emphasis on local schools.

Most large cities have experienced significant white flight during the past two decades, resulting in increasing concentration of Hispanics and blacks in inner cities while many suburbs remain predominantly white. Overwhelmingly, African-Americans are likely to live in metropolitan areas. According to the 1990 census, 84 percent of blacks, compared with 76 percent of whites, lived in metropolitan areas. The majority of all blacks and Hispanics live in just thirty metropolitan areas. Minorities make up 41 percent of central city populations and 18 percent of the suburban population.[10] About half of all blacks, Hispanics, and Asians live in cities of 100,000 or more, compared to only 20 percent of whites. Places with populations under 2,500 are 90 percent white.

While suburbs remain mostly white, there has been a substantial departure of middle- and working-class minority persons from cities since the 1980s. Census figures show that from 1980 to 1990, minorities experienced a higher percentage of growth in suburbs than in central cities. In the 1980s the population of Washington, D.C., declined by about 100,000, and the loss of black households was nearly three times as great as for whites. Hispanic and Asian-American suburbanization occurred in the 1980s at even higher rates than for blacks across the country. Circles of black-majority suburbs exist around Washington, Atlanta, St. Louis, and Chicago. Minorities leaving central cities cite the same reasons as whites for their flight to suburbs—crime, quality of life, property values, and schools. While all-white suburbs are diminishing, some suburbs that exclude all but the superwealthy remain overwhelmingly white. At the other extreme, so-called disaster suburbs such as East St. Louis, Illinois, and Compton, California, are nearly all-minority and very poor. In the chapter reading Neal R. Peirce looks at the decline of inner-ring suburbs and how metropolitan regions should recognize and respond to the problems this has created.

In addition to socioeconomic differences, *political differences* between central cities and suburbs can be identified. From our understanding of socioeconomic factors and their relationship to party identification (see Chapter 3), we would expect cities to be strongly Democratic and suburbs to be strongly Republican. In fact, cities, with their concentrations of union members, ethnic minorities, and blacks, historically have supported the Democratic party in national and local elections. New York City has cast a majority of its votes for every Democratic presidential candidate since Thomas Jefferson. However, as noted in Chapter 10, New York City and Los Angeles have elected Republican mayors in the 1990s; and several other large cities—including Cleveland, Indianapolis, Minneapolis, and San Diego—elected Republican mayors in the 1980s.

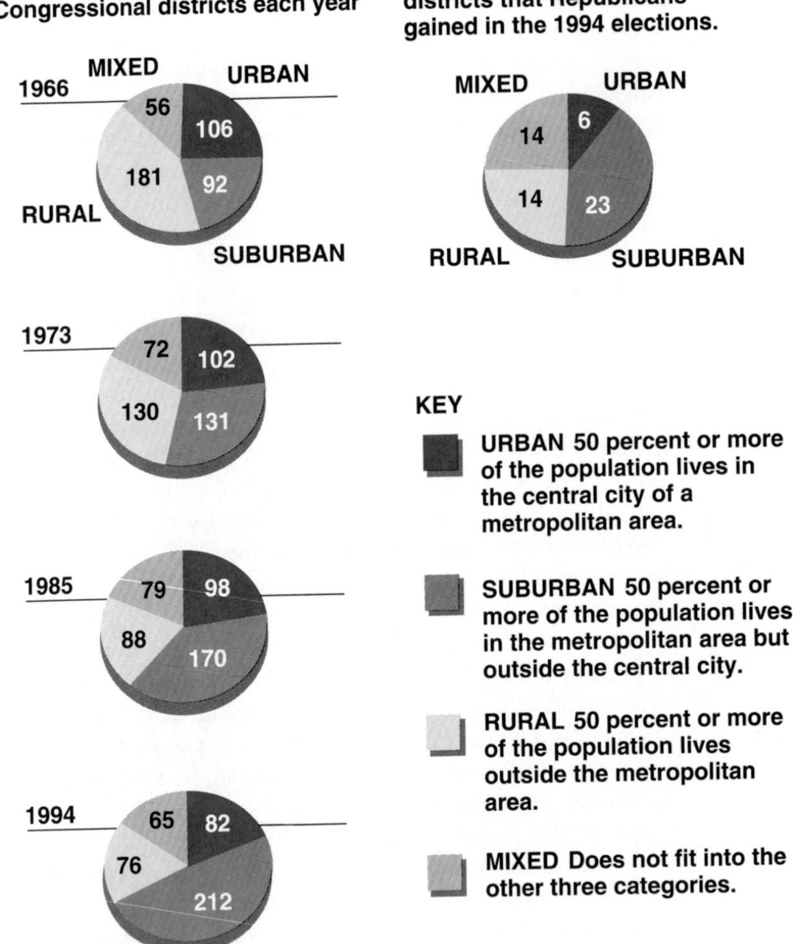

FIGURE 11-1 Changing urban, rural, suburban mix of congressional districts, 1966–1994. (Congressional Research Service, *The New York Times,* December 19, 1995, p. A13.)

Suburban residents typically vote for Republican presidential and congressional candidates. For their city government, they have a strong preference for nonpartisan elections. Suburban councils typically consist of part-time amateurs, and a city-manager form is the government of choice in a majority of suburbs. As suburban communities become more economically and racially diverse, we can expect a decline in the politics of consensus that has guided their public decision making.

Figure 11-1 shows how the type of population in congressional districts changed from 1966 to 1994. Note the significant decline in rural districts and the increase in suburban districts. The 1994 congressional and gubernatorial elections, which brought Republicans to power across the country, clearly showed the political impact of suburban sprawl and the conservative attitudes it fosters.[11] The power of suburbia was especially evident in the South where the large vote helped defeat many Democratic candidates who traditionally have had only token opposition. Despite the diversity of suburbs—from nearly all-white enclaves, to Hispanic communities in California, and black-majority towns in Maryland—many suburban voters in 1994 shared the belief that they had worked hard and they did not want the government taxing them to help those who had not worked as hard.

THE POLITICS OF METROPOLITAN CONSOLIDATION

Differences in the political, social, and economic composition of cities and suburbs have a direct effect on public policy. In many instances people have moved to suburbs to escape the problems of central cities or, increasingly, to escape the problems of inner-ring suburbs. They do not want to contribute tax dollars to help solve other people's social problems. Meanwhile, cities must respond to a host of pressing issues even as their revenue base declines.

As we would expect, city-suburban differences also have a major impact on the fate of proposals for consolidation of metropolitan governments. In most instances, consolidation plans are opposed by both city and suburban officials, who seek to maintain their community's autonomy and their personal political power. Of the two groups, those in suburbs have been the most opposed to unification. However, the support of residents of central cities has also waned. With population of the central cities declining, metropolitan government would come to mean control by white, middle-class suburbanites. The liberal coalitions of labor and blacks that control many city governments would stand to lose considerable power if their political strength were diluted in a metropolitan area. In Cleveland, for example, during the period 1933–1959, voters defeated ten referenda to create various forms of metropolitan government. Over the years, black support declined from 79 percent in 1933 to 29 percent in 1959. White voter support also declined over time, but the fall-off was less dramatic.

Blacks and labor leaders usually oppose consolidation for reasons that are more political, social, and psychological than economic. They contend that the existence of many local governments helps increase citizen *access* to decision making, which produces a greater sense of community and personal effectiveness in dealing with smaller units of government. In such a situation, a variety of groups have the opportunity to make their views heard and to affect public policy.

Fragmentation benefits white, upper-class suburbanites because it allows them to isolate themselves from the problems of cities and to maintain school assignments based strictly on place of residence. In a time when there is strong sentiment for less government, suburban residents may not place a high priority on improved service delivery. At any rate, few are likely to believe that metropolitan government would improve services, and most fear metro government would mean higher taxes. Evidence from metropolitan areas where consolidation has occurred—Miami and Nashville—shows that expenditures have risen.

Suburbia's New Growing-Old Pains

Neal R. Peirce

Could the United States be on the verge of a permanent thaw in the ice age of antagonistic distrust between suburbs and cities that's choked off, for two generations, any meaningful debate about metropolitan governance or sharing of tax bases?

Conventional wisdom says no. Suburbanites long ago decided, we're told, to distance themselves and their tax money from the poverty, crime and minorities of the nation's big cities. As for inner-city blacks and Hispanics, they're supposedly dead set against sharing the political power it took them so long to win.

Conventional wisdom also says that we shouldn't expect much to change. The Berlin Wall may fall, the "Evil Empire" may evaporate, Yasir Arafat and Yitzhak Rabin may shake hands on the White House lawn, but it's foolish, we're told, to expect a rapprochement between America's suburbs and their inner cities.

Fortunately, however, the conventional wisdom may be wrong. A new set of political realities has been emerging across America's "citistate" regions in 1993:

First, large numbers of older working-class suburbs are starting to fall into the same abyss of disinvestment that their center cities did years ago.

Second, entire counties—with scores of suburbs filled with residents who once thought that they'd safely escaped poverty, crime and a host of other urban ills—may be economically imperiled.

And third, the scorecard of winners and losers has shifted radically. Through the 1970s, the lineup was simply center cities against their suburbs. But a careful look at the results of the 1990 census shows that a handful of outer-ring suburbs from coast to coast have been picking up a massive share of new industrial and commercial investment and high-property-taxpaying residents.

The "losers," it turns out, are not just the nation's center cities, but also broad areas of inner-ring suburbs that are now yielding up their most successful businesses and residents to the outer rings.

Thomas Bier of Cleveland State University has painstakingly documented the economic effects of successive rings of outward movement, first from Cleveland, then from its older inner-ring suburbs. Each new ring of housing development on the regional periphery, Bier found, drives down housing prices in Cleveland and its older suburbs and erodes their tax bases and economic viability.

"The wake of decline and urban pathologies that spread behind outmigration," Bier said, "will not stop at the city-suburban line."

With such suburbs as Euclid, Maple Heights and Parma perhaps the most vulnerable, Bier has warned that "over the next 20–30 years, Cuyahoga County may follow the city of Cleveland into distressed fiscal condition, which would in turn further jeopardize the economic condition of the multi-county Cleveland region."

It isn't a pretty picture, and it isn't unique. Look almost anywhere around the regions of the United States and there are constellations of suburbs in deep trouble. They're south of Chicago, south of Los Angeles, west of Minneapolis and northeast of Washington.

Paul Glastris of *U.S. News & World Report* checked data on suburbs from the 1990 census in a cross section of six metropolitan regions. He found that 35 per cent of the suburbs suffered real declines in median household incomes in the 1980s. Glastris quoted Charles Lockwood, a real estate consultant, as saying, "The nation that invented the throwaway city is now creating the throwaway suburb."

St. Louis County, which rings St. Louis, is really two counties, Rob Gurwitt recently observed in *Governing* magazine. In the 1980s, luxury homes and canyons of condominiums sprang up in the county's outer reaches, accompanied by gargantuan office buildings—filled by such corporate giants as Citicorp, International Business Machines Corp. and Hewlett-Packard Co.—astride the freeway. Meanwhile, however, the suburbs of inner St. Louis County lost 8 per cent of their combined population, saw their median household incomes drop and experienced sharp increases in their elderly populations.

The biggest flights of middle-class families in the 1980s, in fact, didn't come out of center cities, but out of the inner-ring suburbs of such cities as Atlanta and Chicago.

"Barrios in Riverside and Oxnard are as devastated as South Central Los Angeles," notes Jane Pisano of the University of Southern California. "There are more poor in Pomona, percentage-wise, than in Los Angeles."

A decade ago, Massachusetts's big socioeconomic split was Boston versus the rest of the state, according to Harry Spence, the administrator of Chelsea. But now, Spence says, urban ills afflict such communities as Brockton, Everett, Lowell and Somerville just as much as Boston.

Admitting that they face many inner-city problems comes hard to many residents of older blue-collar suburbs who struggled to gain a piece of the American Dream—but now see their houses declining or stagnant in value, jobs fleeing to the outer rings, poor people moving into their neighborhoods and crime rising.

In many regions, these neighborhoods are the heart of distressed, rebellious Ross Perot country.

Yet as unlikely as it seems, an alliance of center cities and inner-ring suburbs may be taking shape.

This year, the Minnesota Twin Cities' Association of Metropolitan Municipalities, which represents 70 of the 136 governments in the seven-county Minneapolis-St. Paul metropolitan area, voted unanimously to support an elected Metropolitan Council. The result could be rising pressure to equalize tax wealth across the region.

The Minnesota vote is just one straw in the wind—but possibly a very significant one.

Source: National Journal, Nov. 6, 1993, p. 2675. Reprinted with permission of National Journal.

Among academics, those who support the **public choice** approach argue that metropolitan area residents are best served by a fragmented system in which various communities can offer different sets of services that appeal to various tastes of citizens.[12] Public choice theorists contend that those citizens who are willing to pay more for certain services, such as education and recreation, can choose to live in certain communities and those who prefer lower taxes and fewer services can live elsewhere. This is comparable to a free marketplace where consumers shop for the best products at the most appropriate price. As in business, it is contended that competition among suburban communities will lead to innovation and a greater incentive to produce government services more efficiently.

Critics of public choice theory respond that while this model might work for those free to move within the metropolitan area, many people do not have the ability to "vote with their feet." Family, finances, and jobs may greatly reduce the mobility of many residents. Of course, this is particularly true for the poor and for minorities. Even if people were relatively free to move, it might result in isolated suburbs pursuing narrow goals to benefit their own residents with little concern for resolving area-wide problems.

Those in favor of **consolidation** are most likely to be business and professional people whose perspective is similar to that of early twentieth-century urban reformers. These groups fear that as the central cities are abandoned by the middle class, the poor and less well educated will gain undue political influence. They also believe that metropolitan government would be more efficient because it could achieve the economies of large-scale operations and provide improved public services.

Contrary to conventional wisdom, some supporters of consolidation argue that it will help minorities. They note that while blacks and Hispanics often constitute a majority of voters in large cities, those cities have such weak tax bases that it is nearly impossible for them to respond effectively to the needs of the minority community. These reformers advocate a district system of election in which minority groups would be directly represented in an areawide government. W. W. Herenton, the black mayor of Memphis, advocates his city's merger with predominantly white Shelby County. Without such a change, Herenton believes that Memphis will become a poor black enclave surrounded by rich white suburbs.

Plans for Metropolitan Consolidation

Because opposition to consolidation is so widespread and is based on so many different rationales, it is not surprising that proposals to establish metropolitan governments have failed in nearly 75 percent of the times they have been brought before the voters. However, a metropolitan area need not make the move from extreme fragmentation to rigid consolidation in one giant step. There are several intermediate options available, such as annexation, special districts, and councils of government. David B. Walker outlines seventeen approaches to regional service problems ranging from those that are the most politically feasible and least controversial to those, such as city-county consolidation, that have relatively little likelihood of being adopted.[13] We need to remember that while comprehensive consolidation of municipalities in metropolitan areas is rare, other approaches are relatively easy to accomplish, and consequently, they are found in most metropolitan areas. In the box below, Walker outlines ten current trends in America's metropolitan areas, which he believes point to regionalism as a solution.

Among the "easiest" regional approaches to service delivery, Walker includes informal cooperation between two local jurisdictions; interlocal service contracts between

CURRENT METRO TRENDS

Metropolitan America is experiencing change on at least ten fronts.

1 More metro areas. More metro areas exist today (320 in 1990, with 522 central cities) than ever before, a more than 33 percent increase since 1962.
2 More people in metro areas. Seventy-eight percent of the total population was located in metro areas in 1990, compared with 63 percent in 1962. More people also live in suburban jurisdictions than previously—some 60 percent of total metro population in 1990, compared with 50 percent in 1960.
3 The big are getting bigger and more numerous. Although more than half the individual metropolitan areas have populations of 250,000 or less, more than half of the metropolitan population lived in the thirty-nine metro areas that in 1990 had populations of 1 million or more.
4 The West is as metropolitan as the Northeast, much to the consternation of the "wide, open spaces" westerners. Not surprisingly, the fastest-growing metro areas are in the South and the West.
5 Continued metro government fragmentation. Growth in metro areas has meant further fractionalization of the local governmental map. More of the nation's local governments in 1987 were located in metro areas: roughly 38 percent of the 83,186 total, compared with 36 percent in 1982 and 20 percent in 1972. The average metro area still encompasses about ninety-four governmental units, and there was a slight increase recently in the proportion of larger multicounty metro areas from 55 percent in 1987 to 61 percent in 1989.
6 Increased metro diversity. Compared with their situation in the 1960s, metro areas now are much more diverse in (a) population and territorial size, (b) the mix of private economic functions and the range of public services offered, (c) the respective position of central cities vis-à-vis outside-central-city jurisdictions, (d) the kinds of jurisdictional complexity, and (e) the varieties of regional bodies and processes.
7 Reduced federal aid. Direct federal aid to localities—many of them urban—accounted for 29 percent of all federal grant outlays in FY 1978, an all-time high, but by FY 1991 it was down to 13 percent of the total without much of a concomitant reduction in federal regulations.
8 Reduced rate of growth in state aid. Because non-educational state aid was reduced and other changes were made in state mandates and conditions, metro aid, even when it included federal "pass-through aid," increased by only 105 percent between 1977 and 1987 (compared with a 455 percent jump between 1964 and 1977).
9 Central-city urban America possesses a smaller proportion of the nation's population now than In decades. Its combustible mix of poverty, poor schools, minority alienation, drugs, violence, desperation, babies with single parents, and indigenous examples of some breakthroughs—with or without external help—all suggest a metropolitan challenge that nearly three decades of social experimentation and market-oriented cures have not overcome.
10 Academic cacophony. For officials seeking guidance from the academic experts, theoretical harmony is more elusive than ever; more theories are in vogue as to how metro areas should be run—from public choice (market-oriented) and the more governmental providers the better, to a mixed-servicing approach combining public and private provision of services, to two- and one-tier regional governmental reorganizations. The many faces of reform have produced little real reform at any time.

From: David B. Walker, *The Rebirth of Federalism* (Chatham, N.J.: Chatham House, 1995), pp. 270–272.

two or more local jurisdictions; and joint power agreements in which two or more jurisdictions agree to plan, finance, and deliver a service. About two-thirds of the states permit **extraterritorial powers** in which cities can exercise some regulatory power outside their boundaries in unincorporated areas. This might include zoning and subdivision regulation.

The following plans are included in Walker's categories of "middling" approaches and "hardest" approaches.

Annexation

Throughout the nineteenth century, most growth in metropolitan areas occurred through **annexation.** Because annexation was so common, there was little of the suburban fringe fragmentation that marks present-day metropolitan areas. For example, Philadelphia used annexation to expand from 2 square miles to 136 square miles in 1854, and the city's boundaries have not expanded since then.[14] In 1898 New York City expanded its territory sixfold by adding Brooklyn. By the early 1900s opposition to annexation developed, and large cities in the East and Midwest became surrounded by incorporated suburban communities. Suburban residents wanted to be isolated from large immigrant populations in central cities, and many state legislatures changed annexation laws to require approval by voters in the area to be annexed and by voters in the city.

Annexation has continued to be a useful tool of big-city growth in many Southern and Southwestern states. In part this is because in some states—Arizona, Missouri, North Carolina, Oklahoma, Texas, Tennessee, and Virginia—land may be annexed by action of the city alone or by judicial procedures. Texas permits each city to annex up to 10 percent of its territory without any voter approval. In Oklahoma, Oklahoma City has annexed more than 500 square miles of territory since 1959, and Tulsa added 116.8 square miles in a single annexation in 1966. The largest city in area outside Alaska, where three city-county consolidated areas have over 1,000 square miles, is Jacksonville, Florida. City-county consolidation in 1967 gives Jacksonville 774 square miles. Since 1950, Houston has annexed land to grow from 160 to 540 square miles, and Phoenix grew from 17.1 square miles in 1950 to 420 square miles in 1990. When city-county consolidations are *not* considered, Oklahoma City, with 608 square miles, is the largest city in land area. Houston is second and Los Angeles (469 square miles) is third. In contrast, most older Eastern cities are quite small: Boston has 47 square miles, Pittsburgh 55 square miles. Some Southern and Southwestern states also give cities the power to keep adjacent land unincorporated and available for annexation.

About two-thirds of all cities with populations over 2,500 reported boundary changes in the 1980s.[15] Annexations were down from the past several decades. In part, this is because the suburban fringe has largely surrounded such cities as Seattle, Atlanta, Denver, and Milwaukee, which all had large annexations in the 1950s and 1960s. In Texas, black and Hispanic groups have opposed annexation, arguing that it dilutes their political strength in cities.

Large annexations in the 1980s included San Antonio, which added 73,000 people, Portland, Oregon, which added 52,900 people, and Durham, North Carolina, which annexed 26,000 people, or an amount equal to one-fourth its 1980 population. Denver added 43 square miles, yet lost population in the decade because most of the land annexed was for the construction of a new airport. Cities in Texas, North Carolina, and California accounted for over one-third the total number of people annexed in the 1980s, and they continued to lead the nation in annexation in the early 1990s. Cities in North Carolina were the most active. All seventy cities with more than 5,000 residents added land, and all but two increased population. Cities in nine states—Delaware, Hawaii, Maine, Massachusetts, New Hampshire, New Jersey, Pennsylvania, Rhode Island, and Vermont—either did not annex any territory or annexed less than 1 square mile in the 1980s. The *Municipal Yearbook 1993* reports there were only two boundary changes in all the New England states in the 1980s, compared to 20,550 changes in the South Atlantic states.

Some new suburban cities are incorporated with very large populations. West Valley City, Utah, with 72,000 people, was the largest new city in the 1980s. Other large incorporations were Santa Clarita, California (66,730), and Mission Viejo, California (50,000). Thirty-five new places were incorporated in North Carolina in the 1980s, and thirty-four in California. In a few cases cities detach property from their boundaries. For example, Oklahoma City detached 30 square miles during the 1980s and is still **overbounded**—that is, large amounts of virtually uninhabited land remain within the corporation.

Annexation is viewed as a means by which metropolitan areas can eliminate some conflicts of authority, avoid duplication of services, and promote more orderly growth. As noted, cities annex land undergoing development in order to control that development or protect the environment. Opposition comes from suburbanites who fear higher taxes and wish to remain independent of the central city. In some cases, cities may simply add to their problems by annexing areas that lack a strong tax base and are in need of costly services such as roads, water, and sewers. Often these fringe areas have not imposed any zoning laws, and thus they present special problems of development to city administrators.

Many large cities—such as Boston, Chicago, Detroit, Minneapolis, and Pittsburgh—have become encircled by incorporated areas and have been unable to expand their boundaries. For them, annexation presents no solution to their metropolitan problems. In the Los Angeles area, for example, Beverly Hills continues to resist the annexation efforts of Los Angeles, which completely encircles that affluent suburb (see Figure 11-2). Los Angeles annexed land from 1910 to 1919 to expand its territory fourfold. Pittsburgh is surrounded by nearly 200 municipalities, and there are nearly 100 municipalities in St. Louis County. Although some central cities are able to coerce annexation by withholding services such as water to independent suburbs, cities in most states cannot force annexation against the wishes of suburban residents. In addition, many of the largest metropolitan areas, including New York City, Philadelphia, Chicago, and St. Louis, extend into two or more states, and of course no central city can annex land outside its state's boundaries. There are many metropolitan areas that cross state lines and five (Detroit, San Diego, El Paso, Brownsville, and Laredo) whose boundaries adjoin urban areas outside the United States.

Thomas R. Dye found that annexation efforts have been most successful when the central city has a substantial proportion of middle-class residents.[16] Where there is less

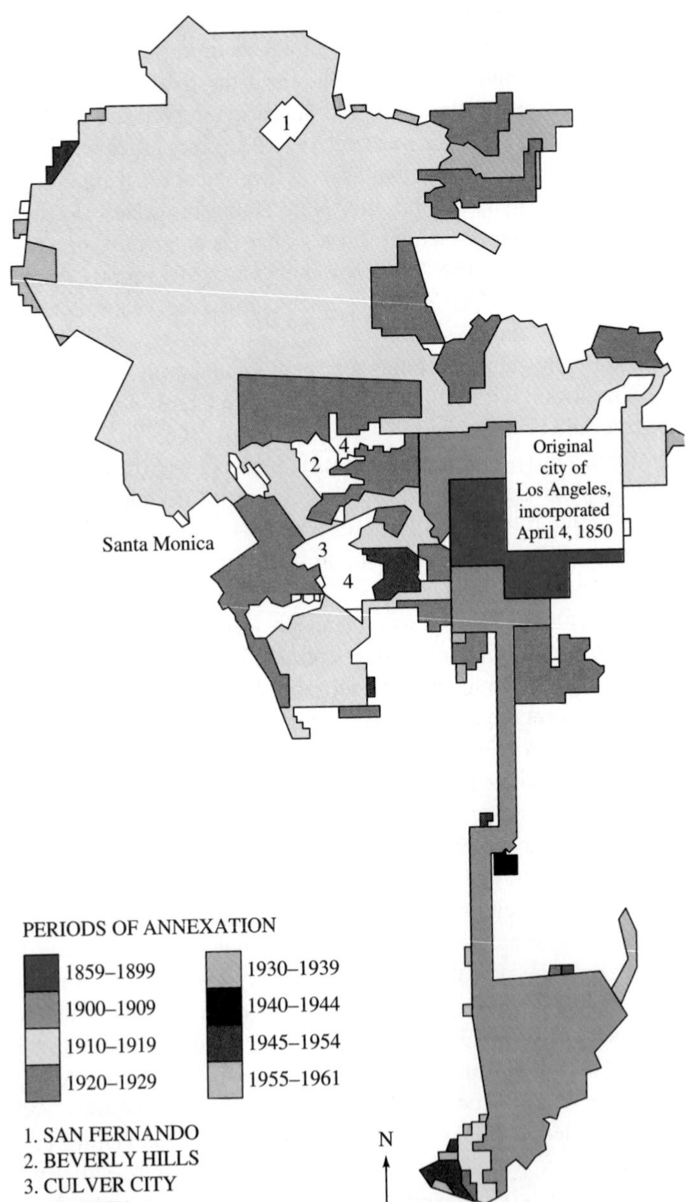

FIGURE 11-2 Annexations by the city of Los Angeles, 1859–1963. [Winston W. Crouch and Beatrice Dinerman, *Southern Metropolis* (Berkeley and Los Angeles: University of California Press, 1963), p. 161. Copyright 1963 by the Regents of the University of California. Reprinted by permission of the University of California Press.]

"social-class distance" between city and suburban residents, suburbanites have less fear of unification. Dye's data suggest that cities with managers are more likely to be successful in annexation than are cities with mayor-council systems of government. Managers tend to put suburbanites at ease, indicating to them that the influence of partisan politics has been lessened in the city. Size and age have only a limited effect on annexation, with success being slightly greater in smaller urbanized areas and in newer areas. Curiously, Dye found that the ease or difficulty of legal procedures was not a clear indication of the degree of success in annexation.

Special Districts

A politically inoffensive way of providing services on a metropolitan-wide or intermunicipal level is to create a special district government to provide a single service. **Special districts** are appealing because they are superimposed on the existing structure of government and leave municipal boundaries untouched. As a result, suburbs receive the services they need without losing their independence. Special districts also have the advantage of bypassing taxation or debt limitations imposed on local units by state law. About half of all existing special districts have been created for fire protection, soil conservation, water, and drainage. Others provide sewer, recreation, housing, and mosquito-control services. Since 1942, the number of special districts has grown from 8,000 to about 30,000 (although school districts may be classified as special districts, they are considered separately by the Bureau of the Census). Recently there has been a significant increase in the number of special districts on the fringes of metropolitan areas. Often these special districts provide a variety of services to suburban residents and become a kind of junior city.[17] Later the area may be annexed by the central city.

Special districts are established under state law and usually require voter approval. In most states, they are governed by a small board, which has taxing and bonding authority. Board members are most often chosen indirectly, rather than being elected directly by popular vote.

In spite of their wide appeal, special districts have many problems. Governing boards have low voter visibility, and in most cases there is little citizen access to their decision making. One result is that contractors and others doing business with special districts (lawyers, bankers, real estate agents) often operate behind the scenes to their own economic advantage. Special districts are frequently established to meet short-range goals. Once created, they lessen the likelihood that long-range planning will be accomplished to meet problems at their most fundamental levels. Because special districts perform only a single function, coordination of government services is made more difficult and district administrators often view public policy from the narrow perspective of what benefits them without considering the overall needs of their community. Special districts usually encompass only a few municipalities within a metropolitan area, so they cannot be viewed as a suitable substitute for metropolitan government.

Kirk H. Porter refers to "disguised" special districts for hospitals or libraries that are coterminous with existing city or county boundaries.[18] Often the main purpose for creating these districts, says Porter, was to get the administration of certain government functions out of the hands of "regular" city officials. The growth of these kinds of special districts has the effect of badly decentralizing government administration. Because there are so many special districts in metropolitan areas, each with the power to impose taxes, some reformers want to eliminate all of them in one grand gesture and set up consolidated city-county governments with full control over the area. Porter recommends a more moderate approach of keeping special districts that extend into two or more jurisdictions (or turning those functions over to the state) and then increasing the authority of cities and counties to administer services within their jurisdictions.

In addition to local special districts, there also are regional districts that are area-wide organizations, usually set up by state law. These include the Chicago Metropolitan Sanitary District, the Bay Area Rapid Transit District (San Francisco), and the Port Authority of New York and New Jersey. These large units require special action by state legislatures, and because of their size they can become very expensive and quite independent of municipal and county governments.

Transfer of Function

In several places, the county has taken over a variety of public services by entering into contractual arrangements with local governments, a process known as **transfer of function.** For example, Erie County in New York (Buffalo area) provides health, hospital, library, and welfare services to communities throughout the county. Nassau County (suburban Long Island, New York) pursues a program of providing services, including police protection, to towns and villages that have a strong tradition of home rule. Los Angeles County also provides a variety of services to the hundreds of communities in an area that includes over 10 million residents. Large cities also may provide services to neighboring communities. For example, more than a dozen suburbs contract with Chicago for their water supply. The permanent transfer of functions, usually to counties but occasionally to special districts, has limited potential because fewer than half the states permit transfers and often voter approval is required.

Councils of Government (COGs)

Nearly 600 **councils of government** (COGs) have come into being since the first one was created in Detroit in 1954. COGs are voluntary regional associations of local governments in a metropolitan area that are concerned about a broad range of problems, such as water supply, transportation, sewers, and airports. Each local government is represented in the COG by its own elected officials. Members of COGs meet to discuss problems, exchange information, and make policy proposals. COGs usually conceive comprehensive plans for metropolitan development.

In 1967, the Twin Cities Metropolitan Council was created to act as a planning, coordinating, and review agency for Minneapolis and St. Paul. Although the council is not a metropolitan government, it does oversee sewers, highways, transit, parks, and airports in a seven-county area that includes 320 separate but overlapping government units, of which 133 are incorporated. The council supervises metropolitan public policymaking through its control of the capital budgets of the operating agencies that provide metropolitan services. Because of its broad authority and taxing power, the Twin Cities Metropolitan Council differs from most councils of government. Although it does not operate public services, it has the power to overrule municipalities, counties, and special districts in its area. John J. Harrigan, a Twin Cities resident, notes that the Metropolitan Council has developed incrementally. As the state legislature has increased the Council's powers, those powers have been tested and then brought back to the legislature for fine-tuning.[19] Because the Metropolitan Council has been bypassed in some of the metropolitan area's biggest projects, including a domed stadium in Minneapolis, Harrigan and William C. Johnson described the Twin Cities model on its twentieth birthday as "looking more and more like a stodgy, mature bureaucratic agency than the dynamic policymaking body it had been for its first decade of existence."[20]

The most ambitious regional authority is the Metropolitan Service District (Metro) for Portland, Oregon, which runs the zoo, the convention center, and performing arts center, and directs regional land use and transportation for twenty-four cities and three counties. Metro originated from a federal planning grant in the mid-1970s. A sixty-five-member citizens' committee studied proposals for regional government and recommended the plan to the Oregon legislature with the provision that it be submitted to area voters. As in the Twin Cities, the Portland COG had existed for several years before the new government was approved by Portland area voters and the Oregon legislature in the late 1970s. Metro has a paid, elected executive officer and twelve elected council members who are paid $23,000 a year: Before 1993 they were paid only a per diem allowance. Under a new charter approved in 1993 Metro has increased planning powers and can impose taxes without voter approval. Regional government created by popular vote succeeded in Portland but failed in Tampa, Denver, and Rochester, which had similar federal grants. Its original approval by Portland voters was due in large part to Oregon's strong tradition of citizen participation. Still, Metro remains largely unknown to most residents in greater Portland. Few know who their Metro councilor is. When they passed the charter reform in 1993, many voters believed they were limiting the regional government's power when, in fact, they greatly increased its taxing authority.[21]

Councils of government have been formed in all metropolitan areas to serve as a focal point to help bring local officials together, particularly for the purpose of coordinating federal grants. The federal government's Model Cities Act of 1966 required cities and counties to clear grant applications with COGs or regional planning agencies. As a result, COGs grew from 35 in 1965 to 352 by 1972 and to 660 in 1980. COGs are not governments because they can only make recommendations and hope for voluntary compliance by member governments. Their weaknesses include a tendency to concentrate on less controversial physical problems, such as sewers and water supply, and to avoid more controversial socioeconomic problems, such as racism and poverty. Also their authority is very limited, since they can seldom compel participation or compliance with decisions. Since COGs are voluntary organizations, members can withdraw if they wish. Because COG officials are also employed by local governments in the area, there often is conflict among them based on their municipal alliance.

In some instances COG membership has been roughly proportional to the population of constituent governments, but this puts smaller suburban communities at a disadvantage.

Because of changes in federal government policy and cuts in federal planning grants in the 1980s, over 100 COGs disbanded. The others have shown more staying power than many predicted. They continue to get federal assistance, and they have gotten more state aid, plus funding from private foundations.

City-County Consolidation

The most serious attempts at establishing metropolitan government in the United States have come in the form of consolidating city and county governments. Although proposals have been introduced in many cities, **city-county consolidation** has been successful in only a few large metropolitan areas—Nashville, Jacksonville, Lexington, and Indianapolis. Voters in Oakland, St. Louis, Portland, Pittsburgh, Memphis, Albuquerque, and Tampa have rejected city-county consolidation referenda. Compared with the other methods of integration, consolidation minimizes more completely the duplication of services and makes possible metropolitan-wide planning and administration. In each instance where such a proposal has been adopted, however, some public services continue to be administered by local units of government whose identities have remained intact. Because many metropolitan areas extend beyond a single county, city-county consolidation offers few possibilities to the nation's largest cities.

In the nineteenth and early twentieth centuries, state legislatures mandated city-county consolidation in New Orleans (1805), Boston, Philadelphia, San Francisco, New York, Denver, and Honolulu (1907). While city-county consolidation was common in the nineteenth century, no consolidations occurred from 1908 through World War II. By the late 1980s the merger of one or more municipalities with a county had occurred in twenty-one communities where the population was more than 10,000. There were three city-county consolidations in Alaska and Louisiana, two in Massachusetts and Montana, and one each in ten other states.[22] Only one consolidation was achieved in the 1980s. In 1991 the city of Athens, Georgia, consolidated with Clark County and another Georgia city-county consolidation was under legal review.[23]

All cases where consolidation has been achieved by a voter referendum have been in the South and West. Five were approved in the 1970s—four in the West. Except in Miami, no referendum has been successful in a city with a population greater than 250,000. In Kentucky in 1982, voters in Louisville and in Jefferson County rejected a city-county consolidation by a margin of only 1,400 out of a total of 175,000 votes cast. Over forty cities operate independently of any county and perform both city and county functions. They include all forty-one cities in Virginia, plus Baltimore, St. Louis, and Carson City, Nevada.

In most cases, proponents of consolidation have been successful only after long battles in which ultimate victory was achieved with the help of unusual political circumstances. Prior political corruption helped gain approval of reform in Jacksonville, Florida, after there were grand jury charges of graft and corruption and the city-county schools lost their accreditation. In metropolitan Nashville, suburban voters feared an aggressive annexation policy waged by the mayor of Nashville.

In 1969, Indianapolis became the first Northern city to become part of a city-county consolidation. It is significant that approval came by state legislative action without a popular vote by the residents of Marion County. UNIGOV (as the consolidation is named) operates under a single mayor and a twenty-nine-member council. To a large extent, its creation was made possible because of Republican control of the appropriate state legislative committees and the political leadership of Richard Lugar, the Republican mayor of Indianapolis and currently Indiana's senior U.S. senator. Approval of UNIGOV also was aided by the preservation of most suburban and county offices as well as special service and taxing districts within the county. Three small municipalities and sixteen townships in Marion County chose not to be included in the consolidated government. As in Nashville and Jacksonville, a large council, elected in a combination of at-large and single districts, provides representation for a wide range of groups within Marion County. Republicans have controlled UNIGOV, winning all mayoral elections and often electing at least twenty members of the council.

Many existing governments have remained separate under UNIGOV. School districts continued to maintain their boundaries, and the county, suburban cities, and special districts continue to elect officials and operate as legal entities. Thus the degree of unification is less than that under most other city-county consolidations.

Two-Tier Government

Two-tier government is a type of consolidation that meets the desire of local governments to maintain their identity within a metropolitan area. A federal relationship is established between cities and a metropolitan government similar to the relationship between the states and the national government. In this arrangement, areawide functions are assigned to the metropolitan government and local functions remain with existing municipalities. The existing governments do not merge.

In the United States, Metro Miami-Dade County is the only two-tier system. Elsewhere, such a system operates in Toronto, Winnipeg, Berlin, and London. The Toronto plan was approved in 1954 by action of the province of Ontario, not the local voters. The metropolitan government in Toronto is responsible for areawide services including parks, freeways, schools, and transit. Local municipalities maintain fire, police, and public health services.

In Miami after World War II, residents were confronted with a host of problems stemming from accelerated growth. In 1957 the voters of Dade County approved a two-tier form of government.[24] Approval came by a slim margin with only 26 percent of those eligible registered to vote. The proposal was supported by the Miami business community, the newspapers, and such good-government groups as the League of Women Voters. Opposition came chiefly from various local public officials and from the wealthier suburbs, such as Surfside and Miami Beach. In metropolitan Miami the usual opponents of unification—organized labor, political parties, and minority groups—all lacked effective organization. As in Jacksonville, the electorate consisted of a large percentage of newcomers to the community. Such a situation is unlikely to exist in any of the older cities of the Midwest or Northeast.

Under a federal-type structure, the twenty-six cities in the metropolitan Dade County area have kept control of many local functions, including garbage pickup, street maintenance, and police and fire protection. The metropolitan government controls such countywide services as transit and welfare. The plan included the establishment of a council-manager form of government for the county. Eight commissioners are elected at large but represent geographical districts. A ninth commissioner, elected at large and representing the entire county, is designated mayor. But the power of the mayor is weak because of the authority of the county manager. As the population of the area has grown to over 3 million, the metropolitan government's responsibilities have increased, because local units have asked the county to take over local functions. Evidence that all has not gone smoothly can be seen in the strong division among commissioners and in the attempt by several of the wealthier suburbs to secede from the metropolitan unit.

The Need to Grow

The failure of city-county consolidation plans to be approved in Northern cities is due largely to the fact that consolidation would shift power toward the Republican party. In many metropolitan counties, suburban residents outnumber those in the central city, and they thus have the potential to control government under a consolidation plan. Edward C. Banfield noted some years ago that in addition to consequences for political parties, metropolitan government "would mean the transfer of power over central cities from the largely lower-class Negro and Catholic elements who live there to the largely middle-class white and Protestant elements who live in the suburbs."[25] Most residents of metropolitan areas are reasonably satisfied with the existing structural arrangements, and they do not wish to give up their independent units of government.

Still, many academics and public officials believe that the ability to expand their borders is the key to success for cities. Most large cities that have been able to expand by annexation in the period since World War II have done well. But, as we have noted, many Northeast and Midwest cities have become surrounded by incorporated communities, and many have not expanded their borders in this century. Former mayor of Albuquerque, David Rusk, has calculated a "point of no return" for cities.[26] This point comes when a city's population has declined 20 percent from its peak, when minority population has exceeded 30 percent, and when per capita income in the city has fallen below 70 percent of that of its suburbs. Cities in this category include Chicago, Philadelphia, Detroit, Cleveland, Buffalo, and St. Louis. Rusk says gimmicks like new convention centers will not turn them around. They must get help from their state legislatures to be able to "stretch" their boundaries (see the Scholarly Box).

Rusk points out that almost *all* metropolitan areas have grown since 1950. Surprisingly, the Detroit metropolitan area grew by 35 percent (over 1 million in population) from 1950 to 1990, even as the city lost about 800,000 people. While inelastic cities, such as Detroit and Cleveland, have lost population, "elastic" cities, such as Houston (area in square miles up 237 percent since 1950) and Columbus, Ohio (up 385 percent), have greatly increased their populations (see Tables 11-2 and 11-3). Elastic cities

TABLE 11-2 ELASTIC CITIES EXPAND THEIR CITY LIMITS; INELASTIC CITIES DO NOT

Metro area	City area (square miles) 1950	City area (square miles) 1990	Percentage change 1950–1990
Houston, Tex.	160	540	237%
Detroit, Mich.	139	139	0
Columbus, Ohio	39	191	385
Cleveland, Ohio	75	77	3
Nashville, Tenn.	22	473	2,051
Louisville, Ky.	40	62	56
Indianapolis, Ind.	55	362	555
Milwaukee, Wis.	50	96	92
Albuquerque, N. Mex.	48	132	176
Syracuse, N.Y.	25	25	0
Madison, Wis.	15	58	275
Harrisburg, Pa.	6	8	29
Raleigh, N.C.	11	88	550
Richmond, Va.	37	60	62

Source: David Rusk, *Cities without Suburbs* (Baltimore: The Johns Hopkins University Press, 1993), p. 17.

TABLE 11-3 ELASTIC CENTRAL CITIES HAVE GROWN; INELASTIC HAVE SHRUNK

Metro area	City population 1950	City population 1990	City population Change 1950–90	Percentage change 1950–90
Houston, Tex.	596,163	1,630,553	1,034,390	174%
Detroit, Mich.	1,849,568	1,027,924	−821,644	−44
Columbus, Ohio	375,901	632,910	257,009	68
Cleveland, Ohio	914,808	505,616	−409,192	−45
Nashville, Tenn.	174,307	488,374	314,067	180
Louisville, Ky.	369,129	269,063	−100,066	−27
Indianapolis, Ind.	427,173	731,327	304,154	71
Milwaukee, Wis.	637,392	628,088	−9,304	−1
Albuquerque, N. Mex.	96,815	384,736	287,921	297
Syracuse, N.Y.	220,583	163,860	−56,723	−26
Madison, Wis.	96,056	191,282	95,226	99
Harrisburg, Pa.	89,544	52,376	−37,168	−42
Raleigh, N.C.	65,679	207,951	142,272	217
Richmond, Va.	230,310	203,056	−27,254	−12

Source: Rusk, *Cities without Suburbs*, p. 14.

SCHOLARLY BOX

STRATEGIES TO STRETCH CITIES

As we have noted, the former mayor of Albuquerque, David Rusk, believes that if cities are to increase in population and expand their economies they must be "elastic."* That is, they need to acquire more territory. Moreover, Rusk contends that fragmented municipalities favor racial segregation. The smaller the community, the more likely it is to serve a narrow and exclusive population. Thus his arguments for metropolitan governance are not simply that it would improve the efficiency of public service delivery (in fact, small units may do this better), but that it would reduce racial and economic segregation and help make central cities vital centers of metropolitan areas.

Rusk recommends the following four ways state governments should act to help "stretch" city boundaries.

1 *Metropolitan government.* It should cover at least 60 percent of the area's population, and it must contain the central city.
   - **a** The most direct way is for the state legislature to empower county governments to be the dominant source of delivery of public services. Ultimately, the urban county would absorb the functions of municipalities and abolish them.
   - **b** As with the consolidation of Indianapolis and Marion County in 1970, state legislatures could consolidate cities and counties. To ease political barriers, some municipalities can be excluded from the consolidation and rural residents can be given fewer services and lower taxes. Because metropolitan areas continue to expand on their borders, legislatures should consider creating consolidated multicounty regional governments.

2 *Annexation.* Although municipal annexation is authorized in forty-one states, most attach severe conditions. Rusk believes that state law should permit municipalities to initiate and carry out annexation, while protecting rural property owners from increased taxes without increased services and from unwanted intrusions in their life styles.

3 *Limit new municipalities.* States should make it difficult for new incorporations near existing municipalities. While nearly all states set limits regarding minimum population, area, and tax base for new municipalities, the limits are usually minimal. About one-third of the states set a minimum distance between existing cities and proposed new incorporations. In New Mexico this is 5 miles. If other states followed the New Mexico standard, they could then focus on strengthening county government without a proliferation of towns and cities. Large cities in a state could be given power over smaller cities by having presumptive authority to annex contested land.

4 *Promote public partnerships.* Rusk recommends that state legislatures authorize joint powers or joint service agreements to allow communities in metropolitan areas to band together to solve problems. While about three-fourths of the states authorize communities to join together to provide a service, such as sewerage treatment, few of these partnerships deal with such controversial issues as housing, schools, and tax disparities. Exceptions include metropolitan districts in Portland, Oregon, and in Minneapolis–St. Paul and suburban communities in Connecticut. In the Twin Cities since 1971, 40 percent of the increase in taxes from commercial-industrial property has been put in a common pool for 188 municipalities in 7 counties. The pool is redistributed to reduce disparities between rich (major suburbs that benefit from shopping malls and office towers) and poor communities. Metro government in Portland can carry out functions given to it by the state legislature. In Connecticut, the state legislature requires suburbs to adopt "inclusionary zoning," so that affordable housing is included in new developments. While the Connecticut law will not result in affordable housing in every suburban neighborhood, it should open suburbs to several economic classes and promote racial dispersal. It should be noted that in a time of downsizing government, none of these strategies require states or cities to spend any money.

*David Rusk, *Cities without Suburbs* (Washington, D.C.: The Woodrow Wilson Center Press, 1993), pp. 90–107.

are able to "capture" suburban growth. As a result, most elastic cities are doing well financially, even though they may be in modest-income areas, while many point-of-no-return cities are doing poorly, even though some are in wealthy areas. Elastic cities are much less racially segregated (only 27 percent of Houston's population is black) than inelastic cities (75 percent of Detroit's population is black) because their central cities are not hemmed in by predominantly white suburbs.

PLANNING

Most nineteenth-century cities in the Midwest and West were "new towns." As such, the layout of streets, the location of parks, and the placement of businesses were planned in detail. However, as city populations rapidly expanded, growth was largely unplanned. Thus by the 1880s, many large cities were crowded, dirty, and unhealthy. The same reform movement that brought changes to the structure and operation of city government (see Chapter 9) also reinstituted planning as a way to beautify cities. Their results in cities such as Chicago were very impressive.

Planners created master plans for the overall development of cities to serve as guides to government officials and private business. In recent years, comprehensive planning has gone beyond earlier concern for a set of maps and land-use guidelines. Planners now consider such matters as population projections, transportation, and sociocultural patterns. Although these plans are not legally binding on communities, most cities take them seriously. In most larger cities there is a planning commission, made up of business people and other residents, and a city planner who reports to the mayor or city manager. Oftentimes the layout of suburbs has been designed by real estate developers. After incorporation, suburbs may develop a master plan and set up planning offices that are similar to those in central cities.

Some suburban communities—such as Petaluma, California; Mount Laurel, New Jersey; and Ramapo, New York—have approved limits on their growth. In a few states, including Hawaii and Vermont, statewide land management plans have been developed. California has a system for coastal management in which a state coastal zone commission has developed a statewide plan and developers must secure permission from regional commissions *and* from local governments in order to build in coastal areas. In Minnesota, the state legislature gave the Twin Cities Metropolitan Council power over the land-use plans of local governments. Each of these plans represents the exception, not the rule. In most metropolitan areas planning is fragmented among local governments and **zoning** has been the major tool to promote orderly growth.

Zoning

Zoning ordinances divide a community into districts (residential, industrial, light industrial, commercial, recreational) and prescribe the uses that can be made of the land in each zone. Such ordinances are enforced by a building inspector, and a zoning board is created to make exceptions to rules or amend their provisions. In many cities, zoning ordinances have been enacted too late, after commercial and industrial establishments have already misused the land. Zoning ordinances that prescribe the height of buildings or the amount of land necessary for home construction have the effect of keeping minority groups out of upper-class suburbs. Since New York City adopted the first zoning ordinance in 1916, all major cities except Houston have enacted some form of zoning.

A particularly controversial use of zoning is when it is used to *exclude* lower-income persons from suburban communities. Zoning can exclude economic groups of people by setting minimum lot sizes and by prohibiting apartments of a certain size or, in extreme cases, prohibiting all apartment buildings. Suburbs also may exclude people through subdivision infrastructure costs that are assessed to builders and passed on to home buyers. As noted earlier, fragmented communities favor racial and economic segregation. Smaller communities tend to promote uniformity, not diversity, and they make areawide planning very difficult. As housing costs have soared in the 1980s and 1990s, even middle-income white people find themselves effectively shut out of many suburban communities.

Even in the absence of metropolitan government, state legislatures, as in Connecticut, can enact **inclusionary zoning** to force developers to include affordable housing in a mix of new homes. The New Jersey Supreme Court ruled in 1975 that all zoning regulations in Mount Laurel were invalid because they failed to provide a range of density levels and building types. The court used a "fair share" concept regarding the location of multifamily housing as well as of houses on small lots. Later, the New Jersey legislature established the Council on Affordable Housing to implement the state's inclusionary zoning policy.

However, in 1977 the Supreme Court ruled that communities are not required to alter zoning laws to provide housing for low-income families. The case involved Arlington Heights, a Chicago suburb, and its refusal to rezone a vacant property surrounded by single-family homes to permit construction of a federally subsidized townhouse development. In supporting the Arlington Heights board of trustees, the Court reasoned that predominantly white communities do not have to make special allowances for integration unless there is proof of purposeful racial discrimination. Thus a zoning ordinance was upheld even though it resulted in a racially disproportionate impact. On a more narrow issue, the Court held in 1995 that cities cannot use single-family zoning to exclude group homes for disabled people, including recovering alcoholics and drug addicts.

Metropolitan Areas

Planning has been extended to a metropolitan-wide basis, in part, because of federal requirements if the area is to receive funding for such projects as airports, housing, recreation, and transportation. Before the 1960s there were relatively few metropolitan planning commissions and their activity was limited to population studies and economic analysis.[27] While the number of planning commissions has increased significantly in the past thirty years, all we have to do is look around most metropolitan areas to see that their impact has been limited. Local politicians like to see immediate economic expansion and often are not interested in how the region will look in another twenty years. Planners can set goals, but they must be implemented by individual communities whose government officials control budgeting and zoning.

RURAL AND SMALL-TOWN AMERICA

Moving beyond the city limits of suburbs, we come to rural America. Although the Bureau of the Census defines "rural" as the population outside incorporated or unincorporated places with more than 2,500 people and/or outside urbanized areas, few people living in communities of 5,000 or 15,000 and located outside metropolitan areas think of themselves as urban. There is general agreement that small-scale, low-density settlements are rural,[28] and the study of rural America usually includes "small towns" with as many as 25,000 people.[29] Even following the census definition, the United States is more rural than we commonly perceive it. For example, forty-four of New York's sixty-four counties in 1990 had less than 50,000 population and are officially designated as rural. In the 1990s, seventy-four congressional districts (plus Vermont and South Dakota) have predominantly rural populations.

While urban-rural differences may be declining nationally as a result of such factors as cable television, access to interstate highways, the use of computers, and increased population mobility, many government officials believe that rural-urban differences are the biggest dividing line in their state's politics. For example, in Oregon, which is divided east from west by the Cascade Mountains, major differences of opinion are evident on such issues as taxation, land use, the environment, government regulation, and gay rights.[30] As a case in point, although Measure 9, an antigay rights initiative in 1992, was defeated statewide 43 percent to 57 percent, it carried twenty of the state's thirty-six counties and narrowly lost in three others. It was approved in virtually all the state's rural eastern and southern counties.

As Foster Church points out, rural Oregonians are distrustful of government at a distance, and they are especially fearful of state- or federal-imposed environmental regulations that can affect their livelihood. At least in Oregon, newspaper endorsements and television advertising seldom affect voting behavior in rural areas, where people are close to their government institutions and where they have direct contact with elected officials. Living in homogeneous communities, rurals often appear less tolerant of diversity in life styles.

While we all know that rural and farming are not synonymous, a romanticized view of rural America plotted with family-owned farms continues to influence public policy. Legislatures are led to believe that if they improve farm life, they will improve rural life. In fact, farming constitutes less than 2 percent of the national economic activity and labor force. Farmers make up less than 8 percent of the rural population, and even among farm families the majority of their income comes from nonfarm employment.

In part because of misconceptions about rural America, unprecedented federal spending on "rural areas" in the 1980s did little to improve their long-range prospects. Both federal and state officials need to understand that the basic problem for rural America is not on farms but in the decline of small manufacturing in rural towns. The out-migration from rural areas in the 1980s came primarily from rural towns, not from farms. States need to find ways to help small towns diversify their economies as they deal with the continuing decline of timber, mining, and fishing industries. For example, while rural Oregonian residents may not be happy about it, with timber towns on the way out and tourism on the way in, one government official noted that "there's going to be less barbed wire sold in this town. And there's going to be more espresso sold in this town."

TABLE 11-4 1995 MOST DANGEROUS STATE

Rank	State	Avg.	Rank	State	Avg.
1	Louisiana	10.21	26	Arkansas	25.71
2	Maryland	11.86	27	Washington	26.36
3	Nevada	13.07	28	Massachusetts	26.57
4	Florida	13.93	29	Ohio	26.64
5	Illinois	14.83	30	Hawaii	26.93
6	Texas	15.36	31	Indiana	27.57
7	Arizona	15.86	32	Virginia	28.93
8	California	16.79	33	Utah	29.14
9	New Mexico	16.86	34	Wisconsin	29.21
10	South Carolina	17.29	35	Idaho	30.50
11	New York	19.29	36	Connecticut	30.57
12	Delaware	19.79	37	South Dakota	30.86
13	Michigan	20.07	38	Montana	31.36
14	Alaska	20.50	38	Pennsylvania	31.36
15	Oklahoma	20.86	40	Wyoming	31.43
16	Tennessee	21.14	41	Rhode Island	31.50
17	Missouri	21.21	42	Minnesota	32.43
18	Colorado	22.00	43	Nebraska	33.50
19	North Carolina	22.21	44	Kentucky	34.36
20	Alabama	22.43	45	Iowa	35.79
21	Georgia	22.50	46	North Dakota	36.79
22	New Jersey	23.36	47	New Hampshire	38.50
23	Kansas	23.67	48	West Virginia	39.79
24	Oregon	25.14	49	Vermont	42.21
25	Mississippi	25.57	50	Maine	43.71

Factors considered:

1 Crime Rate in 1993
2 Violent Crime Rate in 1993
3 Murder Rate in 1993
4 Rape Rate in 1993
5 Robbery Rate in 1993
6 Aggravated Assault Rate in 1993
7 Property Crime Rate in 1993
8 Percent Change in Crime Rate: 1989 to 1993
9 Percent Change in Violent Crime Rate: 1989 to 1993
10 State Prisoner Incarceration Rate in 1994
11 Reported Arrests of Youths 17 Years and Younger as a Percent of All Arrests in 1993
12 Reported Arrests of Youths 17 Years and Younger for Violent Crime as a Percent of All Such Arrests in 1993
13 State-Local Government Expenditures for Police Protection as a Percent of All Direct Expenditures in 1992
14 Full-Time Sworn Officers in Law Enforcement Agencies per 10,000 Population in 1992

Source: Kathleen O'Leary Morgan, Scott Morgan, and Neal Quitno, eds., *Crime State Rankings 1995* (Lawrence, Kan.: Morgan Quitno Corp., 1995), p. iv. The editors believe that the fourteen factors considered provide a sound statistical basis for comparing how safe states are. Each state's ranking for the fourteen categories was determined, and then an overall average was computed.

Beginning in the 1930s, federal legislation was formed around selective agricultural goods, not general social policy for rural areas. As a result, narrow-based commodity interest groups flourished and broad-based rural interest groups were not created. While some regional rural development groups have been created, commodity and agribusiness groups continue to dominate the rural power structure.

For their part, rural communities have not had a sense of common purpose, and their commitment to individualism has made it very unlikely that they would support collective political action. In Chapter 5, we discussed the overrepresentation of rural areas in state legislatures in the early 1960s. Ironically, after the reapportionment revolution rural areas now find themselves underrepresented in state legislatures, and their problems are given less attention than their numbers would suggest.[31]

The loss of general revenue sharing in the mid-1980s was especially damaging to many small towns and counties because it represented a significant proportion of their budgets.[32] Even worse, most small towns have been forced to comply with an increasingly large number of federal and state mandates, and the federal Economic Development Administration cut grants to rural areas significantly in the 1980s. Although the Clinton administration funded three rural empowerment zones and thirty-five rural enterprise communities in 1994, both Democrats and Republicans in 1996 voted for substantial cuts in or the elimination of several rural and farm programs.

Earlier we contrasted the roles of council members in cities with their small-town counterparts. Clearly, there are many differences in towns of part-time versus full-time mayors and council members and the scale of government operations as city populations increase. While rural crime rates have increased in recent years, they remain relatively low. For example, predominantly rural Vermont recorded only three murders in 1994. As shown in Table 11-4, northern rural states generally are the least dangerous places in the United States.

Yet rural America shares a surprisingly large number of similarities with the nation's inner-city neighborhoods. In most cases, both have steadily lost population for the last half century. Education, transportation, and health care problems in these "other Americas" are equally severe.[33] Incomes are lower, there are few doctors, more infants die, and high school dropout rates are higher than in populations not residing in rural areas and inner cities. Although cities have had more influence than rural areas over the public policy agenda, neither has developed an effective constituency to press for change. As a result we do not have a comprehensive urban or rural policy nationally or at the state level.

SUMMARY

While urban sprawl has been developing for nearly a century, it is largely a post-World War II phenomenon. The movement of people and businesses away from central cities has been aided by federal government policies, private business decisions to relocate, and the social problems of cities. The results are politically fragmented metropolitan areas and a concentration of racial minorities in central cities. In the chapter reading Neal Peirce examines the decline of "inner-ring" suburbs, which have suffered the same fate as central cities, as new rings of suburbs attract people and business away from old suburbs, as well as from central cities. Although suburbs have become more diverse, their residents are more likely than central city voters to support Republican candidates and conservative issues. This was particularly evident in the 1994 elections.

In response to increased metropolitan fragmentation, a host of consolidation solutions have been tried. They range from those that are relatively easy to implement, such as joint power agreements, to "middling" approaches, such as annexation and councils of government, to the extremely difficult, such as city-county consolidation. Although city-county consolidation has been opposed by both suburban and central city residents, many urbanists contend that cities must be "elastic" if they are to grow in population and to prosper.

Comprehensive metropolitan planning is a rarity. Zoning has been the most significant technique to limit growth and to manage land use by encouraging an economic mixture of housing units.

Beyond suburbs, 20 percent of Americans live in small towns and rural areas. While rural Americans are distrustful of distant state government and are opposed to intervention in their affairs by city people, they share a surprisingly large number of social and economic problems with the residents of central cities.

KEY TERMS

Annexation The process by which cities incorporate adjacent land into their municipal boundaries.

City-county consolidation The process by which a city and the county in which it is located merge into one government unit. UNIGOV, the consolidation of Indianapolis and Marion County, is an example of such a plan. The goal is to improve the coordination of government functions within a metropolitan area.

Consolidation In metropolitan areas, the uniting of separate, independent government units into a larger, central government.

Councils of government Voluntary associations of governments in metropolitan areas that oversee the delivery of certain services and develop regional planning strategies.

Extraterritorial powers The ability of a city to regulate land use in unincorporated territory adjacent to its boundaries.

Fragmentation The situation existing in most metropolitan areas, in which there are a large number of small, separate government units.

Inclusionary zoning Ordinances that require communities to include a mix of middle- and low-income housing in new developments. This contrasts with *exclusionary zoning* provisions that increase the cost of housing and keep lower-income people out.

Metropolitan areas Large cities and their surrounding suburbs, which are integrated socially and economically. As defined by the Bureau of the Census, a "standard metropolitan statistical area" includes each county, or group of contiguous counties, containing a city with a population of at least 50,000.

Overbounded A condition that occurs when cities have large tracts of virtually uninhabited land within their corporate limits.

Public choice theory Contends that citizens can get the kind of public services they want at the price they want to pay by choosing to live in particular communities.

Redlining When lending institutions literally draw a red line around neighborhoods they consider bad risks and refuse to make loans for home purchases or improvements there. This policy is prohibited by law.

Satellite cities Independent suburbs located on the fringes of metropolitan areas.

Special districts Units of local government created to perform a single service—such as water supply, fire protection, or soil conservation—on a regional basis.

Transfer of function When a city or county performs certain functions, such as supplying water, to other units of local government in its region.

Two-tier government Metropolitan government in Miami where Dade County has assumed certain areawide functions and municipalities continue to provide various local services.

Urban sprawl Uncoordinated residential and commercial growth spreading outward from cities.

Zoning The division of a city or other government unit into districts to regulate the use of land according to residential, industrial, recreational, or commercial classification.

REFERENCES

1 For a look at the classic sociological studies of the 1950s, see David Riesman, *The Lonely Crowd* (Garden City, N.Y.: Doubleday, 1956); and William H. Whyte, *The Organization Man* (Garden City, N.Y.: Doubleday, 1959).

2 John J. Harrigan, *Political Change in the Metropolis,* 5th ed. (New York: Harper Collins, 1993), p. 288.

3 Peter Marks, "Home Rule's Exclusive, Costly Kingdoms," *New York Times,* January 29, 1994, p. A16.

4 Bernard H. Ross and Myron A. Levine, *Urban Politics: Power in Metropolitan America,* 5th ed. (Itasca, Ill.: Peacock, 1996), pp. 311–313.

5 See *How Superstore Sprawl Can Harm Communities* (Washington, D.C.: National Trust for Historic Preservation, 1994); and James Howard Kunstler, *The Geography of Nowhere: The Rise and Decline of America's Man-Made Landscape* (New York: Simon and Schuster, 1993).

6 Edward B. Fiske, "U.S. Says Most of Growth in 80's Was in Major Metropolitan Areas," *The New York Times,* February 21, 1991, p. A-12. Also see Joel Garreau, *Edge City: Life on the New Frontier* (Garden City, N.Y.: Doubleday, 1991).

7 This is classically presented in Robert C. Wood, *Suburbia: Its People and Their Politics* (Boston: Houghton Mifflin, 1958), p. 9.

8 Ira Sharkansky, *The Maligned States* (New York: McGraw-Hill, 1972), p. 137.

9 "Spiffing Up the Urban Heritage," *Time,* November 23, 1987, p. 75.

10 Karen DeWitt, "It's Official: Texans Outnumber New Yorkers," *New York Times,* December 28, 1994, p. A6.

11 Karen DeWitt, "Have Suburbs, Especially in the South, Become the Source of American Political Power?" *New York Times,* December 19, 1994, p. A13.

12 See Vincent Ostrom, Charles M. Tiebout, and Robert Warren, "Organizing Government in Metropolitan Areas," *American Political Science Review* (December 1961), p. 838.

13 David B. Walker, "Snow White and the 17 Dwarfs: From Metropolitan Cooperation to Governance," *National Civic Review* (January–February 1987), pp. 14–27. Also see Walker, *The Rebirth of Federalism* (Chatham, N.J.: Chatham House, 1995), pp. 272–281.

14 Ross and Levine, *Urban Politics,* p. 365.

15 Joel Miller, "Annexations and Boundary Changes in the 1980s and 1990–1991," *The Municipal Yearbook 1993* (Washington, D.C.: International City Management Association, 1993), p. 100.

16 Thomas R. Dye, "Urban Political Integration: Conditions Associated with Annexation in American Cities," *Midwest Journal of Political Science,* November 1964, pp. 430–446.

17 Ross and Levine, *Urban Politics,* p. 363.

18 Kirk H. Porter, "A Plague of Special Districts," *National Civic Review* (Spring–Summer 1994), p. 108.

19 John J. Harrigan, *Political Change,* p. 388.

20 William C. Johnson and John J. Harrigan, "Political Stress and Metropolitan Governance: The Twin Cities Experience," *State and Local Government Review* (Fall 1987), pp. 108–113.

21 Steve Dunn, "Rena Flies Off before the Fireworks Begin," *The Oregonian,* July 25, 1993; and Gordon Oliver, "Metro: Student Becomes Mentor," *The Oregonian,* May 18, 1993.

22 Victor S. DeSantis, "County Government: A Century of Change," in *The Municipal Yearbook 1989* (Washington, D.C.: International City Management Association, 1989), p. 57.

23 Joel Miller, "Annexations and Boundary Changes," p. 108.

24 See Edward Sofen, *The Miami Metropolitan Experiment,* 2d ed. (Garden City, N.Y.: Doubleday, 1966).

25 Edward C. Banfield, "The Politics of Metropolitan Area Reorganization," *Midwest Journal of Political Science,* May 1957, p. 77.

26 David Rusk, *Cities without Suburbs* (Baltimore: The Johns Hopkins University Press, 1993), pp. 75–78.

27 John J. Harrigan, *Political Change,* p. 377.

28 David W. Sears and J. Norman Reid, "Rural Strategies and Rural Development," *Policy Studies Journal* (1992), p. 215.

29 Alvin D. Sokolow, "Small Local Governments as Community Builders," *National Civic Review* (1989), pp. 362–370.

30 Foster Church, "Country Consequences," *The Oregonian,* July 11, 1993, p. 1.

31 Jim Seroka, "Rural Administrative Capacity and Intergovernmental Capacity: Making a Case," *National Civic Review* (1991), p. 177.

32 Alvin D. Sokolow, "Small Local Governments," p. 364.

33 See Oska Gray Davidson, *Broken Heartland: The Rise of America's Rural Ghetto* (New York: Free Press, 1990).

12

FINANCING STATE AND LOCAL GOVERNMENT

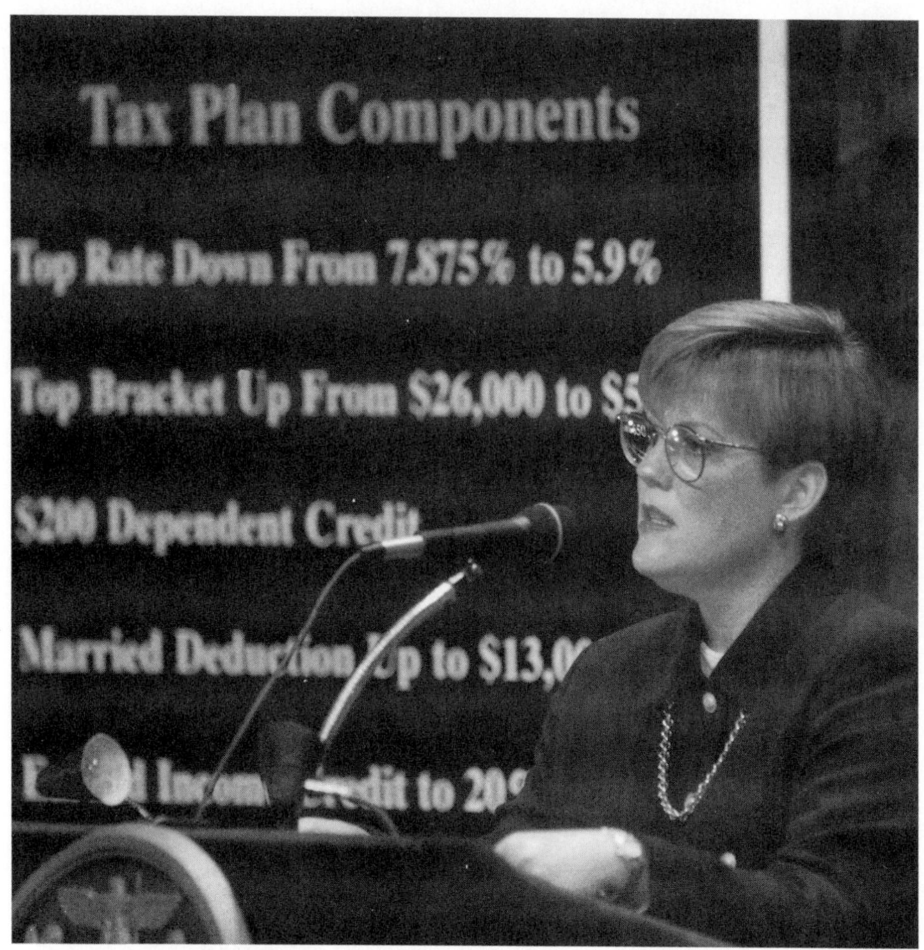

Wojanowicz/The Image Works

How much money do state and local governments raise and spend? This simple question is not as easily answered as it might seem. The most accurate picture of spending can be found in a category called **direct general expenditures,** a rather complicated name that requires some explanation. The word *general* means that almost all expenditures are covered; a few are excluded such as spending on unemployment and worker's compensation, which are financed by government-mandated employer and employee contributions. *Direct* refers to expenditures that are actual payments, that is, money paid to government employees, to contractors that governments buy things from, or to beneficiaries of government programs such as Aid to Families with Dependent Children (AFDC is discussed in Chapter 14). **Intergovernmental expenditures,** are transfer payments from one level of government to another, and are particularly difficult to sort out in arriving at how much money different levels of government spend. It is important to note that these payments are not counted as spending by the

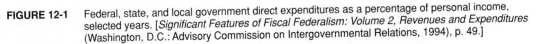

FIGURE 12-1 Federal, state, and local government direct expenditures as a percentage of personal income, selected years. [*Significant Features of Fiscal Federalism: Volume 2, Revenues and Expenditures* (Washington, D.C.: Advisory Commission on Intergovernmental Relations, 1994), p. 49.]

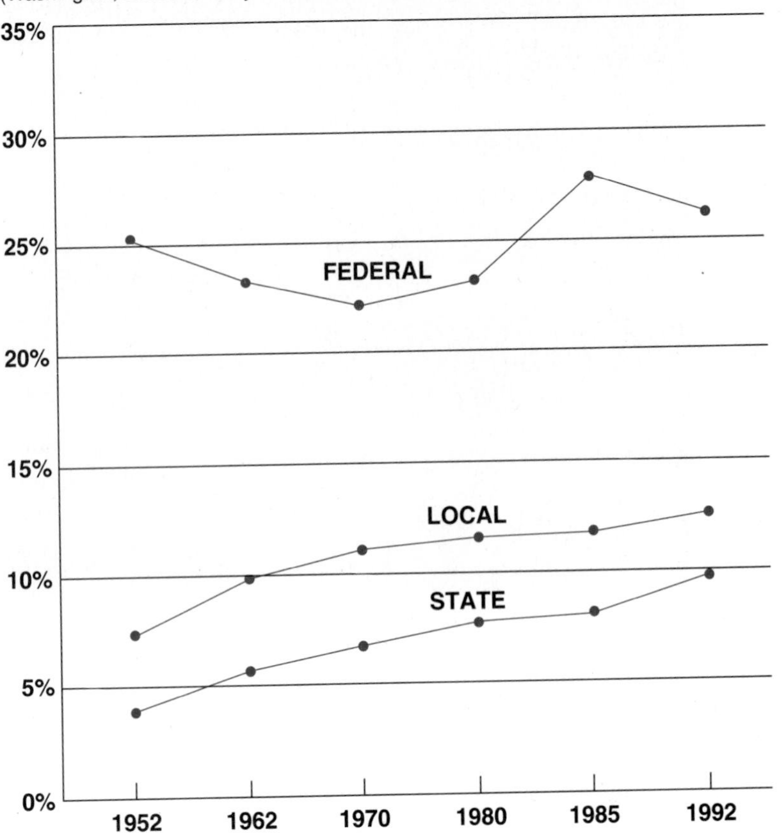

government that transfers the funds. These transfer payments become a source of revenue for the government that receives the money, and an expenditure for the level of government that uses it to make actual payments. Intergovernmental expenditures are an important part of state government spending because states not only receive federal grants and frequently pass the money on to local governments but also have their own programs that transfer funds to local governments.

Direct general expenditures in 1992 for state and local governments totaled $972.2 billion.[1] This total was almost 73 percent of federal direct expenditures ($1.34 trillion) for 1992! Dollars per capita (for each person) are a little easier to comprehend; state government expenditures in 1992 were $1,608 per capita and for local governments $2,207.[2] The comparable figure for the federal government was $5,250.

The real growth of direct expenditures can be obtained by examining Figure 12-1. Federal government expenditures, as a percentage of personal income, are large but have changed little over the years, staying between 22 and 28 percent. Local government expenditures have increased substantially, from 7.3 percent of personal income in 1952 to 12.6 percent in 1992. But the greatest growth is by state governments where expenditures have more than doubled, from 3.9 percent in 1952 to 9.7 percent in 1992!

With the big picture of expenditures as background, the rest of this chapter will focus on limitations on taxing authority, what state and local governments actually spend their money on, a description of the kinds of tax and nontax sources of revenue, how taxes can be evaluated, the property tax revolt, and the problem of matching revenues to expenditures.

LIMITATIONS ON RAISING REVENUE

In their attempts to raise revenue, state and local governments are affected by a number of factors, most fundamentally, by the level of wealth and personal income within their boundaries. Unless poor states and communities increase tax rates to unbearable levels, they simply cannot raise sufficient revenue to provide services comparable to those in more affluent areas (see the Scholarly Box entitled State Wealth and State Taxes).

State and local governments also encounter constitutional limits on taxation. The U.S. Constitution prohibits interference with federal operations by states through taxation, and it protects interstate commerce from direct taxation or undue interference by the states. It also prohibits states from taxing exports and imports without consent of Congress. Perhaps of more importance are state constitutions, which seriously restrict taxing authority by exempting certain kinds of property and by defining the kinds of taxes that can be used.

The most serious limitations are placed on local governments, which have only those powers of taxation that state constitutions have granted them. State constitutions prescribe what taxes local governments may impose, they often establish the amount of taxation, they specify procedures of tax administration, and they outline the purposes for which tax revenues may be used. The only exceptions are in a few states where constitutions contain home-rule clauses (see Chapter 9) giving cities a general grant of power to levy taxes.

SCHOLARLY BOX

STATE WEALTH AND STATE TAXES

State and local governments in Connecticut collected $3,061 per capita in taxes in 1992, while in West Virginia only $1,660 per capita was collected. Connecticut was 41 percent above the national average ($2,178), and West Virginia was 24 percent below. Why do these states differ in the amount of taxes collected?

The first explanation that comes to mind is that Connecticut simply taxes its citizens much more heavily than West Virginia. However, this is not the case. The Advisory Commission on Intergovernmental Relations estimates each state's tax effort, that is, how heavily governments in a state tax relative to other states. The tax efforts of Connecticut and West Virginia are very similar; in fact, both are close to the national average.

Another possible explanation is that Connecticut is simply a wealthier state than West Virginia. In fact, Connecticut, with a personal income per capita of $28,100 (1993), is one of the wealthiest states in the nation. And at the other end is West Virginia, with a personal income per capita of $16,200. This difference affects tax collections because a 5 percent sales tax rate on purchases made by consumers in Connecticut, for example, is going to bring in more revenue because people in Connecticut have more money to buy not only more consumer goods but also more expensive consumer goods. Of course, Connecticut's cost of living is higher, so it probably costs more to deliver public services in Connecticut (higher salaries for government employees and higher construction costs, for example), but even with that there is enough revenue to deliver more and better quality services than in West Virginia. Generally, urbanized and industrial states have greater private wealth, which when taxed at even a moderate rate can produce substantial revenue.

Again, the Advisory Commission on Intergovernmental Relations, with its index of tax capacity, provides some useful information on the relationship between a state's wealth and its ability to generate revenues through taxes. Simply put, **tax capacity** is a measure of a state's ability to raise revenue given its tax base, which is composed of things such as the dollar value of retail sales. Of course, a strong economy also creates a good tax base. The index of tax capacity is arrived at through calculations that assume the same state and local tax system, called a representative tax system, is used in every state.

Table 12-1 contains tax capacity indexes for all fifty states. An index of 100 is the national average. A state with an index of 120 has a revenue-raising ability 20 percent above the national average; this means that given its tax base it can raise 20 percent more in taxes than the average for all states when using the representative tax system. An index of 80 means a state's revenue-raising ability is 20 percent below average.[3]

Generally, wealthier states, as measured by personal income, have a tax capacity index over 100. This is not always the case because some states, Nevada, for example, have an extensive gambling and tourist industry that can be taxed.

Of course, federal spending through grants-in-aid is usually designed to give more money (per capita) to poor states, which may help to reduce some public service inequalities caused by differences in state wealth. Alice Rivlin suggests that a revenue-side approach might be better. This would require states to have a joint tax with the proceeds shared among the states according to a formula that enlarges the revenues of states with less wealth. A joint sales tax at the same rate on a common set of goods and services is one example.[4] A revenue-side approach would be a more direct way to help less affluent states.

During the 1970s and 1980s, state governments were particularly active in imposing **TELs** (tax and expenditure limitations) that place limits on revenue or expenditure increases of local governments. Budgets of municipalities in New Jersey, for example, are limited by the state to a 5 percent increase over the previous year's total appropriations or the percentage change in inflation, whichever is less.[5]

The use of particular kinds of taxes at different levels of government has been strongly influenced by a pattern in which the national government relies heavily on the income tax, state governments make the broadest use of the sales tax, and local

TABLE 12-1 1991 TAX CAPACITY INDEXES

(100 = U.S. Average)

New England		Southeast	
Connecticut	130	Alabama	81
Maine	95	Arkansas	78
Massachusetts	117	Florida	103
New Hampshire	103	Georgia	91
Rhode Island	88	Kentucky	83
Vermont	94	Louisiana	89
Mideast		Mississippi	68
Delaware	125	North Carolina	93
District of Columbia	123	South Carolina	83
Maryland	106	Tennessee	82
New Jersey	119	Virginia	103
New York	103	West Virginia	77
Pennsylvania	96	Southwest	
Great Lakes		Arizona	94
Illinois	102	New Mexico	87
Indiana	90	Oklahoma	87
Michigan	94	Texas	97
Ohio	93	Rocky Mountain	
Wisconsin	90	Colorado	109
Plains		Idaho	82
Iowa	93	Montana	91
Kansas	93	Utah	82
Minnesota	101	Wyoming	134
Missouri	91	Far West	
Nebraska	95	Alaska	178
North Dakota	91	California	115
South Dakota	86	Hawaii	146
		Nevada	128
		Oregon	100
		Washington	108

Source: Significant Features of American Federalism: 1994, Volume 2 (Washington, D.C.: Advisory Commission on Intergovernmental Relations, 1994), p. 182.

governments depend on the property tax. Both state and local governments are making greater use of a revenue source called a *user charge.* All of these revenue sources and recent trends will be described below.

WHERE DOES THE MONEY GO?

Table 12-2 presents an overview of ten major functions on which state and local governments spend the most money. The biggest expenditure item is for elementary and

TABLE 12-2 MAJOR DIRECT GENERAL EXPENDITURES BY STATE AND LOCAL GOVERNMENT, 1992

Function	Expenditure (in billions)	Percent
Elementary and secondary education	$228.9	23.5
Public welfare	154.2	15.9
Higher education	84.3	8.7
Health and hospitals	81.4	8.4
Highways	66.7	6.9
Interest on general debt	55.3	5.7
Police protection	34.5	3.5
Sewerage and solid waste management	32.3	3.3
Corrections	28.6	2.9
Parks and recreation	15.7	1.6
Other spending	190.3	19.6
Total	972.2	100.0

Source: U.S. Bureau of the Census, *Government Finances: 1991–92 (Preliminary Report),* Series GF/92-5P (Washington, D.C.: U.S. Government Printing Office, 1994), p. 1.

secondary education. The operation of the public school system consumes almost 25 percent of state and local spending. The other education category—higher education, which refers to publicly operated universities, colleges, and community colleges—accounts for a little over 8 percent of total expenditures. These two categories taken together make up one-third of state and local expenditures! The second biggest item, 15.9 percent, is for public welfare. This includes, for example, cash assistance to the poor and payments made directly to doctors and hospitals for providing medical care for the poor. Almost as much money is spent on health and hospitals, a little over 8 percent, as on higher education. Health expenditures refer to things such as public health research, immunization programs, and maternal and child health programs. Hospital expenditures are principally for the establishment and operation of hospital facilities.

Although we have lumped state and local spending together, this does not mean that both levels spend equally across all of these functions. State government, through the operation of state prisons, spends two-thirds of the total amount of money that is spent on corrections. On the other hand, local governments are primarily responsible for police protection and spend over 85 percent of these funds. Eighty-five percent of higher education expenditures are made by state government and only 15 percent by local government. A good example of the use of intergovernmental revenue is in elementary and secondary education spending (see Chapter 13) where about 50 percent of the money spent by local government is actually money that is transferred from the state and even the federal government.

WHERE DOES THE MONEY COME FROM?

Intergovernmental expenditures, which have already been defined, are a major source of revenue for state and local government. The other major source of revenue is from

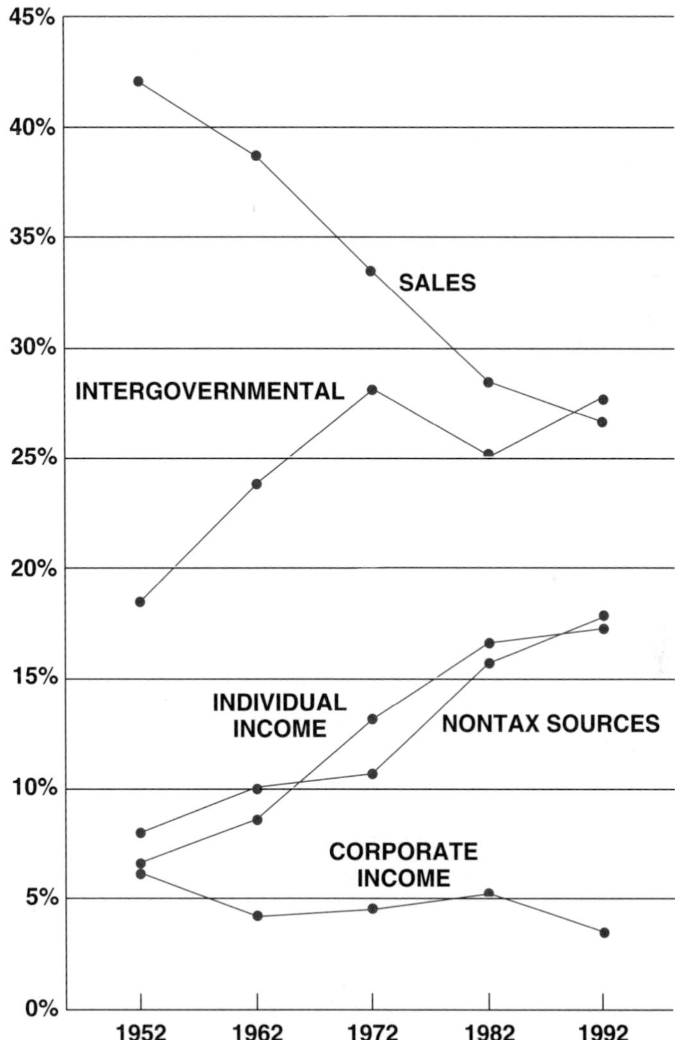

FIGURE 12-2 Percentage distribution of state general revenue by principal sources, 1952–1992. [*Significant Features of Fiscal Federalism: Volume 2, Revenues and Expenditures* (Washington, D.C.: Advisory Commission on Intergovernmental Relations, 1994), p. 65.]

state and local governments themselves (often referred to as "own source" revenue). This comes from taxes such as the income tax (both individual and corporate), the sales tax, the property tax, and nontax revenue such as user charges and state-operated or state-regulated gambling activities. Before examining these taxes in some detail, we will look at their relative importance in generating revenues.

Figure 12-2 shows the principal revenues for state governments over the years. The corporate income tax and the sales tax have declined in importance since 1952. At that time almost half of state revenues came from the sales tax. In terms of proportion of total revenues, the individual income tax and nontax sources have increased the most, with the former having almost a threefold increase. Intergovernmental revenue, almost all of it (94 percent) from the federal government, has become more important, in fact, the single most important source in 1992. Overall, in terms of own source revenue in 1992, the sales tax is still dominant, almost 10 percentage points ahead of the individual income tax and nontax sources.

Figure 12-3 has information on principal revenue sources for local governments. Note first of all that two of the taxes that are important to state governments, individual and corporate income taxes, are missing when we look at local governments. These taxes are rarely used at the local level, at least in part because they are so heavily used by the federal and state governments. The proportion of revenue from property taxes has decreased dramatically, although it is still the most important own source revenue. Nontax sources have increased significantly; the local sales tax has also, but it still represents a relatively small contribution to the total picture, only 6 percent. In 1992, intergovernmental revenue, from both the federal and state governments, provided the largest proportion of revenue to local governments.

Property Tax

At present, the **property tax** is a tax on what is termed *real property,* that is, land and the buildings on it. Because the property tax is almost exclusively a local tax, it is usually administered by the county treasurer. The process includes assessment of property values, determination of tax rates (millage), tax computation, and tax collection. A market approach is frequently used to assess the value of real property. In this approach, a local assessor periodically evaluates all property in a neighborhood by using the value of property that has been sold recently to determine the value of property that has not been sold. Assessors must develop and maintain detailed records of each property. One economist describes the market approach as "similar to neighbors estimating the current market value of their homes based on the sale price of a home on the same street."[6] Tax rates, set by local government officials, are usually expressed in mills; a mill is one-thousandth of a dollar. Thus if a house and the land it is on are assessed at \$100,000 and the mill rate is 20, the tax will be \$2,000 (\$100,000 × 0.020).

In many cities, nearly 25 percent of all property is exempt from property taxes. In Boston, the proportion is as high as 50 percent; in New York City, it is 35 percent. In large part, tax-exempt property is owned by the government or by religious organizations.

General Sales Tax

The **general sales tax** was first used by Mississippi in 1932, shortly after the start of the Great Depression. The property tax was the mainstay of state and local government revenue at that time, but during the Great Depression incomes fell more rapidly than the taxes on the property people owned and many simply could not pay.[7] (During the first three years of the Great Depression, incomes fell by 33 percent and unemployment was at 25 percent!) Foreclosures to pay property taxes were common

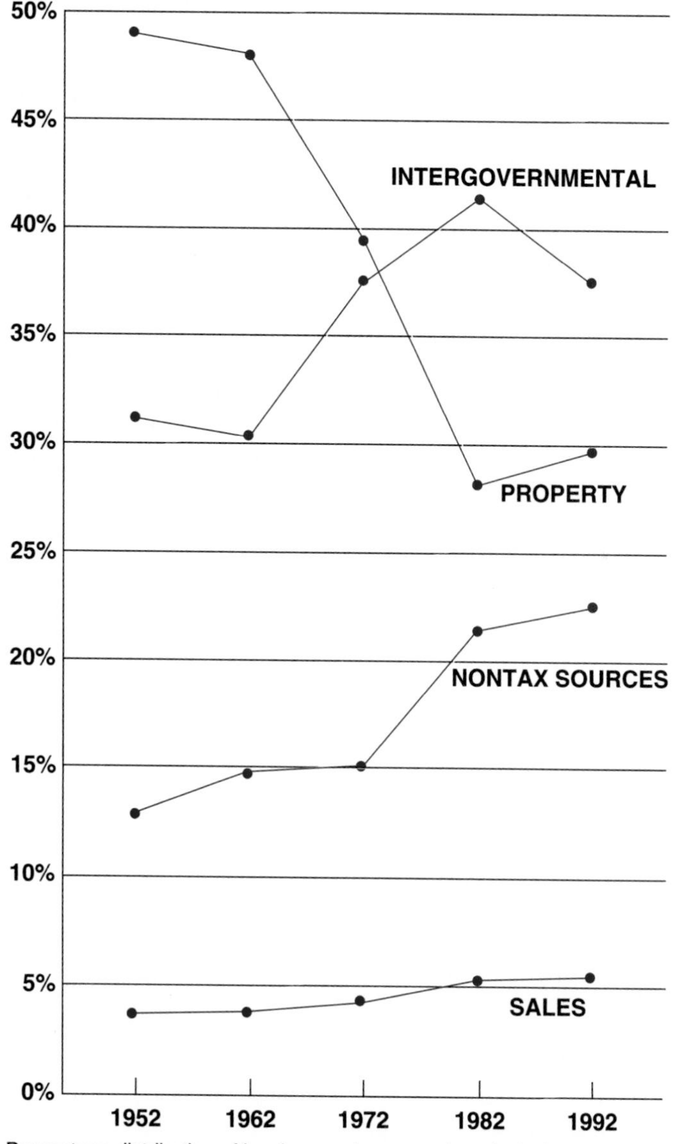

FIGURE 12-3 Percentage distribution of local general revenue by principal sources, 1952–1992. [*Significant Features of Fiscal Federalism: Volume 2, Revenues and Expenditures* (Washington, D.C.: Advisory Commission on Intergovernmental Relations, 1994), p. 67.]

but unpopular. Consequently, twenty-two states, looking for other sources of revenue, quickly followed Mississippi's lead and adopted the sales tax before the end of 1938. During the 1940s and 1950s, more states (ten) decided to use a sales tax; and in the 1960s, with state governments facing increased responsibilities, eleven states adopted it. Vermont was the last (1969). Currently, only five states—Alaska, Delaware, Montana, New Hampshire, and Oregon—do *not* use it.

The sales tax is levied on retail sales, and today the rate ranges from a low of 3 percent (Colorado) to a high of 7 percent (Mississippi and Rhode Island). Almost half of the states have a sales tax rate at 5 or 6 percent. An important element in the sales tax is the tax base, that is, what is actually taxed. The sales tax does not apply to the sale of all goods and services. For example, most states do not tax the sale of food in grocery stores or prescription drugs, and a few even exempt clothing. (However, most states do tax the purchase of nonprescription drugs.) Services are another area that is not usually taxed by states; this includes legal, accounting, and management consulting services as well as barber and beauty services.[8]

Over 30 states authorize local governments to use the sales tax, and about 6,400 do. Of course, the local tax is added on to the state sales tax so local government rates tend to be low, usually 1 or 2 percent. For example, a person making a purchase in Kansas City, Kansas (in 1993), paid 4.90 percent state sales tax, 1.0 percent county tax, and 1.0 percent city tax, for a total sales tax of 6.9 percent.

Income Tax

Forty-three states have a personal income tax, and forty-five have a corporate income tax. Wisconsin was the first state to adopt an income tax, in 1911, two years before the federal government enacted its income tax. Although eight states adopted the income tax shortly after Wisconsin, it wasn't until the Depression of the 1930s that a large number of states (sixteen) adopted it. Beginning in 1961, another eleven states added the income tax; New Jersey was the last (1976). In the late 1950s, many states began for the first time to employ a withholding system to collect income taxes in a manner similar to the federal government. The seven states without an income tax are Alaska, Florida, Nevada, South Dakota, Texas, Washington, and Wyoming.

The **income tax** almost never taxes total income, but rather what is called *taxable income,* the amount left after exemptions, adjustments, and credits have been subtracted.[9] State income tax rates are typically much lower than federal rates. A few states have a "flat tax," which means the rate is the same percentage regardless of income level: Connecticut's rate is 4.5 percent, and Pennsylvania's is 2.8 percent. Although most state income taxes are graduated—that is, the rate of taxation increases as income increases—the rate of increase and the maximum tax vary from state to state but are much less than those in federal tax schedules. The tax rate for Iowa is one of the most graduated; it begins at 0.4 percent and increases to 9.98 percent; this top rate is paid on incomes of $47,700 and higher. Many states have tax rates in the 2 to 7 percent range.

Taxes on the income or profits of corporations also started in Wisconsin, and as other states adopted income taxes, they taxed both personal and corporate income, also. Corporate income tax rates used by the states are also flat or graduated. Corporate income taxes bring in about one-fifth as much revenue as the tax on personal income.

Approximately 3,800 local governments in 13 states also tax income, with especially heavy use in Pennsylvania (over 2,800 local governmental units use it). Rates tend to be low, 1 or 2 percent.

Other Taxes

All states place an **excise tax,** sometimes called a selective sales tax, on particular commodities such as cigarettes, alcoholic beverages, and gasoline. Taxes on cigarettes and alcoholic beverages are often called *sin taxes* because they tax products that people should not use too much of anyhow. The idea is that taxing these products will raise revenue and may help to diminish consumption. The median tax on a pack of cigarettes is 25 cents; Virginia has the lowest at 2½ cents and Massachusetts the highest at 51 cents. Alcoholic beverages are usually taxed on a per gallon basis. Tax on beer, for example, ranges from 6 cents a gallon in Missouri and Wisconsin to 77 cents a gallon in South Carolina.

The tax on gasoline is considered a *benefit tax* in that there is a relationship between public service benefits received and taxes paid. Gasoline taxes are used to finance the construction and maintenance of highways, so people who use the highways the most will pay a greater share of the taxes that finance the highway system. The median tax on a gallon of gasoline is 19 cents; Georgia has the lowest at 7½ cents and Connecticut the highest at 29 cents.

During the 1920s and early 1930s, prior to the adoption of the general sales tax, selective sales taxes brought in about 28 percent of state tax revenue (over 50 percent of this amount was from the gasoline tax).[10]

A variety of other taxes are levied—on admissions to entertainment events, inheritance, stock transfers, gifts, and pari-mutuel betting. In states that have valuable natural resources—such as coal, oil, natural gas, and timber—a **severance tax** is often levied on their extraction and removal. Although about two-thirds of the states employ some form of severance tax, only a few states account for most of the severance tax revenue. In Alaska, North Dakota, Montana, New Mexico, and Wyoming, severance taxes account for 25 percent of all state tax revenue. Fluctuating prices for oil, natural gas, and coal have a strong effect on severance tax revenues. When the price for oil and natural gas declined sharply in the mid-1980s, the accompanying decline in severance revenue caused severe financial problems for the state governments of Alaska, Oklahoma, Texas, and Louisiana.

Nontax Sources

User charges and state-sponsored gambling activities are two examples of nontax revenue. A **user charge** is defined as "a payment to government for a specific good, service, or privilege."[11] The definition implies that the payment will equal the actual cost of the service, but that's not always the case. User charges are employed by both state and local governments. At the local level user charges are various and include fees paid for the following: rides on subways and buses, trash collection, police services at special events, and water and sewerage systems. A fairly recent user charge by many local governments is the impact fee, a one-time fee paid by real estate developers to cover at least part of the cost of extending water and sewer lines and building new streets for a new housing development. The most significant user charges among state governments are the fees (for example, tuition) students pay, frequently with the help of their parents, to attend public-supported colleges and universities.[12] Other familiar charges are tolls for highways and bridges and fees to enter parks and other recreational areas.

With the antitax mood of the 1980s and 1990s, more and more states have turned to gambling activities, especially lotteries, as a source of revenue. Recently, every state has at least considered the revenue benefits of legalized gambling. Between 1982 and 1992 the number of states operating lotteries increased from fifteen to thirty-six. Lotteries are not new in the United States; in fact, they were used in colonial times and during the nineteenth century, but scandals and unethical practices brought federal and state controls. After 1894, when the federal government banned interstate lotteries, no legal lotteries existed in the United States until New Hampshire, hoping to avoid the adoption of a general sales tax, instituted a state-operated lottery in 1964 with New York following a few years later.[13] But it is New Jersey (1971)—by lowering the price of tickets, increasing the number of ticket outlets, giving somewhat better odds, and aggressively marketing the game—that is credited with designing a lottery that proved popular with the public and created more revenue for the state than expected.[14]

In 1992, people spent $19.7 billion buying lottery tickets, and the states and the District of Columbia captured $7.8 billion as revenue. This is a considerable amount of money, but how much does it contribute to a state's total revenue picture? In 1992, lottery revenues averaged only 1.8 percent of own source revenue. The range among the states is from a low of 0.8 percent in California and Iowa to a high of 4.8 percent in Florida.

Today many states are moving beyond lotteries and authorizing casino gambling (see the article entitled "Casinos Get Some Smoother Operators" by Neal R. Peirce). In 1989, only Nevada and New Jersey had casino gambling. By the end of 1993, fourteen states had legalized it in some form. Mississippi law requires casinos to be on water, so they are located on barges or boats docked off the beaches of the Gulf of Mexico and along the Mississippi River. State and local governments are rushing to casino gambling not only because of the promise of additional tax revenue but also for the jobs it will create building and operating the casinos. In a 1994 initiative to allow casino gambling in Florida, pro-casino forces argued that approval of the initiative would create $4.7 billion in new construction, generate 67,000 new jobs paying $26,000 a year to operate the casinos, and reap $720 million more in state and local taxes. Some analysts believe the economic benefits are exaggerated. Casino gambling frequently drains economic activity from other business; for example, in Florida tourists might spend less money attending spring training baseball games and more at casinos. If this happens, a net increase in spending is unlikely. In addition, costs of casino gambling such as increased demands on law enforcement are often underestimated.[15]

Casinos Get Some Smoother Operators

Neal R. Peirce

Corporate America has moved heavily into casino gambling, effectively elbowing the mob aside. And now the big casino operators have begun to repackage one of man's oldest vices as clean family fun.

That's the story told by David Johnston, a reporter for *The Philadelphia Inquirer,* in his new book, *Temples of Chance—How America Inc. Bought Out Murder Inc. to Win Control of the Casino Business* (Doubleday & Co. Inc.).

It's a pretty chilling picture. Johnston tells, for example, of teenagers being welcomed in some of Atlantic City's leading casinos, plied with free drinks and allowed to gamble freely—so long as they're losing. In one case, a 19-year-old was turned over to the police for arrest as an underage gambler after he won a $50,000 slot jackpot.

Since 1989, under guises ranging from historic towns and Indian reservations to Mississippi riverboats and theme parks, casino gambling has expanded from its bases in Nevada and New Jersey to no fewer than 12 additional states: California, Colorado, Connecticut, Illinois, Iowa, Louisiana, Michigan, Minnesota, Mississippi, Missouri, Nebraska and Wisconsin. And wars between the states may be inevitable. In California, for example, the director of the governor's planning and research office recently suggested in a report that the state consider legalizing casino gambling in a few of its "isolated" border towns and in such higher-rolling spots as Palm Springs and Treasure Island in San Francisco Bay. "The Money Californians spend in gambling and related tourism in Nevada," the report said, "is in a very real sense paying for the exodus of California jobs."

"So completely, and quietly, has the trend toward universal casino gambling swept the nation that few people realize that Minnesota now has more casinos than New Jersey," Johnston reports. What's more, public officials are so desperate for fresh revenues that "more casinos managed or owned by state and local governments are a virtual certainty."

This book ought to be required reading for any governor, state legislator, county or city official who might be tempted to go after the "easy" money of casino gambling. In fulsome detail, Johnston relates how gambling—which has found favor with revenue-hungry governments ever since the days of the Continental Congress—has been spreading its tentacles from coast to coast as market-wise corporate America moves in.

In Las Vegas, Beverly Hills (Calif.)-based MGM Grand Inc.'s new casino will include an adjacent theme park with rides and amusements based on *The Wizard of Oz.* Circus Circus Enterprises Inc.'s Excalibur casino in Las Vegas includes huge boardwalk-like arcades for families to play in right off the gambling floor, not to mention an area with trapeze and other circus acts. Beverly Hills-based Hilton Hotels Corp., along with Circus Circus and Los Angeles-based Caesars World Inc., are planning to open a "family entertainment center," anchored by four big casinos, in Chicago. Riverboat casinos up and down the Mississippi are advertised as good fun for the whole family.

Johnston argues that as reprehensible as organized crime was when it dug its claws into Nevada's legalized casino business, "its incompetence at managing a business as complex as casinos limited its profits." By contrast, he writes, "corporate America has access to skilled managers, and it can employ the same marketing clout that sells dandruff shampoo to push casinos and create an appearance of respectability."

Corporations love the casino game because it's one in which the house *always* wins. Hilton's four Nevada casinos bring in more than twice the revenues of its 264 franchise hotels combined. Memphis-based Holiday Corp., which spread nearly 1,600 Holiday Inns across America, sold them off in 1990 to focus (under a new name, Promus Cos. Inc.) on its ultra-profitable casinos. Ramada Inns also shed its hotels to go all-casino.

Such sell-offs are freeing corporations to think about propagating casinos across the nation and around the world. "Their goal," Johnston says, "is to make gambling a routine leisure activity for most Americans, as it has become for 20 per cent of metropolitan Philadelphia residents" with Atlantic City a short ride away.

And central to it all, Johnston contends, is the marketing strategy of "encouraging young adults to gamble often—and on credit—as the beer and cigarette companies aim to make customers for life of people just entering adulthood."

For sheer sophistication, consider the casino industry's computerized "frequent gambler cards." Step up to an Atlantic City slot machine, insert your card and presto!—a video screen greets you by name. Simultaneously, just off the casino floor, your hosts can glance at a computer screen and see information about you and your betting history. Before you can even ask, a waiter or waitress brings your favorite drink.

So it is, Johnston charges, that "the business of chance prospers" even as "America approaches the dawn of a new millennium, its industrial might withering." No wealth is created; the casinos simply "take money from many people and funnel it to the few lucky enough to hold a casino license."

Yet politicians of all ideological stripes keep on touting casinos as job and revenue-producing panaceas. And as often as not, sadly, voters swallow the same line.

Is there any chance to roll back the tide?

Johnston's prognostication is bleak—he thinks we're hooked, for good. But he offers some intriguing reforms on the margin. Some examples: Ban the use of credit by gamblers. Make gambling debts uncollectible and any attempt to collect them a crime. Ban gambling advertising of all kinds. Ban the free alcoholic drinks that unhinge people's common sense. Fine or revoke the licenses of casinos that allow juveniles to gamble.

In light of the real and present perils of compulsive gambling, state and local governments owe us no less than those minimal public safety measures. Will they take Johnston's advice? Or will the collective clout of America Inc.'s casino operators win out? Don't hold your breath.

Source: National Journal, January 2, 1993, p. 39. Reprinted with permission of National Journal.

IS THERE A GOOD TAX?

Criteria

Economists have established criteria for a "good tax." Three of the criteria are especially useful in evaluating state and local taxes: simplicity, fairness, and stability.

Simplicity refers to the ease and cost of administration. Taxes should be inexpensive for governments to collect and easy for taxpayers to comply with.

Fairness is the idea that taxes should be related to an individual's ability to pay. Taxes can be progressive (as income increases, the taxes paid as a percentage of income also increase); proportional (as income increases, the taxes paid as a percentage of income remain constant); or regressive (as income increases, the taxes paid as a percentage of income decrease).[16] The key to understanding these terms is to realize that the *percentage* of an individual's income used to pay taxes is what determines if a tax is progressive, proportional, or regressive. For example, a person who makes $50,000 and pays a state income tax of 5 percent will pay $2,500 in taxes, and a person who makes $25,000 a year will pay $1,250 in taxes. The person who makes less pays less in taxes, but the percentage of income that goes to pay the tax bill is the same, so this would be a proportional tax. Of course, debate surrounds the criterion of fairness, especially whether the income tax should be proportional or progressive.

Stability means that taxes should produce enough revenue to provide basic services regardless of the state of the economy in any particular year. Henry Raimondo argues that "the economic cycle of growth and recession should not produce dramatic government surpluses and deficits."[17] Ideally, taxes should allow for enough revenue growth to keep up with the impact of inflation and population growth. This way decisions about the level of services will not be based on the presence of a budget surplus or deficit.[18]

The tax that usually earns low marks on simplicity is the property tax. All taxes involve some administrative costs, but the record keeping on each property, the hiring and training of assessors, the periodic reassessments, and the handling of appeals make the property tax a more expensive tax to administer. Keep in mind that this process is not centralized in a single large office at the state capital but is being carried out in all of the counties in a state. Applying the criteria of fairness frequently leads to debates among economists. There seems to be agreement that the general sales tax is only modestly regressive because of numerous exemptions.[19] Exemptions on food, prescription drugs, medical services, and other items that people must have mean that the sales tax does not take as large a share of money from low-income people that it otherwise would. The income tax, by its very nature, is likely to be progressive, but most states have only a few rates and frequently there is not much difference between the highest and lowest rate. Generally, state income taxes are only moderately progressive.[20] Most states have only a few rates, and there is not much difference between the highest and lowest rates.

For over twenty years the Advisory Commission on Intergovernmental Relations has asked the public for their opinion of taxes that are widely used in the United States. Some results of these surveys are in Table 12-3. In the first year of the survey (1972) the property tax is clearly viewed as the "worst tax." Also, it is seen as the "worst tax" in 1977, but the margin it has over the federal income tax narrows considerably to only 5 percentage points. In 1982 and 1987, the federal income tax takes the lead as the "worst tax," although the property tax is only a few percentage points behind. In the two most recent surveys, the federal income tax and the property tax are essentially the same. Over the years the state income tax comes out the best on this question and the sales tax also does well.

TABLE 12-3 WHICH DO YOU THINK IS THE WORST TAX—THAT IS, THE LEAST FAIR? (Percent of U.S. Public)

	1972	1977	1982	1987	1992	1994
Federal income tax	19	28	36	30	25	27
Federal social security tax	—	—	—	—	10	12
State income tax	13	11	11	12	9	7
State sales tax	13	17	14	21	16	14
Local property tax	45	33	30	24	25	28
Don't know	11	11	9	13	15	12

Source: Changing Public Attitudes on Governments and Taxes (Washington, D.C.: Advisory Commission on Intergovernmental Relations, 1994), p. 4.

Although economists still debate the fairness of the property tax,[21] it is clear that a sizable portion of the public does not like it. Why is that? One reason is that the value of an individual's home is not always tied to his or her annual income. People may live in areas that are growing rapidly and their property values are increasing dramatically, along with their property taxes, even though their incomes may be increasing modestly at best. Of course, when people retire, their incomes usually drop, but their property values and taxes may continue to increase. As a consequence, many states enacted property tax relief laws. O'Sullivan, Sexton, and Sheffrin define property tax relief as any "measure that reduces property taxes below what they otherwise would be."[22] The principal types are homestead exemptions and circuit breakers; both target specific home owners. **Homestead exemptions,** used in forty-four states and the District of Columbia, are aimed at people who own their home and also are elderly, disabled, or have low incomes. The exemptions exclude from taxation a certain amount of the assessed value of their home. The exemption amount is subtracted from the assessed value of the property before the amount of tax is calculated. **Circuit breakers,** used in thirty-four states and the District of Columbia, limit the percentage of a home owner's income that can be taken in property taxes. As with the homestead exemption, this program is designed to prevent senior citizens on fixed retirement incomes and low-income households from having to sell their homes because of increasing property taxes. The name *circuit breaker* is appropriate because when an individual's property tax exceeds a certain point relative to income, this program "breaks" the load of higher taxes.[23]

These programs do provide some relief to property owners, especially low-income households. States with the highest property taxes tend to have the most generous programs. New Jersey has 2 million beneficiaries, while Oklahoma has under 4,000. Average benefits are $550 in Maryland and $81 in Arizona.[24]

The Property Tax Revolt

Public dissatisfaction with the property tax was particularly acute in California during the 1970s when real estate values doubled and, for many home owners, property tax bills skyrocketed, sometimes as much as 20 to 30 percent per year.[25] Howard Jarvis, using California's initiative process, led a campaign that succeeded in placing **Proposition 13,** a tax-reduction measure, on the 1978 ballot. With a $7 billion surplus in the state's treasury, voters did not believe dire warnings of cuts in services if Proposition 13 passed. Although labor unions, teachers, public employees, the League of Women Voters, and most elected officials urged a no vote, Proposition 13 passed with nearly 70 percent support in a high turnout election.[26] It had three main provisions:

- It limited property taxes to 1 percent of assessed value.
- It "rolled back" assessed values of all property to *1975 assessments.* Annual updating increases were limited to no more than 2 percent per year. However, any change of ownership triggers reappraisal based on current value, usually the purchase price, which results in an increase in taxes for the new owner.
- It prohibited the state from raising any state taxes to make up for lost revenue unless the new taxes are approved by a *two-thirds* vote of the legislature.

The passage of Proposition 13 led to a flurry of tax-cutting activity in more than half the states from 1978 to 1980. Eighteen states approved limitations on taxes and expenditures (TELs, as we called them earlier). The most extreme limits were approved in Massachusetts, Minnesota, and Idaho. As a result of the passage of Proposition 2½, Boston lost about 75 percent of its property tax revenue. Susan Hansen notes that, in general, states with a tradition of using the initiative process were the ones most successful in reducing taxes.[27]

Initially the impact of Proposition 13 was what its supporters wanted; property tax bills declined significantly, and because of the state's budget surplus most public services remained about the same. When the surplus disappeared in the early 1980s, revenue problems began to emerge and continue to plague the state.[28] Like other states, California was affected by the 1981–1982 national recession and the reduction of federal aid. As a result, there were cuts in many state programs and communities began to impose user charges for many services. Also, the provision in Proposition 13 that allows property to be reappraised to current market value only when it is sold means that new property owners may pay taxes as much as ten times higher than those of people owning similar houses that have not been sold and are still protected by Proposition 13. In 1992, the Supreme Court upheld this system.

BORROWING AND DEBT POLICIES

When tax revenue is insufficient to meet general operating costs or when state and local governments wish to finance major capital programs such as highways or schools, money must be borrowed. Although borrowing to meet current expenses is discouraged, long-term borrowing for permanent improvements is standard procedure. Because of unsound financial management in the nineteenth century, state constitutions place narrow limits on borrowing. Limits are placed on the amount of debt that can be incurred, and borrowing decisions are most often made by the voters in referenda, rather than by legislators.

State indebtedness declined in the late 1980s, but it has increased in the 1990s. Older cities in the Northeast tend to have more debt than other cities because of the variety of services they provide and their deteriorating financial base. State debt occurs because capital spending (e.g., building and repairing bridges) necessitates borrowing. States and cities are rated by private agencies, and if they have low ratings (based on their financial condition), they must pay higher rates of interest. Debt also exists because states form government corporations to finance public works projects, and these corporations can borrow money in excess of state constitutional limits.

A part of state and local debt is in the form of short-term bank loans and tax anticipation warrants, which are paid out of current revenue. To pay for capital improvements, which may involve tens of millions of dollars, governments issue bonds (usually referred to as "municipals"). **General-obligation bonds** are backed by the full faith and credit of the issuing government. In approving this kind of bond, frequently by a referendum, the government agrees to increase taxes to pay the interest and ultimately to retire the bond. **Revenue bonds** are supported by the income from a project such as a toll road. In most cases, voter approval is not needed to issue revenue bonds, and they can often be used to extend the total debt of a government beyond constitutional limits. Generally, both types of bonds are attractive investments, especially to wealthy investors, because the interest they pay is exempt from the federal and state income taxes. Since revenue bonds are somewhat more risky than general-obligation bonds, they usually pay a higher rate of interest.

The best means of repayment is to issue serial bonds, in which a certain portion matures each year and is retired from current income. In the past, governments created a "sinking fund" in which they set aside a given amount of money each year to provide sufficient funds to pay off the bond when it matured. In many cases, however, governments dipped into the sinking fund for other purposes or tax revenues dropped and the extra money was not available once current operating expenses were met.

TAXES IN THE 1990s

Short-Term Problems

As noted in Chapter 2, states and localities entered the 1990s in the midst of a financial crisis. An economic recession, which lasted from July 1990 to March 1991, reduced the amount of money generated by state and local taxes. The recession was felt hard in Northeastern states and in California. The economy's effect on state tax revenue can be seen in Figure 12-4.

How did states react to the 1990–1991 recession and its negative impact on revenues? Did they reduce spending? Or did they increase taxes? Actually, most states did both. According to finance expert Steven Gold, total spending by states in fiscal years 1991 and 1992 in real dollars, that is, after subtracting inflation, did not increase at all in 1991 and only a modest 1.5 percent in 1992. This compares to increases in the late 1980s that averaged around 3 percent.[29] But spending reductions were not enough to balance budgets; taxes had to be raised. In 1991 and 1992, eighteen states increased taxes. Many of these increases affected the personal income tax rate. For example, in California the top tax rate of 9.3 percent was increased to 10 percent for taxable incomes over $200,000 and to 11 percent for incomes over $400,000.[30]

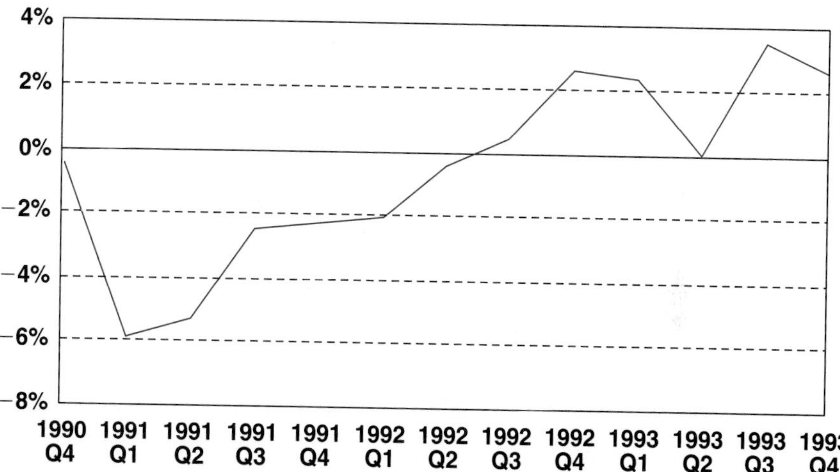

FIGURE 12-4 Fluctuations in state tax collections during and after the recession of July 1990 to March 1991. Changes in tax collections were calculated after the effects of inflation and legislated tax increases were eliminated. [Steven D. Gold, "State Fiscal Problems and Policies," in *The Fiscal Crisis of the States,* Steven D. Gold, ed. (Washington, D.C.: Georgetown University Press, 1995), p. 9. Reprinted by permission of Georgetown University Press.]

One state that did not follow this pattern was Michigan where, under the leadership of Republican governor John Engler, taxes were not increased. Engler's main approach was to cut spending, especially for capital improvements and social services.[31] Actions also were taken to reduce expenditures by privatizing some state services (see Chapter 7).

It is important to note that governors in most states also resorted to what are called "gimmicks," that is, "policies that provide a one-shot injection of revenue or one-time savings on expenditures."[32] Examples include delaying state aid payments to local governments and school districts and delaying state payments to pension funds. Not all of these gimmicks are harmful, but some are. Delaying payments to pension funds simply means that payments will have to be made later; the payment is simply shifted to future taxpayers.[33] Also, many states took advantage of a loophole in the federal government's Medicaid program that allowed a state to appropriate money to hospitals for Medicaid with the understanding that it would not really be spent on Medicaid but returned to the state. The federal government, which splits the cost of Medicaid with the states, then matched this money even though it was not actually used for medical care for the poor. This helped states balance their budgets in the short run, but shifted the cost to the federal government. States received several billion dollars in extra federal aid through this loophole;[34] it was eliminated in 1992.

Long-Term Problems

Economic recessions have occurred in the past, will happen in the future, will adversely affect revenues, and will have to be managed by state governments; these are difficult but basically short-term problems. Some specialists on state taxes, however, see a long-term problem with state tax systems, which they refer to as a **structural deficit.** A structural deficit exists when money produced by the tax system is insufficient "to maintain existing level of services."[35] In other words, the assumption is no longer valid that additional government revenue produced through normal economic growth will maintain the present level of services. A few examples will help to explain this problem.

It has been widely reported that the strength of the American economy is less and less in the manufacturing of tangible goods and more and more in the production of services (see Figure 12-5). The service sector is the fastest growing sector of the American economy. However, the general sales tax, as has been noted, primarily taxes the purchase of tangible goods, not services. As consumption switches from tangible goods to services, sales tax collections fail to grow as much as they should. Personal income tax collections are also affected because of the shift from higher paying manufacturing jobs to lower paying jobs in the service sector.[36]

Another example deals with changes in the way people shop and buy things. The tremendous increase in sales through mail-order catalogs has a negative effect on state tax collections because states cannot tax purchases made by its citizens through catalogs of out-of-state businesses. State and local governments may lose as much as $3 billion annually through these untaxed sales.[37] One can only wonder how much sales tax revenue has been lost by not taxing purchases made over Home Shopping Network!

FIGURE 12-5 Services and tangible goods in the national economy as a percentage of GNP, 1940–1990. [Ronald Snell, ed., *Financing State Government in the 1990s* (Denver, Colo.: National Conference of State Legislatures; and Washington, D.C.: National Governors' Association, 1993), p. 21. Reprinted by permission of the National Conference of State Legislatures and National Governors' Association.]

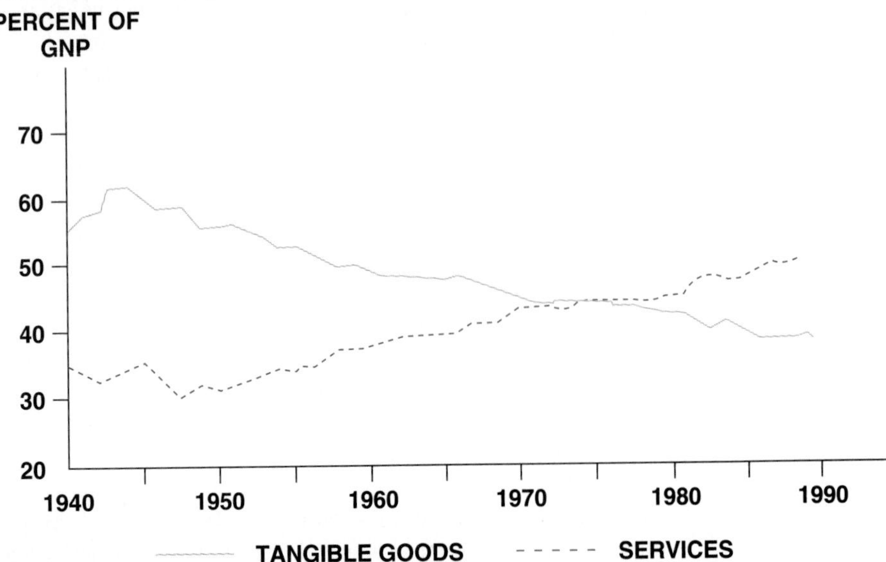

A study sponsored by the National Conference of State Legislatures and the National Governors' Association makes the following conclusion about today's state tax systems:

> State systems are becoming obsolete, inequitable, and unresponsive to changes in the economy. Designed primarily during the 1930s for a nation of smokestack industries in deep economic depression, state tax systems fall short in the 1990s when services are supplanting manufacturing as the economic linchpin, the economy is increasingly global, and new information-based industries appear almost daily.[38]

Local governments are not immune to financing problems, and this is especially true in large cities (population over 300,000). No one can help but notice the differences between life in the cities and life in the suburbs, and most people with decent financial resources conclude that the suburbs are where they want to live. Between 1957 and 1990, the percentage of the U.S. population living in large cities declined from 19.8 percent to 16.8 percent.[39] More important than the decline is the fact that residents of large cities tend to be poor; their 1990 median family income was almost 8 percent lower than the national median.[40] Central cities also have more problems such as higher crime rates and a declining infrastructure that require higher expenditures by city governments. The resulting higher taxes frequently cause businesses and residents in cities to move to the suburbs where taxes are usually lower. The smaller tax base increases the likelihood that taxes will be raised in the cities. If taxes are not raised, then the quality of services declines. Because of the presence of a wider array of problems, cities spend less money on elementary and secondary schools; education expenditures consume "about half of most suburban budgets, but rarely more than a third of most central cities'."[41] Many are caught in a downward spiral that can be reversed only by increased financial assistance from the federal and state governments or arrangements that would allow central cities to share in their suburbs' tax base.[42]

Solving long-term financial problems of state and local government as we move through the 1990s will not be easy. The "reinventing government" approach (see Chapter 7) may yield more efficient delivery of services, but it is unlikely to solve long-term problems of the states and large cities. Public aversion to anything but a decrease in taxes is strong, even if that means a decline in services. Even tax changes that only try to keep revenue growth in proportion to economic growth are unlikely to be viewed favorably by the public.

SUMMARY

State and local governments spend a great deal of money ($972.2 billion in 1992), and their share of total government spending has increased in the last few decades. Close to one-third of these expenditures are used to finance the public school system (elementary and secondary education, as well as higher education). Other significant expenditure items are public welfare, health and hospitals, and highways.

Intergovernmental funds are an important source of revenue for both state and local governments. In terms of their own taxes, the sales tax is the most important source of revenue for state governments and the property tax is the most important source for local governments. Both of these taxes have been declining in their percentage contribution to state and local treasuries over the past few decades, and user charges have been growing in importance. In their search for new revenues, states are operating lotteries and are beginning to authorize casino gambling.

The public consistently gives low ratings to the property tax because many doubt its fairness, one of the criteria used to evaluate different kinds of taxes. Public dissatisfaction has manifested itself in a number of ways, from California's Proposition 13, which dramatically reduced property taxes, to the adoption in most states of property tax relief laws, which reduce property taxes through homestead exemptions and circuit breakers.

State and local government leaders are being challenged to find enough revenues to provide needed public services. Changes in the American economy—such as a shift from higher paying manufacturing jobs to lower paying service sector jobs—are causing a structural deficit whereby existing tax systems do not generate enough revenue to maintain services at the current level. A further challenge is finding revenues to meet the demand for services in large cities that have an inadequate tax base.

KEY TERMS

Circuit breakers A property tax relief law used in many states that limits the percentage of a home owner's income that can be used to pay property taxes. It is designed to help those on fixed incomes, especially the elderly, to stay in their homes even though property taxes are increasing.

Direct general expenditures Government expenditures that include all spending that is an actual payment to a final recipient. Some of the expenditures not included in this category are intergovernmental transfers and unemployment compensation.

Excise tax A selective sales tax on items such as cigarettes, alcoholic beverages, and gasoline. These taxes are frequently paid by manufacturers, wholesalers, or retailers and passed on to consumers in the form of higher prices.

General-obligation bonds Bonds issued by state or local governments that are backed by the full faith and credit of the issuing body. Taxes may have to be increased to pay the interest and principal of the bond.

General sales tax A tax levied on retail sales and paid by the consumer. State tax rates range from 3 to 7 percent and frequently exclude from taxation items such as food purchased in grocery stores and prescription drugs.

Homestead exemptions A property tax relief law used in many states that exempts from taxation a certain amount of the assessed value of a person's home. It is designed to help those on fixed incomes, especially the elderly, to stay in their homes even though property taxes are increasing.

Income tax A tax levied on individual and corporate taxable income, which is the amount left after adjustments, exemptions, and credits are subtracted. State tax rates on individual income are usually in the 5 to 7 percent range.

Intergovernmental expenditures Transfer of funds from one level of government to another. An important source of revenue for state and local governments, these expenditures are not part of a government's direct general expenditures.

Property tax A tax levied almost exclusively by local governments. The amount of tax is determined by assessment of property values (homes and businesses) and the rate at which the property is taxed.

Proposition 13 An initiative passed in California in 1978 that substantially cut property taxes and made it difficult to increase them. Adoption of Proposition 13 was followed by tax-cutting activity in about half of the states.

Revenue bonds Bonds supported from the income earned by such projects as toll roads and bridges.

Severance tax A tax levied on the extraction of scarce natural resources such as timber, oil, coal, and natural gas.

Structural deficit A characteristic of a tax system that does not generate enough revenue to maintain the existing level of government services.

Tax capacity A comparative index that measures a state's ability to raise revenue given its tax base.

TELs Tax and expenditure limitations that place limits on revenue or expenditure increases. State governments frequently adopt laws that place these kinds of limits on local governments.

User charge A payment to purchase a specific service from a state or local government. It is a nontax source of government revenue that has been growing in importance as a source of revenue.

REFERENCES

1 U.S. Bureau of the Census, *Government Finances: 1991–92 (Preliminary Report),* Series GF/92-5P (Washington, D.C.: U.S. Government Printing Office, 1994), p. 1.

2 *Significant Features of Fiscal Federalism: Volume 2, Revenues and Expenditures* (Washington, D.C.: Advisory Commission on Intergovernmental Relations, 1994), pp. 47 and 49.

3 *Significant Features of American Federalism: 1994, Volume 2* (Washington, D.C.: Advisory Commission on Intergovernmental Relations, 1994), p. 177.

4 Alice M. Rivlin, *Reviving the American Dream: The Economy, the States and the Federal Government* (Washington, D.C.: The Brookings Institution, 1992), pp. 142–147.

5 *Tax and Expenditure Limits on Local Governments* (Washington, D.C.: Advisory Commission on Intergovernmental Relations, 1995), p. 44.

6 Henry J. Raimondo, *Economics of State and Local Government* (New York: Praeger Publishers, 1992), p. 138.

7 *Local Revenue Diversification: Local Sales Taxes* (Washington, D.C.: Advisory Commission on Intergovernmental Relations, 1989), p. 3; J. Richard Aronson and John L. Hilley, *Financing State and Local Governments* (Washington, D.C.: The Brookings Institution, 1986), p. 94.

8 Raimondo, *Economics,* pp. 168–171.

9 Ronald John Hy and William L. Waugh, Jr., *State and Local Tax Policies: A Comparative Handbook* (Westport, Conn.: Greenwood Press, 1995), p. 36.

10 Aronson and Hilley, *Financing,* p. 43.

11 Raimondo, *Economics,* p. 206.

12 Aronson and Hilley, *Financing,* p. 157.

13 John L. Mikesell and C. Kurt Zorn, "State Lotteries as Fiscal Savior or Fiscal Fraud," *Public Administration Review* (July–August 1986), p. 311.

14 Frederick D. Stocker, "State Sponsored Gambling as a Source of Public Revenue," *National Tax Journal* 25 (September 1972), p. 437; Raimondo, *Economics,* p. 212.
15 Frank D. Roylance, "Gambling on the Future," *Baltimore Sun,* November 6, 1994, p. 1D.
16 Raimondo, *Economics,* p. 111.
17 Ibid., p. 126.
18 Ronald Snell, ed., *Financing State Government in the 1990s* (Denver, Colo.: National Conference of State Legislatures, and Washington, D.C.: National Governors' Association, 1993), pp. 16–17.
19 Raimondo, *Economics,* p. 180.
20 Ibid., pp. 200–201.
21 See Raimondo, *Economics,* pp. 152–156, for a discussion of two different views of the fairness of the property tax.
22 Arthur O'Sullivan, Terri A. Sexton, and Steven M. Sheffrin, *Property Taxes and Tax Revolts: The Legacy of Proposition 13* (New York: Cambridge University Press, 1995), p. 26.
23 Ibid., pp. 26–27.
24 Ibid.
25 Ibid., p. 2.
26 Susan B. Hansen, "The Politics of State Taxing and Spending," in Virginia Gray, Herbert Jacob, and Robert B. Albritton, eds., *Politics in the American States,* 5th ed. (Glenview, Ill.: Scott, Foresman/Little, Brown, 1990), pp. 355–356.
27 Ibid.
28 Jerry Hagstrom and Neal R. Peirce, "The Quake That Didn't Quit," *National Journal,* May 25, 1988, pp. 1413–1416.
29 Steven D. Gold, ed., *The Fiscal Crisis of the States* (Washington, D.C.: Georgetown University Press, 1995), p. 9.
30 Ibid., pp. 20–23.
31 Robert J. Kleine, "Michigan: Rethinking Fiscal Priorities," in *The Fiscal Crisis of the States,* Steven D. Gold, ed. (Washington, D.C.: Georgetown University Press, 1995), p. 305.
32 Steven D. Gold, *Fiscal Crisis,* p. 47.
33 Ibid.
34 Ibid., p. 30.
35 Ibid., p. 43.
36 Ronald Snell, ed., *Financing,* pp. 21–23.
37 Ibid., p. 42.
38 Ibid., p. 1.
39 Paul E. Peterson, "The Changing Fiscal Place of Big Cities in the Federal System," in *Interwoven Destinies: Cities and the Nation,* Henry G. Cisneros, ed. (New York: W. W. Norton & Company, 1993), p. 188.
40 Ibid., p. 189.
41 Peter D. Salins, "Metropolitan Areas: Cities, Suburbs, and the Ties that Bind," in *Interwoven Destinies: Cities and the Nation,* Henry G. Cisneros, ed. (New York: W. W. Norton & Company, 1993), p. 158.
42 Carol O'Cleireagain, "Cities' Role in the Metropolitan Economy and the Federal Structure," in *Interwoven Destinies: Cities and the Nation,* Henry G. Cisneros, ed. (New York: W. W. Norton & Company, 1993), pp. 176–183.

13

EDUCATION POLICY

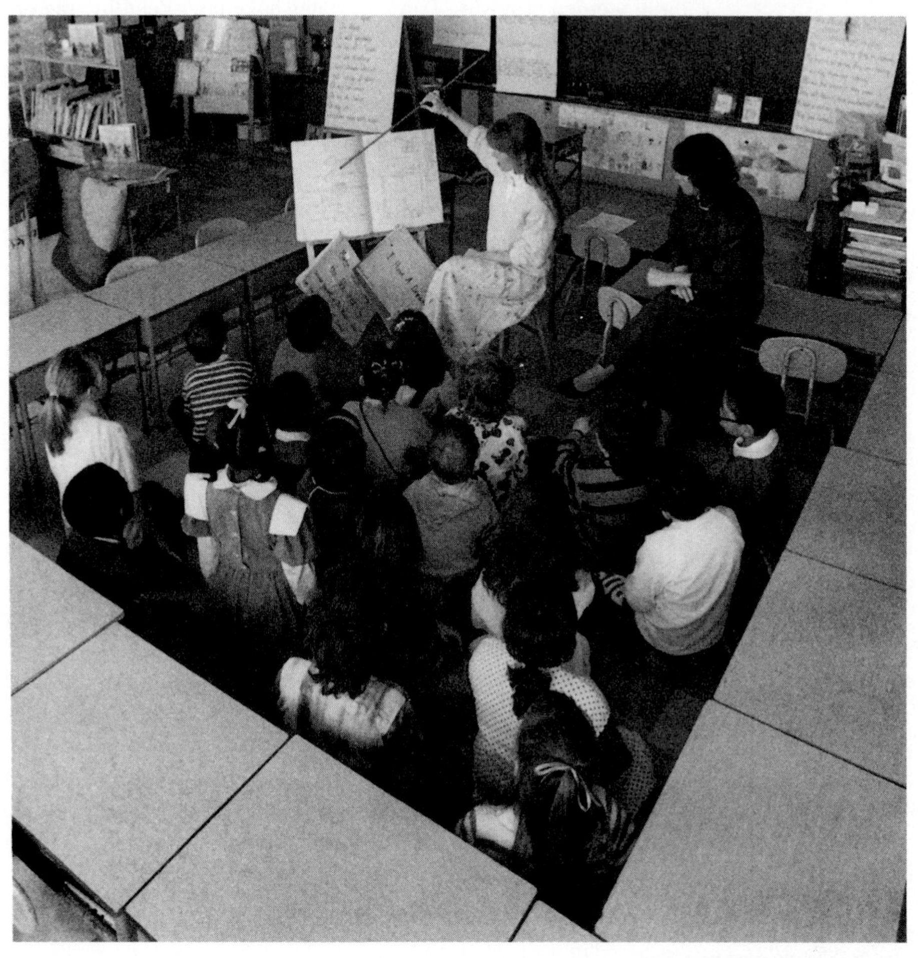

Frank Siteman/The Picture Cube

The U.S. Constitution makes no direct reference to education, but state constitutions almost always specify that education is the legal responsibility of state government. The constitution of Maryland states that the legislature shall "establish throughout the State a thorough and efficient system of Free Public Schools, and shall provide by taxation, or otherwise for their maintenance." Constitutions of almost all states have similarly worded provisions, and all states have laws detailing the organizational structure of public education.[1]

State governments delegate considerable control over elementary and secondary education to local school districts; more recently state government, and to a lesser extent the federal government, has increased its influence in educational policy. State government's importance in providing higher education has grown so much since World War II that state universities and colleges almost overshadow the once dominant private sector.

Education is a gigantic enterprise. In the fall of 1993, 64.5 million persons were enrolled in schools and colleges in the United States. About 3.7 million teachers were employed, and administrative and support staff totaled 4.2 million.[2] (See Figure 13-1.)

This chapter examines the governing and financing of public elementary and secondary schools. School district funding inequities and concerns about the quality of education are discussed as are reforms aimed at improving public schools. Also considered is state government's role in providing opportunities for higher education.

GOVERNING PUBLIC SCHOOLS

The history of public elementary and secondary education in the United States dates from 1647, when Massachusetts towns were required to establish schools. The Northwest Ordinances of 1784, 1785, and 1787—which provided for the sale of land and governance of territory that was later to become the states of Indiana, Illinois, Michigan, Ohio, Wisconsin, and part of Minnesota—required that 1 section (640 acres) in each township of 36 sections be granted to the state for the support of public schools. Connecticut in 1850 was the first state to mandate free education. Mississippi in 1910 was the last. By 1900, most states had compulsory attendance laws and had created a state education officer position, usually called the state school superintendent. It was not until the Elementary and Secondary Education Act of 1965 that Congress approved the first significant federal intervention in local education.

Local Government's Role

Many decisions concerning public schools are made by boards of education in local school districts. Over 90 percent of the more than 16,000 school districts in the United States are classified as **independent school districts,** meaning they are administratively and financially independent of other units of local government. The school board can levy taxes, usually with the approval of the voters, spend money, and hire a superintendent and teachers. In addition, the board oversees the actual operation of schools within its district, but *independent* does not mean that it can do anything it wants. Its policies must be consistent with state and federal laws.

School board members in independent school districts are elected directly by the voters, usually on nonpartisan ballots, in elections held at different times than the more

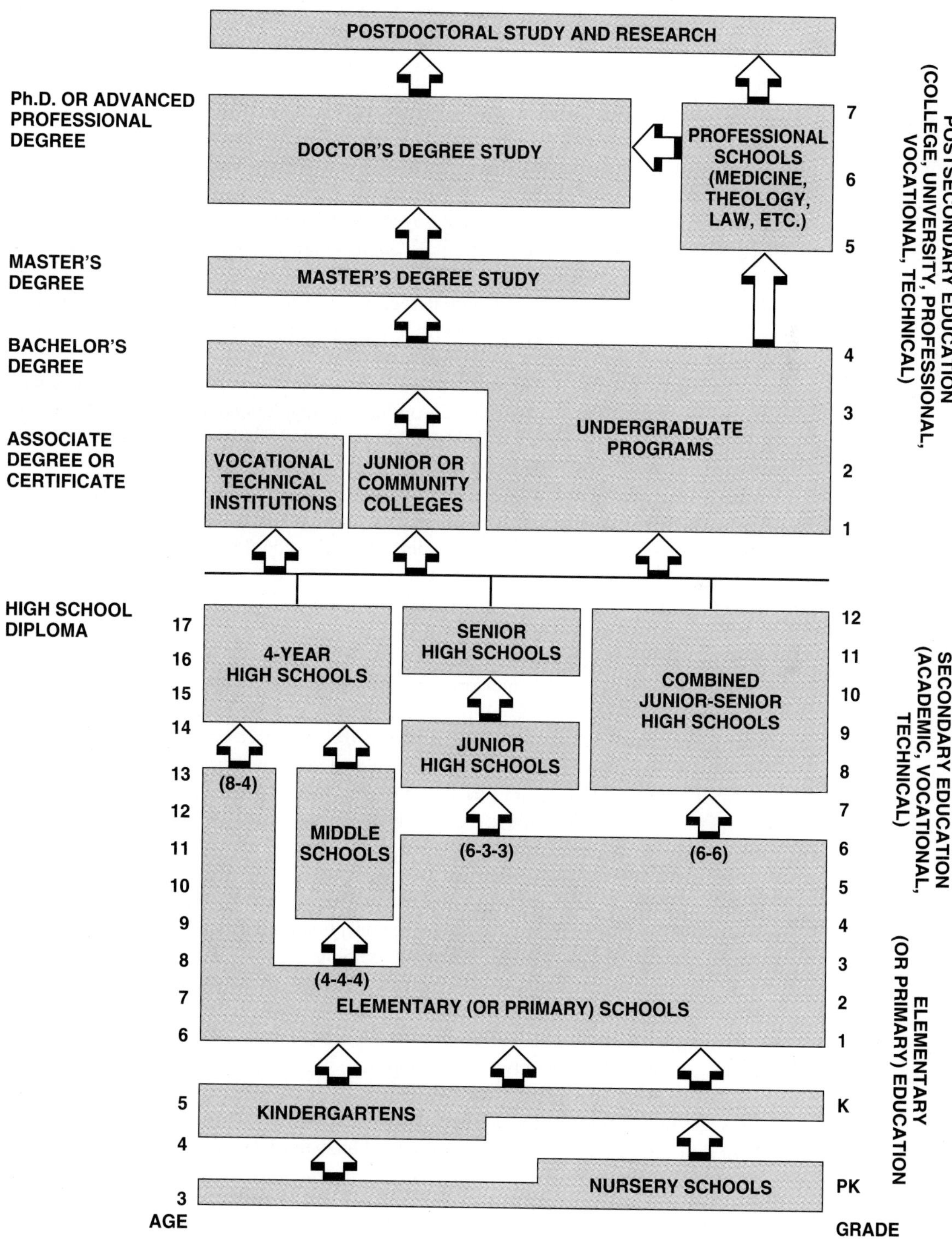

FIGURE 13-1 The structure of education in the United States. [*Digest of Education Statistics, 1994* (Washington, D.C.: National Center for Education Statistics, 1994), p. 7.]

publicized elections for state offices. As a result, school board elections usually have low voter turnout and can be dominated by single-issue groups whose educational concerns may be limited to school policies on sex education or AIDS.[3]

Dependent school districts lack sufficient autonomy or independence in budgetary matters to be considered as a separate government. The school board, even if its members are elected by the voters, reports to another unit of local government such as a mayor or county council. This board has no taxing authority, and its budget must be approved by the governmental unit it reports to. The board may or may not have authority to appoint the superintendent, and even if the board does, it may be influenced by the mayor or other political leaders.

The school district's superintendent is important in determining policies because of his or her expertise in the field of education. The superintendent's relationship to the school board is similar to the relationship between the city manager and council in a small city (see Chapter 9). However, the superintendent typically dominates policymaking to a greater extent than a city manager, and council members typically have more experience than school board members. In most instances, there is little conflict between the board and the superintendent regarding school policy.

State Government's Role

With thousands of school districts, it is easy to lose sight of the fact that school districts work within a legal framework established by state government. Aside from education policymaking responsibilities of governors and legislatures, forty-nine states have a state board of education that is part of the executive branch and is responsible for the general supervision of elementary and secondary education within the state.[4] Members of these boards are usually appointed by the governor, but in a few states they are elected by the voters. As with local school boards, members serve without salary and are not professional educators.

State boards of education appoint the state school superintendent, although in some states he or she will be elected by the voters or appointed by the governor. The state superintendent is important in determining educational policy and heads a state department of education that averages about 300 employees.

Traditional activities at the state level have involved teacher certification and standards for the instructional program. All states have regulations governing teacher certification, that is, how a person becomes qualified to teach, and administer these regulations directly.[5] Frequently, states approve higher educational institutions and programs, and graduates of these programs are automatically certified. State legislatures oftentimes delegate the writing of standards for the instructional program to state boards of education. Minimum standards, which must be followed by local school boards, may be established for curriculum, instructional materials, promotion, and graduation requirements.[6]

Federal Government's Role

The federal role in education is based on actions of the Congress and president in making laws and also on decisions by the Supreme Court. In 1979, a separate Department of Education was created in the executive branch; prior to that there was a Division of Education and even earlier an Office of Education, both housed within a department that had broader responsibilities than just education.

Although our emphasis is on education policymaking at the state and local levels, the federal government plays an important role, also. Early examples are the Morrill Act (1862), which helped states establish colleges of agriculture (the forerunners of many of today's large state universities), and the Smith-Hughes Act (1917), which provided matching funds to assist states in establishing vocational education programs.

Still, it is the **Elementary and Secondary Education Act of 1965** that significantly extended the federal government's role. The most important component of this law, commonly referred to as Title I, provided federal funds to local school districts ($1.06 billion the first year) that had large numbers of children from low-income families. (Children from low-income families are likely to enter school not prepared to learn and have difficulty making normal progress.) Money also was provided for library resources, textbooks, and other instructional materials. Congress, in 1994, reauthorized the Elementary and Secondary Education Act for another five years. President Bill Clinton and some members of Congress wanted to concentrate the money even more on school districts in high-poverty areas, but this effort failed. The present funding mechanism sends money to 90 percent of the nation's school districts.[7]

The federal government's impact on schools is more obvious in the adoption of national policies than in the number of federal tax dollars transferred to the states. A few examples are listed below:

- U.S. Supreme Court decision of *Brown* v. *Board of Education* (1954) declared racially segregated public schools unconstitutional.
- Title IX of the Education Amendments of 1972 forbids sex discrimination in schools receiving federal financial assistance. As a result, courses designed for one sex have been eliminated and the number of girls' athletic programs has increased.
- Education for All Handicapped Children Act of 1975 (frequently referred to as Public Law 94-142) requires schools to provide appropriate public education for handicapped children that meets their special needs.
- A recent Supreme Court decision upheld an Oregon school district's policy of mandatory surprise drug testing of high school students who play sports, opening the way for other school districts to adopt a similar policy.

All of these federal-level policies have had a tremendous impact on how public schools operate.

SCHOOL FINANCING

The Overall Pattern

When it comes to revenues for operating public schools, the dominance of state and local governments over the federal government is clear (see Figure 13-2). State government's share has gradually increased and in 1991–1992 was 46.4 percent, approaching 50 percent of total revenues. The local share, which was close to 60

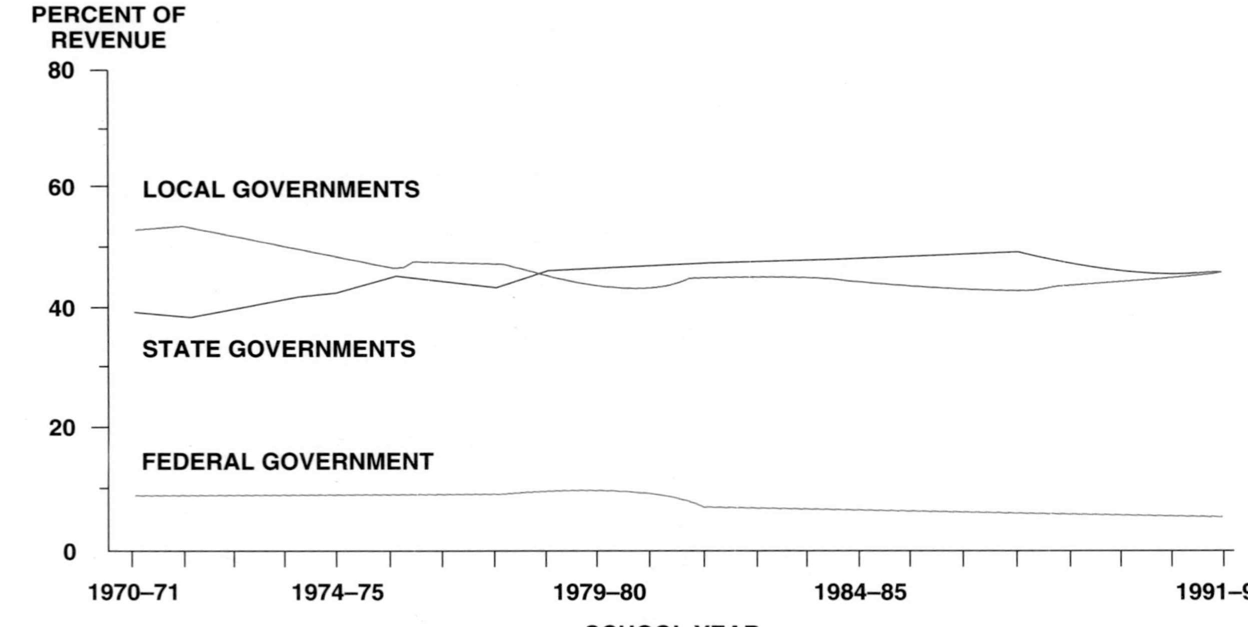

FIGURE 13-2 Source of revenue for public elementary and secondary schools, 1970–1971 to 1991–1992. [*Digest of Education Statistics, 1994* (Washington, D.C.: National Center for Education Statistics, 1994), p. 49.]

percent in 1950, has declined to 44.3 percent. The federal government's contribution has never been particularly large; it peaked just under 10 percent in 1979–1980 and has declined to 6.6 percent. (A little over 2 percent is from miscellaneous sources.)

The pattern of state-local financing varies greatly among the states. At the extremes, Hawaii finances public education almost entirely from state funds, while in New Hampshire the state's share is about 5 percent. In general, political culture is the strongest indicator of the degree of state control.[8] The traditional Southern states have a history of centralized or state control of education. In contrast, the moralistic states of the upper Midwest have stressed local control and financing of schools. But funding in most states is becoming more centralized because of political pressure from special interest groups, greater interest by the governor, and the passage of measures such as Proposition 13 that limit the amount of revenues local governments can collect from the property tax.

Even with the growing importance of state governments in school financing, expenditures by local school districts vary considerably because local revenues come from the property tax. As was noted in Chapter 12, the amount of revenue the property tax raises depends to a great extent on the value of property, or the tax base, in the school district. According to a study based on 1986–1987 data from the U.S. Census Bureau, **funding inequities** result in "rich" school districts and "poor" school districts within the same state, literally existing alongside each other. For example, in Indiana the ten wealthiest school districts spent an average of $4,817 per pupil, and the ten poorest districts spent an average of $2,349 per pupil.[9] Districts with valuable residential, commercial, and industrial property have a rich tax base and can easily raise money to finance higher expenditures than districts with a low-valued tax base. Black school children in inner cities and white school children in rural communities live in districts that tend to have schools supported by low-valued tax bases.

Funding inequities can lead to glaring differences in schools, as revealed in a recent comparison between schools in East St. Louis, Illinois, and New Trier High School in suburban Chicago. For example, students in East St. Louis, most of them black, go to school in old buildings with inadequate heating systems, use outdated textbooks, and have no access to college-level advanced placement courses. The average high school teacher's salary is $38,000. Students at New Trier High School, mostly white, have computer labs, an olympic-sized swimming pool, and eighteen advanced placement courses. The average teacher's salary is $59,000.[10]

Controversy over Unequal Funding

Inequities in school district funding have led to considerable political controversy. Some argue that the kind of education children receive should not depend on the tax base of their school districts; all children should have an opportunity to an equal education. The other side argues that effort to equalize school funding is a "Robin Hood" approach, taking money from rich areas of the state and giving it to poor areas, and will result in a leveling down of schools. This debate has flowed into the court system, as do most issues in American politics. A *national* right to equalized funding for education was denied by the U.S. Supreme Court in *San Antonio Independent School District* v. *Rodriguez* (1973). In upholding the Texas school finance system, the Court argued that education is not a fundamental right protected by the Constitution. (This opinion overturned a lower federal court ruling that the Texas system of school finance did violate the equal protection clause of the Fourteenth Amendment because it discriminated against less wealthy districts. In the San Antonio area, the most affluent school district spent nearly twice as much per year, per pupil, as the poorest district.)

It would seem that this decision would end legal challenges to inequities in education funding; in fact, it has not. Rather than litigating in federal courts, plaintiffs turned to state courts and used as the basis for their suits statements in *state constitutions* concerning the state's responsibility to provide education for its citizens. The most recent count is that twenty-five states are being sued for operating what the plaintiffs call unconstitutional school financing systems.

The Kentucky Supreme Court in 1989 declared the state's educational system unconstitutional. The court said the Kentucky legislature must provide funding that provides each child an "adequate" education and the schools throughout the state must be "substantially uniform," or equal.[11] The Kentucky court did more than simply direct the legislature to correct funding inequities; it also said that the legislature must improve the management and quality of Kentucky's public schools.[12] Supreme courts in a number of states—including Montana, New Jersey, Tennessee, and Texas—have ruled their financing systems unconstitutional.

In Michigan it was the legislature and governor, not the courts, that reformed the school financing system. In an extraordinary action in 1993 the legislature passed, and Governor John Engler signed into law, a bill that repealed all school-operating property taxes at the end of the year, nearly $7 billion and 60 percent of all local property taxes. This meant no money would be available to operate schools in 1994–1995. Michigan's political leaders and voters were forced into a position where they had to change the financing system. The legislature passed a bill that would finance schools primarily from an increase in income taxes. But the legislators and governor gave the voters the opportunity to vote in a referendum on a different plan that would fund most of the money for schools through an increase in the sales tax, from 4 to 6 percent. The voters chose the sales tax increase. Early estimates are that state support for public schools will jump to 80 percent, one of the highest in the nation, and all districts are guaranteed a minimum of $4,200 per pupil to spend. Property taxes were reduced by about one-third, and a cap was created on how much districts can raise local taxes to provide additional support for schools in their districts.[13]

With many states moving toward equalized funding, it is appropriate to ask what its impact will be? Malcolm Jewell, referring to changes in Kentucky, predicts:

> The quality of education might still vary because of the quality of teaching, the availability of skilled teachers, the skill with which resources are utilized, the willingness of local schools and teachers to use experimental techniques and (unfortunately) the level of parental support for students. But it would not vary because of tax resources of the district.[14]

DO PUBLIC SCHOOLS PROVIDE A QUALITY EDUCATION?

Widespread concern for the quality of education in the United States started with a 1983 report from the National Commission on Excellence in Education entitled *A*

Nation at Risk: The Imperative for Educational Reform. In dramatic language the report said:

> If an unfriendly foreign power had attempted to impose on America the mediocre educational performance that exists today, we might well have viewed it as an act of war. As it stands, we have allowed this to happen to ourselves.[15]

Declining SAT scores, especially on the verbal test, and high school dropout rates are favorite indicators of the poor performance of public schools (see Figure 13-3).

More than ten years after this report many Americans are still concerned about the state of our public schools and the public's level of education and about how that affects our ability to compete in an increasingly competitive and international marketplace. A 1992 national study of literacy levels found that nearly half of all adults read and write so poorly that the most difficult tasks they can perform include calculating the difference in price between two items and filling out a Social Security form. They cannot write a brief letter explaining an error on a credit card bill or figure out a Saturday departure on a bus schedule. With the disappearance of well-paying assembly-line jobs, where a high level of reading and problem-solving skills are not as important, a person's ability to make a decent living is closely tied to his or her educational background.[16]

State and Local Reforms

All levels of government have been active in debating and adopting educational reforms, but it is state governments that have seized the initiative. State politicians

FIGURE 13-3 Declining Scholastic Aptitude Test scores, 1966–1967 to 1992–1993. [*Digest of Education Statistics, 1994* (Washington, D.C.: National Center for Education Statistics, 1994), p. 49.]

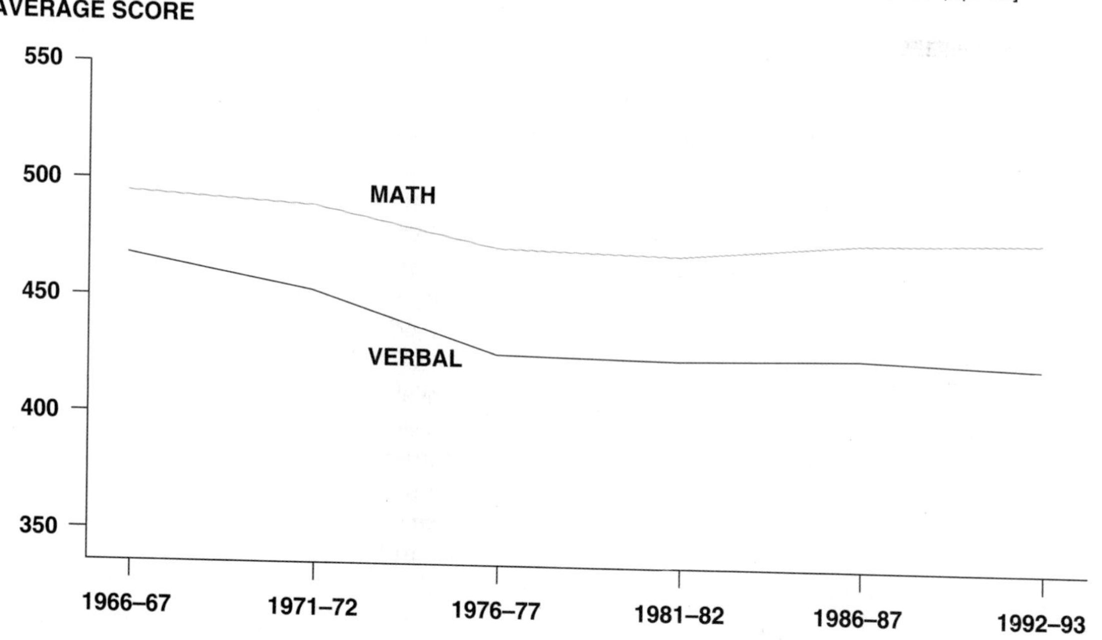

have the authority to solve financing inequities between districts, and they have been sensitive to the demand for **accountability,** that is, the belief that schools should be held responsible for graduating students who have the reading, writing, and calculating skills needed in today's workplace.[17] By the end of the 1980s, nearly all states had tightened curriculum requirements and increased teachers' salaries; many adopted merit pay that allows larger raises for exceptional teachers. New standards such as minimum grade-point average and minimum scores on standardized tests were adopted for college students seeking to enter the teaching profession.

In the 1990s, some states—Alabama, Kentucky, Ohio, and Washington, for example—adopted "comprehensive statewide reforms" where specific goals for student performance are identified, curriculum frameworks to achieve the goals are supported by the state, and tests are developed and administered to measure whether the goals are being met. Teachers and administrators in successful schools will be rewarded, and those in failing schools will be given assistance or may be even penalized.[18]

Many educators and political leaders, including Presidents Ronald Reagan and George Bush, have advocated more radical reforms under the label of **school choice,** meaning that parents and their children could choose any school, public or private, to attend. This market-oriented reform, its advocates contend, would force schools to compete for students. To engage in this competition, public school principals and teachers would be given more freedom to design their own curriculum and teaching strategies. To attract students, schools would have to establish a record demonstrating that their students actually learn. The frequently cited teacher's expression to an uncooperative student that "I get paid, whether you learn this or not" would no longer be true because if a school's students are not performing, its enrollment will drop. And just like a business in the economic marketplace, a school could fail and the principal and teachers would be out of their jobs. Schools, it is hoped, will compete on the basis of quality. Suggestions for financing a market-based school system include a voucher plan whereby schools, again public or private, receive a fixed amount of money from the school district for each student who enrolls.[19]

Objections to school choice are many. Some critics do not want any public money going to private schools, as would be the case under most voucher plans. Others wonder where the "good" schools would come from, especially in big cities where the quality of public schools is uniformly low. Starting a new school, renovating a building, hiring staff, and buying supplies cannot be accomplished overnight.[20] (See "School Vouchers: Bad News, Good News" by Neal Peirce.)

Privatizing, another approach to school reform, is being experimented with in a small number of local school districts, as well as in other government agencies (see Chapter 7). In privatizing, the school board hires a private company to manage a school; the company expects to make a profit in return. EAI (Education Alternatives Incorporated) is one of only a handful of organizations in this new business, initially operating nine schools in Baltimore, Maryland, and one elementary school in Miami Beach, Florida. The Edison Project, a spinoff from Whittle Communications that produces Channel One classroom news shows, has contracted to run three schools in Massachusetts beginning in 1995. EAI and Edison ask for the same amount of money currently spent per pupil and promise improved student performance and increased

School Vouchers: Bad News, Good News

Neal R. Peirce

America's most ambitious school voucher plan to date went down in flames on Nov. 2, 1993. The nay vote on California's Proposition 174, which would have let the parents of 5.5 million children in the state take $2,600 in vouchers to any public or private school of their choice, was a landslide of unexpected proportion—3.3 million against to only 1.5 million in favor.

But if educational establishments across the nation take the vote as an endorsement of doing business as usual, they could be making a big mistake. As California state Sen. Gary K. Hart warned right after the vote, the initiative's decisive defeat "was not a victory but a wake-up call."

Without the massive—and perhaps hard-to-repeat—$12 million negative advertising campaign waged by the California Teachers Association, the vote could have been much closer. The fiscal implications of the ballot initiative were so grave that mainstream Republicans, including Gov. Pete Wilson, opposed it. The measure was sloppily drawn, and many voters in California were clearly worried about a body blow to the state's public education system without commensurate benefits for its children.

But a deep undercurrent of dissatisfaction with the existing public school system, combined with the growing desire of many parents to have more of a say in which schools their children attend, is underscored by the choice, voucher and "charter-school" movements that are gaining popularity in states and cities across the nation.

Other voucher proposals, which would allow public monies to be used for parochial and other private schools, appear to be alive and well in the Connecticut, Florida, Indiana, Kansas, Michigan, New Jersey, Ohio and Pennsylvania legislatures.

Even more significant, however, is the grass-roots action on school choice. Despite bitter opposition from teachers' unions and school boards, 14 states have followed Minnesota's lead in allowing students to select the public schools that they will attend, even if they are in another school district.

What's more, three states—California, Georgia and Minnesota—have launched limited plans to allow panels of parents and teachers to form charter schools, financed by tax dollars, subject to public standards and forbidden to collect tuitions, but in competition with conventional schools.

And the idea of contracting out the operation of whole schools—even entire school systems—to private-sector firms is gaining fast. Last year, for example, a Minnesota-based company, Education Alternatives Inc., took over the operation of nine decaying schools in Baltimore that have a combined enrollment of 4,800 students. The company gets the same $5,918 per pupil that the city's other schools do, and it uses existing teachers under union contract.

Even so, by cutting way back on nonteaching administrative employees, Education Alternatives has found the money to make dramatic physical improvements in the schools it operates, which were formerly plastered with graffiti, riddled with bullet holes and scarred by hundreds of broken windows. The company has equipped the schools with state-of-the-art computers—one for every four students. It's also given teachers some of the instructional tools they have requested (as well as business cards and telephones)—but told them that they'll be held strictly accountable for the quality of their classroom work.

Education Alternatives is running other schools in Florida and is currently negotiating with school systems in Arkansas, California and Wisconsin. Entrepreneur Christopher Whittle's Knoxville (Tenn.)-based Edison Project, which couldn't raise the capital it needed to build a chain of 1,000 low-tuition private schools, is now aiming at management contracts with school districts across the nation.

And in Minneapolis, the school board voted on Nov. 3, 1993, to turn over full management of all city schools to the Public Strategies Group, a consulting firm that specializes in slimmed down, consumer-responsive government organization. The company's president, Peter Hutchinson, a former state finance director and foundation executive, will perform the duties of school superintendent.

The idea of a noneducator from the private sector supervising a city's public school system is viewed as close to revolutionary in educational circles these days. But why not? As Babak Armajani, the chief executive officer of the Public Strategies Group, pointed out, "There is a feeling here in Minnesota and all over the country that the current bureaucratic system of running a school is antiquated."

The harsh fact is that most urban school districts, unlike Minneapolis's, resist change and fail to recognize that parents are rebelling against standardized, top-down, factory-like schools that fail to effectively teach and train their students.

The school choice movement seems likely, as school boards and bureaucracies come under increasing fire, to spread across the country as rapidly as term limits. Moves to contract out the operations of individual schools, or entire systems, seem destined to multiply, too, born of the same impulse to break the monopolistic ways of educational establishments. And chartering new public schools opens the door to competition, inviting the founding of more-responsive and creative schools.

But the public isn't ready to embrace the idea of letting private and parochial schools tap the taxes that are levied to finance public education. Maybe the reluctance stems from a romantic memory of public schools as the great democratic equalizers of American society. Maybe it's rooted in Americans' historic insistence on the clear separation of church and state and on not using public monies to finance sectarian schools.

Whatever the reason, though, the defeat of California's Proposition 174, particularly on the heels of rejection of other voucher proposals by voters in Colorado and Oregon, should bury the idea of vouchers that can be carried outside the public school systems. The real hope lies in today's outpouring of effort to create competition where we want and need it—within the public's own schools.

Source: National Journal, December 1, 1993, p. 2901 Reprinted with permission of National Journal.

---

capital investment in the schools. They hope to make a profit by improved management, for example, contracting out various services and economies of scale in purchasing. In Baltimore, EAI used lower-paid interns to replace unionized teachers' assistants.[21] True privatizing would give the manager authority to hire and fire teachers, but this has been strongly objected to by teachers' unions. Thus far, existing teachers' contracts have been honored. It is too early to tell if privatizing, or "contract management" as some prefer to call it, will succeed. In Baltimore, early reports indicated that EAI provided better janitorial, accounting, and food services, but progress in student performance is not clear. Consequently, the school board renegotiated its contract with EAI to require improvements in student attendance and achievement.[22] The effect of this will never be known because a financial crisis in Baltimore's school system forced the board to ask EAI to accept a $7 million cut in its fees. EAI refused and the board canceled its contract.

Federal Reforms

The reform movement is not entirely a state and local venture. In 1989, President Bush and the fifty state governors convened the President's Education Summit with Governors at the University of Virginia. This conference led to the adoption of six national goals for education, to be achieved by the year 2000. These six goals, now expanded to eight, have been adopted in national legislation known as **Goals 2000: Educate America Act.** The eight goals are listed below:

- *School readiness.* All children will start school ready to learn.
- *School completion.* The high school graduation rate will increase to at least 90 percent.
- *Student achievement and citizenship.* Students will leave grades 4, 8, and 12 having demonstrated competency in English, math, science, foreign languages, civics and government, economics, arts, history, and geography; every school will ensure that all students learn to use their minds well so that they are prepared for responsible citizenship, further learning, and productive employment.
- *Teacher education and professional development.* All teachers will have access to programs for the continued improvement of their professional skills.
- *Mathematics and science.* American students will be the first in the world in math and science achievement.
- *Adult literacy and lifelong learning.* Every adult American will be literate and possess the knowledge and skills to compete in the global economy and to be responsible citizens.
- *Safe, disciplined, and alcohol- and drug-free schools.* Every school will be free of alcohol, drugs, and violence, and will offer a disciplined environment conducive to learning.
- *Parental participation.* Every school will promote partnerships that will increase parental involvement in promoting the social, emotional, and academic growth of children.[23]

Richard Riley, President Clinton's secretary of education and former governor of South Carolina, says that the "federal role is not one of mandating but of encouraging reform"[24] to achieve these goals. The Goals 2000 Act also establishes a National Education Standards and Improvement Council (NESIC) that will develop, among other things, *voluntary* national academic content and student performance standards to show "what constitutes a world-class education."[25] A state, to receive federal funds appropriated to support the Goals 2000 Act, must develop and implement a plan for the improvement of its elementary and secondary education program. This plan, which must be approved by the U.S. secretary of education, will explain the state's strategies for reaching the national education goals. In keeping with local control of education policy, states do not have to adopt national standards but can develop their own as long as they are comparable to those at the national level.

The future of Goals 2000 is uncertain. Two states (Virginia and New Hampshire) have refused to participate. Conservatives in these states argue that it represents too much federal intrusion into the making of education policy, which should be a state and local responsibility. They contend it encourages a "politically correct" curriculum. Efforts are under way in Congress to stop or at least reduce funding.[26]

HIGHER EDUCATION

The Demand for a College Degree

In response to growing demand for higher education, state support for colleges and universities has expanded greatly since World War II. In 1947, about half of all college students were enrolled in state institutions. By 1968, the figure had risen to 71 percent, and by 1990 to over 80 percent (see Figure 13-4). Increased student demand has meant expanded facilities on existing campuses, the creation of new colleges, and a tremendous increase in the number of community colleges. This, of course, was accomplished by a vast expenditure of state funds. In several states, expansion in the 1960s to meet the "baby boom" was followed by declining enrollments in the 1970s and by legislative cutbacks in funding for higher education. Since the 1980s, college enrollment has been inching ahead, while vocational and technical schools have had substantial increases. The percentage of high school graduates who go on to college has also increased, (see Figure 13-5).

Unlike the administration of elementary and secondary schools, state control of colleges is much more diverse.[27] In some states, such as Wisconsin, there is a single governing board for all universities; in other states, such as Illinois, there are several university systems and several boards. In most cases board members are appointed by the governor, although they are popularly elected in a few states. States with several boards usually have a coordinating panel to review operations of all universities.

The quality of public institutions of higher learning has improved significantly during the last fifty years. The University of California (especially at Berkeley and Los Angeles) and other major state-supported universities stand on an equal footing with the best private institutions in their states. Several states have established "centers of excellence" at their major universities, and special funds have been created to hire eminent scholars.

Financing

State funds account for under half the revenue for public colleges, resulting in varying levels of tuition that students pay (see Table 13-1). It is difficult to discern a

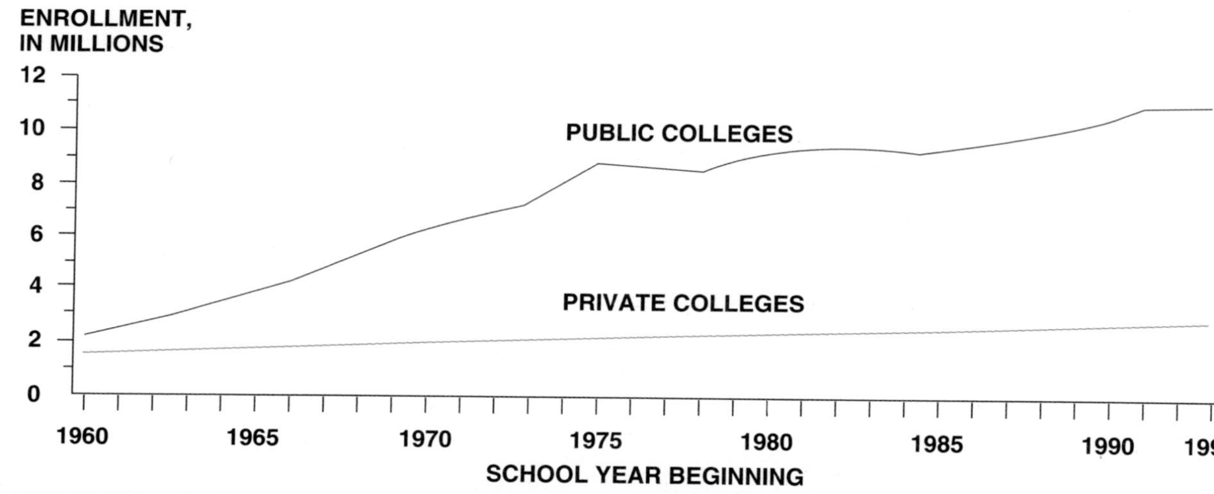

FIGURE 13-4 Enrollment in institutions of higher education, 1960–1961 to 1993–1994. [*Digest of Education Statistics, 1994* (Washington, D.C.: National Center for Education Statistics, 1994), p. 170.]

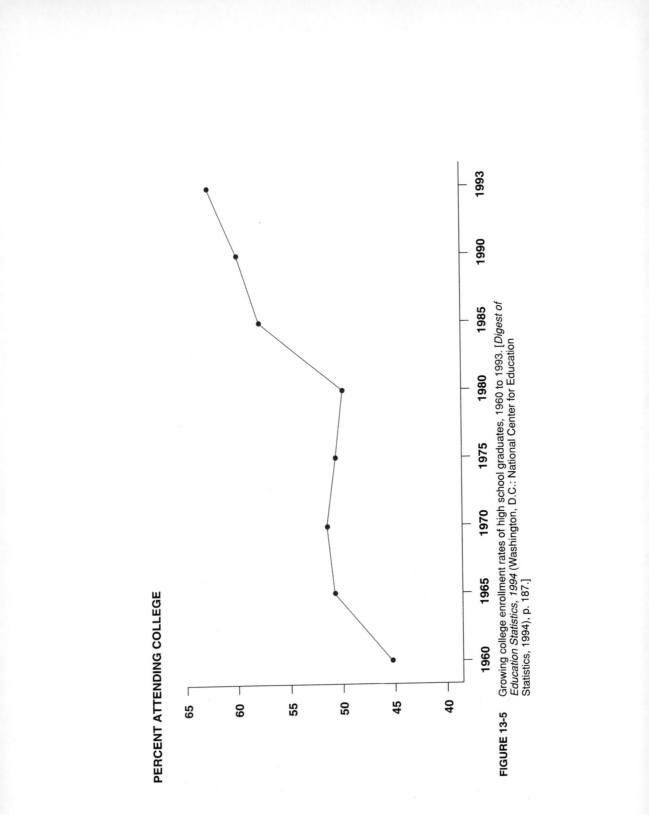

FIGURE 13-5 Growing college enrollment rates of high school graduates, 1960 to 1993. [*Digest of Education Statistics, 1994* (Washington, D.C.: National Center for Education Statistics, 1994), p. 187.]

geographical or regional pattern, although the Northeastern states rank very low in appropriations per student for higher education. In part, this is because well-established private institutions continue to dominate in the Northeast, although Massachusetts made a determined effort to upgrade its state system of higher education until beset by serious financial problems in the late 1980s.

Often there is considerable political conflict among state universities competing for public funds. Faced with serious budget problems, nearly half the states cut their higher-education expenditures in 1991. It was the first time in over thirty years that states appropriated less money for higher education than they had the year before.[28]

Community colleges also offer strong competition for state appropriations. While four-year institutions were coping with cuts in the early 1990s, state support for community colleges was up 13 percent in 1990–1991. Community colleges are popular with state legislators because they emphasize vocational education and also provide an inexpensive way for students to complete their first two years of college close to home before transferring to a four-year institution to complete a bachelor's degree.

Most states give some form of financial assistance to private colleges or to students who are legal residents attending in-state private colleges. Only three states—Arizona, Nevada, and Wyoming, states with few private colleges—do not. Among the more generous states, New York and Illinois have programs for students attending private colleges, and they also make per capita payments to private colleges.

Increasingly, states have developed innovative plans to help parents finance their children's college education. For example, several states allow families to purchase tax-exempt bonds for college savings, and a few offer prepaid-tuition plans at public institutions that allow parents to pay a set sum of money, years in advance, for their children's education.

The Issue of Accountability

Concern over accountability, which has been around for several years in elementary and secondary schools, has reached higher education. Governors and state legislators are asking questions about the efficiency and productivity of colleges and universities. Much of the concern is over program duplication and faculty work load. Legislators in Ohio question, for example, whether their state really needs thirteen Ph.D. programs in history. Faculty work load, in terms of the amount of time spent in the classroom, is a perennial issue. Many citizens and legislators actually believe that a professor who teaches four 3-hour courses is working only 12 hours a week. Of course, the time involved in preparing lectures, grading papers and exams, meeting with students, committee meetings, and research more than fills a 40-hour week. Upon reflection, government officials usually agree that faculty members are not slackers. A more serious issue is how faculty members divide their time between their two most important duties: teaching and advising undergraduate students and doing research. State legislators think professors are spending too much time on research and not enough in the classroom. Legislation has been introduced in a number of states that would increase the amount of time faculty spend on undergraduate education.[29] Public colleges and universities will be forced in the coming years to prove they are using taxpayer funds wisely.

TABLE 13-1 AVERAGE UNDERGRADUATE IN-STATE TUITION AND FEES IN PUBLIC INSTITUTIONS OF HIGHER EDUCATION, 1993–1994

State	Four-year	Two-year
United States	$2,543	$1,114
Alabama	1,983	1,110
Alaska	1,908	1,268
Arizona	1,819	729
Arkansas	1,808	833
California	2,378	345
Colorado	2,262	1,193
Connecticut	3,479	1,398
Delaware	3,684	—
District of Columbia	974	—
Florida	1,784	1,076
Georgia	1,894	972
Hawaii	—	479
Idaho	1,498	914
Illinois	3,029	1,135
Indiana	2,621	1,737
Iowa	2,352	1,612
Kansas	1,921	960
Kentucky	1,913	962
Louisiana	2,182	956
Maine	3,139	1,913
Maryland	3,120	1,676
Massachusetts	4,142	2,361
Michigan	3,481	1,358
Minnesota	2,780	1,858
Mississippi	2,370	939
Missouri	2,475	1,152

SUMMARY

Providing elementary, secondary, and higher education is a major governmental activity. Historically, elementary and secondary education policy has been made by more than 16,000 local school districts, within the general guidelines of the state boards of education, governors, and legislators. The federal government's role was of less importance.

School district funding inequities and public concern over the quality of education in public schools have caused the federal government and especially state governments to become more active participants in the making of education policy. Overall, states are assuming a larger role in financing school systems. They now contribute close to 50 percent of the total revenue for public elementary and secondary schools. And some states, such as Kentucky, have undertaken major reforms to eliminate funding inequities and improve the management and quality of public schools. Almost all states are adopting more and more laws and regulations that school districts must follow. For example, many states have adopted merit pay plans to reward exceptional teachers, have established specific goals for student performance, and have developed tests that measure whether the goals are met. More radical reforms such as school

TABLE 13-1 AVERAGE UNDERGRADUATE IN-STATE TUITION AND FEES IN PUBLIC INSTITUTIONS OF HIGHER EDUCATION, 1993–1994 (*Continued*)

State	Four-year	Two-year
Montana	1,890	1,171
Nebraska	1,939	1,091
Nevada	1,538	822
New Hampshire	3,833	2,261
New Jersey	3,518	1,539
New Mexico	1,731	625
New York	2,921	2,112
North Carolina	1,409	577
North Dakota	2,128	1,634
Ohio	3,259	2,076
Oklahoma	1,645	1,095
Oregon	2,833	1,186
Pennsylvania	4,316	1,671
Rhode Island	3,402	1,546
South Carolina	2,891	1,061
South Dakota	2,288	2,640
Tennessee	1,797	950
Texas	1,503	625
Utah	1,964	1,315
Vermont	5,536	2,793
Virginia	3,639	1,332
Washington	2,337	1,141
West Virginia	1,875	1,247
Wisconsin	2,318	1,557
Wyoming	1,648	872

—Data not reported.

Source: Digest of Education Statistics, 1994 (Washington, D.C.: National Center for Education Statistics, 1994), p. 313.

choice and other forms of privatizing public schools are being discussed and experimented with.

The federal government is encouraging reform through Goals 2000: Educate America Act, which identifies eight national goals for elementary and secondary schools.

States have played an important role in meeting the demand for higher education by creating public two- and four-year colleges and universities. Although state funds on the average account for about half the revenue of public higher educational institutions, the amount of state support and tuition varies considerably from state to state. The quality of public higher education is frequently praised, but more critical questions dealing with efficiency and productivity have been raised recently.

KEY TERMS

Accountability The idea that elementary and secondary schools should be held responsible for graduating students who have the skills needed in today's workplace. In higher education accountability usually refers to efficiency and productivity, specifically program duplication among universities and faculty work load.

Dependent school districts School districts that have no taxing authority and report to another local government unit such as a mayor or county council. Dependent school districts make up about 10 percent of the total number of school districts in the United States; members of their school boards are elected or appointed.

Elementary and Secondary Education Act of 1965 This law significantly expanded the role of the federal government in elementary and secondary education. The most important section of the law, Title I, provided federal funds to local school districts with large numbers of children from low-income families.

Funding inequities Refers to differences in revenues available to school districts to support public education. Because school districts rely on the property tax to raise revenues, districts with a good tax base ("rich districts") can raise and spend more money than districts with a weak tax base ("poor districts").

Goals 2000: Educate America Act An educational reform measure signed into law by President Clinton. It establishes eight national goals for elementary and secondary schools as well as voluntary national academic content and performance standards to achieve these goals.

Independent school districts School districts that are administratively and financially independent of other units of local government. They have taxing authority and their school board members are elected by the voters. Ninety percent of the school districts in the United States are classified as independent.

School choice A market-oriented educational reform that permits parents and their children to choose a public or private school to attend.

REFERENCES

1 Roald F. Campbell and others, *The Organization and Control of American Schools* (Columbus, Ohio: Merrill Publishing Company, 1990), p. 50.

2 *Digest of Educational Statistics, 1994* (Washington, D.C.: National Center for Education Statistics, 1994), p. 1.

3 Jacqueline P. Danzberger and Michael D. Usdan, "Strengthening a Grass Roots American Institution: The School Board," in *School Boards: Changing Local Control,* Patricia F. First and Herbert J. Walberg, eds. (Berkeley, Calif.: McCutchan Publishing Corporation, 1992), pp. 98–99.

4 Campbell and others, *Organization and Control,* p. 81.

5 Ibid., p. 93.

6 Ibid., pp. 91–92.

7 Robert Marshall Wells, "Senate Ends Prayer Filibuster, Clears $12.7 Billion Bill," *Congressional Quarterly Weekly Report,* October 8, 1994, p. 2884.

8 Frederick M. Wirt, "Does Control Follow the Dollar? School Policy, State-Local Linkages, and Political Culture," *Publius* 10 (1980), pp. 69–88.

9 Ibid., p. 749.

10 Jill Zuckman, "The Next Education Crisis: Equalizing School Funds," *Congressional Quarterly Weekly Report,* March 27, 1993, p. 749. In part, this article by Zuckman is based on Jonathan Kozol, *Savage Inequalities* (New York: HarperCollins Publishers, 1992).

11 Malcolm E. Jewell, "The Supreme Court, Kentucky's School," *Comparative State Politics* 10 (August 1989), p. 1.

12 Ibid., pp. 4–5.
13 Robert J. Kleine, "Michigan: Rethinking Fiscal Priorities," in *The Fiscal Crisis of the States,* Steven D. Gold, ed. (Washington, D.C.: Georgetown University Press, 1995), pp. 318–321.
14 Jewell, "Kentucky Schools," p. 3.
15 National Commission on Excellence in Education, *A Nation at Risk* (Washington, D.C.: Department of Education, 1983), p. 5.
16 Mary Jordan, "90 Million Lack Simple Literacy," *Washington Post,* September 9, 1993, p. A1.
17 Campbell and others, *Organization and Control,* p. 82.
18 Paul T. Hill, *Reinventing Public Education* (Santa Monica, Calif.: Rand, 1995), pp. 75–78.
19 A concise statement of the market-based approach to education can be found in John E. Chubb and Eric A. Hanushek, "Reforming Educational Reform," in *Setting National Priorities: Policy for the Nineties,* Henry J. Aaron, ed. (Washington, D.C.: The Brookings Institution, 1990), pp. 213–247.
20 Hill, *Reinventing,* pp. 82–83.
21 Charles Mathesian, "The Precarious Politics of Privatizing Schools," *Governing* 7 (June 1994), pp. 46–51.
22 Jean Thompson and JoAnna Daemmrich, "Mayor Orders Changes in EAI Contract," *The Sun,* March 17, 1995, p. 1A.
23 Richard W. Riley, "Redefining the Federal Role in Education," *Journal of Law and Education* 23 (Summer 1994), pp. 321–322.
24 Ibid., p. 337.
25 Ibid., p. 324.
26 Sarah Lindenfeld, "Goals 2000 Plan Slips from Consensus to Controversy," *The Sun* (Education), July 23, 1995, p. 4.
27 Frederick Wirt and Samuel Gove, "Education," in *Politics in the American States,* 5th ed., Virginia Gray, Herbert Jacob, and Robert B. Albritton (Boston: Scott, Foresman/Little, Brown, 1990), p. 471.
28 Scott Jaschik, "State Funds for Higher Education Drop in Year," *Chronicle of Higher Education,* November 6, 1991, p. 1.
29 Charles Mathesian, "Higher Ed: The No-Longer-Sacred Cow," *Governing* 8 (July 1995), pp. 20–26.

14

SOCIAL WELFARE POLICY

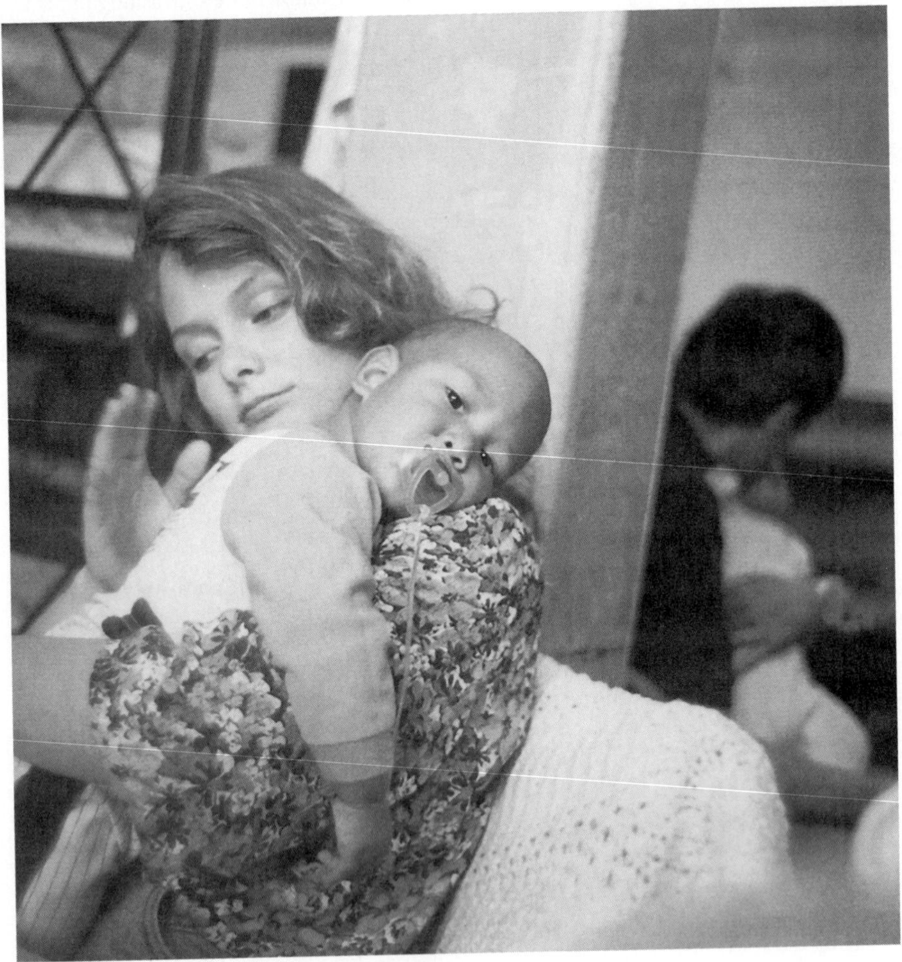

Mark Ludak/Impact Visuals

The greater importance of local and state governments over the federal government in education policymaking is not duplicated in social welfare policy. Local governments traditionally provided services to the poor, but the federal government moved in strongly beginning in 1935, and states have been playing a larger role since the late 1980s. The state role may continue to grow if national welfare reform proposals are enacted into law in the mid-1990s by the Republican-dominated U.S. Congress.

Social welfare policymaking illustrates better than most other policy areas the complex interrelationships that can occur among levels of government in the United States. **Social welfare** policies are those "that directly affect the income, services, and opportunities available to people who are aged, poor, disabled, ill, or otherwise vulnerable."[1] They emerge from a maze of congressional committees, state legislatures, federal and state executive branch agencies, and 1,500 county welfare departments. In recent years, social welfare policy has been in a state of change at both the federal and state levels. In fact, almost anything said about it today may be outdated tomorrow.

Social welfare policy is of three types: public assistance, social insurance, and social services. **Public assistance** programs pay benefits out of general-revenue funds to people who meet a legal definition of "poor." It is these programs that politicians and voters think of when the term *welfare* is used (see the Scholarly Box entitled Who Are the Poor?). Examples are Aid to Families with Dependent Children (AFDC), food stamps, Medicaid, and state general assistance programs. **Social insurance** programs are designed to prevent poverty and are financed by contributions from employees and employers. Employees are then entitled to benefits regardless of their personal wealth. Examples are Social Security, unemployment compensation, and workers' compensation. (Public assistance and social insurance are frequently referred to as income maintenance programs.) **Social services** are provided to those with special needs. Examples are day care, job training, mental health care, and vocational rehabilitation.[2] This chapter focuses on how the poor are identified; it describes major social welfare programs and discusses the welfare reform issue.

MAJOR SOCIAL WELFARE PROGRAMS

A description of a few social welfare programs will help to examine federal, state, and local responsibilities.

Unemployment Compensation

Unemployment compensation, sometimes called unemployment insurance, provides benefits to regularly employed persons who become involuntarily unemployed and are able and willing to accept suitable employment in another job when one is available.[3] In other words, it provides some income to those who are temporarily unemployed. Wisconsin, in 1932, established the first unemployment compensation program in the United States. The Social Security Act, signed into law by President Franklin Roosevelt in 1935, did not establish one national unemployment compensation program but contained a tax incentive to encourage states to establish and administer their own programs, which the states did. Although there are general federal guidelines that a

SCHOLARLY BOX

WHO ARE THE POOR?

Attempts to measure the number of poor people in the United States are complicated by the question of whether poverty should be defined in absolute terms or as relative deprivation. That is, are people poor when their incomes fall below a certain level, or are they poor when measured against an acceptable standard of living in their community? The most widely accepted standard follows the former approach by establishing a **poverty threshold** or poverty line. The Bureau of the Census established the present threshold over thirty years ago. It is adjusted annually for inflation and represents what a family of four needs to spend for an "austere" standard of living (the threshold was $3,100 in 1963 and $14,335 in 1992). It is based on pretax income only and does not include the value of in-kind benefits such as employer-provided health insurance, food stamps, or Medicaid. In 1992, approximately 36.9 million people were below the official government poverty level; this was 14.5 percent of the population (see Figure 14-1).

A recent study by the National Research Council identified a number of problems with the current way of defining poverty. In particular, recent changes in American society are not reflected in underlying assumptions of the poverty threshold. For example, more mothers, whether single or married, are in the labor force and must pay for child care, an expense that was not even considered when the poverty threshold formula was developed thirty years ago. Also, it does not reflect the Social Security payroll tax that lowers disposable income or in-kind benefits that increase disposable income. Suggestions made by the National Research Council include:

- *Setting the poverty threshold.* A poverty-level budget should include the cost of basic goods and services—food, clothing, and shelter, including utilities. This sum should be increased by a modest amount for other goods and services such as personal care, household supplies, and non-work-related transportation, and should be adjusted annually.
- *Defining family resources.* Family resources should include money income and in-kind benefits such as food stamps and subsidized housing. It should exclude income and payroll taxes, if any, child care and other work-related expenses, and medical care expenditures, including health insurance premiums.[4]

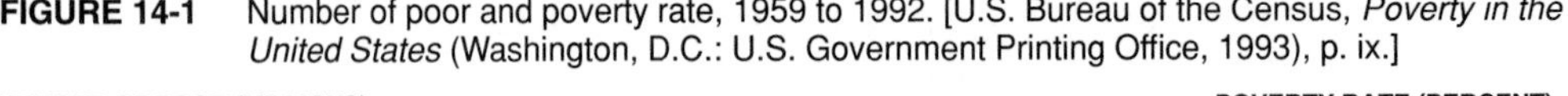

FIGURE 14-1 Number of poor and poverty rate, 1959 to 1992. [U.S. Bureau of the Census, *Poverty in the United States* (Washington, D.C.: U.S. Government Printing Office, 1993), p. ix.]

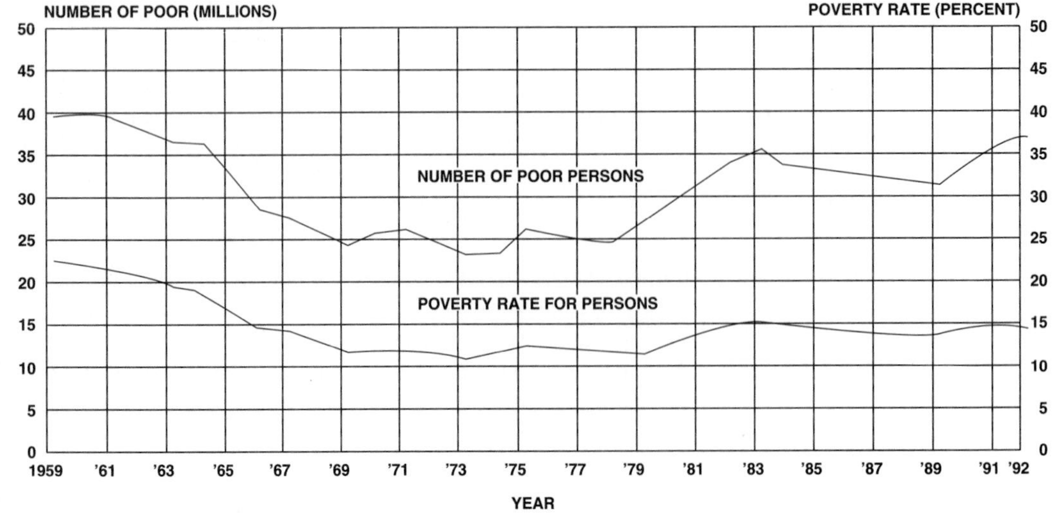

This proposed poverty measure would have two effects: (1) Depending on the data used, the percentage of poor in the United States would increase from 14.5 to 15 or 16 percent, perhaps even to 19 percent. (2) Poverty rates would be higher for families with one or more workers (the "working poor"), higher for families that lack health insurance coverage, and lower for families that receive public assistance.[5]

state must follow, they have some leeway in creating their own unemployment compensation programs. State programs are financed by taxes paid by employers and collected by the states. (The money, however, is deposited in the unemployment trust fund in the U.S. Department of the Treasury!) States determine the amount and duration of benefits, establish eligibility requirements, take claims, and pay benefits. The federal government requires states to operate a program that is "fairly administered and financially secure"[6] and offers other services such as job counseling and placement. Occasionally, during a recession, Congress will authorize and help finance extended benefits for the unemployed who have exhausted benefits under state programs. Unemployment compensation, in even the relatively good economy of 1993, is a large program: Average weekly insured unemployment in that year was 2.6 million persons, and benefit payments totaled $34.0 billion. The average weekly benefit was $180, and the average duration of benefits was 15.9 weeks.[7]

Aid to Families with Dependent Children

Aid to Families with Dependent Children (AFDC), which also originated in the Social Security Act of 1935 as Aid to Dependent Children, provides "cash assistance to poor families so that children can continue to be cared for in their own homes."[8] The vast majority of these children live with their mothers only. AFDC is the largest and most controversial of the federally assisted welfare programs. In 1992, the average monthly number of families on AFDC was about 4.8 million, and the average monthly payment per family was $373, actually a decrease from the 1991 level of $390 (see Table 14-1). States are reimbursed by the federal government up to a maximum amount, and anything beyond that must be financed from their own funds. The federal government pays about 55 percent of total AFDC spending; the remainder comes from the states. But the percentage the federal government pays in each state varies considerably, ranging from 50 percent in several states to a high of close to 80 percent in Mississippi. States with low per capita incomes receive more federal assistance.

Each state determines its own standard of need based on estimates of what it would cost families of various sizes to meet the cost of basic food, clothing, and shelter. States also set benefit levels at whatever they want, but are not required to pay benefits at 100 percent of need.[9] Because of this discretion, benefit payments vary greatly among the states. California, with an average payment of $590 per family in 1992, has

TABLE 14-1 AVERAGE MONTHLY NUMBER OF FAMILIES AND RECIPIENTS AND TOTAL AMOUNT OF PAYMENTS, 1992

State	Aid to Families with Dependent Children					
	Average monthly number of—			Amount of payments		
	Families	Recipients		Total (in thousands)	Monthly average per—	
		Total	Children		Family	Recipient
Total	4,829,094	13,773,319	9,302,846	$21,655,881	$373.71	$131.03
Alabama	51,033	141,915	100,878	81,421	132.95	47.81
Alaska	11,161	33,106	20,985	91,610	683.98	230.60
Arizona	65,457	185,045	128,777	231,821	295.13	104.40
Arkansas	26,760	74,601	53,068	60,596	188.70	67.69
California	819,227	2,341,342	1,628,512	5,813,961	591.41	206.93
Colorado	42,177	123,090	82,231	160,646	317.40	108.76
Connecticut	55,897	157,971	105,823	372,963	556.03	196.75
Delaware	10,907	26,920	18,223	36,274	277.14	112.29
District of Columbia	22,768	60,514	42,456	101,794	372.58	140.18
Florida	236,265	643,647	443,749	673,609	237.59	87.21
Georgia	138,167	392,996	271,818	414,903	250.24	87.98
Hawaii	16,978	51,793	34,575	120,551	591.72	193.96
Idaho	7,462	19,987	13,439	23,545	262.93	98.17
Illinois	228,113	684,395	469,824	918,365	335.49	111.82
Indiana	70,052	201,592	134,475	214,394	255.04	88.63
Iowa	37,038	102,278	66,877	164,243	369.54	133.82
Kansas	29,048	85,321	57,209	117,123	336.00	114.39
Kentucky	83,314	229,410	147,068	212,954	213.00	77.36
Louisiana	91,835	271,616	194,141	188,452	171.01	57.82
Maine	23,771	67,573	42,079	118,088	413.98	145.63
Maryland	80,199	221,482	149,468	336,274	349.41	126.52
Massachusetts	111,908	314,834	208,806	712,112	530.28	188.49
Michigan	225,558	672,661	439,974	1,150,026	424.88	142.47
Minnesota	64,420	193,201	126,059	387,042	500.67	166.94
Mississippi	60,745	176,516	127,230	88,737	121.73	41.89
Missouri	86,383	253,418	166,148	278,289	268.47	91.51
Montana	11,111	32,679	21,165	44,756	335.67	114.13

one of the highest payment levels, while Mississippi has one of the lowest, with an average payment of $120.

Political scientists have looked at the question of why some states use a greater share of state and local funds to augment the federal contribution to AFDC. This is called a state's welfare effort and is the ratio of state and local funds used for AFDC to total state personal income. According to Robert Albritton, a state's income level is not a strong indicator of welfare effort. He sees state population size as the major

TABLE 14-1 AVERAGE MONTHLY NUMBER OF FAMILIES AND RECIPIENTS AND TOTAL AMOUNT OF PAYMENTS, 1992 (Continued)

	Aid to Families with Dependent Children					
	Average monthly number of—			Amount of payments		
		Recipients			Monthly average per—	
State	Families	Total	Children	Total (in thousands)	Family	Recipient
Nebraska	16,662	48,362	32,731	64,738	323.78	111.55
Nevada	12,161	32,999	22,908	39,523	270.84	99.81
New Hampshire	10,670	28,656	18,200	53,485	417.72	155.54
New Jersey	126,574	352,784	241,110	509,788	335.63	120.42
New Mexico	29,486	89,949	58,310	101,810	287.73	94.32
New York	402,969	1,130,712	750,213	2,555,499	528.47	188.34
North Carolina	124,419	320,439	214,011	330,334	221.25	85.91
North Dakota	6,498	18,499	11,978	26,910	345.13	121.22
Ohio	263,432	744,646	486,785	979,125	309.73	109.57
Oklahoma	47,688	137,123	93,501	165,716	289.59	100.71
Oregon	41,531	115,831	76,308	199,436	400.18	143.48
Pennsylvania	201,976	597,613	399,603	921,608	380.25	128.51
Rhode Island	21,470	59,876	39,260	127,097	493.31	176.89
South Carolina	50,549	141,182	100,913	116,973	192.84	69.04
South Dakota	7,231	20,346	14,344	25,250	291.01	103.42
Tennessee	97,877	276,931	188,340	203,629	173.37	61.28
Texas	270,144	766,092	534,443	509,537	157.18	55.43
Utah	18,099	52,273	34,636	74,786	344.34	119.22
Vermont	10,054	28,952	17,703	66,730	553.12	192.07
Virginia	71,763	190,846	130,744	220,526	256.08	96.29
Washington	97,608	277,015	178,196	560,131	478.21	168.50
West Virginia	40,787	118,909	73,624	119,906	244.98	84.03
Wisconsin	81,272	242,205	139,283	454,510	466.04	156.38
Wyoming	6,738	18,974	12,642	26,714	330.38	117.33

Source: Social Security Bulletin, Annual Statistical Supplement, 1994 (Washington, D.C.: Social Security Administration, 1994), p. 344.

determining factor. Albritton suggests that in states with large urban areas, "the size of the pool of persons eligible for welfare assistance appears to have a dynamic effect in determining the proportion of the population admitted to welfare assistance categories."[10] Robert Brown has extended this analysis by examining the effect of political parties on welfare effort. He concludes that state welfare effort is greatest in states where the Democratic party is in control *and* when the coalition of groups supporting the Democratic and Republican parties is class-based, resembling the parties as they existed during the New Deal period of Franklin Roosevelt (in other words, when the

Democratic party draws its support from Catholics, low-income persons, union members, and females, and the Republican party has its strength among Protestants, high-income persons, and college graduates). Brown identifies a number of states that had class-based parties between 1976 and 1988, including Vermont, Massachusetts, New Mexico, Minnesota, Washington, and Oregon.[11]

Benefit levels, as opposed to welfare effort, appear to be closely tied to the wealth of a state and its political culture. States with high benefit levels tend to have moralistic political cultures, and those at the bottom tend to have traditionalistic cultures.

In part, AFDC is controversial because of its cost, which was approximately $22 billion in 1992. Even controlling for inflation, cost has increased dramatically (AFDC cost $12.5 billion in 1980). A more important explanation of why AFDC is at the center of controversy is the public's perception that too many AFDC children are born to unmarried parents, some of whom are even teenagers, and the parents become dependent on AFDC rather than finding a job and supporting themselves. Many of these popular perceptions are not entirely accurate—for example, teenage mothers make up only 8 percent of AFDC parents—but there is enough truth in them that they have fueled a continuing debate on reforming welfare, which will be discussed in the next section.

Food Stamps and Medicaid

The Food Stamp Act passed Congress and was signed into law by President Lyndon Johnson in 1964. Of course, it has been amended many times over the years. The **food stamp program** is designed to improve nutrition in low-income families and, more than unemployment compensation and AFDC, is truly a federal program. Food stamps are coupons that can be redeemed at grocery stores for food. The federal government pays for the entire cost of the coupons and shares the cost of administering the programs with the states. The food stamp program is administered by the Department of Agriculture and state and local welfare offices. National eligibility standards and benefit levels exist. States have much less discretion with this program but are involved in administering it because they certify a person's eligibility. Food stamp recipients usually receive other forms of public assistance; in 1992, 47 percent received AFDC and 6 percent received unemployment compensation, among others.[12] The average number of persons participating in the food stamp program in 1993 was 26.9 million, and food stamp expenditures were $22.8 billion.

Medicaid, established in Social Security amendments of 1965, provides medical assistance for individuals and families with low incomes. In terms of federal-state cooperation, this program resembles AFDC. Both share its costs, which in 1993 totaled $125.8 billion ($72.3 billion paid in federal expenditures and $53.5 billion in state funds). In 1993, 33.4 million people received medical care under Medicaid. Within broad federal guidelines, each state establishes eligibility standards, type of services covered, and the rate of payment for services by health care providers, which is usually below what is charged other patients. (AFDC recipients and children whose families are at or below the federal poverty level are automatically eligible for Medicaid.)

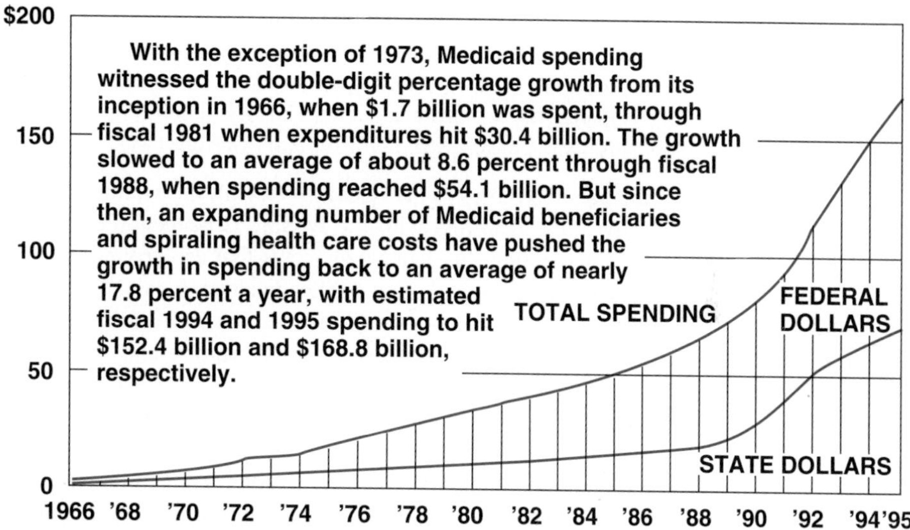

$200
150
100
50
0
With the exception of 1973, Medicaid spending witnessed the double-digit percentage growth from its inception in 1966, when $1.7 billion was spent, through fiscal 1981 when expenditures hit $30.4 billion. The growth slowed to an average of about 8.6 percent through fiscal 1988, when spending reached $54.1 billion. But since then, an expanding number of Medicaid beneficiaries and spiraling health care costs have pushed the growth in spending back to an average of nearly 17.8 percent a year, with estimated fiscal 1994 and 1995 spending to hit $152.4 billion and $168.8 billion, respectively.
TOTAL SPENDING
FEDERAL DOLLARS
STATE DOLLARS
1966 '68 '70 '72 '74 '76 '78 '80 '82 '84 '86 '88 '90 '92 '94'95

FIGURE 14-2 Increase in Medicaid costs (dollar amounts in billions). ("The Blossoming of Medicaid," *Congressional Quarterly Weekly Report,* June 10, 1995, p. 1638. Reprinted by permission of Congressional Quarterly, Inc.)

In terms of social welfare policies, Medicaid is the most expensive welfare program in the United States, and its cost has been increasing rapidly, claiming a growing share of what at best are small increases in states' revenues (see Figure 14-2).

ENDING WELFARE AS WE KNOW IT

"Ending welfare as we know it" expresses the sentiment of many voters and political leaders during the 1990s. Donald Norris puts the problem into some perspective:

> . . . [welfare] is a solution to the problem of poverty, but it is also a persistent problem in itself. For welfare is an inadequate response to the problem of poverty; it is perceived to neither increase income enough to end poverty nor encourage its recipients to stand up and leave it on their own. It invites reform.

Differing Views of the Causes of Poverty

How welfare should be reformed is determined primarily by one's view of the causes of poverty, and three of the more popular explanations are summarized below:[13]

- *Victim of the system.* The poor are no different than the nonpoor; they simply lack the opportunities for education, job training, and decent housing. If they had the opportunities, they would take advantage of them. Poverty is caused by defects in the American economy, which is deficient in well-paying jobs, and an American society that still discriminates against minorities and women.
- *Welfare dependency.* The present welfare system provides people with disincentives to work. They are encouraged to stay on welfare because policies guarantee

a rather generous standard of living if a person takes advantage of available programs, from AFDC to food stamps. Consequently, there is no incentive to work.

Culture of poverty. The value system of poor people disregards traditional values such as the "work ethic, sexual chastity, deferred gratification, and family responsibility,"[14] Poor people will remain poor until they adopt these traditional values.

Liberals tend to associate themselves with the victim of the system view, and conservatives are identified with the welfare dependency or culture of poverty view, or both. It is certainly the latter two views that are driving welfare reform today. However, a recent survey of the public discovered that although most Americans feel poverty is caused more by a lack of individual effort than by circumstances, they also believe that improving and expanding education and job training is the best way to move people off welfare. In fact, a majority favors spending more money in the short run if it would help people leave the welfare system.[15]

Welfare reform has been on everyone's agenda for some time. During the past ten years, two important changes at the national level have affected the states. The first is the Family Support Act of 1988, and the second is simply called Section 1115 waivers.

Family Support Act of 1988

The Family Support Act of 1988 was signed into law by President Ronald Reagan and contains a new program called JOBS (Job Opportunities and Basic Skills). **JOBS** is a "welfare employment program that provides education, training, and employment services"[16] to help AFDC families become economically self-sufficient. States must meet overall participation rates of nonexempt AFDC recipients that start at 7 percent and increase in future years. (Recipients who cannot work because of illness or some other incapacity are exempt.) Federal financial support was increased for state employment programs and child care; the latter is particularly important if single parents are to find jobs. However, states must match federal funds with their own funding, anywhere from 50 to 20 percent. A ten-state study found that use of federal funds in 1991 and 1992 varied considerably, ranging from 100 percent of those available to New York to 30 percent in Tennessee. Most states used 60 to 80 percent of the funds available to them. Tight state budgets in 1991 and 1992 may have hindered some states from obtaining all of their federal allocation, and some states, such as Tennessee, continued a pattern of spending little money on AFDC and welfare employment programs.[17]

It is unknown at this time how successful JOBS will be. What is clear, as Diana DiNitto notes, is that the welfare problem has been redefined "from poverty—being poor and lacking opportunity—to dependency—not having a job and the need for greater incentives to self-sufficiency."[18]

Section 1115 Waivers

Section 1115 waivers are based on an obscure provision in 1962 amendments to the Social Security Act that allows states to experiment with welfare reform through "demonstration projects." States interested in demonstration projects must obtain a Section 1115 waiver from the U.S. Department of Health and Human Services. States were not encouraged to apply for waivers until the Reagan administration, and they did not appear in any great numbers until the Bush and Clinton administrations.[19] Although the waiver process has been slow and cumbersome, by 1995 over fifty demonstration projects were operating in twenty-seven states. These waivers allow states to try things that federal rules would normally prohibit. Wisconsin with seven projects and Illinois with six were early leaders among the states.[20] Demonstration projects have a number of benefits: (1) States have more freedom to create programs for their unique circumstances and to find out what works and what doesn't, (2) states can proceed with welfare reform without waiting for the federal government to act, and (3) innovative and successful state ideas can become part of any national welfare reform.[21] It should be underscored that Section 1115 waivers are not designed for broad-scale reform but for testing new ideas and strategies.

What kinds of programs are states experimenting with? Two in Wisconsin and one in New York have attracted national attention. Wisconsin's Learnfare program reduces AFDC benefits for families with teenagers who do not attend school regularly. If teens fail to attend, and do not have a good reason, they are not counted in determining their family's benefit payment. The goal, of course, is to improve school attendance and increase graduation rates. Wisconsin's other program is called Work Not Welfare. It is used in two counties and requires AFDC recipients to sign an agreement that they will work for their benefits, which are limited to twenty-four months. Recipients must take a job or participate in education and training. Education and training is limited to twelve months after which the recipient must take a job for pay in the private sector or for the government in exchange for benefits.[22]

New York's Child Assistance Program (CAP) is designed as an alternative to AFDC for single-parent families. Waivers from the federal government allow CAP participants who get jobs to keep their welfare benefits (current federal regulations require that benefits be reduced dollar for dollar against earnings). In addition, CAP families receive more intensive and personalized services from a social worker, and the state ensures that the absent parent makes child support payments.[23]

Many of these programs are so new that they have not yet been systematically evaluated. Early evidence in Wisconsin (1992–1993) found that 97 percent of Learnfare teens complied with school attendance requirements, and CAP families have a 27 percent higher income than families not in CAP. What effect these programs will have on welfare dependency is a long-term research question. It is clear, however, that efforts to help welfare recipients find and keep jobs—which may involve training classes, placement services, child care, and additional administrative oversight—are more expensive, at least in the short run, than simply paying benefits.

SUMMARY

The federal government is the principal developer and funder of social welfare programs. But state and local governments are important, also. They assist in financing these programs and play a meaningful role in their administration.

In 1992, the federal government's poverty threshold for a family of four was $14,335. Approximately 36.9 million people, 14.5 percent of the population, were below the official poverty level.

This chapter centered on income-maintenance programs such as unemployment compensation, which provides income to those who have been working but are temporarily unemployed, and Medicaid, which provides medical care for low-income individuals and families. One of the most controversial programs is Aid to Families with Dependent Children.

A continuing issue in American politics is welfare reform. One side argues that the poor are victims of the American system, a system that does not have enough well-paying jobs or has denied them opportunities to better themselves. Others argue that the poor have grown dependent on welfare programs that are too generous or they have adopted a value system that denies traditional values such as hard work and family responsibility.

This debate has produced significant attempts to reform welfare programs, especially AFDC. The JOBS program hopes to reduce the number of families on AFDC by providing services that may help them to become economically self-sufficient, and Section 1115 waivers allow states to experiment with their own ideas on how AFDC can be changed.

KEY TERMS

Aid to Families with Dependent Children (AFDC) Provides cash assistance to poor families so that children can be cared for at home. It is one of the most controversial social welfare programs.

Food stamp program Designed to improve the nutrition of low-income families. Food stamps are coupons, paid for by the federal government, that recipients can redeem at grocery stores for food.

JOBS (Job Opportunities and Basic Skills) A program created in the Family Support Act of 1988 that provides education, training, and employment services to help AFDC families become economically self-sufficient.

Medicaid A federal program adopted in 1965 that provides medical assistance to individuals and families with low incomes. Federal and state governments share in the cost of Medicaid. Within federal guidelines, each state establishes its own program.

Poverty threshold The amount of money a family of four needs to spend ($14,335 in 1992) to maintain an "austere" standard of living. Those below this threshold are officially defined as poor by the federal government.

Public assistance Welfare programs such as AFDC and food stamps that pay benefits out of general-revenue funds to individuals who meet the legal definition of poor.

Section 1115 waiver A provision in 1962 amendments to the Social Security Act that allows states to experiment with welfare reform through "demonstration projects" by exempting these projects from normal federal regulations.

Social insurance Welfare programs such as unemployment compensation and Social Security that are financed by contributions from employees and employers.

Social services Welfare programs that assist those with special needs such as day care for their children and job training.

Social welfare Government policies that affect the income, services, and opportunities available to the poor, disabled, ill, or otherwise vulnerable.

Unemployment compensation Provides financial benefits to employed persons who become involuntarily and temporarily unemployed.

REFERENCES

1 Diana M. DiNitto, *Social Welfare: Politics and Public Policy,* 4th ed. (Needham Heights, Mass.: Allyn & Bacon, 1995), p. 3.

2 Ibid., pp. 3–4.

3 "Unemployment Insurance," *Social Security Bulletin* 56 (Winter 1993), p. 19.

4 Constance and Robert T. Michael, eds., *Measuring Poverty: A New Approach* (Summary and Recommendations) (Washington, D.C.: National Academy Press, 1995), pp. 7–11.

5 Ibid., p. 11.

6 "Unemployment Insurance," *Social Security Bulletin* 56 (Winter 1993), p. 19.

7 *Social Security Bulletin, Annual Statistical Supplement, 1994* (Washington, D.C.: Social Security Administration, 1994), p. 329.

8 DiNitto, *Social Welfare,* p. 167.

9 Clarke E. Cochran and others, *American Public Policy,* 4th ed. (New York: St. Martin's Press, 1993), p. 223.

10 Robert B. Albritton, "Social Services: Health and Welfare," in *Politics in the American States,* 5th ed., Virginia Gray, Herbert Jacob, and Robert B. Albritton, eds. (Glenview, Ill.: Scott, Foresman/Little, Brown, 1990), p. 430.

11 Robert D. Brown, "Party Cleavages and Welfare Effort in the American States," *American Political Science Review* 89 (March 1995), pp. 23–33.

12 DiNitto, *Social Welfare,* p. 219.

13 These categories and descriptions are based on Ted George Goertzel and John Hart, "New Jersey's $64 Question," in *The Politics of Welfare Reform,* Donald F. Norris and Lyke Thompson, eds. (Thousand Oaks, Calif.: Sage Publications, 1995), pp. 122–123. Also useful was Clarke E. Cochran and others, *American Public Policy,* pp. 216–218.

14 Goertzel and Hart, "New Jersey," p. 122.

15 Geoffrey Garin, Guy Molyneux, and Linda Divall, "Public Attitudes Toward Welfare Reform," *Social Policy* 25 (Winter 1994), pp. 44–49.

16 Jan L. Hagen and Irene Lurie, "Implementing JOBS: From the Rose Garden to Reality" 40 (July 1993), p. 523.

17 Ibid., p. 525.

18 DiNitto, *Social Welfare,* p. 185.

19 Kitty Dumas, "States Bypassing Congress in Reforming Welfare," *Congressional Quarterly Weekly Report,* April 11, 1992, pp. 951–952.

20 "Welfare by Waiver," *Public Welfare* (Winter 1995), p. 4.

21 Ibid.

22 These programs are described in Thomas J. Corbett, "Welfare Reform in Wisconsin," in *The Politics of Welfare Reform,* Donald F. Norris and Lyke Thompson, eds. (Thousand Oaks, Calif.: Sage Publications, 1995), pp. 24–25; and Jeffrey L. Katz, "Putting Recipients to Work Will Be the Toughest Job," *Congressional Quarterly Weekly Report,* July 8, 1995, p. 2003.

23 Diane Baillargeon, "New York's Waiver Experiences," *Public Welfare* (Winter 1995), pp. 21–25.

15

CRIME, THE POLICE, AND CORRECTIONS

Librado Romero/New York Times Pictures

Dealing with crime is a $60 billion annual business for state and local governments.[1] Soaring Medicaid and state prison costs have made up the largest increases in state budgets in the 1990s. There were 1.2 million full-time state and local employees in police and correction agencies across the country in the early 1990s. Overwhelmingly, crime control in the United States is the responsibility of states, counties, and cities. The relatively small federal involvement is reflected by statistics that show that New York City's 31,000 sworn police officers are triple the number of FBI special agents. There are more police in the United States than hospital workers or postal workers.[2] In 1994 the United States prison population grew by 1,600 new prisoners a week, and 90 percent of prisoners are in state facilities.

Like other policymaking areas we have discussed, crime and corrections reflect the interaction of officials at all levels of governments. While cities bear the greatest burden of fighting crime, federal, state, and county governments all are involved in passing laws, appropriating money, and making rulings that affect crime fighting at the street level as well as correctional facilities from city jails to maximum security state prisons.

THE POLITICS OF CRIME CONTROL

Although the federal contribution to crime fighting is small, national elections since 1960 have featured presidential and congressional candidates claiming to be the toughest on crime. As evidenced by George Bush's infamous Willie Horton television ad in 1968 (which criticized Michael Dukakis for his role as governor of Massachusetts in implementing a prison furlough program), Republicans generally have been successful in portraying themselves as tougher crime fighters than Democrats. However, in the wake of the 1995 terrorist bombing in Oklahoma City, Democrats were more likely than Republicans to favor policies restricting the activities of paramilitary groups across the country.

Following the 1992 elections, polls showed that Americans placed crime at the top of their concerns and that they expected federal, as well as state and local, officials to do something about it. After twelve years of Republican presidential opposition to stronger gun control, President Bill Clinton in 1993 pledged to secure congressional approval of the so-called Brady Bill. Twelve years after the shooting of James S. Brady in an assassination attempt on President Ronald Reagan, Congress in 1993 passed the first major gun control legislation since 1968. The **Brady Bill** instituted a waiting period of five business days for all handgun purchases. It also raised the licensing fees for gun dealers and required police to be notified of any multiple gun purchases. Approval represented a major defeat for the National Rifle Association, which opposed the waiting period. The NRA has opposed even limited restrictions on gun ownership, fearing these measures will be the first steps toward tighter control.

Strategically, one of the reasons the Brady Bill was approved in 1993 was that it was separated from the more controversial omnibus anticrime bill. Congress spent the first eight months of 1994 debating that crime bill, which was supported by President Clinton. Just before adjourning for the fall election campaign, Congress approved the most extensive federal intervention in history in the area of crime fighting. The omnibus bill authorized $8.8 billion to hire 100,000 police over six years, $7.9 billion in state prison construction grants, and $6.9 billion for crime prevention programs. The bill also created dozens of new federal capital crimes, mandated life in prison for three-time violent offenders, and banned nineteen types of semiautomatic assault weapons. The vote in the House on banning assault weapons was 216 to 214.

Once again, the bill was passed despite strong opposition from the National Rifle Association, which lobbied intensely against the ban on assault weapons. As we would expect, the NRA gets its strongest support from members of Congress who represent rural districts, especially those in the South and West.

Congress traditionally produces crime bills in election years, but the 1994 bill, six years in the making, represents a different level of federal involvement. Republicans charged that the bill had too much pork barrel spending on social programs and that President Clinton politically needed this bill, in any form, to offset the losses of health care legislation. Republicans promised to work for another crime bill that would cut social programs and give local governments more control over how money would be spent. Following the 1995 bombing of the federal building in Oklahoma City, Republicans postponed reconsideration of the assault weapons ban and Senate Majority Leader Bob Dole suggested the NRA needed to "get a little repair job."

Crime was a major issue in several 1994 gubernatorial campaigns. While Governor Mario Cuomo's opposition to the death penalty contributed to his loss in New York, California Governor Pete Wilson used the fear of crime as an effective issue in his reelection campaign. In Texas, both candidates presented themselves as being the toughest crime fighter. Since World War II, several gubernatorial candidates, including Thomas Dewey in New York and James Thompson in Illinois, have used their experience as criminal prosecutors as a springboard to electoral success.

State legislators in the 1990s have responded to voter alarm about crime by passing legislation and supporting ballot initiatives to lock up criminals and keep them behind bars. As indicated in Figure 15-1, polls show people are fed up with crime and view it as the nation's most important problem. Variations of "three strikes and you're out" legislation—the most popular get-tough policy—have been introduced in over thirty states since voters in Washington first approved it in 1993. That policy is discussed at the end of this chapter. "Truth in sentencing" rules that preclude early release for prisoners and laws treating juvenile defendants as adults also have been approved in states across the country. Legislators are pressured by associations of sheriffs and police chiefs, who often favor more gun control, by associations of district attorneys, who seek adjustments in sentencing guidelines, and by associations of public defenders, who seek more funds in the face of federal cutbacks.

Like governors, candidates for mayor and city council also have been running strong anticrime campaigns. Mayor Rudolph Giuliani of New York is a former federal prosecutor, and other former law enforcement officials, such as Frank Rizzo in Philadelphia, have been elected mayor in several large cities.

At the local level, politics has a direct impact on the criminal justice system because we often elect sheriffs, prosecutors, and trial judges. City and county prosecutors have broad discretion regarding whether or not to prosecute, what kinds of crime will be targeted for prosecution, and whether charges will be reduced to less

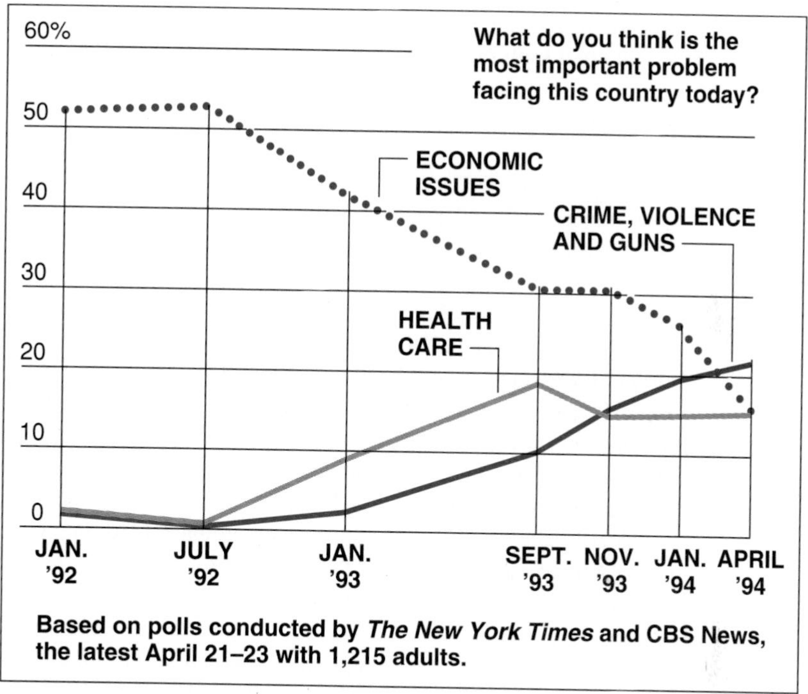

FIGURE 15-1 The nation's changing concerns. (*The New York Times,* May 10, 1994, p. A12.)

serious offenses in order to ensure conviction. Successful prosecution in well-publicized cases can ensure prosecutors' reelection, and it can help them move on to elected political office or to judgeships.

Gun control has been one of the most emotionally charged and politicized crime control issues for nearly twenty years. In 1993 there were 23,271 murders included in the FBI's *Uniform Crime Reports.* Of those, 70 percent involved firearms and 82 percent of the firearms were handguns. The risk of being murdered by a handgun for all people in the United States doubled from 1966 to 1993, and for those aged fifteen to nineteen the rate increased nearly seven times. It is little wonder that there has been a movement to regulate their sale.

Following the passage of the Brady Bill in 1993, it appeared as though gun control advocates might seize the upper hand in this long-standing political battle. However, opposition to the Brady Bill led to a sharp gain in National Rifle Association membership. NRA activity helped elect Republican members of Congress and state legislators in 1994, and it contributed to the defeat of Democratic gubernatorial candidates in New Jersey and Virginia in 1993. NRA figures say that twenty of twenty-five NRA-endorsed candidates for governor and 74 percent of their endorsed candidates for state legislatures won in 1994.[3] In Texas, challenger George W. Bush outdid Governor Ann Richards by supporting the most controversial item on the gun agenda, the right to carry concealed weapons. In 1995, Texas became the twenty-eighth state to permit this. In many states, rural and small-town legislators strongly oppose gun control, arguing that high-crime urban areas are trying to set policy for the whole state.

THE CRIME PROBLEM

The compilation and interpretation of voluminous crime statistics by government officials, the media, and academics can be overwhelming to the general public. These range from the annual *Uniform Crime Reports* by the FBI and various academic reports on incarceration rates and victimization studies to popular magazine articles on the "murder capital" of the United States. Having seen the statistics, we are confronted by an array of questions: Is the crime rate up or down in the 1990s? By how much? Is violent crime increasing? How does the crime rate in the United States compare with that of other countries? How accurately is crime reported? How many people are imprisoned during a calendar year? How does the crime rate vary by region, by age, by gender, by race among young Americans? Then we want to know what *causes* crime and how we can best combat it.

Clearly, the crime rate has risen significantly in the past forty years. Violent crime tripled from 1960 to 1980. Then the crime rate leveled off and declined in the early 1980s, but it increased in the late 1980s. The FBI's total of seven major crimes dropped 3 percent in 1992, 2 percent in 1993, and 2 percent in 1994. Crimes were down in all regions of the country. The rate of violent crimes in 1994 fell to its lowest level since 1989. Violent crimes in 1994 fell in the 9 cities with over one million people, while the overall crime rate increased slightly in the suburbs and rural areas. The bad news is that homicide committed by fourteen- to seventeen-year-old males increased by 165 percent from 1983 to 1994. By the year 2005, as the children of baby boomers age, there will be 23 percent more teenagers than there were in 1995.

Although the rate of crime has fluctuated since the 1980s, the number of people in prison has steadily increased. In 1980 about 200,000 persons were incarcerated, and at the end of 1994 about 1.1 million men and women were in state and federal prisons.

Statistics show that blacks are more likely than whites to commit crimes and blacks are more likely to be the victims of crime. Among black males between the ages of fifteen and thirty-four murder is the most common cause of death. About half of all people murdered each year in the United States are black.

There are several reasons why we should be cautious when reading crime statistics. First, the *Uniform Crime Reports* covers only four types of violent crime (assault, murder, rape, and robbery) and four types of property crime (arson, burglary, larceny, and motor vehicle theft). Most white-collar crimes are omitted. Second, many crimes are not reported to the police. Third, police reports to the FBI may underestimate the amount of crime to make local departments look better. And fourth, while most murders and motor vehicle thefts are reported, other crimes, for various reasons, are vastly underreported to the police. For instance, many victims do not think the police can solve cases, or they don't think crimes are important enough to report, or the crimes (often assault or rape) have been committed by a relative or friend, or the victim fears retaliation from gang members.

TABLE 15-1 STATE AND CITY CRIME RATES

Crime Rate, per 100,000 Persons, 1993		Violent Crime Rate, per 100,000 Persons, 1993	
1 District of Columbia	11,761.1	**1** District of Columbia	2,921.8
2 Florida	8,351.0	**2** Florida	1,206.0
3 Arizona	7,431.7	**3** California	1,077.8
4 Louisiana	6,846.6	**4** New York	1,073.5
5 California	6,456.9	**5** Louisiana	1,061.7
6 Texas	6,439.1	**6** South Carolina	1,023.4
7 Hawaii	6,277.0	**7** Maryland	997.8
8 New Mexico	6,266.1	**8** Illinois	959.7
9 Georgia	6,193.0	**9** New Mexico	929.7
10 Nevada	6,180.1	**10** Nevada	875.2
11 Maryland	6,106.5	**11** Massachusetts	804.9
12 Washington	5,952.3	**12** Michigan	791.5
13 South Carolina	5,903.4	**13** Alabama	780.4
14 Oregon	5,765.6	**14** Tennessee	765.8
15 North Carolina	5,652.3	**15** Texas	762.1
16 Illinois	5,617.9	**16** Alaska	760.8
17 Alaska	5,567.9	UNITED STATES	746.1
18 New York	5,551.3	**17** Missouri	744.4
19 Colorado	5,526.8	**18** Georgia	723.1
UNITED STATES	5,482.9	**19** Arizona	715.0
20 Michigan	5,452.5	**20** Delaware	685.9
21 Oklahoma	5,294.3	**21** North Carolina	679.3
22 Tennessee	5,239.5	**22** Oklahoma	634.8
23 Utah	5,237.4	**23** New Jersey	626.9
24 Missouri	5,095.4	**24** Arkansas	593.3
25 Kansas	4,975.3	**25** Colorado	567.3
26 Massachusetts	4,893.9	**26** Washington	514.6
27 Alabama	4,878.8	**27** Ohio	504.1
28 Delaware	4,872.1	**28** Oregon	503.1
29 Arkansas	4,810.7	**29** Kansas	496.4
30 New Jersey	4,800.8	**30** Indiana	489.1
31 Montana	4,790.0	**31** Kentucky	462.7
32 Connecticut	4,650.4	**32** Connecticut	456.2
33 Rhode Island	4,499.0	**33** Mississippi	433.9
34 Ohio	4,485.3	**34** Pennsylvania	417.5
35 Indiana	4,465.1	**35** Rhode Island	401.7
36 Mississippi	4,418.3	**36** Virginia	372.2
37 Minnesota	4,386.2	**37** Nebraska	339.1
38 Wyoming	4,163.0	**38** Minnesota	327.2
39 Nebraska	4,117.1	**39** Iowa	325.5
40 Virginia	4,115.5	**40** Utah	301.0
41 Wisconsin	4,054.1	**41** Wyoming	286.2
42 Vermont	3,972.4	**42** Idaho	281.8
43 Iowa	3,846.4	**43** Wisconsin	264.4
44 Idaho	3,845.1	**44** Hawaii	261.2
45 Pennsylvania	3,271.4	**45** West Virginia	208.4
46 Kentucky	3,259.7	**46** South Dakota	208.4
47 Maine	3,153.9	**47** Montana	177.5
48 South Dakota	2,958.2	**48** New Hampshire	137.8
49 New Hampshire	2,905.0	**49** Maine	125.7
50 North Dakota	2,820.3	**50** Vermont	114.2
51 West Virginia	2,532.6	**51** North Dakota	82.2

Source: Edith R. Horner, ed., *Almanac of the 50 States, 1995* (Palo Alto, Calif.: Information Publications, 1995), p. 436.

U.S. Cities with High Murder Rate

Cities over 100,000 population with the highest murder rates in 1993 per 100,000 population.

City	Murder rate
1 Gary, Ind.	89.1
2 New Orleans	80.3
3 Washington, D.C.	78.5
4 St. Louis	69.0
5 Detroit	56.8
6 Richmond, Va.	54.5
7 Atlanta	50.4
8 Baltimore	48.1
9 San Bernardino, Ca.	47.1
10 Birmingham, Ala.	45.0
11 Bridgeport, Conn	43.8
12 Jackson, Miss.	41.9
13 Oakland, Calif.	40.8
14 Inglewood, Calif.	39.9
15 Shreveport, La.	38.5
16 Little Rock, Ark.	38.0
17 Newark, N.J.	35.6
18 Kansas City, Mo.	35.1
19 Flint, Mich.	34.3
20 Miami	34.1
21 Cleveland	33.0
22 Baton Rouge, La.	32.8
23 Memphis, Tenn.	32.0
24 Portsmouth, Va.	31.1
25 Los Angeles	30.5

Source: Associated Press, 1993.

David C. Anderson presents an illuminating image of "the criminal funnel" in which 35 million crimes (25 million of them are "serious," that is, they involve violence or sizable property loss) are committed each year in the United States.[4] Anderson's rough numbers suggest that only 15 million of the serious crimes are reported to the police. Of those, the police "solve" 3.15 million cases by arresting 3.2 million people. The courts convict 1.9 million defendants, and 500,000 of them go to prison.

Several factors contribute to the small percentage of convictions. In millions of cases arrests are made, but they are handled as misdemeanors. Several hundred thousand cases are turned over to the juvenile-justice system. Once cases progress to the court stage, many are dismissed for lack of evidence or because witnesses refuse to testify. If convicted, young first or second offenders typically receive probation or suspended sentences.

As indicated in Table 15-1, the crime rate varies by more than a factor of three among the states. In general, North Central states have the lowest crime rate. While seven of the eight states with the highest crime rates are in the South or Southwest, several other Southern states have very low crime rates. Nevada's high crime rate seems to be related to its legalized gambling. Many "conventional wisdom" beliefs about crime are not supported by these statistics. For example, in urban, racially mixed New Jersey (where gambling is legal in Atlantic City) the crime rate is lower than in rural, predominantly white Utah. The state with the highest percentage of blacks (Mississippi) ranks fortieth in the rate of crime. The state of Washington, with its moralistic political culture, has a higher crime rate than Illinois. When *violent* crimes are considered (Table 15-1), the picture changes as some Northern, urbanized states move above the national average. But cities with high murder rates are evenly distributed across the country.

CAUSES OF CRIME

Theories regarding the causes of criminal behavior have been evolving since the eighteenth century when the classical school argued that crime was due to the exercise of free will. Prevention of crime was linked to swift and certain punishment that would offset any gains from criminal acts. Curiously, this corresponds closely to today's predominant crime prevention theory.

Other criminological theories have contended that "criminal genes" cause deviant behavior (biological), that criminal behavior is the result of early childhood experiences (psychological), and that association with criminal subcultures leads people to commit criminal acts (sociological). Social-psychological theories contend that criminal behavior is learned in association with other people within small groups.[5]

Political scientist James Q. Wilson relates crime to biology and the environment, arguing that it is the combination of genetic factors (such as maleness, aggressiveness, body type) and environment (poor family life and inferior schools) that leads to criminal behavior.[6] Wilson and Herrnstein compare crime rates in the United States and Japan and conclude that inherited tendencies toward introversion and the existence of strong families help explain the low crime rate in Japan.

Recently some scholars have added the idea that weather contributes to criminal behavior. It seems that the greater the number of possible explanations, the more difficult it will be for criminologists to develop a "unified" theory that combines a variety of explanations.

Regardless of what causes an individual to perform criminal acts, we can strongly associate violent criminal behavior with young males: Half of the crimes on the annual *Uniform Crime Reports* are committed by males under the age of twenty. Except for larceny-theft, where they constitute about 30 percent of all arrests, women make up less than 15 percent of the arrests for all other *UCR* crimes, and only about 6 percent of all prisoners in the United States are women. Arrest rates in cities with populations over 100,000 are nearly double those in rural areas. About two-thirds of the men charged with robbery and with burglary in the early 1990s tested positive for drugs. About 20 percent of black males between the ages of fifteen and thirty-four have a criminal record.

We should remember that over 90 percent of the crimes do not involve violence, and these are not indexed by the *UCR*. Among them, drunk driving accounts for the single largest number of criminal arrests. And most white-collar crime is committed by middle-aged white men.

POLICE ACTIVITIES AND ORGANIZATION

Although the police make arrests in only about 20 percent of the most serious crimes that are reported to them, the record is not as bad as it first appears. As noted earlier, in millions of cases arrests are made, but the cases are processed as misdemeanors. Thousands more are turned over to juvenile authorities. Millions of urban burglaries are reported to the police largely for insurance purposes, and in most cases there is little hope that arrests will be made. Because urban police are so overworked and because often there are not any credible witnesses, no one seriously expects the police to make arrests in many cases.

What Police Do

In routine patrolling and in responding to calls, police have unusually broad **discretionary authority** (see Chapter 7 for a discussion of bureaucratic authority). Working alone or in pairs, police officers operate with little direct supervision from police administrators. James Q. Wilson notes that police discretion is inevitable, "partly because it is impossible to observe every public infraction, partly because many laws require interpretation before they can be applied at all, partly because the police can sometimes get information about serious crimes by overlooking minor crimes, and partly because the police believe that public opinion would not tolerate a policy of full enforcement of all laws all the time."[7]

One of the results of having so much discretionary authority is that police often decide to handle situations informally, rather than strictly enforcing the law. For example, police may choose to issue a warning instead of an arrest for possession of certain controlled substances. The ways in which police exercise discretion may depend on the background and personality of the officer, the characteristics of suspects (if they are belligerent or if their style of dress is offensive, they are more likely to be arrested), and the nature of the offense (while child sex abuse is unlikely to be overlooked, certain "victimless" crimes, such as gambling and prostitution, may be tolerated).[8]

The ways in which police deal with suspects and with the general public also are tied to **police culture.** There is an informal socialization process among police that produces streetwise cops.[9] Police cynicism leads them to believe that people can't be trusted, that everyone hates cops, and that experience on the street is better than rules set by legislators or judges.

As seen in the 1995 indictment of sixteen police officers in New York City, streetwise cops often are open to corruption: Low pay, a sense of not being appreciated, and constant contact with people breaking the law and reaping financial gain encourage some police to get a piece of the action. Another downside of police culture is that new officers see veterans mistreating racial minorities and using excessive force on many suspects and copy this behavior. The beating of Rodney King in 1992 and revelations of racism in the Los Angeles police force during the 1995 trial of O. J. Simpson severely undermined public confidence in the police. Oftentimes a "code of silence" means that bad cops are not reported by other officers. And most police departments resist the appointment of citizen review boards to monitor their behavior.

Law enforcement takes up only about 10 percent of police time. Most of their shifts are devoted to service (responding to motor vehicle accidents or directing traffic) and to peacekeeping (intervening in family disputes, quieting noisy parties). Of course, if police in cruisers were not "doing nothing," they would not be able to respond quickly to emergencies.

Police discretionary activity and the allocation of their time among the three basic functions noted above are influenced by department policy. Some departments target certain kinds of crime to be enforced, some emphasize the service function, and some reduce discretion by keeping in close communication with officers. In turn, department policy may be strongly associated with the style of the department.

Organizational Styles

In his study of police behavior in eight communities, James Q. Wilson identified three basic styles of operation.[10] In the **watchman style,** police are poorly paid, are locally recruited, and receive minimal initial training. This style emphasizes maintenance of order in public places, rather than law enforcement. The police ignore a certain amount of minor violations and often do not interfere in private disputes, particularly in black neighborhoods. In performing their duty, police officers tend to judge people by "what they deserve." Such a style was characteristic of nineteenth-century police departments.

The **legalistic style** is usually found in cities where police were previously corrupt. Police organization stresses formal, hierarchical authority in which officers are constantly evaluated. There is an emphasis on technical efficiency in which all officers on patrol are under some pressure to produce arrests. In such circumstances, many traffic tickets are issued, juveniles are detained and arrested, and there are substantial numbers of arrests for misdemeanors. Because so many arrests are made, there are inevitable charges, especially by minority groups, of police "harassment."

The **service style** is most often found in homogeneous middle-class communities. Here police seek to protect a well-established public order against occasional threats. Serious matters—burglaries, robberies, assaults—are taken seriously. Minor infractions, particularly when juveniles are involved, are handled more informally. Police are courteous, well-paid, and well-trained. In many cities a kind of evolutionary development can be identified, beginning with the traditional watchman style and moving to a service style.

Community Policing

In recent years the most popular law enforcement reform has been to institute **community policing,** which is a variation of the service style. Under this model the police and the public together become responsible for social order.[11] Since most calls to police are requests for service, much of what officers do is make referrals to social agencies. To do this effectively, police need close, personal connections to neighborhoods. In community policing, they walk beats or ride bicycles as means to develop the trust of members of a community. In turn, residents are encouraged to watch for criminal behavior and report it to the police. As Wilson and Kelling argued in their groundbreaking article on community policing, crime often is linked to a disorderly environment: If trash and graffiti go unattended, it looks as though no one cares about the neighborhood and crime goes up. Thus a major goal of community policing is to help create order.

To be successful community policing needs the support of many governmental agencies, whose activities need to be coordinated with the police. Often it is difficult to get meaningful cooperation when departments are in competition with one another. Community policing may require more police in order to deal effectively with social problems, as well as to fight crime directly. Of course, this means more money when city budgets are tight or are being reduced. In a few instances cities have abandoned community policing in the 1990s and moved to aggressive crime fighting. When it works well, community policing gives many city departments a point of entry into neighborhoods that may have been isolated from city hall.[12] Keeping communities safe is a complex task that requires the cooperation of a host of public and private organizations.

Much of the credit for the recent drop in crime has been given to innovative police work under the umbrella of community policing. The real challenge for police is how well they will be able to respond to the crime potential of 40 million children under 10 years of age in 1995 who will become the largest group of adolescents in a generation.

Because most police work has been reactive—responding to calls for help—little attention has been given to crime prevention. Community policing is part of the "reinventing government" emphasis on giving citizens control over public safety and creating anticipatory government. The standard measures of police efficiency are how quickly they respond to calls and how often they "clear" cases with arrests and convictions. As a result, we hire more police and build more jails while the crime rate continues to grow. In fact, most studies show little connection between the amount of crime and any traditional policy activity.

State and County Law Enforcement

Every state except Hawaii has a law enforcement agency known as the *state police,* the state highway patrol, or, as in Texas, the Rangers. In a quarter of the states, the responsibility of this central police force is limited to highway duties. In the other states, law enforcement responsibilities include aiding local police in making arrests and controlling riots.

Traditionally, the *county sheriff* has been a central figure in American law enforcement. In addition to making arrests, the sheriff maintains the county jail and serves summonses and warrants. In every state except Rhode Island, which does not have counties, the sheriff is elected. While sheriffs continue to play a major role in rural counties, *municipal police forces* have assumed most of the sheriff's law enforcement duties in urban areas. However, sheriffs' offices have become very professionalized in many suburban areas where smaller communities may contract with the county for law enforcement service.

SENTENCING POLICIES

In Chapter 8 we discussed trial court procedures in criminal disputes. We now turn to the last stage in those procedures—sentencing defendants who have been found guilty. Of the 15 million serious crimes reported to the police each year, about 3.2 million criminals are turned over to the courts, 81 percent of them are prosecuted, and about 60 percent (1.9 million) are found guilty.[13] As explained in Chapter 8, most often guilt has been established through a plea bargain, not a trial. Having been found guilty, it is up to judges (and occasionally juries) to determine what punishment best fits the crime. Traditionally, options have included imprisonment, fines, probation, and death. Courts have followed several philosophies to help justify their choice of sentences.

Retribution, the most ancient goal of sentencing, suggests that offenders deserve punishment and that it is proper for society to seek vengeance for crimes that are normally offensive. In earlier societies punishment often was certain, quick, and brutal, even for what appears now to be a minor offense. Nowadays, long terms of imprisonment are justified by saying the offender got what was coming to him.

Deterrence contends that certain, swift punishment of convicted criminals will cause other people not to commit crimes. Because imprisonment is thought to be an especially effective deterrence, this philosophy is compatible with incapacitation.[14] To the extent that crime rates have continued to rise as prison sentences have gotten longer, there are serious questions raised about their deterrent effect. In particular, there has been long-standing debate (discussed later in this chapter) about the deterrent effect of the death penalty for the crime of murder. Many criminologists argue that it is *certainty,* more than severity of punishment, that deters crime.[15] And as we have noted, most crimes in the United States go unreported or no arrest is made.

Rehabilitation became the goal of prison reformers in the 1930s, and it dominated prison philosophy into the 1970s. Rehabilitation was applied to youthful offenders and to adult offenders by Pennsylvania Quakers in the late eighteenth century, but retribution soon came to be the primary goal of adult sentencing in the United States.

As the term *corrections* suggests, rehabilitation seeks to change individual behavior, to make offenders see the evil of their ways, and to prepare them for a productive life outside prison. For those sentenced to prison, there is an emphasis on psychological counseling, education, and job training. It was recommended that prisons should be smaller and they should be located close to cities so that family visits would be more frequent. After their release, rehabilitation called for halfway houses and more parole officers to better supervise the reentry of former prisoners into society. Psychology offered the opportunity to treat offenders at various stages and to "cure" them of their criminal tendencies.

Indeterminate sentencing is closely associated with rehabilitation. Since some offenders are more easily rehabilitated than others, this suggests different punishments for the same type of crime. While some offenders are imprisoned, others will be placed on supervised probation. When prison sentences are handed down, the time will be indeterminate, for example, "not less than five or more than fifteen years." Indeterminate sentencing gives broad discretion to judges in the first instance, and it introduces the possibility that judges will base some sentences on the social characteristics of defendants. Later it permits parole boards to shorten the sentences of inmates for good behavior to the point where persons sentenced for several years might serve only a few months in prison.

Of course, the basic test of rehabilitation is how well ex-prisoners behave after their release from prison. The answer is not well.[16] The **recidivism** rate among former convicted offenders in the 1970s was as high as 90 percent. Instead of rehabilitation, imprisonment seemed more likely to serve as a training ground for future criminal behavior. With the crime rate soaring, sentences neither deterred crime nor rehabilitated criminals.

In response to these realities and in reaction to increased fear of crime, the dominant sentencing philosophy changed to **incapacitation.** This calls for separating people from society, often by long, or at least certain, prison sentences. It is argued that to the extent criminals are taken off the streets, they will not be endangering lives and property. Incapacitation differs from retribution to the extent that its primary objective is not punishment. For example, a convicted criminal can be incapacitated by house arrest using electronic monitoring devices. Still, this philosophy in recent years has supported a "lock 'em up and throw away the key" approach to sentencing.

Incapacitation is closely associated with **determinate** or **mandatory sentences.** This philosophy argues that the punishment should be proportionate to the crime and that those who commit similar crimes should be treated equally. However, there is a recognition that offenders with past records have a greater "social debt" to repay to society and therefore should serve longer sentences than first-time offenders. Since the late 1980s the "get tough on crime" movement has led to increased penalties, has reduced probation, and has established mandatory sentencing guidelines for a variety of criminal offenses. The results include much less judicial discretion and more crowded prisons. Because they do not reward inmates for good behavior, mandatory sentences can be criticized for not encouraging inmates to be part of educational or job skills programs.

The most well-publicized form of mandatory sentencing is the "three strikes and you're out" law that requires persons convicted of committing three felonies to be sentenced to life in prison. This movement began with the passage of an initiative in the state of Washington in 1993, and it quickly spread across the country as legislators responded to public demands to get tough on crime. The federal Omnibus Crime Bill also has a "three strikes and you're out" clause.

Extensive use of mandatory sentencing for drug offenses led to the release of 130,000 inmates in Florida in the late 1980s to make room for drug offenders.[17] In New York, it led to a reduction in the percentage of violent offenders in state prison from 63 percent in 1982 to 34 percent in 1992. Some state legislators are beginning to rethink the consequences of three-strike laws because they are leading to the warehousing of prisoners. Estimates suggest that the California law could increase the state's prison population by 275,000 before the year 2030, and, of course, the state would incur enormous prison construction and maintenance cost. In California, a defendant must have been convicted of one or more violent felonies in the past, but the third felony need not be violent. A 1996 study found that 85 percent of those convicted under the law had most recently committed a nonviolent offense.

PROBATION AND PAROLE

These terms were introduced in the discussion of rehabilitation. **Probation** means that convicted offenders technically are sentenced to prison, but they are placed under the supervision of a probation officer. Probationers may have to pay a fine. They are required to live under a number of restrictions regarding their employment, place of residence, and possession of drugs and firearms. In most instances, probation officers are responsible for too many probationers to provide effective supervision.

Parole is the supervised early release from prison. It has restrictions similar to probation, but its goal is to manage the transition of a prisoner back into society. Evidence shows, however, that the rate of recidivism among parolees is the same as for those released without supervision.[18]

As noted earlier, the use of mandatory sentencing and the decline of rehabilitation as a sentencing goal have substantially reduced the use of probation and parole. Even when parole is used, it is for a much shorter time (just a few months) than in the past. State parole boards have lost much of their power to decide when prison terms will be shortened. Still, there are large numbers of adults on parole and probation. In 1990 there were about 500,000 parolees. Among the states, numbers ranged from 110,000 in Texas and 68,000 in California to 116 in North Dakota and zero in Maine. At the same time, there were over 2.6 million adults on probation. Texas and California led the way with just over 300,000 each, while North Dakota had 1,700 on probation.[19]

CAPITAL PUNISHMENT

The ultimate penalty, of course, is death. This ancient punishment has a brutal history. In biblical Israel, criminals were stoned to death. In Rome, beheading was the preferred method of death, although arsonists were burned and slaves were strangled.[20] In the Dark Ages those suspected of committing certain crimes were submerged in cold water or placed in boiling oil. Early in the nineteenth century 160 crimes were punishable by death in England. The guillotine was invented in France as an efficient way of beheading criminals. In the United States electrocution replaced hanging early in this century as the most common form of capital punishment. More recently, lethal injection has become the most widely authorized form of execution among the states.

The Role of the Supreme Court

From 1930 to 1967 about 3,800 persons were executed in the United States. Executions were halted in 1967 by an order of the U.S. Supreme Court as it waited to decide pending cases challenging the constitutionality of the death penalty. As noted in Chapter 8, the Supreme Court's 1972 decision in *Furman* v. *Georgia* effectively struck down the way in which the death penalty was administered in thirty-seven states, but the Court ruled for the first time that the death penalty did not necessarily constitute "cruel and unusual punishment" as prohibited by the Eighth Amendment. The Court's decision in *Gregg* v. *Georgia* two years later upheld the use of the death penalty as modified by the state of Georgia. Based on the Court's 7 to 2 opinion in *Gregg,* death penalty statutes are constitutionally acceptable if there is a two-stage process in which the jury first considers whether or not the defendant is guilty of murder and then at a sentencing stage the same jury considers any **aggravating** or **mitigating circumstances.** The jury must find the defendant guilty beyond a reasonable doubt of at least one aggravating circumstance, such as the offense was committed for hire, in order to impose the death penalty. Then the state supreme court must review the death sentence. Mitigating circumstances, such as lack of a criminal record or mental condition, are used to support a lesser penalty.

Following *Furman* and *Gregg* the Supreme Court held that *mandatory* death sentences for certain crimes are unconstitutional and that capital punishment for rape is excessive. Later, however, a more conservative Court made it easier for states to execute convicted murderers by supporting the death penalty for persons as young as sixteen years old and for those who are mentally retarded. In addition, the Rehnquist Court has limited the number of prisoner petitions from those sentenced to death, and it has permitted victim impact studies at the time of sentencing to help determine the defendant's "blameworthiness." In 1995 the Court refused to hear an appeal from a prisoner sentenced to death who argued that the seventeen years he had spent on death row constituted cruel and unusual punishment and his death sentence should be lifted.

After years of upholding death sentences, the Court in 1995 ordered a new trial for a convicted murderer in Louisiana saying that the prosecution had failed to disclose important evidence. Also in 1995 the Court gave a Missouri death row inmate a chance to present new evidence he said would prove his innocence. In the Louisiana case

(Kyles v. *Whitley)* three justices noted that the "current popularity of capital punishment" made the Court's oversight role particularly important.

State Responses

While some states did not restore the death penalty after the Supreme Court permitted it in 1976, most states rewrote their laws to comply with the *Furman* decision. In 1995, New York state became the thirty-eighth state to have capital punishment. Because of legal restrictions, imposition of the death penalty is time-consuming, costly, and seldom applied. By 1995, thirteen states with capital punishment statutes had not executed anyone and seven states had executed only one or two people since 1976. California reinstated the death penalty shortly after *Furman,* but it was fifteen years before the first person was executed, and by 1995 only one other person was executed.[21] Across the country, over 2,500 persons were on death row in 1995. Both California and Texas have about 400 convicted murderers who could be executed.

In contrast to California, Texas executed ninety-two persons from 1977 through early 1995. While Texas has by far executed the most people since 1976, Louisiana and Nevada have had higher per capita rates. Just nine Southern states—Arkansas, Alabama, Florida, Georgia, Louisiana, Missouri, North Carolina, Texas, and Virginia—accounted for 226 of the 266 people executed from 1977 through early 1995.[22] Even in Texas, forty-two counties have not put anyone on death row since 1977. Harris County (Houston) accounts for over 25 percent of the state's death row inmates.

One man executed in Texas in 1995 had spent eighteen years on death row. Nationally, the average time between sentencing and death is about eight years. California has an Office of Public Defender that does appellate work for indigent defendants on death row, but it can handle only a small percentage of the death penalty cases. The cost to taxpayers to imprison a defendant for ten years and then execute him may be as high as $2 million dollars. Indeed, even the cost of prosecuting cases in which the death penalty is sought may be so great that small counties often seek to avoid such charges altogether.

As we have noted, capital punishment statistics clearly show that a convicted murderer's chances of being executed vary greatly among the states and within single states. Only one woman (in North Carolina) has been executed since 1977. When the death penalty is sought by prosecutors, it is most likely to be in cases where the victim is an innocent child or older person. Gang shootings and drug-related killings, which are more common, do not elicit the same emotions that call for retribution by the state.

Race and the Death Penalty

The fact that about 40 percent of all persons who have been executed are black has led many to oppose capital punishment on the grounds that it is inherently unfair. Just before his retirement in 1994, Justice Harry Blackmun cited racial inequities as a major reason for his opposition to capital punishment in any circumstances. In 1987, the Supreme Court refused to strike down Georgia's system of sentencing even though a study showed that blacks in Georgia who killed whites were four times more likely to receive the death sentence than blacks who killed other blacks *(McCleskey* v. *Kemp).* As explained in the Scholarly Box that follows, David C. Baldus, in the most authoritative study of racial factors in capital punishment, concluded that racial disparities are due more to the *race of the victim* than to the race of the murderer. When the victim is white, the likelihood that the death penalty will be imposed is more than double than when the victim is black.[23] Black-on-white killings are more common than white-on-black killings, and this, along with the nature of the crimes, helps account for some of the statistical disparities. Still, black Americans face a criminal justice system in which an overwhelming number of prosecutors and judges are white and in which fear of crime by white voters may affect sentencing. The prosecution of O. J. Simpson showed that a defendant's wealth and celebrity status may make it unlikely that prosecutors will seek the death penalty even in a multiple murder case. That case also showed that blacks and whites are likely to have very different perceptions of guilt in cases involving black defendants and white victims.

There has been an age-old debate over whether or not the death penalty *deters* murder. Recent evidence in the states suggests that it does not. For example, the homicide rate in Texas is nearly 1⅔ times the national average. Whether or not it deters murder, public opinion polls in the 1990s have shown that capital punishment is supported by a margin of 3 to 1. If we can't rehabilitate criminals or deter crime very well, at least we can have a sense of retribution and a feeling that murderers have gotten what they deserve. The fact that the United States is the world's only democracy that executes criminals seems to make little difference to the majority of the public and the majority of state legislators and governors.

CORRECTIONS

History of Prisons

The history of prisons in the United States shows we have gone through a great variety of stages, seeking ways to further public safety and punish offenders. While the philosophy of imprisonment has changed from one historical stage to the next and technology has altered prison construction, many of the ideas from past stages continue to influence our thinking about prisons.[24]

In colonial America people were put in jail only to await punishment—flogging or mutilation or hanging—not as punishment. Beginning in 1790, Pennsylvania Quakers created penitentiaries designed to humanize the confinement of prisoners. Inmates were held in solitary confinement, exercise was held in walled yards, and handicrafts were introduced to permit prisoners to work in their cells.[25] As the number of prisoners expanded, solitary confinement became too expensive and group workshops were seen as more profitable than the solitary system of the Quakers. Larger prisons were built throughout the nineteenth century, modeled on the New York State Prison at Auburn, where prisoners were isolated at night and worked in silence during the day. The Elmira (New York) Reformatory, opened in 1876, ushered in the next stage where young offenders were given education and trade training. Although there were high

SCHOLARLY BOX

THE BALDUS STUDY

Warren McCleskey, a black man, was convicted in 1978 of killing a white policeman during a robbery in Fulton County, Georgia. McCleskey had a criminal record, he offered no mitigating evidence, and he was said to have boasted about the killing.

We have noted that the Supreme Court in *McCleskey* v. *Kemp* (1987) upheld McCleskey's death sentence, ruling that he had failed to produce sufficient evidence that *his* death sentence was the result of racist decision making. At best, the five-member majority believed that race was a factor that might have played a role in McCleskey's sentencing, but the facts in his case did not indicate the kind of systemic defects in capital punishment procedures that had been prohibited in *Furman* v. *Georgia* (1972).

The Supreme Court reached its conclusions even though it accepted the validity of a comprehensive study showing that murderers of whites in Georgia were 4.3 times more likely than murderers of blacks to get death sentences.* The now-famous Baldus study examined over 2,000 murder cases in Georgia in the 1970s. It took into account 230 variables that might have explained the sentencing disparities on nonracial grounds. It found, for example, that, like blacks, white murderers with a prior conviction for armed robbery, rape, or another murder were about 4.3 times more likely than those without similar prior convictions to be sentenced to death. The study also found that blacks who killed whites in Georgia were 3 times more likely to get death sentences than whites who killed whites.

The Court's unwillingness to use the Baldus data to overturn McCleskey's sentence prompted a commentator in the *Harvard Law Review* to call the opinion "logically unsound, morally reprehensible, and logically unsupportable."† Among the four dissenters on the Court, Justices Brennan and Marshall would have vacated McCleskey's sentence and all other death sentences in Georgia.

Randall Kennedy points out the irony that most killers of blacks are blacks. One interpretation of the Baldus statistics would be that in order to end arbitrariness and discrimination, killers of blacks should be sentenced to death with the same frequency as killers of whites. If that were the case, then there would be an increase in the number of blacks sentenced to death.‡

Kennedy notes that rather than "leveling up" by executing more people, McCleskey argued that it was unfair to subject killers of whites to a harsher punishment than those who kill blacks. Like Brennan and Marshall, McCleskey's argument would have "leveled down" the system by sentencing to death killers of blacks at the same rate as killers of whites, or by abolishing the death penalty altogether. Currently the latter option seems politically impossible in most states.

rates of recidivism, the ideas of reformatories with indeterminate sentencing and parole continue to be discussed in current debate about prisons.

In the early twentieth century, large prisons—such as Sing Sing (New York), Statesville (Illinois), and San Quentin (California)—became veritable industrial sites behind walls. In the South, prisoners were more likely to work on farms and build public works projects. Curiously, the state of Alabama revived the use of the chain gang in 1995. Money-making prisons were sharply curtailed when labor unions gained political power during the Depression. Since prisoners had more time on their hands, education programs were introduced to keep them busy. Yet prison manufacturing has continued, and the idea of providing meaningful work for prisoners has gained strength in recent years.

Many former industrial prisons, such as Alcatraz (California), shifted to an era of punitive custody during the 1940s. This was followed by the medical model of prisons, which was guided by the principal that clinical treatment could lead to rehabilitation. Prison environments based on therapy featured better living conditions as rewards to improving inmates.

Another remedy, as suggested by Justices Stevens and Blackmun in their dissent, would be to limit the death penalty to those convicted of the worst kinds of homicide. This argument is based in part on evidence from the Baldus study that found race was most likely to be a factor in a "middle range" of homicides where sentencing could go either way. In contrast, the study found that for very serious homicides prosecutors consistently sought and juries imposed the death penalty. A major problem here is how to define a "very serious" homicide. If McCleskey was classified as in the middle, how much more serious would a murder have to be to impose the death penalty?

Another key element identified in the Baldus study was the power of prosecutors to determine charges. In ranking the seriousness of homicides, prosecutors might show racial bias by charging blacks with more serious offenses. The Baldus study found that prosecutors sought the death penalty in 70 percent of the cases involving black defendants and white victims and in 19 percent of the cases involving white defendants and black victims.

Baldus and his associates suggested there has been a failure of states to monitor their systems after *Furman*.[§] Few death sentences have been vacated by state supreme courts because of racial discrimination. Randall Kennedy believes the Baldus statistics showed McCleskey faced an impermissible risk of illicit official conduct. Considering that risk, he felt that in "Georgia's marketplace of emotion the lives of blacks simply count for less than the lives of whites."

The Supreme Court's majority feared that if they upheld McCleskey's claim, they would open up a Pandora's box in which other groups would allege bias in death sentences and the racial argument would be extended to noncapital cases. This position prompted Justice Blackmun to respond that the majority "fears too much justice."

*David C. Baldus, George Woodworth, and Charles A. Pulaski, Jr., "Monitoring and Evaluating Contemporary Death Sentencing Systems: Lessons from Georgia," *University of California Davis Law Review* (Summer 1985), p. 1375.

†"Leading Cases," *Harvard Law Review* (November 1987), p. 119.

‡Randall Kennedy, "*McCleskey* v. *Kemp*: Race, Capital Punishment, and the Supreme Court," *Harvard Law Review* (May 1988), p. 1392.

§See David C. Baldus, Charles A. Pulaski, and George Woodworth, "Arbitrariness and Discrimination in the Administration of the Death Penalty: A Challenge to State Supreme Courts," *Stetson Law Review* (Spring 1986), pp. 133–261.

Since about 1980 American prisons largely have abandoned the goal of rehabilitation. But they are still concerned, as were the Quakers, with returning individual inmates to society in a better frame of mind than when they entered prison. Studies in the late 1970s showed that about 70 percent of young adults paroled from prison were rearrested one or more times for serious crimes within six years. In other words, most were not rehabilitated. The get-tough philosophy of determinate sentencing, stiffer sentences for drug offenders, and tighter parole policies have led to warehousing prisoners in overcrowded facilities in the 1990s. In 1992 drug offenders constituted 30 percent of all newly sentenced inmates, compared to 7 percent in 1980. State prison facilities operated at between 18 and 29 percent over capacity.

Number of Prisoners

In 1994 the number of inmates in all American prisons topped 1 million for the first time in history. About 90 percent of prisoners are in state facilities. These figures do not include local jails, which had about 484,000 prisoners at the end of 1994. There were 373 people in prison for every 100,000 residents in the United States, up from 139 per 100,000 in 1980. This rate is significantly higher than in any other democratic country in the world. As shown in Table 15-2, the incarceration rate varies greatly among the states. In general, Southern states have the highest rates, while New England and North Central states have relatively few people in prison. While the rate of incarceration correlates reasonably well with the violent crime rate (see Table 15-1), several states, such as Oklahoma and Arizona, rank much higher in rates of incarceration than in rates of crime.

Racially, 1,432 out of every 100,000 blacks were in prison, while 203 of every 100,000 whites were inmates. About three-fourths of new prison admissions in 1994 were blacks or Hispanics. In 1994 for the first time, the number of black inmates surpassed the number of whites in the federal and state prisons. Racism and poverty clearly contribute to the high numbers of blacks who are arrested and imprisoned.

More people sentenced to prison, of course, means that states must build more prisons as existing facilities have populations that exceed their capacities (see Table 15-3). The Census Bureau estimates that state spending on prison construction increased 612 percent, adjusted for inflation, from 1979 to 1990. Pushed by the new "three strikes and you're out" law, California officials in 1995 estimated they would need to build 21 new prisons by the year 2000 to house an estimated 240,000 inmates. Texas planned to open a new corrections installation each week during 1995 and 1996. So many prisons are being built that many small towns have become overwhelmed by huge institutions literally in their backyards. In the mid-1990s, voters in several rural California counties rejected plans to construct new prisons in their communities. In Texas, corrections account for nearly 6 percent of state spending, double the national average. New construction averages $18,000 to $25,000 per cell, and it costs about $25,000 a year to maintain a cell. The cost for some maximum security cells can be two or three times higher.

In order to keep costs down, states are building larger prisons (with up to 5,000 inmates each) that will house a wide range of prisoners, from the least to the most dangerous. To help satisfy conflicting political demands to put more people in jail and to keep down state expenditures, many new prisons have a harsh environment—gray walls, no windows, stainless steel tables, and high-voltage wire fences that eliminate the need for patrol. Touch the fence and you're dead.[26]

In the chapter reading, Neal R. Peirce explains the concept of "structured sentencing" by which North Carolina is trying to reinvent government and hold down the cost of punishing convicted criminals.

Privatization of Prisons

Perhaps the most popular (and the most controversial) way to reduce the costs of incarceration is to privatize prisons. Although private prisons were used in colonial America, tales of prisoner abuse led to public management of virtually all prisons and jails until the idea was revived in the 1980s. However, state prisons have a long history of contracting out such services as food and psychological testing to private business.

TABLE 15-2 STATE PRISONER INCARCERATION RATE IN 1994

National Rate = 343 State Prisoners per 100,000 Population*

Rank	State	Rate
1	Texas	545
2	Louisiana	514
3	South Carolina	504
4	Oklahoma	501
5	Nevada	456
6	Arizona	448
7	Alabama	439
8	Michigan	423
9	Georgia	417
10	Florida	404
11	Maryland	392
12	Delaware	391
13	Mississippi	385
14	California	382
15	Virginia	374
16	Ohio	369
17	New York	361
18	Arkansas	355
19	Connecticut	331
20	Missouri	321
21	North Carolina	314
22	New Jersey	307
23	Illinois	302
24	Kentucky	281
25	Tennessee	278
26	Colorado	272
27	Alaska	256
28	Indiana	256
29	Idaho	253
30	Wyoming	247
31	Kansas	239
32	South Dakota	227
33	Pennsylvania	224
34	New Mexico	216
35	Washington	198
36	Montana	192
37	Rhode Island	185
38	Iowa	180
39	Wisconsin	172
40	Hawaii	170
41	Oregon	169
42	New Hampshire	167
43	Massachusetts	165
44	Utah	154
45	Nebraska	148
46	Vermont	138
47	Maine	113
48	West Virginia	106
49	Minnesota	100
50	North Dakota	75
District of Columbia		1,578

Source: U.S. Department of Justice, Bureau of Justice Statistics, press release (October 27, 1994).

*As of June 30, 1994. Includes only inmates sentenced to more than one year. Does not include federal incarceration rate of 30 prisoners per 100,000 population. State and federal combined incarceration rate is 373 prisoners per 100,000 population.

TABLE 15-3 STATE PRISON CAPACITIES, 1992

State or other jurisdiction	Rated capacity	Operational capacity	Design capacity	Population as a percent of: (a) Highest capacity	Lowest capacity
Alabama	14,788	14,788	14,788	111	111
Alaska	2,472	. . .	. . .	116	116
Arizona	. . .	15,520	. . .	106	106
Arkansas	. . .	7,614	. . .	104	104
California	. . .	. . .	57,367	191	191
Colorado	. . .	7,496	6,136	113	138
Connecticut	10,093	11,102	. . .	103	113
Delaware	4,009	3,987	2,928	99	136
Florida	49,939	55,100	37,887	88	127
Georgia	. . .	25,252	. . .	100	100
Hawaii	. . .	2,382	1,566	123	187
Idaho	2,015	2,158	. . .	106	113
Illinois	24,562	24,562	20,818	129	152
Indiana	11,983	13,817	. . .	95	110
Iowa	3,265	3,265	3,265	138	138
Kansas	6,621	. . .	. . .	91	91
Kentucky	9,119	8,923	. . .	107	110
Louisiana	17,131	17,131	17,131	95	95
Maine	1,353	1,353	1,353	112	112
Maryland	. . .	19,804	12,856	101	155
Massachusetts	. . .	. . .	6,999	144	144
Michigan	27,086	. . .	. . .	144	144
Minnesota	3,678	3,678	3,678	104	104
Mississippi	8,557	9,083	9,007	89	95
Missouri	15,630	16,187	. . .	100	104
Montana	1,160	1,465	1,160	106	134
Nebraska	. . .	. . .	1,706	150	150
Nevada	5,743	5,743	4,770	105	127
New Hampshire	1,358	1,576	1,162	113	153
New Jersey	. . .	. . .	14,980	131	131

As discussed in Chapter 7, advocates of all types of privatization argue that public services can be produced more efficiently and at lower cost by private industry. While managing some services, such as trash collection, can be evaluated on a cost-efficiency basis, running prisons raises more complex issues. These include how to ensure the humane treatment of prisoners, how to guard against the possibility of prison contractors keeping inmates in jail longer so that they could make more money, and how to assess legal liability when inmates bring lawsuits. Of course, state on-sight supervision of prisons and careful wording of contracts could prevent more obvious abuses. Moreover, the record in many states shows public management

TABLE 15-3 STATE PRISON CAPACITIES, 1992 *(Continued)*

State or other jurisdiction	Rated capacity	Operational capacity	Design capacity	Population as a percent of: (a) Highest capacity	Lowest capacity
New Mexico	3,427	3,290	3,443	95	99
New York	60,054	57,005	49,543	103	125
North Carolina	17,913	20,900	. . .	98	114
North Dakota	. . .	576	576	81	81
Ohio	. . .	. . .	21,738	177	177
Oklahoma	9,130	12,451	. . .	119	162
Oregon	. . .	6,557	. . .	101	101
Pennsylvania	. . .	. . .	16,713	149	149
Rhode Island	3,292	3,292	3,292	84	84
South Carolina	16,216	16,216	12,527	112	145
South Dakota	1,189	1,130	1,189	125	132
Tennessee	11,119	10,837	11,463	94	99
Texas (b)	57,455	54,459	. . .	106	112
Utah	3,184	2,897	. . .	81	89
Vermont	647	852	647	147	193
Virginia	13,852	13,852	13,852	139	139
Washington	6,190	7,779	7,779	128	161
West Virginia	1,680	1,745	1,730	100	104
Wisconsin	6,342	6,342	6,342	139	139
Wyoming	977	977	977	105	105
District of Columbia	11,087	11,087	8,746	95	121

Source: U.S. Department of Justice, Bureau of Justice Statistics, *Prisoners in 1992* (May 1993).
Key:
. . . — Not available
(a) Excludes inmates who had been sentenced to state prison but were held in local jails because of crowding and who were included in the total prisoner count.
(b) Excludes prisoners housed in contract or other nonfederal facilities.
From: The Book of the States, 1994–95 (Lexington, Ky.: Council of State Governments, 1995), p. 532.

has produced overcrowded prisons, delayed construction of new facilities, poorly maintained buildings, and physical abuse of prisoners. Privately managed prisons have benefited from state and federal mandates to reduce prison overcrowding. A 1995 report in Tennessee showed that private prisons there operated at a lower cost and provided safer services than state-run facilities. However, private firms have largely limited themselves to managing smaller low-security prisons where staff can be kept low.

About half the states permit their corrections departments to contract out the management of prisons, and in the mid-1990s fourteen states had for-profit corporations either building or operating a prison facility.[27] Corrections Corporation of America, the nation's leading for-profit manager of prisons, had twenty-three facilities in seven states in 1994. Since prison management is very labor-intensive, Corrections Corporation saves money because its workforce is not unionized, its workers do not have a

Seeing Prisons through New Prisms

Neal R. Peirce

Are the nation's burgeoning prison systems ready for "reinvented" government? With the population of prison inmates in the United States soaring past one million—more than double what it was in the early 1980s—the question has never been more acute.

The dilemma has most recently been sharpened by a raft of "three strikes and you're out" proposals—voters approved several such measures in November—and the crime bill that Congress approved earlier this year, which gave states an additional $7.9 billion in grants to build prisons. California alone, under legislation approved this year, is spending $3.1 billion on prisons, and the state is headed for a gargantuan $6 billion in yearly outlays on prisons by 2000.

And 1995 will produce new prison politics. Incarceration costs will continue to pose serious threats to school, university and other social budgets. But now, prisons have another potential effect: making mincemeat of all the Republican and conservative talk of cutting taxes and trimming back the size and cost of government.

Enter the North Carolina solution. It's called "structured sentencing" and went into effect in October. It rests on computer-based technology, a healthy dose of common sense and the imperative of controlling costs.

Structured sentencing virtually guarantees that criminals will remain behind bars for the duration—100 per cent of their sentences. Violent and repeat offenders—felons convicted of murder, armed robbery, rape, assault with a deadly weapon—will have no early way "out."

But there's a tradeoff. To stay affordable, the structured sentencing system relies on a radically expanded set of community-based penalties for petty thieves, minor drug law offenders, embezzlers and forgers. These folks will get such punishments as halfway houses, day reporting centers, mandatory drug and alcohol treatment, boot camps, electronic anklet monitors and fines.

The heart of North Carolina's system is a hard-and-fast sentencing grid approved by the state legislature. In sentencing offenders, judges must now match the class of crime a person has been convicted of against his or her prior offenses, with only a limited allowance for mitigating circumstances.

A first-offender burglar, for example, will draw 44–55 months of real time; a first or second-time nonviolent offender may be given a suspended sentence in return for completing an alternative form of punishment such as house arrest or restitution.

For once, there's a rational attempt to sort out punishments between the people society is legitimately afraid of and those it's just angry at. Real sentences mean serving real time, and the public should feel safer. Conversely, lots of petty offenders who've been needlessly sent to prison in the past will be spared that often dangerous experience—yet be obliged to accept alternative punishments with better chances of rehabilitation.

There's more, though, to North Carolina's experiment: The legislature also required that every bill that affects prison space in the state have a cost estimate attached to it.

The importance of such up-front cost accounting became clear earlier this year, after a spate of highly publicized murders. The governor called a special session of the legislature, and angry lawmakers pressed for drastically increased sentences. Some of the bills introduced were tough indeed, adding 3–6 years to sentences for crimes involving a firearm, for example, or up to 10 years for displaying the gun during the crime.

Typically, the sponsors of such bills had next to no idea of what their "solutions" would actually cost. But the computer simulation model used to generate the cost estimates produced sobering news. The more extreme bills, for instance, would have caused the state's inmate population of 23,000 to more than double within a decade.

Result: The legislature settled on a much more modest approach, one that would add fewer than 2,000 prison slots over a decade.

This should create a new culture of legislative crime action, with the costs on the table and the lawmakers knowing the costs to taxpayers of the stiff sentencing measures that they recommend.

Structured sentencing, on its own, isn't the full solution. Neither is the requirement for computer-based modeling or other forms of fiscal analysis. It's the combination of the two that should work—assured sentences as the basis for calculating realistic long-term costs.

This is a big step toward what honest, reinvented government for the times ought to be. And the good news is that many states are now looking to these reforms.

There's a danger, however, that legislatures will fail to come up with enough money for the alternative punishments that are needed to keep minor offenders out of state penitentiaries. Intensive probation, halfway houses, supervised community service—all cost a lot less than prison cells but still involve real money. Financing them doesn't turn legislators into political heroes.

Yet if the alternative punishments don't get adequate support, thousands of petty offenders will get a head start on becoming serious offenders and the new reforms will abort and thousands more prison cells will be necessary. Maybe the computers need to be programmed to project what *that* will ultimately cost taxpayers.

Truly reinvented government will have arrived in the criminal justice arena when the computers can prove how much cheaper and less dangerous it is to prevent crime in the first place. That means helping patch broken families together, providing activities for latchkey kids, reforming schools, offering more-inventive school-to-work programs and the like.

Sadly, too few Americans today believe that such efforts can work. Some politicians cavalierly call them "pork." But North Carolina's initiative at least gives the nation a shred of hope that honesty about prison sentences and costs, coupled with respect for alternative punishments and hardheaded projections, could lead to safer communities—and more-affordable government.

Source: National Journal, Dec. 17, 1994, p. 2988. Reprinted with permission of National Journal.

---

pension plan, and its building designs reduce the number of guards.[28] Private corporations can be most cost-effective when they build a prison, rather than when they come in to manage an existing facility. Elsor Correctional Services—which runs detention centers, halfway houses, and boot camps across the country—was hit by a series of protest actions and lawsuits in 1995 stemming from incidents involving alleged prison abuse and low bidding procedures.

Jails

In addition to state correctional facilities, cities and counties maintain jails in which some defendants are held while they await trial and others serve short sentences for committing minor crimes, such as being drunk and disorderly. Many of these facilities are old and lack adequate recreational and medical services. America's largest jail complex is Rikers Island where 8,200 guards watch over 15,000 inmates on a 415-acre site in the East River of New York City. A year at Rikers costs taxpayers $58,000.[29]

Prison Subcultures

Sociologists have documented an inside world of prisoners **(prison subculture)** that is far more influential on their lives than the formal rules and procedures established by prison officials. Stastny and Tyrnauer described a "traditional" culture at the Washington State Penitentiary with a convict code of behavior, but they also found that minority prisoners had developed a "revolutionary" culture based on radical political slogans.[30] Still, revolutionary inmates tried not to break the traditional rules.

A traditional inmate code of behavior would include the following:[31]

1 *Don't interfere with the interests of other inmates:*
  - **a** Never rat on a con.
  - **b** Don't be nosey.
  - **c** Don't have a loose lip.
  - **d** Don't put a guy on the spot.

2 *Don't quarrel with fellow inmates:*
  - **a** Play it cool.
  - **b** Don't lose your head.
  - **c** Do your own time.

3 *Don't exploit other inmates:*
  - **a** Don't break your word.
  - **b** Don't steal from cons.
  - **c** Don't sell favors.
  - **d** Don't welsh on bets.

4 *Maintain yourself:*
  - **a** Don't weaken.
  - **b** Don't whine.
  - **c** Don't cop out.
  - **d** Be tough.
  - **e** Be a man.

5 *Don't trust the guards or the things they stand for:*
  - **a** Don't be a sucker.
  - **b** Guards are hacks or screws.
  - **c** The officials are wrong and the prisoners are right.

Sexual violence is widespread in prisons, with older inmates preying on naive, younger men. In most cases those who are sexual aggressors do not consider themselves to be homosexuals. Of course, there are others who engaged in homosexual activity before they entered prison, and their sexual contacts may be more voluntary. Racial conflicts are common among prisoners and between black prisoners and white guards.

Inmates have to deal with prison staff, whose behavior may range from demanding subservience from inmates to trying to win inmate friendship by doing special favors, such as bending minor rules. In either case, inmates must learn how best to react to guards. And they must cope with body searches, shakedowns, and a host of strict rules of behavior. In some instances guards may rely on tough prisoners to manage the behavior of other inmates.

As we would expect, a different kind of subculture exists in women's prisons. Although women make up only 6 percent of the nation's prison population, their rate of increase in the past two decades has been more rapid than that of men. More than 50,000 women are imprisoned in the United States, with Oklahoma having the highest percentage (10 percent) of women among its prisoner population. Many sociological studies have found complex "family" structures in women's prisons. Although they are not present everywhere, in some instances there are "husbands" and "wives" and others may play the roles of extended family members—children, grandparents, in-laws.[32] There appears to be much less violence in women's prisons than in men's prisons, and few homosexual contacts are forced. Still, there are accepted roles for women prisoners to play and a definite hierarchy of personal relationships that resemble those in men's prisons.

Court Review of Prisons

Since the 1970s federal district court judges increasingly have stepped in to manage state prisons in response to lawsuits concerning overcrowded, unsanitary, and dangerous conditions. By 1990, forty-five states had been issued federal court orders or litigation was in progress. Typically federal judges name a special master to represent them in managing prison conditions. As we have noted, many states have built new prisons in the 1980s and 1990s, but most quickly have become overcrowded. By spending money, states can improve unsafe and unsanitary prisons, but reducing prisoner abuse by guards requires more of a commitment to reform than just appropriating money.

The Supreme Court held in *Wilson* v. *Seiter* (1991) that prisoners must show a "culpable state of mind on the part of prison officials" in order to be successful in suits charging that prison conditions violate the "cruel and unusual punishment" provisions of the Eighth Amendment. In other words, prisoners must prove that dangerous prison conditions are the result of deliberate indifference by prison officials and are not due simply to the failure of the state legislature to appropriate adequate funds. In due process cases where prisoners may complain about issues ranging from disciplinary hearings to temporary placement in solitary confinement, the Court in 1995 held that only actions by prison officials that impose "atypical and significant hardship on the inmate" should even be considered as possible violations of due process.

The Supreme Court has given prisoners some help in suits where they charge that guards used excessive force. In 1992 the Court ruled 7 to 2 (Justices Scalia and Thomas dissenting) that force might be acceptable when there was a good faith effort to control prisoners, but in the issue at hand the use of force had been malicious and sadistic. In that case a prisoner had been punched and kicked while handcuffed and a supervisor had told the guards "not to have too much fun."

NEW DIRECTIONS IN THE CRIMINAL JUSTICE SYSTEM

Since the early 1970s, computers have become an important part of all police departments, including those in small towns and rural counties.[33] This followed the creation of the Law Enforcement Assistance Administration in 1968, whose tasks included technological assistance to state and local governments to aid their fight against crime. Computers have given police easy access to nationwide crime information, and they permit checks on stolen vehicles through machines installed in patrol cars. Police can use large computer databases to cross-reference information and to identify suspects. For example, computer models can be used to track the activities of gang members. Of course, police must deal with increasingly sophisticated criminals who commit high-tech crimes.

As highlighted in the 1995 trial of O. J. Simpson, law enforcement officials are developing the technology to use DNA profiling to identify suspected criminals. Only a few human cells from hair or blood samples can be used to provide genetic material to compare with those of the alleged offender. As we saw in the Simpson trial, this technology is not foolproof and defense attorneys are quick to challenge its authenticity.

As more convicted criminals are being sent to prison and overcrowding has become a major problem in virtually all state prison systems, states have been experimenting with numerous alternatives to traditional imprisonment. These include boot camps for young offenders, "shock" incarceration, house arrest, electronic monitoring, and community service or restitution.

As an alternative to traditional prisons, several states have experimented with **boot camps** to scare younger offenders "straight." These camps are based on the military model of discipline and rigorous physical training. Inmates who accept the regimen are released in a relatively short time, while others may be transferred into the regular prison system if they are noncooperative or if they choose to leave the boot camp. While these facilities appeal to those who want to get tough with criminal offenders and yet keep prison populations down, evidence suggests they have little impact on recidivism.[34]

Shock incarceration began in Georgia in the early 1980s and spread quickly across the country. In many instances, it resembles boot camps where young offenders are placed in a highly regimented program for a short time and then released under some kind of supervision. In other cases, older first-time offenders can be "shocked straight" by a short period of incarceration. Other alternatives to traditional imprisonment include a kind of house arrest in which offenders are monitored by electronic devices on their ankles. Criticisms of house arrest include concern about offenders who are risks to commit violent acts and concern that they are being coddled by staying in their homes. Community service may be done without any time being served in jail, or it may be mixed with a sentence that requires the offender to spend weekends in jail.

It is curious that alternatives to imprisonment are being sought at the same time that there is an outcry across the country to "lock 'em up and throw away the key." In fact, get-tough reforms have led to overcrowded prisons, and they have created serious, unintended consequences for our criminal justice system.

Earlier we noted that about a dozen states have passed "three strikes and you're out" laws. California has especially tough provisions that require those with a serious or violent felony conviction on their record to receive twice the normal sentence when they are convicted of a second felony and to receive twenty-five years to life for a third felony conviction. By early 1995 California officials reported that many defendants in felony cases were refusing to plea bargain, and the courts in many areas were clogged with trials. Jails were filling up and nonviolent offenders were being given early releases.[35] A few cities stopped all civil trials in order to deal with criminal cases. The California three-strikes law does not distinguish among 500 crimes that are felonies. As a result, one three-time loser was sentenced to twenty-five years to life after being convicted of stealing a pizza.

Criminologist Jerome Skolnick believes that three-strike laws will not significantly reduce violent crime because most of these offenses are committed by young men aged thirteen to twenty-three. By the time they are jailed for their third offense, they are, says Skolnick, in the twilight of their criminal careers. Keeping aging prisoners in jail will become, in Skolnick's words, "the most expensive middle-age and old-age (housing and medical care) entitlement in the history of the world."[36] While legislators are lobbied by crime victims groups, who want them to get tough with criminals, and some city and county officials lobby to have new correctional facilities located in their jurisdictions, only a few civil rights groups lobby for more humane treatment of prisoners.

Those, like David Broder, who accept Skolnick's point of view suggest that states and cities should put their emphasis on crime prevention—dealing with drug and alcohol abuse and reducing access to handguns—rather than on building more prisons. However, it is very difficult for government officials to devise comprehensive solutions to complex problems. Getting at the roots of problems takes time, money, and long-term commitment. Oftentimes elected officials lack all three. As a result, they settle for short-term solutions that may be politically popular but, in the long run, may make things worse.

As we noted in Chapter 7, the theme of prevention is stressed by Osborne and Gaebler as they seek to reinvent government in many areas. In regard to crime, they note that governments seldom "tie police, court, or prison funding to outcomes, such as arrest rates, conviction rates, recidivism rates, or customer satisfaction surveys. They just shovel more money in as the inputs—the number of crimes, the number of cases, the number of inmates—rise."[37] They recommend the creation of funding formulas that encourage police to do strategic planning and to invest in prevention. Governments find it easier to measure arrest rates and police response time to crime scenes than to determine how well police and others in a community have prevented crimes from occurring.

Earlier we discussed community policing as the most widespread reform of local law enforcement. Privatization of prisons also was discussed as a possible way for states to save money. Both of these policies need further evaluation and longer-term monitoring. Community policing is a concept that could be trivialized as mere jargon or convenient buzzwords that are used to give the appearance of change when real reform has not occurred.

State and local officials need to be on guard against unintended consequences of programs, such as "three strikes and you're out." In the area of crime prevention it is easy to become cynical because public policies have not deterred crime nor have they succeeded in rehabilitating criminal offenders. As a result, many have concluded that at least if they are locked up for longer periods of time criminals will commit fewer crimes against the general population.

SUMMARY

The high rate of crime in the United States has become a major political issue in elections at all levels of government. State legislators have responded to public demands by passing a host of bills to "get tough with crime." These include "three strikes and you're out" and mandatory prison sentences. The unintended consequences of these measures are discussed at the end of the chapter. Gun control and the role of the National Rifle Association have been at the forefront of the anticrime debate, whose intensity went up after the 1995 bombing of the federal building in Oklahoma City.

Official statistics underestimate the total amount of crime in the United States, in large part, because many crimes go unreported. Of those reported, only a small percentage result in convictions or imprisonment. Various theories of the causes of crime have been put forth, but a "unified" theory does not exist.

On the job, police have an unusually high amount of discretion. Police behavior can be influenced by the type of organizational structure of their departments. The use of community policing, in which officers are encouraged to develop the trust of members of local communities, is the newest approach to improving police effectiveness.

In addition to controlling crime by policing, criminal sentencing has sought to reduce crime by deterring others or by rehabilitating criminals in the hope of reducing recidivism. Responding to political pressure, the goal of sentencing in the past decade has largely been to incapacitate criminals. Sentencing may also include probation and parole, both of which have been reduced as part of the get-tough policy. Of course, capital punishment is the ultimate criminal sentence. A series of Supreme Court decisions involving the death penalty are reviewed, and the Scholarly Box examines the effects of race on the imposition of the death penalty.

Rising crime rates and the use of longer and more certain prison sentences have resulted in exploding prison populations. Building and maintaining prisons are a major expense for state and county governments. States have responded to the added financial demands by privatizing some prisons and by constructing more secure, austere facilities. Besides building more prisons, states also use a variety of alternatives to traditional incarceration. These include boot camps and electronic surveillance.

KEY TERMS

Aggravating circumstances At the sentencing stage a jury may consider certain factors, such as the use of a gun in the commission of a crime, that make the behavior more serious and lead to a longer sentence.

Boot camps Prisons in which military-type discipline is used to scare young first offenders straight.

Brady Bill Gun control bill passed in 1993 requires a five-day waiting period to purchase handguns, and it requires gun dealers to report certain purchases.

Community policing Model for police behavior that stresses the development of greater trust between the police and members of neighborhoods; residents are encouraged to report criminal acts to the police.

Determinate sentencing Removes much judicial discretion by setting specific terms for specific crimes.

Deterrence Sentencing aimed at preventing similar criminal acts by others.

Discretionary authority Broad latitude of choice within legal bounds for public employees; it is particularly broad for police officers.

Incapacitation Separating people from society, often by long, or at least certain, prison sentences.

Indeterminate sentencing By not setting an exact time of incarceration, it gives judges discretion to fit the sentence to the characteristics of the crime and of the criminal.

Legalistic style A style of police operation that is characterized by a concern for technical efficiency. The police force is formally organized, and there is strong pressure on officers to make arrests.

Mitigating circumstances At the sentencing stage a jury may consider certain factors, such as the fact that the crime was a first offense, and impose a milder penalty than normal.

Parole Following release from prison, individuals spend a transition period under supervision.

Police culture Informal relationships among police, who often believe they are disliked by the general public.

Prison subculture The world inside prisons in which there are traditional codes of inmate behavior that are enforced by inmates.

Probation Rather than being sent to prison, convicted criminals are required to live under a set of restrictions and to report to a probation officer.

Recidivism The likelihood that convicted criminals will return to criminal behavior following completion of their sentences.

Rehabilitation Sentencing whose aim is to reform criminals and return them to society as better persons.

Retribution Sentencing that seeks to punish criminals for acts that society finds normally offensive. This could be called "just deserts."

Service style A style of police operation that is characterized by a concern to treat serious threats to the peace seriously, but to handle minor violations more informally. Often found in affluent suburbs, service style police are courteous, well-paid, and well-trained.

Shock incarceration Short incarceration intended to scare first-time offenders straight.

Watchman style A style of police operation that is characterized by a concern to maintain order, rather than to closely enforce laws. Watchman style police forces are marked by low pay, local recruitment, and minimal initial training.

REFERENCES

1 For state and local government expenditures and employee statistics, see Morgan, Morgan, and Quitno, eds., *State Rankings 1994* (Lawrence, Kan.: Morgan Quitno Corp., 1994), pp. 68, 70, 72, 74.

2 Wesley G. Skogan, "Crime and Punishment" in Virginia Gray and Herbert Jacob, eds., *Politics in the American States,* 6th ed. (Washington: Congressional Quarterly Press, 1996), p. 365.

3 Charles Mahtesian, "The NRA Rides Again," *Governing* (March 1995), p. 20.

4 David C. Anderson, "The Criminal Funnel," *New York Times Magazine,* June 12, 1994, pp. 56–58.

5 Edwin Sutherland, *Principles of Criminology* (Chicago: J. B. Lippincott, 1947), pp. 6–7.

6 See James Q. Wilson and Richard J. Herrnstein, *Crime and Human Nature* (New York: Simon & Schuster, 1985).

7 Frank Schmalleger, *Criminal Justice Today,* 3d ed. (Englewood Cliffs, N.J.: Prentice-Hall, 1995), p. 204.

8 James Q. Wilson, *Varieties of Police Behavior* (New York: Atheneum, 1973), p. 7.

9 See Jerome H. Skolnick, *Justice without Trial: Law Enforcement in a Democratic Society* (New York: John Wiley, 1966).

10 James Q. Wilson, *Varieties of Police Behavior,* Chapters 5–7.

11 James Q. Wilson and George Kelling, "Broken Windows," *Atlantic Monthly* (March 1982), pp. 29–38.

12 Rob Gurwitt, "Cops and Community," *Governing* (May 1995), p. 24.

13 David C. Anderson, "The Criminal Funnel," p. 57.

14 Frank Schmalleger, *Criminal Justice Today,* p. 369.

15 James Q. Wilson, *Thinking about Crime* (New York: Basic Books, 1975), pp. 174–175.

16 See Robert Martinson, "What Works: Questions about Prison Reform," *Public Interest* (1974), pp. 22–54.

17 Rhonda Reeves, "The Federalization of Crime and Justice in the United States," *The Book of the States 1994–95* (Lexington, Ky.: Council of State Governments, 1994), p. 526.

18 Bureau of Justice Statistics, *Annual Report, 1987* (Washington: Bureau of Justice Statistics, 1988), p. 70.

19 Morgan, Morgan, and Quitno, *State Rankings,* pp. 66–67.

20 Herbert A. Johnson, *History of Criminal Justice* (Cincinnati: Anderson, 1988), p. 36.

21 Sam H. Verhovek, "Across the U.S., Executions Are Neither Swift Nor Cheap," *New York Times,* February 22, 1995, pp. 1, 12.

22 Tamar Lewin, "Who Decides Who Will Die? Even within States, It Varies," *New York Times,* February 23, 1995, pp. 1, 13.

23 Erik Eckholm, "Studies Find Death Penalty Often Tied to Victim's Race," *New York Times,* February 24, 1995, p. A6.

24 For a history of prisons, see Frank Schmalleger, *Criminal Justice Today* pp. 447–469.

25 In a word, prisoners were to be penitent and wrestle with the evil in their souls. This was the way they would be rehabilitated. "Reformatories" were established in the late 1800s, and now we use the term *corrections* to refer to prisons—different words, different approaches, but the same unattainable goals.

26 Penelope Lemov, "Roboprison," *Governing* (March 1995), pp. 24–29.

27 Penelope Lemov, "Jailhouse, Inc.," *Governing* (May 1993), p. 44.

28 Anthony Ramirez, "Despite a Checkered Past, the Future Is Looking Brighter for the Private Prison Industry," *New York Times,* August 14, 1994, p. 6.

29 As reported in the television documentary, "Lock Up: The Prisoners of Rikers Island" (1994).

30 See Charles Stastny and Gabrielle Tyrnauer, *Who Rules the Joint? The Changing Political Culture of Maximum-Security Prisons in America* (Lexington, Mass.: Lexington Books, 1982).

31 From Inez Cardozo-Freeman, *The Joint: Language and Culture in a Maximum Security Prison* (Springfield, Ill.: Charles C. Thomas, 1984), pp. 480–541. Also see Eugene Ray, *Dictionary of Prison Slang,* Federal Bureau of Prisons, Computer Printout (November 30, 1986).

32 See Rose Giallombardo, *Society of Women: A Study of Women's Prisons* (New York: John Wiley, 1966). Also see Jean Harris, *They Always Call Us Ladies* (New York: Scribners, 1988).

33 Alana Northrup, Kenneth L. Kraemer, and John L. King, "Police Use of Computers," *Journal of Criminal Justice* (Vol. 23, No. 3, 1995), pp. 259–275.

34 Rhonda Reeves, "The Federalization of Crime," p. 527.

35 Fox Butterfield, "California's Courts Clogged in Wake of 'Three-Strikes' Law," *New York Times,* March 21, 1995, p. 1.

36 Quoted in David Broder, "When Tough Isn't Smart," *Washington Post,* March 23, 1994, p. A21.

37 David Osborne and Ted Gaebler, *Reinventing Government* (Reading, Mass.: Addison-Wesley, 1992), p. 320.

16

ECONOMIC DEVELOPMENT AND ENVIRONMENTAL PROTECTION POLICIES

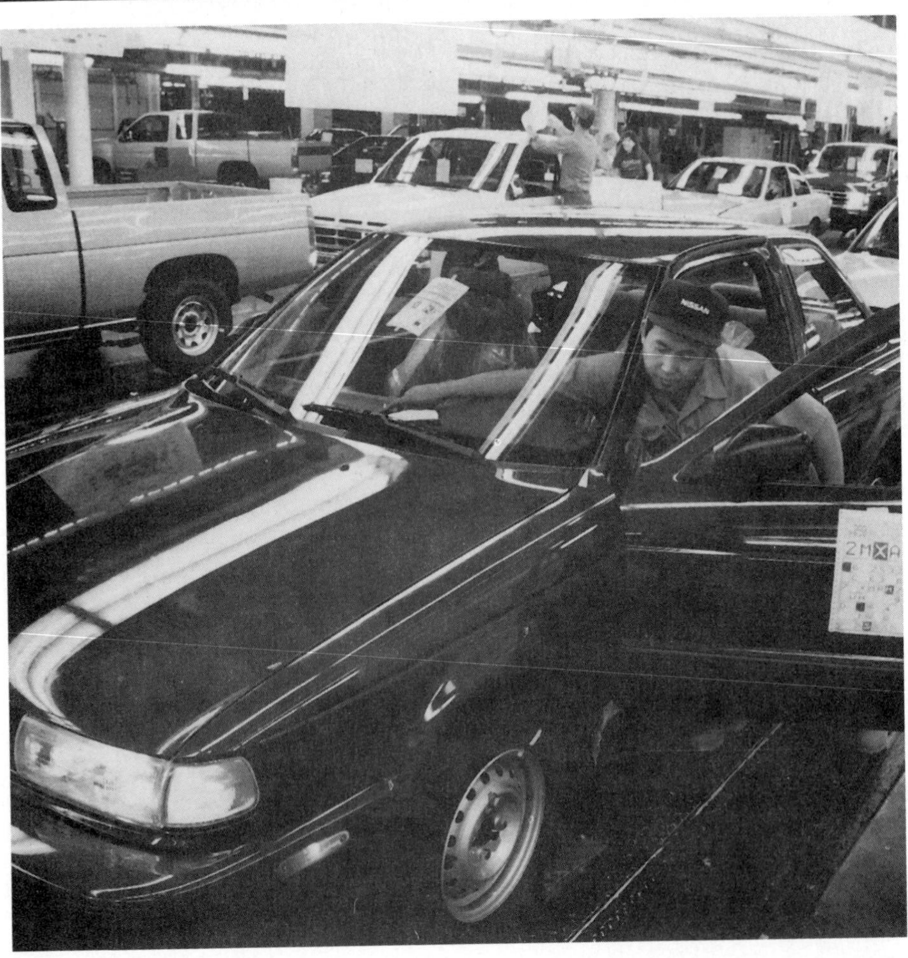

Dan Loftin/AP/Wide World Photos

At a glance, policies affecting the economy and the environment would appear to be completely dominated by the federal government. After all, state and local governments do not have a Federal Reserve Board to set interest rates; they are not allowed, legally, to carry budget deficits that could help stimulate their economies during a recession; and they cannot threaten, as President Bill Clinton did in 1995, to place a tariff on luxury import automobiles to force another nation (Japan) to buy more American automobiles and automotive parts. Economic policies are identified with the federal government in Washington, D.C. Environmental policies are perceived in the same way. The major environmental laws—the Clean Air Act, Clean Water Act, and Endangered Species Act—passed the U.S. Congress and were signed by the president. And it is federal agencies—the Environmental Protection Agency and the Fish and Wildlife Service, for example—that we associate with the administration of these laws. It is true that the federal government is the dominant actor in these policies, but state and local governments play an important role, also.

ECONOMIC DEVELOPMENT

At various times in American history, states have taken an active role in stimulating economic growth. Perhaps the best known period is the early nineteenth century when state governments financed a transportation network, especially canals, that opened up states in the interior of the country (Illinois, Indiana, and Ohio) to trade with the Northeast and South. The state of New York spent $7 million to build the Erie Canal, the most successful of many similar ventures by state governments.[1]

Southern states, during the early part of the twentieth century, adopted policies to diversify their agricultural economies by attracting Northern industry. Mississippi created a Balance Agriculture with Industry program, which lured companies from the North by offering tax incentives and low labor costs. At the same time, as discussed in Chapter 14, many states were adopting laws to protect their workers by providing unemployment insurance and workers' compensation programs.[2]

During the post-World War II period, a vibrant American economy dominated the world for at least twenty-five years, economic growth was reasonably widespread within the United States, and generally there was little state intervention to promote economic growth. The fact that investment decisions were made by private businesses free to locate in any state was of little importance. During the late 1980s, however, increasing economic competition from abroad and slow growth in the national economy created a situation that continues today, where "state effort to sustain growth could be instrumental for economic progress."[3]

State governors now rank economic development as important as more traditional state issues, such as education, welfare, and highways. **Economic development policies,** as defined by Gray and Eisinger, are those that "encourage new business investment in particular locales in the hopes of creating or retaining jobs and enhancing and diversifying the tax base."[4] The importance of private investment is illustrated in Figure 16-1.

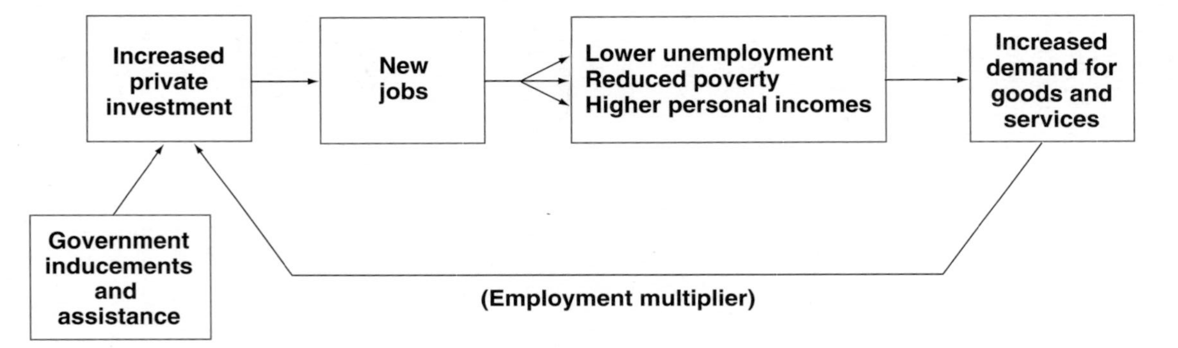

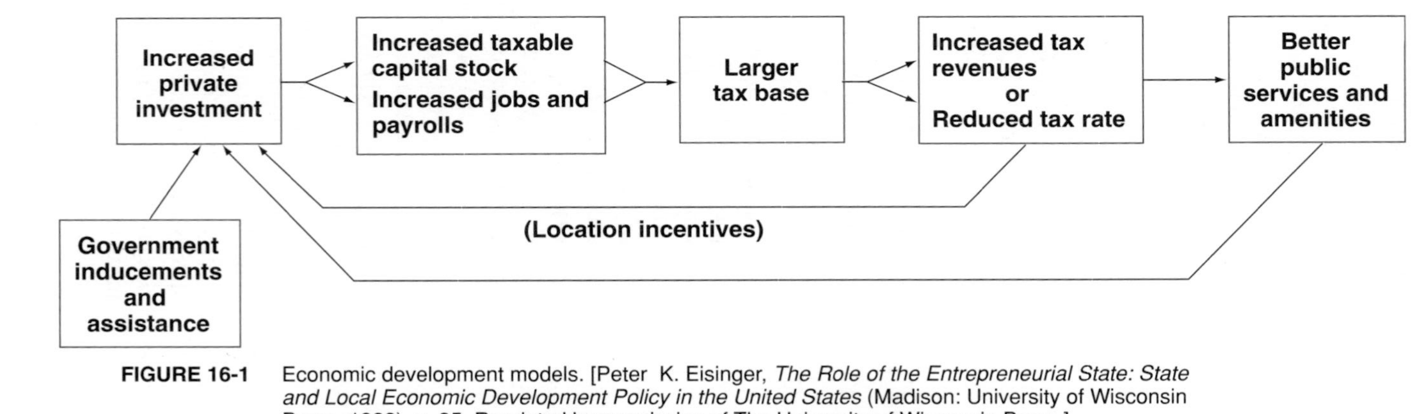

FIGURE 16-1 Economic development models. [Peter K. Eisinger, *The Role of the Entrepreneurial State: State and Local Economic Development Policy in the United States* (Madison: University of Wisconsin Press, 1988), p. 35. Reprinted by permission of The University of Wisconsin Press.]

Location Incentives and Bidding Wars

The demand for businesses that provide factory or service jobs exceeds the supply, resulting in competition between state and local governments that causes them to offer businesses incentives to maintain existing industries or to induce out-of-state business to relocate or build branch plants within their boundaries. John Jackson calls this the **maintenance/attraction strategy.**[5]

An example of this approach is the use of **tax incentives,** which give tax breaks to recruit and retain businesses. In the past ten years, the number of states using tax incentives for job creation increased from twenty-seven to forty-four.[6] The nature of this incentive varies from state to state; North Carolina offers a $2,800 income tax credit for every new manufacturing job created above a threshold of nine. The creation of specific jobs is only one item that qualifies for tax breaks. Others include the purchase of equipment and machinery, raw materials used in manufacturing, and money spent on research and development. The total number of different tax incentives offered is over fifteen, although all of them are not used by every state. Local governments frequently exempt a new business from the local property tax for a number of years, an incentive known as tax abatement. Property tax abatement is the most popular incentive used by local governments.

Financial incentives are low-interest loans that have the backing of state or local governments. More than forty states offer loans for plant construction, purchasing equipment, existing plant expansion, and establishing plants in areas of high unemployment.

Both of these incentives lower a business's costs, which should translate into increased sales and profits.[7] Generally, states in the South have the highest number of tax and financial incentives to attract businesses.

Unfortunately, today's global economy, where jobs can move abroad almost as easily as they move from state to state, has intensified competition. States and communities are now putting together **customized incentives,** a package of a large number of firm-specific incentives used to recruit a major new business or retain an existing one. Customized incentives are usually associated with a bidding war where one state after another ups the ante hoping to win a new automobile manufacturing plant or an equivalent prize (see Figure 16-2). In this environment, companies see a chance to ask for more and more. Recently, Intel Corporation made available to states interested in a new computer chip factory a 104-item wish list of the kind of incentives they were looking for. (Intel called it an "ideal incentive matrix.") In addition to the usual tax and financial incentives, the list included an item requesting immediate resident status for its employees and dependents so that they could take advantage of lower in-state college tuition.[8]

In 1993, states and cities vied for a new Mercedes-Benz plant that would build sport-utility vehicles. At first, 170 cities and 30 states were in the running. It then narrowed to 64 sites in 21 states, then 11 states, and then 7 states, with Alabama emerging as the winner.[9] Alabama's incentives package, which totaled over $250 million (some estimates were as high as $300 million), included the following:

- Plant site paid for by the Tuscaloosa County commission and cleared by the Alabama National Guard.
- A $5 million welcome center for visitors to the plant paid for by the state.

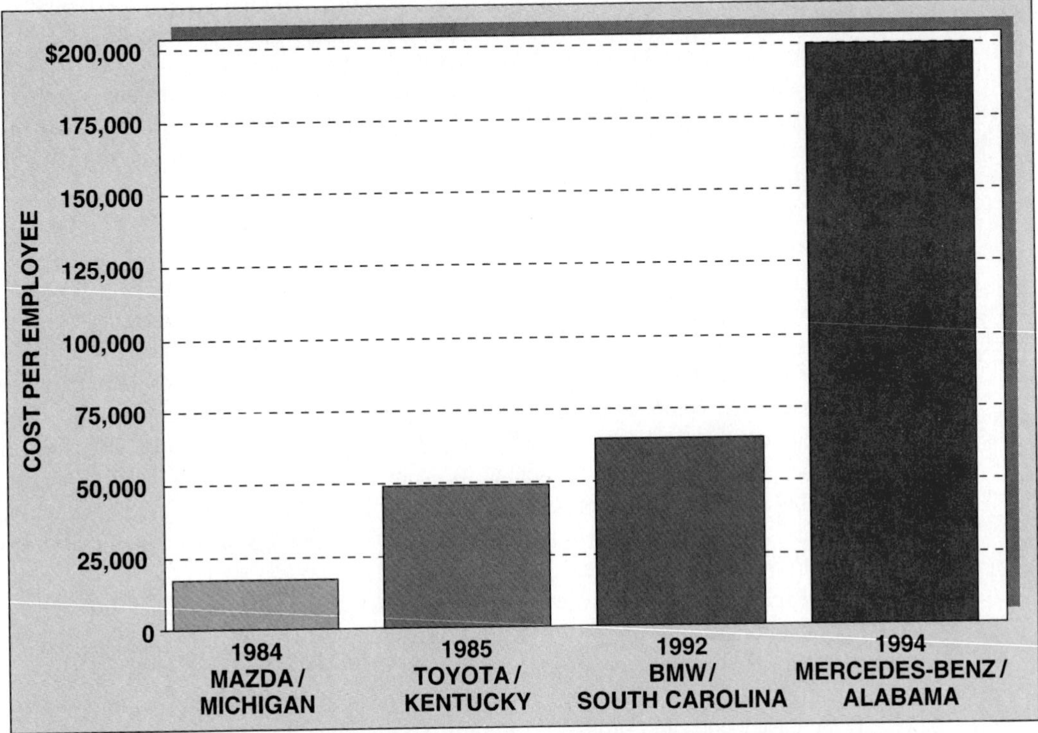

FIGURE 16-2 Increasing costs of customized incentives packages for automobile manufacturing plants. [Data for this figure are from Charles J. Spindler, "Winners and Losers in Industrial Recruitment: Mercedes-Benz and Alabama," *State and Local Government Review* 26 (Fall 1994), p. 202.]

- Twenty-five years of state corporate tax breaks and tax credits.
- Exemption from local property taxes.
- Employee training costs, including salaries during the training period, and construction of a training facility were paid for by the state.[10]

Bidding wars may occur when a business threatens to leave its present location. In 1989, NBC television was thinking of moving to New Jersey; in return for staying in New York City NBC received $100 million in tax breaks and other concessions. A few years later, CBS obtained $50 million in incentives for staying in the city. ABC, which apparently was not seriously thinking of moving, negotiated a $26 million package by promising to create 185 additional jobs.[11]

With the rising cost of these incentives, some observers are questioning whether the economic benefits a state and its citizens receive from the acquisition of a new facility actually outweigh the costs. States are being cautioned that before offering an expensive package of incentives they should look at it from the perspective of cost-benefit analysis. (See the essay by Neal R. Peirce.) But this is hardly an exact science. What benefits does the Mercedes-Benz plant offer the state of Alabama and its citizens? Once the plant is built, it will employ 1,500 workers making about $12

The When, How and Why of Wooing

Neal R. Peirce

Phoenix—This sun-soaked city is embroiled in a heated controversy over a proposed downtown baseball stadium. The basic issue is who will pay for the stadium—private investors led by Jerry Colangelo, the president of the Phoenix Suns, or taxpayers?

Colangelo's group and several county supervisors think that it would be fine to raise the $240 million in capital that's needed to build the stadium through a quarter-cent boost in the local sales tax.

Lots of taxpayers, though, believe that they'd be taken to the cleaners through a rental agreement that would provide a slim 1.5 per cent return on the county's investment. County officials are feeling the heat and show signs of backing off the deal.

By contrast, government officials and lawmakers in most states have only to whisper "jobs" for the public to acquiesce in transferring huge sums to subsidy-hungry firms—and not just owners of major league sports teams, but also big industries. Last year, for example, Mercedes-Benz of North America Inc. got a stunning $253 million offer to put its new U.S. plant in Alabama. To snare a 400-worker Dosasco Steel plant, Kentucky anted up $140 million in incentives—an all-time record that translates to $350,000 per job.

Are states giving up "the seed corn of their tax base"?

That's the real danger, according to George Autry, a veteran economic development expert. State officials and lawmakers are obligating funds, he said in a recent interview with a reporter for the *Raleigh* (N.C.) *News & Observer,* that they'll need to provide the "necessary infrastructure to keep their states progressing—the roads, the schools, the security, the water and sewer."

Maybe it's time to ask: Do any incentives to business represent a good investment for taxpayers?

A very qualified yes to that question has emerged from a dispassionate study of business incentives conducted by Mary Jo Waits of Arizona State University's Morrison Institute for Public Policy. The study was prepared for the Arizona Commerce Department and the Greater Phoenix and Tucson Economic Councils.

More important to businesses than incentives, the study found, are a high-quality work force, good access to markets and reasonable operating costs.

But if subsidies are to be considered, Waits said, they should be based on clear goals—quality jobs, plant modernization, upgrading technology and worker skills—"and not just to win competitive bidding wars for companies."

A state or locality, she suggested, should decide on explicit guidelines by which to judge any deal—"rigorous cost-benefit analysis," she said, "is the bottom line."

Yet only two states—Illinois and Indiana—have formalized such cost-benefit analysis.

Once a firm is given a subsidy, Waits suggested, it needs to be held accountable for what it produces in return. States and localities should be prepared to press for "clawbacks"—reducing, canceling or recovering public subsidies if a company doesn't provide as many jobs as it promised or tries to skip town after accepting public aid.

As an example, a court has blocked General Motors Corp. from closing its Willow

Run plant in Ypsilanti, Mich., because GM had accepted years of tax abatements Ypsilanti offered to keep the plant in place.

The Arizona study stops just short of what may be needed the most on the subsidy front: a strong dose of democracy and sunshine—ways to let the public in on what the deals are, and their pros and cons, before state or local officials sign off on them.

Who's to say, for example, that the public subsidies greasing the way for a new manufacturing plant are the best way to spend taxpayer dollars? Waits reported that if Arizona were to invest in job training to upgrade skills, so as to boost the average Arizona worker's earnings by $100 a year, the state's economy would benefit as much as if 6,000 new jobs were brought in. And the state wouldn't suffer the burden on its roads, schools and other public services caused by a burgeoning population.

Behind that lies a simple but basic point: In economic development, the premium ought to be on improving the livelihoods and quality of life of existing residents, and not just on growth for growth's—or some big company's—sake.

The ideal is a government that bargains sensitively and smartly in the interest of its citizens—unswayed by flashy newspaper headlines and simplistic appeals of numbers of jobs over quality of jobs.

Admittedly, there are intangibles in the equation. Is it worth subsidizing a sports stadium, for example, in the hope of drawing a major league team that might raise a city's profile and prestige?

But realistic cost-benefit analyses can illuminate most of the arguments over subsidies. And if government itself is too often too politicized, under too much pressure to evaluate each proposal coolly and effectively, why not think of a partnership between universities and newspapers?

Jointly, the academicians and a state or city's news media could produce some realistic sets of yardsticks by which to judge proposed deals. They could analyze investments that are alternatives to the ones that politicians come up with, or give in to. They could, in short, do the public's homework—and strengthen the hand of citizen and public-interest groups—in decisions that are typically rife with overclaims and confusion.

Such collaboration, of course, wouldn't stop the debate over which cost-benefit analysis is the most realistic. And it wouldn't stop newspapers from reporting any and all debate on a subsidy issue.

But it would slow down the freight train of half-cooked deals and give proposed subsidies a sanitizing dose of clear-eyed inspection.

Source: National Journal, February 26, 1994, p. 488. Reprinted by permission of National Journal.

---

an hour for the first two years and after that $16 an hour. Unfortunately, there is no way of knowing with any certainty who will fill these jobs. Will they be filled with unemployed workers living in Alabama, or will they be filled by unemployed autoworkers from other states? Additional jobs created by the presence of Mercedes-Benz, called "spin-off" jobs, were estimated at 10,000 to 11,000. However, some of these jobs may go to Atlanta, Georgia, where automobile manufacturing suppliers already exist.

What costs are involved for Alabama and its citizens? A number of costs to the state or local government such as purchasing the site and conducting training sessions involve an exact amount of money that is easily known. Taxes not collected because of various tax breaks can be estimated with some reliability. Development "impact costs" are difficult to estimate and are sometimes simply ignored. What will it cost to provide water and sewer services, schools, and police and fire protection for workers and their families who move to Tuscaloosa County to work in the new plant?[12] Because benefits are particularly difficult to estimate, states should be careful in offering incentives packages that exceed a realistic appraisal of benefits.

The increasing expense of head-to-head competition in the bidding wars has caused some state leaders to call for a truce. The National Governors' Association adopted *voluntary* guidelines that encourage governors to improve the general business climate in their states rather than using customized incentives packages. Under these guidelines, incentives packages would be used primarily to encourage investment in economically depressed areas of a state.[13]

Alternative Approaches

A few states are following a different strategy to promote economic development. Gray and Eisinger describe the shift this way: "Previously states tried to attract existing firms to the state; now they try to develop new growth opportunities for local entrepreneurs and businesses."[14] Jackson calls this a **creation strategy** that relies on increasing the availability of capital for entrepreneurs, educating the workforce, and promoting innovation.[15] This approach may help take states out of the bidding wars because political leaders will focus on their state's economy as it is, evaluating strengths and weaknesses, establishing economic goals, and building on economic strengths. In Pennsylvania, for example, the Ben Franklin Partnership program provides matching state funds to encourage local businesses and universities to work "together on research that might result in a marketable (or improved) product or process."[16] State-sponsored venture capital funds, which are used to give financial backing to high-risk companies in the early stages of developing and marketing a new product, exist in over thirty states. Many states also are actively seeking overseas markets for local firms.

David Osborne emphasizes another approach to economic growth. He suggests that in today's world of high-tech industries and global competition, states must have, among other characteristics, a skilled, educated workforce, an intellectual infrastructure of first-rate universities and research facilities, and an attractive quality of life.[17] In other words, the expenditure of public revenues on traditional government functions is important in the long run in determining a state's or a community's economic prosperity. The Corporation for Enterprise Development has devised a report card that measures states in some of these areas (see Table 16-1).

Although the importance of private investment to state and local governments is clear (see Figure 16-1), the overall economic effect of their efforts is more problematic (see the Scholarly Box entitled Do State Economic Development Programs Work?). Nevertheless, the political payoffs of aggressively seeking new businesses to

TABLE 16-1 A REPORT CARD ON THE DEVELOPMENT CAPACITY OF THE STATES*

State	Grade	State	Grade
Alabama	D	Montana	B
Alaska	D	Nebraska	C
Arizona	B	Nevada	D
Arkansas	F	New Hampshire	C
California	B	New Jersey	A
Colorado	A	New Mexico	D
Connecticut	A	New York	C
Delaware	A	North Carolina	C
Florida	C	North Dakota	C
Georgia	C	Ohio	B
Hawaii	B	Oklahoma	F
Idaho	B	Oregon	A
Illinois	A	Pennsylvania	B
Indiana	D	Rhode Island	C
Iowa	C	South Carolina	D
Kansas	D	South Dakota	D
Kentucky	D	Tennessee	C
Louisiana	F	Texas	C
Maine	D	Utah	A
Maryland	B	Vermont	C
Massachusetts	A	Virginia	B
Michigan	C	Washington	A
Minnesota	A	West Virginia	F
Mississippi	F	Wisconsin	B
Missouri	C	Wyoming	C

*The Development Capacity index is one of three indexes used by the Corporation for Enterprise Development to assess each state's economy. The Development Capacity index measures a state's capacity for growth and recovery from economic adversity. It is a broad-based index that takes into consideration the education and skill levels of a state's workforce, availability of capital for business's needs, technology resources, and infrastructure.

Source: The 1995 Development Report Card for the States, 9th ed., (Washington, D.C.: Corporation for Enterprise Development, 1995), pp. 1–2, 5, 163. Reprinted by permission of the Corporation for Enterprise Development.

locate in a state or city mean that it is unlikely bidding wars will end. Quite simply, governors and mayors find the good press and possible increased voter support to be compelling reasons for aggressively seeking new businesses. For example, Indiana Governor Evan Bayh used a $290 million incentives package to attract a United Airlines maintenance facility to Indianapolis in spite of the fact that during the election campaign he criticized his opponent for an expensive incentives package used to land a foreign carmaker!

The Effect of Political Culture

State economic problems cause states to adopt economic development programs, but political culture is an important determinant of the kind of programs they adopt. Research by Keith Boeckelman and Russell Hanson examines several hypotheses concerning the effects of political culture.[18] Boeckelman concludes that moralistic states

SCHOLARLY BOX

DO STATE ECONOMIC DEVELOPMENT PROGRAMS WORK?

The answer to this question would certainly be yes, if the abundance of economic development programs offered by state governments were an indicator of success in achieving desired goals. Political scientists and economists, however, differ in their answers to this question. Their conclusions could hardly be more mixed.

Ronald Hy and William Waugh examined site selection decisions made by new and expanding businesses and concluded that tax and financial incentives are not as important as other factors such as market access, community characteristics, and availability of transportation networks. According to Hy and Waugh the "effect of tax incentives is that firms are often rewarded for behaving as they would have without tax incentives."[19] At best, tax incentives serve as a tiebreaker in those cases where two or more locations are equal on all other factors.

On the other hand, Paul Brace's detailed study of state-level development policies between 1968 and 1989 established that they can make a significant contribution to a state's economic health. States had little effect on their economies between 1968 and 1982. But between 1983 and 1989, development policies had a positive effect on growth in per capita personal income.

What accounts for these mixed conclusions? In part, this is due to a number of complex research problems associated with attempts to link state economic development policies to growth in the state economy. First, researchers frequently select different indicators of state economic performance, and this may account for some of the differences in their findings. Per capita personal income, nonagricultural employment, value added by manufacturing, and total gross state product are just a few of the indicators that have been used. Second, to a large degree the economic performance of all states is tied to the direction the national economy is going. It is hard to imagine state development policies that could completely offset the effects of a national recession or other national trends. For example, Pennsylvania is considered aggressive in keeping and attracting high-paying factory jobs. It uses grants, offers guaranteed loans, and pays for employee job-training programs. In addition, and equally important in the eyes of plant owners and managers, Pennsylvania obtains quick approval of permits for plant construction, access roads, and sewers, along with appropriate environmental clearances. Nevertheless, Pennsylvania still lost about 10 percent of its factory jobs between 1989 and 1994. But this decline was about half the loss experienced by other states in the Northeast (New York's loss was 19.8 percent).[20]

Given diverse findings and the complexity of the research problem we must be cautious in drawing firm conclusions concerning the effect of state economic development policies.

are less likely to offer tax and financial incentives that primarily serve business interests and are more likely to focus on the protection of workers (workers' compensation benefits and efforts to encourage labor-management cooperation) and programs that are part of the creation strategy mentioned above. Hanson also finds evidence that moralistic states, with their concern for the "good society," for example, protect the interests of workers with liberal minimum wage and workers' compensation laws.

In states with individualistic political cultures, governing is conceived of as a marketplace. Government is more directly concerned with commercial considerations and economic matters, and it engages only in activities that are specifically demanded of it. Business leaders are well organized to make demands, and resulting policies favor the use of incentives, which means states emphasize a maintenance/attraction strategy for economic development. Loans for building plants and purchasing equipment and machinery, whether made directly or guaranteed by the state, are prominent incentives.[21]

Traditionalistic states, which include most Southern states, regard governing as an activity solely for those at the top of the social structure who use their power to preserve their elite position. Development policies were designed (1) to provide businesses with low labor costs through the adoption, for example, of "right-to-work" laws that made labor union organizing difficult and (2) to offer tax incentives such as tax exemptions for new equipment and machinery. Many policies that kept labor costs low prevented labor from organizing and gaining power, and thus threatening the position of the existing elites. However, since the mid-1980s traditionalistic states have abandoned some of their policies that were against the interests of labor. Hanson suggests that economic changes and growth in these states are beginning to "alter traditional social structures, loosening the hold of elites on public policy, and increasing the number and power of groups previously excluded from politics."[22] Of course, the traditionalistic political culture of these states may change as a result.

ENVIRONMENTAL PROTECTION

The Tragedy of the Commons

The problem of protecting the environment is often illustrated this way: Imagine a pasture that is used by cattle for grazing and is open to all who own cattle; in other words, the pasture is held in common. It is to be expected that a herdsman will try to keep as many cattle as possible on the commons so as to maximize his profit. And the herdsman will continue to add cattle because he will receive all proceeds from the sale of an additional animal, and the cost of overgrazing that results from more and more cattle is shared by all the herdsmen. Garrett Hardin argues that the same decision to add cattle is made "by each and every rational herdsman sharing a commons."[23] This is the **tragedy of the commons** because eventually the pasture will be overgrazed and become depleted. In other words, short-term economic self-interest results in actions that harm the environment and even long-term economic interests. The problem with pollution is similar: "Self interest often encourages businesses and people to pollute."[24] An owner of a manufacturing plant faced with installing expensive pollution control equipment will decide that the small improvement in air quality from a single act is not worth the large reduction in profits caused by purchasing the equipment. One way to deal with this situation is to pass laws that require the installation of pollution control equipment.

Federal Environmental Protection Laws

Prior to the first Earth Day in 1970, environmental protection was primarily a state and local responsibility. In the late nineteenth century, Chicago and Cincinnati had laws regulating smoke emissions, and the first state law regulating air quality was passed in Ohio about the same time. In 1952, Oregon was the first state to pass statewide air pollution legislation and to establish an air pollution control agency. Generally, however, state and local governments paid little attention to environmental protection. Increased public concern about the issue caused the federal government to assume a leadership role in the early 1970s that led to the passage of two significant laws: the Clean Air

Act of 1970 and the Federal Water Pollution Control Act of 1972 (usually called the Clean Water Act). Both laws, as amended, are basic to environmental protection today.

Evan Ringquist describes the role of federal and state governments by identifying five government activities in environmental policymaking: setting goals and standards, designing and implementing programs, monitoring and enforcement, research and development, and funding.[25]

The federal government tends to dominate in *setting goals and standards.* For example, the Clean Air Act required the U.S. Environmental Protection Agency to set uniform, nationwide emission standards for a number of hazardous air pollutants. The Clean Water Act, however, did not take a strong top-down approach. The federal goal was to classify most waterways as suitable for recreational activities (or "fishable-swimmable," as it is usually called), and states were given authority to define specific water quality standards to meet this goal. Actually, the air quality standards are not completely uniform either because many states have enacted standards that exceed those of the federal government. In 1991, eleven Northeastern states and the District of Columbia adopted California's strict standards for new car emissions. On the other hand, a few states have laws that prohibit exceeding federal air quality standards.

States play a larger role in *designing and implementing programs* and *monitoring and enforcement* of regulations. This means that states, to some extent, can determine techniques to achieve federal goals and standards, monitor air and water quality, inspect facilities, and levy fines when violations are discovered. In 1988, states completed 28,000 air pollution control inspections, while the U.S. EPA completed only 2,800.[26] Through the process of implementing these laws, states have occasionally developed innovative ideas. For example, states pioneered the "bubble" concept of air pollution control. This approach, rather than strictly regulating each emission source, allows an imaginary bubble to be placed over a plant, and as long as emissions within the bubble do not exceed air quality standards, the plant's owners can decide how to best regulate each source of emissions. Perhaps the standards can be met by installing very sophisticated pollution control equipment on one emission source and less sophisticated equipment on others. With the bubble concept, it may be possible to meet air quality standards at less cost to the plant's owner.[27] Also, some states, Minnesota and New Jersey, for example, have an "environmental bill of rights," which allows citizens to file enforcement suits against polluting firms.[28]

The last two activities are *research and development* and *funding.* Questions about acceptable levels of pollution and the best strategies to control pollution still do not have definitive answers, and research continues to be important. Few states have elaborate research programs, and most of the research money comes from the federal government. In 1989, the U.S. EPA spent $770 million on research; states spent only $33 million.[29]

Federal funds to state and local governments for environmental protection peaked at close to $550 million in 1975, declined during the 1980s, and then increased slightly to $400 million in 1992. Even though states had budget problems of their own during the late 1980s and early 1990s, state spending on the environment increased between 1986 and 1991 (see Figure 16-3). A few states such as Arizona found innovative ways to fund environmental programs. Arizona enacted a $1.50 sur-

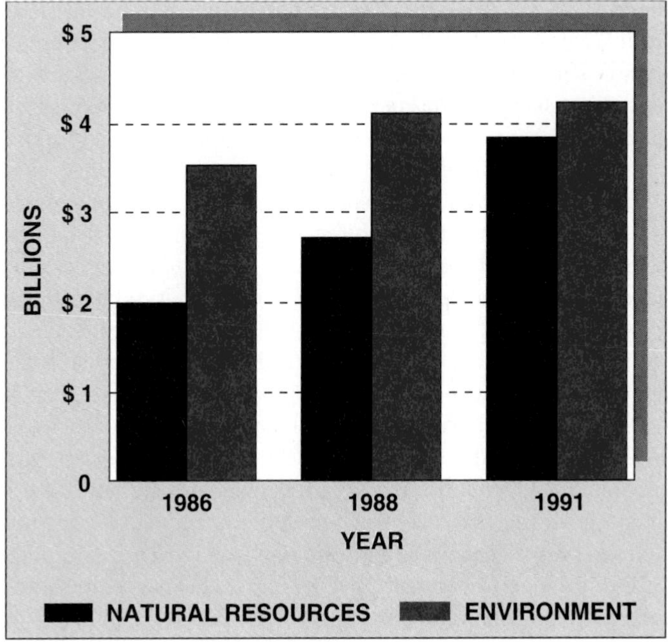

FIGURE 16-3 State expenditures on environment and natural resources (in 1987 dollars). [DeWitt John, *Civic Environmentalism: Alternatives to Regulation in States and Communities* (Washington, D.C.: CQ Press, 1994), p. 57. Reprinted by permission of Congressional Quarterly, Inc.]

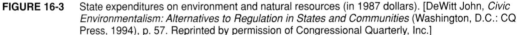

charge on annual motor vehicle registrations to provide money for air pollution control improvements.

Still, it should be remembered that in the most important activity—setting goals and standards—it is the federal government that is dominant and not the states. States are important in administration and are playing a greater role in funding, but the states have been following the federal government's lead.

Problems developed in the late 1980s and early 1990s, as the term *environmental mandates* (see Chapter 2) was increasingly used by state and local government officials to describe new and amended federal environmental laws and the EPA's regulations interpreting them. The Safe Drinking Water Act, for example, requires local governments to test drinking water by 1995 for over 100 health-threatening contaminants; if the level of contaminants exceeds standards, the water must be treated to remove them. Estimates to monitor and treat only lead and copper contaminants for 1995 are $490 million, and close to a total of $1.4 billion for all of the contaminants that presently have standards.[30]

But what's all the fuss? Doesn't everyone want safe drinking water? First, the federal government is not helping to pay for the growing cost of compliance. It is simply passed on to state and local governments, and their officials fear that taxpayers won't want to pay the increase in taxes that will be required. Estimates in Ohio in 1992 ranged from $2,000 to $3,000 per household over the next decade to comply with mandates that were in effect at that time. That is a considerable sum of money, but it is possible the public would be willing to pay if the mandates were reasonable and justifiable. This leads to a second point: State and local officials argue that mandates are not always reasonable. The Safe Drinking Water Act requires testing for contaminants that are unlikely threats to many water supplies or sets standards that are unrealistically high. For example, all drinking water was to be tested for an agricultural chemical that is known to be used only on Hawaiian pineapple fields! (The EPA has since waived this rule.) If the federal government cannot help pay for compliance, it should at least offer greater flexibility to state and local officials so that they "can address the greatest risk first rather than spending their energies in protests about high-cost, low-payoff mandates."[31] (See the essay by Tom Arrandale.)

Civic Environmentalism

The approach to environmental protection that has just been discussed is frequently referred to as command-and-control regulation. In general terms, this regulatory approach frames "rules of behavior that are applied to specific individuals or organizations through an enforcement process."[32] Quite recently, another approach has emerged. It is called **civic environmentalism,** which is the idea that in some instances "communities and states will organize on their own to protect the environment, without being forced to do so by the federal government."[33] It is a bottom-up approach to environmental protection. A leading expert on civic environmentalism, DeWitt John, has identified the key features of civic environmentalism by examining environmental initiatives in Iowa, Florida, and Colorado.

First, civic environmentalism *focuses on unfinished business* in environmental protection—those pollution issues that are not receiving adequate attention from the federal government. Examples are **nonpoint pollution,** pollution that comes from many sources and covers a large area such as fertilizer runoff from agricultural activities and runoff from urban storm water systems. (Point pollution comes from a single, easily identifiable source, such as a smokestack.) Other examples are pollution prevention (trying to prevent at least some pollution before it occurs rather than trying to clean up after it happens) and ecosystem protection (concern for an entire ecosystem rather than protecting a single species or controlling a single polluter).[34]

Nonpoint pollution is an important issue in Iowa where large quantities of herbicides and chemical fertilizers are used to increase corn yields. Iowans have taken steps to reduce the use of these chemicals, thereby protecting the drinking water supply from contamination. Florida's Governor J. Lawton Chiles led the way in negotiating an end to a three-year battle between local, state, and federal officials over water quality in the Everglades. The result was an agreement on initial plans to protect and restore the Everglades. In Colorado, the state's Public Utilities Commission made a commitment to energy conservation by encouraging "demand-side" management from companies generating electric power. (Reducing demand for electricity reduces the amount of electricity produced, which reduces pollution from the generation of electricity, especially from coal-fired electric power plants.) Demand-side management means utility companies encourage consumers to take measures to use less electricity, which they would normally see as counter to their interests because less consumption could reduce company profits.

Federal Micro-Managing Isn't the Answer

Tom Arrandale

This country clearly needs to overhaul how governments go about protecting the environment. But when the chairman of the U.S. House Public Works Committee labels the U.S. Environmental Protection Agency an "environmental Gestapo," you've got to wonder how constructively the conservatives now running Congress really have thought about making pollution control work better. EPA needs shaking up, but government-bashing invective and piecemeal deregulation schemes don't amount to reasonable environmental policy.

It would be a shame if Congress meanwhile misses a chance to make more meaningful change in how pollution-control programs operate. The National Academy of Public Administration, a congressionally chartered research organization, set the stage this spring by recommending some common-sense restructuring of EPA's regulatory role. In a report titled *Setting Priorities, Getting Results,* a panel of public policy thinkers concluded that the nation cannot make progress improving the environment much longer unless both Congress and EPA "change—in some cases radically—the way they do business" in managing pollution-control efforts. With the costs to governments and business climbing steadily, the panel concluded that "the only sensible public policy is to set the right priorities and pursue them intelligently" to deal with pollution as efficiently and effectively as possible.

That's precisely what EPA and state environmental agencies can't do the way current environmental statutes are constructed. Banning unfunded mandates, ordering up inconclusive risk assessments and demanding artificially precise cost-benefit tests for every regulation won't solve the basic problem. The time has come to replace prescriptive federal laws and rigid EPA rules with what NAPA terms "accountable devolution" of real pollution-control power to states that prove they're ready to do the job.

That will require several steps: First, EPA needs to integrate its splintered air, water and waste programs and start setting pollution-control priorities. Second, state governments should be trusted to target what they consider their most serious threats without second-guessing by EPA's regional offices. Third, businesses and local governments need the chance to find creative ways to meet the nation's pollution-control goals.

There's still a need for baseline environmental standards so states won't be tempted to compete for jobs by lowering regulatory requirements. But you can argue that some state agencies already do a better job than EPA in protecting environmental quality within their borders. Most others are ready to upgrade their own programs, but they need EPA's help through funding and technical assistance that's not tied to separate federally mandated programs.

The current EPA administrator, Carol M. Browner, deserves credit for experimenting with sharing more authority. Along with state agency heads who make up the Environmental Council of the States, Browner in May signed an agreement to negotiate state-by-state environmental performance plans. The process would reward the strongest state programs with greater autonomy while EPA focuses its attention on the laggards.

As part of the deal, EPA will ask Congress for authority to streamline regulations so states can combine federal air, water and other program grants to fund multi-media regulatory efforts. Regulators also will explore new ways to judge how well states are performing without resorting to the kind of "bean counting" that now merely totes up how many permits they've issued, how much they've collected in fines or how many polluters they've taken to court. As the states take over, it's going to be more critical than ever to find methods to measure environmental progress meaningfully.

State agencies would also do well to nurture a political consensus on environmental priorities, perhaps by conducting comparative risk assessments that bring the public as well as scientists into the process. And EPA and ECOS agree that federal regulators need to stay on guard against backsliding—when, for instance, a new governor starts gutting previously effective programs. That may be happening right now in New York, where ousted regulators accuse Governor George E. Pataki of turning the state Environmental Conservation Department over to industry lobbyists and campaign aides.

The public wants fairer, more consistent environmental regulation, but that doesn't mean they'll tolerate more pollution close to home. Instead of empowering the states, U.S. House leaders so far seem content to continue micro-managing environmental policies from Congress, this time to give favored industries a break while inventing more procedural hurdles that would gum up the process for everyone else. If we're lucky, the Senate will listen to NAPA instead and consult the experienced Republican governors who have been running effective state pollution-control programs. The states can give the country better, not lesser, environmental protection, and it's time for the feds to let go.

Source: Governing, July 1995, p. 104. Reprinted with permission.

Second, civic environmentalism makes *extensive use of nonregulatory tools* such as educating the public at large about environmental concerns, technical assistance and grants along with tax credits, and loans to correct pollution problems. The Groundwater Protection Act in Iowa emphasized educating farmers about new ways of cultivating and rotating crops as well as reduced use of chemicals. Funds were provided to help farmers pay for improvements that would reduce chemical pollution of waters. This nonregulatory approach may be better than command-and-control regulation when there are a large number of polluters (90 percent of Iowa is farmland and there are 100,000 farmers) and when it is difficult to monitor how much pollution each individual contributes such as in groundwater contamination.[35]

Third, *interagency and intergovernmental cooperation* is emphasized because environmental problems usually involve many governmental agencies and little can be accomplished without cooperation. In Florida, agencies regulating the Everglades included the South Florida Water Management District, the state Department of Environmental Regulation, as well as the governor, and various individuals at the federal level including the superintendent of Everglades National Park and the secretary of the interior. It is unlikely that a single agency can improve most environmental problems, especially those dealing with ecosystems; long-term relationships and trust among these groups are needed.

Fourth, *alternatives to confrontation* are sought in an attempt to ameliorate the white hat–black hat arguments between environmentalists and polluters over who is responsible for a particular environmental problem. To do this, both sides need to agree that there is a problem. If this can be accomplished, negotiations may bring some success in protecting the environment.

Fifth, a *new role for the federal government* will be created. With states providing leadership on the "unfinished business" agenda, the federal government should assist by continuing to provide information from environmental research and more funds for environmental protection. Both can help states initiate new programs.

Civic environmentalists, however, do not want the federal government out of the environmental protection business entirely. They see the bottom-up approach of civic environmentalism as a complement to existing federal laws and regulations.

SUMMARY

Today, the federal government plays the key role in making policies affecting the economy and the environment. Within this context, and in recent years, state and local governments have become more active in adopting economic development policies. State governments also play a vital role in the implementation of federal environmental laws and are beginning to create their own initiatives to protect the environment.

State and local governments adopt economic development policies to encourage business investment in their particular state or community. This is an important issue throughout the United States because of stagnant personal incomes, business downsizing, and global economic competition. The traditional approach to economic development is the maintenance/attraction strategy that uses a variety of tax and financial incentives to attract new businesses and keep existing ones. Increasing competition for private investment, especially large manufacturing plants, has caused bidding wars between states. A newer approach to economic development, called a creation strategy, provides resources for local entrepreneurs and businesses to develop new products or processes that have the potential for growth. Although governments spend considerable time and money on economic development programs, scholars disagree as to their exact economic effect.

Political culture helps to determine the kind of development programs a state adopts. Moralistic states are more likely to have programs that place less emphasis on tax and financial incentives to business and more emphasis on the creation strategy and programs that protect the interests of workers. Individualistic states are more responsive to the demands of business and favor the use of tax and financial incentives. Traditionalistic states have used tax incentives and have adopted laws that provided less protection to workers so that labor costs could be kept low. In recent years, however, some traditionalistic states have provided more protection for workers, which may be an indication of possible significant change in their political culture.

State government's role in environmental protection has been primarily in designing and implementing programs, along with monitoring and enforcing them, to achieve federally determined goals. State governments have been required by Congress to spend more and more of their own funds on environmental protection. Nevertheless, in the late 1980s many state and local officials started to protest the growing presence of environmental mandates from the federal government. These mandates sometimes appeared unreasonable to them, and the costs to implement these programs were difficult to bear in light of tight state budgets.

In part, civic environmentalism is a response to the command-and-control regulatory approach to protecting the environment. Civic environmentalism emphasizes state and local initiatives to solve some environmental problems, especially nonpoint pollution.

KEY TERMS

Civic environmentalism When communities and states organize on their own to protect the environment, without being forced to by the federal government.

Creation strategy An economic development strategy used primarily by state governments that emphasizes financial assistance to local entrepreneurs and businesses to develop new or improved products.

Customized incentives A package containing a large number of tax, financial, and other incentives to recruit a major new business or retain an existing one. Customized incentives are usually associated with a bidding war.

Economic development policies A general term used to refer to a variety of policies adopted by state and local governments to encourage business investment within their boundaries. The goal is to create or retain existing jobs as well as enhance and diversify the tax base.

Financial incentives Low-interest loans guaranteed by state or local governments and used to recruit and retain businesses. Loans are for a number of purposes, including plant construction and the purchase of equipment.

Maintenance/attraction strategy An economic development strategy of state and local governments that emphasizes the use of incentives to maintain existing businesses and to recruit new ones from out of state.

Nonpoint pollution Pollution that comes from many sources and covers a large area such as fertilizer runoff from agricultural activities and runoff from urban storm water systems.

Tax incentives Tax breaks offered by state and local governments to recruit and retain businesses. Tax incentives are given frequently for the purchase of plant equipment and the creation of new manufacturing jobs.

Tragedy of the commons The idea that rational actions taken to pursue economic self-interest may result in harming anything people hold in common such as water and air. For example, owners of a manufacturing plant are unlikely to eliminate air or water pollution from their plant voluntarily if it requires the installation of expensive pollution control equipment that increases the cost of production and reduces profits. It is rational, in terms of the owners' economic self-interest, to decide that the small improvement in air and water quality achieved from eliminating pollution from their single plant is not worth the cost.

REFERENCES

1 Paul Brace, *State Government and Economic Performance* (Baltimore, Md.: Johns Hopkins University Press, 1993), p. 19.

2 Ibid., pp. 24–25.
3 Ibid., p. 31.
4 Virginia Gray and Peter Eisinger, *American States and Cities* (New York: HarperCollins Publishers, 1991), p. 282.
5 John E. Jackson, "Michigan," *The New Economic Role of American States,* R. Scott Fosler, ed. (New York: Oxford University Press, 1988), pp. 105–111.
6 The Council of State Governments, "State Business Incentives," *State Trends and Forecasts* 3 (June 1994), p. 3.
7 Charles J. Spindler, "Winners and Losers in Industrial Recruitment: Mercedes-Benz and Alabama," *State and Local Government Review* 26 (Fall 1994), p. 192.
8 Charles Mahtesian, "Romancing the Smokestack," *Governing* (November 1994), p. 37.
9 Council of State Governments, "State Business," p. 12.
10 Spindler, "Winners and Losers," p. 194.
11 Mahtesian, "Romancing," p. 39.
12 Spindler, "Winners and Losers," pp. 196–199.
13 Council of State Governments, "State Business," pp. 18–19.
14 Gray and Eisinger, *States and Cities,* p. 286.
15 Jackson, "Michigan," pp. 105–111.
16 David Osborne, *Laboratories of Democracy* (Boston, Mass.: Harvard Business School, 1990), p. 49.
17 Ibid., pp. 4–11.
18 Keith Boeckelman, "Political Culture and State Development Policy," *Publius* 21 (Spring 1991), pp. 49–62; Russell L. Hanson, "Political Cultural Variations in State Economic Development Policy," *Publius* 21 (Spring 1991), pp. 63–81.
19 Ronald John Hy and William L. Waugh, Jr., *State and Local Tax Policies: A Comparative Handbook* (Westport, Conn.: Greenwood Press, 1995), p. 224.
20 Jay Hancock, "Pa. Offers Lessons on Attracting, Keeping Industry," *Sun* (Baltimore), July 30, 1995, p. 1E.
21 Hanson, "Cultural Variations," p. 77.
22 Ibid., p. 81.
23 Garrett Hardin, "The Tragedy of the Commons," *Science* 162 (December 1968), p. 1244.
24 DeWitt John, *Civic Environmentalism: Alternatives to Regulation in States and Communities* (Washington, D.C.: CQ Press, 1994), p. 283.
25 This discussion relies heavily on Evan J. Ringquist, *Environmental Protection at the State Level* (Armonk, N.Y.: M. E. Sharp, 1993), pp. 67–76.
26 Ibid., p. 73.
27 Walter A. Rosenbaum, *Environmental Politics and Policy* (Washington, D.C.: CQ Press, 1985), pp. 292–293.
28 Ringquist, *Environmental Protection,* p. 73.
29 Ibid., p. 74.
30 Tom Arrandale, "A Guide to Environmental Mandates," *Governing* 7 (March 1994), pp. 82–83.
31 John, *Civic,* p. 293.
32 Ibid., p. 309.
33 Ibid., p. 7.
34 Ibid., pp. 260–261.
35 Ibid., p. 10.

APPENDIX

HISTORICAL DATA ON THE STATES

State or other jurisdiction	Source of state lands	Date organized as territory	Date admitted to Union	Chronological order of admission to Union
Alabama	Mississippi Territory, 1798 (a)	March 3, 1817	Dec. 14, 1819	22
Alaska	Purchased from Russia, 1867	Aug. 24, 1912	Jan. 3, 1959	49
Arizona	Ceded by Mexico, 1848 (b)	Feb. 24, 1863	Feb. 14, 1912	48
Arkansas	Louisiana Purchase, 1803	March 2, 1819	June 15, 1836	25
California	Ceded by Mexico, 1848	(c)	Sept. 9, 1850	31
Colorado	Louisiana Purchase, 1803 (d)	Feb. 28, 1861	Aug. 1, 1876	38
Connecticut	Fundamental Orders, Jan. 14, 1638; Royal charter, April 23, 1662 (e)	. . .	Jan. 9, 1788 (f)	5
Delaware	Swedish charter, 1638; English charter, 1683 (e)	. . .	Dec. 7, 1787 (f)	1
Florida	Ceded by Spain, 1819	March 30, 1822	March 3, 1845	27
Georgia	Charter, 1732, from George II to Trustees for Establishing the Colony of Georgia (e)	. . .	Jan. 2, 1788 (f)	4
Hawaii	Annexed, 1898	June 14, 1900	Aug. 21, 1959	50
Idaho	Treaty with Britain, 1846	March 4, 1863	July 3, 1890	43
Illinois	Northwest Territory, 1787	Feb. 3, 1809	Dec. 3, 1818	21
Indiana	Northwest Territory, 1787	May 7, 1800	Dec. 11, 1816	19
Iowa	Louisiana Purchase, 1803	June 12, 1838	Dec. 28, 1846	29
Kansas	Louisiana Purchase, 1803 (d)	May 30, 1854	Jan. 29, 1861	34
Kentucky	Part of Virginia until admitted as state	(c)	June 1, 1792	15
Louisiana	Louisiana Purchase, 1803 (g)	March 26, 1804	April 30, 1812	18
Maine	Part of Massachusetts until admitted as state	(c)	March 15, 1820	23
Maryland	Charter, 1632, from Charles I to Calvert (e)	. . .	April 28, 1788 (f)	7
Massachusetts	Charter to Massachusetts Bay Company, 1629 (e)	. . .	Feb. 6, 1788 (f)	6
Michigan	Northwest Territory, 1787	Jan. 11, 1805	Jan. 26, 1837	26
Minnesota	Northwest Territory, 1787 (h)	March 3, 1849	May 11, 1858	32
Mississippi	Mississippi Territory (i)	April 7, 1798	Dec. 10, 1817	20
Missouri	Louisiana Purchase, 1803	June 4, 1812	Aug. 10, 1821	24
Montana	Louisiana Purchase, 1803 (j)	May 26, 1864	Nov. 8, 1889	41
Nebraska	Louisiana Purchase, 1803	May 30, 1854	March 1, 1867	37
Nevada	Ceded by Mexico, 1848	March 2, 1861	Oct. 31, 1864	36
New Hampshire	Grants from Council for New England, 1622 and 1629; made Royal province, 1679 (e)	. . .	June 21, 1788 (f)	9
New Jersey	Dutch settlement, 1618; English charter, 1664 (e)	. . .	Dec. 18, 1787 (f)	3
New Mexico	Ceded by Mexico, 1848 (b)	Sept. 9, 1850	Jan. 6, 1912	47
New York	Dutch settlement, 1623; English control, 1664 (e)	. . .	July 26, 1788 (f)	11
North Carolina	Charter, 1663, from Charles II (e)	. . .	Nov. 21, 1789 (f)	12
North Dakota	Louisiana Purchase, 1803 (k)	March 2, 1861	Nov. 2, 1889	39
Ohio	Northwest Territory, 1787	May 7, 1800	March 1, 1803	17

HISTORICAL DATA ON THE STATES *(Continued)*

State or other jurisdiction	Source of state lands	Date organized as territory	Date admitted to Union	Chronological order of admission to Union
Oklahoma	Louisiana Purchase, 1803	May 2, 1890	Nov. 16, 1907	46
Oregon	Settlement and treaty with Britain, 1846	Aug. 14, 1848	Feb. 14, 1859	33
Pennsylvania	Grant from Charles II to William Penn, 1681 (e)	. . .	Dec. 12, 1787 (f)	2
Rhode Island	Charter, 1663, from Charles II (e)	. . .	May 29, 1790 (f)	13
South Carolina	Charter, 1663, from Charles II (e)	. . .	May 23, 1788 (f)	8
South Dakota	Louisiana Purchase, 1803	March 2, 1861	Nov. 2, 1889	40
Tennessee	Part of North Carolina until land ceded to U.S. in 1789	June 8, 1790 (l)	June 1, 1796	16
Texas	Republic of Texas, 1845	(c)	Dec. 29, 1845	28
Utah	Ceded by Mexico, 1848	Sept. 9, 1850	Jan. 4, 1896	45
Vermont	From lands of New Hampshire and New York	(c)	March 4, 1791	14
Virginia	Charter, 1609, from James I to London Company (e)	. . .	June 25, 1788 (f)	10
Washington	Oregon Territory, 1848	March 2, 1853	Nov. 11, 1889	42
West Virginia	Part of Virginia until admitted as state	(c)	June 20, 1863	35
Wisconsin	Northwest Territory, 1787	April 20, 1836	May 29, 1848	30
Wyoming	Louisiana Purchase, 1803 (d,j)	July 25, 1868	July 10, 1890	44
Dist. of Columbia	Maryland (m)	. . .	. . .	. . .
American Samoa	Became a territory, 1900			
Guam	Ceded by Spain, 1898	Aug. 1, 1950	. . .	. . .
No. Mariana Is.	. . .	March 24, 1976	. . .	. . .
Puerto Rico	Ceded by Spain, 1898	. . .	July 25, 1952 (n)	. . .
Republic of Palau	. . .	Jan. 1, 1981	. . .	. . .
U.S. Virgin Islands	Purchased from Denmark, March 31, 1917			

(a) By the Treaty of Paris, 1783, England gave up claim to the 13 original Colonies, and to all land within an area extending along the present Canadian border to the Lake of the Woods, down the Mississippi River to the 31st parallel, east to the Chattahoochee, down that river to the mouth of the Flint, east to the source of the St. Mary's, down that river to the ocean. The major part of Alabama was acquired by the Treaty of Paris, and the lower portion from Spain in 1813.

(b) Portion of land obtained by Gadsden Purchase, 1853.

(c) No territorial status before admission to Union.

(d) Portion of land ceded by Mexico, 1848.

(e) One of the original 13 Colonies.

(f) Date of ratification of U.S. Constitution.

(g) West Feliciana District (Baton Rouge) acquired from Spain, 1810; added to Louisiana, 1812.

(h) Portion of land obtained by Louisiana Purchase, 1803.

(i) See footnote (a). The lower portion of Mississippi also was acquired from Spain in 1813.

(j) Portion of land obtained from Oregon Territory, 1848.

(k) The northern portion of the Red River Valley was acquired by treaty with Great Britain in 1818.

(l) Date Southwest Territory (identical boundary as Tennessee's) was created.

(m) Area was originally 100 square miles, taken from Virginia and Maryland. Virginia's portion south of the Potomac was given back to that state in 1846. Site chosen in 1790, city incorporated 1802.

(n) On this date, Puerto Rico became a self-governing commonwealth by compact approved by the U.S. Congress and the voters of Puerto Rico as provided in U.S. Public Law 600 of 1950.

Source: The Book of the States 1994–95 (Lexington, Ky.: Council of State Governments, 1994), pp. 633–634.

Federally Owned Land, 1991

1. Nevada	82.9%
2. Alaska	67.9
3. Utah	63.9
4. Idaho	61.7
5. Oregon	52.4
6. Wyoming	48.9
7. Arizona	47.2
8. California	44.6
9. Colorado	36.3
10. New Mexico	32.4
United States	28.6
11. Washington	28.3
12. Montana	28.0
13. District of Columbia	26.1
14. Hawaii	15.5
15. New Hampshire	12.7
16. Michigan	12.6
17. Minnesota	10.5
18. Wisconsin	10.1
19. Florida	9.0
20. Arkansas	8.2
21. West Virginia	6.7
22. Virginia	6.3
23. North Carolina	6.3
24. Vermont	6.0
25. South Dakota	5.7
26. Missouri	4.7
27. Mississippi	4.3
28. North Dakota	4.2
29. Kentucky	4.2
30. Georgia	4.0
31. Tennessee	3.7
32. South Carolina	3.7
33. Alabama	3.3
34. New Jersey	3.1
35. Maryland	3.0
36. Illinois	2.7
37. Louisiana	2.6
38. Delaware	2.2
39. Pennsylvania	2.1
40. Indiana	1.7
41. Oklahoma	1.6
42. Nebraska	1.4
43. Texas	1.3
44. Ohio	1.3
45. Massachusetts	1.3
46. Iowa	0.9
47. Maine	0.8
48. Kansas	0.8
49. New York	0.7
50. Rhode Island	0.3
51. Connecticut	0.2

Persons Born in State of Residence, 1990

1. Pennsylvania	80.2%
2. Louisiana	79.0
3. Iowa	77.6
4. Kentucky	77.4
5. West Virginia	77.3
6. Mississippi	77.3
7. Wisconsin	76.4
8. Alabama	75.9
9. Michigan	74.9
10. Ohio	74.1
11. Minnesota	73.6
12. North Dakota	73.2
13. Indiana	71.1
14. North Carolina	70.4
15. South Dakota	70.2
16. Nebraska	70.2
17. Missouri	69.6
18. Tennessee	69.2
19. Illinois	69.1
20. Massachusetts	68.7
21. Maine	68.5
22. South Carolina	68.4
23. New York	67.5
24. Utah	67.2
25. Arkansas	67.1
26. Texas	64.7
27. Georgia	64.5
28. Oklahoma	63.5
29. Rhode Island	63.4
United States	61.8
30. Kansas	61.3
31. Montana	58.9
32. Vermont	57.2
33. Connecticut	57.0
34. Hawaii	56.1
35. New Jersey	54.8
36. Virginia	54.2
37. New Mexico	51.7
38. Idaho	50.6
39. Delaware	50.2
40. Maryland	49.8
41. Washington	48.2
42. Oregon	46.6
43. California	46.4
44. New Hampshire	44.1
45. Colorado	43.3
46. Wyoming	42.6
47. District of Columbia	39.3
48. Arizona	34.2
49. Alaska	34.0
50. Florida	30.5
51. Nevada	21.8

Personal Income, per Capita, in Current Dollars, 1993	
1. District of Columbia	$29,438
2. Connecticut	28,110
3. New Jersey	26,967
4. New York	24,623
5. Massachusetts	24,563
6. Maryland	24,044
7. Hawaii	23,354
8. Alaska	22,846
9. Nevada	22,729
10. New Hampshire	22,659
11. Illinois	22,582
12. Washington	21,887
13. California	21,821
14. Virginia	21,634
15. Colorado	21,564
16. Delaware	21,481
17. Pennsylvania	21,351
18. Rhode Island	21,096
19. Minnesota	21,063
20. Florida	20,857
United States	20,817
21. Michigan	20,453
22. Kansas	20,139
23. Wisconsin	19,811
24. Nebraska	19,726
25. Ohio	19,688
26. Wyoming	19,539
27. Vermont	19,467
28. Missouri	19,463
29. Oregon	19,443
30. Georgia	19,278
31. Indiana	19,203
32. Texas	19,189
33. Maine	18,895
34. North Carolina	18,702
35. Tennessee	18,434
36. Iowa	18,315
37. Arizona	18,121
38. South Dakota	17,666
39. Idaho	17,646
40. North Dakota	17,488
41. Montana	17,322
42. Alabama	17,234
43. Kentucky	17,173
44. Oklahoma	17,020
45. South Carolina	16,923
46. Louisiana	16,667
47. New Mexico	16,297
48. West Virginia	16,209
49. Utah	16,180
50. Arkansas	16,143
51. Mississippi	14,894

Public Aid Recipients, as Percent of Population, 1992	
1. District of Columbia	13.3
2. Mississippi	11.8
3. California	10.7
4. Louisiana	10.2
5. Kentucky	9.8
6. West Virginia	9.7
7. New York	9.0
8. Michigan	9.0
9. Ohio	8.7
10. Tennessee	8.6
11. Georgia	8.5
12. Rhode Island	8.0
13. New Mexico	8.0
14. Illinois	7.9
United States	7.6
15. Maine	7.6
16. Massachusetts	7.5
17. Vermont	7.2
18. North Carolina	7.2
19. Alabama	7.1
20. Wisconsin	6.9
21. Washington	6.9
22. Pennsylvania	6.9
23. Missouri	6.8
24. Florida	6.8
25. Arkansas	6.8
26. South Carolina	6.7
27. Alaska	6.7
28. Oklahoma	6.4
29. Arizona	6.4
30. Texas	6.3
31. New Jersey	6.1
32. Maryland	6.0
33. Connecticut	6.0
34. Hawaii	5.9
35. Minnesota	5.7
36. Montana	5.4
37. Wyoming	5.2
38. Oregon	5.2
39. Delaware	5.2
40. Iowa	5.0
41. Indiana	5.0
42. Colorado	5.0
43. Virginia	4.8
44. South Dakota	4.6
45. Kansas	4.6
46. North Dakota	4.3
47. Nebraska	4.2
48. Utah	3.8
49. Nevada	3.6
50. New Hampshire	3.4
51. Idaho	3.2

Source: Edith Horner, ed., *Almanac of the Fifty States* (Palo Alto, Calif.: Information Publications, 1995).

STATE STATISTICS

State or other jurisdiction	Land area: In square miles	Land area: Rank in nation	Population: Size	Population: Rank in nation	Percentage change 1980 to 1990	Density per square mile
Alabama	50,750	28	4,040,587	22	3.8	79.62
Alaska	570,374	1	550,043	49	36.9	0.96
Arizona	113,642	6	3,665,228	24	34.9	32.25
Arkansas	52,075	27	2,350,725	33	2.8	45.14
California	155,973	3	29,760,021	1	25.7	190.80
Colorado	103,729	8	3,294,394	26	14.0	31.76
Connecticut	4,845	48	3,287,116	27	5.8	678.40
Delaware	1,955	49	666,168	46	12.1	340.82
Florida	53,997	26	12,937,926	4	32.7	239.60
Georgia	57,919	21	6,478,216	11	18.6	111.85
Hawaii	6,423	47	1,108,229	41	14.9	172.53
Idaho	82,751	11	1,006,749	42	6.6	12.17
Illinois	55,593	24	11,430,602	6	0.0	205.61
Indiana	35,870	38	5,544,159	14	1.0	154.56
Iowa	55,875	23	2,776,755	30	–4.7	49.70
Kansas	81,823	13	2,477,574	32	4.8	30.28
Kentucky	39,732	36	3,685,296	23	0.7	92.75
Louisiana	43,566	33	4,219,973	21	0.3	96.86
Maine	30,865	39	1,227,928	38	9.1	39.78
Maryland	9,775	42	4,781,468	19	13.4	489.17
Massachusetts	7,838	45	6,016,425	13	4.9	767.60
Michigan	56,809	22	9,295,297	8	0.4	163.62
Minnesota	79,617	14	4,375,099	20	7.3	54.95
Mississippi	46,914	31	2,573,216	31	2.1	54.85
Missouri	68,898	18	5,117,073	15	4.1	74.27
Montana	145,556	4	799,065	44	1.6	5.49
Nebraska	76,878	15	1,578,385	36	0.5	20.53
Nevada	109,806	7	1,201,833	39	50.1	10.95
New Hampshire	8,969	44	1,109,252	40	20.5	123.67
New Jersey	7,419	46	7,730,188	9	5.0	1,041.97

STATE STATISTICS *(Continued)*

No. of representatives in Congress	Capital	Population	Rank in state	Largest city	Population
7	Montgomery	187,106	3	Birmingham	265,968
1	Juneau	26,751	3	Anchorage	226,338
6	Phoenix	983,403	1	Phoenix	983,403
4	Little Rock	175,795	1	Little Rock	175,795
52	Sacramento	369,365	7	Los Angeles	3,485,398
6	Denver	467,610	1	Denver	467,610
6	Hartford	139,739	2	Bridgeport	141,686
1	Dover	27,630	2	Wilmington	71,529
23	Tallahassee	124,773	8	Jacksonville	635,230
11	Atlanta	394,017	1	Atlanta	394,017
2	Honolulu	365,272	1	Honolulu	365,272
2	Boise	125,738	1	Boise	125,738
20	Springfield	105,227	4	Chicago	2,783,726
10	Indianapolis	731,327	1	Indianapolis	731,327
5	Des Moines	193,187	1	Des Moines	193,187
4	Topeka	119,883	3	Wichita	304,011
6	Frankfort	25,968	8	Louisville	269,063
7	Baton Rouge	219,531	2	New Orleans	496,938
2	Augusta	21,325	6	Portland	64,358
8	Annapolis	33,187	22	Baltimore	736,014
10	Boston	574,283	1	Boston	574,283
16	Lansing	127,321	5	Detroit	1,027,974
8	St. Paul	272,235	2	Minneapolis	368,383
5	Jackson	196,637	1	Jackson	196,637
9	Jefferson City	35,481	15	Kansas City	435,146
1	Helena	24,569	5	Billings	81,151
3	Lincoln	191,972	2	Omaha	335,795
2	Carson City	40,443	9	Las Vegas	258,295
2	Concord	36,006	3	Manchester	99,567
13	Trenton	88,675	6	Newark	275,221

(table continued on following page)

STATE STATISTICS (*Continued*)

State or other jurisdiction	Land area: In square miles	Land area: Rank in nation	Population: Size	Population: Rank in nation	Percentage change 1980 to 1990	Density per square mile
New Mexico	121,365	5	1,515,069	37	16.2	12.48
New York	47,224	30	17,990,455	2	2.5	380.96
North Carolina	48,718	29	6,628,637	10	12.7	136.06
North Dakota	68,994	17	638,800	47	–2.1	9.26
Ohio	40,953	35	10,847,115	7	0.5	264.87
Oklahoma	68,679	19	3,145,585	28	4.0	45.80
Oregon	96,003	10	2,842,321	29	7.9	29.61
Pennsylvania	44,820	32	11,881,643	5	0.1	265.10
Rhode Island	1,045	50	1,003,464	43	5.9	960.27
South Carolina	30,111	40	3,486,703	25	11.7	115.79
South Dakota	75,896	16	696,004	45	0.8	9.17
Tennessee	41,220	34	4,877,185	17	6.2	118.32
Texas	261,914	2		3	19.4	64.86
Utah	82,168	12	16,986,510	35	17.9	20.97
Vermont	9,249	43	1,722,850	48	10.0	60.84
Virginia	39,598	37	562,758	12	15.7	156.26
Washington	66,581	20	6,187,358	18	17.8	73.09
West Virginia	24,087	41	4,866,692	34	–8.0	74.46
Wisconsin	54,314	25	1,793,477	16	4.0	90.07
Wyoming	97,105	9	4,891,769	50	3.4	4.67
Dist. of Columbia	61	. . .	453,588	. . .	–4.9	9,884.40
American Samoa	77	. . .	606,900	. . .	44.8	607.44
Guam	210	. . .	46,773	. . .	25.6	634.06
No. Mariana Islands	179	. . .	133,152	. . .	158.8	242.15
Puerto Rico	3,427	. . .	43,345	. . .	10.2	1,027.90
Republic of Palau	177	. . .	3,522,037	. . .	24.8	85.44
U.S. Virgin Islands	134	. . .	15,122	. . .	5.4	760.90
			101,809			

STATE STATISTICS *(Continued)*

No. of representatives in Congress	Capital	Population	Rank in state	Largest city	Population
3	Santa Fe	55,859	3	Albuquerque	384,736
31	Albany	101,082	6	New York City	7,322,564
12	Raleigh	207,951	2	Charlotte	395,934
1	Bismarck	49,256	3	Fargo	74,111
19	Columbus	632,910	1	Columbus	632,910
6	Oklahoma City	444,719	1	Oklahoma City	444,719
5	Salem	107,786	3	Portland	437,319
21	Harrisburg	52,376	10	Philadelphia	1,585,577
2	Providence	160,728	1	Providence	160,728
6	Columbia	98,052	1	Columbia	98,052
1	Pierre	12,906	7	Sioux Falls	100,814
9	Nashville	488,374	2	Memphis	610,337
30	Austin	465,622	5	Houston	1,630,553
3	Salt Lake City	159,936	1	Salt Lake City	159,936
1	Montpelier	8,247	8	Burlington	39,127
11	Richmond	203,056	3	Virginia Beach	393,069
9	Olympia	33,840	18	Seattle	516,259
3	Charleston	57,287	1	Charleston	57,287
9	Madison	191,262	2	Milwaukee	628,088
1	Cheyenne	50,008	1	Cheyenne	50,008
1 (a)	. . .	. . .	. . .	. . .	. . .
1 (a)	Pago Pago	3,519	3	Tafuna	5,174
1 (a)	Agana	1,139	18	Dededo	31,728
. . .	Saipan	38,896	1	Saipan	38,896
1 (a)	San Juan	426,832	1	San Juan	426,832
. . .	Koror	9,000	1	Koror	9,000
1 (a)	Charlotte Amalie, St. Thomas	12,331	1	Charlotte Amalie, St. Thomas	12,331

Source: U.S. Department of Commerce, Bureau of the Census.
Key:
. . . — *Not applicable*
(a) Delegate with privileges to vote in committees and the Committee of the Whole.
From: The Book of the States 1994–95 (Lexington, Ky.: Council of State Governments, 1994), pp. 635–636.

INDEX

INDEX

Boldface entries indicate pages on which key terms are defined in the text.